My Thus Far

Sahar Zahraee

Presentation by *BookLeaf Publishing*

Web: www.bookleafpub.com

E-mail: info@bookleafpub.com

ISBN: 9789357691109

First edition 2022

DEDICATION

I dedicate this to my loved ones: my dearest family and the people dearest to me that are nothing less than family. Everything I am is because of you, and everything I do is for you.

ACKNOWLEDGEMENT

Thank you to my family for creating an aquarium of beautiful thoughts and values in my head. Thank you to my family — not by blood but by love, Alyssa and Mannat — for giving me so much goodness and love. You have all ensured my happiness for an eternity. I am the luckiest.

Last but not least, I would like to acknowledge every life that has ever graced mine in any way, shape, or form. It is the collective impression your souls have made on mine that has made me who I am. Thank you.

PREFACE

There's a room in my mind and the atmosphere in there is still. It's warm and chilly at once— the air, crisp like an autumn morning. It smells like the ground does after an endless night of rain, and it smells like home and my mother's cooking. There's the sound of a fireplace crackling, in it, the same fire is burning, the one that burned during our first Christmas in our new home on Music Lane. There's the sound of water, the same sound from the fountains in our front yard. The room is lit a warm orange glow, just as my study is, soft Persian rugs beneath my feet. On the walls, there are moving images and memories of every beautiful encounter I have ever had. In my heart, there's a palace where my most loved ones live. They live there forever, and nothing can ever upset them, not even me. There's a desk in the room and a large library of every book I've ever read and every word I've ever heard. On my desk, there are piles of every line I've ever said and written, organized by their sincerity, the sincerest at the top, facing me. There is a large garden in my abode, from which fragmented emerald light pours into the room through a mosaic glass window. It's drizzling.

The surface of a lake blurs blue grey. The fog makes distant trees look like a dream.
Nothing touches this room. It exists at the center of my mind and is ever expansive. While anything can doubt my logic and cause stormy chaos in my mind, this oasis cannot be distorted. It is safe here. It is warm here. My loved ones are with me. The world can touch and offend my physical self and my thinking self, but who I really am and what I really treasure will always be safe in this room. My thoughts may be vulnerable, but my soul is not. I spend the most time with my soul. In this room.

We all have a place within us that should never be touched, should never be moved, by the force of anyone else's soul.

Here is my consolation: everything I feel that brings me unhappiness does not come from my inner place. It comes from what I have thought I needed to feel. It comes from the fear I taught myself. It is my very own, and I can dissolve it. As lost as we may feel, half of the confusion is a result of us ignoring the little sense of truth in the bottom of our hearts that we know how it is we must feel. I am using every poet, author, director, musician, philosopher, confidante, advisor, friend, and family that has ever graced my life, as my shovel. But with it, I will dig in a land that no one has ever been on and unveil something that no one has ever seen or heard. This will be my unique answer. My philosophy. The meaning in my life. My thus far.

This is to the new me, the same me that I was before I convinced myself otherwise.

When It Rains It Pours

To them, I owe the world,
But the world says she's not mine to give,
So indebted I will remain forever,
A debt that beside me now, will outlive.

It was duty not yours to drizzle,
Yet purpose you made to flood,
And so with the soul you've made of me,
I place you above all I will ever love.

A Walk Under the Clouds

Music is the language of the heart,
And poetry is the music of language.
The ears accept one,
And the eyes, the other.

The mouth relays both,
The hands record both.
The feet move in joyous synchronicity,
As the lips relax into a smile.

In that moment,
The sidewalk has no start, no finish.
The clouds move over my head, and I am
anchored in time.
My world becomes a little smaller.

The trees become a tender green and sway
slightly as if to say, 'Hi,
Thank you for spending your moment with us.'
The grass is the Earth's love for the skies,
Reaching high towards the Sky to grasp its
beloved.

The water, nothing but a gift from the Sky for
the Earth.

And the wind? A hug from the world, for me,
Pleading me to see the life around me,
To hear it speak.

To realize that reality
Is all but a figment of our imagination.
That reality and fantasy are both born of the same mind
And separated by nothing but the desire to communicate with one another.

That reality exists to communicate with others
And fantasy exists to communicate with ourselves.

Oh, to be poetic in a tongue that is not ours.
To be profound in a language that does not capture our essence.

How else to resolve the incongruity
But to join the heart and the mind,
With music and poetry,
To make fantasy our reality.

Fragrant Deeds

Jaanam, my life, there is a beautiful garden somewhere,
A garden long forgotten by man.
It is said the scent of this garden drives the sane to their insanity,
And the insane to their sanity.

Eshqam, my love, there is a beautiful garden somewhere,
Where no two flowers nor two petals are alike,
Each possessing its own unique hue.
The blossoms drink from the same soil and nurture the same air.

Azizam, my dearest, there is a beautiful garden somewhere,
Where freedom is the sunlight all the leaves turn towards,
Peace, the rain they feed from,
Wind, the opposition that strengthens their roots.

Nafasam, my breath, there is a beautiful garden somewhere,
That needs no announcement nor praise,

The roots of which reach the very heart of the earth,
And the petals, the very soul of the skies.

Nazaninam, my sweet, this garden's splendor sets it apart from all others,
For it is the only home of an eternity's worth of resilience,
The birthplace of the spirit's songbird,
And the burial ground of every dawn's morning dew.

Maaham, my moon, its exceptionality is such
That during the darkest and longest night of the winter,
The stalks stand so tall together that
Even the moonlight can nourish their breaths and the stars can retain their dreams.

Asalam, my honey, during the darkest and longest night of the winter,
The deprived blooms release a fragrance that eludes no soul on Earth,
And like so, the garden long forgotten
Draws all eyes and ears to its lovely flowers and its songbird's melodies.

Golam, my flower, the heavenly garden reminds us of an unforgettable message —

True beauty needs no praise,
For its divine fragrance speaks for itself,
And its voice permeates all receptive souls.

My love, while you may forget this beautiful garden exists,
May its fragrant message never escape you.

Soul

My being different from you all is not what
makes me beautiful.
My being just like you all is what makes us all
beautiful.

To learn tenderness from one,
And assertiveness from another.
Humility from one,
Pride from another.
Beauty from one,
Bitterness from another.

I want nothing more than to follow the shadow
of all those before me.
To walk the steps that have been walked many a
time before,
And place my feet in the imprints of your
footsteps,
And learn that the path of life can be endlessly
beautiful,
Until I too,
Become a forgotten fragment of this world's
mythical history.

Fragments that may be found hundreds of years from now,
In the corner of someone's heart,
In another's hand,
In another's eye,
In the water that quenches your thirst,
In the wind that tousles your hair,
In the trees of the land where I was buried,
And as words of advice shared between a mother and her son.
Perhaps as a story of someone who once was,
Or wasn't.
They won't be sure.

Childhood

I hope you didn't listen
When they told you these were the best years of
your life.

I hope you didn't understand
When they told you the world of the grown-ups
is sorrowful and grey.

I hope you weren't hurt
When your childhood washed away.

If you were,
I hope you find hope again.
In your mother's smile,
In your best friend's laughter,
In your father's hugs,
And in your brother's loving gaze.

I hope you know the gifts of childhood never
leave.
To anyone who has ever sought something
unprecedented,
To all that currently exists and was once
extraordinary,
The joys of childhood never left.

I hope you are free
To live with joy and childlike wonder.

I hope you know,
Just because a door is open,
Doesn't mean the room beyond has a place for
you.

Your greatest years were never destined.
Nothing ever comes of ranks and lists,
In placing people above and below each other
When our world is, after all, circular,
And the ground beneath our feet, level,
When all that is certain is birth and death,
And both are vowed for everyone.

I hope you know that the world is nothing more
than your mind's best guess,
And unrestrained emotions,
Unwarranted laughter,
Infinite art,
And boundless fantasies,
Are accessories at your disposal.
So color your mind as you please.

Who you really are,
Is in how you choose to see the world.

I hope you choose to see joy.

Coffee for Comfort, Flowers for Breath, and Me for Myself

Would murky coffee offend me if each sip were
delectable?

Would your friend's friendships hurt you if
quality were more important than quantity?

Would you feel humiliated every time you
misspoke if you believed in values more
important than intelligence?

What does a flower care about its beauty,
When it exists for the deeper cause of exhaling
air for life?
Flowers do not bloom for what you see.

Petals or not, fragrant or not, planted or potted,
What meaning does this carry,
To a flower that does its best when unspotted?

The human condition is such that we simply care
too much
And too much of everything do we wish to be,

Holding all revered titles too tightly in our clutch.

But,

If we were to make our values clear
And care for only what is worth caring for,
Nothing could hurt our sense of why we are here.

So, listen to me, dearest brothers and sisters.
Yes, the world is your oyster,
And you are capable of fashioning boundless pearls.

But when you greet me,
If you wish to praise me,
Only do so for the most valuable pearls.

While I've clashed with pressures to have this and that,
At one point, red lips and long hair,
At others, grace and intellect,
I've finally found my most enduring resolve in my heart.

That though beauty and brains may one day fail me,

What never will fail is my will to be sincere and kind,
And for only my heart's principle will I accept your admiration.

Silence

In silence, there is beauty.
Be quiet, and watch the room come alive.

The weaver of dreams is silent,
For it is in silence that dreams are born.

Silence is giving way to life.
A moment in the imbalanced tug-of-war,
Where you let go of the rope,
Just long enough,
To know your opponent's strength.

A moment,
Where you stop sprinting to notice the stillness of life around you,
Where you turn off the lights to see the stars,
Where you let go of your desperate demand to live life,
and let life live you.

The most important lessons are learned in silence.
The most enlightening ideas are molded in silence.
The purest emotions are exchanged in silence.

The weaver of dreams is silent.
Be silent,
And dream.

Butterflies

When you're upset,
And your stomach quivers,
As though a butterfly is resisting its cage,
Just remember,
That something relentless in you needs to flutter.
Let it be nothing else than your heart,
And let it leave your chest each dawn.

Let it take flight,
To an awaiting castle in the sky
That will gift it the flickers of unfamiliar fables,
Before it returns, wings tired and eyes grateful,
To rest inside your chest again each dusk.

Each time you're upset,
Look forward to a new dawn with a new
awareness,
Waiting for you.

To worry is to fear loss,
To fear hitting the ground.
Know that you are lucky,
To have so much to lose,
and so far to fall.

Today

I spent 90 minutes waiting to ask a question.
I spent just as long to see a little bunny crawl out of the bush it ran into when it first saw me.
I spent twice as long waiting on an email.

Am I waiting too long for a chance to live my life?
Has everything until now been my waiting?

But,
I can't wait two minutes for a response.
And I can't wait two seconds to react to my thoughts.

Maybe,
Waiting is for the Impatient
Because otherwise, you're not waiting.
You're just living,
And life happens when it does
And moments pass us when they do
And if you looked for them,
If you felt loss after they were gone,
Then you were waiting.
And like me,
You are Impatient.

What you really need to know is —
Oh,
I gotta go now,
The bunny just crawled out.

Prejudice

She smiles at me lovingly,
But weaves her next words cunningly.

What else does our culture teach,
But to praise my beauty though she believes it isn't deep?

I find it hard to be angry at this stranger's betrayal.
What more could I expect from someone who thinks all others have failed?

Her handcuffs are rather golden bangles, she bluffs,
But I know she has no choice than to accept them as such.

The truth would make waste her 60 years.
So the truth that there are other truths is of her greatest fears.

The truth that what she cannot see
Can still indeed come to be.

All because those shimmering handcuffs
Convinced her that she cannot understand us.

Identifying Self Before Faith

It is a natural human instinct to minimize our sight
Because when one person is taught a single truth,
They see their experiences through the filter of that truth.

But if a child is left to witness life free of any compulsory beliefs,
Before learning the beauty of faith, then maybe we can create a world of people who see less differences between each other.

To love is good,
To hurt is bad,
These are truths we all know.

But those of us born by the book believe it to be our only source,
We attribute all we know to faith,
And wholeheartedly believe we would not know without faith.

But the devout and I both know
That love is good,

And hate is bad.

Life gives us several means of arriving in the same location.
But those of us who take the train
Can be unaware of other methods of travel.

And so, we close our eyes from most opportunities
And give God's text more importance than Man's
When Man is just another one of God's stories.

My children will find their raw emotions first,
Without the help of any preceding principles.
And when they discover
All of their friends,
Their family,
Their beloved,
Their acquaintances,
Their contemporaries,
In the same waiting room at the end of the tunnel,
They will realize that the beauty of life and all its knowledge cannot be
given a shape, nor a color, nor a plot, nor a message, nor a sound,
nor any indication of form through our senses.

And any way of experiencing life,
Through faith,
Or not,
Is beautiful all the same.

I Don’t Like You

I don't wish to offend you when I tell you how
harmful I find your beliefs.
After all, if this is your truth, why should my
dissent offend you?

If there is any truth at all, it is maybe this:
That if we accept there is no single truth,
Then we will never again find offense in
anyone's heart,
In anyone's truth.

We will never again find a reason to abolish
those that contradict our truth,
Because their truth is no threat to ours.
Contradiction is no threat to us.

For the air contradicts the ground every time a
storm is born,
The Moon contradicts the Sun every time an
eclipse shadows the land,
The land contradicts the ocean every time our
cities quake,
And the Universe contradicts its planets every
time a meteor strikes.

But,
This is all natural, you might say,
Just the way our world turns.
If such is your response, you are undoubtedly correct.

Because,
When the truth of one element contradicts the truth of another,
This is nature.

So many truths.
So many contradictions.
This is nature.

So why does my truth,
Urge you to war?

If you still find offense by my words, then ask yourself
Why my submission to your beliefs is necessary
For you to maintain the strength of your faith?

Yes,
I don't like you,
But that shouldn't matter at all.

Thunder

Hands hopeful for the day you feed me as my
hand has fed you,
Eyes hopeful for the day you tend to my wounds
with the ache my decades have felt for yours,
So that you may lock eyes with me,
And hold my hands,
And recognize the frightening thunder,
Was just our hearts beating together.

So don't be scared.
I am no different from your mother,
And a mother to you my mothers have been.

You place me at your knees on the ground
When I am more fitted for the crown on your
head,
But don't be scared.

When even the ground one day does all it can to
pull me up,
I'll keep my knees where your knees are,
Above the ground,
But below your heart,
As equals.

Arrows and Shields

The biggest mistake you can ever make
Is thinking they meant to hurt you.

No.
They dodged an arrow,
Without thinking
That you might be standing in their shadow.

Few people in this world find joy in hurting
others.
Most are trying to escape themselves.

So,
If you were hurt today,
Rest assured.

What hurts most is thinking they meant it.
What helps most is trusting,
they didn't.

To Wish Upon a Shooting Star

Waiting,
Eyes gazing hopefully out the window,
In search of the twinkling lights above and below us,
The large world making us feel small.

Flying,
Together deep into an ocean of clouds,
As strangers sharing a space in the skies with the stars,
For just a short time.

A child cries in her mother's arms behind me,
A teenage girl listens to her favorite band across the aisle.
A young boy sleeps soundlessly next to me.
A businessman types away at his laptop in front of me.
I hold a book that promises me happiness.

Dreaming,
Alongside each other for just a little while,
In pursuit of different paths,
But together just for now,

As strangers sharing a destination.

Wishing,
Upon the stars, that our one lives are our best lives,
We are all looking forward,
These strangers and I.

And
Somewhere not far away,
There is a child pointing to the sky,
Mistaking us for a star.

Homeland

How strange is a homeland.

So strange that
Without stepping on the soil,
I can feel the steps of my people shaking the streets.

Without seeing the people,
My eyes still shed the tears of their grief.

Without understanding the script,
My blood flows in cadence to the rhythm of my mother tongue
And burns with the power of its chants.
So much so that my other tongue can speak my mind but never my heart.

And while my heart beats in another land,
It pulls and aches with the cries of my people.
So much so that no temptation nor obligation can distract it.

What a strange bond it is indeed.

Or is it so strange?

To be reborn of the same matter, the same dust,
the same air,
And expect no connection?

That even when separated
We are one being scattered around the universe,
I don't find that so hard to believe.

That our homeland is less about the land and
more about the people.
We, the people, who are the land, in flight for
just a moment, before we settle.

Before the dust settles,
Before we are born again,
As another one of each other.

We, our homeland.
Is it really so strange after all?

Furnace of Friendship

Most of us are born with a furnace in our soul.
To light the fire,
Then to keep it alight,
We are in constant pursuit for that which ignites.

Our furnace is lit in pleasant company,
Each joyous moment worth a fleeting flame,
Lit in love and passion,
And extinguished in pain.

Then there are those very few of us who,
Rather than an empty hearth,
Carry the very source of fire
On this Earth.

It is rare to meet those who set your soul afire.
How lucky am I,
To have you in this life
To admire.

My soul always lit
With the fire of your existence,
Like a moth to a flame,
I will follow you any distance.

Know this,
My dearest flame,
That until the last rain,
My every breath will be in your name.

The Wish Fulfilled

There was an unfulfilled yearning,
The cause of restless wandering.

Unbeknownst to me but understood by above
Who created you in the image of dreams,
My love.

To my home away from home,
To intoxication without wine,
To love given freely without invitation,
To admiration that inspires change,
To endless support that gives me certainty,
To blazing warmth,
To a heart I don't need to win over as it has
already vowed itself mine,
To your always awaiting arms,
To you,
My wish,
Thank you for being mine.

Shadow

What is a sibling,
But your reflection in the water inverted?
Molded after you,
In praise of you,
But flowing through a different medium.

What is a sibling,
But the time it takes between perception
And comprehension?
From when the sun rises
And thrusts its light outwards,
To when we grasp it no less than
8 minutes after.

To my brother,
Who is grown but still young,
Passionate but not yet directed,
Michievous but still innocent,
Short tempered but oh so loving,
I love you.

May you grow to see the Earth for all its beauty,
And discount the bad for all that is good.
May you grow in the shadow of our father and mother,

For no shadow is warmer and more reliable.
And may I be worthy enough to be a guide,
For the rarest moments when you need one,
Else an anchor for all the rest.

My Forever Father

Money comes and goes,
Relationships come and go,
Fortune comes and goes,
And sometimes with it, happiness too.

Please,
Don't measure your fatherhood
By the number of trips,
And the price of such gifts,
Or the number of relatives surrounding us,
Because life flies past us,
And such things are to the ability of every father,
When life is kind.

But,
Your wisdom,
Your time,
Your love,
Your tender hugs,
Your loving smile,
Your heart of gold,
All while life was stacking its burdens on your back,
Have never gone,
And will never go,

And these are the gifts few fathers can give.

So please be sure of your worth,
That though you are not the head of the world in this lifetime,
You are the life I place on my head in this one and all the next.
I am proud of you, and I cherish you.

To you,
My eternal guide,
Without whom the world would be but wouldn't endure.
May I be your daughter in every existence.

Moonlight

If God is the Sun,
My Mother is the Moon.
The brightest reflection of Life itself,
As resilient as the creator itself,
Ever-present with indifference to night or day,
Host of the skies,
And home to the stars.

Behold her,
For she is beauty in the absence of sight,
Warmth in the absence of the ancestral flame,
Loveliness that forever strikes but never
scorches.

Glimpse at her infinitely,
For her beauty never exhausts nor empties.

If covered by clouds, the clouds illuminate her
dignity.
If shadowed by the leaves, the water mirrors her
face.

The guide of the night,
Luring out the distressed from their darkness,

Soothing them into sweet slumber with dusk's lullaby.

As we circle the Sun for it is the giver of Life,
The Moon circles us for she is the gifter of Meaning.
What is left of Life without Meaning?

Mother,
My proudest achievement was not of my doing.
My pride is in being your daughter.

After my form has circled the sun abundantly
And lays itself to rest,
May I sprout as a tree that reaches tirelessly towards your light.
May my branches house the nightingale that'll sing in everlasting worship of you.
May the tree nourished from my body be made an eternal oud that strums your praises by the hands of innumerable devotees.

May I forever,
Be adorned,
By your moonlight.

www.ingramcontent.com/pod-product-compliance
Lightning Source LLC
Chambersburg PA
CBHW062203160726
48282CB00027B/973

* 9 7 8 9 3 5 7 6 9 1 1 0 9 *

Devotion and Dissent in Indian History

Edited by

Vijaya Ramaswamy

Foundation Books is an imprint of Cambridge University Press India Pvt. Ltd.

314 to 321, 3rd Floor, Plot No.3, Splendor Forum, Jasola District Centre, New Delhi 110025, India

www.cambridgeindia.org

First published 2014
Reprint 2018

Printed in India at Thomson Press (India) Ltd.

ISBN 978-93-82993-19-3 Hardback

To the memory of those in the shadow of
whose loss this book has come out:
My mother Sethu
My sister Manju Akka
&
My niece Saumya.
All these women were, in a sense, devout dissenters.

Contents

List of Tables and Figures

Table

Figures

Foreword

During the three days from 11 March to 13 March 2010, a rich and remarkable scholarly event was held on the campus of Jawaharlal Nehru University (JNU), New Delhi. It was a major international conference devoted to a critical examination and discussion on a wide variety of the forms of religious devotion and sectarian practice and, more provocatively, to the various types of dissent that these forms have engendered over the *longue durée* of Indian history. The event, conceived and organized by Professor Vijaya Ramaswamy of the Centre for Historical Studies at JNU and hosted by the Centre, brought together scholars – both Indian and foreign – who were experts in many different religious and linguistic traditions as these traditions have evolved in different regions of the subcontinent from antiquity through the medieval period and down to modernity.

The conference – the papers presented at which appear in the present volume – represented an original and productive turn in the study of the history of religious movements over time in South Asia. It focused scholarly attention specifically on the frequently overlooked currents of dissent within and against several major, mainstream religious movements and organizations that are often represented as the uncontested, if not the exclusive, representatives of their respective faiths in India and throughout the Indian diaspora. In highlighting the phenomenon of dissent, the conference thus productively focused the attention of the scholars in attendance, and one would hope, of those who have the opportunity to read the present collection of the proceedings, on some less fully examined aspects of Indian religions. These include the countercurrents, disputes and debates that have characterized religious belief and practice in many different movements from ancient Buddhism and medieval South Indian Virashaivism to early modern dissent in Islam, Sikhism and the Syro-Malabar Catholic Church of Kerala. In a similar vein, several papers discussed religious syncretism and attempts to forge new, specifically Indian, forms of religiosity as types of religious dissent.

By thus probing dissent as a feature common to a variety of religious traditions, the papers presented in the conference and the additional scholarly essays included in the present volume will encourage scholars to renew and rethink their understanding of some of the major religions – both indigenous to and exogenous of India – as they have evolved and developed over time, and also help to creatively undermine rigid notions of what constitutes the core or essence of any given religious movement in South Asia, or for that matter, anywhere.

The conference, inaugurated under the Chairmanship of Professor Kunal Chakrabarti, then Chair of JNU's Centre for Historical Studies, opened with an inaugural session in which Professor Ramaswamy set forth the theme entitled 'Locating Devotion in Dissent and Dissent in Devotion', as will be adumbrated in her learned introduction to the present volume. Following the inaugural session, there were seven additional sessions presided over and moderated by a series of scholars representing JNU and other universities in India and abroad.

The theme of religious dissent is an interesting and very timely one as recent years have seen, on many fronts, an increasing interpolation of religious ideologies into the social and political life of contemporary societies. This phenomenon has had a profound impact both at the national and global levels. On the global stage, for example, there has been renewed discussion on international relations in the framework of Samuel P. Huntington's controversial concept of the 'clash of civilizations'. Huntington believed that there is no such thing as a unified global civilization but that, instead, there are a number of mutually antagonistic civilizations and that much of what characterizes at least some of these different civilizations consists of a number of mutually irreconcilable foundational religions. Thus, it has been argued that there are distinct Islamic, Hindu and Western (read Christian) civilizations that can, at best, coexist only in an uneasy tension with one other.

Although there is much evidence to contradict Huntington's thesis, it has led some conservative thinkers and politicians in the West and in India to posit irreconcilable fissures, based essentially on religious difference, that separate the supposedly distinct civilizations of the West and the East. Such views, however, inevitably ground themselves in forms of essentialism that ignore or erase the multiple different views and schools of thought that characterize all major religious systems originating in Europe and Asia and construct these systems as unchanging, monolithic forms of belief and practice. It is in this context that the critical scholarly investigation of religious dissent and difference becomes both apposite and necessary.

The question of religious devotion and dissent is of particular significance within the boundaries of the modern nation-state. Intra-religious dissent and sectarianism is, of course, a critical issue in a number of countries and, in some, has resulted in ongoing tension and religiously motivated violence. This can be seen, for example, in the case of tensions between Sunni and Shia communities in a number of predominantly Islamic countries and in countries that constitute themselves as religious states in which religious dissent comes to be seen as heresy and may be punished as a criminal offence.

It is, however, in large, secular and democratic nations, which are highly diverse ethnically, culturally and religiously, that the questions of devotion and dissent have been thrust into the clearest light through the intersection of religion and politics. Perhaps the most outstanding examples of this are India and the United States (US). In the latter, recent decades have witnessed dramatic shifts in mainstream attitudes towards many social phenomena. These, in turn, have sparked powerful reactions on the part of groups that align themselves with the more socially conservative Christian churches and communities, while more progressive churches have taken strongly opposing views. Such changes are most obvious in the areas of beliefs and practices in the areas of gender, women's rights, sexuality and reproduction. As social practice and law continue to change rapidly with regard to such issues as gay marriage, the ordination of gay and female clergy and abortion rights, some groups suffer a form of what Alvin Toffler first called 'future shock', the perception that there has been too much change in too short a period of time. Differing views on such matters, often posed in the framework of devotion to and dissent from inherited forms of orthodoxy and orthopraxis, have inevitably spilled into the political arena. Conservative groups strongly oppose increasing permissiveness in these areas and contend that they undermine the moral and spiritual foundations of what they insist is a Christian nation, while liberal churches and secular groups support such developments as evidence of progress towards equality for women and LGBT groups. For conservatives, religious orthodoxy is equated with national identity, which inheres in and is defended by 'real' or 'authentic' Americans, while those with more liberal social and religious views are seen as antipathetic and somehow alien to all that constitutes American culture and civilization.

India, too, has witnessed this kind of religious, political and social tension in recent years as globalization and modernity clash with traditional views and social practices. This can be seen, for example, in the violent opposition of conservative religious and political groups to liberalizing trends in the same areas of women's rights, sexuality and sexual orientation that have sparked controversy in the West. This can also be seen in the repeated instances of resistance to social phenomena, such as Valentine's Day celebrations, international beauty contests and the emerging clubbing and dating culture of middle-class urban youth. As in the US, conservative groups have decried these phenomena as alien to all that is real and authentic to the Indian nation. The difference between the 'Real America' of an imagined rural 'heartland' and the more liberal urban youth culture posited by conservative religious leaders and religiously focused politicians in the US is similar to that recently proposed by one of the leaders of the *Rashtriya Swayamsevak Sangh* (RSS) in the wake of the infamous Delhi gang rape incident. In that case, a distinction was made between Bharat, a nostalgically imagined, traditional, pious and village-based heartland, and India, a modern, permissive and essentially godless urban periphery.

Such ideological, social and political clashes are, in many ways, more poignant and more interesting than inter-faith or communal tensions. For they are not about the things that divide different religions but rather concern those differences that divide groups belonging to the same religion. In many cases, such dissent, sometimes amounting to schism, may be about power, that is to say, about control of or access to the religious hierarchy; in others, it may be concerned with issues of doctrine or practice, while in yet others, it may simply reflect what Freud referred to as 'the narcissism of small differences', a phenomenon found among ethnic and religious groups as well as individuals that serves to bolster and preserve a vital sense of uniqueness and superiority.

In the light of these ongoing and still unresolved issues that separate differing communities within such highly diverse religions such as Christianity, Islam and Hinduism in many countries around the globe, a scholarly project that seeks to examine and understand the reciprocally linked phenomena of devotion and dissent is an important and timely one. This volume marks a new and important step in what must be an ongoing journey of exploration into the roots and varying expressions of religious devotion, diversity and dissent in both pre-modernity and modernity alike.

In aid of advancing our knowledge of the many varieties of religious dissent, the scholars who gathered for the conference presented a broad spectrum of inquiries into the various kinds of religious dissent and their motivations across many diverse religious traditions of India, including Vaishnavism, Shaivism, Islam, Sikhism and Christianity, from medieval times down to the present day. In what follows, I will discuss some of the issues and themes of that intense and broad-ranging gathering of scholars of various religions. In so doing, I hope that I may stimulate further fruitful discussion of this critically important subject and this open-ended project.

One of the most common motives for various forms of religious dissent is the desire on the part of a segment of a community of faith to remedy what it sees as its domination and disempowerment by members of religious or clerical elites who may control access to the priesthood, to holy shrines and temples and deny it to some adherents of the faith in question. For this reason, much of the research presented at the conference and much of the discussion among those present focused on this critical area. A prime example of how spiritual and religious dissent often proceeds from the experience of exclusion by clerical elites can be found in the origins and motives of the Kabir Panth, one of the best known of the anti-elite, *nirguṇa bhakti* movements to emerge in the fifteenth and sixteenth centuries. As discussed in the contribution of David Lorenzen, the Panth was itself grounded in dissent against the rigid socio-religious hierarchies and orthodoxies that characterized the principal religious traditions, Hindu and Muslim, as they existed in the era in which Kabir lived and in which his and other non-caste-based *panth*s emerged in North India. In his discussion, Lorenzen takes on and contests a number of theories concerning the origins and nature of Kabir's particular form of dissent and spiritual egalitarianism as they have been propounded by scholars such as Dumont, Moffat, Barthwas, Dvivedi and Vaudeville. Lorenzen argues instead for the views of Agarwal and concludes by noting that the impetus towards dissent that drove the formation of such movements as the Kabir Panth – that is, the rigid anti-egalitarian and caste/class-based socio-religious structures of pre-modernity – has, at least to a great extent, been weakened in the era of the foundation of the modern Indian state on the principles of religious and civil tolerance and equality.

The social aspect of religious dissent and how it often militates towards a more egalitarian spiritual community and society in modernity is further illuminated by the contribution of Yogesh Snehi. He provides an interesting diachronic study of the popular Sufi shrines of Punjab and how, in post-partition India, they have become the sites not only for veneration of the *pir*s but also for vigorous dissent in making strong claims for caste mobility and for a specifically Hindu–Muslim syncretism. Many of these spiritual seekers and saints wrote songs that dissented from the rigorous caste structures of Hindu society by urging that all groups, rich and poor, belonged to one spiritual community. These tensions between prosperous spiritual elites and impoverished communities of faith are the crux of the discussion of the struggle for social justice on the part of Dalit communities in Kerala with special reference to figures such as Narayana Guru and Ayyankali. This discussion is extended and enriched by Professor Udaya Kumar who draws our attention more closely to

Narayana Guru and the particular nature of his idiom of egalitarian spiritual discourse.

The way in which religious dissension often arises from social discontent is evident in the number of cases in which dissenting movements begin among the disenfranchised and downtrodden caste groups, generally referred to in modernity by the term 'Dalit'. Professor Raj Kumar Hans illustrates how this phenomenon can occur even within such an ostensibly egalitarian and originally dissenting religious movement such as Sikhism. He brings out the little-studied history of the dissent represented within Sikhism by Dalit saint poets such as Jeevan Singh, Sadhu Wazir Singh, Giani Ditt Singh and Sadhu Daya Singh, all of whom ultimately contributed significantly to the corpus of Sikh religious poetry.

Professor Sumanta Banerjee, together with writer and researcher Surojit Sen, contributes significantly to the discussion on marginalized groups in their study of the situation of the contemporary fakirs of West Bengal whose lives and music follow the Sufi ideal of devotion to and unity with a god who resides within the human soul. As in the case of the Chishti Sufis in the era of Nizam-ud-Din Auliya, the modern fakirs have, since the eighteenth century, faced hostility and persecution on the part of the orthodox clergy for their songs, which express their dissent against what they see as the oppressive social regimes of the orthodoxy. Disturbingly, the two scholars report that they receive no protection by the state in the face of harassment and violence. Several of these cases open up a wider discussion of what happens to successful movements of dissent over time. For, looked at from a broad historical perspective, many great religious movements themselves began as forms of dissent only to become established orthodoxies in their own right. This can be seen in the origins and history of Christianity, which began as an egalitarian and anti-ritualistic Jewish devotional sect and spread to form a large number of established churches around the world, many of which themselves become the targets of dissent as, for example, the Roman Catholic Church at the time of the Protestant Reformation. Drawing examples from the non-conformist Nath Siddha and Charpatnath traditions of medieval Punjab, Professor Mahesh Sharma shows how dissent is a dynamic rather than a static phenomenon. This, in turn, raises the question as to what it means when dissent itself becomes a form of dogma and then may inspire successive waves of dissent.

Socially based dissent in Indian religion has not always been directed against Indian spiritual authorities. In some cases, it was derived not so much from caste-based inequalities as from ethnic disparities. In the case of what might be viewed as a form of religious proto-nationalism, Professor Pius Malekandathil presents us with the engaging history of the struggles between Indian clergy and European missionaries for control of the South Indian Saint Thomas Christian Church in eighteenth century Kerala. His research is based on a fascinating travelogue entitled *Varthamanapusthakam*, composed in the 1790s by Father (Fr) Thomas Paremakkal as an account of his travels with his friend Mar Joseph Kariyattil to Madras, Africa, South America and Europe. The motive for the trip was largely to inform the Pope in Rome of the discrimination and persecution that Kerala Christians were suffering at the hands of European Carmelite missionaries and to challenge the authority of the latter. Dissenting from the top-down authoritarianism of the European church and its European missionaries, Fr Paremakkal argued for a return to an earlier and more culturally syntonic form of church governance in the form of more democratic institutions such as the *yogam*s or representative bodies.

The issue of religious syncretism as a special form of dissent, as raised by Snehi, is an interesting one. Efforts to bridge the divisions that divide two different faiths have a long and complex history. They may be classified as dissent in that they seek to contest the exclusivist claims frequently made by the authorities of various religious traditions. Attempts to break down these rigid distinctions amount to, in effect, dissension directed towards two religious hierarchies. The best-known example of such a move from Indian religious history is Emperor Akbar's top-down effort to promote his syncretic *Din-i-Ilahi*, a 'Divine Faith' that would somehow bridge the gulf between Hinduism and Islam. The failure of his approach points to the difficulty of such attempts at syncretism. A more modern example of this is provided by Gispert-Sauch and Cornelius Ekka who discuss the fascinating career of the Brahmo Samajist, educator and freedom fighter Brahmabandhab Upadhyay, who converted from Hinduism to Catholicism and considered himself to be a 'Hindu-Christian'. Upadhyay's efforts to create a syncretic and specifically Indian form of Christianity were not much more successful than the efforts of Akbar. They led to both his persecution by the authorities of the Catholic Church and to rejection by his former Hindu friends and colleagues. His life illuminated the delicate and often difficult area of religious syncretism, which can be seen as dissent on the part of the orthodox establishments of both religions in question.

As suggested earlier in the brief discussion on contemporary socio-religious dissention and controversy in India and the US, one of the other great sources of dissent, along with class and caste-based discrimination and disempowerment, is the denigration and exclusion based on gender. Many of the major world religious traditions are deeply rooted in strongly patriarchal social systems, and their spiritual practices and clerical hierarchies are reflections of these systems. As a result, many religious communities assign an inferior role to women or may exclude them entirely from the ranks of religious officiants. This can be seen in the history of the monastic orders of Buddhism, Hinduism and Jainism in India; the early exclusion of women from learning or even hearing the Vedas; and in the contemporary tensions within the highly patriarchal Catholic and Anglican churches over the exclusion of women from the priesthood.

This critical issue lies at the heart of a number of examples of religious dissent in India. Drawing on the *vachana*s of the medieval Virashaiva saints, several of whom were women, Professor Ramaswamy opens an interesting discussion on the seminal role of erotically oriented mysticism in the theology of the Lingayat movement. Resultant social tensions were the result of the different registers of the domain of spirituality and that of a largely patriarchal social order. It was also, equally, a consequence of shifting attitudes towards gender relations within a cathartic devotional movement like Virashaivism.

The JNU conference, so excellently conceived and organized by Professor Ramaswamy, and raising as it did so many seminal issues regarding the social, political, spiritual and gender-based sources of dissent in the religious traditions of India, thus constituted a significant contribution to the study of the complex religious history of India from antiquity to modernity spanning many of the languages, regions and spiritual traditions of the vast subcontinent. It is hoped that the present volume, under her editorship, will serve to bring the stimulating presentations of the participants to a far wider audience than those who had the good fortune to attend.

Robert P. Goldman
Department of South and Southeast Asian Studies
University of California, Berkeley

Preface

I am grateful to the many women I have interacted with in the course of three decades of my research on spirituality. Of them, it can be truly said that dissent from orthodox understandings of religion, and the shattering of liminalities in the spiritual domain, was the warp and weft of their very existence. Although my study focused on women, this would be equally true of spiritual masters like Ramakrishna Paramahamsa, Ramana Maharshi, Narayana Guru or the Sufi masters, Bulleh Shah or Lalon Fakir.

One of my early interactions was with Gomati Rajangam of Varanasi, an erudite Sanskrit and Hindi scholar and author of a commentary on the *Kasi Khandam.* Niece of the Tamil poet and nationalist leader Subramanya Bharatiyar, Gomati was married into an affluent family. The untimely demise of her husband brought home to the young woman all the travails and cruelties of widowhood. She told me that she travelled ticketless to Kasi, believing that it was better to die in Kasi than live the ignoble life imposed on her by the male relatives who robbed her of all the property. She lived on for the next 75 years in her chosen place on the Kedarghat of the Ganga and her everyday life was a celebration of the presence of god.

In the case of Gomati Rajangam and many like her, both men and women, dissent was not an oppositional category to be juxtaposed against norms but the very definition of true spirituality. In the three decades I have spent encountering and interacting with such figures, either in the Himalayas, on the river banks of Rishikesh and Varanasi or in the hermitage of Ramanashramam in Tiruvannamalai, this truth has been borne upon me and my heart goes out to these 'devout dissenters' with overflowing gratitude.

My forays in spiritual encounters and interactions led me eventually to frame a course which invited students to write term papers from the areas of their own intellectual engagement with this issue. The result of these classes was the recording of a rich tapestry of vibrant spiritual/devotional movements which went beyond stereotypes. My warm gratitude therefore goes out to the MA batches in the Jawaharlal Nehru University (JNU) from 2009 onwards who did this course with me.

My classroom engagements led me to organize an international conference on 'Devotion and Dissent in Indian History'. The present volume brings together some of the essays presented at this conference as also some fresh ones.

My academic engagements in recent months have perforce been intermeshed with personal soul-searching as I lost my mother, my sister and my niece within a couple of months. As I sit down to work, my vision is at times blurred by tears. It is to these dear departed ones that this book is dedicated. I would like to thank Devaki Khanna (my student), Dr Ranjeeta Dutta and the editorial team of Cambridge University Press, India for giving the book its final shape.

Vijaya Ramaswamy

Introduction

Locating Devotion in Dissent and Dissent in Devotion

A Thematic Overview

Akka Mahadevi, a prominent figure of the Veerashaiva Bhakti movement of the twelfth century Karnataka.
Image courtesy: Vijaya Ramaswamy

Introduction

Vijaya Ramaswamy

Religion has played a Janus-faced role in historical societies all over the world. Religion, on the one hand, has served as the instrument of fundamentalist forces in religion, strengthening and reinforcing canonical stereotypes. It also has the dubious distinction of providing moral justification for acts of violence and terror in the name of religion. On the other hand, religion, especially spirituality, has also been a palpable phase of liberation theologies, such as Protestantism. It has been perceived as a cathartic force providing openings for voices of dissent and resistance. In contrast to sectarian movements which have been fundamentalist in terms of their ideology and locked in schisms and conflicts with those who worshipped 'differently', dissent movements within devotional streams were characterized by the qualities of universalism, humanism and love which cut across communal, caste and gender lines.

Beginning from Marx, the entire Marxian tradition has situated religion within the framework of society. An exemplar of this ideological position in the Indian context is D.D. Kosambi, the doyen of Marxist Indian historians. Many of his essays, such as 'The Social and Economic Aspects of the Bhagawad Gita' and especially the sub-essay 'The Social Function of Bhakti', reflect the firm location of religion as a socio-economic precipitate and *bhakti* as a reflection of the feudal order. To quote a typical passage:

> The essence of fully developed feudalism is the chain of personal loyalty which binds retainer to chief, tenant to Lord and baron to king or emperor. Not loyalty in the abstract but with a secure foundation in the means and relations of production: land ownership, military service, tax-collection and the conversion of local produce into commodities through the magnates...To hold this type

> of society and its state together, the best religion is one which emphasizes the role of bhakti, personal faith, even though the object of devotion may have clearly visible flaws.[1]

Kosambi's essay, 'The Social Functions of Bhakti', thus clearly reflects the firm location of religion as a social precipitate and *bhakti* as a reflection of the medieval feudal order. The Marxist position on devotion and devotional movements can also be seen in Nandi[2] and Veluthat and Narayanan[3], to name only some important books and essays that reflect the classic Marxian frameworks which places religion and devotion squarely within the material realm, socio-economic dimensions of feudalism and the politics of exploitation.

What the present set of essays attempt to do is to critique the Marxian position on the role of religion in society. This does not mean that the essays deny the Marxist position altogether or attempt to replace it with another dogma of dissent as an essential component of religion. What the anthology seeks to achieve is to provide a counter-perspective to the well-known and well-trodden school of Marxist historiography which locates religion firmly within the existing socio-economic order. However, I have not conceived of a tailored closure to these two positions and there are essays in the present volume, such as Gunasekharan's essay (Chapter 5) on the Siddhas, which explore and eventually reject the notion of devotion as being embedded in dissent, both religious and social.

Despite the image of Janus which I have invoked, conjuring up a vision of religion oscillating between the bipolarities of 'strangulation' and 'liberation', many of the essays here are engaged with the ambivalences which characterize the role of religion in various societies at different points of time. I have invoked the Janus-faced imagery of religion not in order to juxtapose religious conformism and religious dissent but to counter the almost monodimensional representation of religion within the 'secular' tradition as 'intellectually bankrupt' and coloured by fundamentalist ideology. Even at the popular level, religion is imaged as reflecting orthodox and fundamentalist ideologies, be

---

[1] D.D. Kosambi, *Myth and Reality: Studies in the Formation of Indian Culture* (Bombay: Popular Prakashan, 2005), 31–32.

[2] R.N. Nandi, *Religious Institutions and Cults in the Deccan* (Delhi: Motilal Banarsidass, 1973); *Social Roots of Religion in Ancient India* (Calcutta and Delhi: K.P. Bagchi and Co., 1986).

[3] M.G.S Narayanan and Kesavan Veluthat, 1978 'The Bhakti Movement in South India' in S.C. Malik, ed. *Indian Movements: Some Aspects of Dissent, Protest and Reform*, Simla, The Indian Institute of Advanced Study, 32–45.

it the Islamic 'jihad' or its counterpart 'Hindutava'. It is thus seen as counter to secularism. The entire aim of this volume is to 'complicate' the issue of devotion and dissent in Indian history. The Janus imagery is intended to bring into focus the rich tapestry of grey which distinguishes the location of religion in Indian society. Clearly, the idea here is not to project an oversimplified model of 'conformity versus non-conformity' since many of the essays deal precisely with the presence of non-conformity in seeming conformity and vice versa.

Devotion and Dissent: A Historical Contextualization

The entire tradition of devotionalism in India bears testimony to the complex relationship between conformism and non-conformism, between intense devotion and outspoken dissent, resulting in images which are neither black nor white but extremely rich tapestries of grey ranging from the very dense to the almost translucent. Some of the essays in this volume seek to explore these shades of grey, while others attempt to juxtapose the twin notions of devotion with conformism against dissent embedded in devotion. As was made clear at the outset, while being alert to the ubiquitous presence of grey in the long and sometimes tortuous course taken by these devotional movements, the purpose of this volume is to track dissent in devotion rather than conformism in devotion.

Buddhism arose in the sixth century BC as a heterodox movement challenging Brahmanical hierarchies, especially in the context of caste. However, the Buddhist position on gender was much more ambivalent. Buddhism initially refused entry to women nuns on grounds situation within a typically patriarchal discourse and the Buddha is said to have told his chief disciple, Ananda, that Buddhism would be short-lived if women were to enter the religious order.[4]

However, these images of women as impediments to spirituality get complicated by the many voices of dissent within the Buddhist tradition itself.[5]

---

[4] *Mahanibbana Sutra* in *Dialogues* (London: Luzac and Co., 1966), Book II, 154 vide Diana Paul, *Women in Buddhism – Images of the Feminine in Mahayana Tradition* (Berkeley: University of California Press, 1979), 7–8. The ambivalent attitude towards women is even more explicit in the *Bhikkuni Khanda* of I.B. Horner, trans., *Vinaya Pitaka* (London: Luzac and Co., 1963).

[5] Charles Luk, ed. and trans., *Vimalakirtinirdesa Sutra* (Berkeley and London: Shambala Publications, 1972); Alex Wayman and Hideko Wayman, trans., *Srimaladevi Simhanada Sutram* (The Lion's Roar of Queen Srimala) (Delhi: Motilal Banarsidass, 1990).

The *Vimalakirtinirdesa Sutra,* a Mahayana text belonging roughly to the fifth century AD, makes the point that maleness or femaleness is immaterial in the attainment of salvation. The goddess, by her supernatural powers, changes the spiritual seeker Sariputra into a likeness of herself, that is, she herself takes on the form of Sariputra. She tells him:

> Sariputra, if you can change into a female form then all women can also change into men. Just as you are not really a woman but only appear to be female in form, they are fundamentally not women. Hence the Buddha said, 'All things are neither male nor female.'[6]

Similar fuzziness characterized the place of women within Jainism. A brilliant analysis of the ambivalence within the various sectarian streams in Jainism is to be found in Padmanabha Jaini's *Gender and Salvation: Jaina Debates on the Spiritual Liberation of Women.*[7] In the present anthology, the dissent within Buddhism has been tracked by K.T.S. Sarao in the context of Buddha's leading disciple Devadatta's points of departure from the path and ideology of the Buddha (Chapter 2).

The best examples of the cathartic forces within religion would be the many devotional movements within the broad trope of the Bhakti movement, which covers the period from the seventh to the seventeenth centuries. Devotion and dissent have gone hand in hand within many of the religious movements in India, such as the Bhagavata movement of the Tamil country; the Virashaivite or Lingayat movement of Karnataka; and the Varkari movements of Maharashtra, which is not to say that these movements did not have the strongly orthodox elements within them. The chequered path to *bhakti* within the Bhagavata movement, imbued by notions of devotion, dissent and caste dominance, is reflected in one of Champakalakshmi's early essays written in 1996.[8]

The beginnings of the devotional movements can be traced to the Bhagavata movement in South India commencing around the seventh century with the Nayanars and the Alvars. The Vaishnavite Alvars and the Shaivite Nayanars came largely from the lower castes. Tiruppanazhwar was a Panar by caste

---

[6] Luk, *Vimalkirtinirdesa Sutra*, VII, 78.

[7] Padmanabha S. Jaini, *Gender and Salvation: Jaina Debates on the Spiritual Liberation of Women* (Berkeley: University of California Press, 1991).

[8] *Devotion* and *Dissent* to *Dominance*: The Bhakti of the Tamil Alwars and Nayanars', 135–63 in R. Champakalakshmi, 2011. *Religion, Tradition and Ideology: Pre-colonial South India,* Oxford Collected Essays (Delhi: *Oxford University Press*).

and Vaishnavite hagiographical tradition clearly locates him as an outcaste. Tirumazhisai Azhwar seems to have had low-caste origins. Among the Nayanars, Nandanar (Paraiya – landless agriculturists), Kannappa Nayanar (Vedar – hunter), Tirukurippu Nayanar (Vannar – washerman) and some others were either low castes or outcastes. While the Advaita (Vedantic monism) of Shankara, the Vishishtadvaita of Ramanuja and the Dwita (dualism) of Madhava represented the orthodox streams within devotionalism, a movement like the Srivaishnavism of Ramanuja also had a fairly prominent low-caste presence such as Pillai Uranga Villi Dasar and Maran Eri Nambi.

The visibility and audibility of non-Brahmanical groups within these movements is however complicated by two aspects. First, upper-caste non-Brahmins, who were both powerful and affluent, were very much a part of the Bhakti movement which ipso facto takes away the seemingly 'subaltern' character of these movements. Second, upper-caste/Brahmanical (if not Brahmin) forces were clearly involved in the writing of the lives of these saintly figures, as exemplified by the *Periyapuranam*, the hagiographies of Shaivite saints compiled by Chekkizhar Peruman in the twelfth century.

Aspects of Brahmanical as well lower-caste/outcaste dissent within the Bhagavata movement of the Alvars and Nayanars is encapsulated in this anthology in the two biographical essays by Ranjeeta Dutta (Ramanuja Dasar; Chapter 4) and T.S. Satyanath (Kannappa Nayanar; Chapter 3).

The spiritual realm has provided unexpected spaces for the marginalized voices in our collective social past. The voices of the 'Dalit' saints are clearly audible in the Virashaivite or Lingayat movement in twelfth century Karnataka. Although the movement was pioneered by Basavanna, a Brahmin, many of the Shiv *sharana*s and Shiv *sharane*s (male and female Lingayat saints respectively) came from the working class, and quite a few of them belonged to the untouchable castes like the Medara and Madivala (basket makers and washermen). A recent anthology of the *vachana*s of Lingayat saints brings to the fore the anxieties and socio-spiritual responses of the downtrodden to the religious and social dominance of the upper castes.[9] The Virashaivite movement was also remarkable for the accommodation of women within it.[10] In the case of women, spiritual self-expression cut across caste divides since women's

[9] H.S. Shivaprakash, *I Keep Vigil of Rudra: The Vachanas* (Delhi: Penguin Books, 2010).

[10] Leela Mullatti, *The Bhakti Movement and the Status of Women* (Delhi: Abhinav Publications, 1989); Vijaya Ramaswamy, *Divinity and Deviance: Women in Virasaivism* (Delhi: Oxford University Press, 1996).

spiritual emergence encounters and challenges gender oppression which cuts across both class and caste. In their quest for transcendence, women, consciously or unconsciously, shatter social and patriarchal limits. My own essay in this anthology seeks to locate women within the Virasaivite movement focusing on the centrality of the love motif (Chapter 6).

The Dasara movement of sixteenth century Karnataka represented by such voices as that of Kanakadasa, belonging to the Kuruba or shepherd caste, indicates that marginalized voices did not always go unheeded or unrecorded. The vibrancy of the Dasa musical compositions arises from poetic self-expression, which clearly ignores or deliberately cuts across caste hierarchies.

The Varkari movements in the neighbouring state of Maharashtra were spread over five centuries from the thirteenth to the seventeenth. Beginning with the Mahanubhava movement under Chakradhar, the devotional movements in this region entered their classical phase under the Varkari saints like Jnandev, Chokhamela, Namdev, Janabai and Muktabai. The last Varkari saint in the classical stream was Tukaram. The final phase of the Bhakti movement in Maharashtra was under Samartha Ramdas (said to be the guru of the Maratha chief Chatrapati Shivaji) in the seventeenth century. The medium of communication of ideas and popular devotion was spoken Marathi and the mode of dissent was best seen in the annual surge towards Pandarpur which was a confluence cutting across caste and gender divides. A recent work on untouchable saints records the significance of saints like Chokhamela, his wife Soyrabai and others within the Varkari movement.[11] Rohini Mokashi-Punekar's essay, 'Dissenting Voices: Continuities in the Varkari Tradition' (Chapter 7) fleshes out these elements of dissent within the Varkari tradition which Jayant Lele, in his thought-provoking Marathi essay, described as 'revolutionary'.[12]

Raidas, Kabir and other saint poets reflect the powerful nature of lower caste and Dalit presence in medieval North Indian society and the cultural churning that played a catalytic role in social change. The writings of Kabir, Dadu and Raidas overturned Brahmanical superiority by upholding the principle of monism and humanism. It must however be pointed out that this humanism seems to have encountered a roadblock when it came to dealing with women's issues. Here their attitudes were clearly ambivalent. The devotional verses of Tulsidas are less radical and much more in tune with societal ordering. David

[11] Eleanor Zelliot and Rohini Mokashi-Punekar, *Untouchable Saints: An Indian Phenomenon* (New Delhi: Manohar, 2005).

[12] Jayant Lele, 'Varlari Sampradayateel Krantikarak Aashay', *Samay Prabodhan Patrika*, no. 117, 1991.

Lorenzen's insightful essay on dissent in Kabir and the Kabir Panth reflects this cultural churning in society (Chapter 8).

Both women (cutting across caste–class distinctions) and Dalits have also made radical entries into devotional movements, such as Sikhism in the Punjab region, in the late medieval period. The circular movement of Sikhism into the patriarchal fold, partially if not wholly, does not take away its radical potential in its early years. An interesting essay on the Dalit presence in the devotional movements in Punjab is by Raj Kumar Hans. His essay, 'Devotion and Dissent of Punjabi Dalit *Sant* Poets', records the presence of these marginalized voices in the realm of religion during the colonial period (Chapter 9).

What predominates in *bhakti* and Sufi literatures is a spirit of radicalism that informs spiritual liberation. This social dissent and radicalism is most clearly perceivable in the poetry of both women and low-caste/outcaste saints. Sufism, which in India has, broadly speaking, constituted the popular phase of Islam, is exemplified by two essays in the present anthology: Yogesh Snehi's essay, 'Dissenting the Dominant: Caste Mobility, Ritual Practice and Popular Sufi Shrines in Contemporary Punjab' (Chapter 13); and the essays on the fakir movement of Bengal conceived of as complementary pieces and authored by Bannerji and Sen (Chapter 11). Sumanta Bannerji provides the historical overview of the fakirs who were persecuted by the British regime, because their mystical socio-religious and political non-conformism made them a bigger threat than the clearly identifiable dissenters. Surojit Sen, who has lived among the fakirs, focuses on their ideological dissent essentially through the mode of fakir music exemplified by such saintly figures as Lalon Shah (Lallon Shah). Raziuddin Aquil's essay on music as a mode of dissent within the Islamic tradition complements Surojit Sen's piece on fakir music (Chapter 12).

Morphology of Dissent

Dissent within devotional movements has manifested itself consistently in mysticism both of language and body – the former revealing itself in outpourings which being 'mystical' sound 'nonsensical' if weighed against the patriarchal idiom or 'the language of the Father'. The language of dissent in physical terms was usually couched in 'bridal mysticism' cutting across caste and gender. That is, both male and female saints averred themselves to be brides of god. Mysticism, going beyond religion, aspires to an intimate union with the divine. This union has 'love' at its core.

It is necessary to add that bridal mysticism cuts across gender divisions and male saints also regard themselves as the brides of the Lord. When male saints adopt the path of mystic love to attain union with the godhead, they often resort to transvestism. Therefore, although the language of erotic love is common to both male and female saints, men in the adoption of this mode resort to the female voice in order to assume what patriarchal society dubs the feminine qualities of erotic love and passion. Some outstanding examples of 'male' bridal mysticism can be seen in Kabir in medieval North India, in Nammalvar and Tirumangai Alvar within the Vaishnavite Alwar tradition and Manikkavachagar in the Shaivite tradition.

Tirumangai Alvar says that while he is languishing for God, even the soft breeze feels like a burning gale. The body loses weight and his (her?) bracelets drop down. The crisis is reached when Alwar is consumed by flaming love.[13] He decides on the ancient practice of *madal eruthal* to expose the cruelty of his beloved. Nammalvar similarly threatens God if He/She does not accept the plea for union. There seems to be a blurring of gender identities here and not merely gender crossings. While the saint's words suggest a 'woman in love', the ancient Tamil practice of *madal eruthal* is associated with men. In this practice, any man whose love has been spurned, mounts an ass and parades his love in front of his beloved, usually ending his own life. It is clear here that just like the saint himself, God is also both male and female. In fact, Nammalvar in one erotic poem talks of 'communing' with Her (God) 'in the nakedness of her beauty'.[14]

Male bridal mysticism within the Christian tradition is exemplified in St John of the Cross. In his book, *Living Flame of Love*, the saint writes:

> In that sweet drink of God, in which the soul is imbibed in him, she most willingly and with intense delight surrenders herself wholly to him, in the desire to be totally his and never to possess in herself anything other than him. God causes in this union the purity and perfection necessary for such surrender. And since he transforms her in himself, he makes her entirely his own and empties her of all she possesses other than him.[15]

---

[13] Tirumangai Alvar, II:7:VIII:1,3,5 etc., vide Vijaya Ramaswamy, *Walking Naked: Women, Society, Spirituality in South India*, Second Revised Edition (Shimla: Indian Institute of Advanced Studies, 2007), 128.

[14] Ibid.

[15] (C, 27, 6) sic. The bridal mysticism of St John of the Cross is very well discussed in Richard P. Hardy, 'Embodied Love in John of the Cross', in *Carmelite Studies VI: John of the Cross*, ed. Steven Payne, OCD and accessed 2 November 2009,

In the present anthology, mine perhaps is the only essay which specifically focuses on love as a powerful mode of dissent, drawing upon 'women in love', within the Virashaivite tradition (Chapter 6).

Music as a mode of expression of both creativity and protest has always occupied an uneasy space in orthodox Islam, while it is an essential component of Sufi ideology. An oral tradition of the period of Emperor Aurangzeb says that the musicians of Delhi, frustrated at the ban on music and the use of musical instruments, took out a symbolic funeral procession on the streets of Delhi. The essay, 'Music and Related Practices in Chishti Sufism: Celebrations and Contestations', by Raziuddin Aquil incisively analyzes these tensions and their resolutions (Chapter 12).

It is interesting that within the *bhakti* mode, transgression and transcendence have often gone together. This might seem an oxymoron since those who seek transcendence or liberation do not really concern themselves with social protest and tangentially with transgression. Nevertheless, the lives of many saints bear testimony to the fact that they have covertly or overtly challenged the social order, whether class and caste hierarchies, or patriarchy or any other mode of social or political oppression, which has stood in the way of their spiritual quest. Walking naked is one of the most powerful examples in which spiritual transcendence and social transgression share a symbiotic relationship.

The ultimate act of dissent against social order and moral codes was the act of walking naked by both men and women within the devotional mode. While male nudity or the Digambara saint gained a certain degree of acceptance and institutionalization through certain orders of the Naga sects or the Dashanami orders, the nakedness of women saints was seen as social transgression of the worst kind. The interesting combination of transgression and transcendence can be seen in women like Akka Mahadevi or the fourteenth century Kashmiri saint, Lal Ded. Lalla (Lallesvari) of Kashmir danced naked and sang in her *vak*:

> Lalla, think not of things that are without
> fix upon thy inner self thy thought
> so shall thou be freed from doubt
> dance then, Lalla, clad but in the skys
> Air and sky, what garment is more fair?
> cloth, says custom, (but) does that satisfy?[16]

---

http//www.ispublications.org. The article is based on his major work, *Search for Nothing: The Life of John of the Cross* (New York, NY: Crossroad, 1982). Published by Washington Province of Discalced Carmelites, Inc.1992.

[16] Prem Nath Bazaz, *Daughters of the Vitasta* (New Delhi: Pamposh Publications, 1959), 133.

It is a historical truism to state that society has often felt the need to dissent against dissenters when a movement that originates as a challenge to an oppressive social order itself settles down into a condition of social and moral stasis. This constant critiquing of a radical movement that has lost its edge happens from both within and without. The Nath Sampradaya, like the Virashaivite movement, was, in its initial phase, perceived as a radical socio-religious movement but the very fact of its condensation into a *sampradaya* or traditional order meant that it had lost its radical edge. Mahesh Sharma's essay, 'Protest and Counter-protest: The Nath Siddhas and Charpatnath', reflects this dialectical process in society.

The Language of Dissent

It is important to note that mysticism and mystical language in its monotheistic manifestation could go beyond the language of love, which is still within the realm of human comprehension, into the language of unintelligible symbolisms and metaphors, what psychoanalysts would equate with the 'semiotic', the language of 'mother desire'. In a world structured in patriarchal language, the language of mystics would be equated with the 'gibberish of the mad, the retarded and the schizophrenic.' Women mystics like Janabai speak of 'the bride coming out of the bridegroom', 'an ant flying up and swallowing the sun', etc. The language of Allamma Prabhu, the Virashaivite Shiva *sharana*, is known for its mysticism and esoteric quality.

Another feature of the language of dissent is the flaunting of shamelessness, a characteristic that one encounters in many of the saint poets, especially women like Andal, Lal Ded, Janabai and Meerabai. Just as Chokhamela, Soyrabai, Janabai, Tukaram and others represent the dissenting elements within the Varkari movements, Meerabai, Raidas and Kabir constitute important facets of dissent and protest within medieval religious movements in the northern belt.

Meera represented one kind of defiance when she walked on the streets and sang and danced exulting that 'Meera dances with anklets on her feet, defiant of worldly censure or family shame'. In an era when only dancing girls danced with anklets on the feet, for someone like Meera – who was a Rajput princess and supposed to live behind the veil – to dance in a like manner was radical deviance indeed! In her celebrated composition which begins with '*Pag gunguroo bandh* Meera *nache re*', literally 'Meera dances with anklets on her feet', she says:

> I will dance for Giridhar
> I care not for worldly shame or family pride.

Elsewhere, she acknowledges that 'By keeping company with saints, I have lost the respect of society'. [17] To quote Meera:

> Rana to me even this shame seems sweet
> Let anyone insult or laugh
> I walk with firm unfaltering steps
> When I talk with saints, wicked people rebuke me
> But Meera's Lord is Giridhar Gopal
> May the wicked feed the kitchen flames ('*durjan jale angiti*')[18]

It is noteworthy that even now, in parts of conservative Rajasthan, especially Mewar, Meera does not enjoy social respectability and the singing of her songs is not encouraged.

Raidas was a *chamar* by caste whose profession was working with leather or animal hides. Yet, Raidas' devotion led to a complete inversion of social hierarchies and ritual pollution. To quote Raidas:

> In whatever family a good Vaishnav is found,
> Whether they be high caste or outcaste, lord or pauper,
> The world will know the one by his flawless fragrance.
> Whether one is Brahmin or Vaisya, Shudra or Kshathriya
> Dom, Chandal or Malech,
> Through the worship of the Lord, one becomes pure, and
> liberates the self and both family lines;[19]

The language of dissent is clearly visible within the Siddha tradition of South India as well as the Nath Sampradaya of the northern belt, especially the region referred to as Himachal Pradesh today. Mahesh Sharma's essay (Chapter 10) however looks at dissent within dissent movements, like the Charpatnath movement. Both Mahesh Sharma and Gunasekharan, who writes on 'Dissent Within: Dissent and Devotion in Tamil *Cittar* Tradition' (Chapter 5), point out how dissent itself became dogma in course of time and had in its turn been challenged.

---

[17] 'Anklets on the Feet: Women Saints in Medieval Indian Society', *The Indian Historical Review,* vol.XVII, Nos 1–2, 60–89, 60.

[18] Vijaya Ramaswamy, 1991, 'Anklets on the Feet: Women Saints in Medieval Indian Society', *The Indian Historical Review,* vol.XVII, Nos 1–2, 60–89, 84.

[19] Anne Murphy vide Eleanor Zelliot and Rohini Punekar-Mokashi, *Untouchable Saints: An Indian Phenomenon* (Delhi: Manohar Publishers, 2005), 197.

Transvestism and androgyny as stages in spirituality can be located somewhere between erotic sublimation at the lower level and gender transcendence at the highest level. Akka Mahadevi, in describing herself as 'female though in name', claims that she is actually 'the male principle'. Basavanna in a revealing *vachana* says:

> Look here, dear fellow:
> I wear these men's clothes
> only for you.
> Sometimes I am man
> Sometimes I am woman.[20]

Socio-Religious Dissent

The voice of resistance comes in the voices of women and low-caste saints within and outside devotional movements. It is noteworthy that the entire notion of the *bhakta kula* or community of devotees undercuts social hierarchies and simultaneously, transcends it. A beautiful verse by the Shaivite Nayanar saint of the twelfth century called Tirunavukkarasar or Appar explains this position thus in a *Tevaram* hymn:

> With all bodily blemishes, ugly,
> Inflicted with leprosy,
> The Pulaya skinning the cow and eating its flesh
> If he is devoted to Him who is adorned
> with Ganga in his locks,
> To him I will offer my prostrations.[21]

Texts of Virashaivism are most useful in understanding and mapping the textual tradition of religious dissent. Virashaivism or the Lingayat movement originated in twelfth century Kalyana in Karnataka under Basavanna, a Brahmin, but was anti-caste and stridently anti-Brahmanical. It also gave both visibility and audibility to women and the lower castes, especially craft groups.

Devara Dasimayya mocks at spurious asceticism: 'What is the use of shaving your head unless you shave your mind of its impurities? It is like a cat quietly

---

[20] A.K. Ramanujan, *Speaking of Siva,* Harmondsworth, London, Penguin, 1973, vachana:703, 87.

[21] *Tevaram*: 7182 vide Ramaswamy, *Walking Naked*, 114.

"meditating" in a monastery, no sooner a rat is sighted in the corner than it pounces on its prey! What mistake the hair on your head have done for you? Shave off the evil desires of your mind, first! What use is the saffron robe unless your mind is pure?'[22]

Virashaivism makes very strong anti-Brahmanical and anti-caste statements. Some of the most virulent anti-Brahminical statements come from Kalavve:

> In thirty-two lakhs of years in Kritayuga
> they, (the Brahmins) killed elephants for homa (sacrificial fire)
> In sixteen lakhs of years in tretayuga
> they killed buffaloes for the sacred fire
> In the eight lakhs of Dvapara yuga
> they offered into the fire horses
> In the four lakhs of the kaliyuga
> they now offer goats (hota)
> Brahmins have killed so many
> although as every Shiva bhakta knows
> 'anoraniyan mahatomahiyan' God is smaller than the smallest, larger than the largest.
>
> (*note:* This line is a straight upanishadic utterance and reveals the strong sanskritic–Agamic influence on Virasaivism)
> Therefore one who offers salulations to Brahmins will be born as a pig for eighty four lakhs of years (!) (Kalavve: V: 12 in Hiremath: 216: 101)[23]

Within Islam, the voice of dissent, which goes in tandem with humanism and a love that transcends religion and community, is encountered in many of the Sufi cults, although some of them chose to institutionalize themselves and align with the state whether the Deccani sultanates or the Turko-Afghan state in the North or the Mughal state. After the demise of Hazrat Muhammad, institutional Islam (Shariat) took to the task of world domination by converting people to Islam through religious wars. As a counterpoint, *marfat* or non-institutional Islam reached far and wide in search of human love by spreading the message of love and compassion. The Sufis conveyed their dissent through unorthodox styles of living; through music and dance and, above all, through their mystical spiritual poetry.

---

[22] Devara Dasimayya, vachana, Shivamurthy Shivacharya, *Religion and Society at Crossroads* (Virasaivite Mutt, Sirigere, Karnataka,1990), 44.

[23] The translation quoted here is from Ramaswamy, *Divinity and Deviance*, 55–56.

I would like to conclude this section on foregrounding of 'Devotion and Dissent' by quoting the *Paichalur Padigam* which are verses attributed to woman saint of the fifteenth century known only as 'Uttiranallur Nangai'. She was a pariah woman who married a Brahmin and when the Brahmin community came to punish the erring couple with death, she responded with the most powerful verses of dissent in medieval times. I shall quote just two of them:

Brahmins of the village gather
build a wall[24].
Dip in the river
and pour ghee on fire:
Like frogs in the rain
croak the four Vedas.
Do they then gain deliverance
O elders of paichalur?

Neem and Sandalwood
smell distinct when they burn.
But the smell of the burning Brahmin
you cannot tell.
Does fire smell different
When the unwashed Pulaya[25] burns?
The stuff that burns
and the flames that burn__
How do they differ
O elders of Paichalur?[26]

Trope of Devotion, Dissent and Social Reform in Colonial India

The nineteenth and twentieth centuries in Indian history can be described as years of political and social transition. Politically, these years saw the launching of movements towards an anti-colonial struggle in India. The freedom struggle

---

[24] The (high) wall refers here to the *vedi* or sacrificial platform. Since only Brahmins could sit near the *vedi*, the 'wall' kept the 'others' out.

[25] The 'Pulaya' are untouchables and placed below all the four castes and are therefore 'outcastes'.

[26] The Tamil text is from M. Arunachalam, *Tamizh Ilakkiya Varalaru* (Mayavaram, Tanjavur: Gandhi Vidyalayam Publications, 1969), 359–60. The translation is by the author.

took different forms in different regions. While Tamil politics came to be dominated by the anti-Brahmin movements of leaders like Periyar and the linguistic nationalism of Maraimalai Adigal and Neelambikai Ammaiyar in the 'Tani Tamizh Iyakkam', in Bengal, it was marked by the reformist zeal of the Brahmo Samaj and the spiritual force of Ramakrishna and Vivekananda. In Maharashtra, the Prarthana Samaj of Ranade and the Dalit movement of Jyotirao Phule took the lead in the anti-imperial struggle and social reform. The entire Indo-Gangetic belt countered Christian conversions and Brahmanical ritualism through the launching of the Arya Samaj movement under Swami Dayananda Saraswati. Although the anti-Brahmin movement of Periyar and the burgeoning communist parties rejected theism, the era of social reform, pegged on the notion of dissent against orthodoxy, was largely coloured by a strong sense of religiosity/spirituality.

Narayana Guru and Sri Chattambi Svamigal, who are iconized as leaders of the Ezhava movement, exemplify the combination of spiritual power with the zeal for social reform. Narayana Guru occupies a very special place in Kerala's history. He is not only a blazing spiritual figure but an icon of socio-religious reform within the caste ridden Kerala society in the nineteenth century. Since Narayana Guru belonged to the Ezhava community, his spiritual career was seen as being symbolic of the larger issue of Dalit uprising in the region. Sree Narayana Dharma Paripalana (SNDP) Yogam was organized for the propagation of Sree Narayana Dharma in 1903. However, Narayana Guru was perceived by one stream of his followers as the votary of a more universal message. Narayana Guru's message of 'One human race, one religion and one God' clearly transcended caste, community and religious boundaries. Communists saw in his egalitarian philosophy a pale reflection of their own ideology. Some recent scholars have shown the flaws in his so-called egalitarianism and located him within the social tensions of his age. How then does one read Narayana Guru? I have here chosen an essay by Omana (Chapter 17) which is very much within the devotional stream led by Narayana Guru even while it outlines his socio-religious role as dissenter and reformer. A brief but telling counterpoint to this insider perspective is provided by Udaya Kumar who locates Narayana Guru within a much more critical discourse of caste hierarchies, social tensions and ideological/spiritual negotiations (Chapter 16).

Equally significant is the ideological and social departure of indigenous groups within larger missionary or proselytizing movements in Christianity within India. Two essays in the present anthology focus on the challenge to

Christianity from within its orders in the Indian context. Father (Fr) Gispert-Sauch, himself an ordained priest, talks about the dissent in the Christian church of colonial Bengal in the context of the life of Brahmabandhab Upadhyay, who was a converted Christian but chose his own path to spirituality, which ran counter to Christian theology (Chapter 14). The other essay by Pius Malekandathil enters this particular discourse through his analysis of a Malayalam travelogue written in the 1790s (Chapter 15). This essay, 'Narratives of Travel, Voices of Dissent and Attacks on the Colonial Church Fabric of the European Missionaries: A Study of the *Varthamanapusthakam*', provides a perspective on religious discourse and internal dissensions from colonial Kerala. The author, Fr Thomas Paremakkal, was delegated by the St Thomas Christians of Kerala to let the Pope and the Queen of Portugal know how the Indian Christians of the St Thomas Church were being brutalized and killed by the white Christian missionaries who perceived a threat to their power from the indigenous democratic institutions like *yogam* and *mahayogam.* This incisive essay documents the struggle of Kerala Christians to remain both 'Indian' and 'Christian'.

By Way of Ending the Beginning

The trope of essays brought together in this volume connect, in myriad ways, the twin themes of 'devotion' and 'dissent'. What holds this divergent collection together is the powerful presence of both individual dissenters and cathartic dissent movements. This is intrinsically different from the path of conformism, which dissolves not only dissent but even the dissenter. I cannot do better than quote here the lead essay by Professor Arvind Sharma which spells out the kaleidoscope of perceptions and perspectives, which cover the notions of both devotion and dissent. Sharma states in his introduction in the context of devotion as unquestioning surrender to God, 'The ultimate thrust of this version of devotion cuts deep, for it implies that not only *dissent*, but the *dissenter* also stands dissolved'.

The hagiographies of Ramanujan, Tukaram or Narayana Guru depict them not only as towering spiritual figures but as the focus of social and religious dissent. However, the relevance of their lives as markers of dissent is rendered much more complex by the fact that the interpretation of their lives has varied through the passage of time and varying locations in social space, depending on who is mediating and recording their lives. Thus, Brahmanical representations of their lives were different in their interpretation of the main events in their lives. The emergence of different diametrically opposed readings of the life of saints can be seen in the stories about Kannappa Nayanar, who has been discussed in this collection by Satyanath (Chapter 3), and Raidas and Nandanar, the conflicting versions of whose lives are to be found in the 'Zelliot and Mokashi-Punekar 2005' edited anthology on untouchable saints. These multiple readings of hagiographies suggest that dissent or conformism eventually lies 'in the eye of the beholder'.

With these 'post-modernist' observations by way of winding up this longish introduction to these essays, I invite readers to critically read and enjoy this book.

References

Arunachalam, M., *Tamizh Ilakkiya Varalaru* (Tamil) (Mayavaram, Tanjavur: Gandhi Vidyalayam Publications, 1969).

Bazaz, Prem Nath, *Daughters of the Vitasta* (New Delhi: Pamposh Publications, 1959).

Bhikkuni Hardy, Richard P., 'Embodied Love in John of the Cross', in *Carmelite Studies VI: John of the Cross*, ed. Steven Payne, OCD and accessed 2 November 2009, http//www.ispublications.org. The article is based on his major work, *Search for Nothing: The Life of John of the Cross* (New York, NY: Crossroad, 1982). Published by Washington Province of Discalced Carmelites, Inc. 1992.

Champakalakshmi, R. *Religion, Tradition and Ideology: Pre-colonial South India.* Oxford Collected Essays (Delhi: Oxford University Press, 2011).

Hardy, Richard P., *Search for Nothing: The Life of John of the Cross* (New York, NY: Crossroad, 1982).

Horner, I.B., trans. Cullavagga, *Bhikkuni Khanda* in *Vinaya Pitaka* vol. V (London: Luzac and Co, 1963).

Jaini, Padmanabha S., *Gender and Salvation: Jaina Debates on the Spiritual Liberation of Women* (Berkeley: University of California Press, 1991).

Kosambi, D.D., *Myth and Reality: Studies in the Formation of Indian Culture* (Bombay: Popular Prakashan, 2005).

Lele, Jayant, 'Varlari Sampradayateel Krantikarak Aashay' (Marathi). *Samay Prabodhan Patrika*, no. 117, Diwali, 1991.

Luk, Charles, ed. and trans. *Vimalakirtinirdesa Sutra* (Berkeley and London: Shambala Publications, 1972).

Mullatti, Leela, *The Bhakti Movement and the Status of Women.* Delhi: Abhinav Publications, 1989.'The Bhakti Movement in South India'. In *Indian Movements: Some Aspects of Dissent, Protest and Reform*, edited by S.C (Malik. Shimla: Indian Institute of Advanced Study, 1978).

Nandi, R.N., *Religious Institutions and Cults in the Deccan* (Delhi: Motilal Banarsidass, 1973).

______. *Social Roots of Religion in Ancient India* (Calcutta and Delhi: K.P. Bagchi and Co., 1986).

Ramanujan, A.K., *Speaking of Siva* (Harmondsworth, London: Penguin, 1973) vachana: 703, p.87.

Ramaswamy, Vijaya, 'Anklets on the Feet: Women Saints in Medieval Indian Society', *The Indian Historical Review,* vol.XVII, Nos 1–2, 60–89, 60.

Ramaswamy, Vijaya., *Divinity and Deviance, Women in Virasaivism* (Delhi: Oxford University Press, 1996).

______. *Walking Naked: Women, Society, Spirituality in South India*, Second Revised Edition (Shimla: Indian Institute of Advanced Studies, 2007).

Shivamurthy Shivacharya, *Religion and Society at Crossroads,* Virasaivite Mutt, Sirigere, Karnataka, 1990, p. 44.

Shivaprakash, H.S., *I Keep Vigil of Rudra: The Vachanas*. Delhi: Penguin Books, 2010.

Wayman, Alex and Hideko Wayman, trans. *Srimaladevi Simhanada Sutram* (*The Lion's Roar of Queen Srimala*) (Delhi: Motilal Banarsidass, 1990).

Zelliot, Eleanor and Rohini Punekar-Mokashi., *Untouchable Saints: An Indian Phenomenon* (Delhi: Manohar Publishers, 2005).

CHAPTER 1

Parsing of Devotion and Dissent

Arvind Sharma

Introduction

This imaginative theme will, of course, be parsed in several ways in the essays that follow but what intrigues me about it is the various ways in which it can be parsed.

Dissent without Devotion

To begin with, one could speak of dissent without devotion. And to this category would belong, surprisingly, both the atheists and the transtheists of the Indian religious scene. Thus, we have dissent sans devotion when the atheist denies the very existence of God and thereby of devotion to Him. But even here we may be need to be careful, for one must distinguish between what is personal or impersonal in its ultimate formulation, and the personal or impersonal quality of the devotion towards the object of that devotion, whether personal or impersonal. Four possibilities emerge. First, the possibility that the object of the devotion is personal in nature and our attitude towards it also personal: as when we pray to a god or goddess with devotion – the very core of *bhakti*. Second, the possibility that the object of devotion is impersonal and our attitude towards it is also impersonal. Thus, nirvana, as the *summum bonum* of Buddhism, is something Buddhists would be devoted to but, at least in Theravāda Buddhism, the goal is impersonal in nature and the attitude of the seeker after it is also impersonal, the way a scientist may approach an object of investigation. Similarly, in Advaita Vedanta, the ultimate reality is pure consciousness and one seeks to 'know' it. This knowing is not in the nature of personal knowledge, although it is a person who acquires this liberative knowledge. These first two cases are fairly straightforward and align easily with aspects of the doctrines of *bhakti* yoga and *jñana* yoga as found in Hinduism.

What is somewhat counterintuitive is the third possibility that one may entertain a personal attitude towards what is impersonal. If one is devoted to truth, for instance, as Mahatma Gandhi is said to have been, then truth is not a personal object, it is an impersonal entity. Yet, it is possible to entertain a personal attitude towards it, such as being devoted to it or loving it. Often our ideals tend to be impersonal in nature, such as truth, or justice or even one's country, but the attitude entertained towards them by us could be quite personal in nature. The fourth possibility is even more intriguing: the possibility that one may entertain an impersonal attitude towards a personal entity. A judge in a court, for instance, dispenses justice to persons while viewing them impersonally. An *advaitin* could also accept the existence of god but exhibit an impersonal attitude towards god. A discussion on dissent without devotion leads us in these directions.

Devotion without Dissent

If we now reverse the statement and speak not of dissent without devotion but devotion without dissent, then new configurations arise. The quintessential idea of surrender to God in devotion belongs here, which in a sense is the essence of *bhakti* or of *prapatti* when it is distinguished from *bhakti*. The main point is that one surrenders one's ego to God and that this encapsulates 'devotion without dissent' because it is the ego which dissents from God. As Saint Nammalwar says: 'I was in a maze, clinging to "I" and "mine"; I wandered without knowing myself. On realizing myself I understand that I myself and you and that "mine" (that is, my possessions) is only Yours.'[1] Perhaps a romantic analogy might help clarify the point. There is a famous verse which runs:

> *yadeva rocate mahyam tadeva kurute priyā*
> *iti vetti na jānāti tat priyam yat karoti sā*
>
> My beloved does whatever pleases me.
> So she thinks; she does not seem to know that whatever she does pleases me.

This is the high point at which a devotee stops asking for things from God and begins to welcome whatever God seems to be doing to him or her, as a gift from God. The famous woman mystic of Islam, Rābi'ah (c. 713–801),

[1] Cited in Arthur Osborne, ed., *The Teachings of Bhagavan Sri Ramana Maharshi in His Own Words* (Tiruvannamalai, India: Sri Ramanasramam, 1971), 207.

put it this way: 'My Lord, if I worship you in fear of fire, burn me in hell. If I worship you in desire for paradise, deprive me of it. But if I worship you in love of you, then deprive me not of your eternal beauty.'[2]

The ultimate thrust of this version of devotion cuts deep, for it implies that not only dissent, but the dissenter also stands dissolved: 'If one surrenders completely there will be no one left to ask questions or to be considered.'[3]

The two terms of reference may also be paired, not merely as 'dissent without devotion' and 'devotion without dissent' but also as dissent as devotion and devotion as dissent.

Dissent as Devotion

There are many ways of relating to God according to the doctrine of *bhāva*s in Hindu theism. A *bhāva* is an emotive attitude, which one might adopt towards God, of which no less than 19 are listed.[4] Thus, one may adopt the attitude of a

---

[2] Mahmoud M. Ayoub, 'The Islamic Tradition', in *World Religions: Western Traditions*, ed. Willard G. Oxtoby (Toronto: Oxford University Press, 1996), 433. The following story provides a good example of devotion without dissent: 'There was a man who was intensely devoted to Sri Rama and he believed that nothing could happen in the world without His Will and that His Will was the ultimate cause for every action of his and every step that he took. Once he was passing through a forest when he found dacoits returning with booty after committing a dacoity. Seeing him, they told him to carry their booty and placed a heavy load upon his head. He went with them but a party of policemen came and when the dacoits saw them coming, they ran away in different directions leaving him behind with the booty on his head. The police arrested him and brought him to the police station and after a trial he was sent to jail. When he was released after his term of imprisonment he came home in his village. The people of the village asked why he had been absent for such a long period. He said, "Everything has happened by Rama's Will. By Rama's Will I passed by a lonely road in a forest and by Rama's Will I was seized by a band of dacoits and asked to carry their booty. By Rama's Will the police came and the dacoits ran away, leaving me behind. By Rama's Will I was arrested, tried, and sentenced and by Rama's Will, having served my term, I have been released and have come home."' See Swami Sambuddhananda, *Vedanta through Stories* (Bombay: Sri Ramakrishna Ashram, 1959), 192–93.

[3] Also, see Osborne, *Teachings of Bhagavan Sri Ramana Maharshi*, 205: 'Surrender can never be regarded as complete so long as the devotee wants this or that from the Lord. True surrender is the love of God for the sake of God and nothing else, not even for the sake of salvation.'

[4] T.M.P. Mahadevan, *Outlines of Hinduism* (Bombay: Chetana Limited, 1971), 91.

servant towards God, known as *dāsya-bhāva*, of which Hanuman is a celebrated example. Or one could adopt the attitude of a parent towards a child, called *vātsalya-bhāva*.

> Kausalyā had the Lord Himself as her child in the form of Rāma. The love of Yaśodā to Kṛṣṇa was of the nature of *vātsalya*. *Śanta-bhāva* is the converse of *vātsalya*; it is the feeling of a child to its parent. Dhruva and Prahlāda are the classical examples.[5]

Now, one such attitude one may adopt towards God is *dveṣya-bhāva* or the attitude of hostility, which characterizes those who dissent from God, that is, come into deliberate conflict with Him. This is also supposed to be salvific and seems to provide a good example of dissent as devotion. Benjamin Walker explains this *bhāva* as follows:

> *dveshya-bhāva*, (dvesha, 'hatred') the attitude of an atheist or god-hater towards god, as Śiśupāla king of Chedi to Kṛishṇa; this notion is based on the Tantrik belief that an intense feeling towards the deity may even be expressed in hatred for him, since this implies a belief (albeit concealed) in god's terrible rage and power.[6]

Dissent in Devotion, Devotion in Dissent

This category of 'dissent in devotion ' can be further refined by identifying two other possibilities within it: (a) devotion in dissent; and (b) dissent in devotion. A good example of devotion in dissent is provided by the sage Uttaṅka in the Mahabharata. He was a devotee of Krishna who accepted Krishna as an incarnation, and was unhappy with Krishna on account of the fact that he could not prevent the Mahabharata war from occurring (just as many Indians were unhappy with Mahatma Gandhi for failing to prevent the partition of India). Krishna had to explain to him that sometimes all that an incarnation can do is damage control, revealing his cosmic form as he took leave of him.[7]

Dissent in devotion would also represent moments when a devotee teases God, complains to God or protests against God while remaining a devotee.

---

[5] Ibid.

[6] Benjamin Walker, *The Hindu World, Vol. I* (New York: Frederick A. Praeger, 1968), 138.

[7] This case has been discussed in detail by Bimal K. Matilal, see Jonardon Ganeri, ed., *The Collected Essays of Bimal Krishna Matilal* (New Delhi: Oxford University Press, 2002), 99–100.

It might take a mild or severe form. Tukaram (1598–1649) provides a good example of the mild version:

> That we fall into sin is thy good fortune: we have bestowed name and form on thee; had it not been we, who would have asked after thee, when thou wast lonely and unembodied? It is the darkness that makes the light shine, the setting that gives lustre to the gem. Disease brought to light Dhanvantari; why should a healthy man wish to know him? It is poison that confers its value on nectar; gold and brass are high or low compared with each other. Tuka says, know this, O God, that because we exist, Godhead has been conferred on you.[8]

A more severe form of it is found in the following verses of Janabai, who served in the household of Namdev (thirteenth/fourteenth century).[9]

> O God I have lost your love
> And will not serve you again,
> There is nothing special about you
> Your vanity turns me away
> Why should I fear your anger?
> Your strength depends on me
> O Hari, now you are powerless
> I've finally caught the thief[10]

Perhaps the state of separation or *viraha* can be described as one of 'emotional dissent', at an extreme point in which suffering is hard to endure, so much so that two women mystics, Kanhopatra from fourteenth century Maharashtra and Andal from ninth century Tamil Nadu, compare themselves to food for wild animals. Kanhopatra writes:

> When a roving jackal
> steals the food of a lion,
> it is the great
> who is put to shame.

---

[8] See S. Radhakrishnan, *The Hindu View of Life* (New Delhi: Indus, 1993 [1927]), 23.

[9] Sarah Sellergren, 'Janābāī and Kānhopātrā: A Study of Two Women Saints', in *Images of Women in Maharashtrian Literature and Religion*, ed. Ann Feldhaus (Albany, NY: State University of New York Press, 1996), 226. In one *abhaṅga*, she raises troubling questions of how directly Namdev's theories of equality among the *bhakta*s were translated into his real life (ibid.).

[10] Ibid., 223.

Says Kānhopātra,

> I offer my body
> at your feet,
> protect it,
> at least for your title[11]

Andal writes:

> My swelling breasts I dedicated
> to the Lord who holds
> the sea-fragrant conch –
> if there is but a whisper
> of giving me to a mortal,
> I shall not live, O Manmatha –
> would you permit a roving jackal
> to sniff and make its own
> the sacrificial foods
> the Brahmins offer
> to celestial Gods?[12]

Devotion as Dissent

It is interesting to consider the Bhakti movement itself as representing dissent from the regnant philosophy of Advaita Vedanta. It has been pointed out by spokespersons of even the Advaita Vedanta tradition that while Shankara 'is an absolute non-dualist in his metaphysics, he had great faith in bhakti or devotion to a personal God'.[13] The significance of his following prayer to Vishnu will not be lost on the reader:

> *satyapi bhedāpagame nātha tavāham na māmakīnas tvam*
> *sāmudro hi taraṅgaḥ kvacana samudro na tāraṅgaḥ*

> Oh Lord, even after realising that there is no real difference between the individual soul and Brahman I beg to state that I am Yours and not that You are mine. The wave belongs to the ocean and not the ocean to the wave.[14]

---

[11] Ibid., 229.

[12] Ibid., 230.

[13] S. Radhakrishnan, *The Brahmasūtra: The Philosophy of Spiritual Life* (New York: Harper Brothers, 1960), 37.

[14] Ibid., 38.

Advaita Vedanta abolishes the ontological difference between the individual and the ultimate reality; *bhakti* dissents from this and insists on maintaining a distinction. This point is made with great finesse by Nammalwar in the *Tiruvāymoḷi* (8.1.9):

It's true
even I am you
even the unbearable hell
of this world
is you:
this being so
what's the difference?
One may go to paradise
and reach perfect joy
or go the other way
and fall into hell
yet I being I
even when I remember
I am you
I still fear hell:
lord in perpetual paradise
let me be at your feet.[15]

Echoes of this sentiment can be heard in more modern times as well. As Jane I. Smith notes:

> In Advaitic sadhana Ramakrishna had to give up Mother...And yet Ramakrishna continued to the end of his life to worship Mother Kali in the most intensely devotional of ways, even to the point of being willing to give back, as it were, the full experience of nirvikalpa samadhi: 'O Mother, do not plunge me in the knowledge of Brahman and take away my consciousness!' he pleaded at a moment of intense illness not long before his death. 'I am but thy child. I have fears and anxieties! I do want my Mother! A thousand salutations to Brahma-Jnana. Give it to him who wants it, O Mother.' Paradoxes of logic can certainly be truths of mysticism...[16]

[15] A.K. Ramanujan, trans., *Hymns for the Drowning: Poems for Viṣṇu by Nammāḷvār* (Princeton: Princeton University Press, 1981), 39.

[16] Jane I. Smith, 'Sri Ramakrishna's Approach to Religious Plurality', in *God of All: Sri Ramakrishna's Approach to Religious Plurality*, by Claude Alan Stark (Cape Cod, MA: Claude Stark, Inc., 1974), 189–90.

Dissent can take many forms. One could speak of critical dissent, as when the poet advises one to keep a critic in one's own house;[17] veridical dissent, when one is prepared to dissent even from God, if God is economizing on the truth, as in the case of Nakkīran;[18] pious dissent, when two devotees compete for having their throat cut;[19] divine dissent, considering the way Shiva responds to the way the Brahmin treats Kannapar's offerings,[20] or even double divine dissent, when Shiva intervenes to prevent Kannapar from immolating his remaining eye;[21] medical dissent, or dissent on medical grounds, when God takes his own time to cure a disease, as in the case of Appar;[22] familial dissent, experienced by so many devotees, but specially by Bahinabai (seventeenth century);[23] political dissent, as in the case of Basavanna;[24] sectarian dissent, as between Vaishnavas and Shaivas; and so on.

Most would agree, however, that perhaps the most significant dimension of dissent represented by *bhakti* is social dissent in the context of the hierarchical structures of Hinduism, which privilege the twice-born over others and men over women.[25] The theme of devotion and dissent therefore needs to be particularly

---

[17] I have a *dohā* attributed to Raskhān in mind, which may be roughly translated as: 'Keep your critics close by, with their hut in your courtyard. They cleanse without soap and water.' (Professor Vijaya Ramaswamy, personal communication).

[18] See Kamil Veith Zvelbeil, *Tamil Literature* (Wiesbaden: Otto Harrassowitz, 1974), 184. I am indebted to Dr Saraswati Sainath for this reference.

[19] Dennis D. Hudson, 'Violent and Fanatical Devotion among the Nāyaṉars: A Study in the Periya Purāṇam of Cekkiḻār', in *Criminal Gods and Demon Devotees: Essays on the Guardians of Popular Hinduism*, ed. Alf Hiltebeitel (Albany, NY: State University of New York Press, 1989), 393–394.

[20] Ibid., 381–382.

[21] Ibid.

[22] See Mary McGee, 'Bahinābāī: The Ordinary Life of an Exceptional Woman, or, the Exceptional Life of an Ordinary Woman', *Journal of Vaishnava Studies* 3(4): 111–47. Also, see Hudson, 'Violent and Fanatical Devotion', 402, note 33.

[23] See A.K. Ramanujan, *Speaking of Śiva* (New York: Penguin Books, 1973), 61–63; also, see Gavin Flood, *An Introduction to Hinduism* (Cambridge: Cambridge University Press, 1996), 171–72 and Norvin J. Hein, 'Caitanya's Ecstasies and the Theology of the Name', in *Hinduism: New Essays in the History of Religions*, ed. Bardwell L. Smith (Leiden: E.J. Brill, 1976), 16–20.

[24] Hudson, 'Violent and Fanatical Devotion', 397–399.

[25] See John Stratton Hawley and Mark Juergensmeyer, *Songs and Saints of India* (New York: Oxford University Press, 1988), 9–23; Eleanor Zelliot, 'Chokhāmeḷā: Piety and Protest', in *Bhakti Religion in North India*, ed. David N. Lorenzen (Albany, NY:

pursued in this context. This was an age in which the husband was to be looked upon as a God; an equation which got turned around in *bhakti* into looking upon God as one's husband. A major example here is provided by the sixteenth century Meerabai.

> Krishna's Bride
> My only Lord is Giridhar Gopāl
> None else, none else, in this false world;
> I have forsaken my family and friends,
> I sit among saintly souls,
> I have lost regard for worldly fame and honor.
> My heart swells at the sight of the godly,
> It shrinks at the sight of the worldly.
> I have watered the creeper of God's love with my own tears.
> Churning the curds of life, I have taken out the butter, and thrown away the rest.
> The King, my husband, sent me a cup of poison:
> I drank it with pleasure.
> The news is now public, everyone knows now
> That Mīrābāī has fallen in love with God!
> It does not matter now: what was fated to happen, has happened.[26]

Meerabai's whole life is virtually a study in dissent and devotion.[27]

References

Ayoub, Mahmoud M., 'The Islamic Tradition'. In *World Religions: Western Traditions*, edited by Willard G. (Toronto : Oxford University Press, 1996).

Embree, Ainslie T., ed. *The Hindu Tradition* (New York: Random House, 1972).

Flood, Gavin, *An Introduction to Hinduism* (Cambridge: Cambridge University Press, 1996).

Ganeri, Jonardon, ed. *The Collected Essays of Bimal Krishna Matilal* (New Delhi: Oxford University Press, 2002).

State University of New York Press, 1995), 212–220; and Eleanor Zelliot, 'Women Saints in Medieval Maharashtra', in *Faces of the Feminine in Ancient Medieval, and Modern India*, ed. Mandakranta Bose (Delhi: Oxford University Press, 2000), 192–200.

[26] See Ainslie T. Embree, ed., *The Hindu Tradition* (New York: Random House, 1972), 253.

[27] Nancy M. Martin-Kershaw, 'Mīrābāī: Inscribed in Text, Embodied in Life', *Journal of Vaishnava Studies* 3(4): 5–44.

Hawley, John Stratton and Mark Juergensmeyer, *Songs and Saints of India* (New York: Oxford University Press, 1988).

Hein, Norvin J., 'Caitanya's Ecstasies and the Theology of the Name'. In *Hinduism: New Essays in the History of Religions*, edited by Bardwell L. Smith (Leiden: E.J. Brill, 1976).

Hudson, Dennis D., 'Violent and Fanatical Devotion among the Nāyaṉars: A Study in the Periya Purāṇam of Cekkiḻār'. In *Criminal Gods and Demon Devotees: Essays on the Guardians of Popular Hinduism*, edited by Alf Hiltebeitel (Albany, NY: State University of New York Press, 1989).

Mahadevan, T.M.P., *Outlines of Hinduism* (Bombay: Chetana Limited, 1971).

Martin-Kershaw, Nancy M., 'Mīrābāī: Inscribed in Text, Embodied in Life'. *Journal of Vaishnava Studies* 3(4): 5–44.

McGee, Mary, 'Bahinābāī: The Ordinary Life of an Exceptional Woman, or, the Exceptional Life of an Ordinary Woman'. *Journal of Vaishnava Studies* 3(4): 111–147.

Osborne, Arthur, ed., *The Teachings of Bhagavan Sri Ramana Maharshi in His Own Words* (Tiruvannamalai, India: Sri Ramanasramam, 1971).

Radhakrishnan, S., *The Brahmasūtra: The Philosophy of Spiritual Life* (New York: Harper Brothers, 1960).

______. *The Hindu View of Life* (New Delhi: Indus, 1993 [1927]).

Ramanujan, A.K., *Speaking of Śiva*. New York: Penguin Books, 1973.

______, trans. *Hymns for the Drowning: Poems for Viṣṇu by Nammāḷvār* (Princeton: Princeton University Press, 1981).

Sambuddhananda, Swami, *Vedanta through Stories* (Bombay: Sri Ramakrishna Ashram, 1959).

Sellergren, Sarah, 'Janābāī and Kānhopātrā: A Study of Two Women Saints'. In *Images of Women in Maharashtrian Literature and Religion*, edited by Ann Feldhaus (Albany, NY: State University of New York Press, 1996).

Smith, Jane I., 'Sri Ramakrishna's Approach to Religious Plurality'. In *God of All: Sri Ramakrishna's Approach to Religious Plurality*, by Claude Alan Stark (Cape Cod, MA: Claude Stark, Inc., 1974).

Walker, Benjamin, *The Hindu World,* Vol. I. New York: Frederick A. Praeger, 1968.

Zelliot, Eleanor, 'Chokhāmeḷā: Piety and Protest'. In *Bhakti Religion in North India*, edited by David N. Lorenzen (Albany, NY: State University of New York Press, 1995).

______. 'Women Saints in Medieval Maharashtra'. In *Faces of the Feminine in Ancient Medieval, and Modern India*, edited by Mandakranta Bose (Delhi: Oxford University Press, 2000).

Zvelbeil, Kamil Veith, *Tamil Literature* (Wiesbaden: Otto Harrassowitz, 1974).

CHAPTER

2

Dissent and Protest in Early Indian Buddhism with Special Reference to Devadatta

K. T. S. Sarao

The Buddha and Devadatta were cross-cousins. Devadatta and Bhaddakaccānā/Bhaddakaccā were respectively the son[1] and daughter of Sākyan Suppabuddha and Amitā.[2] Amitā was the sister of the Buddha's father, Suddhodana.[3] The Buddha's mother, Māyā/Mahāmāyā, and stepmother, Pajāpatī Gotamī, were Suppabuddha's sisters.[4] According to the Pāli texts, Bhaddakaccānā was married to Prince Siddhattha, the would-be Buddha.[5] Devadatta entered the

---

[1] However, some texts like the *Mahāvaṃsa* and the *Dhammapada Aṭṭhakathā* show Devadatta as the son of Suppabuddha's brother, Amitodana, and thus, the brother of Ānanda. See the *Mahāvaṃsa* (London: PTS, 1908) (henceforth *Mhv*), ii, 22; the *Dhammapada Aṭṭhakathā* (London: PTS, 1906–15) (henceforth *DhA*), iii, 44.

[2] At one place in the *Vinaya Piṭaka*, she is called Godhī. See the *Vinaya Piṭakaṃ* (London: PTS, 1879–83) (henceforth *Vin.*), ii, 189.

[3] The *Paramatthadīpanī* (London: PTS, 1891–1977) (henceforth *ThaA*), i, 105; the *Papañcasūdanī* (London: PTS, 1922–38) (henceforth *MA*), I, 289.

[4] See G.P. Malalasekera, *Dictionary of Pāli Proper Names, Vol. 2* (New Delhi: Oriental Reprint, 1983) (henceforth *DPPN*), *s.v.* Māyā.('check under the word 'Māyā' in the Dictionary of Pāli Proper Names prepared by G.P. Malalasekera.')

[5] The *Buddhavaṃsa* (London: PTS, 1974) (henceforth *Bu*), XXVI, 15; the *Manorathapūraṇī* (London: PTS, 1956–1973) (henceforth *AA*), I, 204; *Mhv*, ii, 24. Though her name is generally given as Rāhulamātā, in some later Pāli texts, she is also called by various other names. For instance, she is called Yasodharā in the *Madhuratthavilāsinī* (London: PTS, 1946) (henceforth *BuA*), 245. In some of the *Jātakas*, she is called Bimbādevī. See, for example, *The Jātakas* (London: Trübner & Co., 1877–97) (henceforth *J*), ii, 392f or Bimbāsundarī (*J*, iv, 478).

Saṃgha when the Buddha visited Kapilavatthu shortly after Enlightenment.[6] He appears to have begun his career quite impressively as a monk. During the very first *Vassāvāsa* that followed his entry into the *Saṃgha*, Devadatta acquired the power of *iddhi*, possible to those who are still of the world (*puthujjanika-iddhi*).[7] According to the account, as a result of this achievement, the prestige of Devadatta grew tremendously and he came to acquire great respect within the *Saṃgha*. In fact, elsewhere in the Pāli *Nikāya*s, Devadatta is praised as a quintessential example of an ideal monk, who had the right views and preached the correct *dhamma*.[8] Sāriputta lavished praises on him saying: 'Godhīputta is of great psychic power, Godhīputta is of great splendour'.[9] The Buddha also praised Devadatta and included him amongst those eleven Elders[10] who were particularly praiseworthy. In fact, the Buddha went so far as to call Devadatta and the others as the ones who had 'put away evil, who have destroyed the fetters, the wise ones'.[11]

But after this, we are told, Devadatta began to have evil designs.[12] He is shown in the Pāli texts as a person who became not only jealous of the Buddha's fame but also became eager for gain and fame. Thus, it is pointed out, Devadatta began to entertain ambitions to win lay converts and satisfy his desire for honour and material gain. To attain this objective, Devadatta decided to enlist the support of the crown prince, Ajātasattu. Devadatta manifested himself to the latter as a young boy clad in a girdle of snakes. Ajātasattu was tremendously impressed with Devadatta's display of his supernatural powers and became his loyal patron, showering all kinds of favours on him.[13] Thereafter, Devadatta began to smell real power and conceived the idea of becoming the leader of the *Saṃgha* in the Buddha's place. But at this point, his psychic powers are said to have diminished.[14]

---

[6] *Vin*, ii, 182–202; iii, 172–175.

[7] *Vin*, ii, 183.

[8] The Aṅguttara *Nikāya* (London: PTS, 1885–1900) (henceforth *A*), iv, 402.

[9] '*mahiddhiko godhiputto, mahānubhāvo godhiputto*' (*Vin*, ii, 189).

[10] Sāriputta, Mahāmogallāna, Mahākassapa, Mahākaccāna, Mahākoṭṭhita, Mahākappina, Mahācunda, Anuruddha, Revata, Devadatta and Ānanda. See *The Udānaṃ* (London: PTS, 1885) (henceforth *Ud*), I, 5.

[11] Ibid.

[12] The *Saṃyutta Nikāya* (London: PTS, 1884–98) (henceforth *S*), ii, 156.

[13] *Vin*, ii, 184.

[14] Ibid., 184ff; *Vin*, iii, 171f, 174f; iv, 71; *A*, iii, 123, 402; ii, 73; iv, 160; *J*, i, 113, 142, 185, 490; iv, 37, 158; v, 333ff; vi, 129f.

According to the *Cullavagga* account, almost immediately after Devadatta joined the *Saṃgha*, the Buddha was warned by the *devaputta* Kakudha about Devadatta's desire to deprive him of the leadership of the *Saṃgha*.[15] But the Buddha is not troubled by such reports as he felt that such actions of Devadatta would only be counterproductive.[16] For the fulfilment of his desire to take up the leadership of the *Saṃgha*, we are told, Devadatta approached the Buddha and pointed out to him that as the latter was getting old, he should let the former assume leadership of the *Saṃgha*. The Buddha immediately rejected his request and snubbed him for entertaining such thoughts.[17] Devadatta left dejected and threatened revenge. The Buddha, thereafter, told the monks to carry out the following formal act of information against Devadatta in Rājagaha:

> whereas Devadatta's nature was formerly of one kind, now it is of another kind; and that whatever Devadatta should do by gesture and by voice, in that neither the Awakened One nor Dhamma nor the Order should be seen, but in that only Devadatta should be seen.[18]

The act being carried out, the Buddha asked Sāriputta to inform against Devadatta in Rājagaha. When Sāriputta expressed hesitation because he had formerly spoken in praise of him, the Buddha allowed that just as Sāriputta's former praise had been true, now his condemnation will be equally true.[19] When Sāriputta proclaimed the act of information in Rājagaha against Devadatta, it resulted in protests by some of the lay devotees of Devadatta who accused the followers of the Buddha of being jealous of Devadatta's gains and honours.[20]

After the above-stated incident, according to the Pāli texts, Devadatta turns into a completely anti-social character and a criminal. He makes up his mind to murder the Buddha. For this purpose, he approaches Ajātasattu so that he can assassinate the Buddha and usurp the leadership of the *Saṃgha*. Ajātasattu agrees and provides him with assassins. Hence, a conspiracy – known as the Abhimārapayojanā Conspiracy in the Pāli texts – was hatched to have archers

---

15 *Vin*, ii, 184.

16 Ibid., 187–188.

17 Ibid., 188; The *Majjhima Nikāya* (London: PTS, 1888–1896) (henceforth *M*), i, 393.

18 *The Book of the Discipline* (London: PTS, 1938–1966) (henceforth *BD*), v, 264–265.

19 *Vin*, ii, 189.

20 Ibid., 190.

shoot the Buddha fatally.[21] But the assassins are dissuaded from their intended act by the charisma, insight and kindness of the Buddha.[22] Thereafter, Devadatta tries to kill the Buddha by rolling down a boulder on to him from a hilltop. Though the boulder is miraculously destroyed, splinters from the boulder draw blood from the Buddha's foot. At this, the Buddha remarks: 'You have produced great demerit, foolish man, in that you, with your mind, malignant, your mind on murder, drew the Tathāgata's blood'.[23]

After this incident, the monks become very worried about the Buddha's safety, but the latter tells them not to worry as a Buddha cannot be killed before his time by a person such as Devadatta.[24] Now, Devadatta sets a mad killer elephant on the Buddha, but the Buddha tames the elephant through his loving kindness.[25] According to these sources, attempts to kill the Buddha led to an outrage and public unpopularity of Devadatta. Ajātasattu was compelled by the force of public opinion to withdraw his patronage from Devadatta, whose gain and honour, anyway, had decreased.[26] However, according to Pāli Buddhism, these plans of Devadatta to harm the Buddha were the result of the Buddha's evil deeds in previous births.[27] In any case, despite the hatred shown by Devadatta towards him, the Buddha on his part did not harbour any ill will towards him.[28]

After having failed to kill the Buddha, Devadatta, along with four other companion monks (Kokālika, Koṭamorakatissa, Khaṇḍadeviyāputta and Samuddadatta), goes to the Buddha and requests him that the following five austere (*dhuta*) practices be imposed on the *Saṃgha* and that their violation be treated as sinful:

1. Monks should dwell all their lives in the forest (*āraññaka*); whoever should carry himself to the neighbourhood of a settlement, sin (*vajja*) would sully him.
2. Monks should, all their lives, obtain alms by begging (*piṇḍapātika*); whoever should accept invitations for meals, sin would sully him.

---

[21] *J*, i, 141; vi, 130f; *DA*, i, 154.

[22] *Vin*, ii, 190–193.

[23] Ibid., 193.

[24] Ibid., 194.

[25] Ibid., 194–194.

[26] The *Samantapāsādikā* (London: PTS, 1947–1975) (henceforth *VA*), iv, 811.

[27] The *Apadāna* (London: PTS, 1925–1927) (henceforth *Ap*), ii, 300–301.

[28] The *Milindapañha* (London: Williams and Norgate, 1880) (henceforth *Mil*), 410.

3. Monks should, all their lives, wear robes made of discarded clothes (*paṃsukūlika*); whoever should accept a robe given by the laity, sin would sully him.
4. Monks should, all their lives, dwell at the foot of a tree (*rukkhamūlika*); whoever dwell under a roof, sin would sully him.
5. Monks should, all their lives, abstain completely from fish and flesh (*macchamaṃsaṃ na khādeyyuṃ*); whoever should eat fish and flesh, sin would sully him.[29]

As pointed out by Mukherjee,[30] it is quite strange indeed to note that even after the various attempts made by Devadatta on the life of the Buddha (including injuring him), he was not expelled from the *Saṃgha*. So much so, he even went over to the Buddha as a monk and demanded the imposition of these five austere practices.[31] As a justification for demanding the imposition of these practices, Devadatta is said to have appealed to the Buddha in the following words:

> Lord, the lord in many ways speaks in praise of desiring little, of being contented, of expunging (evil), of being punctilious, of what is gracious, of decrease (of the obstructions), of putting forth energy. Lord, these five items are conducive in many ways to desiring little, to contentment.[32]

The Buddha leaves the option to the monks and enjoins Devadatta not to bring out a schism in the *Saṃgha*:

> Whoever wishes, let him be a forest-dweller; whoever wishes, let him dwell in the neighbourhood of a village; whoever wishes, let him be a beggar for alms; whoever wishes, let him accept an invitation; whoever wishes, let him wear rags taken from the dust-heap; whoever wishes, let him accept a householder's robes. For eight months, Devadatta, lodging at the foot of a

---

[29] *Vin*, iii, 171.

[30] B. Mukherjee, *Die Uberlieferung von Devadatta, dem Widersacher des Buddha, in den kanonischen Schriften* (Munich: J. Kitzinger, 1966), 120. See also Mukherjee's book's review in D. Seyfort Ruegg, *T'oung Pao*(journal), Second Series, Vol. 54, Livr. 1/3 (1968).

[31] But some non-Theravādin texts reverse these incidents and put them in different chronological order, thus making them look more logical. Mukherjee considers these to be, in all likelihood, unhistorical accretions.

[32] *BD*, i, 296.

tree is permitted by me [i.e., except during the rains]. Fish and flesh are pure in respect of three points: if they are not seen, heard or suspected (to have been killed for him).[33]

However, Devadatta in turn, according to the account, accuses the Buddha of being prone to luxury and abundance, especially because 'people esteem austerity.'[34] Devadatta then goes ahead (in the *Uposatha* ceremony) through the formalities of creating the first schism in the *Saṃgha* and leaves for Gayāsīsa along with 500 supporting monks.[35]

According to the commentary of the *Dhammapada*, then onwards, Devadatta tries to imitate the Buddha by keeping two chief disciples by his side.[36] Among his followers, Devadatta also has some prominent personalities like the nun Thullanandā who upheld Devadatta as a stalwart in the *sāsana*.[37] The Buddha sends Sāriputta and Moggallāna to Devadatta's camp. After arriving, though these two seem to have approved of Devadatta's *dhamma* but when Devadatta goes to sleep, they convince the 500 'wayward' monks to return to the Buddha. Kokālika then wakes up Devadatta and reveals the bad news to him. Devadatta is so shocked by the events that hot blood gushes out of his mouth and he falls

[33] Ibid., 298.

[34] *Vin*, iii, 171–172.

[35] Vesālī was the scene of the Second Buddhist Council in which the issue of the Ten Extravagances (*dasavatthūni*) was raised and a large number of monks belonging to the Vajjian clan (known as Vajjiputtaka/Vajjiputtiyā) who were practising these 'extravagances' were expelled from the *Saṃgha*. As a consequence, the Vajjiputtakas formed a separate sect, the Mahāsaṃghikas. It is interesting to note that the same Vajjiputtakas seceded from the *Saṃgha* under the leadership of Devadatta (*Vin*, ii, 199f). Buddhaghosa, as a matter of fact, actually identifies the heretics as belonging to the same party (*VA*, i, 228). It is also important to remember here that, initially, the Vajjiputtakas were supported even by Kāḷāsoka, the King. See, for instance, *Mhv*, iv, 7ff; See, for instance, W. Geiger (ed.), *The Mahāvaṃsa*, London: Pali Text Society, 1908.iv.7ff; B.C. Law (ed. and trans), *The Chronicle of the Island of Ceylon or the Dīpavaṃsa*, the *Ceylon Historical Journal*, 7, 1958: 1–266).iv.44. (This famous Buddhist journal, published from Colombo, was edited by S.D. Saparamadu in the 1950s. In this journal in 1958 the entire Pali original of the Sri Lankan chronicle *The Dīpavaṃsa* along with its translation (ed. and trans. B.C. Law) was published under the title *The Chronicle of the Island of Ceylon or the Dīpavaṃsa).*

[36] *DhA*, i, 122.

[37] *Vin*, ii, 66, 335.

fatally ill.[38] The Buddha subsequently remarks that Devadatta would fall into *Niraya* Hell. However, when Devadatta breathes his last nine months later, he makes a dying statement that he has no refuge other than the Buddha:

> In him, who of the best is far the best.
> The god of gods, the guide of gods and men,
> Who see'th all, and bears the hundred marks
> Of goodness,- 'tis in him I refuge take
> Through all the lives that I may have to live.[39]

Though Devadatta falls into *Niraya* Hell, he is assured that after a 100,000 aeons, he would be born as a *paccekabuddha* by the name of Aṭṭhissara.[40]

Interestingly, as one moves away from the Buddha chronologically,[41] the criticism of Devadatta becomes more and more scathing. Thus, in the different commentaries of the *Nikāya*s, and later texts such as the *Jātaka*s, Devadatta is depicted as the quintessential example of a wicked person. The *Dhammapada* commentary gives graphic details of the tortures inflicted on Devadatta in Avīcī.[42] The same text also mentions that when people heard of the death of Devadatta, they were so happy that they held a great festival.[43] As many as eighty-nine (that is, more than 16 per cent) *Jātaka*s primarily focus on the condemnation of Devadatta. In all the references, he is shown as the Buddha's arch rival who constantly competed with him and tried to usurp the leadership of the *Saṃgha* from him. The different stories portray him as performing a variety of pernicious deeds and as an inveterate evildoer who was driven by ambitious and hateful intentions. The *Jātaka*s clearly portray him as the object of hatred of Buddhists. The table prepared on the basis of information available in the *Jātaka*s is self-explanatory (Table 2.1).

---

[38] To this account given in the *Vinaya Piṭaka*, is added in the *Jātakas* (*J*, i, 491) and the *Dhammapada Aṭṭhakathā* (*DhA*, i, 143), the incident of Kokālika kicking Devadatta in the chest.

[39] Ibid., 147; *Mil*, 111. Translation from the *Questions of King Milinda* (henceforth *Milinda*) (Oxford: Oxford University Press, 1890, *Sacred Books of East*), XXXV, 167.

[40] *Mil*, 111; *DhA*, i, 125. However, according to the *Saddharmapuṇḍrīka* (chapter XI, stanza 46), Devadatta would be born as a Buddha by the name of Devarāja.

[41] For later and early portions of the Pāli *Tipiṭaka*, see K.T.S. Sarao, *Origin and Nature of Ancient Indian Buddhism*, Reprint (Delhi: Delhi University, 2003), 43–48.

[42] *DhA*, i, 147.

[43] Ibid., 126–127.

Table 2.1: Devadatta's character as depicted in the Pāli Jātakas

Nature of the Character of Devadatta	*Jātaka No.*
A fake ascetic	11, 277, 492
A person of bad principles, a bad leader and a bad companion	12, 26, 397
A pretender, an ungrateful person, a plotter, a traitor, a drunkard and a murderer.	21, 57, 58, 72, 110, 111, 112, 131, 142, 143, 160, 168, 174, 204, 206, 208, 210, 220, 221, 241, 308, 329, 335, 342, 350, 358, 364, 389, 404, 407, 416, 445, 448, 452, 457, 471, 472, 473, 482, 500, 505, 508, 516, 517, 530, 533, 546
A liar, low, mean, unwise, double-faced, inefficient, dishonest, shameless, self-destructive, criminal-minded, disobedient, unjust, harsh and cruel person.	1, 3, 10, 113, 139, 141, 150, 184, 193, 194, 209, 224, 231, 240, 294, 295, 313, 353, 357, 367, 422, 438, 466, 503, 506, 514, 518, 543, 547
Heretical, deserter, schism-creator, jealous and anti-Buddha.	122, 222, 243 , 326, 474, 544
A wicked man who attempted human sacrifice.	542

Some of the close relatives of the Buddha from his wife's side also appear in a bad light. Sākyan Daṇḍapāṇi is said to have preferred Devadatta to the Buddha.[44] He was the brother of Suppabuddha and thus, the brother of Buddha's mother and paternal uncle to both Devadatta and Bhaddakaccānā.[45] It has been pointed out in the *Madhupiṇḍika Sutta* of the *Majjhima Nikāya* that once Daṇḍapāṇi met the Buddha and questioned him on his teachings. But being dissatisfied by the Buddha's explanation, he left abruptly and 'shook his head, pulled out his tongue, made three wrinkles on his forehead' contemptuously.[46] The *Dhammapada Aṭṭhakathā* points out that Sākyan Suppabuddha was angry with the Buddha because he had not only deserted his daughter in renouncing life as a householder but had also turned hostile to his son Devadatta after ordaining him as a disciple in the *Saṃgha*.[47] In the fifteenth year of his ministry,

---

[44] *MA*, i, 298.

[45] Northern Buddhist sources mention Daṇḍapāṇi as Prince Siddhattha's father-in-law (W.W. Rockhill, *Life of the Buddha and the Early History of His Order: Derived from Tibetan Works*, Reprint [London: Kegan Paul International, 2003], 20).

[46] *M*, i, 103.

[47] *DhA*, iii, 44. Devadatta's enmity towards the Buddha is also shown as being based on the same reasons as that of Suppabuddha.

the Buddha revisited Kapilavatthu, and there his father-in-law, Suppabuddha, in a drunken fit, refused to let the Buddha pass through the streets. Seven days later, he was swallowed up by the earth at the foot of his palace.[48]

Different personalities associated with Devadatta also face the brunt of criticism, and this criticism becomes sharper as time goes by. Kokālika draws maximum flak amongst all of Devadatta's associates. The early Pāli texts do not say much by way of criticism of Kokālika and simply point out that whenever anyone criticized Devadatta, Kokālika was always ready to defend him.[49] However, the incident of Devadatta being kicked by Kokālika[50] is added in the later portions of Pāli literature. The criticism against him becomes quite virulent in the *Jātaka*s where he is not only portrayed as an accomplice of Devadatta but is also held to ridicule. We are told that when Devadatta's gains diminished, Kokālika went about praising him, his birth, accomplishments and holiness, and many believed him.[51] His character is compared to a jackal who tried to imitate lions;[52] an ass in the lion's skin;[53] the talkative tortoise who lost his life because he could not keep his mouth shut;[54] the crow who praised the jackal (Devadatta);[55] the young cuckoo who lost his life because he would not keep quiet;[56] and the talkative tawny-brown *brāhmaṇa*.[57] It is pointed out in another *Jātaka* story[58] that once he expressed unhappiness because he had never been asked to recite the *sutta*s; so, the monks decided to fulfil his wish. He took his favourite soup, and at sundown, wearing a blue lower robe and an outer robe of white[59] and carrying a beautifully carved fan, he appeared in the assembly.

---

[48] Ibid. See also I.B. Horner, 'The Earth as a Swallower', Supplementum, Vol. 23, in *Essays Offered to G.H. Luce by His Colleagues and Friends in Honour of His Seventy-fifth Birthday, Vol. I: Papers on Asian History, Religion, Languages, Literature, Music Folklore, and Anthropology* ed. Ba Shin (Ascona: Artibus Asiæ, 1966), 151–159.

[49] *Vin*, iii, 174.

[50] *DhA*, i, 143; J, i, 491.

[51] *J*, ii, 438f.

[52] Ibid., 65ff, 108.

[53] Ibid., 110.

[54] Ibid., 175.

[55] Ibid., 438.

[56] *J*, iii, 102.

[57] *J*, iv, 242.

[58] *J*, ii, 65f.

[59] See the violation regarding meal-timing (BD.ii.335–337) and dress (Vin.i.46, 49, 196, 198, 253, 283, 285, 289, 306, ii.267, iii.11, v.117)'.

But when he tried to recite, he began to sweat and lost his nerve. Thereafter, we are told, the monks became aware of the fact that his claim to learning was but pretence. This story obviously contradicts his portrayal in the *Vinaya* as a furious defender of Devadatta. But Thullanandā held him, Devadatta, Khaṇḍadeviyāputta, Samuddadatta and Kaṭamorakatissa as eminent disciples (*mahānāgā*) and rated them above Sāriputta, Moggallāna and Mahākaccāna.[60]

Thullanandā, who was known for her knowledge of the *dhamma*, was a clever preacher. However, Thullanandā too faces criticism for supporting Devadatta. She appears to have had charge of a large number of nuns, all of whom are shown as following her in various malpractices.[61] She is also accused of once using a false pretense to keep away monks from good food so that these friends of hers and their colleagues could have it.[62] In the *Suvaṇṇahaṃsa Jātaka* and the *Vinaya Piṭaka*, she is shown as greedy for possessions and often misappropriated gifts intended for other nuns.[63] She is also shown as being fond of the company of men, and frequenting streets and crossroads unattended so that she might not be hindered in her intrigues with them.[64] She is also accused of having regarded with sympathy such women who succumbed to temptation and having tried to shield them from discovery.[65] Further, she is accused in the later texts for bribing dancers and singers to sing her praises. She is shown as someone fractious and someone who could brook no rival, and especially hated Bhaddā Kapilānī Therī,[66,67] It has further been pointed out that she was an ardent admirer of Ānanda[68] and once when Mahākassapa called him a 'boy,' she is said to have become very upset and soon after left the *Saṃgha*.[69] She is also criticized for befriending Ariṭṭha when he was cast out of the *Saṃgha*.[70] The *Khuddakapāṭha Aṭṭhakathā* mentions Khaṇḍadeviyāputta, another associate of Devadatta, in a list of wicked persons.[71] In a late portion

[60] *Vin*, iv, 66.

[61] Ibid., 211, 239–240, 280.

[62] Ibid., 335.

[63] *J*, i, 474ff; *Vin*, iv, 245–246, 258.

[64] Ibid., 270, 273.

[65] Ibid., 216, 225, 230–231.

[66] Ibid., 283, 285, 287, 290, 292.

[67] Ibid., 248, 250.

[68] Her criticism may partly be explained by the fact that Ānanda, too, was criticized by a section of the *Saṃgha* on the eve of the First Council.

[69] *S*, ii, 219ff.

[70] *Vin*, iv, 218.

[71] The *Paramatthajotikā,* Vol. I (London: PTS, 1915) (henceforth *KhpA*), 126.

of the *Saṃyutta Nikāya*, Koṭamorakatissa is mentioned as one of the monks about whom dissatisfaction was expressed to the Buddha as well as by two *paccekabrahmā*, Subrahmā and Suddhāvāsa.[72]

However, Devadatta does not stand totally condemned in the Pāli literature. As many as three *sutta*s have been named after him in the Pāli *Tipiṭaka*. Once mention is also made of the text of a sermon delivered by Devadatta and when this was reported to Sāriputta, he used it as an occasion for a talk to the monks.[73] In some of the references, he is mentioned as an impeccable saint whose achievements were not only acknowledged by other saints like Sāriputta but also by the Buddha himself. For instance, the *Aṅguttara Nikāya* mentions him as the one who had the right view and could preach the correct *dhamma*.[74] Sāriputta and Ānanda are known to have acknowledged his great psychic power and majesty, which the Buddha also affirmed.[75] As pointed out earlier, the Buddha once not only praised Devadatta but also called him, along with ten other Elders, as the one who had 'put away evil...(and)...destroyed the fetters'.[76] In one reference in the *Vinaya Piṭaka*, in which he is condemned, he is also mentioned as the one who meditates in solitude.[77] In the same text, he is mentioned as an eloquent teacher, who 'gladdened, rejoiced, roused, delighted the monks far into the night with talk on *dhamma*'.[78] Some found in him a ready friend who was at their service both in prosperity and adversity.[79]

How does one reconcile with such a contradictory description? In one of the dilemmas, discussed in the *Milindapañha*, Devadatta is depicted as a mixture of good and evil.[80] Here, King Milinda asks Nāgasena:

> But, venerable, Nāgasena, your people say that Devadatta was altogether wicked, full of wicked dispositions, and that the Bodhisatta was altogether pure, full of pure dispositions. And yet Devadatta, through successive existences, was

---

[72] *S*, i, 148.

[73] *A*, iv, 402f.

[74] Ibid., 402.

[75] *Vin*, ii, 189. See R.A. Ray, *Buddhist Saints in India: A Study in Buddhist Values & Orientations* (New York: Oxford University Press, 1994), 162.

[76] *Ud*, i, 5. Strangely, the name of Devadatta is missing from the same list in *M*, iii, 78–89.

[77] *Vin*, ii, 184.

[78] *BD*, v, 280.

[79] '*Devadatto amhākaṃ maṅgalāmaṅgalesu sahāyo udakamaṇiko viya niccappatiṭṭhito*' (*DhA*, i, 65).

[80] *Mil*, 200–205.

> not only quite equal to the Bodhisatta, but even sometimes superior to him, both in reputation and in the number of his adherents.[81]

Nāgasena replies:

> Devadatta...was a protection to the poor, put up bridges and courts of justice and rest-houses for the people, and gave gifts according to his bent to the Samaṇas and Brāhmaṇas, to the poor and needy and the wayfarers, it was by the result of that conduct that, from existence to existence, he came into the enjoyment of so much prosperity. For of whom, O king, can it be said that without generosity and self-restraint, without self-control and the observance of the Uposatha, he can reach prosperity?[82]

A critical review of all the references appears to indicate that stories regarding Devadatta being an opponent of the Buddha since childhood are only later additions. There does not appear to be any historical truth in them. The differences between the Buddha and Devadatta appear to have arisen out of some serious issues which may have been personal and/or related to the functioning of the *Saṃgha*. It certainly cannot be denied that after the death of the Buddha and with the passage of time, the positive side of the character of Devadatta is overshadowed by the vitriolic condemnation as most of this condemnation appears in later Buddhist literature.[83] The statements of some of the contemporaries of the Buddha also seem to point to the fact that criticism of Devadatta was not justified. For instance, Nigaṇṭha Nātaputta is quoted by Pāli texts as saying that it was unfair to malign Devadatta as incorrigible (*atekiccho*).[84] So much so that once even Ānanda, who was a constant companion of the Buddha, is said to have been unsure about the criticism of Devadatta.[85]

The episodes relating to Devadatta have been analysed systematically by Mukherjee[86] and Bareau[87] and both of them have pointed out quite persuasively

---

[81] Ibid., 200. Translation from *Milinda*, 284.

[82] *Mil*, 204. Translation from *Milinda*, 291.

[83] See Ray, *Buddhist Saints in India*, 176, fn. 32.

[84] *M*, i, 392–393.

[85] For instance, when monks once asked Ānanda whether the Buddha's predictions regarding the results of Devadatta's crimes were based on actual knowledge, he furnished them with no answer at all until he had consulted the Buddha (*A*., iii, 402).

[86] Mukherjee, *Die Uberlieferung von Devadatta*.

[87] A. Bareau, 'Étude du bouddhisme', *Annuaire du Collçge de France* (1988–1989): 533–547.

that the episodes maligning Devadatta are a fabrication of later times. Devadatta's positive character becomes darker and darker as time goes by and one can discern an attempt to whitewash the positive side of his character as more and more blame is heaped on him. He is, thus, accused of being filled with greed, pride and ambition and of attempting various crimes, to set himself in the Buddha's stead, to induce Ajātasattu to kill his father, to himself murder the Buddha and so on, all in spite of his (in some accounts) previously saintly character. All this appears to be part of a plot whose agenda it was to tarnish his character.[88] It appears, as argued by R.A. Ray, Devadatta was not an evildoer but a realized master and that the most important reason for the vilification was his strict identification with forest Buddhism as it did not go well with settled monasticism.

> It is not just that he practices forest Buddhism, is a forest saint, and advocates forest renunciation. Even more, and worse from the viewpoint of his detractors, he completely repudiates the settled monastic form, saying in effect that he does not judge it to be authentic at all.[89]

He considered this 'as a form of laxity, a danger for the future of the community and of Buddhism altogether'.[90] His unwavering advocacy of the five austere practices may also be seen in the issue of leadership whereby Devadatta may have shown interest in taking up leadership after the Buddha's death considering that he believed and wanted to keep Buddhism austere against settled monasticism. As pointed out by Bareau, the only issue that could be accepted as historically true is that Devadatta proposed to the Buddha that the five austere practices be made obligatory, which the Buddha rejected; and thereafter, Devadatta affected schism in the *Saṃgha* by leaving along with 500 bhikkhus; and later, these bhikkhus were won back by Sāriputta and Moggallāna.[91]

That Devadatta was not so bad, after all, has also been pointed out in some of the texts of other Buddhist traditions. It has been pointed out in the *Sarvāstivāda-Vinaya* that for 12 years after his admission into the Order, Devadatta conducted himself with faultless deeds and thoughts. He read and recited the *sūtra*s, lived according to proper discipline and strove in his practice of dhamma.[92] In the

---

[88] Ibid., 542.

[89] Ray, *Buddhist Saints in India*, 171.

[90] Bareau, 'Étude du bouddhisme', 542.

[91] Ibid., 540ff.

[92] Mukherjee, *Die Uberlieferung von Devadatta*, 120.

Saddharmapuṇḍrīka Sūtra, Devadatta is depicted in a former life as a forest renunciant who assisted Buddha Sākyamuni to Buddhahood,[93] and the Buddha calls him his 'spiritual friend' (*kalyāṇamitra*),[94] in effect his teacher. It was through training under Devadatta as his teacher, the Buddha tells us, that he was able to perfect the qualities by which he eventually became a Buddha.[95] In future times, the Buddha continues, Devadatta will be greatly revered and honoured and shall become no less than the greatly revered *Tathāgata* Devarāja, who shall lead innumerable beings to Enlightenment. His relics will not be divided and shall be kept in a single gigantic *stūpa* worshipped by gods and humans. So holy will this *stūpa* be that those who circumambulate it, may hope for realization as an *arhant*, a *pratyekabuddha* or a Buddha. Finally, in the future, a great blessing shall come to those who hear about Devadatta: for those hearing this chapter of the *Saddharmapuṇḍrīka Sūtra* and gaining from it shall be liberated from rebirth in the three lower realms.[96]

It appears that the schism created by Devadatta was successful and Sāriputta and Moggallāna were either unsuccessful in winning back all those dissident monks who had left with Devadatta for Gayāsīsa or perhaps Devadatta succeeded later in recruiting some of his own. This fact is proved by a story related in one of the *Jātaka*s. According to this story, Ajātasattu built a monastery for Devadatta and sent 500 pots of such luxurious food that even some of the followers of the Buddha would steal themselves to taste it.[97] Thus, it seems that not only that Devadatta continued to have his own followers, but he even continued to have the support of Ajātasattu. Over seven centuries later, Faxian saw, near Sāvatthī, a community of disciples following Devadatta who rendered homage to the three previous Buddhas but not to the Sākyamuni Buddha.[98] Similarly, Xuanzang saw three monasteries in Bengal where the followers

---

[93] H. Kern, trans., *Saddharma-Puṇḍrīka or the Lotus of the True Law*, Sacred Books of the East, no. 32 (Oxford: Clarendon Press, 1884), chapter XI, stanza 46.

[94] Ibid.

[95] Ibid.

[96] Ibid.

[97] *J*, i, 186, 508. Interestingly, Devadatta, who left the *Saṃgha* on account of disagreement with the Buddha because the latter refused to implement the five austere practices, is himself accused in later portions of the Pāli literature of having indulged in violation of the same. Examples such as luxurious food being served at his monastery and his attempts to imitate the Buddha appear to be part of the smear campaign.

[98] S. Beal, *The Travels of Fah-hian and Sung yun* (London: Trübner, 1869), 82.

of Devadatta were in residence.[99] Xuanzang also saw a cave known as the Devadatta *samādhi* that was located near Rājagaha.[100] It is suggested that the reason for Devadatta's schism was indeed his adherence to certain austerities, which the mainstream community from which he and his group seceded were not willing to follow. These references also reveal the great success of Devadatta and his tradition, which was in existence at least up to a thousand years after its separation from mainstream Buddhism.[101] However, Ray believes that Devadatta's schism actually took place after the death of the Buddha.[102] This appears a little far-fetched. Not only that Devadatta predeceased the Buddha, but the tradition of Devadatta's differences with the Buddha is also well-grounded in all the traditions. Thus, it is hard to believe that Devadatta's parting of ways with the *Saṃgha* took place after the *Mahāparinibbāna*. The argument in the *Dhammapada Aṭṭhakathā* that Devadatta's resentment against the Buddha was for reasons similar to Suppabuddha's, who did not forgive the Buddha for abandoning his daughter,[103] does not appear to be true of Devadatta, a realized master.

The five austere practices must be seen as *raison le plus décisif* for the parting of ways between the Buddha and Devadatta. Prior to that, it was at most a playful cross-cousin rivalry, sans animus, that existed between the Buddha and Devadatta. And the only motive that may have influenced Devadatta, at least till the issue of the five austere practices, was this playful cross-cousin rivalry, a desire to surpass his cousin. However, non-resolution of this issue may have led to the frosting of relationship between the two: Devadatta being an advocate of stricter ascetical practices as against the Buddha's greater patience and forbearance in matters of discipline. In all probability, when with the passage of time the memory of the practice of playful cross-cousin rivalry disappeared, this frosting of relationship was misinterpreted as bitter enmity, thus the idea of fighting becoming its vital ingredient, ultimately culminating

[99] Thomas Watters, trans., *On Yuan Chwang's Travels in India,* Vol. 2 (London, 1904–1905), Second Indian Edition (Delhi: Munshiram Manoharlal, 1973), 191.

[100] Ibid., 155.

[101] Bareau, 'Étude du bouddhisme', 544; Ray, *Buddhist Saints in* India, 172; É. Lamotte, *Histoire du Bouddhisme Indien: Des Origenes á l'ére Śaka* (Louvain: Bibliothéque du Muséon, vol. 43, Louvain, Publisher: L'Institut Orientaliste de Louvain, 1958), 374. Also, see É. Lamotte, 'Le Buddha insulta-t-il Devadatta?', *Bulletin of the School of Oriental and African Studies* 33 (1970): 107–115.

[102] Ray, *Buddhist Saints in* India, 172.

[103] *DhA*, iii, 44f.

into antagonism of the Evil One against the Good One.[104] It is quite conceivable that the main body of the *Saṃgha* found it necessary to utilize Devadatta as a scapegoat, ridding the *Saṃgha* of its contradictions by imputing the insoluble problems of the community to him.[105]

References

Ref no	*Text*	*Editor/editors/translators*
#1	*The Dhammapada Aṭṭhakathā*	H.C. Norman (ed.)
#2	*The Vinaya Piṭakaṃ*	H. Oldenberg (ed.)
#3	*The Paramatthadīpanī*	F.L. Woodward (ed.)
#3	*The Papañcasūdanī*	J.H. Woods, D. Kosambi, and I.B. Horner (eds.)
#5	*The Buddhavaṃsa*	N.A.Jayawickrama (ed.)
#5	*The Manorathapūraṇī*	H. Walleser and H. Kopp (eds.)
#5	*The Madhuratthavilāsinī*	I.B. Horner (ed.)
#6	*The Jātaka*	V. Fausböll (ed.)
#8	*The Aṅguttara Nikāya*	R. Morris and E. Hardy (eds.)
#10	*The Udānaṃ*	P. Steinthal (ed.)
#12	*The Saṃyutta Nikāya*	M.L. Feer (ed.)
#17	*The Majjhima Nikāya*	V. Trenckner, and R. Chalmers (eds.)
#18	*The Book of Discipline*	I.B. Horner (trans.)
#26	*The Samantapāsādikā*	J. Takakusu and M. Nagai (eds.)
#27	*The Apadāna*	M.E. Lilley (ed.)
#28	*The Milindapañha*	V. Trenckner (ed.)
#35	*The Chronicle of the Island of Ceylon* or the *Dīpavaṃsa*	B.C. Law (ed. And trans.)
#39	*The Questions of King Milinda*	I.B. Horner (Trans.)
#71	*The Paramatthajotikā*	H. Smith (ed.)

Mahāvaṃsa. London: PTS, 1908.

Dhammapada Aṭṭhakathā. London: PTS, 1906–1915.

Vinaya Piṭakaṃ. London: PTS, 1879–1883.

The *Paramatthadīpanī*. London: PTS, 1891–1977.

[104] See A.M. Hocart, 'Buddha and Devadatta', *Indian Antiquary* 52 (1923): 267–272 and Kalipada Mitra, 'Cross-cousin Relation between Buddha and Devadatta', *Indian Antiquary* 53 (1924): 125–128.

[105] Yoshihiro Matsunami, 'Conflict within the Development of Buddhism', *Japanese Journal of Religious Studies* 6(1–2) (1979), Proceedings of the 1978 Tokyo Meeting of the Conference Internationale de Sociologie Religieuse, March–June, 338.

The *Papañcasūdanī*. London: PTS, 1922–1938.

Malalasekera, G.P. *Dictionary of Pāli Proper Names*, Vol. 2 (New Delhi: Oriental Reprint, 1983).

Buddhavaṃsa. London: PTS, 1974.

Manorathapūraṇī. London: PTS, 1956–1973.

The *Madhuratthavilāsinī*. London: PTS, 1946.

The *Jātakas*. London: Trübner & Co., 1877–1897.

The *Aṅguttara Nikāya*. London: PTS, 1885–1900.

The *Udānaṃ*. London: PTS, 1885.

The *Saṃyutta Nikāya*. London: PTS, 1884–1898.

The *Majjhima Nikāya*. London: PTS, 1888–1896.

The Book of the Discipline. London: PTS, 1938–1966.

The *Samantapāsādikā*. London: PTS, 1947–1975.

The *Apadāna*. London: PTS, 1925–1927.

The *Milindapañha*. London: Williams and Norgate, 1880.

Mukherjee, B. *Die Uberlieferung von Devadatta, dem Widersacher des Buddha, in den kanonischen Schriften*. Munich: J. Kitzinger, 1966.

Ruegg, D. Seyfort . *T'oung Pao*, Second Series, Vol. 54, Livr. 1/3 (1968): 164–168.

Chronicle of the Island of Ceylon or the Dīpavaṃsa.

Ceylon Historical Journal 7 (1958): 1–266.iv.44

Questions of King Milinda. Oxford: Oxford University Press, 1890, *Sacred Books of East*.

Sarao, K.T.S. *Origin and Nature of Ancient Indian Buddhism*, Reprint (Delhi: Delhi University, 2003).

Rockhill, W.W. *Life of the Buddha and the Early History of His Order: Derived from Tibetan Works*, Reprint (London: Kegan Paul International, 2003).

Horner, I.B. 'The Earth as a Swallower', Supplementum, Vol. 23, in *Essays Offered to G.H. Luce by His Colleagues and Friends in Honour of His Seventy-fifth Birthday, Vol. I: Papers on Asian History, Religion, Languages, Literature, Music Folklore, and Anthropology* (Ascona: Artibus Asiæ, 1966, 151–159).

Paramatthajotikā, Vol. I (London: PTS, 1915).

Ray, R.A. *Buddhist Saints in India: A Study in Buddhist Values & Orientations* (New York: Oxford University Press, 1994).

Bareau, A. 'Étude du bouddhisme', *Annuaire du Collçge de France* (1988–1989): 533–547

Kern, H., trans., *Saddharma-Puṇḍrīka or the Lotus of the True Law*, Sacred Books of the East, no. 32 (Oxford: Clarendon Press, 1884).

Beal, S. *The Travels of Fah-hian and Sung yun* (London: Trübner, 1869).

Watters Thomas, trans., *On Yuan Chwang's Travels in India,* Vol. 2 (London, 1904–1905), Second Indian Edition (Delhi: Munshiram Manoharlal, 1973).

Lamotte, É. *Histoire du Bouddhisme Indien: Des Origenes á l'ére Śaka* (Louvain: Bibliothéque du Muséon, vol. 43, Louvain, 1958).

______. 'Le Buddha insulta-t-il Devadatta?', *Bulletin of the School of Oriental and African Studies* 33 (1970): 107–115.

Hocart, A.M. 'Buddha and Devadatta', *Indian Antiquary* 52 (1923): 267–272

Mitra, Kalipada. 'Cross-cousin Relation between Buddha and Devadatta', *Indian Antiquary* 53 (1924): 125–128.

Matsunami, Yoshihiro 'Conflict within the Development of Buddhism', *Japanese Journal of Religious Studies* 6, nos 1 and 2 (1979), Proceedings of the 1978 Tokyo Meeting of the Conference Internationale de Sociologie Religieuse, March–June, 329–345.

CHAPTER

3

Devotion and Dissent in Hunter's *Bhakti*

*Kannappa in Hagiography, Sthalapurāṇa and Iconographic Representations**

T. S. Satyanath

Introduction

Did the spider study the Vedas?
or the snake consult law books?
Did the elephant labour at spiritual disciplines?
or the hunter intone a mantra?
Can learning be the source,
of our awakening?
No! To worship your feet
with devotion,
O god of Kāḷahasti,
would be enough for everything,
that lives![1]

1 *Śrīkālahastīśvara-śatakamu*, verse 13; see Hank Heifetz and Narayana Rao, Velcheru. 1987. tr. *For the Lord of the Animals-Poems from the Telugu, The kāḷahastīśvara Śatakamu of Dhūrjaṭi* (Delhi: Oxford University Press).

* This essay is based on one of the chapters of my doctoral dissertation. I am grateful to Professor Vijaya Ramaswamy for incorporating it in the current volume.

This poem, from Dhurjati's *Śrīkālahastīśvara-śatakamu*, a seventeenth century Telugu text, rightly creates an interesting intertextuality between *bhakti* poems, hagiographies and the *sthalapurāṇa* of Kalahasti and Kannappa. The reference to the animals associated in the *sthalapurāṇa* and to the hunter, *Bhakta* Kannappa, in a single verse, not only establishes an intertextuality between the *sthalapurāṇa* and hagiographic traditions but also creates an equation between the *bhakti* of the hunters, animals and animal-like *bhakta*s. The first four lines of the verse question the futility of orthodox learning as the spider, snake, elephant and the hunter *bhakta* did not have any such knowledge. Subsequently, it states in a declarative tone that the learning need not have to be the source of awakening. Then, while negating all such orthodox approaches to the realization of God, the poem upholds the belief that devotion, even performed sacrilegiously, could liberate everything that lives on the earth. The poem epigrammatically captures the discussion and analysis that has been done in this essay within an ambivalent trend of a subservient devotion and subversive revolt in operation simultaneously that has been variously conceived as counter-structure,[2] dissent[3] and non-*āgamic*, *pratilōma*.[4]

To start with, the essay undertakes a depiction of the hunter saint Kannappa in hagiographic traditions that are available in the Sanskrit, Tamil, Kannada and Telugu languages, to study the change and variation within the hagiographic traditions. Some of these depictions are in the *bhakti* poems composed by the saint poets belonging to different Shaiva sectarian groups[5] and some of them are in the form of hagiographies and *sthalapurāṇa*s. It has been suggested that the change and variation that we notice temporally, spatially and socially are symptomatic of the changes that took place in the ideological and social aspects of life in medieval South India. An attempt has also been made to explore the changes that took place within the iconography of the hunter *bhakta* to further substantiate the point just made.

---

[2] A.K. Ramanujan, *Speaking of Śiva* (Harmondsworth: Penguin, 1973).

[3] R. Champakalakshmi, 'From Devotion to Dissent and Dominance: The Bhakti of the Tamil Alvars and Nayanmars', in *Tradition, Dissent and Ideology: Essays in Honour of Romila Thapar*, ed. R. Champakalakshmi and S. Gopal (Delhi: Oxford University Press, 1996).

[4] T.S. Satyanath, 'Hunter's Bhakti: Kannappa(n) in Hagiographic Traditions' (Unpublished PhD thesis, University of Delhi, 2006).

[5] T.S. Satyanath, 'Bhakti of Hunters, Animals and Animal-like Bhaktas: Implications for Comparative Dravidian Literature', *Dravidian Studies* 1(2) (2003): 61–86.

Kannappa: The Hunter *Bhakta*

Kannappa, the hunter *bhakta*, has traditionally been considered as the earliest of the sixty-three Nayanars. The hagiographies record that he worshipped the *linga* in the Shiva temple of Kalahasti with the offerings of flowers tucked into his curly hair, meat tasted by him and water which he carried in his mouth. When one of the eyes of Shiva started to bleed, Kannappa plucked out his right eye with an arrow and fixed it to the god. When the other eye of Shiva started bleeding too, Kannappa prepared to pluck out his other eye, raising his sandal-clad foot and placing it against the eyebrow of Shiva to mark the exact spot. At this juncture, Shiva intervened by stopping Kannappa with his own hands, gave his eyes back and showered his grace on his hunter *bhakta*. Although several versions of the story are available from hagiographies, most of them show the pattern that is briefly outlined here. Though Kannappa is not included in the list of seven Nayanars who are credited with singing poems in praise of Shiva, he has been revered and praised by some of these Nayanars in their poems.

Kannappa's story is important in the hagiographic tradition because he was a *bhakta* belonging to a hunting community. References to kingdoms of the hunters occur not only in the famous inscriptions of the Gupta King, Samudragupta, but also come from the epics, the *Ramayana* and the *Mahabharata*. There is a Jaina story in Prakrit in which a *kirāta* king becomes a follower of Mahavira, the founder of Jainism (Nagarajayya 1997: 61)[6] Despite such references, the hunters were probably not an integral part of the agrarian system during the early centuries of the first millennium. However, the recognition of the *kuranci* (mountainous region) as one of the five *tiṇai*s in early Tamil literature suggests that the forest dwellers were already in the process of getting incorporated into the agrarian world and its belief system. Kannappa's mode of worship of Shiva broke all the rules of ritual purity prescribed by the *āgama*s, when he makes the ritual offering of raw meat, bathes the God from the water he had carried in his mouth and puts his sandal-clad foot on the eyes of the *linga* to offer his eyes. The hagiographies portray the episode as if everything in the story happened according to the desire of Shiva, and this was to test and demonstrate the devotion of the hunter *bhakta* to the world.

[6] H.P. Nagarajayya, *Jaina Kathakosa* (Hampi: Kannada University, 1997).

Nomenclature of Kannappa

The way the hagiographic tradition has constructed the name of the hunter *bhakta* throws certain insights into the process of understanding the story of Kannappa. Early references from Tamil mention his name as *tiṇṇa(n)*. He is referred to by the same name in the *Periya-purāṇam* of Sekkilar, a Tamil hagiography belonging to the twelfth century. The hunter *bhakta* gets his name Kannappa because of his deed – offering his eyes to Shiva. In Dravidian languages, the word *kaṇ* designates the eye (DED. 1209). Harihara, the earliest hagiographer in Kannada (c. AD 1200), refers to him as Kannappa. Shadakshari's *Basavarāja-vijaya* (AD 1677), another hagiography in Kannada, also refers to him as Kannappa. The earliest Telugu hagiographer, Palkuriki Somanatha (c. AD 1280), refers to him as *uḍumūri kannappa*. A Kannada folk version, narrated by the Myasa Bedas, a hunting community that migrated to Karnataka during the sixteenth century AD, has been called *beḍara kannayyana kathe* or 'the story of Bedara Kannayya'. Most of the Kannada and Telugu hagiographies refer to him as Kannappa. It appears that rather than his real name, which suggested his heroism as a hunter, the devotional aspect of his worship, that is, the offering of his eyes, has become the popular name of the saint in hagiographic traditions.

The Sanskrit versions of the story too appear to literally translate the word in giving a name to him suggesting the direction of movement of the story. Thus, he is addressed as *netrārpaka* or 'the one who offered the eyes' in Upamanyu's *Śivabhaktya-mahātmyam* and *Śivarahasyam*. Similarly, in *Bhaktivilāsa*, ascribed to the legendary sage Agastya, Kannappa has been referred as *nayanārpaṇa*, the one who offered his eye. However, it is interesting to point out that he has also been given the name *dhīra* (Sanskrit), 'courageous', in the works of Upamanyu and Agastya just mentioned. This could be due to the fact that he is also addressed as *tiṇṇa* in Tamil, which carries the same meaning as *dhīra*. Almost all Sanskrit works that mention his name have been a part of the *Skanda-purāṇa* , which itself is a later text, most probably composed after the composition of the early hagiographies in Tamil, Kannada and Telugu.

Most of the *bhakti* poems in Tamil, Kannada, Sanskrit and Telugu actually stress his offering of his eyes and the hunter's profession rather than actually naming him. This suggests the important role of sacrificial acts in the hagiographic tradition.

Kannappa in Hagiographic Traditions

In this section, I have attempted to outline the details regarding the depiction of Kannappa in Tamil, Kannada and Telugu hagiographic traditions. Although there is only one version of hagiography in Tamil, *Periya-purāṇam* by Sekkilar, in Kannada, there are about fifteen versions and in Telugu, there are about six versions. It would be beyond the scope of this essay to undertake a detailed description and a comparative study of all the versions available. Hence, a brief outline of the salient features of the story of Kannappa common to all the hagiographies has been given here and a structural analysis of the hagiography has been provided.

> *Tinna*, a wild tribesman, was a devotee of Sri Kalahasthisvara. He used to offer raw meat to the god in worship, after tasting it himself to make sure that it is tasty. He would also bring water in his mouth and offer it as a ritual bath for the god. He also carried flowers tucking them to his curly hairs to offer them to the god. Another devotee, a Brahmin priest, who regularly offered worship in the temple, used to find the temple desecrated. The priest used to clean up the shrine everyday and performed worship with appropriate *āgamic* rituals. But everyday *Tinna* returned, swept away the flowers and leaves with his footwear and offered his worship. This went on for four days. On the fifth night the god appeared to the priest in a dream and directed him to hide himself behind the *linga* the next day so that he could see the love of a true devotee. He said that he esteemed the tasted meat and the polluted water that *Tinna* offered Him more than any other kind of offering. Accordingly, the next day, priest hid himself behind the *linga* and when *Tinna* arrived to offer his worship witnessed the great offering. As god had resolved to test *Tinna*'s devotion and demonstrate it to the world, blood began to flow out from one of the eyes of the *linga*. *Tinna* was struck with grief looking at what was happening to his god. Though he tried to stop the bleeding from all the medicines that he knew, he could not stop the bleeding. Thereupon, he removed one of his eyes with an arrow and placed it on the bleeding eye of the god. The bleeding in the affected eye stopped, but blood started coming out from the other eye. *Tinna*, in desperate grief, resolved to take out his second eye too. In doing so, he placed his left foot clad with sandal on the eye of the *linga* and was about to pluck his other eye with an arrow. The god appeared and stopped him from plucking his second eye, embraced him and said since he had offered him his own *kannu*s 'eyes', he would hereafter be known as Kannappa, the one who offered the eyes. The god also assured that Kannappa would ever stand by the side of the god. This is how there is an image of Kannappa in the sanctum sanctorum at Kalahasti.

The versions differ slightly with regard to certain features. We can only look at a few of them to demonstrate the nature of such variations by taking the earliest versions from Tamil, Telugu and Kannada.[7] One such variation is the way in which the priest of the temple has been treated in the hagiographies. In *Periya-purāṇam*, the priest of the temple is a Brahmin and his name is Civakōcari. Though shocked by the imprint of sandals, pugmarks of dogs, meat and strange wild flowers on the head of the god, he patiently sweeps and cleans the entire premises and, after due purificatory rites, worships the lord according to tradition. He has been praised as a pious man and a great *bhakta* of Shiva.

In the *Basava-purāna* version, the priest is an ascetic and after noticing what Kannappa had offered to the god, thinks that it must be the action of a barbarous person. He throws away the pieces of meat, performs a five-nectar (*pancāmṛta*) ritual bath, takes water from *linga*'s feet and sprinkles it all over the temple, reciting the Vedas. The ascetic also says, 'He hunts animals, and I am an ascetic. This is a fight between unequals', and narrates the episode of a fight between the spider and the elephant, in which the spider kills the elephant. After the ascetic watches Kannappa offering his own eyes and Shiva appearing before him, he praises Kannappa for his innocence, courage and power and prostrates before him. In the Kannada versions, the depiction of the Brahmin, however, becomes problematic. In fact, the Virashaiva tradition in general depicts Brahmins in a negative image. This has been discussed in detail next. In Harihara's *Kaṇṇappana-ragaḷe*, the priest has been referred as a *śiva-brāhmaṇa*. His devotion to god has been said to be a pseudo one. When Parvati asks Shiva about his devotion, Shiva says:

> The Brahmin looks like a clear water from outside,
> but his heart is muddy, Oh Gauri.
> The Brahmin worship looks sweet,
> but his heart is poisonous, Oh Gauri.[8]

---

[7] A detailed comparison of similarities and differences between *Periya-purāṇam* and Harihara's *Kaṇṇappana-ragaḷe* and Surangakavi's *Triṣaṣṭi-purtana-cāritra* could be seen in the introduction in R.C. Hiremath, *Surangakaviya Trisasti Puratana Caritra* (Dharwar: Karnataka University, 1973).

[8] *pārvan-aggavaṇi tiḷi mana kadaḍu ele gauri,*
pārvan-arcane-y-inidu mana-v-ati viṣam gauri. (Ibid., 275, lines 407–408)

The Brahmin priest even gets ready to kill Kannappa with a dagger.[9] There are also differences with regard to the way Kannappa gets rewarded in the end. Whereas in *Periya-purāṇam* Shiva hugs Kannappa and keeps him in proximity forever, Palkuriki Somanatha says that Shiva and Kannappa kept looking at each other and still continue to do that even today. The Kannada version of Harihara says that Shiva took Kannappa to his abode and gave him the *gaṇa-padavi*, to stay eternally with Shiva. However, each of these details has their own specific function with regard to the narration of specific ideology.

A comparison of the hagiographies reveals that certain actions of the entire episode might be partly narrated or sometimes completely missing in different versions. Whereas the *Periya-purāṇam* does not contain the *bhakti* of the animal devotees referred in the *sthalapurāṇa* version, namely, the spider, the snake and the elephant, it is narrated differently in the *Basava-purāṇa* version.[10] In the latter one, there is no reference to a snake at all. Instead, the spider and the elephant cross each other's path of worship and fight. There is also no reference to the web catching fire from the votive lamp and the spider hurling on it to extinguish it. Kannada versions of hagiography usually avoid incorporating the episode of the animal devotees, which the Telugu *sthalapurāṇa* ceremoniously celebrates. The version available in Dhurjati's *Śrīkāḷahasti-māhātmyamu* goes one step ahead and gives the stories of the previous birth for the three animals, and some versions also give a *purāṇic* lineage for the three animals. There are also disagreements among the versions regarding the specific animal's meat that was offered to Shiva by Kannappa. While some versions say it was wild boar's meat, other versions say it was rabbit's meat. There are also versions which say that it was deer's meat. What specific and functional role does each of these variants play for the narratives in which they become an integral part, and the significance they have on the communities that share such epistemologies, however, needs a detailed and thorough study of variations from a comparative perspective.

---

[9] In the folk version of the Myasa Bedas of Karnataka, the Brahmin priest first loses his cool for the *bilva* leaf heap that Kannappa has put all over inadvertently and cleans the entire premises. He then performs the worship, offers the ritual food to the God and goes back with the *prasāda*.

[10] Although several poems in Dhurjati *Śrīkālahastīśvara-śatakamu* refer to this story in brief, a detailed account of it is given later.

There is one aspect of the story about which hagiographies are unanimous. This aspect is central to the understanding of the story of Kannappa's offering of the flowers tucked into his hair, the water from his mouth and the tasted meat to Shiva. The hagiography and the episodes that get integrated into it have shown two concerns that are central to South Indian Shaiva *bhakti*. In fact, the two issues emerge from the sacrilegious mode of worship that Kannappa performs to Shiva. The first one is the identification and incorporation of a *bhakta* from a marginalized, non-agrarian community and his sacrilegious modes of worship. The second concern is to create a confrontation between the *āgamic* and the non-*āgamic* modes of worship and accommodating the non-*āgamic* modes of worship along with their polluting and extremely violent aspects incorporated into the temple traditions.

Medieval Indian Hindu society's attempts to preserve and sustain caste segregation was made possible through forbidden food exchange and forbidden matrimonial alliances across castes. Accordingly, food and bride exchange rules are exactly alike, making caste an endogamous unit. However, regarding food exchange, there were certain relaxations. Whereas the cooked (*pakva*, Sanskrit) food was forbidden for exchange across castes, except in the form of giving it as alms (*bhikṣā*, Sanskrit) and in the form of *prasāda*, 'leftover from food offered to god', the raw (*kaccā*) food was acceptable to some extent. The pastoralist products like milk, yogurt, buttermilk and ghee were thus exchanged without any restriction.

Pointing out the focus of the stories about the hunter's *bhakti*, Shulman observes as follows:

> The story in its present form demonstrates a theme common to many devotional movements – the superiority of crude but sincere worship over more conventional, 'orthodox' forms. Bhakti makes acceptable even the anathema of offering food and water that has come into contact with saliva. Kannappar's offering is the reversal of the idea of *prasāda* as the gift of the deity: the god grants the reminder of the offering, which in this context is sacred that impure, and which express a relationship of servant and lord between the worshipper (the recipient of *prasāda*) and the deity who grants it. In the Kannappar's story, it is the simple devotee who offers impure food to the god, but the polluted is accepted and even preferred because it is offered in love.[11]

---

[11] Shulman, D., *Tamil Temple Myths: Sacrifice and Divine Marriage in the South Indian Shaiva Tradition* (Princeton: Princeton University Press, 1980), 136.

There is a need to interrogate and rework the concept of *prasāda* and its implications for understanding the hagiography. In general, saliva is a polluting agent and everything that comes in contact with it results in pollution, which is inauspicious. However, it is not considered as polluting under certain circumstances. The concept of consuming the leftover food offered to the god or the holy men is a practice widely prevalent among several religious sects of Hinduism. However, the conceptual framework of consumption of *prasāda* entails the grace of the god on the one hand, and a mutual obligatory binding between the god and the *bhakta* on the other. In several *bhakti* sects, *prasāda* entails accepting God's saliva in the form of food that has been offered to God. The aspect of acceptance of saliva is also central to the family as a unit and is permissible only between the husband and wife on the one hand, and the mother and offspring on the other. It is interesting to note that the husband and wife and the mother and child share the food between them that has come into contact with saliva not only in reality but also ritualistically.[12] In addition, they also share a mutually obligatory relationship between them, similar to the one that is found between the god and his *bhakta*. In fact, the *bhakta* as a wife and as a child are two most celebrated themes in *bhakti* literature. What is fascinating about Kannappa's episode is that whereas the saliva exchange within the family is hierarchical and unidirectional, implying a unidirectional flow of body fluids from husband to wife and from mother to the child, the direction of flow is reversed in the case of Kannappa. As Kannappa's mode of worship reverses the direction of the flow of body fluids – the flowers that he had tucked into his hair is offered to God,[13] water contaminated by Kannappa's mouth is sprinkled on God's body, his partly eaten meat is offered to the god – it creates an inverse world order and threatens the order that prevailed within the orthodoxy. Such reversals create a *pratilōma* system, an inverse world order, which, in turn, creates and defines new types of interpersonal relationships in a society or sectarian community.

[12] Among the Brahmins of Karnataka, a marriage feast called *bhūmada ūṭa* is arranged in which the newly wed couple eat and feed each other from the same banana leaf. A similar ritual is observed at the time of *upanayana* (sacred thread) ceremony in which the mother and son eat food for the last time together from the same banana leaf.

[13] In the Vaishnava hagiography of the Alvars of Tamil Nadu, Andal offers the flowers that she had put on her head to Vishnu. This act has continued as a ritual practice and even today, the flowers are offered first to Andal and taken subsequently to Vishnu for offering.

The dynamics of food and saliva consumption for *bhakta*, couple and god in terms of *anulōma* (orthodox) and *pratilōma* (counter) systems, as structures and counter-structures, have been schematically represented in Figure 3.1.

Kannappa's offering of the tasted meat or performing the ritual bathing to Shiva, in which saliva – the highest polluting agent – is involved, gets repeatedly sanctified in hagiography. One of the web versions of the story compares the saliva to the ghee that is offered to *agni* in sacrificial rites on the one hand, and to honey that is poured over the food to sweeten it on the other.

> To provide the maximum tasty food to the Lord he tasted the cooked meat to select the exotic pieces. Like the ghee that is given to the tongues of flame in the sacrificial rites that reaches the *devas*, the food he tasted was enjoyed much by the Lord. The hunter poured honey to the food he selected, to make it more tasty (www.saivam.org).[14]

It has been further claimed that the water Kannappa used to bring in his mouth for the anointment of Shiva has been said to be more sacred that the holy waters of Ganga.

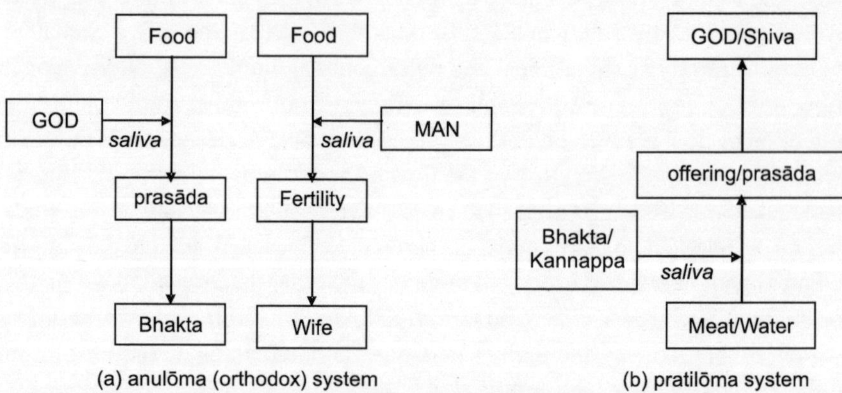

Fig. 3.1: A Schematic Representation of Food as Prasāda/Leftover for *Bhakta*, Couple and God[15]

It is said that Shiva's body became more auspicious after accepting the sacrilegious mode of worship by Kannappa. In fact, the hagiography goes one

[14] Available at www.saivam.org. 'The History of Kannappa Nayanar', no author, accessed 27 July, 2013.

[15] *Dynamics of Food and Saliva consumption for Bhakta, Couple and God.* Satyanath (2006: 175) Satyanath, T.S. *Hunter's Bhakti: Kannappa(n) in Hagiographic Traditions* (Unpublished PhD Thesis, University of Delhi, 2006).

step ahead and says that Shiva became what he is because of the contact of the saliva of Kannappa. His body was purified; he became superior to the universe; he gained immortality; he surpassed the sacred texts; transcended all taboos and his body became as sacred as his head, where the sacred Ganga dwells.

> Moon bearer became popular when he was touched by the water from Kannappa's feet. The one who destroyed Rati's husband had his body purified by Kannappa's leftovers. Because he drank Kannappa's gargle water, the destroyer of the three demon cities became superior to the whole universe. By eating Kannappa's *prasāda*, Parvati's husband gained immortality. By eating that *prasāda*, the god surpassed the knowledge of the *veda*s and *śāstra*s. By eating food that was polluted by Kannappa's saliva Shiva transcended all taboos. Because the *linga* was polluted by Kannappa's saliva, his entire body gained the same status as his head.[16]

It is not only the canonization of the counter-structure that we see here. The fact that the ritualization process of such a counter-structure was already complete by the thirteenth century AD is evident from how Palkuriki Somanatha declares towards the end of the story of Kannappa that he is narrating: 'Even today in that city, Three eyes is anointed with the water he has first washed Kannappa's mouth. Mṛḍa still never eats anything unless it has been first offered to Kannappa.'[17]

There is another interesting transaction that takes place between Shiva and Kannappa that needs to be problematized here. It is the exchange of body parts and has significant implications for the understanding of not only the story of Kannappa in hagiography but also the stories of the animals associated with the *sthalapurāṇa*. In a way, Kannappa's eyes being fixed to Shiva creates a sort of unity between Shiva and Kannappa. Moreover, Shiva grants a new pair of eyes to Kannappa. The exchange of eyes between Shiva and his *bhakta*, leading to the mutual sharing of the body parts, creates symmetry between Shiva and Kannappa. Whereas Kannappa is worshipped in the sanctum of the temple at Kalahasti, Shiva becomes a hunter elsewhere, as Kirata Shiva in the Indrakila episode of the Mahabharata, and according to the local traditions, Kannappa is Arjuna reborn. Scholars have pointed out that Kirata Shiva episode appears to be a South Indian interpolation into the text of the *Mahabharata*. There is a

---

[16] V. Narayana Rao, trans., *Shiva's Warriors: The Basava Purana of Palkuriki Somanatha* (Princeton: Princeton University Press, 1990), 119.

[17] Ibid., 120.

long passage in Palkuriki Somanatha that appropriately brings out the unification and symmetry between the two. This process needs to be highlighted further. Uma (Parvati) notices that Shiva and Kannappa started to look alike: 'they were equally beautiful as they looked into each other's eyes. And they seemed to have become one with each other. Kannappa's eyes and Black Throat's eyes looked like twins.'[18] Making use of a hyperbole, Somanatha further observes, 'It was equally valid to say that all four eyes belonged to Kannappa or all four eyes belonged to Ishvara'.[19] Finally, suggesting the greatness of the act of offering of the eyes by Kannappa, and thereby underscoring the significance of the process of incorporating the *bhakti* of the hunters and their community into agrarian *bhakti*, Somanatha says, 'the brilliance of the four eyes dimmed the eye on Shiva's forehead'.[20] The deed of the *bhakta* getting celebrated at the expense of the greatness of God Himself is a characteristic feature of many hagiographies of the Shaivism of South India. The exaggerative statement of Somanatha rightly underscores the analysis done here by making the *purāṇic* version of the third eye of Shiva's mythology look dim due to the brightness of the counter-structure constructed by the hagiographic version of Kannappa's story.

The significance of Kannappa offering his eyes to Shiva without any expectation and with pure devotion has been further highlighted by comparing his act to others, in particular to Vishnu who has done something similar to it. It is interesting to point out that Vishnu himself offered one of his eyes to Shiva and in turn, got the discus as a reward for his offering. Although the story is not popular among the hagiographers, Nayanars appear to have been familiar with the episode. Appar's poem refers to it as follows:

> While Vishnu,
> smearing himself liberally with the sacred ash,
> was worshiping Lord Civan daily,
> with one thousand lotus flowers.
> One day he found himself short of one flower,
> And made up the shortage with one of his eyes;
> For that act of ardour,
> the Lord bestowed on him the discus.
> The same Lord of conflicting deeds,

[18] Ibid., 118.

[19] Ibid.

[20] Ibid.

bestows His grace on humanity,
while seated at Veezhimizhalai,
in the temple,
which Vishnu brought down there from heaven,
in gratitude for Lord Civan bestowing on him the discus.[21]

Vanmikanathan further observes that the act of Vishnu's offering of one of his eyes to Shiva to get rewarded by the discus actually pales in front of unselfish compassion and the compelling feeling of empathy expressed by Kannappa.[22] He quotes Manikkavachagar's *Tiruvācakam* in support of his observation:

What is the story behind the gracious bestowal,
of the godly disc,
which split the body of the stormy petrel
of a Salandharan –
on goodly Narayanan on that day?
Note that on fortunate Narayanan
gouging out his eye
and placing it on a flower at the feet of Haran
He bestowed the disc on him.[23]

Such stories also reflect the tensions that prevailed between Shaivism and Vaishnavism, which eventually were appropriated and interpreted in hagiographies and *Purāṇas*. Hagiographies in this sense are sites for debates and controversies, and it is through their appropriation that sectarian communities effectively and convincingly constructed structures and counter-structures and generated the discourses of medieval *bhakti*. Hagiographies are actually attempts of incorporation and canonization of ideological pressures that are exerted on traditions and reflect the processes of change that are constantly in operation within a given tradition. Accordingly, the process of incorporation and canonization is never complete and as long as we do not see such changes as degeneration and inappropriate developments, there is always ample room to view them as continually evolving systems reflecting the dynamic changes that the traditions are undergoing within themselves.

---

[21] Appar, IV, 64. See Vanmikanathan. G. 1985. *Periya Puranam: A Tamil Classic On The Great Saiva Saints of South India by Shekkizar*. Chennai: Sri Ramakrishna Math.

[22] Ibid.

[23] Ibid. Vanmikanathan (1985: 518)

Kannappa in *Sthalapurāṇa* Traditions

The study of the story of Kannappa in hagiographic traditions demonstrated that rather than the conventional type of *bhakti*, it is the sacrilegious acts and the extreme violence and cruelty that is involved in such devotion that become central to the construction of hagiographies. The analysis also demonstrated the processes of constructing counter-structures to dominant orthodoxy, thereby carving out niches in the tradition to accommodate the counter-structures of hagiographic traditions. *Sthalapurāṇa*s, as legendary tales associated with the sacred geography of gods and their *bhakta*s, not only provides space and power for the characters associated with them but also play an important role in the dissemination of the ideologies and counter-ideologies constructed by the sects and temples, through its sacred geography and hagiography. It is for this reason that we need to look at the *sthalapurāṇa*s.

There is another specific reason for the need to study the *sthalapurāṇa*s of Kalahasti in particular. It is interesting to note that by the time Palkuriki Somanatha composed *Basava-purāṇa*, an element of the *sthalapurāṇa* of Kalahasti had already been incorporated into the hagiography by referring to the rivalry between the spider and the elephant in worshipping Shiva. In hagiography, and in several *bhakti* poems in Telugu, an intertextuality develops between the hagiographic tradition and the *sthalapurāṇa* tradition. All these aspects are going to be looked into in detail in this section.

Dhurjati's *Śrīkālahastīśvara-śatakamu*

Dhurjati, claimed to be a prominent poet of medieval Telugu literature, lived during the middle part of the sixteenth century AD (1480–1545). Tradition claims that he lived in the temple town of Kalahasti. There are also scholars who say that he belonged to seventeenth century and only visited the temple and composed his two works on Kalahasti temple.[24] Traditionally, Dhurjati has been considered as one among the eight great poets, *aṣṭadiggajamulu* or 'the eight guardian elephants', and a major poet in a galaxy of poets patronized by the Vijayanagara court during the period of Krishnadevaraya. He wrote two important works: *Śrīkāḷahasti-māhātmyamu*, a *bhakti prabandham* containing the *sthalapurāṇa* in Telugu; and *Śrīkālahastīśvara-śatakamu*, a composition in praise of Shiva in the genre of *śataka* in Sanskrit. *Śataka* is a genre of 100 short poems on a specific theme. In addition, many *cāṭu* poems available in popular lore have been claimed to be written by Dhurjati.

[24] Heifetz and Narayana Rao, *For the Lord of the Animals*.

There are several poems in *Śrīkālahastīśvara-śatakamu* in which there are references either to Kannappa or to the animal *bhakta*s mentioned in the *sthalapurāṇa*. In the genre of *bhakti* poems, there is a particular sub-genre called *nindā stuti* (praise in the guise of censure), where the saint poets accuse the god either for having done something which he is not expected to do for a *bhakta* or for accepting his *bhakta*s only when they did such a deed. Many such deeds that appear in poems of this type actually constitute sacrilegious acts that are not accepted within the *āgamic* mode of worship. The overtone of such praises suggests a hidden admiration for having let something take place, which otherwise would not have been possible. As Kannappa's mode of worship is considered highly sacrilegious, Dhurjati (in verse 17) ridicules Shiva that he had a craving for meat, which refers to the story of Kannappa. However, the ridicule is for the fact that having a deer in hand, a sword in the other hand to cut it, Ganges water on the head, fire in the eye and a skull as a vessel to cook it, it is not befitting for Shiva to have accepted the meat that has been tasted offered by Kannappa.[25]

> If what you had was a craving for meat,
> how could that have been any trouble,
> when you hold a deer on the palm of a hand,
> with another arm raising a sharp sword,
> and fire alive inside your third eye,
> and water of the Ganges in your hair,
> to be well cooked in the bowl of that skull that you carry?
> Was it fitting for you then, O God of Kāḷahasti,
> when that tribesman,
> offered you meat he had soiled
> with his own spit by tasting it,
> for you to have accepted
> and to have eaten?[26]

The glaring aspects of Kannappa's offering to Shiva constitute meat, that too meat tasted by the devotee; the bathing of Shiva by the water that he has carried in his mouth and placing his sandal-clad foot on the head of the *linga*. Dhurjati's verse, given next, praises Shiva who accepted such an unusual worship and in turn, rewarded the devotee with the great honour that he deserved. In a sarcastic tone, the poet says that he and the other *bhakta*s are unable to understand the majesty of Shiva.

---

[25] The description appears to present Shiva in *kāpālika* form.

[26] Ibid., verse 17.

He gave you food soiled by his tasting it,
in the cup of a folded leaf.
He bathed you,
with a jet of water out of his mouth.
And yet you made Kannappa
Worthy of all this great honour with which
he glows!
O God of Kāḷahasti,
we cannot understand
the majesty in which you move.[27]

It has already been pointed out that extreme violence and cruelty marks South Indian Shaiva *bhakti* in general, and the episodes associated with Kalahasti in particular. There is a direct reference to the fierce violence involved in the *bhakti* of the spider, snake and elephant. Dhurjati, as a *bhakta*, complains that despite his mind being full of thoughts of such devotion-filled violence, he has not been able to find Him and by implication, salvation.

Those fortunate beings,
whom you once anointed as kings,
of the realm of Freedom
and I are alike!
Yes! You ask how?
Like them – the spider,
the young cobra,
and the elephant in rut,
my thoughts are filled with fierce violence!
The only difference,
is that I have not found you,
in mind,
O God of Kāḷahasti![28]

In the previous section, there is a discussion on the exchange of eyes between Shiva and his *bhakta*, leading to the mutual sharing of the body parts that creates symmetry between Shiva and Kannappa. Interestingly, the verse given below further substantiates the point discussed there. If the hunter shares his eyes with Shiva, the elephant shares its skin as Shiva's robe and the snake shares itself with Shiva as an ornament around his neck. The poet thinks that it

[27] Ibid., verse 85.
[28] Ibid., verse 38.

is appropriate that as they share their body or body parts with Shiva, they were rightly given salvation. But he is puzzled by the very fact that the spider did not do such an act and has been imaged on the *linga*, despite getting an honour similar to that the other two animals got. Hence, he requests the presiding deity of Kalahasti to explain to him the reason behind the spider being accepted by Shiva. The spider's story appears to be earlier as compared to the snake and elephant, and this is clearly evident from the fact that it has been mentioned in Palkuriki Somanatha's *Basava-purāṇa* and that of the snake and elephant appear for the first time in the works of Dhurjati.

The first verse of *Śrīkālahastīśvara-śatakamu*, which appears to be in a distress and tone of surrender, however cannot hide the pleasures of enjoyment that the author is attempting to discard now, that too half-heartedly. The helplessness expressed due to old age and wearing of the body's physical strength and lack of interest in erotic desire appear to glorify the happy past rather than the poet's distress in the present. At the same time, like many of the accusing verses that we have seen, the poem does not reflect any element of *nindā* in that sense.

> My chest has been worn away,
> by the breasts of women rubbing against it.
> My skin has been roughened,
> with love scars from their nails.
> Lost in the straining of passion, youth
> has gone.
> My hair has started falling out,
> I am sick of it all.
> I can't go on in this circling world,
> God of Kāḷahasti, make me desire less.[29]

The superiority of the saints and their unique devotion has been considered to be far more superior compared to the deeds that are prescribed as virtuous in codes during the medieval period. Consider the following verse, which says that such virtuous deeds are not capable of leading one to the world attained by the great saints even though they have done deeds amounting to sacrilege. It is interesting to point out that giving donations, building a temple, constructing a reservoir (irrigation tank), growing a forest, were all considered as acts of merit. In fact, these acts are the characteristic aspects of the medieval agrarian system in which *bhakti* sects emerged and flourished.

---

[29] Ibid., verse 1.

Those who father a son or –
of equal merit – give charity,
build a temple,
pay for the marriage of a Brahmin,
deservedly receive the dedication of a fine poem,
dig out a reservoir for the flow of water,
or make a forest grow.
Even such people,
who've lived well,
cannot go to the world,
earned by those who have served you,
O God of Kāḷahasti.[30]

The discussion done so far clearly demonstrates the nature of intertextuality that exists between the hagiographic, *bhakti* poem and *sthalapurāṇa* traditions. It also reveals that such intertextuality gradually increases as one moves from the tenth century to the seventeenth century AD, suggesting the tilt that the representations are taking. Whereas references to animal episodes of the *sthalapurāṇa* are conspicuously absent in *tēvārams*, and only the spider episode is found in the *Basava-purāṇa* of Palkuriki Somanatha, *Śrīkālahastīśvara-śatakamu* of Dhurjati is densely interspersed with episodes from Kannappa and the animal episodes of the *sthalapurāṇa*. Based on the points discussed hitherto, a detailed study of the *sthalapurāṇa* of Kalahasti is attempted next.

In an earlier section, while analyzing the representations of Kannappa in hagiographic traditions, a reference has already been made to the pollution due to body fluids and body parts and the role they play in the hagiography through constructing a *pratilōma* model of counter-structure. This analysis applies equally well to the construction of the *sthalapurāṇa* of Kalahasti. There is a striking resemblance in the mode of worship performed by the hunter *bhakta* and the animals, the spider, snake and elephant. Just like the meat tasted by Kannappa and the water carried in his mouth contains the polluting agent saliva, the spider's web woven by its mouth, snake's jewels that it carried in its mouth and the water that the elephant carried in its trunk, all contain saliva and become symptomatic of the worship that Kannappa offered to Shiva. Thus, a structural similarity gets established between the animals' mode of worship and that of Kannappa. Such similarities, by implication, extend the mutual obligations that we see between Shiva and the hunter *bhakta* to Shiva and the animal *bhakta*s of the *sthalapurāṇa*. In fact, for this reason, the hagiography and the *sthalapurāṇa*

[30] Ibid., verse 101.

become complementary to each other. The intertextuality that has been pointed out between the two and Dhurjati's verses from *Śrīkālahastīśvara-śatakamu* substantiates this point further.

There are interesting similarities between the hagiography and the *sthalapurāṇa* with regard to the object that the devotees offered to Shiva. Whereas Kannappa offered his own eyes, the animals offer their own lives to Shiva. This is apart from the fact that the spider offered its own home, the web, and the snake offered the jewels. Interestingly, in Dhurjati's version, the story of the animals appears before the story of Kannappa. In fact, the story of the spider is located in the *kṛta-yuga* where dharma is followed at its best (it rests on all four legs) and then, in gradually decreasing order of dharma, come the stories of the snake, the elephant and Kannappa.

The mode of *bhakti* of the animal devotees and the hunter *bhakta*, portrayed in the hagiography and the *sthalapurāṇa*, stand in striking contrast with the ritual traditions performed at the temple in Kalahasti. The local traditions narrate that Shiva in the form of *linga* remains untouched even by the priests, the *abhiṣēka* is performed without touching the *linga* by hand, and other offerings such as sandal paste, flowers and sacred thread, which involve touching the *linga*, are offered to the *utsava mūrti*, the deity taken out for ritual procession, rather than to the main *linga*. At the same time, hagiographies and the *sthalapurāṇa* narrate that Kannappa as well as the animals not only touched the *linga* but also secreted their body fluids on it and offered their body parts to Shiva. Above all, the ritual of anointing Shiva with the water that has touched the image of Kannappa, which continues even today, is suggestive of the ritual and religious space that the sacrilegious mode of worship of the hunter *bhakta* and his larger community, the non-agrarian communities, managed to earn over a period of time. In order to further substantiate this point, there is a need to look at the way the iconography of the hunter *bhakta* has changed over the centuries.

Kannappa in Iconographic Representations

In this section, I will make an attempt to demonstrate an interesting correlation between the social/political changes in South India during the post-tenth century and the sculptural changes in the representations of Kannappa. A look at the iconic representations of Kannappa available in Dahejia[31] reveals how the changes in political and cultural history of South India during the medieval

[31] Vidya Dahejia, *Slaves of the Lord: The Path of Tamil Saints* (Delhi: Munshiram Manoharlal, 1988).

period – leading to the emergence and prominence of left-hand castes (*iḍangai*, artisan and servicing castes) on the one hand, and the non-agrarian pastoralist, nomad and hunter communities on the other, that gets reflected in *bhakti* poems, hagiographies and *sthalapurāṇa* – could also be seen in iconographic representations. Dahejia expresses her frustration over the fact that there is a general lack of correspondence between the textual traditions that prescribe iconography (architectural texts) and the actual iconography itself. She further notices that maximal and unusual variations come from a period which pre-dates the compilation of the codes for the representations of Nayanars. However, if we consider the fact that many of these texts describing the formulaic prescriptions for the representation of Nayanars actually belong to a time that is much later, at least three to four centuries after the first set of images appeared, then the situation starts looking clear. The first set of prescriptions and the canonized version of iconography seem to have appeared around the eleventh century AD. This is exemplified by inscription of the Chola King, Rajaraja I, which makes a reference to the installation of the idols of the Nayanars in the temple complex of Brihadeshvara temple at Tanjavur. According to prescriptions, the iconography of Kannappa should have the following details: 'matted locks piles high; palms joined; bow in crook of arm; quiver of arrows against back; often bearded'.[32] However, many of the images of Kannappa that pre-date the canonization process do not follow these prescriptions. Except for a small period soon after the canonization, which provided prescriptions of iconography, we again find a variation in the iconographic representations of Nayanars. This, however, needs to be understood in the light of the discussions done in the present study, the presence of non-agrarians in the agrarian system.

The earliest image of Kannappa, according to Dahejia, is 'holding his eye ball in his outstretched hand',[33] as shown in Figure 3.2. The image is from Tiruvalankadu and belongs to the eleventh century AD. The description and image rightly represent the act for which Kannappa has been repeatedly praised in *tēvāram*s. The iconic representation is also consistent with the Nambi Andar Nambi's verse poem from tenth century AD.

> … gouged out with deadly dart,
> his flower-like right eye
> and applied it (on the wounded eye).[34]

---

[32] Ibid., 158.

[33] Ibid., 147.

[34] Nambi Andar Nambi's *Tiruttoṇḍar-tiuvandāti*, verse 20, Vanmikanathan's (1985) translation.

Fig. 3.2: Kannappa Holding his Plucked Eyeball in Hand from Tiruvalankadu: Eleventh Century
Source: Dahejia.[35]

However, a majority of the images of Kannappa that belong to the subsequent period (post-eleventh century AD), after the formulaic prescription codes have been established and canonized, depict him as follows: 'with palms together, holding the bow in the crook of his arm', as shown in Figures 3.3 and 3.4.

Fig. 3.3: Kannappa with Folded Hands from Darasuram Temple: Twelfth Century
Source: Dahejia.[36]

[35] Dahejia, *Slaves of the Lord*.

[36] Ibid.

Fig. 3.4: Kannappa with Folded Hands from Tiruvenkadu: Eleventh Century
Source: Dahejia.[37]

These representations, apparently, are according to the formulaic prescription of codes. Figure 3.3 is from Darasuram temple and belongs to the twelfth century AD. The latter one (Figure 3.4) is from Tiruvenkadu and belongs to the eleventh century AD, though the bow in the crook of his arm is missing.

But most of the representations of Kannappa that appear after the fourteenth century AD, in particular during the Vijayanagara period and subsequent to it, depict him with his left or right foot raised against the *linga*, to mark the place of the *linga*'s damaged eye, so that he can insert it correctly, as shown in Figures 3.5 and 3.6. The first one is from Virinchipuram and belongs to the sixteenth century AD. The second one is from Kovilpatti and belongs to the same century. These types of images of Kannappa are not only available in higher frequency but also have a higher visibility by depicting them in places like the pillars of the temple, suggesting a greater and higher visibility of the representation. The point that hagiographies are trying to make, namely, the sacrilegious mode of worship, could be clearly visualized in this representation.

[37] Ibid.

Fig. 3.5: Kannappa with His Left Leg on the Head of the *Linga* from Virinchipuram: Sixteenth Century
Source: Dahejia.[38]

Fig. 3.6: Kannappa with His Right Leg on the Eye of the *Linga* from Kovilpatti: Sixteenth Century
Source: Dahejia.[39]

---

[38] Ibid.

[39] Ibid.

In fact, the change and transformation of Kannappa's iconography in three phases, as just outlined in this section, actually correspond to the socio-political changes and the changes in the hagiography and *sthalapurāṇa* outlined earlier. It has been suggested in the study that the change and variation within the *bhakti* tradition that we notice temporally, spatially and along social levels are symptomatic of the changes that took place in the ideological and social networks that were operating in medieval South India. Thus, the *bhakti* poems, hagiographies, *sthalapurāṇa* and iconography not only seem to develop intertextualities but also converse together as though they are in a chorus, incorporating the ideological, social and political changes that took place during the post-tenth century period in South India. Thus, *bhakti* in South India is ambivalent in nature; on the one hand, it demonstrates intense and subservient devotion and on the other, accommodates sacrilegious, non-*āgamic* and *pratilōma* systems suggesting a dissent.

References

Adluri, S.M.R. 1988. Website on Telugu literature: www.engr.mun.ca/~adluri/telugu/index.html.

Burow, T. and M.B. Emeneau. *A Dravidian Etymological Dictionary* (Oxford: Clarendon Press, 1962).

Champakalakshmi, R. 1989. Religion and Social Change in Tamil Nadu (c. A.D. 600–1300). In *Medieval Bhakti Movements in India*, ed. by N.N. Bhattacharya. (New Delhi: Munshiram Manoharlal), 135–163.

Champakalakshmi, R. 'From Devotion to Dissent and Dominance: The Bhakti of the Tamil Alvars and Nayanmars'. In *Tradition, Dissent and Ideology: Essays in Honour of Romila Thapar*, edited by R. Champakalakshmi and S. Gopal (Delhi: Oxford University Press, 1996).

Dahejia, Vidya. *Slaves of the Lord: The Path of Tamil Saints* (Delhi: Munshiram Manoharlal, 1988).

Doniger, W. 'The Scrapbook of Undeserved Salvation: The Kedara Khanda of the Sknada Purana', in *Purana Prennis: Reciporocacity and Transformation in Hindu and Jaina Texts* (Albany: State University of New York Press, 1993).

Heifetz, H. and V. Narayana Rao. *For the Lord of the Animals – Poems from the Telugu: The Kalahastishvara Shatakamu of Dhurjati* (Delhi: Oxford University Press, 1987).

Hiremath, R.C. *Surangakaviya Trisasti Puratana Caritra* (Dharwar: Karnataka University, 1973).

Nagarajayya, H.P. *Jaina Kathakosa* (Hampi: Kannada University, 1997).

Narayana Rao, V., trans. *Shiva's Warriors: The Basava Purana of Palkuriki Somanatha* (Princeton: Princeton University Press, 1990).

Ramanujan, A.K. *Speaking of Śiva* (Harmondsworth: Penguin, 1973).

Satyanath, T.S. 'Bhakti of Hunters, Animals and Animal-like Bhaktas: Implications for Comparative Dravidian Literature'. *Dravidian Studies* 1(2) (2003): 61–86.

______. 'Hunter's Bhakti: Kannappa(n) in Hagiographic Traditions' (Unpublished PhD Thesis, University of Delhi, 2006).

______. 'Tellings and Renderings in Medieval Karnataka: The Episode of Kirata Shiva and Arjuna'. In *Decentring Translation: India and Beyond*, edited by Judy Wakabayashi and Rita Kothari, (Amsterdam: John Benjamins, 2009), 43–56.

Shulman, D. *Tamil Temple Myths: Sacrifice and Divine Marriage in the South Indian Shaiva Tradition* (Princeton: Princeton University Press, 1980).

Stein, B. *Peasant State and Society in Medieval South India* (Delhi: Oxford University Press, 1980).

Vanmikanathan. G. 1985. *Periya Puranam: A Tamil Classic On The Great Saiva Saints of South India by Shekkizar* (Chennai: Sri Ramakrishna Math).

Wagoner, P.B. *Tidings of the King: A Translation and Ethnohistoriacl Analysis of Rayavacakamu* (Honolulu: University of Hawaii Press, 1993).

CHAPTER

4

Devotion and Dissent

The Biographical Process of Ramanuja in Shrivaishnava Tradition and History

*Ranjeeta Dutta**

Amongst one of the greatest religious personalities of India, Ramanuja has an enduring reputation of a social reformer who dared to defy the Brahmanical orthodoxy of his times by democratizing temple worship for the marginalized castes of society. One of the radical steps he is supposed to have taken in this direction was to shout out the *dvaya* mantra, exclusively meant for the *brahmins*, from the top of the temple tower at Tirukkottiyur so that everyone, irrespective of their caste status, could hear, learn and recite it. Thus, such occurrences in the life of Ramanuja have delineated him as a rebel saint who dissented against the Brahmanical convention, caste hierarchy and political order of the day, and simultaneously evolved the Vishishtadvaita exegesis, developing a structure of devotion that involved large sections of society in the attainment of salvation and direct accessibility to the divine.

Hence, the association of Ramanuja with dissent and devotion has been the central belief of the Shrivaishnava community of South India, for whom Ramanuja was the founder, who organized the community and gave it an

* I wish to thank Vijaya Ramaswamy for her patience while I inordinately delayed the submission of my essay. I am grateful to the library staff at the Indian Institute of Advanced Studies (IIAS), Shimla, who cooperated with me in providing the references. This paper presented in the Conference in 2010 was a part of the ongoing work that I completed and submitted to the Institute in April 2011.

exegetical basis through the Vishishtadvaita Vedanta. Thus, one knows about Ramanuja's life, his beliefs, his catholicity and compassion. We know what his biographers tell us: in this case, the hagiographies whose authors were located in a particular context and, through Ramanuja's attitude of dissent and devotion, were putting forward a certain vision for the Shrivaishnava community and attempting to create a particular kind of collective consciousness within the community.

This essay discusses certain narratives of dissent and devotion in the Shrivaishnava hagiographies or the *guruparampara*s that have become well known in the biographical accounts of Ramanuja in modern times. It will be emphasized here that the theme of dissent and devotion in general for the lives of the early Shrivaishnava saints, the Alvars and later *acharyas*, like Ramanuja in particular, had implications for the Shrivaishnava community identities. Like all religious communities, Shrivaishnavism drew its initial impetus from the religious experience of its saints. The hagiographies, while documenting the biographies of these saints – in this case, Ramanuja – also delineated the history of Shrivaishnavism and its community. Enmeshed with this portrayal of history were the issues of community consciousness, caste, identities, the notion of a tradition and consolidation of the community – all of which were largely influenced by the contemporary socio-political context, from the twelfth to the seventeenth century. Ramanuja's protest against the social hierarchy was linked to the accessibility to the temple, performance of the temple rituals and idea of service, that is, *kainkarya* and the philosophy of Vishishtadvaita, which was meant to be comprehensible to an ordinary devotee. These themes in the hagiographies, structured as counter-hegemonic, became an integral part of the Shrivaishnava historical memory that was circulated through the institutionalization of certain rituals and activities in temples. Thus, the process of canonization of Ramanuja was implicit in these narratives and the texts that contained them. In the course of their interaction with various contexts and moments in history, they not only emerged as a part of the Shrivaishnava received tradition, but entered the nineteenth century discourse on the social reform movements that were engaged in using the resources of the past to emphasize upon a well-developed lineage of social reformers in Indian history. In this connection, Ramanuja was a 'philosopher' and a 'social reformer'. He is not only supposed to have engaged in intellectual polemics with his liberal ideas of *mokṣha* (salvation) and *prapatti* (complete surrender to god), but was also a 'social reformer' who protested against the social hierarchy of his times and fought for the poor and the oppressed. Such a representation made him an ideal for the nineteenth century reform movements. Swami Vivekananda commented in his paper, 'The Historical Evolution of India':

> The movement of Sankara forced its way through its high intellectuality, but it could be of little service to the masses, because of its adherence to strict caste laws, very small scope for ordinary emotion and making Sanskrit the only vehicle of communication. Ramanuja, on the other hand, with a most practical philosophy, a great appeal to the emotions, an entire denial of birthrights before spiritual attainments and appeals through popular tongue, completely succeeded in bringing the masses back to the Vedic religion.[1]

Interestingly, such a delineation continues till day, and has not only influenced the contemporary Shrivaishnava tradition but has also been in circulation in the secular public domains as subjects of secular biographies, theatre and comics like the Amar Chitra Katha, newspaper articles, chapbooks and films.[2] Therefore, while discussing the theme of devotion and dissent in the hagiographies, this essay also discusses the complexities in the narratives and the manner in which the latter conceptualized them evolving a particular kind of religiosity which primarily centred on who an ideal Shrivaishnava should be.

Tradition and Community: Devotion and Dissent as a Metaphor

The delineation of Ramanuja protesting against the established systems – social, political and religious – is a dominant motif in the *guruparampara* texts. This section discusses, at length, two hagiographical themes of dissent

---

[1] As quoted in, i. Swami Ramakrishnananda (trans. from Bengali by Swami Budhananda). 1986. *Life of Sri Ramanuja*. Madras: Sri Ramakrishna Math

[2] Some of the well-known modern biographies on Ramanuja are: M. Narasimhachary, *Sri Ramanuja* (New Delhi: Sahitya Akademi, 2007); Swami Ramakrishnananda (trans. from Bengali by Swami Budhananda). 1986. *Life of Sri Ramanuja*. Madras: Sri Ramakrishna Math; and Kandadai Seshadri, *Srivaishnavism and Social Change* (Calcutta: K.P. Bagchi and Co., 1998). For further references on academic researches of this kind, see G. Lakshamma, *The Impact of Ramanuja's Teachings on Life and Conditions in Society* (Delhi: Sundeep Prakashan, 1990). For children's books, see *Ramanuja: A Great Vaishnava Saint* (Mumbai: Amar Chitra Katha, 1974), 715. For theatre and films, see Indira Parthasarathy, *Ramanujar: The Life and Ideas of Ramanuja*, trans. T. Sriaman, critical introduction by C.T. Indra (New Delhi: Oxford University Press, 2008) and *Ramanuja*, directed by G.V. Iyer.

that highlighted the beginnings as well as the establishment of Ramanuja as the *acharya* of the community. One is related to his early life as a *shishya* when despite being a devoted disciple, he protested against his *guru*, Yadavaprakasha, who was renowned for expounding upon the Advaita philosophy of Shankara. Second is the theme of protest against the established *varna* hierarchy which occurs at various moments of his life starting from the time of his life as a married man to his being initiated into the Shrivaishnava community and finally, becoming a part of the *acharyic* lineage which involved a significant control over the resources and activities of the Ranganathasvami temple at Srirangam. These two motifs, while questioning the existing established systems, put forth an alternative structure of religious and social norms that articulated the ideas of Vishishtadvaita, Shrivaishnava devotion and social practice and became the basis of changing and expanding the organization and institutional establishment in the temples of the Shrivaishnava community.

According to the Shrivaishnava tradition, the appointment of Ramanuja as the *acharyic* head of the community was divinely preordained. The hagiographical texts inform us that Ramanuja was born in a well-known Brahmin family in a Brahmin settlement named Shriperumbudur.[3] The narratives go to great lengths in describing the intellectual expertise of the Brahmins of Śhrīperumbudūr, who were also followers of the Vedanta tradition.[4] Ramanuja was born in the *asuri kula*, supposedly an erudite and elite Brahmin lineage. His father, Asuri Keshavacharya, was an expert in performing *yajna*s.[5] While describing

[3] Garudavahana Pandita, *Divyasuricaritam*, ed. Pandita Madhvacharya, T.A. Sampathakumaracharya and K.K.A. Venkatachari (Bombay: Ananthacharya Research Institute, 1978), Chapter 17, *Shlokas* 1–10, 354–357.

[4] Ibid., Chapter 17, *Shlokas* 1–10, 354–357. Vedanta is a system of thought that is based on the *Upanishads*. However, there are different schools of Vedanta reflecting different interpretations of the *Upanishads*.

[5] In another version, Ramanuja is shown to be already born in a Shrivaishnava family. According to this version, his maternal uncle was Shrishailapurna, who was in the lineage of Yamunacharya, the *acharya* preceding Ramanuja in the *gururparamapara* tradition. While searching for suitable grooms for his two sisters, Bhumidevi and Shridevi, Shrishailapurna met two young men, Keshavacharya and Kamalanayanabhaṭṭa, from Bhūtapurī (Śhrīperumbudūr) and Maduramaṅgalam respectively, and was impressed by their depth of Vedic learning. After initiating them into the Shrivaishnava community through the rituals of uttering the mantra, and branding them with conch and discus, Śrīśailapurṇa got Keśavācārya married to his elder sister, Bhūmidevī, and Kamalanayanabhaṭṭa to his younger sister, Śrīdevī. After sometime, to Keśavācārya and Bhūmidevī was born a son, who was

the extraordinary qualities of Ramanuja, the narratives tell us that he was an incarnation of Adiseshsa, the thousand-hooded snake on which Vishnu sleeps. According to the texts, such an incarnation was imperative as Vishnu felt that proper religious ideas and practices were not being followed on the earth. Hence, to restore order and live among his Bhagavata devotees, Adiseshsa, being God's loyal servant, took the form of Ramanuja. Such a divine connection is introduced early in the narratives foregrounding the fact that we would be told about an extraordinary individual who had no parallels. In addition, the idea of *avatara* or incarnation representing God's accessibility and transcendence and the notion of devotion represented by Adisessha and Ramanuja are introduced. Another version tells us that Ramanuja was born to dispel the incorrect understanding of the Vedanta and propagate the correct understanding, presumably the Vishishtadvaitic interpretation.[6] Ramanuja's initiation, that is, rice taking, boring of the earlobes, tonsure and investiture with the sacred thread, was performed according to the Brahmanical norms. The texts inform us about his prodigious intellect. The precocity of Ramanuja was evident when at an early age, he mastered the Vedas. Soon thereafter, he was married.

It is at this stage in the life story that the texts introduce an important trope of the *guru–shishya* relationship. This relationship not only introduces the Shrivaishnava worldview on dissent and devotion but also initiates the audience into the notion of *acharyic* lineage. The texts point out that in order to acquire further knowledge, Ramanuja came to Kanchi and after

named Ramanuja, and Kamalanayanabhaṭṭa and Śrīdevī also had a son, Govinda. For details, see V. Varadachariar, ed., *Yatirāja-Vaibhava of Āndhrapūrṇa* (Vaṭuka Nambi) (Madras: M.C. Krishnan, 1978,), Chapter 17, Shloka 1, 354.

[6] Ibid., Shlokas 6–7, p.6. Vishishtadvaita of Ramanuja proposes that the sentient souls (*jīvas*) and the non-sentient objects (*achetna*) are as real as Brahman (that is, the Supreme Being), but both of them are only a *visheshana* or an attribute of the Brahman and hence, are not independent of the Brahman. Brahman has innumerable divine qualities and attributes, that is, it is *saguna*. This is discussed in contradiction to Shankara's Advaita that emphasizes that the Brahman is *nirguna* or unqualified and god, individual souls and the world are mere appearances or illusion due to an indefinable principle of *māyā* that is real or unreal. The Vishishtadvaita of Ramanuja and Shankara's Advaita, both being different schools of the Vedantic expositions, are always discussed on a comparative basis in the discipline of Indian philosophy. For instances, see S.M. Srinivasa Chari, *Advaita and Viśiṣṭadvaita* (Delhi: Motilal Banarsidass, 2004[1961]).

worshipping Lord Varadaraja, he became the disciple of Yadavaprakasha as he wished to study the Vedanta. Ramanuja's *guru*, Yadavaprakasha, was a famous *advaitin*.[7] In the course of his learning, he often questioned his *guru's* Advaitic interpretation of the Upanishads and countered the arguments by 'Sadvaita' interpretations.[8] According to the *Divyasuricaritam*, he was utilizing those *shrutis* for expounding Sadvaita (Vishishtadavaita) that were already being made the reference point for the Advaita interpretations, especially by his teacher, Yadavaprakasha, whose reputation was already well established. This brought him into direct opposition with Yadavaprakasha. This tension between the teacher and the disciple represented the contradictions between the Vishishtadvaita and Advaita systems of philosophy, where the latter was well established. This is reflected in the narratives that discuss the interface between Ramanuja and Yadavaprakasha, which will be discussed shortly. The texts further inform us that while Ramanuja was a student, his fame spread far and wide as someone who could counter the Advaita Vedanta with alternative interpretations. This reputation impressed Yamuna who was then the *acharya* of the Shrivaishnava community with its centre at Srirangam. Along with his chief disciples, Yamuna arrived at Kanchipuram, worshipped Lord Varadarajaswami and saw Ramanuja from a distance in the company of his *guru*, Yadavaprakasha, and other fellow disciples and wondered as to when Ramanuja would be his own student. He prayed to Varadaraja:

> I take refuge in that boon-giving Deity by a fraction of whose grace the deaf hear, the lame move swiftly, the dumb speak, the blind see and a barren woman becomes the mother of a son…O Lotus-eyed One, O Lord Of lakshmi, do You bring Ramanuja to your faith by bestowing Your grace upon him.[9]

---

[7] The *smarta* Brahmins usually follow the Advaita tradition of Shankara. They worship five deities – Vishnu, Shiva, Parvati, Ganesha and Surya. However, the *smartas* are not initiated into any of these religious traditions but may have their leanings towards these religious traditions. Similarly, Ramanuja's family, despite being *smartas*, had Vaishnava leanings.

[8] Garudavahana Pandita, *Divyasuricaritam*, op,cit., *Shlokas* 11 and 12, 357–358. The term mentioned is *Sadvaita*. Here, it is mentioned as Vishishtadvaita and should not be confused with Madhava's Dwita.

[9] Anantacharya's *Prapannamritam*, Chapter VII, Shlokas 30–31 in Swami Ramakrishnananda (trans. from Bengali by Swami Budhananda). 1986. *Life of Sri Ramanuja*. Madras: Sri Ramakrishna Math, 96.

Finally, unable to meet Ramanuja, Yamuna went back to Srirangam. This interlude in the narratives on the *guru–shishya* relationship at this point was probably an intention on the part of the hagiographers to show that even before Ramanuja was aware, the Shrivaishnava community, with Yamuna as its *acharya*, had decided to incorporate Ramanuja as an *acharya* into the community. This justified the fact that even though Ramanuja was not born a Shrivaishnava, his induction as an *acharya* was pre-decided. Thereafter, the sequence of events in these texts focus on the tensions between Yadavaprakasha and Ramanuja, finally culminating in Ramanuja leaving his *guru* and joining the Shrivaishnava community.

The narratives first highlight Yadavaprakasha's failure and Ramanuja's success in dealing with practical situations of devotion, like relieving the king's son from the affliction of a *brahmarakhshasa*:

> While he (Ramanuja) was a disciple of Yadavaprakasha, during that time the king's son was afflicted by a *brahmarakhsasa*. The king was told about Yadavprakasha's occult power and therefore he invited Yadavaprakasha and his disciples to relieve his son. As soon as Yadavaprakasha saw the son and the possession of *brahmarakshasa* over him, he immediately started chanting the *mantras*. On hearing Yadavaprakasha chanting the *mantras,* the *brahmarakshasa* was besieged with rage and ridiculed Yadavaprakasha and declared him completely ignorant. The *brahmarakshasa* asserted that he knew about all the past births of Yadavaprakasha and himself. In the course of the argument that ensued, Yadavaprakasha challenged the *rakshasa* to reveal all about their respective past births. The *rakhsasa* informed that, 'In the past birth you were a chameleon (lizard) living near the banks of a pond in an *agrahara*, named Madurantaka. When some learned Vaishnava men were on their way to participate in the festivals, they stopped here, rested and ate. Their leftover rice was consumed by you. As a result of the consumption of these sacred leftovers, you were redeemed and hence were born in a human form in this birth. I was a *brahmana* who along with other *brahmanas* performed the *yajnas*. In one of the *yajnas*, I erred and with the result I was reborn as a *brahmarakshasa*.'
>
> Pointing towards Ramanuja, the *rakshasa* then said, 'This incarnation of *sesha* (the snake on which Vishnu is resting), who has been sent on this earth to protect mankind has power over me. If he asks me to leave the body of this bot , I will immediately obey. In fact, his sweet words will release me from this body and will give me *moksha* or salvation.' After saying this, the *brahmarakshasa* fell at the feet of Ramanuja. Thereafter, Yadavaprakasha ordered Ramanuja to command the *rakshasa* to leave the body of the prince. Ramanuja obeyed his guru and commanded politely the aggrieved *brahmarakshasa* to leave the body, the sign being the breaking of a branch of the *pipal* tree. The *rakshasa*

> left the body of the prince and while going broke the branch of the *pipal* tree. The king was happy and rewarded Ramanuja lavishly. Thereafter, Ramanuja gave all the endowments to his *guru*.[10]

Such a story states the superiority of the Vishishtadvaita philosophy as well as the extraordinariness of Ramanuja. In fact, the story ridicules the Advaita followers through Yadavaprakasha and upholds the Vishishtadvaita followers through Ramanuja. Such an account of success in the narratives sets the tone for further tensions between the *guru* and the disciple. There are several incidents in the different hagiographical versions on the intellectual incompatibility between Ramanuja and Yadavaprakasha. The breaking point came when Ramanuja, with all humility, corrected his *guru*, Yadavaprakasha, over an interpretation of a *shruti* text.

One day, when Ramanuja was massaging Yadavaprakasha with oil, a *shishya* came to Yadavaprakasha to clarify a particular doubt over a passage in the *Chandayoga Upnaishad*. This passage had a word *kapyasam*, the meaning of which was not clear. Taking the word to mean the posterior of a monkey, Yadavaprakasa explained the passage as follows: 'The two eyes of the golden Purusha, that is the lord, are like two lotuses which are red like the posterior of a monkey.'[11] On hearing this interpretation, Ramanuja was very upset and hot tears, like flames of fire, rolled down from his eyes onto the thigh of Yadavaprakasha who asked Ramanuja as to what was his problem. Ramanuja expressed his grief over his teacher's 'unbecoming explanation' and said that he never expected this from a wise person like Yadavaprakasha.

---

[10] Garudavahana Pandita, *Divyasuricaritam*, Chapter 17, *Shlokas* 16–31, 351–364. This is an approximate translation done by me.

[11] Swami Ramakrishnananda, *Life of Sri Ramanuja, op.cit.,* 81. The *Divyasuricaritam*, one of the earliest hagiographies, does not mention the specific verse from the *shruti*s. It only mentions that Yadavaprakasha interpreted one sentence of *shruti* incorrectly, which pained Ramanuja so much that he started crying. When the hot tears fell on the thighs of Yadavaprakasha, the latter became angry. Enraged with Ramanuja's audacity, he asked him to leave for he had no desire to teach him (Ibid., 32–33). Ramanuja, along with his wife, left for Kanchi and started worshipping Varadarajaswami, by doing *kainkarya* of offering the water from the pond, which he himself brought (Ibid., 34). Hearing this news, Yamuna was very happy, and in order to bring Ramanuja to his order, he sent another learned man, Mahapurna, with his *Stotraratna* to Kanchi. There is no story of Yadavaprakasha attempting to take his life and Ramanuja's rescue due to Govinda's intervention. See, Chapter 17, *Shlokas* 32–37, 364–366.

Yadavaprakasha replied, 'My boy, I am also very much grieved at your audacity… Well, can you interpret the passage in any better manner?'[12] When Ramanuja said he could, Yadavaprakasha responded sarcastically, 'Fine, very good….I see, you like to climb higher than Sankaracharya.'[13] Then Ramanuja provided an alternate explanation that *kapyasam* means 'blossomed by sun' and the passage would then read as, 'The eyes of that Purusha within the golden solar orb are as lovely as the lotuses blossomed by the rays of the sun'.

Subsequently, further disagreements arose over the meaning of Brahman. According to Yadavaprakasha, Brahman was truth, intelligence and infinitude. Ramanuja disagreed and said that the Brahman was endowed with the quality of truth and attribute of intelligence and infinitude. Yadavaprakasha became so annoyed with this interpretation that he asked Ramanuja to leave his *ashrama.* Interestingly, some of the narratives inform us that the rivalry was so intense that Yadavaprakasha conspired to take Ramanuja's life. According to these versions, Yadavaprakasha, under the pretext of taking a pilgrimage to the holy banks of Ganga in Benares, planned to kill Ramanuja. While passing through the forest, his fellow disciple and cousin, Govindabhatta, revealed to Ramanuja the evil designs of Yadavaprakasha. In order to save his life, Ramanuja remained behind in the forest, while the others proceeded on the pilgrimage. However, Ramanuja's feeling of helplessness did not last long. Soon, he encountered a hunter and his wife who offered to take Ramanuja safely back to Kanchi. Further, we are told that this hunter and his wife were none other than Vishnu and his consort, Lakshmi. Somewhere along the way, Ramanuja went to bring water from the well for the thirsty couple. But when he came back, he found that they had disappeared and from where he was standing, he could see the temple towers of the city of Kanchipuram. Consequently, Ramanuja realized that he was saved by none other than the divine intervention of Vishnu[14].

Finally, Yadavaprakasha became Ramanuja's disciple. This was on his mother's insistence who told him to become a *tridandin* like Ramanuja and follow the latter's interpretation of the Vedas. Listening to this, he decided to circumambulate the earth. Then God told him that he should circumambulate Ramanuja, which is equivalent to circumambulating the earth. However, Yadavaprakasha was sceptical about this dream and went to Kanchipuram and requested the latter to beseech the lord with his request of circumambulating

---

[12] Ibid

[13] Ibid.

[14] For details, see, Swami Ramakrishnananda, *Life of Sri Ramanuja, op.cit.,* 80–81; *Divyasuricaritam,* Chapter 17, *Shlokas* 33–34, 364–365.

the earth. However, the lord told Ramanuja that he had indeed come to Yadavaprakasha's dream and without any fear, Yadavaprakasha should do what he had told him to do.. Finally, with all respect and love, Yadavaprakasha went round Ramanuja, took *sanyasa* under him and then became his disciple .[15]

The motif of this *guru–shishya* relationship was characterized by the ambivalent attitudes of devotion and dissent. The dissent against an established system of Advaita within a traditional *guru–shishya* method of disseminating knowledge was associated with the organization of the community, conversion and consequent spread of Shrivaishnavism. The latter commentaries on Ramanuja's works invariably attempted to show that Vishishtadvaita, by upholding the qualities of a *saguna* Brahman, was (comprehensible for) easily comprehended by an ordinary devotee than Advaita, which emphasized upon *nirguna* Brahman, an abstract and abstruse concept. Earlier hagiographies are not so vivid in their description of the Yadavaprakasha–Ramanuja rivalry. The texts from fourteenth century onwards are graphic. Could it be because with the emergence of the Vijayanagara Empire in the fourteenth and fifteenth century, and the increasing political power of the Shringeri *matha* that was Advaita in orientation, the Shrivaishnava hagiographers' presentation of the rivalry implied competition over royal patronage and acquiring religio-political power?[16] Thus, Ramanuja's years of youth were spent in Kanchipuram, which was then an important religious and trading centre.

Dissent against the Varnasramadharma

The second theme that will be discussed is that of dissent against the established *varnasramadharma.* One of the most important social concerns of the hagiographies was related to the question of caste. Caste attributes were presented as secondary to that of faith. As mentioned in the beginning of this essay, the irrelevance of caste was highlighted in the narratives of Ramanuja flouting the orthodox norms by proclaiming the *dvaya mantra*, exclusively meant for the *Brahmins*, aloud from the temple tower at Tirukkottiyur, for everybody to hear. This episode is one of the most popular episodes that has consolidated the image of Ramanuja as a social reformer. Further, there are large numbers of narratives that portray his attitude towards caste hierarchy in a radical manner. The hagiographies relate accounts of how his wife, who was

---

[15] *Divyasuricaritam*, Chapter 17, *Shlokas* 72–76, 378–379.

[16] *Divyasuricaritam*, op. cit., Chapter 17, Shlokas 17–31, 359–364. This is an approximate translation done by me.

socially conservative, behaved in a discriminatory manner towards Ramanuja's non-Brahmin teachers, Tirukacchi Nambi (Kanchipuram) and Mahapurna. Ramanuja is said to have been so upset with his wife that he consequently became a renunciate. The narratives further highlight his broadmindedness in seeking and pursuing Tirukacchi Nambi and Tirumalai Nambi, who were non-Brahmin, to become his teachers. His fame as a saint who disregarded caste barriers, and made the access to god and attainment of salvation possible for everybody, appears to have been drawn from an image that was already prominently portrayed in Shrivaishnava hagiographies.

According to the narratives, he went beyond mere metaphysics and introduced institutional reforms in the temple to incorporate non-Brahmin participation in the ritual as well as the organizational aspects of temple worship. The 'Code of Udaiyavar', as described in detail in the *Koil Olugu*, the chronicle of the Ranganathasvami temple at Srirangam, broadened the social base of the community by encouraging non-Brahmanical participation in temple affairs. The hagiographical narratives associate this with the catholicity of Ramanuja.[17] The *guruparampara*s state that Ramanuja took the bold step in Melukote to declare the outcastes as 'Tirukkulattar', meaning people belonging to the family of Lakshmi, the divine mother, and accommodated them in the temple organization. These people belonging to the hunting community had helped Ramanuja ward off dacoits in the forest while he was returning from Delhi, bringing back the festival image of the Narayanaswami temple at Melukote that had been looted earlier by the Sultan of Delhi. Ramanuja is said to have had a large following from all sections of society. For example, Ramanuja's followers comprised 700 *sanyasin*s, 12,003 *ekangi*s and 3,000 *korramai* (that is, women followers).[18]

However, in reality, it appears that the non-brahmin groups who were made a part of the temple organization were not accorded any priestly functions. Their activities were to be mainly confined to:

> Decorating with followers the *tirumandapas* during festivals and the *Alagiyamanavalan tirumandapa* daily; making garlands and offering them for the starting of procession; raining (see) flowers (on special occasions); proceeding in two rows holding censers, two folded cloths, eight gold torches and twenty silver torches and waving two pieces of cloth; forming a rear batch,

---

[17] Ibid., 142.

[18] The numbers of the disciples vary in various hagiographical texts. However, this variation is minor and of no consequence.

> with hands folded behind the row by the waists reciting the last two lines of each stanza; bearing the Ramanuja sword and acting as the bodyguard of the *Jiyars* and the Shrivaisnavas.[19]

That Ramanuja and other Shrivaishnava *acharya*s as well as the *mathadhipati*s were *brahmins* was no coincidence. In fact, till day, the *acharya*s and the heads of the *matha*s are always *brahmins*. Thus, the *brahmin* affiliation was always an integral part of the Shrivaishnava community. This elitist Brahmanical base was responsible for the initial limitations of the Shrivaishnava community in the pre-twelfth century AD. However, Carman, who appears, in my opinion, to be sceptical about the agency of Ramanuja in the temple reforms, concludes that Ramanuja's temple management policy was more liberal than what had existed before and it was this '*relative* liberalism' with reference to caste differences within the Shrivaishnava community that is emphasized in the stories.[20]

The philosophy of Vishishtadvaita, by its association with the Vedic texts, was structured within a highly Sanskritized framework, not comprehensible to the common man, and thus, it was left for the later-day Shrivaishnava hagiographers and theologians to evolve a Tamil tradition through the structuring of the canonical literature, and finally attempt to merge the Tamil and Sanskritic traditions in the personality of Ramanuja.[21] However, a careful observation would reveal that Ramanuja's *bhakti* was more intellectual than popular. The heavy Sanskritic bias cannot be ignored. In Ramanuja's *Shribhashya*, a commentary on the *Brahmasutra*, while answering the question who is to be permitted salvation, it is stated clearly in the comments on the first *sutra* that a Shudra is 'not qualified for knowledge of Brahman' and that 'The prohibition of learning [the Vedas] thus implies the prohibition of understanding and whatever depends on it'. 'It is the Advaitin that Ramanuja accuses of permitting, by the logic of his philosophy, that a Shudra can gain an understanding of this ultimate nature and knowledge of Brahman. Ramanuja appears to reject this idea totally'.[22]

---

[19] The *Koil Olugu*, op.cit., 46. *The Chronicle of the Srirangam Temple with Historical Notes*. V.N. Hari Rao ed. (Madras: Rockhouse and Sons, 1961).

[20] John Braisted Carman, *The Theology of Rāmānuja: An Essay in Interreligious Understanding* (Bombay: Anantacharya Indological Research Institute, 1981), 37.

[21] For instance, see N. Jagadeesan, 1977. *History of Srivaishnavism in the Tamil Country (Post Ramanuja)* (Madurai: Koodal Publishers. op.cit).

[22] Friedhelm Hardy, 'The Formation of Shrivaisnavism', In *Charisma and Canon. Essays on the Religious History of the Indian Subcontinent*, ed. Vasudha Dalmia, Angelika Malinar and Martin Christof (New Delhi: Oxford University Press, 2001), 52.

One of the important aspects of devotion was the notion of *prapatti*, that is, unconditional surrender to God by a devotee whose caste status was of no consequence. The catholicity of Ramanuja is further highlighted by showing that *prapatti* was an integral part of his philosophy. According to Hardy:

> While in Ramanuja it is the *bhakti-yoga*, which includes meditation that allows a person to achieve liberation, among the later authors this *bhakti yoga* is either contrasted as an extremely difficult method – of which only the privileged few are capable – with the 'easy' means of *prapatti*; or it is rejected outright as a sign of human arrogance vis-à-vis the availability of divine grace. By virtue of being human, every one has access to *prapatti*. This now has the potential of being turned into most radical and revolutionary social programme. Indeed the outlines of such a programme were produced in the *Acaryahrdayam*, by Alagiya Manavala Perumal Nayanar. Here the religion of *prapatti* presents itself as a total replacement of the Vedic tradition. Of course such an extreme position found few followers, at least in practice .[23]

Whether Ramanuja addressed the theological concept of *prapatti* and what were his views on it and how he saw it vis-à-vis the *bhakti yoga* became a major issue of contention in the schism of the Shrivaishnava community into the Vatakalai, the northern sect, and Tenkalai, the southern sect. To the Vatakalais, *bhakti* and *prapatti* were two different goals. Status by birth, knowledge and capability were prerequisites for *bhakti*, whereas *prapatti* did not require any qualifications and could be attained by any ordinary human being. It followed that *bhakti yoga* was the main *sadhana* and *prapatti* was just an *anga* (that is, an auxillary). According to the Tenkalais, since *bhakti* required individual effort, it was inferior to *prapatti*, which was effortless and depended on total surrender to God. Hence, a devotee seeking salvation and refuge in God should first have the desire to accept God's protection with total faith in Him.[24] Therefore, the Vatakalais felt that a devotee should follow either *bhakti* or *prapatti* as an *upaya* with the *angas*, and for achieving both, human effort was essential. The issue of the life pattern of *prapanna* (that is, the devotee) was related to the notion of *kainkarya* (or service to the god). According to the Vatakalais, *kainkarya*

---

23 Ibid.

24 For the one fruit – attainment of the Lord – he has taught: 1) the path of *bhakti* which is difficult because...it is accompained by means of the *angas* of *parma*, *jnana* etc, ever many births and 2) the path of *prapatti*, which is easy because, it is performed once and for all, upon ceasing all one's own activity...Thus, the grace of the Lord must be the *upaya* and not *bhakti* or *prapatti*, *Mumuksupati* of Pillai Lokacaraya.

was to be performed according to the *shastric* rules. Steeped in his own world of deeds (that is, *karma*), man committed many sins. Hence, God's redemption and compassion was needed for the peace of the soul. Further sin was to be avoided as it would nullify all efforts and incur God's displeasure. To obtain forgiveness, *prapanna* should follow certain *prayashchitta* (atonement) rules. The Tenkalais did not give importance to the *shastric* injunctions for performing the *kainkarya*. In fact, *prayaschitta* was not required at all and it was assumed that God would forgive and protect his devotee from all his sins, even those committed after *prapatti* and *kainkarya*.

Thus, enmeshed with the idea of *prapatti* was the issue of caste and a particular religious attitude based on sectarian orientations. The Vatakalais represented the Sanskritic tradition. Kanchipuram in Tamil Nadu was their institutional centre and Vedanta Desika (AD 1268–1369) their spiritual preceptor. They gave preference to the Sanskrit Vedas over the Dravida Vedas, that is, the Tamil hymns of the Alvars. Therefore, they were considered Brahmanical and conservative in their outlook. The Tenkalais, on the other hand, represented the Tamil tradition. Srirangam in Tamil Nadu was their centre and Manavala Mamuni (AD 1370–1442) their religious leader. Since the Tenkalais regarded the Dravida Vedas as their scriptures, they were considered to be more broad-based than the Vatakalais and had a large non-Brahmanical following.

Perhaps Ramanuja never intended to address the lay devotee. Rather his concern was to evolve a coherent theological base for Shrivaishnavism, thereby making it ideationally significant for the community, through an intellectually well-articulated and emotionally more appealing philosophy and theology vis-à-vis others, particularly the *advaitins*. The principles of *varnasramadharma* were never questioned in any of his works. Neither did Ramanuja intend to do so. For, the caste identity was the primordial identity and a complete rejection of it implied the disruption of the social order. A social revolution was not what Shrivaishnavism needed. It required a strong base with a legitimizing force of the *Brahmins*. In fact, the attribution of *prapatti* to Ramanuja was a reaction to the viewpoint that *prapatti* has been marginalized in Ramanuja's scheme of religious doctrine. The Shrivaishnava theologians, in their own way, resolved this controversy by showing that *prapatti* as a concept was central in Ramanuja's *Gadyatrayam*.[25]

---

[25] K.K.A. Venkatachari, 1978, *The Manipravala Literature of the Srivaisnava Acaryas*. Bombay: Anantacarya Indological Institute; Robert C. Lester, 'Rāmānuja and Srivaisnavism: The Concept of *Prapatti* or *Sarnagati*', *History of Religion* 5(2) (1966): 266–82.

The hagiographical narratives themselves reflect a discomfort in dealing with the issue of rejecting the caste hierarchy. The tone of the narratives was, in many ways, conservative. According to them, after escaping from the persecution of the Chola ruler, Ramanuja came to the Hoysala kingdom in Karnataka and took refuge in a forest. The hunting community there was kind and hospitable to him. The narratives assert that

> the hunters did not ask for undue favours. Rather they were anxious to find a Brahmin who could feed the *acharya*. The *Gururparamparai Prabhavam* says that they brought honey and millet which were not ritualistically pollutant. No cooked food served by the hunters was eaten by the *acharya* and his men. In fact, he received hospitality from one Kongupiratti who was a brahmin woman who had once received *mantradiksa* or initiation from Ramanuja at Srirangam.[26]

One of the texts states Ramanuja's own inhibitions in rejecting the caste hierarchy:

> Alavandar spotted Maraner Nambi as spiritually advanced soul and hence included him in the pantheon of his disciples. When Maraner Nambi took on the disease of his master out of sheer devotion, he suffered much and was ministered to by Mahapurna who brought him the prasadam food from the Srirangam temple. When he died, Maha Purna had no hesitation in cremating him according to the *Brahmamedha* rites which are accorded only to the brahmins. Ramanuja was embarrassed by the radical length to which his preceptor Maha Purna went in flagrantly violating caste codes. He protested to Mahapurna, worried about the social implications of such an act. There was a significant exchange between Maha Purna and Ramanuja in which the latter expressed the anxiety that while he was trying to keep the fence in shape and maintain social order, Mahapurna was doing away with the cultural fabric of the society.
>
> Maha Purna stressed on transcending the barriers of caste. He said he was not for half measure. He reminds Ramanuja of the impressive line of exceptions in Hindu epics and Puranic literature. 'Am I superior to Rama, the Hero of Ikshvaku race? Is Maraner inferior to the bird Jatayu, for whom Rama performed the *brahmamedha*? Am I greater than Dharmaputra? Is Maraner lower than lower than Vidura to whom the same *samskara* were administered?'[27]

---

[26] C.T. Indra, 'Hagiography Revisited', in *Rāmānujar: The Life and Ideas of Rāmānuja*, by Indira Parthasarathy, trans. T. Sriaman (New Delhi: Oxford University Press, 2008), xi–liii.

[27] Alakondavilli Govindacharya, *Sri Rāmānujacharya: The Exponent of the Visishtadvaita Philosophy*, Reprint (Chennai: Sri Nrisimhapriya Trust, 2004), 144.

The theme of caste and its treatment was, in many ways, a response to the context of that time. In the post-Ramanuja period, the social milieu underwent a transformation. The rise of the non-Brahmin landed class, the emergence of the merchants and the migration of the Telugu warriors and landed magnates to the Tamil region led to the evolution of a distinct Shrivaishnava non-Brahmin identity. Since these groups were powerful and influential, they emerged as major benefactors of the temples and the sectarian leaders. A network of redistribution and exchange between the non-Brahmin and Brahmin elite groups developed that brought into the temple arena the former and provided a regular channel for patronage to the latter. Hence, caste affiliations got interwoven with the community–class paradigm. That is, Srivaishnavism became the integrative factor between the Brahmin and the non-Brahmins, when powerful sections of both the caste groups joined in an interactive/productive relationship. The presence of non-Brahmins in the community influenced the Shrivaishnava discourse on society. New concepts like *ubhaya* Vedanta, that is, dual Vedas; the Tamil Vedas, that is, the *Prabandham*; and the Sankrit Vedas and *prapatti* were evolved, which were all inclusive. Tamil came to be emphasized along with Sanskrit. Some of the Brahmanical religious leaders like the Kandadais and Periya Jiyar at Tirupati had non-Brahmins as their disciples. Referred to as *ekaki*s, *ekangi*s and *sattada* Shrivaishnava, these non-Brahmanical groups figured prominently as the recipients of several shares in temple offerings.

Perhaps the central concern of the hagiographers was to explicate the Shrivaishnava tradition of the *ubhaya* Vedanta not only from a theological point of view but also as the ideological basis of the institutional networks of the temples and the *matha*s, both of which provided an arena of interaction for the community. Thus, the dissemination of this *ubhaya* Vedanta tradition was expressed in the narratives through the issues of: superiority of the Vishishtadvaitic philosophy; lineage and community organization; and the consolidation of the temple and *matha* network. These issues were portrayed primarily in the profile of Ramanuja as the *acharya* and the organizer of the community. It should be noted that the successive *acharya*s were also portrayed in a similar manner, but the narratives on Ramanuja credit him with a seminal role that had no parallel.

Thus, the representation of a past through the biographical delineation of Ramanuja in the *guruparampara* texts influenced the religious attitudes of the Shrivaishnava community for whom Ramanuja was the most revered *acharya*. The *guruparampara*s, developing as scriptures of the community and despite their sectarian affiliations of Vatakalai and Tenkalai, reiterated the normative notion of a single homogeneous uniform community in the charismatic portrayal of Ramanuja. Uniformity became the dominant theme in all the sectarian hagiographies that provided the respective sects with a lineage. The origin of the lineage in most of cases was traced to Ramanuja. In this manner, each sect with its lineage claimed to represent the uniform Shrivaishnava community. Projection of a uniform community became important for establishing claims in the competitive spheres of resource control in the temples. It represented an integrative framework, whereby devotees could be from any section of society. Therefore, the concept of uniformity made the caste ascription secondary to that of a community.

The representation of caste and a radical social past associated with Ramanuja had an impact that went beyond the community boundaries. This image became so popular that various religious communities from the thirteenth to the seventeenth centuries considered Ramanuja as their founder and the most revered saint. In this context, Ramanuja has been considered as the preceptor of Ramanand who, in turn, was supposed to be the guru of Kabir. Ramanuja is also considered to be the founder of yet another sect called the Ramanujis who rose to prominence in the nineteenth century. Both the Ramanandis and the Ramanujis, located in Vrindavan in the Braja region, have a large following from the marginalized sections of the caste hierarchy. Interestingly, both these communities do not identify Ramanuja with Vishishtadvaita Vedanta, but as a saint who disregarded caste barriers and made the access to God and attainment of salvation possible for everybody, an image that was already prominently portrayed in Shrivaishnava hagiographies. This catholicity of Ramanuja endures till date and is considered as a precursor of modern social reformers like Periyar and B.R. Ambedkar.[28]

Complexities and Contradictions: Devotion and Dissent in the Hagiographies

Thus, the ideas of dissent and devotion had complexities, a part of which has just been outlined. Another aspect of the complex nature of dissent and devotion was that it was gendered. The hagiographies, while discussing the theme of unflinching devotion to God and surrender, use the motif of marriage and association in a complex way. Any male devotee aspiring to be a disciple of Ramanuja and a Shrivaishnava was given a place in the temple organization and other community activities. But the devotion of a woman had to be reconciled

[28] Vaali, *Rāmānuja Kavyam* (Chennai: Vanathi Publishers, 2003).

within the marital structure of the household. Any deviant religious attitude on the part of a woman led to her being deprived of her marital status. This is best reflected in the accounts of Ramanuja's life itself. The narratives repeatedly point out that Ramanuja's compassion towards Shudras and having Shudra teachers, like Tirukacchi Nambi and Maraner Nambi, was not acceptable to his wife who insulted his teachers' wives and quarrelled with Ramanuja over this. Her elitist attitude and arrogance about being a Brahmin became the basis of subsequent marital discord. Finally, a tired Ramanuja left home and became a *sanyasin*. Some accounts say that he took his wife to her parent's house on the pretext of visiting them and left her there, never to bring her back, and became a renunciate. One of the important qualifications of an *acharya* of a Shrivaishnava *matha* is that he should have been a householder but on acquiring office, he must be a *sanyasin*. Could it be that, on one hand, this qualification of a renunciate was to compete with the established Shaiva and Advaita order where the religious orders were based on strict celibacy, and on the other, the position of a householder was retained to confirm with the Brahmanical convention of a *grihasta* as opposed to that of an ascetic? Could it be that the transgression from this Brahmanical norm had to be legitimized and what better way it could be than through an agency of a cantankerous wife who came in the way of her husband's devotion? Ramanuja's wife's attitude is constantly contrasted with Kuresa's wife, Andal, whose unflinching devotion to her husband won her an administrative position in the temple at Srirangam for a short time. Perhaps, through the narratives of the two women, the hagiographers were trying to convey to the followers that deviance meant excommunication from the faith and devotion implied accommodation within the community and its institutional structures.

While on the one hand, the unattached status of a male devotee was acceptable, in the case of a female devotee, her spousified status had to be presented. This becomes evident in the story of Tulukka Nacciyar, whose unflinching devotion to Vishnu could only be accommodated by virtue of her being his spouse, a process in which Ramanuja was shown to be instrumental.

Ramanuja imbued with indomitable zeal, travels to various places, converts people to Shrivaisnavism, and revitalizes the derelict Shrivaisnava temple centres. He never wavers in his aim, not even in the time of crisis. One such crisis is the persecution of the Shrivaisnavas by a Shaivite Chola ruler. Ramanuja flees in disguise and arrives at Tonnur in Karnataka, the capital of the Hoysalas. Here, Ramanuja cures the Hoysala ruler's daughter who has been mentally afflicted for a long time. Impressed with Rāmānuja's skills, the ruler, Vishnuvardhana, a Jaina, converts to Shrivaisnavism. After establishing Ramanuja's credibility in the Kannada context, the texts introduce the Tulukka Nacciyar myth. One day, Vishnu appears before Ramanuja in a dream and reveals that the God of Yadugiri (Melukote), Sampatkumara, is lying buried under an ant hill, waiting to be consecrated. The myth informs us that Yadugiri was already a Vaishnavite centre. With the help of the ruler, Ramanuja clears the forest at Yadugiri, builds a temple and installs the idol in it. However, he finds that the festival image or the *utsava murti*, Ramapriya, is missing and the festivals in the temple therefore cannot resume. Vishnu appears again before Ramanuja and reveals that the image is with the Tulukkan Sultan in Delhi.Then, along with other Shrivaishnavas, Ramanuja reaches Delhi and meets the Sultan. At the Sultan's behest, the royal treasury is searched but the image is not found. Finding himself at a loss, Ramanuja appeals to Vishnu who informs him that the idol is with the *Sultani*, that is, the princess. During the day, the idol is her plaything and at night, it is transformed into God himself and becomes her lover. When Ramanuja invokes the God, the *utsava murti* walks out of the princess's bedroom, comes to him and sits on his lap. Ramanuja is delighted and calls him Selvapillai, my little boy. Against the wishes of the princess, Ramanuja takes away the idol. Pining for her lover and unable to bear the separation, the princess follows the God, braving many hardships on the way. On reaching the temple site, the *Sultani* merges with the God. At the behest of the God, Ramanuja installs her image in a separate shrine and names her Tulukka Nacciyar, that is, the Turkish consort. Thereafter, with the restoration of Selvapillai, the festivals of the temple commence.[29]

Transgression within the marital structure was never entertained. While presenting this theme, the narratives always highlighted the role of Ramanuja as a guru who was the saviour of a woman's honour. Once, Ramauja and his disciple, Anantacharya, were travelling to Tirupati.[30] On the way, they decided to rest in the house of a poor Shriviashnava, Vardhacharya, who lived in a village named Ashtasahasra. When Ramanuja and Anantacharya came to Vardhacharya's house, he was not there. Finding no male member in the house, Yatiraj (Ramanuja) went inside the house to announce his arrival. Wearing a torn cloth after her bath, Lakshmidevi, Vardhacharya's wife, was drying her wet garments in the sun. Since she could not appear in front of the *guru*, she clapped

[29] For details, see, Ranjeeta Dutta, 2003. 'The Politics of Religious Identity: A Muslim Goddess in the Srivaisnava Community of South India', *Studies in History*, 19 (2): 157–184; 164–165.

[30] For details, see, Swami Ramakrishnananda, *Life of Sri Ramanuja, op.cit.*, 174–117.

her hands apprising him of her state. Instantly, Yatiraj threw in from outside his upper garment. Covering herself with that, she came out and welcomed them. Since there was no food in the house, she decided to go to a wealthy merchant in the neighbourhood. This merchant had been trying to woo her for a long time with wealth. She justified her approaching him by thinking that 'Why should I not be blessed by serving my *guru*, at the cost of this body of bones, blood and filth?'[31] She promised the merchant that she would come after serving the guru. On being apprised of the situation, Ramanuja was impressed and gave Lakshmidevi and Vardhacharya some *prasadam* to be given to the merchant. On partaking of the *prasadam*, the merchant was transformed completely and regarded Laksmidevi as his mother. The lady was astonished and delighted. All her troubles were now over. Witnessing this glory of her blessed guru, her joy matched her devotion. When she recounted to her husband all that happened, he also experienced the same joy. Both of them came to their guru along with the merchant and prostrated before him. Thus, the woman was saved from transgressing from the path of a loyal wife at the behest of Ramanuja.

To conclude, this essay has attempted to analyse the complex nature of devotion and dissent in relation to Ramanuja and the Shrivaishnava community. It should be noted that dissent remained largely within the framework of Brahmanical tradition and did not transgress significantly like the Virashaiva and other Shaiva traditions did in South India. The hagiographical narratives, while treating the themes of caste and *bhakti*, attempted to project a departure from the erstwhile organization of the community that was conservative and put forth the basis of new organization through the figure of Ramanuja that attempted at a broader social base. However, while using the motif of dissent, they created their own orthodoxies that further consolidated the Brahmanical norms of caste and gender.

Ramanuja's Vishishtadvaita is credited with an emphasis on the accessibility to the divine grace by any devotee, irrespective of his caste status. This idea of devotion, or *bhakti*, was supposed to have been institutionalized on his initiatives making the worship in the temple and participation in the temple organization possible for the marginalized castes of society. Such delineation has been crucial for the Shriviashnava identity that has continuously engaged with rearticulating itself against the Advaita philosophy of Shankara claiming a distinctive community characteristic of being egalitarian and thus liberal in outlook. The basis of such a belief has been the narratives in the *guruparampara*

---

[31] Ibid, 175.

texts, *stotra*s and the commentaries that have interpreted and reinterpreted the exegetical ideas of Ramanuja, and most importantly the Tamil hymns of the Alvars, all of which are regarded as sacred and hence have a scriptural status for the Shrivaishnavas. The conviction that everybody belongs to the community as a Vaishnava, whatever be the social status, may appear to an outsider as a contradiction to the internal stratification within the Shrivaishnava community that assigns the Brahmins the superior status followed by a hierarchy more or less resembling the *Dharamashastric* norms of the *varnasramadharma* with regional specificities. But this contradiction is not even acknowledged by the followers who emphasize the presence of various caste groups as the unique hallmark of the inclusivistic nature of the Shrivaishnava community. The reference point of these ideas, as stated earlier, has been the inspiring life story of Ramanuja. He is revered as unique for, despite his Brahmanical status, he dissented against the established social norms and strove to create a broad social base. The focus is on his exemplary attitude in general, and related to it, his compassionate attitude has generated unmitigated devotion towards him.

The community's perception of Ramanuja, which has always been a part of the Shrivaishnava received tradition, has impressed upon the modern secular genres of biographies and various writings. Ranging from the modern period of the nineteenth century to the contemporary period of the twenty-first century, these writings have often, unquestioningly replicated the sacred exaltation of Ramanuja in their respective analysis of religion and philosophy. In these works, the comparison with Shankara and his philosophy is invariable, and inevitably, Shankara's Advaita is always referred to as more intellectual and Ramanuja's Vishishtadvaita's appeal is perceived in its comprehensibility to an average devotee. In the nineteenth century context of the social reform movement, this juxtaposition of Shankara and Ramanuja projected the latter as a precursor of modern social reforms.

The seamless continuation of these ideas in the modern biographies of Ramanuja, school textbooks, academic researches in the universities, books for children, newspapers, theatre and films reflects the ways in which the cultural memory of a particular religious community is shared, acquires a universal dimension and enters the realm of the popular. In an article that featured on the entertainment page of a national daily of great repute, the following was written about Ramanuja:

> How does one describe Sri Ramanuja? Scholar nonpareil? Ideal disciple? Sterling leader? Intense *bhakta*? The very personification of humility? Friend of the marginalised? Bold reformer far ahead of his times? Hero of the spirit?

> The great Vaishnava Acharya transcends all such compartmentalisations. In fact, the very fort walls of Srirangam echo his words; the streets remain sanctified by his touch, long, long after he has withdrawn from the physical. His dedication to temple ritualism went hand in hand with his intensely practical outlook. He was the one who brought about a complete integration of people belonging to various castes and creeds. The manner in which he functioned while looking after the Srirangam temple reveals the ideal administrator as well.[32]

Articles such as these have often been printed in various national dailies, clearly indicating a wide readership. Cast within the framework of the Bhakti movement, which has often been regarded simplistically as a protest against the caste hierarchy, the portrayal of Ramanuja's unflinching devotion to God, in this case Vishnu, inspiring his dissent against the Brahmanical domination and shaping his worldview towards the marginalized caste, has an appeal in the Indian society in general, and the Tamil society in particular, where caste identities still dominate and influence social interactions and political configurations.

The hagiographical narratives of the Shrivaishnava community on Ramanuja in relation to the issue of social hierarchy developed and travelled through many layers of history to enter the modern biographical domain, thus collapsing the distinction between the hagiographies and biographies and merging the sacred and secular that have often been viewed as mutually exclusive categories. It needs to be pointed out that the narratives on the trope of Ramanuja and the social system have never been unanimous in their representations at any point of time. Even during the twelfth and thirteenth centuries, following closely after Ramanuja's death, the narratives that circulated in oral as well as in written forms varied. These variations were influenced by the form of the particular genre of religious literature and the intentions of the authors and the social groups they were representing. When analysed closely, it seems that these different versions not only registered the diverse perceptions of Ramanuja's attitude towards the *varnasramadharma* but also reflected the varying social attitudes of the hagiographers and authors and the frameworks within which they operated.

Further, it also needs to be pointed out that the tropes discussed in these texts with reference to Ramanuja and caste were a part of the larger ongoing Shrivaishnava discourse on the relevance of the social status for achieving salvation. These discussions were debated upon in the commentaries that

---

[32] Prema Nanda Kumar. 2005. *The Hindu*: Friday, May 13. Entertainment page.

often attempted to trace the genealogy of their interpretations to the ideas of Ramanuja himself. Consequently, there were diverse elucidations of Ramanuja's Vishishtadvaita and these then emerged as frames of reference. Therefore, neither do the hagiographical narratives have a unilateral, unitary approach to the delineation of Ramanuja's activities with reference to the issues of caste and social and ritual practices, nor do the commentaries register a homogenous, undivided opinion about Ramanuja's ideas of grace and salvation that is *prapatti* and *moksha*. Interestingly, none of these complexities are discussed or represented in the modern biographies, films, plays and newspapers, and even if they do, they are expressed in an unproblematic and simplistic manner subordinated to the unilinear discourse of 'social reforms' and the association of Ramanuja with it. Some modern works show that the notion of the 'social reform' was a nineteenth and twentieth century construct that aimed to create a gallery of great men in history that became crucial for nationalism and nation making. Within this scheme of ideas, inclusion of complexities and contradictions in the representations of the great men was avoided or not taken cognizance of, thereby creating an impression of an unproblematic monolithic received tradition. Though sometimes the alternate discussions manifest, but within the text itself, these are evened out with an explanation that is always in congruence with the delineation of Ramanuja as a 'social reformer'.

References

Chari, S.M. Srinivasa. *Advaita and Viśiṣṭadvaita* (Delhi: Motilal Banarsidass, 2004 [1961]). Garudavahana Pandita. *Divyasuricaritam*. Edited by Pandita Madhvacharya, T.A. Sampathakumaracharya and K.K.A. Venkatachari (Bombay: Ananthacharya Research Institute, 1978).

Govindacharya, Alakondavilli. *Sri Rāmānujacharya: The Exponent of the Visishtadvaita Philosophy*, Reprint (Chennai: Sri Nrisimhapriya Trust, 2004).

Hardy, Friedhelm. 'The Formation of Shrivaisnavism'. In *Charisma and Canon. Essays on the Religious History of the Indian Subcontinent*, edited by Vasudha Dalmia, Angelika Malinar and Martin Christof (New Delhi: Oxford University Press), 41–61.

Indra, C.T. 'Hagiography Revisited'. In Indira Pathasarathy, *The Life and Ideas of Ramanuja*, Translated by T. Sriaman (New Delhi, Oxford University Press, 2008).

Lakshamma, G. *The Impact of Rāmānuja's Teachings on Life and Conditions in Society* (Delhi: Sundeep Prakashan, 1990).

Lester, Robert C. 'Rāmānuja and Srivaisnavism: The Concept of *Prapatti* or *Sarnagati*', *History of Religion* 5(2) (1966): 266–282.

Narasimhachary, M. *Sri Rāmānuja* (New Delhi: Sahitya Akademi, 2007).

Parthasarathy, Indira. *Rāmānujar: The Life and Ideas of Rāmānuja.* Translated by T. Sriaman. Critical introduction by C.T. Indra (New Delhi: Oxford University Press, 2008).

Ramakrishnananda, Swami. *Life of Sri Rāmānuja*, Fourth Edition (Madras: Sri Ramakrishna Math, 1986).

Ramakrishnananda, Swami. *Life of Sri Rāmānuja.* Translated by Swami Budhananda (Madras: Sri Ramakrishna Math, 1986).

Rāmānuja: A Great Vaishnava Saint (Mumbai: Amar Chitra Katha, 1974).

Rāmānuja directed by G.V. Iyer.

Seshadri, Kandadai. *Srivaishnavism and Social Change* (Kolkata: K.P. Bagchi and Co., 1998).

Vaali. *Rāmānuja Kavyam* (Chennai: Vanathi Publishers, 2003).

Varadachariar, V. ed. *Yatirāja-Vaibhava of Āndhrapūrṇa* (Vaṭuka Nambi) (Madras: M.C. Krishnan, 1978).

Kumar, Prema Nanda. *The Hindu*, Friday, 13 May 2005, Entertainment.

CHAPTER

5

Dissent Within

Dissent and Devotion in Tamil Cittar Tradition

S. Gunasekaran

Introduction

The Bhakti movement in South India initially emerged as a dissent tradition against the orthodox Vedic Brahmanism and stood for social equality. But at a certain point in time, *bhakti* became an ideological instrument in the hands of ruling elites and justified social inequalities. For the sake of its survival, the radical flavour of the Bhakti movement gradually receded to the background and the movement came to depend upon the patronage of ruling elites. The essay explores how the *cittar* or *siddha* tradition, which nurtured radical views against social injustice, came to fill the vacuum created by the degenerate Bhakti movement and of how such voices dissent eventually gave birth to an alternative value system and a new mode of devotion. It is argued that the *cittar* tradition cannot be studied alone as a theological response to *bhakti* but there is a need to understand how it represented the overall contemporary discontent of the common man against the socio-political institutions created by the *bhakti* ideology. Hence, the essay also studies epigraphic references to people's resistances against socio-political institutions and thus looks at their relevance to the dissents in *cittar* literatures.

Bhakti and Ideological Subjugation

The picture of society indicated in the early Tamil literatures shows us that kin relations and the ideology of heroism defined the early social formation. But the dominant scenarios of early social formation withered away by the beginning of the first millennium AD. The characteristics and practices of early social formation, such as predatory politics, cattle raids and warfare, sharing food with commoners and even kinship bonds in production, had lost their grip. Conversely, a new social formation, structured by the ethos of plough agriculture, began to develop.[1] As production activity was modelled more on the agrarian economy, values and institutions of the agrarian social relations were produced and reproduced. This led to the growth of composite social relations in which the state and religion were integral.[2] The composite ruling class that appeared at different times, in different regions, exhibited a relatively uniform structure and successfully subjugated the masses, converting them to a condition of meagre productive forces. Religion in the Brahmanistic form of *bhakti* operated as an ideological tool and provided justification for the appropriation of the surplus production and additional labour values. In the new material context, hierarchy in the social structure had analogous relations with the hierarchy of landownership and that of access to religious worship.

The consolidation of the state, an exploitative institution of the newly emerging social relations, became viable only through the integration of local tribal elements into Vedic Brahmanism. In the course of this integration, both Vedic Brahmanism and indigenous tribal elements lost their natural characteristics and formed the base for a new religious mode of *bhakti*. The emerging religious ideology facilitated the execution of the state authority without necessary deployment of coercive forces.[3] The promotion of the

---

[1] The dissolution of classical chiefdoms and the consequent emergence of the state are studied as a triumphant development of relations of plough agriculture by overpowering the influence of agro-pastoral productive relations. The period of the Kalabarars is viewed as a period of struggle between these two incompatible modes of production. Rajan Gurukkal, 'Aspects of Great Transformation of Ancient Kerala' (Paper presented in a conference on 'Revisiting Transition', held at Jawaharlal Nehru University, 6 March 2007), 2. Also, see Burton Stein, *Peasant State and Society in Medieval South India* (New Delhi: Oxford University Press, 1994), 76–77.

[2] The mutually beneficial relationships between dominant landlords and Brahmins have been established by several studies. The traders in the medieval period are considered to have emerged from the land-controlling groups. R. Champakalakshmi, 'The State in Pre-modern South India: A Historiographical Re-assessment' (Paper for symposium on 'State in Indian History', Indian History Congress, 61st Session, Kolkata, 2001), 7.

[3] R. Champakalakshmi, 'Urban Processes in Early Medieval Tamil Nadu', in *The City in Indian History, Urban Demography, Society, and Politics*, ed. Indu Banga (New Delhi: Manohar Publications for Urban History Association of India, 1991), 53–54.

Brahmadeya settlements and the construction of monumental temples were the two associated processes that assisted in the ideological legitimization and the consolidation of the state. Temples in particular became centres of all these new developments. More than a religious institution, they functioned as a business hub for the state, local chiefs, landlords, traders, Brahmins, etc. The temples became symbolic representations of the state and the authorities of power. Also, at the local level, temples remained as effective means for the members of the composite ruling class (landlords and wealthy merchants) to exercise their power and legitimize their authority. In a way, as chief patrons, they became the custodians of temples. The more people allowed themselves to be subjugated to a temple in the name of devotion, the more they ended up legitimizing the authority of its patrons.

As mentioned, the purpose of the ruling class and the state was served by the emerging dominant ideology of *bhakti* Brahmanism.[4] As *bhakti* penetrated more deeply among of the masses, the power of the ruling elites became more stable. Providing a psychological basis for social acceptance of exploitation, *bhakti* emphasized voluntary enslavement to a particular deity or God. At the level of society, it encouraged voluntary submission to the powerful, while in the context of family, it legitimized the authority of the patriarchy.[5] 'It glossed over the material reality of the conditions of domination by inventing other-worldly explanations for the social contradictions'.[6] In fact, the Bhakti movement in South India is itself considered to be a protest movement against the orthodox Vedic Brahmanism and social inequalities.[7] But it led to an inverse development of legitimizing social inequalities. The *bhakti* discourses were 'so imposing that these elements of protest and dissent could be articulated only through its discursive practices that neutralized them through the strategy of containment'.[8]

---

[4] The phrase 'bhakti Brahmanism' is used as an opposition to the Vedic Brahmanism and an alternative to 'bhakti Hinduism' used by Burton Stein.

[5] N. Muthumohan, *Indiath Thathuvangalain Aracial* (Politics of Indian Philosophies) (Chennai: Parisal, 2005), 41;.

[6] Rajan Gurukkal, 'Aspects of Great Transformation', 10.

[7] R. Champakalakshmi, 'From Devotion and Dissent to Dominance: The Bhakti of the Tamil Alvars and Nayanars', in *Tradition, Dissent and Ideology*, ed. R. Champakalakshmi and S. Gopal (New Delhi: Oxford University Press, 1996), 136; ; Glenn E. Yocum, 'Shrines, Shamanism, and Love Poetry: Elements in the Emergence of Popular Tamil Bhakti', *Journal of the American Academy of Religion* 41(1) (1973), 5.

[8] Rajan Gurukkal, 'Aspects of Great Transformation', 10.

The presence of Brahmins and Vedic rituals was highly evident in the heroic society. But a significant aspect was that they had not yet evolved as a state apparatus or as institutions of the ruling class. Furthermore, they had not penetrated much amongst the local masses and altered the basic structure of society. Rather this task was successfully accomplished by Brahmanism spread through the ideology of *bhakti*, particularly by a group of Shaivite and Vaishnavite hymnists with large-scale support from the landed elites. *Bhakti* discourses and practices integrated the local folk elements with Vedic Brahmanism, giving birth to a new 'popular mode of religious expression'. In fact, the composite features found in *bhakti* Brahmanism reflect the varied interests of the aforesaid composite ruling class.[9] The incorporation or assimilation of secular traditional folk culture and institutions in Vedic Brahmanism happened to the extent of incorporating only certain popular elements in their folk practices, thus ensuring their subordination within *bhakti*.[10] The convergence resulted in two significant aspects. First, the folk practices were given complicated meanings and interpretations in line with Vedic Brahmanical texts. For example, the indigenous concept of 'love' between men and women, or among human beings, had now taken the shape of personal love between men and the Supreme Being (God). Folk deities such as Murugan and Mayon were incorporated within the pantheon of Vedic literature.[11] The folk tradition of herostone worship by ancestors provided a basis for the temple and temple-centred rituals.[12] Indigenous knowledge of music, dance, medicine,

---

[9] According to Ramanujan and Cutler, 'Early Bhakti movements, whether devoted to Siva or Vishnu, used whatever they found at hand, and changed whatever they used – Vedic and Upanisadic notions; mythologies, Buddhism; Jainism; conventions of Tamil and Sanskrit poetry; early Tamil conceptions of love, service, women and kings; folk religion and folksong; the play of contrasts between Sanskrit and the mother tongue'. See A.K. Ramanujan and Norman Cutler, 'From Classicism to Bhakti', in *Essays on Gupta Culture*, ed. Bardwell L. Smit (Delhi: Motilal Banarsidass, 1983), p177. It seems that *bhakti* was consciously constructed to safeguard the interests of the emerging ruling class. For relevant discussions, see Ganapathy Subbaiah, 'Dakshinapatha: Where Does the Path Lead Us?' (Presidential Address, Indian History Congress, 57th Session, Calicut, 2007), 15–19.

[10] Certain folk elements like 'animal sacrifices and excessively erotic religious customs' were excluded. Stein, *Peasant State and Society*, 85.

[11] Murugan and Mayon came to be known respectively as Subramanya and Krishna. P.T. Srinivasa Iyengar, *History of the Tamils: From the Earliest Times to 600* AD. (Madras: University of Madras, 1929), 76–77.

[12] Champakalakshmi, 'From Devotion and Dissent to Dominance', 138.

literature and even the system of courtesanship were developed as institutions and consequently, became part of the Brahmanic tradition of *bhakti*. Second, since *bhakti* Brahmanism became the exclusive domain of the ruling landholding elites, Brahmins and state rulers, a section of the masses were isolated from the mainstream.

For instance, though the religious ideology of *bhakti* was propagated using the vernacular language as a medium, the literary tenure of the language became unintelligible and beyond the understanding of the common masses. Since indigenous practices were given complicated meanings and interpretations, they were also no longer accessible to the masses. Therefore, despite the fact that the ideology of *bhakti* emerged as a 'popular mode of religious expression' of the Tamils, it did not express the collective consciousness of the people as a whole. But it remained as a hidden structure of social relations of production and subjugated a larger section of people in favour of a few.[13] This subjugation can also be viewed in terms of voluntary acceptance or assimilation into the popular religious ideology. The difference is very narrow, but its implication is significant since it helped the consumption of a large-scale material surplus and labour power.

Therefore, in the medieval South Indian context, any dissent movement concerning social changes and welfare of the downtrodden was to be waged against the ideology of *bhakti* Brahmanism; the authority of the temple, the monopoly of landlords, traders and Brahmins; the lavish and extravagant lifestyle of the upper strata, caste oppression, tax burdens, etc. Particularly, the temple and Brahmanism became prime targets of attack as they represented the state and its ideology. Brahmins, who gave ideological justification for the caste/class oppression, had to face resistance and became the subject of severe criticism.

Multiple Voices of Dissent: Reading on Inscriptional References

The inscriptions on the temple walls are primarily records of land transactions and endowments. In a way, they represent the consciousness of the upper strata. Their purpose was not to document the resistance or the voice of the

[13] *Bhakti* has been viewed as being congenial to the developing feudal social structure in South India. See M.G.S. Narayanan and Kesavan Veluthat, 'The Bhakti Movement in South India', in *Feudal Social Formations in Early India*, ed. D.N. Jha 1987, Chanakya Publications, New Delhi, 348–375.

suppressed, but to justify how these different howls of protest disturbed the interests and institutional practices of the ruling section of society. Therefore, the references that can be culled from inscriptions with regard to resistance are limited and partial.

Seen through the inscriptions, most of dissents emerged from people who belonged to the middle and lower stratum of the social hierarchy. The category of dissenters varied from tenant cultivators and temple servants to agricultural labourers or the Paraiyas. The resistances were generally directed against Brahmins, state authorities, hegemonic landlords and the temple. Most of the protests were triggered against oppressive taxation. Evidently, ordinary peasants suffered due to overtaxation, particularly when landholding relations determined the entire socio-political scenario. The demand for more taxes on whatever was taxable – from land to buffaloes – by a number of agencies had a severe impact on different sections of people. In case of non-payment of taxes, the inscription phrases show that the tax collectors were allowed to break clay pots and to confiscate the bronze pots (*mankalam udaithum venkalam yeduthum)* from people. The authorities that had the power to collect the taxes varied from region to region. However, most of the revenue went into the temple's custody and to local chiefs, rather than to the king and the state.

References found in inscriptions throw light on incidents, such as the refusal to pay taxes, action for reduction of taxes and campaigns in opposition to certain taxes and arbitrary taxation laws.[14] Some of the popular modes of protests by peasants were: refusal to sow; abandoning the entire village uncultivated; and protesting against landlords.[15] An oppressive tax on cows and buffaloes was challenged through denial of payment. On certain occasions, taxes were lowered because of protests from cultivators.[16] The Gauda peasants of Karnataka are said to have protested against the transfer of the land rights of their village to Brahmins.[17] A Telugu–Chola inscription throws light on the peasants' protests against the Brahmin usurpers when they lost their land rights to the Brahmins.[18]

---

[14] Cited in M.D. Rajkumar, 'Struggle for Rights during Later Chola Period', *Social Scientist* 2(6–7) (1974), 29–35.

[15] Ibid., 30.

[16] Ibid.

[17] Cited in R.N. Nandi, 'Growth of Rural Economy in Early Feudal India' (Presidential Address, Indian History Congress, 45th Session, Annamalainagar, 1985), 72.

[18] Ibid.

As stated earlier, different agencies were involved in taxation and tax collection. All those who had power to dominate began to exploit the ordinary peasants and extract as much as possible from their production. A considerable portion of the cultivable and fertile lands were granted tax-free (*iraili*) to Brahmins and to the temple. Big landlords were also not necessarily subjected to any tax regulations and as a result, the entire tax burden fell on the small peasants. Further, there was no specified channel through which the surplus production would flow into the hands of the ruling class. The state authorities, temple managers, Brahmins and landlords practised different means and mechanisms to expropriate surplus production from peasants. From medieval epigraphic materials, we learn that the peasants had requested the members of *sabha* to take necessary action against people who were illegally claiming a share in their production. They were determined not to cultivate land unless their grievances were redressed.[19]

Brahmins did not engage in production directly. Whenever they were granted lands, special arrangements were made for the settlement of agricultural labourers to cultivate these lands. This forced the labourers to settle in the lands granted and come under the direct exploitation of Brahmins. Furthermore, the land granted could be either in the form of *kudinengia* or the *kudineenga* categories. In the case of the former, the old peasants were forcibly evicted from their land, and in the latter, they were allowed to stay on as tenants.[20] A rare reference in the inscriptions shows that the people of Paraiya, a community of agricultural labourers, had revolted against oppressive landlords and Brahmins for better emoluments. 'As a result of this heroic struggle, which encompassed 24 villages, people of lower castes such as *Paganeri* and *Paraiya* who were cruelly oppressed and denied human rights, were able to wrest a few rights from their oppressors'.[21]

A similar incident from Sri Vellipputtur during the Vijayanagara period is also mentioned, when Pallars and Paraiyars revolted and gained certain social rights in favour of their community. It is said that the people of oppressed communities such as Pulaiyar, Paraiyar and Cerumar – the traditional agricultural workers

---

[19] Cited in N. Vanamamalai, 'Consolidation of Feudalism and Anti-feudal Struggle during Chola Imperialist Rule' (Proceedings of the Second International Conference Seminar of Tamil Studies, Madras, 1968), 242.

[20] R. Tirumalai, *Land Grants and Agrarian Reactions in Cola and Pandya Times* (Madras: University of Madras, 1987), 42–47; Vanamamalai, 'Consolidation of Feudalism', 240.

[21] Rajkumar, 'Struggle for Rights', 31.

with the status of agrestic slaves or serfs in medieval society – must be the descendants of the early peasants who lost their lands. The caste system, based on birth and marriages, made self-improvement nearly impossible for such people by the restricting their movements to the village and forcing them to remain illiterate.[22]

The Brahmins and other social groups, whose patronage was necessary to the temple administration, began to claim higher status. They gained several social privileges. Further, they began to construct their exaggerated history, often situating their origin in Brahmanical mythology. A caste could become part of Brahmanical tradition, distancing itself from tribal status, by connecting its genealogy with certain mythical figures in the religious texts. This tendency became quite popular, particularly amongst the middle social hierarchical castes. According to inscriptions, Kammalas, Kaikolars, Idaiyars and Devaradiyars, among others, received special social rights.[23] Inscriptions from Kadthur inform us about the king's special order to the then Kongu Kammalar to allow them to enjoy certain social privileges. Thereby they were entitled to blow double conches in their rituals, to use *patha rakzhai* (footwear) and to plaster or cement their houses. In another inscription, the Kaniudiyar Thatchar (carpenter), Thattan (metal worker) and Kollar (smith) were allowed by the king to blow double conches on special occasions. The Kaikolar and Devaradiyar who lived in Thirumadaivalakam were given the right to sell or mortgage their land. There are numerous similar references, but presumably the demands for special rights vary from one section to another. While the castes in the middle order demanded the right to use *patha rakzhai*, the Sanar and Pulaiyars in certain places had to fight for their right to cover the upper portion of their body.[24] This conscious conferment of certain rights and social privileges to certain castes created a

[22] M.G.S. Narayanan, 'Role of Peasants in the Early History of Tamilakam in South India', *Social Scientist* 16(9) (1988), 17–34.

[23] For a detailed discussion of these inscriptional texts, see S. Gunasekaran, 'State, Society and Economy: An Evolutionary Study of the Kongu Region in Western Tamil Nadu (6th to 16th Century CE)' (PhD thesis submitted to Centre for Historical Studies, Jawaharlal Nehru University, New Delhi, December 2007), 122–123.

[24] Nadar and Pulaiyar communities of Tamil Nadu and Kerala had to fight for the right to cover the upper portion of their body. As a result of this historic struggle, popularly known as *tholseelai porattam*, in the 1850s, the communities were able to liberate themselves from age-long feudal oppression. For details, see K. Natchimuthu, *Kerala Samuka Neethi Porattankal* (Social Reform Movements in Kerala) (Palayamkottai: Centre for Ambedkar Studies, St. Xavier's College, 2005), 23–32.

situation of competition. The middle castes began to engage in conflicts among themselves to secure a high status in the social hierarchy. Thus, it helped the upper castes like Brahmins and Vellalars to be free from any disagreements.

Nonetheless, the supremacy of Brahmins and Vellalars was challenged through the confederation of castes into *Idangai* and *Valangai* categories. While there were fierce conflicts between these social divisions, sometimes the castes of two different divisions came together to fight against the dominant Brahmins and landholding Vellalars, whose social status was above the *Idangai* and *Valangai* divisions. It is important to underline here that in both cases, their prime targets were the Brahmins and the temple. For instance, a thirteenth century inscription states that there was a clash between the *Idangai* and *Valangai* castes. During this incident, 'the village was burnt down, the sacred places destroyed, and the images of deities and the treasures of the temple looted'.[25] Peasants, small traders and artisans of the *Idangai* and *Valangai* groups together resisted the forcible collection of certain taxes. They further declared corporal punishment on those who helped the state and the Brahmin landlords in collecting taxes and maintaining revenue records.[26] In a similar incident, the *Idangai* and *Valangai* castes arrived upon a common agreement for collective resistance against the oppressive taxes of *Idangavari* and *Inavari*.[27] It is said that 'the toiling people of the "right hand" and the "left hand" united in an assembly, called to oppose this practice and decided not to cooperate in any way with Brahman and *Vellalar* landlords and officials'.[28]

People committed self-immolation as a protest against land authority.[29] A dancing girl hanged herself from the temple tower, claiming her right to cultivate in *jeevitha* land.[30] A Brahmin house was set afire in a clash regarding temple rights. A temple, whose walls contained inscriptions denying the cultivation rights of some peasants, was demolished.[31] During the time of Rajaraja I, the main deity of a temple had to be shifted to another place for fears of public revolt. In fact, with their power and monopoly, the inscriptional documents

[25] Cited in Stein, *Peasant State and Society*, 174.

[26] Cited in Nandi, 'Growth of Rural Economy', 254.

[27] Cited in Vanamamalai, 1962.

[28] Rajkumar, 'Struggle for Rights', 34.

[29] Vanamamalai, 'Consolidation of Feudalism', 242.

[30] Ibid. For the relevant discussion, see D.N. Jha, 'Editor's Introduction', in *Feudal Social Formations in Early India*, ed. D.N. Jha (New Delhi: Chanakya Publications, 1987), 22.

[31] Rajkumar, 'Struggle for Rights', 33.

were manipulated in favour of local Vellalar landlords and Brahmins. The declaration of the power and rights deeds inscribed on the temple walls had to be protected since there were always protests and attempts to destroy them. It is said that the rulers maintained a special army named *maditsevakar* to guard the temple walls.

The response of the state to crush these protests has also been referenced a few times. A government order was issued declaring that there should not be any outrage against Brahmins and Vellalar landlords.[32] The protesters were threatened with imposition of severe fines. Sometimes, the king would send his army to bring the situation to normalcy. The damaged inscriptional deeds were replaced with new ones, and sometimes the same documents were placed at different places.

These isolated incidents of protest indicate that there had been growing discontent among the masses over Brahminical orthodoxy, state oppression and the monopoly of the upper classes. The dissenters neither had power nor possessed any mechanism to register or spread their voices. Since the inscriptions remained as 'class texts', it is presumable that a good number of attacks and outbursts might have gone unnoticed. Nonetheless, a tradition of dissent popularly known as *cittar* tradition, which developed in this particular material condition, seemed to have radically advocated for the cause of the oppressed and questioned the ideological premises on which oppressive institutions had developed and functioned.

Cittars: The Intellectual Voice of Dissent

Tamil *cittar* tradition has a long history from Tirumular of the seventh century.[33] There were no specific relations among *cittar*s who lived at different times, except that they all dissented against various forms of oppression. In

---

[32] Ibid., 31; Stein, *Peasant State and Society*, 180.

[33] Subramaniya Bharathi, a modern revolutionary Tamil poet and thinker, claimed, 'I am one of the Siddhas of this land'(S.Murugesan, *Bharathi Kanda Cittarkal,* Chennai: Kurinji Publication, 2007), 8–12. Likewise, the origin of the ideas of Ayothidasar and Periyar E.V. Ramasamy can be traced to the medieval literature composed by *cittar*s. See D. Dharmarajan, 'Samukappini: Cittar Marapilirunthu Oru Samukap Porali' (Social Ills: A Social Activist from Cittar Tradition) (Paper presented in seminar on 'Siddhas of Tamil Nadu', Folklore Department, St. Xavier's College, Palayamkottai, August 2006), 41–66.

general, those who spoke in favour of the dominated and the voiceless were identified as *cittar*s. The ideological discourses of the *cittar*s differed from one another but were determined primarily by the prevailing socio-economic conditions of their time. The word *cittar* is interpreted differently but in the present discussion, the interpretation is restricted within the context of 'radicalism' or 'dissension'. Further, the discussion is primarily confined to the literary compositions of three *cittar*s, namely, Sivavakkiyar, Pattinattar and Pampatti Cittar, who lived in between the tenth to the sixteenth centuries CE.[34]

The elements of dissent in Tamil literatures can be observed right from the beginning of the classical period. The early texts like *Tirukkural*, *Naladiyar*, *Manimekalai* and *Chilapathikaram* carry certain extent of resistance. Similarly, few a *bhakti* hymns and texts in Tirumular's *Tirumandiram* speak against the social hierarchy based on caste divisions. However, in these literatures, there are no direct radical attempts towards social reform, caste annihilation or questioning meaningless rituals. For instance, though the elements of dissent and protest were found in the *bhakti* cult propagated by Shaiva and Vaishnava saints, these were 'temporary, partial and counterproductive'. Ultimately, they helped in the exploitative assimilation of indigenous folk into a caste hierarchy, and thus further facilitated the consolidation and extension of Vedic Brahmanism in a new form. In fact, in the context of the rapid spread of agriculture and the development of a composite ruling class, the conversion of the insipid dissent tradition into a means for social suppression was inevitable. At a certain point in time, the growth and survival of the Bhakti movement was entirely dependent upon the patronage extended by the authoritarians of the ruling class.

In the case of Tirumular, the deviation from the *bhakti* literary tradition is quite clear, but unlike later *cittar*s, he was not a vocal opponent of *bhakti* and temple-centred malpractices and oppression. However, there still are a number of aspects that distinguish Tirumular from the other Shaiva scholars. Probably, this is what connects him with the *cittar* tradition. It is also said that during Tirumular's time (he is dated between the seventh to tenth centuries AD), direct confrontation with *bhakti* was not needed as it was yet to develop as an ideological instrument of the ruling class. Therefore, Tirumular's prime

34 There is no unanimous opinion about the date of Tamil *cittar*s. For relevant details, see K. Meenakshi, 'The Siddhas of Tamil Nadu: A Voice of Dissent', in *Tradition, Dissent and Ideology*, ed. R. Champakalakshmi and S. Gopal (New Delhi: Oxford University Press, 1996), 116–119; R. Venkatraman, *A History of the Tamil Siddha Cult* (Madurai: NS Ennes Publication, 1990), 42–74.

concern was to revivify the indigenous tradition in the context of the growing encroachment of Vedic–Puranic traditions.[35] It is in this context that the literary compositions of medieval *cittar*s deserve special attention.

Sivavakkiyar's questions extend classical examples to the ideological paradigm in which the Tamil *cittar* tradition was anchored. He asked: is there any distinguishing mark between the flesh, or skin or bone? Do you find any difference when you sleep with a Pariah or a Brahmin woman? You ate no venison yet are not the threads on your bosom made of deerskin? You ate no mutton yet do you not perform your sacrifices with sheep's flesh? Do gods ever become stone?[36] After asking these questions, Sivavakkiyar expressed his sense of exasperation by saying, 'What I can do but laugh'. Caste differentiation had been a major concern and contention for all *cittar*s. Though in *bhakti* tradition, the stories of Nandanar and Tirupanan Alwar, who belonged to the lower castes, express a sense of equality, these constructions were meant to bring the people of thc Paraiyar and Panar castes into the sphere of *bhakti* Brahmanism and ensure their service to the landlords and Brahmins. The mingling of these communities was never encouraged as, in actuality, the Brahmin remained the Brahmin and thc Pana or Paraiya rcmaincd thc Pana or Paraiya.[37] Also, the mild criticism of *bhakti* hymnists over the social hierarchy initially and their 'occasional calls for egalitarianism or universal brotherhood' were neither a part nor a reflection of their social philosophy.[38] Several songs of *cittar*s show that thcy confrontcd these existing social values constructed by '*bhakti* Brahmanism' and propagated alternative values that stand for non-caste, as against caste; *onre kulam* (one humanity) versus caste inequality; intra-caste marriage versus inter-caste marriage and inter-caste marriage versus intra-caste marriage. For instance, Pampatti Cittar denounces caste and pronounces, 'we will set fire to the caste divisions, challenge the street division (based on caste)

[35] Pa. Seyaprakasam, 'Cittar Ilakkiyankal Kattum Samuka Muranpadukalum Theervukalaum', (Social Issues and Solutions as They are Shown in Cittar Literatures) (Paper presented in seminar on 'Siddhas of Tamil Nadu', Folklore Department, St. Xavier College, Palayamkottai, August 2006), 74.

[36] Sivavakkiyar *Patal*, 126, K. Meenakshi, trans.,'The Siddhas of Tamil Nadu: A Voice of Dissent', in .Champakalakshmi and S.Gopal (ed), *Tradition, Dissent and Ideology* New Delhi: Oxford University Press, 1996), 129.

[37] M.G.S. Narayanan and Kesavan Veluthat, 1987, 368.

[38] M.G.S. Narayanan and Kesavan Veluthat, 1987, 366.

and have marital relations with untouchable families'.[39] Pattinattar, describing his austere lifestyle, says, 'I dared to beg from families of all castes'.[40]

In fact, both the rulers and the Brahmins patronized each other. While the economic prosperity of the Brahmins had a direct relationship with the socio-economic power of the rulers, the power of rulers largely depended upon the existence of Brahmins and their ideological support.[40] It was strongly believed by the medieval dissenter that the underlying causes for all societal problems and caste differentiations were Brahmins, their virtually meaningless rituals, temple and idol worship and the influence of Vedic and Puranic elements. As stated elsewhere, the temple symbolized the state. The rulers were treated at par with the deities. Both the deity and the king were identified as *ko* and *perumal*, while the word *kovil* was meant for both the temple and the king's palace. *Adiyon* is a common word to denote both the devotees of deities and the servants of rulers. Therefore, 'the ritual of worship is conceived on the same pattern as the ritual of service to the king'.[41] The *bhakta*s (servants) were the base for both the temple and the king to consolidate their power. It is also important to note that a similar pattern was followed at the lower levels of the power hierarchy. The radical approach of *cittar*s against the institution of the temple and the Brahmin seems to be significant in this context. Despite differences in their use of language, personal beliefs and thought contents, all *cittar*s unanimously expressed a sense of anti-Brahmin, anti-Veda and anti-temple rituals. They emphasized moral and rational values, following the self-discipline path of intellectuals rather than fake religious priests and an adherence to reason and rationality rather than blind beliefs and rituals.

Sivavakkiyar calls the temple worshippers fools and says, 'you do puja repeatedly, when the puja itself is within you'.[42] What is implied here is that perfect happiness lies within one's 'self'. Thus, it is better to shape the 'self' and develop moral thinking and humanistic behaviour, rather than worship

---

[39] Pampatti Cittar *Patal*, 123. The reference numbers for Pampatti Cittar Patal (song of Pampatti Cittar) used in this article are based on A. Angamuthu, Cittar Patalkal Vilakka Urai (Chennai: Komugi Publications, 2003).

[40] Pattinattar Patal: Pothupatal (general song), see Pe.Narayanasamy, 2000, 51.

[41] Narayanan and Veluthat, 2000, 402.

[42] Sivavakkiyar *Patal,* standard texts on Sivavakkiyar patal (songs of Sivavakkiyar patal) follow uniform serial number as per the order given in original work of Sivavakkiyar (written in palm leaves), therefore generally scholars give reference to patal no (song number) than the page number of the edited/printed texts., 35, K. Meenakshi, trans., 1996, 130.

God and offer puja. In the same sense, he also asks when 'God is within you, does the stone ever speak?'[43] He argues that it is not necessary to run to distant places to worship when *adinathan* is within one's self and suggests that there is no need for cow worship or the Vedas. Thus, according to him, reciting the Vedas is a waste of time.

Sivavakkiyar's anger continues unabated when he says:

> Oh Brahman, who recites vedic mantras! Will these mantras help you when you die? You recite the four Vedas but do not know the *gnapadam.* Even if you recite the four Vedas and follow all *shastras*, you cannot realize god. Everyday, after taking holy dip, you set the *homa* fire, pour ghee and recite vedic mantras, but what is the use? You are unable to realize that both fire and water are within you. What are temples? What are holy tanks? All are but in the mind. Without realizing yourself, you say god is in bricks, in *karunkal* (granite) and in *senmpu* (copper). Even if you recite the Vedas, mark your body with sacred ashes and grunt the name of god, you cannot realize the Supreme Being. Oh poor, who offer rituals to a stone! Can god ever become a stone? Oh fools, who take holy dip in the morning and evening! What benefit will a toad that always lives in the same water receive? Oh liar, who teaches Vedic scriptures! Let me know what is *nizhtai*? What is knowledge? You *Pattar*, who say god emerged from a pillar, what is the use of *homa kundam, vedas,* and thread knitted clay pot? You split a stone, use one part for steps and sculpt the other as sacred god. Carrying the vedic texts, you mumble lies, you do not understand birth and death. With impure heart, you praise god.[44]

What Sivavakkiyar has attempted to do is to visualize the real practicable human world, rather than the external heavenly world. As stated earlier, symbols like Ganga, Vedas, Brahmin and cow were treated as sacred, and they remained as means of suppression and exploitation. Rajendra Chola, for example, mobilized manpower for his expedition to conquer the north and bring the holy water of Ganga.[45] As evident from the inscriptions, these sacred objects were used to threaten people who disobeyed the agreements displayed in the

---

[43] Ibid., 497, K. Meenakshi, trans., 1996, 130. The reference number for Sivavakkiyar Patal (song of Sivavakkiyar) used in this article is based on Aru. Ramanathan, 2005. *Sitthar periya gnanakkovai ena vazhankum sitthar patalkal.* 1st edition (Chennai: Prema publications, 1959).

[44] Sivavakkiyar Patal: 13, 14, 34, 35, 130, 184, 312, 494, 497, 420.

[45] George W. Spencer, *The Politics of Expansion, The Chola Conquest of Sri Lanka and Sri Vijaya* (Chennai: New Era Publications, 1982), 42–45.

inscriptions. Similarly, pilgrimage to various holy centres and taking a dip in holy rivers was propagated as a way to salvation, for warding off evils and pollution and to escape from sins. Against this background, Pampatti Cittar, who also shared the values expressed by Sivavakkiyar, proclaimed that the *Chatur Veda* or the six categories of religious treatises, mantras, Puranas, etc, are just rubbish. He argued in favour of a teacher who can teach the fake religious preacher to know the right path of true religion. He argues: Does the chiseled stone god have any sense? Even if one constructs a temple in every village and offer prayer, he cannot see God. One may wander in several places, take bath in all holy rivers, but sins cannot be washed away. He further states that religion and caste differentiation are meant for ordinary people but not for a true teacher and for those who have renounced the world and are enlightened. Prayer will not bring knowledge and hence, there is no use of going on pilgrimage, but renouncing one's desires will lead to God.[46] Similar expressions are also quite frequent in the songs of other *cittar*s. For instance, Kaduveli Cittar has ridiculed the projection of the Ganges and Kasi rivers as sacred. The songs of Kudhampai Cittar expose the depraved nature of Vedic *ahamic* rituals and the Brahmanical belief in ill-omens.[47]

The approach of *cittar*s towards temple and temple-related rituals was not just religious rhetoric or a theological response to Brahmanism, but it was also a strong protest against the oppression by the state and the ruling class, represented by landlords and merchants. Though we rarely find references to direct attacks on rulers and the landed ruling class, the *cittar* literature opposed these groups and their social practices. It severely criticized the lavish lifestyle, inhuman practices, hunger for power and money, lust for women and sex and all other bodily desires of wealthy men in society. Invariably, all *cittar*s strongly advocated virtuous conduct, modesty and truthfulness. More than anything else, the shaping of the 'Self' was considered primary for social change. Pattinattar, for instance, criticizes the immoral characters of unwanted men in society:

> they go for unnecessary fighting and dispute, do more harm than good and help others also to do the same, they give nothing to poor but waste their time and money to satisfy their lustful desires with prostitutes...Since they are of no use for society, why should they live in this world?[48]

---

[46] Pampatti Cittar *Patal*, 92–94, 117, 118.

[47] Kudhampai Cittar *Patal*, 22.

[48] Pattinattar Patal: Yekampamalai 18, 19.

The songs of Pampatti Cittar and Sivavakkiyar severely condemn irrational practices in the name of religion. Some expressions of Pampatti Cittar that question the lavish and selfish lifestyle of wealthy people are 'Will elephants, grand army, car, etc., protect one from death? The grand-pillared palaces will not accompany a person after his death. Will they take along the mounted gold when the *yeman* (God of Death) come to take them? Does the mattress, made of cotton and flowers, have any use in crematorium?'[49] Sivavakkiyar on his part says:

> Oh! You built huge houses and protect it with tall doors but poor you, you are unable to protect yourself being taken by *yeman*. What would happen to the luxury of having herds, wealth, family and palaces when *yeman* calls you on? Will herds of cow and goats, elephants, armory, crores of wealth back you when you resist *yeman*?[50]

Sivavakkiyar was against social discriminations based on *thumai* (menstrual blood), *yetchil* (spittle) and *pulal* (meat) on the grounds of impurity. He questions the need to prohibit women from entering temples during their menstrual cycle. He says:

> In mother's womb, baby grows when *thumai* (menstrual blood) ends. This is common to all castes. Even the Brahmans who recite Veda are born out of *thumai*. You did not mind when you were born with *thumai*, then how can this be an obstacle in accessing God? To realize the Supreme Being, one should realize the fact that humans are born from *thumai*. Oh, Fools! You take bath to ward off *theettu* (impurity). You recite Veda after taking dips in water like a tortoise. Can you not understand that the body is a creation of *thumai?* Men and women, lower caste and upper caste – all were the same when they were in the form of *thumai*.[51]

The term *yetchil* has been used more or less in a similar context. According to Brahmanical rituals, the food tasted before offering to God and food prepared by a lower caste are considered unacceptable for puja. Lower castes can supply only raw materials for cooking. Sivavakkiyar confronts, 'the Vedas you recite are spit, the mantras they contain are spit…there is nothing anywhere in the world that is not spit'; 'You say the water swirling in your mouth is spit, are not then

---

[49] Pampatti Cittar *Patal*, 40–45.

[50] Sivavakkiyar Patal: 22, 24, 80, 82, 240.

[51] Sivavakkiyar Patal: 48, 49, 132, 134, 135, 136, 137, 195, 205, 212.

the Vedas formed in your mouth also spit?'[52] There are several other songs in which *yetchil* has been used to ridicule Vedic rituals and social discrimination.[53]

Social hierarchy was also maintained through the division of social groups based on whether they consume meat or not. Sivavakkiyar asks,

> You always isolate yourself from *pulal* (meat), don't you know, the body, where the Supreme Being reside, is made of *pulal?* Don't you know that mother's milk, you grew up drinking, is full of blood. You do not eat fish, deer, goat and cow meat, but don't the fish live in the water where you take your dip daily? Isn't the sacred thread that you wear around you made of deer skin? And, don't you throw goat meat in your *yagam*?[54]

It is said that during the early days of the Bhakti movement, there was a visible elevation in the status of women who were targets of many discriminatory practices of Vedic orthodoxy. Women like Mangaiyarkkarasi, Andal and Karaikkal Ammaiyar emerged as spiritual personalities. Their contributions to the *bhakti* discourses were equal to that of male spiritual leaders. In the beginning, the *devadasi* system remained a source of liberation from family life and nurtured several educated women. However, during later times, 'the *devadasis* degenerated into common prostitutes'.[55] References show that women faced tough times during the medieval feudal period. It is interpreted that in one of his songs, Thirugnana Sambanthar encourages his followers to molest beautiful Jain women.[56] Traditions state that people had to migrate from one place to another due to sexual harassment against women by the Chola kings. A Pandya king, according to Marco Polo's account, had several wives. This king took captive beautiful women into his harem at will – he had forcibly captured the wife of his own brother. According to another account, the Vijayanagara King, Devaraya I, sent out his military to forcibly bring to him a beautiful girl from an ordinary peasant family.[57] It is to be noted

---

[52] Ibid., 41 and 42; translation by Glenn E. Yocum, '*Civavakkiyar's* Abecedarium naturae', *Journal of the American Oriental Society,* 144(3), 1994, 363–382.

[53] Sivavakkiyar Patal: 48, 49, 132, 134, 135, 136, 137, 195, 205, 212.

[54] Cited with detailed discussion in A. Sivasubramaniyan, 'Adithala Makkal Meethana Paliyal Vanmurai' (Sexual Harassment on Subaltern), in *Navavin Araichi*, (44–45) (1993), 218.

[55] M.G.S. Narayanan and Kesavan Veluthat, 1987, 372.

[56] Ibid., 213–215.

[57] Sivasubramaniyan, A., 1993, 214.

that until the nineteenth century, women who belonged to Sanar and Pulaiya communities were prohibited from using upper garments.[58]

The institution of prostitution was encouraged basically to serve the sexual desires of landlords and wealthy men attached to temples. Sometimes, a *devadasi* committed suicide due to her disagreements with her patron landlords. In general, enjoying life with courtesans and prostitutes was a mark of status and power for wealthy men. It was practised at all levels of society. It is in this context that *cittar*s seemed to have deviated from the existing literary traditions by protesting against the greedy desires of the wealthy people. In their songs, the unwanted glorification of women and their bodily beauty, which represented the social values of patriarchal society, is clearly absent. They lamented the inability of people in power to control their desires and deplored the social norms and values that stood for subordination and exploitation of women.

In fact, *cittar*s have been criticized for their negative approach to women and family life. Some of the *cittar* songs go on to liken women to the 'devil', regarding them as 'evil'. However, these expressions are to be approached from the point of their emphasis upon 'renouncing the desire to wealth and sex' and of their stand to oppose the elites and their lavish life. In this sense, the *cittar*s were self-critics. They blame women out of frustration – for not being able to control their personal sexual desire. Pattinattar, for example, expresses his suffering: 'the ghost came in the disguise of a woman, caught hold of me, frightened by eyes, charmed by breasts, pushed me into the sore of pit, snatched away my wisdom'.[59] He also says, 'budding breast would spoil my life, tender eyes would take my sprit,'[60] narrating how he ran like a stray street dog after harlots.[61] He finally advises his heart not to long for the delight in women.[62] Pampatti Cittar says that he is able to refrain from portraying women as peacocks, koals, rubies, deer, honey, light, flowers, sweet, lightening, valuable, blossoms, etc.[63] Though similar examples are numerous in various songs of *cittar*s,[64] there were also several instances where they had expressed great respect for women and their role in society. Sivavakkiyar stressed that sex is a natural instinct and there

[58] Natchimuthu, *Kerala Samuka Neethi Porattankal*, 28.

[59] Pattinattar Patal: Yekampamalai – 23.

[60] Pattinattar patal: Yekampamalai – 23, Muthalvan Muraieedu – 18.

[61] Pattinattar Patal: Nenjodu Pulamapal – 1.

[62] Pattinattar Patal: Nenjodu Pulamapal – 4.

[63] Pampatti Cittar *Patal*, 76.

[64] Kovil Thiruagaval – 1–22, Yekampamalai 1–25.

is nothing wrong in leading a family life. As cited earlier, Sivavakkiyar had also used the signifier *thumai* to emphasize the equality between men and women.

Altogether, the medieval dissenters envisaged a new idea of humanism by magnifying the objective reality of 'human'. It is argued that *cittar* discourses were primarily a theological alternative to *bhakti*. Similarly, some say, 'it was a cult of few mystics mainly concerned for the spiritual development of people, though it represented diverse ideas and opinions on socio-religious sentiments'.[65] But the ideological dogmas of *cittar*s seem to have emerged out of their genuine concern for divergent social issues. Since most social issues were either produced or justified by the dominant ideology, any dissenting voices against such issues ultimately produced an alternative set of ideas. Presumably, there was hardly any interaction among the *cittar*s as they lived in different times and different places. Therefore, radical ideas were not consciously framed and *cittar*s did not intend to create an organized movement. But these individual voices indicate a certain social context and express certain common features. In fact, that is what unifies them.

The songs of *cittar*s were probably addressed to the people. The songs did not try to invoke any ideological dispute with the practitioners and preachers of *bhakti*. The main objective of *cittar*s was to awaken people who were excluded from the *bhakti* ideology or who were forced to accept their subordinated position in society. Liberating them from their deprived position was to make them understand the irrational as well as illogical values expressed through *bhakti*. Therefore, the nullification of Brahmanical values was essentially done through messages to people, to kindle their mind and strengthen their confidence not to believe in such values. For instance, some of the songs were composed in the form of a chorus – as people speaking out against caste distinctions and the institution of temples.[66] Therefore, one can perceive that there was a certain degree of mass mobilization, but in a limited sense. Most of the radical *cittar*s, whom I have referred to predominantly in this discussion, belonged to the period between the tenth and the sixteenth centuries. Likewise, as discussed earlier, it was also a period of numerous spontaneous revolts emerging from various sections of people. Though we do not have any direct evidences to consider the radical thoughts of *cittar*s behind such revolts referred to in inscriptions,

[65] G. Rajagopal, *Beyond Bhakti: Steps Ahead* (Delhi: B.R. Publishing Corporation, 2007), 103.

[66] Pampatti Cittar *Patal*, *Akaparru Neekal*, 12.

the ideological formulations of *cittar*s were certainly intended to represent this contemporary popular sentiment.

It is significant to note that *cittar*s operated at the time when Brahmanism was at its peak with the collaborative support of the state and the ruling class. In fact, any attempt to ridicule Brahmins, Brahmanical rituals, temples, etc., was considered to be against the state and the ruling class. Therefore, *cittar*s could have faced severe opposition from different fronts, including the state. The social history of medieval South India is a history of caste formation, emulation and disputes. With the aim to control power and gain socio-political privileges, the behavioural rules of each caste, interaction mechanisms and the context in which they can be used are clearly defined and strictly followed.[67] In such a social scenario, any dissenting voice against caste and caste-based social division was unwanted and needed to be crushed. One can therefore presume that a considerable section of the population was not in favour of *cittar*s and their ideological propaganda. Though some *cittar*s openly attacked Brahmanism and caste-based hierarchy, others had composed songs with puns. On the face, they had a simple message for the people, while its underlying meaning remained against those who propagated Brahmanism.

In addition to *cittar* songs, there are several other literatures that belong to the medieval period and which have also registered similar voices of protest. For instance, Kabilar *agaval* and the *Pallu* literatures also speak against social hierarchy in its various forms. But these literatures have not yet been subjected to scholarly investigation.

The Alternative Value System: Devotion in *Cittar* Tradition

The alternative values proposed by *cittar*s seem to have emerged from their strong empathy with people at the periphery of the social hierarchy and their everyday sufferings. It seems that their progressive thoughts stemmed from their own personal experiences. Such social thoughts can only be developed by those who are really concerned about humanity and by those who can genuinely listen to the voice of the people. The denial of temple rituals and idol worship can also be interpreted in this line. When Sivavakkiar says: 'What are temples? What are bathing tanks? Fools who worship in temples and tanks! Temples

[67] Gerald D. Berreman, 'Caste as Social Process', *South Western Journal of Anthropology* 22(4) (1967): 363.

are in the mind, tanks are in the mind' – he is not just ridiculing the core ideals of the *bhakti* tradition, but showing an alternative way to people whose entry into the temple premises and use of public tanks was prohibited on the grounds of pollution and impurity. It is evident that even during the modern period, entry into temples and access to public tanks remained a great challenge to the lower castes. Since most of the *cittar*s hailed from the lower castes, they could have had more immediate knowledge about peoples' sufferings in the temples, which were centred on social hierarchical systems. The emphasis upon 'realizing mind' and realizing the strength of one's own being rather than any Super Being, emerged specifically from this particular social context. *Cittar*s are said to have mastered magical and supernatural power (*cittadal*).[68] This can also be interpreted as an attempt to show the power of montals.

The concern over annihilating inhuman practices, specifically the caste/class differentiation, was deeply imbedded in every aspect of *cittar* discourses. They countered the dominant ideology, which divided society based on castes and religion, by proposing 'one humanity and one god'. The denial of the belief in rebirth was also to deny caste based on birth.[69] They visualized a personhood freed from all social biases and superstitious beliefs and campaigned for human values based on self-realization and decontamination of one's mind and attitudes. It was a very rational and humane approach. To them, 'if the mind is in the right disposition, it is unnecessary to utter the *mandiram*'. Since man himself is a god, himself a supreme being, the powerful person in society is the one who realize his strength, the power within him. Rather than religious scriptures, a knowledgeable person or a wise man can guide humanity.[70] Their teachings were quite practicable as well as accessible to everyone in society.

Man is seen as the centre of all his actions and beliefs. They believed that the world is real, not illusory. There is no other universe than the human universe, where man determines his actions. Their radical endeavour demanded reason for every human action and stressed on the practicability of human beliefs. By laying the foundation for human self-realization, they developed a hope for social equality. Through self-realization and self-emancipation, a person shapes his own real world, where everyone is equal. The 'person' is a practical human, who gives up his superstitions, his illusions and has gained reason instead. He

[68] K. Narayanan, *Cittar Thathuvam* (Philosophy of Siddhas) (Chennai: Tamil Puthakalayam, 1988), 40–47.

[69] N. Ganapathy, *The Philosophy of Tamil Siddhas*, Second Edition (New Delhi: Indian Council of Philosophical Research, 2004), 195.

[70] Ibid.

is an able person who is capable of solving his own problems and who reveals his human nature. He is a self-deriving human who estranges from the desires of accumulation of wealth and possesses alternative values that are against the one that stands for separation of men from men.

References

Angamuthu, A. *Cittar Patalkal Vilakka Urai* (Chennai: Komugi Publications, 2003).

Ramanathan, Aru. 2005. *Sitthar periya gnanakkovai ena vazhankum sitthar patalkal.* 1st edition (Chennai: Prema Publications, 1959).

Narayanasamy, Pe. *Pattinattar Patalkal* (Chennai: Pavai Publications, 2000).

Murugesan, S. *Bharathi Kanda Cittarkal* (Chennai: Kurinji Publication, 2007).

Berreman, Gerald D. 'Caste as Social Process'. *South Western Journal of Anthropology* 22(4) (1967): 351–370.

Champakalakshmi, R. 'Urban Processes in Early Medieval Tamil Nadu'. In *The City in Indian History, Urban Demography, Society, and Politics*, edited by Indu Banga (New Delhi: Manohar Publications for Urban History Association of India, 1991), 47–68.

———. 'From Devotion and Dissent to Dominance: The Bhakti of the Tamil Alvars and Nayanars'. In *Tradition, Dissent and Ideology*, edited by R. Champakalakshmi and S. Gopal. (New Delhi: Oxford University Press, 1996), 135–63.

———. 'The State in Pre-modern South India: A Historiographical Re-assessment'. Paper for Symposium on 'State in Indian History', Indian History Congress, 61st Session, Kolkata, 2001.

Kurtz Conald V., 'Legitimation of Early Inchoate States', in Henri J.M. Claessen and S. Peter Skalnik ed, *The Study of the State* (The Hague: Mouton Publications, 1981).

Dharmarajan, D. 'Samukappini: Cittar Marapilirunthu Oru Samukap Porali' (Social Ills: A Social Activist from Cittar Tradition). Paper presented in seminar on 'Siddhas of Tamil Nadu', Folklore Department, St. Xavier's College, Palayamkottai, August 2006.

Ganapathy, T.N. *The Philosophy of Tamil Siddhas* (New Delhi: Indian Council of Philosophical Research, 2004).

Gunasekaran, S. 'State, Society and Economy: An Evolutionary Study of the Kongu Region in Western Tamil Nadu (6th to 16th Century CE)'. PhD thesis submitted to Centre for Historical Studies, Jawaharlal Nehru University, New Delhi, December 2007.

Gurukkal, Rajan. 'Aspects of Great Transformation of Ancient Kerala'. Paper presented in a conference on 'Revisiting Transition', held at Jawaharlal Nehru University, 6 March 2007.

Hall, Kenneth. *Trade and Statecraft in the Age of Colas*, Elmira, New York, 1978.

Jha, D.N. 'Editor's Introduction'. In *Feudal Social Formations in Early India*, edited by D.N. Jha (New Delhi: Chanakya Publications, 1987), 3–41.

Koventhan. T., *Cithar Patalkal* (Chennai: Poompukar Publication, 1987).

Meenakshi, K. 'The Siddhas of Tamil Nadu: A Voice of Dissent'. In *Tradition, Dissent and Ideology*, edited by R. Champakalakshmi and S. Gopal (New Delhi: Oxford University Press, 1996), 111–134.

Muthumohan, N. *Indiath Thathuvangalain Aracial* (Politics of Indian Philosophies) (Chennai: Parisal, 2005).

Nandi, R.N. 'Growth of Rural Economy in Early Feudal India'. Presidential Address, Indian History Congress, 45th Session, Annamalainagar, 1985.

Narayana Veluppillai. M., *Pattinathar Vazhvum Vakkum* (Chennai: Narmatha Publication, 1999).

Narayanan, K. *Cittar Thathuvam* (Philosophy of Siddhas) (Chennai: Tamil Puthakalayam, 1988).

Narayanan, M.G.S. 'Role of Peasants in the Early History of Tamilakam in South India'. *Social Scientist* 16(9) (1998): 17–34.

Narayanan, M.G.S. and Kesavan Veluthat. 2000.

Natchimuthu, K. *Kerala Samuka Neethi Porattankal* (Social Reform Movements in Kerala). Palayamkottai: Centre for Ambedkar Studies, St. Xavier's College, 2005.

Periya Gnakkovai Pathinen Cithar Patalkal, T. Rathnanayakar & Sons, Chennai, 1961.

Rajagopal, G. *Beyond Bhakti: Steps Ahead.* Delhi: B.R. Publishing Corporation, 2007.

Rajkumar, M.D. 'Struggle for Rights during Later Chola Period'. *Social Scientist* 2(6–7) 29–35 (1974).

Ramanujan, A.K. and Norman Cutler. 'From Classicism to Bhakti'. In *Essays on Gupta Culture*, edited by Bardwell L. Smit, 177–214 (New Delhi: Motilal Banarsidass, 1983).

Roy, Kumkum. 'Some Problems in Constructing Varna Identities in Early North India' in Dev Nathan, *Tribe to Caste*, Indian Institute of Advanced Studies, Shimla, 1997.

Seyaprakasam, Pa. 'Cittar Ilakkiyankal Kattum Samuka Muranpadukalum theervukalaum' (Social Issues and Solutions as They are Shown in Cittar Literatures). Paper presented in seminar on 'Siddhas of Tamil Nadu', Folklore Department, St. Xavier's College, Palayamkottai, August 2006.

Sivasubramaniyan, A. 'Adithala Makkal Meethana Paliyal Vanmurai' (Sexual Harassment on Subaltern). In *Navavin Araichi*, (Journal) nos 44 and 45 (1993).

Spencer, George W. *The Politics of Expansion, The Chola Conquest of Sri Lanka and Sri Vijaya* (Chennai: New Era Publications, 1982).

Srinivasa Iyengar, P.T. *History of the Tamils: From the Earliest Times to 600 AD* (Chennai: University of Madras, 1929).

Stein, Burton. *Peasant State and Society in Medieval South India* (New Delhi: Oxford University Press, 1994).

Subbaiah, Ganapathy. 'Dakshinapatha: Where Does the Path Lead Us?' Presidential Address, Indian History Congress, 57th Session, Calicut, 2007.

Tirumalai, R. *Land Grants and Agrarian Reactions in Cola and Pandya Times* (Chennai: University of Madras, 1987).

Vanamamalai, N. 'Consolidation of Feudalism and Anti-Feudal Struggle during Chola Imperialist Rule'. Proceedings of the Second International Conference Seminar of Tamil Studies, Chennai, 1968.

Venkatraman, R. *A History of the Tamil Siddha Cult* (Madurai: NS Ennes Publication, 1990).

Yocum, Glenn E. 'Shrines, Shamanism, and Love Poetry: Elements in the Emergence of Popular Tamil Bhakti'. *Journal of the American Academy of Religion* 41(1) (1973): 3–17.

______. '*Civavakkiyar's* Abecedarium Naturae'. *Journal of the American Oriental Society*, 114,3, 1994.

CHAPTER

6

Women in Love

Mysticism and Eroticism in Virashaivism

Vijaya Ramaswamy

The fragrance mingling in the breeze
Like pleasure in intercourse given freely where there is love;
This is the path of bhakti,
Is it not, Nastinatha?[1]

Love is central to the path of devotion. In striking contrast to sectarian and communal schisms and conflicts which are hate driven, the path of devotion has been marked by love that is intensely physical and at the same time, transcendental. Humanism and universal compassion are often the most pronounced features of the devotional way of religion. The chief moods of *bhakti* are union (*sayujyam*) and separation (*viraha*). This, on the one hand, results in love poetry that is often characterized by *viraha* or separation and unrequited love. On the other hand, devotional poems in the love mode can be passionately sensual and filled with the ecstasy of union. Scholars of religion and spirituality term the intense love of the devotee for God as 'bridal mysticism', although bridal mysticism is only one, albeit the most sensual, of the many ways in which the devotees relate to the Supreme. Karaikkal Ammaiyar, whose love for Shiva is expressed in praise of his cosmic dance on the cremation grounds of Tiruvalangadu, is a striking example of love that is couched in the metaphor of the terrible with the saint herself as the ghoulish figure presiding over the cremation ground. Here, love is passionate but horrific and awe inspiring rather than sensual.

[1] Shiva Sharane Goggavve, in Vijaya Ramaswamy, *Divinity and Deviance: Women in Virasaivism* (New Delhi: Oxford University Press, 1996), 97.

This essay seeks to explore women's love within the context of Virashaivism, a twelfth century devotional movement, which, for over a century, sought to act as a spiritual catalyst and social leveller in medieval Karnataka. The essay foregrounds notions of the feminine as well as the emotion of love in relation to the feminine, encompassing in its trope the assumption of the 'feminine' by male saints in expressing their love for the divine and in seeking union with the godhead.

Love and the 'Feminine' in the Spiritual Realm

The 'feminine' has a very special place in the spiritual realm. Devotion itself is portrayed in the form of *viraha*, the separation of the woman from her beloved. In the *nayaka–nayika bhava*, the individual soul (*jeevatma*) is almost always feminine and the supreme soul (*paramatma*) is masculine. Since this intense spiritual urge which imitates the sexual urge can come only if one is a woman (according to a particular ontological construct), it is fairly common to find male saints, like Kabir in the north or Nammalvar, Tirumangai Alvar and Manikkavachagar in the south, gendering themselves as feminine in the *bhakti* mode. The identification of woman as body-centred, and the close association of unbridled sexuality and desire with the feminine, is again essentially a male epistemological construct.

The gendering of spirituality within the patriarchic mode can be read in two ways. In one sense, the woman uses the male epistemological construct to her advantage by sublimating her weakest points and turning them into her strength. The qualities of 'desire' and 'lack', the notion of woman being 'body-centred' is turned by the saint into passion, very often erotic, for the divine. This notion comes to occupy a certain degree of centrality in the Lacanian theory of psychoanalysis, and more particularly in Julia Kristeva's feminism. Kristeva finds that the effort, especially by mystics, to recover 'desire' lying submerged in the unconscious, involves a rejection of the symbolic (read patriarchal) language structure and their orientation towards the pre-Oedipal, semiotic language. It is in this sense that Kristeva talks of the language of 'madness, holiness, poetry'.[2]

St Augustine, in his *Confessions*, referred to 'concupiscence' which approximates to ardent sexual desire in the Lacanian sense. The notion of 'concupiscence' locates sexual desire as much in the male psyche as it does in the female psyche. Saints, male as well as female, relocate their desire or the

[2] Julia Kristeva, 'Signifying Practice and Mode of Production', *Edinburgh Review* I (1976), 64–77.

feeling of 'lack' in a divine symbol, whether it is the phallic symbol of Shiva or any other symbol, which becomes the sole object of their passion. Since both erotic desire and passion are associated with the female, within the 'Law of the Name of the Father', even males resort to transvestism and gender crossing in their spiritual quest. Men speaking in women's voice are not the exclusive feature of Hindu devotional streams alone, but are also to be found among the male Christian mystics like St John of the Cross who looked upon himself as the bride of the Lord. In the spiritual path, both the female and the male, speaking in a female voice, emphasize qualities which are considered 'feminine', such as submission, surrender, blind love and loyalty, in relation to the Lord, their 'husband'. Seen within the paradigm of patriarchal epistemology, such men and women taking on 'feminine' attributes reinforce patriarchy, instead of rejecting or subverting it. Here again, it is the egoless, self-effacing, sacrificing 'bride of the Lord' who is glorified. She constitutes almost a mirror image of the earthly 'pious' housewife to whom her husband is 'God'. As an ancient Tamil proverb puts it, 'The husband is the woman's palpable, perceptible God' (*kanavane kankanda daivam*). It is within the patriarchal mode and male epistemological constructs that the notions of dominance and subordination, the empowerment of one gender in contradistinction to the disempowerment of the other gender, occupy a seminal place. This essay, however, endeavours to show that women within Virashaivism actually cut at the roots of the patriarchial structure.

Understanding 'Passionate' Love in the Spiritual Domain

While bridal mysticism cuts across gender lines, passionate love, in all its intensity and abandon, has been associated more often with the feminine rather than the masculine. A.K. Ramanujan, in an interesting essay, makes the conjecture that '*bhakti* itself appears as feminine' in nature in contrast to Vedic sacrifices which may be considered masculine in ethos, personnel and language.[3] Thus, in the *bhakti* mode, before God, both female and male saints take on a female personality. It is due to the close association between femininity and spirituality that the Virashaivite women saints, in their passionate expressions of love, enjoy a distinct advantage over their male counterparts. Basava had to metamorphose himself into a woman and a bride vis-à-vis his *ishta linga*, Koodala Sangama, while no such effort was required on the part of the female mystics. An evocative love poem by a male devotee within the Virashaivite

[3] A.K. Ramanujan, 'On Women Saints', in *Collected Essays of A.K. Ramanujan*, ed. Vinay Dharwadker (New Delhi: Oxford University Press, 1999), 270.

tradition has been quoted in a recent translation of *vachanas*.[4] Here is the beautiful translation of Urilingadeva's passionate *vachana*:

In my great rapture
Of making love with my darling
I can't tell myself from the worlds
While making love with my love
I can't tell myself from my darling
After making love with Urilingadeva
The god of the burning member
I can't tell whether it is me, him
or something else.[5]

A striking feature of Virashaivism is the oft-repeated aphorism, '*Sharane Sati, Linga Pati*' meaning the *sharane* or spiritual aspirant is the eternal bride and Shiva the eternal bridegroom. Exemplifying this, Akka Mahadevi writes:

You are my husband and I, your wife,
I have none else, O Lord.
Falling in love with you, I came
I followed you.
When every passerby is grabbing my hands,
Tell me, O husband
How can you stand it?
O master Chennamallikarjuna,
When strangers are dragging away
The woman leaning on your arms,
O king of compassionate ones,
Is it proper to stand aside and look on?[6]

Social dissent was a logical precipitate of the passionate love that these women had for Shiva. Social transgression invariably went hand in hand with their quest for mystical union. Thresholds were crossed, patriarchal norms destroyed and social and moral codes spurned. In fact, Akka Mahadevi, who offered the ultimate affront to the highly conservative twelfth century society

---

[4] H.S. Shivaprakash, *I Keep Vigil of Rudra* (New Delhi: Penguin Books, 2010), 168.
[5] Ibid.
[6] Akka Mahadevi, AV20, in Ibid., 110.

of medieval Karnataka, is said to have walked naked from her marital home. Mahadevi writes in her *vachana*:

> Like a silkworm weaving her house with love,
> From her marrow, and dying in her body's threads,
> Winding tight, round and round, I burn, desiring
> What the heart desires, O Mallikarjuna![7]

Situating Dissent in Virashaivism: A Historical Overview

Virashaivism, the history of which can be traced back to more than 800 years, emerged as a major religious force during twelfth century CE in the southern part of India. The Virashaivite or Lingayat movement, which originated in Karnataka, was the predominant factor in overturning Brahmanical superiority and to some extent, even patriarchal values. Ironically, the greatest living force behind the movement was Basava, who belonged to an orthodox Brahmin family and went through the sacred thread ceremony, so vital to establishing Brahmin identity, at the age of eight years. However, at the age of sixteen years,[8] he discarded the sacred thread, renounced his Brahmin identity and in course of time, emerged as the leader of the radical heterodox Virashaivite movement. In this movement, the traditional paradigms got inverted. The female, with her powers of creation and nurturing, became more important than the male; and the lower castes, devoid of the trappings of wealth, status and power, were deemed to be nearer God than Brahmins and other upper castes. The Virashaivite doctrine of Shakti Vishishtadvaita gave a superior place to women and Siddharama held that 'the woman is Kapilasiddha Mallikarjuna himself'.[9]

Political chaos, religious schisms and an oppressive social structure foregrounds the Virashaivite movement in Karnataka. Kalyana, which witnessed the resurgence of this movement, was controlled by the Western Chalukya and the Kalachuri dynasties in turn. Myriad religions like Shaivism, Shaiva Sidhanta, Vaishnavism and Shakta, besides Jainism and Buddhism, found

---

[7] A.K. Ramanujan, *Speaking of Siva* (New Delhi: Penguin Classics, 1973), 116.

[8] According to Harihara, the author of *Basava Raja Deva Ragale*, written just fifty years after Basava's death. p.XXXIII of S.C.Nandimath, *A Handbook of Virasaivism,* (Varanasi and Delhi: Motilal Banarsidass, 1979).

[9] S.C. Nandimath, L.M.A. Menezes and R.C. Hiremath, *Sunyasampadane,* Vol I (Dharwar: Karnataka University, 1965), 127.

patronage among the rulers depending on the politico-social compulsions and the personal predilections of the monarchs.

The prevailing socio-economic structure in early medieval Karnataka was dominated by the Brahmin landlords. The *Brahmadeya*s necessarily had to have a large non-Brahmanical population which sustained it, composed of cultivators (since the Brahmins would not touch the plough), craftsmen and menials. These groups faced the prospect of double exploitation both by the Brahmin landlords and by the state in the form of oppressive taxes.[10]

As has been argued by so many Western as well as Indian scholars, there was a strong nexus between the ruling class and the Brahmins. The Chalukyas as well as the Kalachuris, who in turn occupied the region of Kalyana which was the seat of Virashaivism, believed in the construction of temples which would sanctify their royal power and provide them with a support base. Brahmin priests were the greatest beneficiaries of the huge endowments in land and money made to these temples. The Chalukyas of Badami built no less than seventy-two temples in their capital, Ayyavole, between the fifth and the seventh centuries.[11] It has been estimated that within a span of the two centuries preceding the emergence of Virashaivism, Shaivites constructed 450 temples and the Vaishnavites some 100 temples in Karnataka. While the ruling class lent its patronage to the temples and priests, the priests and Brahmin beneficiaries of the *Brahmadeya*s endowed the kings with legitimacy and ritual authority.

The domination of Brahmins in society logically implies the dominance of the patriarchal structure, a situation where the Vedic Brahmanical structure determines the ascriptive and prescriptive roles of women and the lower castes. Thus, the lower castes and women, who were in fact so crucial to the successful working of the economy, became marginalized so far as their status within the society was concerned.

The connection between economic exploitation and socio-ritual oppression by the ruling class–Brahmin coalition, leading to a socio-religious protest movement like Virashaivism, is historically and logically tenable. Historians of Virashaivism, like R.N. Nandi, have also tried to link the movement with the breakdown of feudalism and the revival of crafts and commerce in terms of the classic model provided by Henry Pirrene. It is fairly apparent from inscriptional and literary evidence that the social base of the Lingayat movement largely comprised of traders and craft groups like weavers, tanners, the *panchala* or

---

[10] R.N. Nandi, 'Feudalism in South India', *Social Science Probings* (1984), 33–59.

[11] K. Ishwaran, *Religion and Society among the Lingayats of South India* (New Delhi: Vikas, 1983), 23.

group of five smiths and untouchable craftsmen like the Madara or Madivala, that is, basket makers and washermen.[12] Ishwaran, another well-known historian of Virashaivism, pointed out that: 'The Lingayat religious movement was born in the context of a divided and exploitative society in order to challenge it in the name of equality, individual freedom and communitarian commitment.'[13] A *vachana* of Molige Mahadevi voices this dissent in mystical terms:

> Molige Mahadevi writes:
> That light which emanates in space
> Shines equally on stone, iron, brass
> The Linga in my palm
> Your light, that light
> Why is it invisible to me?
> Is it my fault or your deception?
> Be thou in me
> Immadi Nishkalanka Mallikarjuna .[14]

By the middle of the twelfth century, Virashaivism had begun to gain currency in Karnataka as an alternative to Brahmanism. The message of Basavanna's dissent movement in Kalyana against the evil discriminations of caste, creed and sex spread across the country and attracted hundreds and thousands of like-minded and right-thinking people, including women. People from all parts of the country and from all walks of life who believed in the oneness of mankind thronged Kalyana. Farmers, untouchables, pariahs, potters, tanners, weavers, washermen, fishermen, shoemakers, barbers, merchants, hunters and even Brahmins flocked together in the firm bond of humanitarian concerns. The movement, however, had a notably large Sudra following.

Many of these began to challenge the state and Brahmanical authority and the caste order even in their individual capacity. Madivala Machchyya, a washerman, and Sivanagimayya, an untouchable, refused to observe caste pollution and exulted at the liberating influence of Virashaivism. Caste opposition took a tragic turn when two of the Lingayat followers, Madhavayya, a Brahmin, and Haralayya, a Harijan, decided to perform an inter-caste marriage between their son and daughter. The orthodox lobby brought pressure to

---

[12] R.N. Nandi, *Social Roots of Religion in Ancient India* (Kolkata and New Delhi: K.P. Bagchi and Co., 1986), 158.

[13] Ishwaran, *Religion and Society*, 31–32.

[14] Molige Mahadeva, in R.C. Hiremath, *Ippattelu Shivasharaneyara Vachanagalu* (in Kannada) (Dharwar: Karnataka University, 1968), V: 20: 12.

bear on King Bijjala who had failed to balance the contending faiths of the Kalamukhas, orthodox Brahmanism and heterodox Virashaivism. Succumbing to pressure, he ordered the blinding and execution of the two men who had dared to break caste taboos. This event, in CE 1167, led to grim reprisals, and three Virashaivite followers – Molla, Bomma and Jagadeva – murdered the Kalachuri King, Bijjala, and Kalyana was in a state of political and religious turmoil. Thousands of Lingayats were butchered and the survivors scattered in all directions. Many of their *vachana*s or poetic outpourings were burnt.

The broad span of the entire Virashaivite movement was from the twelfth to the seventeenth centuries. The period witnessed tumultuous political changes. The Chalukyas of Kalyana rose and fell and were succeeded by the Kalachuris. The supremacy of the Kalachuris in the Karnataka region was to prove crucial to the political nurturing of the Virashaivite ideology since Basaveshwara, referred to reverentially as Basavanna, was a minister under Bijjala, the Kalachuri King. The egalitarian thrust of the Virashaivite movement threatened to upset the applecart of Brahmanical orthodoxy which lobbied hard to recapture its religious and political dominance. Royalty was caught in the crossfire of social flux and a resistant orthodoxy. The bloodbath that followed left many Virashaivites dead and the rest went underground. Basava fled Kalyana for Koodala Sangama. He went into self-imposed exile and died a disillusioned man.

The *vachana*s of the twelfth century reflect the agony and ecstasy of those years which, for the Virashaivite community, were both the 'spring of hope and the winter of despair'. While there were virtually no *vachana*s written during the period from the thirteenth to the fifteenth centuries, the earliest compilations began in around AD 1430 with Mahalinga and Kalmatada Prabhudevaru and continued into the sixteenth century. The best of such compilations was the *Śunya Sampadane*, compiled in c. 1400 by Shivaganaprasadi Mahadevaiah, which has now been translated into English.[15] What was salvaged from these *vachana*s enables us to locate the passionate love/devotion and social dissent in these *vachana*s.[16]

---

[15] S.S. Bhoosnoormath and L.M.A. Menezes, *Sunyasampadane,* Vols II, III and IV (Dharwar: Karnataka University, 1968, 1969 and 1970).

[16] The corpus of literature on the history of Virashaivism, Lingayat ideology and the morphology of dissent within the movement is prolific and well recorded. For a broad understanding of the ideological and political problematic of medieval Karnataka, I would suggest a reading of the introduction by Ramanujan in his *Speaking of Siva* and Shivaprakash's introduction in his *I Keep Vigil of Rudra*, ix–lxxviii.

Situating Women and the Feminine in Virashaivism

The language of the custodians (primarily Brahmanical) of society in the twelfth century was no different from the dominant male patriarchal voice that had been heard in the preceding centuries. Two eleventh and twelfth century inscriptions from Chennapatna and Nagaamangala *taluka*s, respectively, from the region of Karnataka, refer to the '*suputrah*' or the good son as '*kula dipakah*', meaning light of the family.[17] One, however, encounters eloquent silence on the birth of daughters. The inferior status of women, which was by now well established in theory and practice, was reinforced by commentators like Mallanna. A woman was considered impure because of her monthly menstruation. Her powers of procreation and attraction were looked upon as the greatest deterrents to man's spiritual progress.

It was in this patriarchal, gender-oppressive atmosphere that Virashaivism rose. Some of the traditional images of women seem to have crept into Basavanna's *vachana*s during the earlier phase of his evolution. This, however, is only conjecture since any chronological ordering of Basavanna's *vachana*s is impossible. A classic example of traditional female imagery in his *vachana* is the following verse:

> To give me birth, Maya bore me – as mother.
> To delight me, Maya was born – as my daughter.
> to embrace me, Maya shared my bed – as my wife.
> So many different ways she has,
> Maya,
> to worry and trouble me;
> Not in my power to unhinge this Maya;
> And you are amused,
> O Koodalasangama Deva![18]

In this metaphorical *vachana*, illusion is equated with the many facets of woman but never with father, son or husband. In another *vachana*, he says:

> Her speech is like dark sugar:
> but I have seen, O lord, strong poison in her heart;

[17] B. Lewis Rice, ed., *Epigraphica Carnatica, Vols IV and VI*, Mysore Archaeological Series (Mysore: Department of Archaeology, 1889–1955), 57 and 94, respectively.

[18] K.V. Zvelebil, *The Lord of the Meeting Rivers – Devotional Poems of Basavanna* (New Delhi: Motilal Banarsidass, 1984), V: 15: 8.

she will invite one lover with her eyes;
another man is hidden in her heart;
O lord of the Meeting Rivers, listen,
One must not trust the woman – thief of men![19]

Some of Basavanna's *vachana*s thus seem to echo the commonly held view of women as the dangerous 'Other' in a patriarchy. However, the majority of the verses, both by Basavanna and other male Virashaivite saints, make it impossible to locate their *vachana*s within the discourse of patriarchy. Basava often refers to himself as a woman, whether as a loving bride or a cuckolding wife:

Let the whole world know: I have got a mate.
I'm a married woman.
Married to one am I.
the lord of the Meeting Rivers
is my man
I've got a mate.[20]

One of the most startling usages of the female imagery is by Basavanna in his *vachana* addressing his *ishta linga*, Koodala Sangama, as a prostitute who demands more and more from his devotee:

I take the water of your feet,
I take the offering that you have blest.
I say
My honour, life and wealth
are yours;
Will our lord of the Meeting Revers
love me for empty words –
even as a sinful prostitute
who takes her nightly fee?[21]

These verses indicate that in Basavanna, there is an overturning of the traditional societal values. In the light of these later verses, it is likely that his references to woman as *maya*, as a treacherous and cunning enchantress, are not blanket statements but particularized in the context of the male spiritual

---

[19] Ibid., V: 110: 25.

[20] Ibid., V: 503: 74.

[21] Ramanujan, *Speaking of Siva*, V: 468: 81.

aspirant for whom any contact with the other gender would be a distraction. It is in this sense that one must look at the previously quoted verse of Basava which says, '...she will invite one lover with her eyes, another man is hidden in her heart...One must not trust the woman – thief of man'![22] Akka Mahadevi's *vachanas* bear out this assumption that 'maya' or delusion is not really gender specific. Completely demolishing the correspondence that has been established between woman–*maya*–temptation, Akka Mahadevi states:

To an ascetic, Maya takes the shape
of a female ascetic; to a monk
she is a nun, a man
to a woman, a woman to a man
O chenna Mallikarjuna, I am not
one to fear this Maya of thine.[23]

According to Virashaivism, man and woman differ from each other at the psychological level only. But at the metaphysical level, they are one and the same principle, that is, *atman*, the pure consciousness.[24] Jedara Dasimayya says:

The son of the slave in Channaayya's house, (untouchable)
The daughter of the maid in Kakkayya's house (butcher)
Those two went to the fields for dung
and fell together.
I'm the son born of these two.
The Lord of the Meeting Rivers is my witness.[25]

Shakti Vishishtadvaita lies at the root of Lingayat philosophy and is, in fact, used as an alternative name for Virashaivism. According to this, while Shiva by himself is a pure principle in a state of rest, the entire creation takes place through his symbiotic relationship with *parama shakti* or *maya* who herself emanates from him. This completely overturns the Brahmanical and patriarchal notions of caste pollution and gender inequality since nothing which emanates

---

[22] Zvelebil, *The Lord of the Meeting Rivers*, V: 110: 25.

[23] Menezes and Angadi, 1973, 145, cited in Leela Mullatti, *The Bhakti Movement and the Status of Women* (New Delhi: Abhinav Publications, 1989), 34.

[24] The *Svetasvatara Upanisad* also corroborates this view when it says: '*tvam stri tvam puman asi tvam kumara uta va kumari*' (IV: 3), that is, 'You are woman, you are man, you are the boy and the girl too'.

[25] Zvelebil, *The Lord of the Meeting Rivers*, V: 345: 57.

from the pure can be impure. Expressing this radical worldview of Virashaivism, Akka Mahadevi states:

> As long as woman is woman, then
> a man defiles her;
> As long as a man is man,
> a woman defiles him.
> When the mind's taint is gone, is there,
> room for the body's taint?
> The entire world is mad
> because of this adventitious taint.
> Look you, good sir,
> For the great spouse
> called Chenna Mallikarjuna, my lord,
> The whole world is a wife (emphasis mine)[26]

Thus, women within Virashaivism had almost all the rights to a spiritual life with one notable exception. They were not conceded the *Jangama* status, which meant that women could neither conduct priestly ceremonies nor become head of a Virashavia *mutt* or religious organization.[27] This exception indicates the subtle layer of inequality hidden behind Virashaivite egalitarianism. In fact, towards the latter part of the twelfth century, this inequality surfaces not only in terms of gender but also in terms of caste hierarchies.

Eroticism and *Sati–Pati Bhava* in the Shiva *Sharane Vachanas*

Virasaivite saints –whether rebels or housewives – had a strong tendency to perceive themselves as brides of the lord. It would be necessary to point out here that the two are not being suggested to be mutually exclusive categories. Elements of rebellion have been as strongly present in married women as in those who opted out of marriage and became open rebels against the system. The distinction between the two categories, however, lies in the fact that walking out

26 Menezes and Angadi, 1970, 151, cited in Mullatti, *The Bhakti Movement*, 34.

27 Perhaps even this right was accorded to them in principle, although it seems to have been historically inoperative. In the present century, Mate Mahadevi has broken this unwritten convention by qualifying as a *Jangama* and becoming head of a Lingayat *mutt* in Devangere in Karnataka. Interview with Mate Mahadevi (Mahipalpur, Delhi, 1999). This notable exception, nevertheless, merely substantiates the prevalent convention.

of a marriage on the part of some women, such as Akka Mahadevi (or Lal Ded of Kashmir), was a second-order rebellion since they had initially accepted the yoke of marriage. Therefore, it would be logical to talk of a further split even within the 'housewives' category which could have rebels as well as conformists in the context of the social norms of marriage and family. In the case of the married women, this involved: (a) rejection of their worldly husband; and (b) the identification of Shiva as their groom or *pati*.

The oral tradition regarding Akka Mahadevi's renunciation of her marriage comes to us from the chronicler poet, Harihara, who may have been a contemporary of Basava. In walking out naked form King Kausika's place, her long hair covering her, she transgressed all social boundaries.

Yet Akka Mahadevi re-affirmed her marital status before the Lingayat spiritual council, the Anubhava Mantapa, when she declared her mystical union with Siva and justified her nudity.

> Riding the blue sapphire mountains
> Wearing moonstone for slippers
> Blowing long horns
> O, Siva!
> When shall I
> Crush you on my pitcher breasts?
> O Lord Chennamallikarjuna,
> When do I join you
> Stripped of body's shame
> And heart's modesty?[28]
> In our embrace
> the bones should rattle
> in a welding, the welding mark
> even should disappear.
> The knife should enter totally
> When the arrow enters, even
> the feathers should not be seen[29]

While male nudity, despite being unusual, is not socially cathartic in its impact, female nudity results in social ostracism on the one hand, and religious and social catharsis on the other. It is perhaps the most powerful expression

[28] Ramanujan, *Speaking of Siva*, V: 317:136.

[29] H.M. Chennaiah, 'Akka Mahadeviya Vachanagala Prativavidhana' (in Kannada), *Jigyasa* (Mysore: Suruchi Prakashana, 1974), 39.

of dissent. In some hagiographies and iconic images, Akka Mahadevi is represented as a naked saint. In her own words:

> To the shameless girl
> Wearing Mallikarjuna's light, you fool,
> Where is the need for cover and jewel?[30]

Akka Mahadevi proclaims her marital status as that of the bride of Mallikarjuna and interestingly, confines all earthly husbands to the kitchen fires.

Along with Akka Mahadevi, Ayidakki Lakkhamma, a married saint, provides some explicit examples of the *sati–pati* relationship:

> When the seed is falling
> on the face of the blossom
> Can there be a back and front
> to the blossoming face?
> If you forget it and
> if I realise it, can
> there be different bodies?
> When the root vanishes
> the blossom remains.
> For this union can there be
> any other name but *sati-pati*?[31]

Satyakka, an unmarried saint, visualizes Shiva as her groom and tries to enlist the help of her (imaginary) relatives in drawing him towards her. She calls Shiva 'Gandaru Ganda', 'The man among men', and says that Shiva is the only man for her:

> Siva is within me
> These's no space within
> my heart for speech or thought
> It is filled with Him.
> I am in love with
> the only man without blemishes.
> Despite me he has taken possession of me.[32]

---

[30] Ramanujan, *Speaking of Siva*, V: 124: 129. V: 124: 129.
[31] Ayidakki Lakkhamma, V: 20, in Hiremath 1968, V: 89: 44.
[32] Satyakka, V: 17, in Hiremath 1968, V, 148–171.

In a couple of verses, she reveals to her mother that she is being wasted away by the arrows of Manmatha (god of love) and her youth is being wasted without Shiva.[33] In the next verse, she requests her uncle (Bhava) to intercede with her bridegroom, Shiva, on her behalf. She accuses Shiva of being proud and headstrong because he has conquered many demons and ruined the Daksha *yajna* by cutting off Daksha's head and replacing it with that of a sheep (reference to a mythology concerning Shiva's consort, Sati, and her father, Daksha, who had insulted his son-in-law and was duly punished). Satyakka concludes:

> Having given myself to Him,
> I cannot give myself to anyone else.
> Bring that heartless Siva to me
> I wish to embrace Shambu Jakkesvara.[34]

The love for God sometimes expressed itself in unusual ways in terms of worldly relationships. Kadire Remmavve, a married woman who apparently left her husband and took to spinning for her livelihood, uses language that is both vituperative and contemptuous towards her spouse:

> All husbands (men) are
> destroyers of enemy forces
> My husband crushes
> the petals of my mind
> Other husbands are hunters of elephants
> My husband is the hunter of my mind .[35]

Using very raw sexual imagery, Remmavve writes:

> All wives wash and give to their husbands
> I do not give my husband, he does not need
> All husbands have seeds
> My husband has no seeds.
> All husbands are up above
> My husband below, I'm above him![36]

---

[33] Satyakka, V: 19 in Hiremath1968, V: 150: 73.

[34] Satyakka, V: 20, in Hiremath1968, V: 151: 73.

[35] Kadire Remmavve, V, in Hiremath 1968, *Ippattelu Shivasharaneyara Vachanagalu*, V: 192: 90.

[36] Ibid., 193: 91.

Here, the Shiva *sharane* seems to be referring, knowingly or unknowingly, to the inversion of the sexual posture which one comes across in certain sects of tantricism. Akka Mahadevi writes in one of her *vachana*s:

> I love the handsome one:
> he has no death
> decay or form
> no place or side
> no end, nor birthmarks.
> I love him, O mother, listen,
> So my Lord, Chenna Mallikarjuna
> is my husband.
> Take these husbands who die,
> decay, and feed them
> to your kitchen fires![37]

Virashaivite saints use very strong sexual imagery in the context of their union with the Supreme. When men like Basava use similar imagery, they first have to take on femininity and then think of God as male, but for women, the metaphors of sexual union come naturally. They are also much more powerful in their expression than their male counterparts, sometimes startlingly intense and bold. The influence of the 'Shaktas' and of tantricism is perceivable in this characteristic of Virashaivism. The sexual imagery makes no effort at subtlety. This kind of boldness has no parallel among the male mystics.

Women in Love and Households Divine and Profane

The household, in the perception/s of saintly 'wives', who could be both male and female, existed both within and without. There was a metaphorical inner world which these wives inhabited where the household featured prominently. God, whether envisaged as male or female, was very much a part of this metaphysical household. The saint related to this divine household usually as a bride or wife, but also as mother, lover/paramour, etc. This household was clearly not a seamless one with well-defined parameters. This imagined household with fuzzy boundaries and changing relationships is therefore quite unlike the physical household with its liminalities marked by patriarchal borders of codes and conduct.

[37] Ramanujan, *Speaking of* Siva, V: 283: 134.

Basavanna says in another *vachana*:

Let the whole world know I have got a mate
I'm a married woman.
Married to one am I
Lord Koodala Sangama[38]
Is my man.
I've got a mate.

This verse is cast in the classic mould of patriarchal imaging with protection and social legitimacy being found in marriage. However, this seemingly straightforward meaning is complicated by the fact that its author is a male!

Whether they were fulfilling their role as housewives or rebelling against role models by crossing the borders of marriage and household, many women saints had a strong tendency to perceive themselves as brides of the Lord. It would be necessary to point out here that the two are not being suggested to be mutually exclusive categories. Elements of rebellion have been as strongly present in married women as in those who opted out of marriage and became open rebels against the system. The distinction between the two categories however lies in the fact that walking out of a marriage on the part of some women, such as Akka Mahadevi (or Lal Ded of Kashmir) was a second-order rebellion since they had initially accepted the yoke of marriage. Therefore, it would be logical to talk of a further split even within the 'housewives' category, which could have rebels as well as conformists in the context of the social norms of marriage and family. In the case of the married women this involved: (a) rejection of their worldly husband; and (b) the identification of Shiva as their groom or *pati*. The oral tradition regarding Akka Mahadevi's renunciation of marital ties come down to us from Harihara who was almost contemporaneous with Basava. It is believed that she scorned king Kausika's sexual advances towards her by walking out naked from the king's palace with her long hair as her only covering. Before the Lingayat spiritual council, the Anubhava Mantapa, she declared her mystical union with Shiva:

The Guru became the giver
The Lord Linga became the bridegroom;
and I became the bride.
All this the world knows

[38] Zvelebil. *The Lord of the Meeting Rivers – Devotional Poems of Basavanna*, (Delhi: Motilal Banarsidass, 1984) V: 503: 74.

the innumerable devotes are my parents
Hence Chenna Mallikarjuna is my husband O Prabu,
I have nothing to do with the husbands of this world![39]

The Virashaivite saint Gangambike, again, uses sexual imagery in describing her relationship with the Shiva *sharana*, including her son Chenna Basava:

My body united with Chenna Basavanna
In the field.
My mind dissolved
Into Sanganna Basavanna's truth
My life-breath merged with Allamma Prabhu's intellect.
Since I have given all of myself to these three
having nothing, being nothing,
My true dwelling place
Is the lotus heart of
Chenna Sangayya, beloved of Basavanna.[40]

Love, Mysticism and Transcendence

It is noteworthy that the language of mystics cuts across all boundaries, including gender boundaries. As Kristeva points out in her analysis of subjectivity in poetics, the language of 'madness and mysticism' transcends gender and the symbolic language structure.[41] The mystical experience (in the case of both men and women) is beyond the experiential field of physical existence, and thus becomes a transcendental/metaphysical moment, which no language can unlock. However, in their urge to communicate this incommunicable experience, the mystics are compelled to use the existent language structure, although their vocabulary is dominated by the semiotic, the pre-Oedipal language of signs rather than by the 'symbolic' language system emerging out of the socially acceptable language structure grounded in patriarchy. In this whole process of communication of mystical experiences, both male and female mystics sound mad, unintelligible and yet strangely enough, echo each other in their use of

39 H. Thipperudraswami, *Soul Unto the Sublime* (Hubli: Sri Jagadguru Gangadhara Dharma Pracharaka Mandala, 1982), 195.

40 Ramaswamy, 1996, 77.

41 Julia Kristeva, *The Revolution in Poetic Language* (New York: Columbia University Press, 1984) and *Tales of Love*, trans. Leon S. Roudiez (New York: Columbia University Press, 1987[1983]).

metaphors. Bridal mysticism, for instance, cuts across gender distinctions. Many of these mystics use the metaphor of camphor and fire to describe the state of divine union. The state of merging in the divine is also expressed in erotic mysticism by both men and women saints.

A good example of mystic eroticism is the following verse by Akka Mahadevi. She expresses the *sati–pati bhava* in mystical and almost violent imagery:

> On a frame of water, raising a roof of fire,
> Spreading the hailstones for the bridal floor-bed,
> A husband without head,
> married a wife without legs,
> My parents gave me to an inseparable life,
> They married me to Lord Chenna Mallikarjuna.[42]

However, the sexual relationship is not the only one in which the emotion of love expresses itself in the bhakti mode. Another conspicuous imagery is that of the nurturing woman, the mother, and this is often in contrast to the image of the barren women which, in the mystic terminology, implies spiritual barrenness and not necessarily physical barrenness. Basava's wife, Gangambike's verses are notable for the image of herself as the spiritual mother and Shiva as her child:

> That formless which is constant
> in the mind and speech of Basava
> That which even in the process of
> perception disappears into the void.
> This has been the success of Allamma's love!
> This being determined, my heart craves at the loss.
> My child (Siva) has not gone anywhere
> My Chenna Basava! come to the
> breast of Gangambike.[43]

This verse is a clear rejection of the principle of *shunyata* or emptiness in the adoption of which the Virashaivite philosophers like Basava and Allamma were probably influenced by the Madhyamika school of Buddhism. Instead, the women seem to prefer the feminine relationship of love and nurturing.

---

[42] Thipperudraswami, *Soul Unto the Sublime*, 222–223.

[43] Gangambika, 2, in Hiremath, *Ippattelu Shivasharaneyara Vachanagalu*, V: 173: 83.

One of the recurrent metaphors in Virashaiva philosophy is that of the tiger and the deer in the sense of the merger of irreconcilable opposites. Gangambike, however, brings the mother image even into this metaphor:

> In the vast expanse
> One tiger swallowed a calf
> But the tiger did not go
> back to the forest
> Seeing the calf,
> the tiger became a mother
> What does this mean ?[44]

Here, the tiger represents worldly aspirations and the calf represents spiritual energy, and spiritualism overcomes and alters the very character of worldliness.

In what appears to be a series of startling relationship reversals, Akka Nagamma talks of her brother, Basava, as if he were her husband and says, 'Since Basava's death, I have become a widow without ornamentation'.[45] Elsewhere she says, she has just given birth to Basava who is, in fact, 'her face, her voice'.[46] At the same time, she states that her body has merged or united with that of Chenna Basava (her son!) in the open field and become pure! It is therefore clear that the mysticism of these saints, in fact, transcends all gender relationships, although it is couched in terms of worldly ties.

In the Shakti Vishishtadvaita of Virashaivism, from bridal mysticism, the Shiva *sharana* and Shiva *sharane* sometimes become androgynous. A notable example of this is Akka Mahadevi who claims she is 'female in form but male in principle'. However, the most striking example of androgyne is the following *vachana* of Basava:

> Look here, dear fellow:
> I wear these men's clothes
> Only for you.
> Sometimes I am man
> sometimes I am woman.
> O Lord of the meeting rivers
> I'll make wars for you
> but I'll be your devoted bride.[47]

---

[44] Gangambika, V: 4, Ibid., V: 175: 84.

[45] Akka Nagamma, V: 12, Ibid., V: 171: 82.

[46] Akka Nagamma, V: 8, Ibid., V: 167: 80.

[47] Ramanujan, *Speaking of Siva*, V: 703: 87.

The ultimate step from bridal mysticism to androgyny is transcending gender itself. Prabhudeva, in stating Akka Mahadevi's unique spiritual attainments, says:

> Shedding her corporal traits,
> She has become united with Linga...
> She has become
> herself, the Supreme light,
> I say hail to the majesty
> of Mahadeviyakka, who has,
> shedding the sense of self and other
> Become one with the Linga itself,
> In Guhesvara Linga.[48]

From sublimation of sexuality to an androgynous state marks a distinct development in spiritual evolution. Sexual transcendence, however, constituted the highest stage in the spiritual journey. From the sublimation of worldly love, Akka Mahadevi passes on to transcendence. At this level of sexual transcendence, the pangs of separation and passion both cease to be. Akka Mahadevi writes:

> the Guru gave a spear
> called Linga into the hands
> of one fully-concentrated.
> I fight, I win
> a man called Kama (love)
> Krodha (anger) and others were
> defeated and ran away.
> Since the spear was buried deep
> inside me and vanished (from sight)
> Inside the palm I have caught
> the Linga of Chenna Mallikarjuna.[49]

I would like to conclude with a verse from Akka Mahadevi since the *vachana*, in fact, sums up the spiritual journey of these women in love:

> I cannot say,
> it is God or the Union with God.

---

[48] Prabhudeva, *Shunya Sampadane*, IV: XVI: 58. Allamaprabhu's verse in *Shunyasampadane,* ed. S.S. Bhoosnoormath and Menezes. L.M.A., Vol.IV, Karnatak University, Dharwar, 1970, V: 16: 338.

[49] Chennaiah, 'Akka Mahadeviya Vachanagala Prativavidhana', in *Jigyasa* (Mysore: Suruchi Prakashana, 1974) 38.

I cannot say,
it is meeting or separation
I cannot say,
it has happened or not happened,
I cannot say,
it is me or you
On getting merged
In the Supreme Being of Chennamalikarjuna
There's nothing that I can say ![50]

References

Bhoosnoormath, S.S. and L.M.A. Menezes. *Sunyasampadane,* Vols II, III and IV. (Dharwar: Karnatak University, 1968, 1969 and 1970).

Ramaswamy Vijaya, *Divinity and Deviance: Women in Virasaivism,* Oxford University Press, Delhi, 1996, p.97.

Grosz, Elizabeth, *Jacques Lacan: A Feminist Introduction*, Routledge, London and New York, 1990.

Hastings, James (ed.), *Encyclopaedia of Religion and Ethics*, T.T. Clark, London, 1915, Vol. VIII.

Hiremath, R.C., *Ippattelu Shivasharaneyara Vachanagalu* (in Kannada). Dharwar: Karnataka University, 1968.

Ishwaran, K., *Religion and Society among the Lingayats of South India.* Delhi: Vikas, 1983.

Kristeva, Julia, 1976. 'Signifying Practice and Mode of Production', *Edinburgh Review* I (1976): 64–77.

———. *The Revolution in Poetic Language*. New York: Columbia University Press, 1984.

———. *Tales of Love*. Translated by Leon S. Roudiez. New York: Columbia University Press, 1987 (1983).

Menezes, Armando and S.M. Angadi., *Vachanas of Akka Mahadevi*. Dharwar: Shri Manohar Apasahib Adke, 1973.

Michael, Blake, R., 'Women of the Sunyasampadane: Housewives and Saints in Virasaivism, *Journal of the American Oriental Society*, 103(2), 1983.

Mullatti, Leela. *The Bhakti Movement and the Status of Women* (New Delhi: Abhinav Publications, 1989).

Nandi, R.N., *Religious Institutions and Cults in the Deccan* (New Delhi: Motilal Banarsidass, 1973).

[50] Akka Mahadevi, V: 278 Sri Taralabalu Jagadguru Brihanmath, ed. *Religion and Society at Crossroads: Lingayats* (Karnataka: Lingayat Mutt, Chitradurga, 1990), V: 46: 63.

———., 'Feudalization of the State in Medieval South India', *Social Science Probings*, 1(1), March 1984, 33–59.

———. *Social Roots of Religion in Ancient India* (Kolkata and Delhi: K.P. Bagchi and Co., 1986).

Nandimath S.C., *A Handbook of Virasaivism* (Varanasi and Delhi: Motilal Banarsidass, 1979).

Nandimath, S.C., L.M.A Menezes and R.C. Hiremath. *Sunyasampadane,* Vol. I. (Dharwar: Karnataka University, 1965).

Ramanujan, A.K., *Speaking of Siva* (New Delhi: Penguin Classics, 1973).

———. 'On Women Saints'. In *Collected Essays of A.K. Ramanujan*, edited by Vinay Dharwadker, 270–278 (New Delhi: Oxford University Press, 1999).

Rice, B. Lewis, ed. *Epigraphica Carnatica*, 12 vols. Mysore Archaeological Series (Mysore: Department of Archaeology, 1889–1955).

Shivaprakash, H.S., *I Keep Vigil of Rudra* (New Delhi: Penguin Books, 2010).

Thipperudraswami, H., *The Virasaiva Saints – A Study*, (Mysore: Rao and Raghavan, 1968).

Thipperudraswami, H., *Soul Unto the Sublime* (Hubli: Sri Jagadguru Gangadhara Dharma Pracharaka Mandala, 1982).

Zvelebil, K.V., *The Lord of the Meeting Rivers – Devotional Poems of Basavanna.* (New Delhi: Motilal Banarsidass, 1984).

CHAPTER

7

Dissenting Voices

Continuities in the Varkari Tradition

Rohini Mokashi-Punekar

Varkari Tradition

A continuous religio-socio-literary phenomenon, such as the Varkari tradition, which can be traced back to the late thirteenth century at least, may be seen in categories that have been termed as 'a history of cultural memory' or 'mnemohistory'.[1] The public memory of traditional societies is constructed from a dynamic version of the past that cares not so much for historical accuracy or fact, as for the continuing significance that the past holds for the present. The relationship of the present to the past is dynamic and is constantly shaped by the interpretations of several texts and narratives, written and oral, which live on in a kind of a living debate, extending over centuries. Chronicles of pre-colonial Indian figures, especially those from the domains of religious and devotional sects, and the literary works attributed to them, are not recorded in ways that are amenable to biographical reconstruction, but live in the collective memory of communities. Sanctified and mythologized in hagiographies, these lives may be said to be socially constructed.[2] The contours of the life of a

---

[1] See Jan Assmann, *Religion and Cultural Memory: Ten Studies*, trans. R. Livingstone (Stanford: Stanford University Press, 2006). Jan Assmann, *Moses the Egyptian: The Memory of Egypt in Western Montheism* (Cambridge: Harvard University Press, 1997), 1–22, uses categories such as 'mnemohistory' and 'discourse history' to investigate the history of cultural memory. Also cited in Christian Lee Novetzke, *Religion and Public Memory* (New York: Columbia University Press, 2008).

[2] Richard Eaton, *A Social History of the Deccan, 1300–1761: Eight Indian Lives*, The New Cambridge History of India, Vol. 1, Part 8 (Cambridge: Cambridge University Press, 2005), 5.

proto-historical figure take shape from the values and norms that constitute that community.[3] In a sense then, if one were to trace the lives of two poet saints from the Varkari *sampradaya*, separated from each other by a couple of centuries, yet connected in ways that this essay hopes to explore, the narrative would also be a reconstruction of the culture of the community that had kept the memories of these lives alive.

First, however, a brief note on the Varkaris. One of the largest and oldest religious traditions of the Deccan region, the Varkari community worships the deity Vitthal at the shrine of Pandharpur in southern Maharashtra. A salient characteristic of this tradition is the *vari*, the pilgrimage to the spiritual centre at Pandharpur: etymologically, 'varkari' means one who performs the *vari*. Another intrinsic feature is the body of poetry in the form of *abhanga*s produced by the many poet saints, a majority of whom are householders, through the last seven centuries. This poetry is routinely sung and performed in *kirtans* on the pilgrimage as well as in *bhajan* groups. A third feature is the predominantly non-Brahmin, sometimes anti-Brahmin character of the tradition.[4] Of the four major poets in this tradition, two are Brahmins, the stories of whose lives interrogate caste structures. Jnanadev, the son of an outcaste Brahmin, who in retaliation to the orthodox Brahmins of his thirteenth century world caused a buffalo to recite the Vedas, and Eknath of sixteenth century Paithan, a seat of Brahmanical learning, who befriended untouchable Mahars and transgressed orthodox norms of social and literary propriety. The other major poet saints are non-Brahmin Sudras: Namdev, a tailor, and Tukaram, a farmer, both of whom question caste and social stratification. Counted in this community of poet saints are several women belonging to the Brahmin, Sudra and Mahar castes, as well as a courtesan; a host of other male figures belonging to the many Sudra labouring castes of Maharashtra; and the untouchable Mahar, Chokhamela, who was never allowed entry into the Pandharpur temple and whose poems question his literal and metaphoric position on the threshold.[5]

Historians claim that the cult of Vithoba, which plays a significant role in Maharashtrian culture, has evolved from pastoral origins. The transformation of the Desh region in Maharashtra from a predominantly pastoral to an agricultural

[3] Irina Glushkova, 'Norms and Values in the Varkari Tradition', in *Intersections: Socio-cultural Trends in Maharashtra*, ed. Meera Kosambi (New Delhi: Orient Longman, 2000).

[4] Eaton 2005: 132.

[5] Rohini Mokashi-Punekar, *On the Threshold: Songs of Chokhamela* (New York: AltaMira Press, 2005).

economy went along with changing traditions of worship. Pastoral deities, such as Mhaskoba and Khandoba, were assimilated into the pan-India pantheon of gods, initially into Saiva theology and later, with the increasing social prominence of Vaishnava Brahmins in the agrarian society, into Vaishnavism. Therefore, though Varkari poets have worshipped Vitthal as a *swarup* of Vishnu or as a form of Krishna from the late thirteenth century, the deity has a pastoral history as well as clear associations with Shaivism. In fact, Vitthal is also known as Pandurang, another name for Shiva; Pandharpur's most ancient temple is Shaiva in character and Vitthal's headgear is in the form of a *linga*.

The changing conceptions of Vitthal corresponded to the increasingly agrarian nature of Maharashtrian society and the resulting growth in the caste system with its ideas of social category and Brahmanical hierarchy. Yet, Vithoba keeps in touch with his pastoral origins as seen in the open and egalitarian nature of Varkari devotion, and the camaraderie and equality that characterize the community.[6] The practice of caste differences is clearly perceived as a social construct in the poetry of the Varkari saints, and even Vithoba appears helpless in the face of its almost impregnable hierarchy. This is most clearly seen in Chokha's poems. Vithoba is a personal god who is accessible to everyone; the iconography of the idol standing on a brick, arms akimbo, plays out the story of Sage Pundalik. Vitthal came to meet Pundalik, who was engrossed in the care of his parents. Too busy to meet him, Pundalik threw a brick for the god to stand on, for the river was swollen. Vitthal eternally waits for his devotee on the brick, thus subverting normative hierarchy between god and devotee. The *abhangas* of the poet saints emphasize the importance of the Varkari community and the community of the poet saints for the expression of individual *bhakti*. Like all *bhakti* literatures, the poetic expression is in the medium of the vernacular, available to all classes from the linguistic region. In fact, the use of Marathi in literary expression and the mapping of the sacred on to the territorial, which took place through the *vari*, may said to have constructed the linguistic region, a phenomenon that sees the conceptual fusing of region, language and devotional religion. It is useful to remember that the pilgrimage is regular and simultaneous, and routes to Pandharpur criss-cross almost the entire region of Maharashtra, as *palkhi*s of various saints begin from several different places and converge onto Pandharpur. Even as Sheldon Pollock contests the prevalent view underscoring

---

[6] Eaton 2005: 140; Vijaya Ramaswamy, 'Women "In", Women "Out"', in *Organizational and Institutional Aspects of Indian Religious Movements*, ed. J.T. O'Connell (Shimla: Indian Institute of Advanced Studies, 1999), 253.

the role of religion in the vernacularization of medieval India,[7] yet it is clear that for the Varkari poets, Marathi retains an enabling power.

Dilip Chitre, noting the significance of vernacular Marathi for the Varkaris, remarks that these poets 'made language a form of shared religion and religion a shared language'.[8] The seventeenth century Brahmin poetess, Bahinabai, constructs an image for four centuries of continuity and describes Varkari tradition and the legacy of its devotional poetry in the metaphor of a temple: Jnanadev laid the foundation; Namdev constructed the walls; Eknath built the central pillar of the edifice; and Tukaram crowned its spire.[9] This vivid metaphor conveys an extraordinary variety of meanings: the institutional self-awareness of the Varkari tradition as well as a fluid continuity through the centuries; *bhakti* as a shared and collective endeavour; and poetry as the vital element and medium of that sharing across time and space. Implicit in the metaphor is the significance of the lives of the poet saints and how these lives are remembered down the years as a significant aspect of *bhakti*.[10]

The following two sections of this essay attempt to trace the continuities of dissent through the remembered life and poetry of two Varkari poet saints: Chokhamela and Eknath, respectively.[11] Chokhamela was a fourteenth century Mahar poet saint, a contemporary of Namdev and even Jnanadev according to some sources.[12] His *abhanga*s, compiled in a critical edition by S.B. Kadam, record perhaps the first Dalit voice in Indian history, questioning as he does his position in caste hierarchy and the Brahminical rules of purity and pollution that keep him out of the place he most longs to be in, that is, Vithoba's

---

[7] Sheldon Pollock, 'The Cosmopolitan Vernacular', *The Journal of Asian Studies* 57(1) (1998), 27.

[8] Dilip Chitre, *Says Tuka* (New Delhi: Penguin India, 1991), xvii.

[9] Ibid., xxvi.

[10] I draw on the arguments made by Novetzke in his book, *Religion and Public Memory*. In this excellent study on Namdev, Novetzke examines the ways in which devotional traditions remember the lives and the works of the poets within these traditions, in addition to the 'theology' itself, as significant ways of practising *bhakti*.

[11] Eleanor Zelliot, one of the foremost scholars on the Mahar movement and the history of Varkari forms of protest, has written several papers on Chokhamela and Eknath, examining their lives and poetry as modes of legitimacy for social change in the modern times. The emphasis of the present essay is on the continuities between the two poets on the one hand, and between the Varkaris and modern social movements of Maharashtra on the other.

[12] R.D. Ranade. *Pathway to God in Marathi Literature* (Mumbai: Bharatiya Vidya Bhavan, 1961[1933]), 149.

shrine. The stories of Chokha's life, that the eighteenth century biographer Mahipati narrates, also tell us of his ostracism by the officiating Brahmins of the Pandharpur temple. However, the hagiography goes beyond the poems in narrating to us the loving favour shown to Chokha by Vitthal. Eknath was the prolific sixteenth century Brahmin scholar poet, who is the author of several scholarly works as well as *abhanga*s and *bharud*s in the performative tradition. Mahipati's life of Eknath revolves chiefly around his befriending Mahars and the many remembered instances of social transgression of caste rules. Some forty-seven *bharud*s of Eknath are spoken through the allegorical persona of a Mahar. This Mahar comments, advises and satirizes the contemporary society of Paithan, a busy and cosmopolitan city of sixteenth century Maharashtra. Incorporating translations, the following sections will track the continuities of protest through the figure of the Mahar, both real and metaphorical, in the poetry of Chokhamela and Eknath.

Chokhamela

The *samadhi* of Chokhamela is at the foot of the great door to the temple in Pandharpur. In death as in life, Chokha could never go inside the temple. His poems express devotion for Vitthal and speak with anguish about his own position. As is customary in the Varkari tradition, Chokhamela was a householder, and the fact that his wife, son, sister and brother-in-law also were saints and poets is also not unusual for the many poet saints in the Maharashtrian area. But the very volume of their poetry, and their extraordinary consciousness of their caste status, gives us considerable insight into the ethos of the time as well as their own devotion to Vitthal.

The stories that live on in the collective memory of the Varkaris speak powerfully of Chokha's usual place at the great door of the temple worshipping Vitthal from afar, and the god's divine favour in bringing him into the innermost shrine. In a wonderfully vivid *kirtan*, Mahipati, the eighteenth century pre-eminent biographer of the Varkari saints, narrates one such story, which perhaps draws from and has contributed to the pool of stories that makes up the sacred biography of Chokha. Mahipati's *Bhaktavijay*, composed in 1762, is a textual commentary, but this written form bears clear marks of its performance origins in the way it communicates to its readers. For his biography of Chokha, he draws on hagiographical material in poems attributed to Namdev, who in a way was the very first biographer of the fourteenth century Varkari poets.[13] According to

[13] Novetzke, *Religion and Public Memory*, 120.

Mahipati , Chokhamela's home was Pandharpur; he would bathe in the Bhima, circumambulate the whole city and then prostrate himself in front of the main door of the great Pandharpur temple of Vitthal.[14] He could not go into the temple. However, one night, the Lord of Pandharpur himself took Chokhamela by the hand and 'lovingly led him into the innermost shrine' .[15] A Brahmin priest heard Chokhamela talking to the god, and thought, selfishly, according to Mahipati, 'If a man of low caste can touch the god on whom are garments and ornaments, then our duties as Brahmins will cease'. [16] The Brahmin told Chokhamela to go to the other side of the Chandrabhaga river (the name for the Bhima as it runs past Pandharpur) lest the lord keep bringing him into the temple. Chokhamela protested that the Ganga is not polluted by low castes, nor is the holy earth defiled, but he left the temple domains and worshipped from afar. Chokha looked for a spot straight in front of the temple, on the other side of the river, and he built there a pillar for lights, which was incidentally seen till recently. Vitthal came to him there and dined with him. Soyra, his wife, who was serving them food, spilled some curds on the god, and a nearby Brahmin who heard Chokhamela talking to god about the accident came near and slapped Chokhamela on the mouth. But when the Brahmin went into the temple, he found curds spilled on Vithoba's clothing and the cheek of the god was swollen. And so, the Brahmin repented and took Chokhamela by the hand into the temple.[17]

While the narrated story does not figure in any of Chokha's poems, there is another well-known story that also forms the theme of a poem attributed to the saint, and is included in the Kadam edition of his poems[18]. One day, Chokha was standing at the door of the temple from morning till late in the evening. Towards nightfall, the priests locked up the doors and went away. As Chokha stood there, Vithoba himself came out and led him by the hand to the innermost sanctum, where he lovingly held him to his breast. The night was spent in the

---

[14] Mahipati, 1762. *Bhaktavijaya,* 377–378.

[15] Ibid., 379.

[16] Mahipati, 1762. *Bhaktavijaya: Stories of Indian Saints.* trans. Justin E. Abbot and N.B. Godbole, 2 vols., nos. 9 and 10, in *The Poet Saints of Maharashtra* Series, Poona, 1933, 1934. Reprint (New Delhi: Motilal Banarsidass, 1982), 379.

[17] Some parts of this section describing Mahipati's narrative are drawn from the 'Introduction' in Eleanor Zelliot and Rohini Mokashi-Punekar, eds, *Untouchable Saints: An Indian Phenomenon* (New Delhi: Manohar, 2005).

[18] Kadam, S.B. 1969. *Shri Sant Chokhamela: Charitra ani Abhang* (Mumbai: Shabdalaya Prakashan. Reprinted by Bhalchandra Nemade, 1998), 162.

union of the *bhakta* with the god, after which Vithoba playfully removed his *tulsi* garland (a garland made of basil seeds which the Varkaris wear as a mark of their identity) and put it around Chokha's neck. When the day dawned, he led him out of the temple, still with the garland. Chokha, in a state of bliss, lay down on the sands of the river in a trance. At the temple, the priests discovered that Vithoba's gold necklace had disappeared and went into a rage over the fact that the temple and deity were polluted and the necklace stolen. Search parties found Chokha with the gold necklace around the neck. He was tied to the bullocks and about to be dragged to death but for the animals that stood their ground, despite the whip lashing them. The story ends with Vithoba revealing himself to the entire company, holding the bullocks by the horns.

The poem, however, dramatizes Chokha's plea to Vithoba in the midst of his humiliating position. The incensed priests lashing the whip, the bullocks, the crowd of people are frozen in the background; what is voiced are Chokha's anguished words to his god. The poem makes no mention of Vitthal's public revelation; it, nevertheless, makes an ambiguous reference to a secret shared between them.

They thrash me, Vithu,
now don't walk so slow.
The pandits whip,
    some crime,
    don't know what:
How did Vithoba's necklace come round your throat,
they curse and strike
and say I polluted you.
Do not send the cur at your door
    away,
    giver of everything.
    You,
Chakrapani,
yours is the deed.
With folded hands
Chokha begs
I revealed our secret,
don't turn away.[19]

[19] All translations of Eknath and Chokhamela are mine unless indicated otherwise. The translations of the *abhanga*s of Chokhamela are taken from Mokashi-Punekar, *On the Threshold*, abhanga 82.

This poem is one of a few others that dramatize situations. The collection of Chokhamela's *abhanga*s, of which some poems must be latter-day interpolations, reveals deprivations and humiliations as well as bliss. They work towards an awareness that it is not only divine love that empowers him but also, perhaps more importantly, *his* devotion that empowers Vithoba. Some poems subtly play up the paradox that Vithoba, the holiest of the holy, touches, eats with and embraces him, Chokha – the impure untouchable – a loving favour not extended to the putatively holy Brahmin priests. Chokhamela's poetry, in short, quietly reverses normative understanding of divinity and social structure. This is the voice of a Mahar who speaks as a Mahar; and the Mahar is both a devotee and a dissenter.

Consider, for instance, the following poems that satirize Brahmanical notions of pollution:

> Five elements compound the body impure;
> all things mix, thrive in the world.
> Then who is pure and who impure?
> The body is rooted in impurity.
> From the beginning to the end,
> endless impurities heap themselves.
> Who is it can be made pure?
> Says Chokha, I am struck with wonder,
> can there be any such beyond pollution?[20]
> Vedas and the shastras
> polluted; puranas inauspicious,
> impure; the body, the soul
> contaminated; the manifest
> Being is the same.
> Brahma polluted, Vishnu too;
> Shankar is impure, inauspicious.
> Birth impure, dying is impure:
> says Chokha,
> pollution stretches
> without beginning
> and end.[21]

---

[20] Ibid., *abhanga* 279.

[21] Ibid., *abhanga* 282.

The living memory of Chokha's poems, and the stories of his life which are regularly evoked in performances, such as *kirtans* and *bhajans*, testify to the continuities of protest articulated through means which are within the folds of Varkari spiritual practices. Other poet saints, too, sing of Chokha's social marginalization and Vitthal's special love for this devotee: contemporaries such as Namdev, Janabai, various saints in Chokha's family, as well as Eknath in the sixteenth century and Tukaram in the seventeenth century. Dissent is an important component of devotion for the Varkaris: inclusive love such as *bhakti* cannot condone social exclusiveness. It is also the memory of past dissent and the preservation and remembering of this in continuing traditions of performance that seems to ignite future articulations of radicalism through the many centuries of Varkari protest. However, does the dissent ever translate into praxis? We must turn to the radical Brahmin poet saint Eknath in order to consider this question.

Eknath

As Wendy Doniger has observed recently, oral and written traditions interact throughout Indian literary history.[22] There seems to exist in literary cultures of India, an enormously productive relationship between oral recitations of written texts and written versions of works by persons who may have been literate or illiterate. A case in point is Chokhamela's poetry whose author was undisputedly unlettered. A charming song by Janabai, the Sudra nurse and disciple of Namdev, who sings of the fourteenth century community of poet saints in several *abhanga*s attributed to her, delineates a long list of poets and their scribes among which figure Chokha and Ananta Bhatt, his Brahmin scribe.[23] This is an intriguing bit of literary information: a lowly Mahar poet and his Brahmin amanuensis. Varkari poetry seems to have developed, from its beginning, a fascinating legacy of orality and literacy, which is continued in future generations through both these means .[24] The erudite poet, Jnanadev, and the unlettered *kirtankar*, Namdev, both mark the inception of the tradition, and in Eknath, the sixteenth century pre-eminent author of scholarly compositions

22 Wendy Doniger, *The Hindus: An Alternative History* (New Delhi: Penguin Viking, 2009), 33.

23 Cited in Novetzke, *Religion and Public Memory*, 78.

24 See the chapter on 'Public Performance and Corporate Authorship' in Novetzke (ibid.) for a detailed study of the *kirtan* as performance and mode of memory, 74–99.

and popular folk drama, and the performer of *kirtans*, this legacy is most significantly present in fertile combination.

Recent historical studies suggest that the traditional historiography of the early modern Deccan is, to a certain extent, a prisoner of modern politics.[25] The period between the early fourteenth century and the late seventeenth century, in Marathi historiography, is characterized as one of Muslim conquest and Hindu subjugation. The last of the Yadava rulers, Ramchandra, ruled from 1272 to 1309, but the Yadava kingdom became a tributary state of the Khalji Empire centred in Delhi as early as 1294 and was formally annexed to the Delhi Sultanate in 1317. Since then, the region of Maharashtra was consecutively under the Tughlaq dynasty, the Bahamani Sultanate, the Deccan Sultanates and then the rule of the Mughals till the accession of Shivaji in 1674. Marathi literary histories categorize the two centuries between Namdev and Eknath as the Dark Age, clearly indicating by the epithet an assumed understanding of the destructive impact of Islamic forces on Hindu cultures. However, the prodigious literary output attributed to Eknath (1533–1599) around the third quarter of the sixteenth century suggests, according to Novetzke, not the end to the literary decline, but the returning to written forms; for literature had continued to be composed in the performance art tradition during the putative Dark Age.[26]

Eknath, in many ways, is an extraordinary and liminal figure.[27] A Brahmin scholar poet in the *sastric* tradition, he is equally at home in the non-Brahmin linguistic register of the subaltern. He is the author of several translations and commentaries upon Sanskrit philosophic works, a Marathi version of the Ramayana, a narrative of the marriage of Rukmini and Krishna and a commentary on the eleventh *skanda* of the *Bhagwata Purana*, known as the *Eknathi Bhagwat*. He is especially known for his critical edition of the *Jnaneswari* and is remembered today for a genre of *kirtan*, known as the Eknathi *kirtan*, which 'invested in worldly metaphor and the plight of the "common

[25] Eaton 2005, 103.

[26] Novetzke, *Religion and Public Memory*, 140–41; S.G. Tulpule, *Classical Marathi Literature, Vol. X*, The History of Indian Literature Series (Wiesbaden: Otto Harrassowitz, 1979), 345.

[27] Novetzke, *Religion and Public Memory*, 140; Eleanor Zelliot, 'Eknath's *Bharuds*: The Sant as a Link between Cultures', in *The Sants: Studies in a Devotional Tradition of India*, ed Karine Schomer and Hugh McLeod (New Delhi: Motilal Banarsidass, 1987), 91; 'Chokhamela and Eknath: Two *Bhakti* Modes of Legitimacy for Modern Change', in *From Untouchable to Dalit: Essays on the Ambedkar Movement* (New Delhi: Manohar, 1992), 14.

man" rather than in mythological story-telling'.[28] He is also the author of several thousand *abhanga*s and some 300 *bharuds*, a genre of drama poem, meant to be performed as some kind of impromptu skit rather than sung primarily for non-Brahmin populations. The *bharud*s employ Marathi peppered with Arabic, Telugu and Kannada words, which is a language register closer to Dakhni.[29] This register as much reveals the plural and multicultural world of sixteenth century Deccan, as it does Eknath's empathy for the subaltern and the plurality of his experiences and outlook.

Born in Paithan, a busy holy city within the Ahmednagar Sultanate, on the trade route from the north to the south, famed for its silk sari, the *paithani*, the householder–scholar Eknath was the great-grandson of Bhanudas, a devout Varkari, credited with bringing back the Vithoba idol from neighbouring Karnataka. His guru was Janardanswami, who was said to have held a military/administrative post in the fort at Daulatabad, a capital town of the Sultanate. Some studies link Janardan with Sufism, and claim he was a member of a Sufi order. Even if these links cannot be proved, they indicate cross-cultural influences; *bhakti* and Sufism cannot have been exclusive categories in sixteenth century Maharashtra. A significant number of stories in Mahipati's life of Eknath narrate his encounters with Muslim fakirs or with aspects of Islam. Since Eknath 'signs' off his *abhanga*s with the signature 'EkaJanardan', the ties between Eknath and his guru seem to have been strong and are indissoluble for all posterity. So, not only was Eknath a scholar in the Brahmanic way, he was fully ensconced in the Varkari tradition and lived in an environment where there was a strong Sufi presence.[30]

To these affiliations must be added Mahipati's stories of Eknath's compassion for the Mahars and other marginalized sections. Mahipati narrates several such hagiographic instances where the Brahmin scholar comes to the aid of the lowly Mahars. At a *sraddha* once, Eknath invited Brahmins to his house for the feast. The aroma of the food reached the untouchable Mahar and his wife sweeping the lane outside, who told themselves that they could never have such a sumptuous meal since even the leftovers, which they could claim as their right, would be buried on this occasion. Overhearing this, Eknath invited all

[28] Novetzke, *Religion and Public Memory*, 142.

[29] Vidyut Bhagwat, 'Hindu–Muslim Dialogue: A Rereading of Sant Eknath and Sant Shaikh Muhammad', in *Marga: Ways of Liberation, Empowerment and Social Change in Maharashtra*, ed. M. Naito, S. Kotani and H. Kotani (New Delhi: Manohar, 2008), 77–93.

[30] Eaton 2005; Bhagwat 2008.

the untouchables in the town to the feast serving the food himself. The angry Brahmins excommunicated Eknath, but Lord Krishna, who worked in Eknath's house disguised as a poor Brahmin servant, said, 'Serve the feast to the ancestors anyway'. When the Paithan Brahmins witnessed the splendid heavenly ancestors feasting, they said to him, 'You are indeed the avatar of Vishnu'.[31]

Another story narrates Eknath accepting the invitation of a pious *bhakta*, Ramya Mahar, to dine at his home. Seeing Eknath going towards the Mahar area, the Brahmins went to check on him and saw him eating at both places: his own home as well as the Mahar's house. Vitthal himself had taken Eknath's form and dined with Ramya Mahar.[32] It is said that a poor and starving Mahar who had done his time in jail for thieving was taken in by Eknath and his wife, who took care of him and converted him from a life of crime to one of devotion.[33] Yet another story concerns a small Mahar boy who found himself alone at noon on the hot sands of the bank of the Godavari. Eknath picked up the wailing child and returned him to his mother, realizing only on reaching his poor home that he was a Mahar boy. Mahipati is careful to add that Eknath went back to the river and bathed with all his clothes on. No one saw Eknath doing this act of kindness, but the deed became known and a learned Brahmin who was afflicted with leprosy was told by god that he would become whole of limb again if Eknath were to transfer his good deed to the Brahmin. Putting some water into the Brahmin's palm, Eknath smiled and the Brahmin was cured.[34]

If the stories show Eknath's compassion and liberality, his poetry in the popular register corroborate the same. His *abhanga*s are in the Varkari tradition, which rests on the assumption, as in all *bhakti* traditions, that for God there is no distinction of caste or creed. We may see here an *abhanga* attributed to Eknath that shows God one with the working castes; the poem also unites the regional saints from Maharashtra with pan-India figures of devotion:

> God baked pots with Gora,
> drove cattle with Chokha,
> cut grass with Savata Mali,
> wove garments with Kabir,
> colored hide with Ravidas,
> sold meat with butcher Sajana,

---

[31] Mahipati, *Bhaktavijaya*, 176–181.

[32] Ibid.,139–149.

[33] Ibid., 166–169.

[34] Ibid., 201–204.

melted gold with Narahari,
carried cow-dung with Janabai
and even became the Mahar messenger of Damaji.[35]

Eknath also sang of Chokha's devotion in another *abhanga*.[36] However, it is in his *bharud*s that one can see Eknath's strikingly unconventional interventions on behalf of the marginalized. The *bharud*s are poems classified as *upadesa rupake*: didactic metaphors in collections of Marathi *bhakti* poetry. They are allegories, spoken sometimes through the persona of a human type: low-caste, low-status characters, including the physically challenged, sometimes an animal or a bird, a game, a government document, a festival, a rite or any other aspect of the colourful plural world of Eknath's times. They are in a dramatic form, suitable for enactment, generally through dialogue or monologue. In colloquial everyday language, they quite clearly address non-Brahmin audiences, including Muslims and migrant foreigners such as Habshis,[37] and are meant for didactic purposes. While there are several *bharud*s with women as the speaking metaphoric persona and these include women of upper castes, no orthodox Brahmin or peasant ever constitutes the allegorical centre of Eknath's *bharud*s. Containing references to Vedantic philosophy and stories from the epics and the Puranas, the *bharud*s attempt to teach, frequently through humour and satire, ethical behaviour and devotion to God. A number of other poets have used the *bharud* form,[38] but none in such a wide-ranging fashion, so that the *bharud* is associated largely with Eknath in Marathi literary history. Eknath's *bharud*s are not an expression of his devotion, but show a consistent endeavour to use the form to present a plural view on any subject which suits their didactic purpose. Being allegorical, the *bharud* works on two levels; under the surface narrative, lies the second and more philosophical level of meaning, which is analogous to the surface level. The simplest *bharud*s see an easy correspondence between the two levels; the more complex work at several layers of meaning.

---

[35] Zelliot, 'Chokhamela and Eknath', 22.

[36] Zelliot and Mokashi-Punekar, *Untouchable Saints*, 26.

[37] See Eaton, *A Social History of the Deccan*, for a fascinating account of Turkish and Ethiopian migrants in medieval Deccan. Eknath has a wonderful *bharud*, which is a *samvad* between a Hindu and a Turk, translated and analysed by Zelliot. Several *bharud*s of Eknath have itinerant Muslims and Habshis as the central allegorical persona.

[38] Zelliot, 'Chokhamela and Eknath', 15.

A large proportion of the *bharud*s – forty-seven in all – employ the persona of a devout Mahar. This is a significant number; this is, in fact, the largest number of poems dedicated to a single subject, revealing Eknath's consciousness of and preoccupation with the Mahars. Eknath uses the typical *johar* motif: the traditional manner in which Mahars were supposed to greet their superiors in caste. The allegorical foundation of these *bharud*s is worked through with the employment of a different kind of language that underscores the enigma and/or absurdity of the paradoxical situation presented in the drama poem. This form of paradoxical expression is termed as *ulati-bhasa*, or inverted and upside down language.[39] The peculiar quality of the form and language of the *bharud* will be clear if Chokhamela's *johar abhanga*s were to be contrasted with Eknath's *johar bharud*s. Both poems employ the speaking Mahar saluting the village superior. Chokha's poem has emotional power and is hard-hitting with its combination of satire and poignancy presented through the figure of Chokha as he is, a Mahar:

> Johar, *mai-baap*, johar.
> I am the mahar of your mahars.
> I am come,
> starved
> for your leavings.
> The servant of your servants
> waits with hope.
> I have brought, says Chokha,
> my basket
> for your leavings.[40]

The poem may be read at two levels: one, devotional (where Vitthal is the one greeted; it may be noted the Varkaris typically address Vithhal as father and mother: *mai–baap*); and the other, social (where the upper-caste person is addressed), and it is through the gap between the two levels that the poem works the satire. However, there is no trace of didacticism in Chokhamela's *abhanga*, nor is it spoken through another person.

We may contrast this *abhang* with a *bharud* of Eknath using the *johar* motif.

---

[39] Crow Jr., R. W. 'The Bharuds of the Marathi Sant Eknath'. Unpublished PhD thesis submitted to the University of Pennsylvania, 185.

[40] Mokashi-Punekar, *On the Threshold*, 69.

Johar *mai-baap*, Johar.
Johar to all the saints.
I am the Mahar of Ayodhya city,
Johar to the the court of Lord Rama.
Lord Rama rules Ayodhya,
I am a lowly
servant there; but many jobs
I have to do.
I wake early in the morning
and ask Sita for food.
I sweep the court and
throw the dirt outside.
I run ahead to announce
Lord Rama when he enters the court.
In truth, Eka-Janardana offers
Johar *mai-baap*.[41]

This *bharud* uses the improvised allegory of a Mahar, who is actually shown to be a servant of Lord Rama's court in Ayodhya. A servant of the lord, the Mahar narrates his duties, which seem to be a reflection of his duties in this world.[42] In a way, the Mahar's position has not changed even in the eternal kingdom; yet, he is redeemed, in the sense that he is in close proximity with the God himself, and is empowered to come to this world as his messenger, a gift which the upper caste in the village have not received. The *mudrika* at the end of the *bharud* offers yet another meaning: Eknath himself is the Mahar, the devoted servant of the lord.

In the next *bharud*, the Mahar who has come from the eternal kingdom, the *nirguna* city, not only warns the powerful upper-caste chief about his wrong-doing but also teaches him the inevitability of rebirth if he does not mend his ways.

I am the Mahar of Nirgun City;
Johar, I bow at your feet.
Patil Sir, your rule over the village,
has swollen your head with arrogance.
Your tenants are sullen;

[41] Ibid., *abhanga* 3864, 533.

[42] For the traditional duties of the Mahar, see A.R. Kulkarni , 'The Mahar Watan' in Meera Kosambi ed. *Intersections: Socio-Cultural Trends in Maharashtra* (New Delhi: Orient Longman, 2000), 121–140.

your official has turned against you.
Things don't look good: you
are in a bad way. Eighty four hundred
thousand cycles to cross.
Eka-Janardana's Mahar
touches the feet of the saints.[43]

One way of reading the *bharud* is to see it addressed to the village headman and his lack of control over his affairs, which is daring critique coming from a Mahar. But another allegorical meaning is indicated. The extended allegory is allusive of another reality underlying conscious everyday experience. So, the town could be understood to mean the mortal being, the tenant the body and the official the fickle mind. Eknath often uses numbers as ellipses or synechoche[44] without esoteric numerological intent. Here, the numeral 840,000 thousand refers to the endless number of births one must go through in the cycle of *samsara*. Quite obviously, the untouchable Mahar has transcended the cycles of birth, while the arrogant headman still belongs to the earthly realm.

It is believed that Eknath often composed his *bharud*s orally, performing them during the course of his *kirtans*. As seen earlier, the relation between the written and oral forms of composition may not have been sharply independent, but one of dynamic interaction. Perhaps Eknath composed and performed these *bharud*s throughout his active career as a *kirtankar*.[45] *Bharud*s on the same subject, such as the *johar* poems, share the same idiom and sometimes the same phrases and refrains. This feature may indicate that these *bharud*s are '"formulaic variations" on a fluid text' rather than distinct new compositions.[46]

The potentially subversive themes of the *bharud*s show that Eknath had a considerable reputation that could weather their controversial nature. One of the most popular *bharud*s, and also the boldest, is a dialogue between a Mahar and a Brahmin, where the Mahar gives the arrogant Brahmin lessons in true spirituality.

Brahmin: Hey you, impudent Mahar!
Mahar: What Sir! How do you talk?
Brahmin: Ho! Is your father such a big man?
Mahar: Your mother–father's same as mine.

---

43 Ibid., *abhanga* 3862, 533.

44 Crow, 192.

45 Ibid., 211.

46 Ibid., 212.

Brahmin: Listen, don't you crap!
Mahar: We are all from the same eternal Absolute.
Brahmin: What! You know nothing of the Absolute.
Mahar: Search your own soul and find the answer.
Brahmin: I know very little of my own self.
Mahar: Seek the refuge of the Saints.
Brahmin: How will the Saints help?
Mahar: You will stay clear of the eighty-four hundred thousand cycles.
Brahmin: How do you know all this?
Mahar: This is the blessing of Eka-Janardana .[47]

The Mahar in Eknath's *bharud*s plays a metaphoric role. Eknath empowers the Mahar by giving him a voice and a privileged space to observe and critique. While his social position in the poem is similar to his traditional role, the Mahar of the *bharud* is a detached and objective commentator, attuned as he is to a reality beyond the earthly one. This Mahar is an empowered messenger who is able to critique, ridicule and satirize existing social reality. Even if the critique is intended for spiritual purposes, it is fashioned through a daring subversion of social norms. It is clear that Eknath was able to perceive the world from the perspective of the Mahar, and even if he did not advocate a revolution against existing caste hierarchy, his compassion and generosity showed the way of reform.

Caste and Gender

Hierarchies of caste are more often than not articulated through gender, and as several studies reveal, gender is the primary axis on which caste stratification rests in modern Indian society; this can be seen in the imposition of restrictions on upper-caste women and in the double marginalization to which Dalit women are subjected.[48] The foregoing analysis of the history of dissent within the Varkari tradition has not accounted for perspectives on gender. Not that there are no women's voices here. In fact, from the thirteenth century onwards, there have been several women poet saints in this tradition, as seen in the introductory part of this essay. Among the lower-caste women poets in the

---

47 Mokashi-Punekar, *On the Threshold*, *abhanga* 3863.

48 Some seminal studies are by Uma Chakravarty, *Gendering Caste: Through a Feminist Lens* (Calcutta: Stree, 2003) and Anshu Malhotra, *Gender, Caste and Religious Identities: Restructuring Class in Colonial Punjab* (New Delhi: Oxford University Press, 2002).

fourteenth century, Chokhamela's wife, Soyra, and his sister, Nirmala, speak of their Mahar caste and its location in the caste hierarchy, and though one long poem narrates Soyra's travails of being married to a householder *bhakta*, such as Chokhamela who is always lost in devotion to Vitthal, no poem questions his centrality in the family.[49] In frank and intimate tones, a Sudra, Janabai, said to be Namdev's nurse, who was also the hard-worked serving woman in his home, going by the accounts in her poetry of the endless housework she did there, expresses her confidence in Vitthal's love and concern for her.[50] In the fifteenth century, Kanhopatra, the courtesan, sings of the vulnerability of her position; her poems precipitate an acute sense of the fragility of her being caught between her devotion to Vitthal and the demands of her profession that force her away.[51] Together with Muktabai and Bahinabai who were Brahmin, these remembered women's voices from the past form a continuum of protest.

Recent research on contemporary autonomous Dalit women's organizations has stressed the need to locate these modern social initiatives not as an isolated phenomenon, but within the lineage of women's solidarities formed during Satyashodhak and Ambedkerite movements under the radical leadership of Jyotiba Phule and Bhimrao Ambedkar in nineteenth and twentieth century Maharashtra, respectively.[52] The two important social movements of the 1970s,

---

[49] See 'Soyrabai and Nirmala' in Zelliot and Mokashi-Punekar, *Untouchable Saints*, 157–168. One of Soyra's poems is translated thus by Eleanor Zelliot 2003:

The Brahmins of Pandhari (p.160) harassed Chokha;
God was surprised at this.
Everyone gathered at Chokha's house;
Wealth and Power stood at the door.
Rangoli at the entrance, flags on the gate,
Joyous *kirtan* of the Vaishnavas.
The celebration was like Divali and Dussehra
Soyra waves the lights of *arati* before Chokha.

[50] Sarah Sellergren, 'Janabai and Kanhopatra: A Study of Two Women Sants', in *Images of Women in Maharashtrian Literature and Religion*, ed. Anne Feldhaus (Albany: SUNY, 1996), 213–38. Both Sellergren and Zelliot point out that though the inclusion of women *sant*s in the Varkari tradition attests to the egalitarian nature of the movement, yet the everyday working out of equality must have been complicated.

[51] Ibid.

[52] Sharmila Rege, 'Dalit Women Talk Differently: A Critique of "Difference" and Towards a Dalit Feminist Standpoint Position', *Economic and Political Weekly* 33(44) (1998), 39–46.

the Dalit movement and the women's movement, excluded the urgent concerns of Dalit women; the former subsumed questions of patriarchal domination of lower-caste women under caste marginalization and the latter addressed gender issues from the perspective of upper-caste women. However, Guru points to the sustained efforts of Dalit women through women's organizations who have been vocal on the cultural landscape in post-independence India.[53] Using the traditional poetic forms of the *ovi* and *palana* (the *abhanga* belongs to this common pool of folk poetic forms), Guru draws attention to the way Dalit women voice their political awareness of regional and national issues in some parts of Maharashtra.

Rege's path-breaking contribution to the study of Dalit women's movements traces the contemporary organizational initiatives by Dalit women to social movements in colonial Maharashtra.[54] However, it is a pity that these protests and the poetic forms in which they are articulated have not been connected to the longer and living history of resistance, which is the Varkari tradition. Muktabai and Tarabai Shinde, who challenged social structure and cultural norms that rest on patriarchy and upper-caste male hegemony, write from within the Satyashodhak movement, and Phule, its founder, was deeply influenced by Tukaram though he disavowed Brahmanical Hinduism.[55] Maharashtra has had a long tradition of women who were active in public life;[56] it remains to be studied what role a countercultural phenomenon, such as the Varkari tradition, played in the long, continued and historical questioning of caste and gender disparity in the region that has come to be named as Maharashtra in recent history. Studying the trajectory of women's voices from the present to the medieval times would be a rewarding area of research. Though aware that caste is deeply imbricated in gender, this study attempts to look at the continuities of protest against caste in the poetry of Chokhamela and Eknath.

---

[53] Guru Gopal, *Dalit Cultural Movement and Dialectics of Dalit Politics in Maharashtra* (Mumbai: Vikas Adhyayan Kendra, 1998).

[54] Rege, 'Dalit Women talk Differently'.

[55] For an insightful analysis of Phule's contribution to the lower caste and Dalit movements in Maharashtra, see G.P. Deshpande, ed., *Selected Writings of Jotirao Phule* (New Delhi: Leftword Books, 2002), 7.

[56] Ramchandra Guha, ed., *Makers of Modern India* (New Delhi: Penguin, 2010), 130. This book includes what can be termed as the first feminist tract in India by Tarabai Shinde.

Caste and Performance Traditions

Germane to this discussion is the current debate on the nature of caste. Questions on whether caste is an intrinsic and immutable feature of Indian society or it has changed through its long history have become significant issues of debate in recent scholarship. Fresh perspectives shaped by post-colonial theory have uncovered new material and interpretations of these that have challenged 'Orientalist' studies on caste, such as Dumont's *Homo Hierarchicus* which has been perceived, in a way, as the most typical of such scholarship.[57] Influenced by post-structuralist modes of enquiry into the nature of putatively timeless essences, studies inspired by Said contend that caste was 'metonymically indexed', as it were, as essential Indian reality.[58] Contemporary historians such as Cohn, Dirks and Bayly attempt to convince, in different ways and with varying degrees of success, that caste is not a religious mode of hierarchical social organization based on purity and pollution, but in fact a colonial invention. While their claims that the various state apparatuses which the British created reconfigured caste seem tenable, yet, statements such as caste was a 'conscious design of British colonial policy' invented to facilitate colonial rule attempt to stretch, in a manner of speaking, a definite hunch into a hyperbole.[59]

For Indian sociologists cued into the everyday of Indian social and political reality, the concerns have been different. In the 1960s, M.N. Srinivas's analysis of the field view of caste engendered the concept of Sanskritization to indicate a process of social change and mobility, followed by related ideas such as Kshatriyaization and Rajputization. The role of caste in electoral politics in recent decades has given rise to seminal studies on how caste is kept alive today by the communities most marginalized by its practices.[60] Earlier, Indian responses to Dumont fashioned a more complex analysis of the caste structure that accommodated a greater number of variables than the ones provided by

---

[57] Louis Dumont, *Homo Heirarchicus: The Caste System and its Implications* (Chicago: Chicago University Press, 1970).

[58] Revisionist historiography in contemporary research attempts to question the origin of certain academic truths. Caste was seen as the most significant reality of India in Western scholarship on India. Nicholas Dirks, 'Castes of Mind', *Representations* 37 (1992), 56, attempts to debunk the foundations of such thinking.

[59] Nicholas Dirks, *Castes of Mind: Colonialism and the Making of Modern India* (Princeton: Princeton University Press, 2001), 249.

[60] Rajni Kothari, 'Rise of the Dalits and the Renewed Debate on Caste', *Economic and Political Weekly* 29(26) (1994), 1589–1596.

his simple and rather attractive binary of purity and pollution.[61] However, very little work is available that connects sociological studies of caste in history with the actual voices available from the literary history of various linguistic regions; no sociological analysis has been done of the voices of the poet saints, whose accents carry over through the centuries as living testimonies of their anguish and their dissent. Literary histories are repositories of these voices that have been kept alive in memory through performance traditions, which include oral and written narrations. It is not to argue that caste has been some uniform, historical, pan-India essence: differing social accounts in the poetry from different regions would corroborate how political dispensations changed the fortunes of some communities.[62] It is important though to pay attention to the cultural memory of caste disparity as remembered through the songs of the figures whose voices have been circulating through history.

Continuities of Dissent

Untouchable, non-Brahmin and Brahmin, all Varkari poet saints condemn caste. However, though continuous and long-standing, dissent in the Varkari tradition has never advocated dismantling the caste structure. Chokha's dissent is contained by his devotion. He also sees, in some poems, his karma in past births as the cause of his present social position. Through several instances recorded of his life and his didactic poetry, Eknath points to reforming social reality. His teachings aim to reappropriate, for non-Brahmins and the untouchables, ideas from sacred Brahmanical texts, such as the Bhagavad Gita and the Bhagavat, and to critique upper-caste arrogance.

---

[61] T.N. Madan, J.P.S. Uberoi, R.S. Khare and Veena Das are some Indian sociologists who attempted to read Dumont in a more nuanced and grounded fashion. For a concise collection of readings on the Indian responses to Dumont, see R.S. Khare, ed., *Caste, Hierarchy and Individualism: Indian Critiques of Louis Dumont's Contributions* (New Delhi: Oxford University Press, 2006).

[62] For instance, Kanakadasa in the sixteenth century was a lower-caste poet saint who hailed from the adjoining linguistic region of what would be today's Karnataka. Kanaka belonged to the shepherd community, but his father and he were in charge of a small fort and in command of battalions of soldiers, and therefore people of some importance in the Vijayanagara kingdom. Kanaka had some education and though he too faced caste discrimination, his poems show him as a man of some social standing, at least till the empire lasted.

We must remember the insightful point made by D.R. Nagaraj that these *bhakti* poets, the conscience of their regions, made cultural interventions in the spiritual aspirations of a community.[63] They did not see caste as a problem in the political field, which was perhaps possible only in the context of the nation-state. Their notion of society was cultural and spiritual. The figure of the Mahar as evoked by Varkari poetry dissents, but is never revolutionary, and could thus have little interest for the more radical protest movements of the nineteenth and the twentieth centuries. Neither the non-Brahmin movement nor the Mahar movement of Maharashtra was able to draw directly from the history of 'traditional' dissent in Maharashtra. Yet, perhaps the long cultural memory of such dissent informs these more radical movements. What is perceived as a break with the past is perhaps not really a break at all but only a continuation in the political field of the earlier forms of dissent in the cultural and spiritual domains. Other regions of India have seen *several* non-Brahmin movements and organizations of the untouchables for social and political equality. Tamil Nadu, in particular, has an earlier and successful history of the non-Brahmin movement. Only Maharashtra, however, has been able to mobilize *both* non-Brahmin and untouchable movements, which may indicate a diverse set of social and economic factors that prepared the soil, so to speak, for radical change.[64] Among these factors, the precipitation of a tradition of dissenting voices may surely be counted as a significant cultural legacy.

References

Kulkarni A.R., 'The Mahar Watan' in Meera Kosambi ed. *Intersections: Socio-Cultural Trends in Maharashtra* (New Delhi: Orient Longman, 2000), 121–140.

Assmann, Jan. *Moses the Egyptian: The Memory of Egypt in Western Montheism* (Cambridge: Harvard University Press, 1997).

______. *Religion and Cultural Memory: Ten Studies*. Translated by R. Livingstone (Stanford: Stanford University Press, 2006).

Bayly, Susan. *Caste, Society and Politics in India from the Eighteenth Century to the Modern Age* (Cambridge: Cambridge University Press, 1999).

Bhagwat, Vidyut. 'Hindu–Muslim Dialogue: A Rereading of Sant Eknath and Sant Shaikh Muhammad'. In *Marga: Ways of Liberation, Empowerment and Social Change in Maharashtra*, edited by M. Naito, S. Kotani and H. Kotani (New Delhi: Manohar, 2008).

[63] D.R. Nagaraj, *The Flaming Feet: A Study of the Dalit Movement in India* (Bangalore: South Forum Press, 1993), 3.

[64] Zelliot,'Chokhamela and Eknath', 33.

Chakravarty, Uma. *Gendering Caste: Through a Feminist Lens*, (Kolkata: Stree, 2003).

Chitre, Dilip. *Says Tuka* (New Delhi: Penguin India, 1991).

Cohn, Bernard. *Colonialism and its Forms of Knowledge: The British in India* (Princeton: Princeton University Press, 1996).

Crow Jr., R. W. 'The *Bharuds* of the Marathi Sant Eknath'. Unpublished PhD thesis submitted to the University of Pennsylvania in 1988.

Deshpande, G.P., ed. *Selected Writings of Jotirao Phule* (New Delhi: Leftword Books, 2002).

Dirks, Nicholas. 'Castes of Mind'. *Representations* 37 (1992): 56–78.

______. *Castes of Mind: Colonialism and the Making of Modern India* (Princeton: Princeton University Press, 2001).

Doniger, Wendy. *The Hindus: An Alternative History* (New Delhi: Penguin Viking, 2009).

Dumont, Louis. *Homo Heirarchicus: The Caste System and its Implications* (Chicago: Chicago University Press, 1970).

Eaton, Richard. *A Social History of the Deccan, 1300–1761: Eight Indian Lives*. The New Cambridge History of India, Vol. 1, Part 8 (Cambridge: Cambridge University Press, 2005).

Glushkova, Irina. 'Norms and Values in the Varkari Tradition' In *Intersections: Socio-Cultural Trends in Maharashtra*, edited by Meera Kosambi (New Delhi: Orient Longman, 2000), 47–58.

Guha, Ramchandra, ed. *Makers of Modern India* (New Delhi: Penguin, 2010).

Guru, Gopal. 1995. 'Dalit Women Talk Differently', *EPW*, October 14–21, 2548–2549.

______. *Dalit Cultural Movement and Dialectics of Dalit Politics in Maharashtra* (Mumbai: Vikas Adhyayan Kendra, 1998).

Kadam, S.B. *Shri Sant Chokhamela: Charitra ani Abhang* (Mumbai: Shabdalaya Prakashan, 1969. Reprinted by Bhalchandra Nemade, 1998).

Khare, R.S. ed. 2006. *Caste, Hierarchy, and Individualism: Indian Critiques of Louis Dumont's Contributions* (New Delhi: Oxford University Press).

Kosambi, Meera. *Intersections: Socio-Cultural Trends in Maharashtra* (New Delhi: Orient Longman, 2000).

Kothari, Rajni. 'Rise of the Dalits and the Renewed Debate on Caste'. *Economic and Political Weekly* 29(26) (1994): 1589–1596.

Kulkarni, A.R. 'The Mahar Watan' in *Intersections* 121–140.

Mahipati. *Bhaktavijaya: Stories of Indian Saints*. trans. Justin E. Abbot and N.B. Godbole, 2 vols., nos. 9 and 10, in *The Poet Saints of Maharashtra* Series, Poona, 1933, 1934. Reprinted (New Delhi: Motilal Banarsidass, 1982).

Malhotra, Anshu. *Gender, Caste and Religious Identities: Restructuring Class in Colonial Punjab* (New Delhi: Oxford University Press, 2002).

Mokashi-Punekar, Rohini. *On the Threshold: Songs of Chokhamela* (New York: AltaMira Press, 2005).

Nagaraj, D.R. *The Flaming Feet: A Study of the Dalit Movement in India* (Bangalore: South Forum Press, 1993).

Novetzke, Christian Lee. *Religion and Public Memory* (NewYork: Columbia University Press, 2008).

Pollock, Sheldon. 'The Cosmopolitan Vernacular'. *The Journal of Asian Studies* 57(1) (1998): 6–39.

Ramaswamy, Vijaya. 'Women "In", Women "Out"'. In *Organizational and Institutional Aspects of Indian Religious Movements*, edited by J.T. O'Connell (Shimla: Indian Institute of Advanced Studies, 1999).

Ranade, R.D. *Pathway to God in Marathi Literature* (Mumbai: Bharatiya Vidya Bhavan, 1961 [1933]).

Rege, Sharmila. 'Dalit Women Talk Differently: A Critique of "Difference" and Towards a Dalit Feminist Standpoint Position'. *Economic and Political Weekly* 33(44) (1998): 39–46.

Sellergren, Sarah. 'Janabai and Kanhopatra: A Study of Two Women Sants'. In *Images of Women in Maharashtrian Literature and Religion*, edited by Anne Feldhaus, 213–38 (Albany: SUNY, 1996).

Srisakalsantgatha, 1967 [1923]. First volume. Collected by Srinanamaharaj Sakhre, edited by Kashinath Anant Joshi. Pune: Srisantwangmaya Prakashan Mandir.

Tulpule, S.G. *Classical Marathi Literature, Vol. X*. The History of Indian Literature Series (Wiesbaden: Otto Harrassowitz, 1979).

Zelliot, Eleanor. 'Eknath's *Bharuds*: The Sant as a Link between Cultures'. In *The Sants: Studies in a Devotional Tradition of India*, edited by Karine Schomer and Hugh McLeod (New Delhi: Motilal Banarsidass, 1987), 91–110.

______. 'Chokhamela and Eknath: Two *Bhakti* Modes of Legitimacy for Modern Change'. In *From Untouchable to Dalit: Essays on the Ambedkar Movement* (New Delhi: Manohar, 1992), 3–32.

Zelliot, Eleanor. 'A Medieval Encounter Between Hindu and Muslim: Eknath's Drama-Poem *Hindu-Turk Samvad*' in *India's Islamic Traditions, 711–1750*. Richard M. Eaton ed. (New Delhi: OUP, 2003 [1982]).

Zelliot, Eleanor and Rohini Mokashi-Punekar, eds. *Untouchable Saints: An Indian Phenomenon* (New Delhi: Manohar, 2005).

CHAPTER

8

Dissent in Kabir and the Kabir Panth

David N. Lorenzen

Over the years, my interest in the Kabir Panth and Kabir has often centred on the social dimensions of the beliefs and practices that they have advocated and, more specifically, on the dissent they have expressed against the more dominant socio-religious ideology of *varnashramadharma.*[1] In general, I

[1] See David N. Lorenzen, 'The Kabir Panth and Social Protest', in *The Sants: Studies in a Devotional Tradition of India*, ed. K. Schomer and W.H. McLeod (New Delhi: Motilal Banarsidass, 1987a), 281–303; 'The Social Ideologies of Hagiography: Sankara, Tukaram and Kabir', in *Religion and Society in Maharashtra*, ed. M. Israel and N.K. Wagle (Toronto: Centre for South Asian Studies, University of Toronto, 1987b), 92–114; 'Traditions of Non-caste Hinduism: The Kabir Panth', *Contributions to Indian Sociology* 21(2) (1987c), 264–283; *Kabir Legends and Ananta-das's Kabir Parachai* (Albany: State University of New York Press, 1991); ed., *Bhakti Religion in North India: Community Identity and Political Action* (Albany: State University of New York Press, 1995); *Praises for a Formless God: Nirguni Texts from North India* (Albany: State University of New York Press, 1996); 'The Life of Kabir in Legend', in *Studies in Early Modern Indo-Aryan Languages, Literature and Culture*, ed. Alan Entwistle and Carol Solomon (New Delhi: Manohar, 1999), 209–226; 'A *Vajrasuci* in Hindi', in *The Banyan Tree: Essays on Early Literature in New Indo-Aryan Languages, Vol. 1*, ed. Mariola Offredi (Delhi: Manohar, 2000), 441–55; 'Bhakti', in *The Hindu World*, ed. S. Mittal and G. Thursby (New York: Routledge, 2004), 185–209. A number of essays have been republished in David N. Lorenzen, *Who Invented Hinduism? Essays on Religion in History* (New Delhi: Yoda Press, 2006). Several of these essays also appear in Hindi translation in David N. Lorenzen, *Nirgun Santon ke Swapna*, trans. Dhirendra Bahadur Singh (New Delhi: Rajkamal Prakashan, 2010).

have argued in favour of the view that the social and religious dissent that Kabir and his followers have fostered has had important consequences, even though there never existed much chance for them to break the hegemony of upper-caste dominance. The present essay will criticize some of the arguments that have been used by other scholars to largely discount the importance of the socio-religious dissent promoted by Kabir and his followers against the *varnashramadharma* ideology. The essay will also discuss some of the ideas about Kabir's socio-religious ideology presented by Purushottam Agrawal in his new book, *Akath Kahani Prem ki: Kabir ki Kavita aur unka Samay*.[2] First, however, I need to, very briefly, review a few of the salient features of the dissent found in the compositions of Kabir and the Kabir Panth.

Kabir's compositions are remarkable for his insistence on the necessity for both religious and social reform. He attacks not only superficial and superstitious religious rituals in both Hindu religion and Islam but also the sacred authority of religious texts: the Vedas, the Puranas and the Koran. He also attacks the pretensions to social superiority of high-class persons, particularly Brahmins and *kazis*, often with amusing but quite vicious satire. Today, he would undoubtedly be hauled before a court of justice for his insults to both the Hindu and Muslim religions and for fomenting religious conflict.

The Kabir that most people are now familiar with is the Kabir of popular *bhajans*, songs whose lyrics were mostly composed in his name long after his death. In these *bhajans*, the element of sharp socio-religious dissent is partly muted, although by no means totally absent. To get an idea of the radical nature of Kabir's message, it is better to turn to the songs of the older collections – most notably those of the Sikh *Adi Granth*, the Dadu Panthi *Kabir-granthavali* and the Kabir Panthi *Kabir-bijak*.[3] Here, I will cite only one example, a song

---

[2] Purushottam Agrawal, *Akath Kahani Prem ki: Kabir ki Kavita aur unka Samay* (New Delhi: Rajkamal Prakashan, 2009).

[3] It is, however, interesting that the small number of songs (forty-eight) common to all (or almost all) the oldest manuscripts that W. Callewaert (Kabir 2000) used for his *Millennium Kabir* mostly contain very little social and religious dissent. Since Callewaeart could not find any very old manuscripts of the *Kabir-bijak*, he did not include this text for establishing his short list of forty-eight songs. Many of Kabir's most critical songs are in the *Bijak*. On the other hand, the large collections of early Kabir songs in the *Adi Granth* and the Dadu Panthi *Kabir-granthavali* also contain many critical songs. Perhaps the only explanation for the lack of such songs in Callewaert's short list is that this is simply an accidental artifact resulting from the small number of songs in the short list.

that is found in both the *Kabir-bijak* (*ram.* 39) and the *Kabir-granthavali* (*ram. ashtapadi* 3):

> He who taught the Muslim creed (*kalaman*) in the Kali age
> Was unable to seek out the power of the creation.
> According to karma, the actor performs his actions.
> The Vedas and the Muslim books are all worthless.
> According to karma, one became an avatar in the world.
> According to karma, one fixed the Muslim prayers.
> According to karma, circumcision or the sacred thread.
> Neither the Hindu nor the Turk knows the secret.
> Water and air were joined together,
> And all this turmoil was created.
> When *surati* is absorbed in the Void,
> On what basis can our caste be told?

The literature of the Kabir Panth is less known than the compositions of Kabir himself (although many popular *bhajans* attributed to Kabir probably originated among the sadhus of the Panth). Much of the Kabir Panthi literature takes the form of hagiographical legends about events in the life of Kabir. The earliest versions of these legends seem to be those found in the *Kabir Paracai* of the Ramanandi author, Anantadas (c. 1590), and in Priyadas's AD 1702 commentary on Nabhadas's *Bhaktamal*.[4] Neither Anantadas nor Priyadas were Kabir Panthis, but it remains likely that the legends first appeared among the followers of Kabir (whether or not they belonged to an organized Kabir Panth). Most of these legends involve confrontations between Kabir and representatives of either royal authority (kings and sultans) or religious authority (Brahmins, *kazi*s and mullahs).

One of the most popular of the legends tells how the people of Benaras – led by Kabir's own mother and various *kazi*s, Baniyas and Brahmins – went to complain about Kabir's activities to the Sultan, Sikandar Lodi. Sikandar promised to punish Kabir, but various efforts to do so miraculously failed. Sikandar finally had to apologize to Kabir and became his disciple. The social and religious dissent embodied in this legend, and most of the other legends about Kabir, is never very far from the surface.

---

[4] See Lorenzen, *Kabir Legends and Ananta-das's Kabir Parachai* and 'The Life of Kabir in Legend'. The former contains an edition and translation of the *Kabir Paracai.*

At one stage in my research on the Kabir Panth, I had the opportunity to make a catalogue of the manuscripts found in the collection of the Kabir Chaura Math library in Benaras. Among these manuscripts, two texts are of particular interest from the point of view of socio-religious dissent. Neither of the texts is explicitly identified as a Kabir Panthi text, but their presence as manuscripts in the Kabir Chaura library is obviously significant.

One is a Sanskrit text known as the *Saracandrika* (one copy with a Hindi commentary and one without). A version of this text was published in 1989.[5] The text is a collection of verses taken from various Puranas and other Sanskrit texts. The purpose of many of these verses is to argue that all persons of all castes have a right to salvation thanks to the virtues of *bhakti* religion and God's grace in the Kali Yuga. One such verse is as follows:

> Even a Candala is the best of munis,
> If he is centered on *bhakti* to Brahma.
> But without *bhakti* to Vishnu,
> Even a Brahmin (*dvija*) is the lowest of Dog-eaters (*svapaca*).[6]

This sort of dissent obviously concerns principally the religious or spiritual rights of low-caste persons (most notably, their right to salvation), not their civil rights (that is, their rights to equal justice and social, economic and political opportunity, or even their right to change their religion). Kabir himself goes much further than this when he attacks both religious and social pretensions to superiority head-on.

Here, a comparison with Europe Enlightenment is interesting. In late seventeenth and eighteenth centuries in Europe, two of the first and most notable pleas for religious toleration were made by John Locke and Voltaire. In both cases, the main arguments stressed that they were making a plea for *religious* equality and toleration, not a plea for equal civil rights between either persons of different religions or of different social classes. The first important Enlightenment text to expand the plea for equal rights to both the religious and civil spheres was probably Lessing's play, *Nathan the Wise*.[7]

The second text found in the Kabir Chaura manuscript collection relevant to the discussion of socio-religious dissent is a Hindi translation or adaptation of a

---

[5] *Gramtha-sara-candrika* (Fatepur, Shekhavati: Shri Sarasvati Pustakalay, 1989).

[6] Ibid., 6–7; attributed to *Padma Purana.*

[7] Lessing, Gotthold Ephraim, *Nathan the Wise.* Translated by William Taylor (Lexington, KY: Classic Drama Book Company, 2010).

Sanskrit text known as the *Vajrasuci Upanishad*.[8] Some of you may be familiar with this text. It was included, somewhat mischievously, by Radhakrishnan in his edition–translation of the eighteen principal Upanishads.[9] The history of the text goes back to a Buddhist text in Sanskrit known simply as the *Vajrasuci*, which is attributed to the first century scholar, Ashvaghosha. This text was reworked into the *Vajrasuci Upanisad* by a Hindu author – sometimes identified as the famous philosopher, Shankaracharya – at an unknown date. The date of the Hindi version is also unknown.

What makes this text, in its various versions, interesting is that it embodies a more or less systematic philosophical argument against the ontological basis of caste distinctions. If a person claims to be a Brahmin, the text argues, where can we locate the essence of this Brahminhood? Is it found in the *jiva*, the body, the *jati* or the *varna*? Or is Brahmanhood based on karma or on dharma? The text deconstructs each of these possibilities and concludes that the only real Brahmin is the person who knows Brahman, no matter which caste he (or perhaps even she...) may have been born into.

Several modern scholars have argued strongly against the importance and seriousness of socio-religious dissent in India, not only with regard to Kabir and the Kabir Panth but also with regard to low-caste Hindu religion in general. Louis Dumont and, following his lead, Michael Moffat have claimed that low-caste Hindu religious groups basically 'replicate' the beliefs and practices of high-caste (that is, Brahmin-led) groups.[10] According to this theory, lower castes create their own sets of rules about social and religious practices based on the same central concerns about the limits of the pure and impure and the importance of hierarchy that lie at the heart of Brahmanic socio-religious ideology. In this way, very low castes set up a social pecking order among themselves that replicates the more general pecking order of *varnashramadharma*-based society as a whole. Similarly, low-caste groups

[8] A short study and translation of the Hindi version of the text in the Kabir Chaura collection is found in Lorenzen, 'A *Vajrasuci* in Hindi'.

[9] See S. Radhakrishnan, ed. and trans., *The Principal Upanisads* (London: George Allen and Unwin, 1953), 935–938. The best edition of the Sanskrit text is that found in Sujitkumar Mukhopadhyaya, *The Vajrasuci of Asvaghosa* (Santiniketan: The Sino-Indian Cultural Society, 1950).

[10] Dumont, Louis. *Homo Hierarchicus: The Caste System and Its Implications* (Chicago: University of Chicago Press, 1980). Original French edition published in 1966. Moffat, Michael. *An Untouchable Community in South India* (Princeton: Princeton University Press, 1979).

create their own temples and religious officiants based on the model of upper-caste temples staffed by Brahmins.

This theory proposed by Dumont and Moffat bears more than a passing resemblance to the concepts of 'dominant ideology' and 'hegemony' that are found among Marxist thinkers, from Marx himself to Antonio Gramsci. Marx argued that the ideas of the ruling class are the dominant ideas of each epoch, and Gramsci extended this to emphasize the acceptance of the power of the ruling classes by the lower classes that they ruled. Nonetheless, most Marxist thinkers of voluntaristic Leninist sympathies, including Gramsci, allowed for the possibility of effective dissent against dominant ideologies and hegemony, though they often claimed that this would require a violent revolution. This dissent could come both from the proletarian class, whose material interests were aligned with such dissent, and from a section of the bourgeoisie that would join the proletarian movement and serve as its vanguard and spokespersons.

My own opposition to the ideas of Dumont and Moffat follows a similar voluntarist argument. In my view, it is in fact possible for individual thinkers and spokespersons to challenge the hegemony of dominant beliefs and practices and lead movements against them, even if the economic, political and ideological dominance of wealthier and more powerful groups puts strong limits on the amount of dissent that can be tolerated short of a violent revolution. These strong limits, at times, may force potentially dissenting subaltern groups into a pattern of replicating the ideas and institutions of dominant groups, but this is clearly not always the case.

A somewhat similar argument against the possibility of dissent, or at least against original new expressions of dissent, has been made, in the specific case of Kabir, by various scholars who have argued that Kabir's socio-religious ideas can only be explained with reference to the socio-religious ideas he inherited from his own family traditions. This argument was essentially initiated in the 1940s by two scholars: P.D. Barthwal and H.P. Dvivedi.[11] They argued that Kabir's religious and social ideas were largely determined by a family culture that must have been closely associated with the Nath Sampradaya of the Nath yogis, overlaid by a veneer of Islam acquired through the family's probably recent conversion to Islam. The major part of Kabir's socio-religious ideas, they claim, must have been inherited from the Nath and Islamic traditions of

[11] See P.D. Barthwal, 'Hindi Kavita mem Yog-pravah', in *Yog-pravah* (Varanasi: Shri Kashi Vidyapith, 1946[1930]), 54–78; *Traditions of Indian Mysticism: Based upon Nirguna School of Hindi Poetry* (New Delhi: Heritage, 1978[1936]); also, Hajari Prasad Dvivedi, *Kabir* (New Delhi: Rajakamal Parkasan, 1971[1942]).

his family. Roughly, this same argument has been adopted by several more recent scholars.[12]

In his new book on Kabir, Purushottam Agrawal has shown that this argument based on Kabir's family background has some interesting consequences that Barthwal, Dvivedi and others did not directly recognize.[13] One consequence is that the argument makes it very difficult to explain why it is that the most obvious association between Kabir's ideas and earlier traditions is with the non-orthodox Vaishnavism preached by his predecessors Namdev and Ramananda, and not Islam or yoga. More specifically, most of these scholars have rejected the possibility that Kabir could have been directly associated with Ramananda, whom tradition unanimously claims to have been Kabir's guru.

According to Agrawal, this family background argument is ultimately based on an intellectual hubris that reserves the right of independent thinking to contemporary university professors, and not even all of them. Agrawal's view is that Kabir was – as much as anyone can be – a highly independent thinker who experimented with several different religious ideologies present in late fifteenth century Benaras, and created his own new religious message out of an original intellectual synthesis of religious ideas available. In this synthesis, the sort of Vaishnavism proposed by Namdev and Ramananda was a particularly important ingredient. Agrawal accepts that Kabir was also influenced by the Naths but argues that Nath influence made only one of several contributions to Kabir's thought.

Agrawal convincingly argues that the scholarly consensus that claims that Ramananda was an orthoprax and conservative Brahmin who wrote and preached primarily in Sanskrit is, in fact, simply a myth spread in the early twentieth century by Ramanandi Sampradaya intellectuals as part of their competition with – and ultimately their separation from – the South Indian Srivaishnavas. According to Agrawal, much stronger evidence suggests that the real historical Ramananda was more likely the Hindi Ramananda who wrote Hindi songs similar to those of Kabir and was the guru of low-caste disciples like Kabir, Raidas, Pipa, Dhanna and Sen. Even this Ramananda, however, should be seen more as a precursor of Kabir rather than as a dominant influence. Kabir, in Agrawal's view, was his own man.

Another counter-argument that has been used against accepting the importance of low-caste dissent against dominant religious beliefs and practices

---

[12] See especially, Charlotte Vaudeville, *Kabir, Vol. 1* (Oxford: Clarendon Press, 1974).

[13] Agrawal, *Akath Kahani Prem ki*, 158–177.

is the theory that such dissent, when it appears, is mostly a blowing off of steam against oppression and has little further significance. Richard Eaton, for instance, has used this argument in order to minimize the importance of social dissent as a motive for conversion to Islam in pre-British India. Eaton characterizes 'the "religion of social liberation" theory' as one that claims 'that the Hindu caste system is a rigidly discriminatory form of social organization and that the lowest and most degraded castes, recognizing in Islam an ideology of social equality, converted to it en masse in order to escape Brahmanical oppression'.[14]

Basing himself in part on Louis Dumont's ideas about a low-caste replication of a dominant ideology of hierarchy in Indian society, Eaton argues against the 'religion of social liberation' theory that it:

> commits the fallacy of reading [equalitarian] the values of the present into the peoples or events of the past. Are we to assume that before their contact with Muslims, the untouchables of India possessed, as though they were familiar with the writings of Rousseau or Jefferson, some innate notion of the fundamental equality of all men denied them by an oppressive Brahmanical tyranny? To the contrary, it seems that Hindu society of medieval India was more influenced by what Louis Dumont calls the principle of *homo hierarchicus,* or of institutionalized inequality ...

Kabir, of course, lived well after Islam had already been well established in North India, but as one of the first low-caste poets whose verses have survived, there is hardly any doubt that he had a vision of basic human equality, without any necessity of his having read Rousseau or Jefferson.

A related and more important argument that Eaton and others use against the 'religion of social liberation' theory is that the conversion of low-caste persons to Islam – or in our case the Kabir Panth – has little or no effect on the everyday life of the converts. Eaton comments:

> Moreover, even if it were true that Islam had been presented as an ideology of social equality, there is abundant evidence that former Hindu communities failed upon conversion to improve their status in the social hierarchy and that, on the contrary, they simply carried over into Muslim society the same practice of birth-ascribed rank that they had had in Hindu society.[15]

---

[14] Richard M. Eaton, 'Approaches to the Study of Conversion to Islam in India', in *Religious Movements in South Asia, 600–1800*, ed. David N. Lorenzen (New Delhi: Oxford University Press, 2004[1985]), 109.

[15] Ibid.

In other words, even in the unlikely event that the low-caste converts had some idea of social equality, in practical terms, their conversion gained them virtually nothing.

When this argument is applied to the strong social and religious dissent expressed in Kabir's songs and verses, it is essentially claiming that this dissent is no more than a fantasy consolation for the insults and injuries suffered by low-caste persons in the course of their daily life in an oppressive society. Apart from this consoling function, it has no further significance. To me, this negative judgement seems not only implausible but also simply wrong.

One must, of course, accept the fact that economic and political realities impose strong limits on the amount of socio-religious dissent that Indian society has been willing to tolerate. Nonetheless, the 'conscious raising' embodied in the dissent found in Kabir's compositions has important practical consequences, both as a way of instilling a healthy amount of self-esteem in his followers and as a necessary prerequisite for any successful effort at social uplift. It is undoubtedly true that most Kabir Panthis in contemporary India have not been able to escape from the grinding poverty and poor educational levels that are the common inheritance of most low-caste persons. Nonetheless, I strongly suspect that, on average, they have done better than their caste fellows who are not followers of the Kabir Panth. Outside of India, Kabir Panthis – most of whom were originally indentured labourers brought to Trinidad, Guyana and Mauritius – have achieved a measure of economic success in their new countries not shared by most Kabir Panthis in India.

In the Sikh Panth, we have a vivid example of a religious movement that has made remarkable social, economic and political gains both in India and abroad. Kabir's songs and verses, of course, form a sizeable and integral part of the Sikh *Adi Granth*. Kabir's ideas also made an important contribution to the ideas found in the compositions of Guru Nanak and the other Sikh gurus. Would the success of the Sikh movement have been possible without Kabir's intellectual and religious influence on it? Any answer to this question has to remain quite speculative. One has to admit that the Sikhs had certain advantages that the Kabir Panthis did not have. Most importantly, a higher percentage of Sikhs traditionally had access to some education, most notably among the Sikhs belonging to the caste of Khatris, and a higher percentage of Sikhs managed to become landowning peasants, most notably among the many Sikhs belonging to the caste cluster of Jats. The military traditions of many Sikhs probably also contributed to the success of their community. Nonetheless, it seems to me obvious that the Sikhs were also helped in their rise to economic and political power by the ideology of social dissent fostered by Kabir's ideas.

The relative lack of economic and political success of the followers of the Kabir Panth as compared to that of the Sikhs, undoubtedly, probably stems largely from the Kabir Panthis' average lack of the educational, landowning and military advantages, and also possibly from their weaker sense of community identity. In recent years, however, there have been some signs of change. Nowadays, the Kabir Chaura branch of the Kabir Panth is being led by a strong personality, Acharya Vivekdas, who is attempting to put new life into the Panth through a great variety of projects that aim to attract people to the Panth and to Kabir's socio-religious message. Unlike most Hindu religious intellectuals, Vivekdas's political and social views are basically leftist, although they are now much less radical than when he took part in the Naxalbari movement as a boy. When he discusses social and political questions, his emphasis is on the contributions of Kabir and other *nirguni sant*s to social uplift and consciousness raising among the poor and oppressed; on their opposition to the social privileges of Brahmins and other high-caste people; on the similar hopes of the Indian independence movement and on the need to renew the now largely broken social promises of this movement. In a 2009 essay, published in a new edition of his edited volume, *Kabir Sahitya ki Prasangikta*, Acharya Vivekdas writes:

> Medieval *sants* initiated the *bhakti* movement. They opened a front against Brahmanism and prepared the model of a popular movement. By means of the bhakti movement the *sants* sent in motion the enterprise of giving birth to the empowerment of the poor, the oppressed, those left behind and without hope and gave them new life...Many sharp-tongued *sants* were born among the oppressed classes. The selfishness of the fanaticism and exclusivism of *varnashrama-dharma* had attempted to keep the majority of the people in ignorance of the truth.[16]

Vivekdas argues that if we follow the *sant*s, human unity and equality can still be achieved. Citing a song of Kabir, he comments:

> Mahadeva and Mohammad, Brahma and Adam, are all messengers of this [truth]. If any differences among them are nothing, only a difference of names, then how can there be opposition between Hindus and Muslims? We all live on this earth. In this matter, Kabir Sahab set before us a great ideal and pervasive doctrine...In reality this spiritual awakening gives birth to the spirit of independence which becomes the cause of enmity against those who commit

[16] Vivekdas, Acharya, ed., *Kabir Sahitya ki Prasangikta*, Second Edition (Varanasi: Kabirvani Prakashan, 2009), 240.

> crimes and oppress us. The oppressors want nothing to do with the spiritual unity of oppressed peoples...The medieval Sants understood this quite well and initiated a strong movement against those oppressors. This movement was a reawakening of social change and spiritual consciousness. On it were laid the foundations for nation-wide equality and unity.[17]

One can, of course, still argue that the modern struggles in India for the social uplift of the oppressed and downtrodden and equal human rights owe more to Rousseau, Jefferson and other thinkers of the European Enlightenment than to Kabir and the *sant*s, but this is clearly not the opinion of Acharya Vivekdas and his followers. In this matter, there is little doubt that Nehru and perhaps even Gandhi and Ambedkar were more influenced by European thinkers than by indigenous thinkers and poets like Kabir and the *sant*s. Nonetheless, there is also little doubt that the less Western-educated followers of the nationalist movement were more aware of, and influenced by, the pleas for human justice and equality coming precisely from these same indigenous thinkers and poets.

Another important argument about the role of dissent in Kabir put forward by Agrawal is that the religious and social ideologies of Ramananda and his disciples, and of their successors, in the *nirguni* current of religious poets, including the Sikhs and Dadu Panthis, were representative and instigators of an early, pre-colonial modernity that thrived under the Mughals, but then, mostly fell apart and lost most of its influence under the peculiar sort of colonial modernity imposed by the British colonial administration.[18] Referring back to what Sheldon Pollock has called the 'vernacular millennium', which began in about 1100, Agrawal writes:

> During the vernacular millennium, European and non-European societies were moving in the direction of modernity, each in its own way. Indian society was not a society without history as Hegel thought. Like the Europe of that time, India was travelling on the path of history. Europe and India were similar. The difference between them was that because of European imperialism, the spontaneous, integral development of Indian and other non-European societies met an obstacle. In colonized societies like India, indigenous (*deshaj*) modernity was blocked. As a result of the colonial situation, modernity took the form of a sharp break from tradition instead of a surge integral to the flow of tradition. Between tradition and modernity there rose up a dissociation or rupture of sensibility (*samvedana-vichchhed*). This dissociation of sensibility stands at the root of many of the problems of these societies. In the context

[17] Ibid., 244.

[18] Agrawal, *Akath Kahani Prem ki*.

> of Kabir, because of this dissociation of sensibility baseless things were given the rank of 'historical truths'. One such baseless thing was to regard Kabir as a marginal voice.[19]

For me, modernity is much too elusive a concept to have much analytical utility. Nonetheless, the central idea of Agrawal's argument seems clear and persuasive. He is suggesting that from about 1100 to about 1750 or 1800, society in India was developing in a manner that was separate from Europe but also similar in ways that we associate with the movement towards modern institutions and ideologies. The developing institutions and ideologies that Agrawal implicitly seems to be invoking are those of a less hierarchical society; a more religiously tolerant society; a more bureaucratic state with a deeper penetration into the lives of its members and (hopefully) a greater concern for their welfare; a wider distribution of scientific and humanistic knowledge (both literate and oral); and a better organized economic and commercial system using improved technology. In these ideas about modernity, Agrawal is not concerned with the more negative elements of modern life such as massive race-based slavery, religious inquisitions, more systematic military atrocities and the lack of traditional moral concern for kinsmen and fellow local residents.

The main value of Agrawal's argument is that it places the social and religious dissent of Ramananda (fl. c. 1450–1500), Kabir (fl. c. 1470–1520), Dadu (1544–1603), Guru Nanak (1469–1539) and their followers at the centre of the development of pre-colonial Indian society and not on the margins of this development. Agrawal clearly regards the early 'indigenous modernity' (*deshaj adhunikta*) fostered by Ramananda, Kabir and their fellows as basically a good thing, and here I fully agree.

What I am less in agreement about is Agrawal's implied estimate of a similar speed and depth of the overall modernizing trends in Europe and India. Imperialism was not simply a manifestation of the greed and search for glory of European kings, popes, merchants and military adventurers. It was a product of profound changes in European institutions – political, economic, scientific, religious and social – during the centuries after the near collapse of European civilization in the wake of the Black Death plagues of the second half of the fourteenth century.

The construction of huge historical generalizations is, of course, a highly controversial pastime. Nonetheless, I do think that one can conclude that after about 1450, Europe increased the rate of modernizing its commercial,

---

[19] Ibid., 30.

political, scientific, military and humanistic institutions so that by at least 1700, and probably much earlier, most of these institutions had a decisive advantage over their counterparts in India. The dramatic European advances in scientific knowledge and secular humanist thought during the sixteenth, seventeenth and eighteenth centuries are, of course, well known.[20] Scientists such as Copernicus (1473–1543), Kepler (1571–1630), Galileo (1564–1642) and Newton (1642–1727), and humanists such as Machiavelli (1469–1527), Erasmus (1469–1536), Montaigne (1533–92), Spinoza (1632–77), Hobbes (1588–1679), Locke (1632–1704), Voltaire (1694–1778) and Diderot (1713–84), merely represent some of the leaders of this revolutionary transformation of human knowledge and religious outlook. The technology and commercial policies that allowed the industrialization of Europe in the nineteenth century was largely built on these earlier developments.

India certainly had its own leading intellectuals during the period between 1450 and1750, but fewer of them seem to have had research interests similar to the European scientists and secular humanists. Future historical research such as the work that Charles Needham did on Chinese science may modify this picture, but the contrast between India and Europe in this period is clearly more than simply the result of a lack of scholarly interest in medieval Indian scientists and secular humanists.[21] The comments of Tapan Raychaudhuri about the low level of technology in the Mughal period apply, I think, equally well to Indian natural science in this period: 'In striking contrast to India's pre-eminence as an exporter of manufactured goods, her technology was remarkably backward in comparison with the other advanced civilizations of the period, especially western Europe and China'.[22]

---

[20] I am using the term 'secular humanist' in a general way to refer to a wide range of intellectuals whose main concerns were neither with natural science nor with theology. Some of these persons (including scientists) are often classed as 'humanists' in the more technical sense of the intellectuals of the European Renaissance (c. 1400–1600) who wrote about non-religious topics, often topics related to the revival of knowledge about pre-Christian Greek philosophy. On these Renaissance humanists, see Jacques Lafaye, *Por amor al griego: La nación europea, señorío humanista (siglos XIV–XVII)* (México: Fondo de Cultura Económica), 2005.

[21] Needham, Joseph. *Science and Civilisation in China.* 6 volumes (Cambridge: Cambridge University Press, 1954–2000).

[22] Tapan Raychaudhuri, 'Non-Agricultural Production, 1: Mughal India', in *The Cambridge Economic History of India: Volume I: c. 1200–c. 1750*, ed. Tapan Raychaudhuri and Irfan Habib (Cambridge: Cambridge University Press, 1982), 291.

The well-known Indian scholars who perhaps best fit the labels of scientists and secular humanists in this period include the historians Abu'l Fazl and Abdu'l Qadir Bada'uni, the astronomers who worked under Raja Jai Singh II of Rajasthan between 1722 and 1739 when he constructed his famous astronomical observatories; the logician–philosophers of the *navya–nyaya* school who wrote after Gangesha (c. 1350); and philosophical grammarians such as Bhattoji Dikshita (c. 1590), Konda Bhatta (c. 1640) and Nagesha Bhatta (c. 1714).[23]

Agrawal's argument for an indigenous Indian early modernity depends on an implicit comparison of Ramananda, Kabir, Guru Nanak and Dadu Dayal as early modern intellectuals somewhat analogous to (and on average, somewhat earlier than) Machiavelli, Montaigne, Spinoza and Hobbes. Similarly, Agrawal seems to be implicitly comparing the freedom of thought and religious tolerance permitted and fostered by the Lodi sultans and the Mughal emperors, most notably Akbar, with the patronage and toleration of scientists and secular humanists by European monarchs and popes.

Can we claim that these implicit comparisons are convincing or plausible? In general, I think we can. On the other hand, there are some obvious important differences that should be noted. Taken together, many of these differences can help explain why the early modernity of India was relatively unsuccessful when compared to the early modernity of Europe. Furthermore, at least in terms of intellectual change, early modernity in India fell behind that of Europe well before British colonization of India took place, that is, well before about 1750.

At the risk of making even more controversial wide historical generalizations, I want to argue that the main differences between the intellectual development of early modern Europe and early India can be traced to two basic causes. First, the writings of early European secular humanists and scientists tended to be less religious than those of their Indian counterparts, even in cases where the Europeans were religious in their personal life and sometimes wrote about religious topics. In the period 1450–1750, many intellectuals in both Europe and India criticized existing religious institutions and customs. Here, Kabir is certainly an excellent example. In Europe, however, many of the more radical humanists and Enlightenment thinkers wrote directly against religion itself

---

[23] On *navya–nyaya*, see B.K. Matilal, *The Navya–Nyaya Doctrine of Negation: The Semantics and Ontology of Negative Statements in Navya–Nyaya Philosophy* (Cambridge, MA: Harvard University Press, 1968). On the philosophical grammarians, see H.G. Coward and K. Kunjunni Raja, *The Encyclopedia of Indian Philosophies: The Philosophy of the Grammarians,* Vol. 5 (New Delhi: Motilal Banarsidass, 1990).

and not just against existing religious institutions. Here, Spinoza and Diderot are good examples. As Jonathan Israel has shown in his recent work on the radical Enlightenment in Europe, the number of such radically anti-religious intellectuals was in fact quite large and very influential.[24] I do not think they had many similar Indian counterparts.

A second important difference between intellectuals in early modern Europe and early modern India was that European intellectuals tended to be somewhat less dependent on direct financial patronage from kings and popes than their Indian counterparts. Many European intellectuals were associated with universities that were at least partly independent of both the state and the church.[25] Many important European universities had already been founded in the eleventh and twelfth centuries. These included Bologna, Paris, Salamanca and others. The traditional curriculum in these universities was usually divided into four faculties: arts, theology, medicine and law. Although most of these universities were initially tied to the Catholic Church, most of their students aimed at secular careers in law, medicine, business and government. During the period 1400–1600, these universities increased dramatically in size and number, broke many of their ties with the church and accepted increasing numbers of humanist professors who tended to reject traditional scholastic theology, even those like Erasmus who had a religious vocation. By about 1600, many secular-minded mathematicians and scientists had found employment in these universities, the most famous example being Galileo. In 1732, a Catholic missionary to China founded a Chinese College (Naples, Italy) to teach Chinese language and Chinese culture, the first European institution dedicated principally to the study of Asia. Today, this has become the state-financed Università degli Studi di Napoli 'L'Orientale'. By the mid-eighteenth century, university chairs in Sanskrit language had been created in several existing French and German universities.

---

[24] Jonathan Israel, *A Revolution of the Mind: Radical Enlightenment and the Intellectual Origins of Modern Democracy* (Princeton: Princeton University Press, 2010), presents a convenient summary of his more detailed discussions in earlier books.

[25] Convenient discussions on the development of European universities can be found in Willis Rudy, *The Universities of Europe, 1100–1914: A History* (Rutherford: Associated University Presses, 1984) and in Hilde de Ridder-Symoens, ed., *Universities in the Middle Ages* (Cambridge: Cambridge University Press, 1992) and ed., *Universities in Early Modern Europe, 1500–1800* (Cambridge: Cambridge University Press, 1996).

At a somewhat later date, particularly in eighteenth century Europe, other relatively independent institutions for intellectuals developed, including debating salons (chiefly in France); coffee houses; commercial (and sometimes clandestine) publishing houses; secret societies, such as those of the freemasons and scientific societies, such as the Royal Society of London founded in 1660. Direct patronage by church and state remained important for most European intellectuals, but such institutions of the incipient 'public sphere' made it possible for many intellectuals to live and work more independently.

In India, on the other hand, most highly educated intellectuals remained employed directly in royal courts, temples, *maths*, *khanaqahs* and madrasas. Semi-independent universities were fewer and smaller than their European counterparts. Similarly, more independent, 'public sphere' intellectual institutions, such as commercial publishing houses, coffee houses, debating salons, secret societies and scientific societies, evidently were less influential in early modern India. Under an enlightened and generous ruler such as Akbar (ruled 1556–1605), the lack of independent sources of financing for a life as a scientist or secular intellectual perhaps did not matter much, but Akbar was certainly unusual in the way he patronized open religious and intellectual debate. Most Indian rulers of the period were less generous and much less intellectually curious and tolerant. None of Akbar's successors among the Mughal emperors continued equally enlightened policies in this regard, and his great grandson Aurangzeb is, of course, well known for his attempts to impose orthodox, conservative Islamic norms on the intellectuals patronized by the imperial court.

All this leaves the independent religious and intellectual traditions of *nirguni* poets and thinkers such as Ramananda, Kabir, Guru Nanak and Dadu somewhat out on a limb. All were relatively free of the need to be financed either by the royal court or by established religious institutions like temples, but all were evidently dependent on alms and contributions from lay followers who expected to receive a religious message, not a lecture about atheism, history or political philosophy. It is also clear that Ramananda, Kabir, Guru Nanak and Dadu were, in fact, personally religious thinkers and, with the possible exception of Ramananda, were not deeply learned in the niceties of Hindu scholastic theology, mathematics or natural science. They fostered a radical religious and social message among their followers, but this alone – even if their message had received more royal support and even if European imperial powers had not intervened in Indian affairs – probably could not have given the early indigenous modernity of India the ability to compete on an equal footing with eighteenth century Europe.

Whatever might hypothetically have happened if the Indian indigenous modernity fostered by Kabir and other *nirguni* poets had been allowed to develop further, the failures of this indigenous modernity made the impact of colonial modernity, in the form of European scientific and philosophical thought, much more disruptive to Indian society and culture than the modernity that otherwise might have been. Agrawal is undoubtedly correct to suggest that in early modern India, there was once a possibility that a radical intellectual and social movement could evolve out of the compositions of Kabir and other *nirguni* poets, but Agrawal's arguments about why and when this potential largely failed to be realized seem less convincing.

Turning to present-day India, moreover, it remains to be seen whether or not Kabir's ideas still have the potential to be used as an important resource for a new radical intellectual and social movement. As far as the present-day Kabir Panth is concerned, despite efforts to foster intellectual independence and social uplift on the part of a few contemporary leaders, there remain the sizeable obstacles of the great weight of more orthodox Hindu tradition and the long-established vested interests of Indian society. Another obstacle is the gradually diminishing role of religion in modern society, the very gradual process of secularization. Whatever one wants to make of the recent rise of fundamentalist religious movements – Christian, Islamic, Jewish and Hindu – throughout the world, I think it is fairly obvious that, today, religious beliefs and practices generally play a smaller role in the daily life of most people, including most Indians, than they once did, and I am pretty sure that this is also the case for most other traditional Hindu sects in North India. New Hindu sects have undoubtedly arisen in this period, but they seem to me to be mostly superficial and probably ephemeral movements even in the case of the strongest ones such as those of Sai Baba and Osho.

In these circumstances, what will happen to the Kabir Panth in the future? My rather pessimistic guess is that, over time, the influence of the Panth over the lives of its followers and the total numbers of these followers will continue to decline. In terms of legal rights, both religious and civil, many of the battles of low-caste persons that Kabir fostered have already been won through the creation of the modern Indian nation-state and constitution. Nonetheless, it is also obvious that in practice, most of the economic, social and even religious disabilities of the Kabir Panth's low-caste followers still remain. Whether or not Kabir Panthi reformers like Archarya Vivekdas will be able to strengthen the community and have a significant impact on the social, political, economic and religious uplift of its members remains an open question.

References

Barthwal, P.D. 'Hindi Kavita mem Yog-pravah'. In *Yog-pravah*, 54–78 (Varanasi: Shri Kashi Vidyapith, 1946 [1930]).

———. *Traditions of Indian mysticism: Based upon Nirguna School of Hindi Poetry* New Delhi: Heritage, 1978 [1936]).

Coward, Harold G. and K. Kunjunni Raja. *The Encyclopedia of Indian Philosophies: The Philosophy of the Grammarians,* Vol. 5 (New Delhi: Motilal Banarsidass, 1990).

Dumont, Louis. *Homo Hierarchicus: The Caste System and Its Implications* (Chicago: University of Chicago Press, 1980). Original French edition published in 1966.

Dvivedi, Hajari Prasad. *Kabir* (New Delhi: Rajakamal Parkasan, 1971 [1942]).

Eaton, Richard M. 'Approaches to the Study of Conversion to Islam in India'. In *Religious Movements in South Asia, 600–1800*, edited by David N. Lorenzen (New Delhi: Oxford University Press, 2004 [1985]), 105–127.

Gramtha-sara-candrika (Fatepur, Shekhavati: Shri Sarasvati Pustakalay, 1989).

Israel, Jonathan. *A Revolution of the Mind: Radical Enlightenment and the Intellectual Origins of Modern Democracy* (Princeton: Princeton University Press, 2010).

Kabir. *The Millennium Kabir Vani: A Collection of Pad-s*. Edited by Winand M. Callewaert, with Swapna Sharma and Dieter Taillieu (New Delhi: Manohar, 2000).

Lafaye, Jacques. *Por amor al griego: La nación europea, señorío humanista (siglos XIV–XVII)* (México: Fondo de Cultura Económica, 2005).

Lorenzen, David N. 'The Kabir Panth and Social Protest'. In *The Sants: Studies in a Devotional Tradition of India*, edited by K. Schomer and W.H. McLeod, 281–303 (New Delhi: Motilal Banarsidass, 1987a).

———. 'The Social Ideologies of Hagiography: Sankara, Tukaram and Kabir'. In *Religion and Society in Maharashtra*, edited by M. Israel and N.K. Wagle, 92–114 (Toronto: Centre for South Asian Studies, University of Toronto, 1987b. Also republished in Lorenzen, 2006).

———. 'Traditions of Non-caste Hinduism: The Kabir Panth'. *Contributions to Indian Sociology* 21, no. 2 (1987c): 264–83. Also republished in Lorenzen, 2006.

———. *Kabir Legends and Ananta-das's Kabir Parachai* (Albany: State University of New York Press, 1991).

———, ed. *Bhakti Religion in North India: Community Identity and Political Action* (Albany: State University of New York Press, 1995). This book contains my essays, 'The Historical Vicissitudes of Bhakti Religion' (pp 1–32) and 'Lives of Nirguni Saints' (181–211).

———. *Praises for a Formless God: Nirguni Texts from North India* (Albany: State University of New York Press, 1996).

______. 'The Life of Kabir in Legend'. In *Studies in Early Modern Indo-Aryan Languages, Literature and Culture*, edited by Alan Entwistle and Carol Solomon (New Delhi: Manohar, 1999), 209–226. Also republished in Lorenzen, 2006.

______. 'A *Vajrasuci* in Hindi'. In *The Banyan Tree: Essays on Early Literature in New Indo-Aryan Languages, Vol. 1*, edited by Mariola Offredi, 441–455 (New Delhi: Manohar, 2000).

______. 'Bhakti'. In *The Hindu World*, edited by S. Mittal and G. Thursby, (New York: Routledge, 2004), 185–209.

______. *Who Invented Hinduism? Essays on Religion in History* (New Delhi: Yoda Press, 2006).

______. *Nirgun Santon ke Swapna*. Translated by Dhirendra Bahadur Singh (New Delhi: Rajkamal Prakashan, 2010).

Matilal, Bimal Krishna. *The Navya-Nyaya Doctrine of Negation: The Semantics and Ontology of Negative Statements in Navya-Nyaya Philosophy* (Cambridge, MA: Harvard University Press, 1968).

Moffat, Michael. *An Untouchable Community in South India.* Princeton: Princeton University Press, 1979.Agrawal, Purushottam. *Akath Kahani Prem ki: Kabir ki Kavita aur unka Samay* (New Delhi: Rajkamal Prakashan, 2009).

Mukhopadhyaya, Sujitkumar. *The Vajrasuci of Asvaghosa* (Santiniketan: The Sino-Indian Cultural Society, 1950). Contains the Sanskrit texts of Aśvaghosa′s *Vajrasūcī* and the *Vajrasucy-upanisad*, each based on several manuscripts, and a translation of the former text.

Needham, Joseph. *Science and Civilisation in China.* 6 volumes (Cambridge: Cambridge University Press, 1954–2000).

Radhakrishnan, S., ed. and trans. *The Principal Upanisads* (London: George Allen and Unwin, 1953).

Raychaudhuri, Tapan. 'Non-Agricultural Production, 1: Mughal India'. In *The Cambridge Economic History of India: Volume I: c. 1200–c. 1750*, edited by Tapan Raychaudhuri and Irfan Habib (Cambridge: Cambridge University Press, 1982), 261–307.

Ridder-Symoens, Hilde de, ed. *Universities in the Middle Ages* (Cambridge: Cambridge University Press, 1992).

______, ed. *Universities in Early Modern Europe, 1500–1800* (Cambridge: Cambridge University Press, 1996).

Rudy, Willis. *The Universities of Europe, 1100–1914: A History* (Rutherford: Associated University Presses, 1984).

Vaudeville, Charlotte. *Kabir,* Vol. 1 (Oxford: Clarendon Press, 1974).

Vivekdas, Acharya, ed. *Kabir Sahitya ki Prasangikta*, Second Edition (Varanasi: Kabirvani Prakashan, 2009).

CHAPTER

9

Devotion and Dissent of Punjabi Dalit *Sant* Poets

Raj Kumar Hans

The making of the Punjabi society, a frontier society, for the last 3,000 years has been a fascinating story of complex paradoxes. If the Punjab served as a theatre of warfare, it has also been an abode of sages, seers and *sant* poets. Perpetual political and ideological contestation did not necessarily close the doors to meditative contemplations. Even if the established religions, including the new ones, could not avoid sectarian manifestations, the universal spirituality kept the doors open for egalitarian inclusiveness cutting across all divisive lines. If the rise of Sikhism as a new religious ideology was a popular expression of egalitarian urges and came to offer respectable space to the untouchables from the sixteenth to the eighteenth century, it also degenerated to Brahmanical caste praxis by the mid-nineteenth century. Meanwhile, the Dalit *sant* poets, as part of the tradition, offer a seemingly paradoxical response of devotion and dissent. We have four major Punjabi Dalit poets emerging from the last quarter of the seventeenth century to the first quarter of the twentieth century who were soaked in the contemplative world of knowledge and spirituality, while seeking an egalitarian and just society. The Punjabi Dalit literary tradition begins with Bhai Jaita alias Jeevan Singh (c. 1655–1704), who became part of the guru's household as he had carried the severed head of Guru Teg Bahadur from Delhi to Anandpur, and in his late years, composed a devotional epic poem, *Sri Gur Katha*, around Guru Gobind Singh's life at the turn of the eighteenth century.[1] Our second saint poet,

[1] Bhai Jaita's family had three generations long association with Sikh religion, and his father, Sadanand, an accomplished musician, became a life-long companion to Guru Teg Bahadur as Mardana had been to Guru Nanak. In fact, Jaita had grown up

Sadhu Wazir Singh (c. 1790–1859), attained the status of *Brahmgyani*[2] and prolifically composed philosophical, spiritual and social poetry. The next Dalit writer, Sant Ditta Ram alias Giani Ditt Singh (1850–1901), emerged as poet, polemicist, journalist, orator and ardent Sikh missionary and left behind around fifty books to his credit.[3] Our last Dalit intellectual poet for the purpose of this

as part of the guru's household due to his father's proximity to the ninth guru. It was in this context that, when Bhai Jaita brought the severed head of Guru Teg Bahadur and presented it to the young Gobind in 1675, the latter was so overwhelmed with emotions that he embraced Jaita warmly and pronounced, '*Ranghrete Guru ke Bete*' (Ranghretas, the untouchables, are guru's own sons). Jaita had turned out to be a fearless and daring Sikh warrior endearing himself so much to the tenth guru that he was declared the '*Panjwan Sahibzada*' (fifth son) in addition to his own four *sahibzada*s. He was killed in a fierce battle with Mughal armies in 1704. It is worth noting that his epic composition has eluded the notice of scholars of Sikh literature and history whose efforts to unearth the literature and materials pertaining to the Sikh tradition are otherwise remarkable. The manner in which Bhai Jaita had been integrated not only in the Sikh religion but also in the family of Guru Gobind Singh, it is understandable any other identity would have been meaningless to him. His devotion to the Sikh gurus and their philosophy was complete, subsuming his identity as Ranghreta into his identity as a Sikh as he says: '*Jayayte taranhar gur, taar diye ranghretde, Gur paras ne kar diye, ranghrete gur betde.* (O! Jaite, the saviour guru has saved the ranghretas. The pure guru has adopted ranghretas as his sons). For details, see Samsher Singh Ashok, *Mazhbi Sikhan da Itihas*, Second Edition (Amritsar: Bhai Chatar Singh Jeevan Singh, 2001), 76–89. His composition, *Sri Gur Katha*, was first published in Naranjan Arifi's *Ranghrehtian da Itihas (Adi Kal ton 1850 Tak)*, Part I (Amritsar: Literature House, 1993). Baldev Singh also gives this poem at the end of his novel, *Panjwan Sahibjada* (Ludhiana: Chetna Prakashan, 2005); also, see Giani Nishan Singh Gandiwind, *Shaheed Baba Jeevan Singh: Jeevan, Rachna te Viakhia* (Amritsar: Bhai Chatar Singh Jeevan Singh, 2008),

2 *Brahmgyani* is the one who has realized and attained knowledge of the supreme cosmic power, the 'Brahaman, the one non-personal, all-pervading, ineffable Reality'. See Charlotte Vaudeville, 'Sant Mat: Santism as the Universal Path to Sanctity', in *The Sants: Studies in a Devotional Tradition of India*, ed. Karine Schomer and W.H. McLeod (New Delhi: Motilal Banarsidass, 1987), 26. 21–24

3 Ditt Singh was born in an untouchable Ramdasia (Chamar) caste. He studied Gurmukhi, prosody, Vedanta and *Niti Sastra*, and learnt Urdu. He started his apprenticeship as a preacher and teacher and earned the title of Giani (the knowledgeable) during his teens. For his autobiographical notes, see *Mera ate Sadhu Daya Nandji da Sambad,* Lahore: Khalsa Press, 1900 (Dialogue between Dayanand and Me), n.d. Also, see Dr Karnail Singh Somal, *Bhai Ditt Singh Gyani:*

essay, Sadhu Daya Singh Arif (1894–1946), came to master the Gurmukhi, Urdu, Persian, Arabic and Sanskrit scripts and languages with the help of several non-formal teachers who were stunned by his sharp intellect. Not only did he study me Vedas, Puranas, Granth Sahib and Koran, he also read a wide range of secular literature and had also reached the stage of *Brahmgyani* like Sadhu Wazir Singh, which is apparent from his assuming the title of 'Arif' as much as it comes from his own compositions.

All our four Dalit poets have a complex relationship with Sikhism. While Jaita reflects complete devotion not only to the ninth and tenth gurus because of his lived experience but also to the Sikh philosophy, Wazir Singh goes

---

Jeevan, Rachna te Sakhshiat (Life, Works and Personality of Bhai Ditt Singh Gyani), Second Edition (Amritsar: Singh Brothers, 2005). He recievel his spiritual instructions at the hands of Gubakash Singh Gulabdasi of Teur village in Ambala district and started preaching in his teens, and at about the age of 17 years, he shifted to the main Gulabdasi centre at Chathianwala, near Kasur, in Lahore district. For the details on the sect, see Gian Inder Singh Sevak, 'Gulabdasi Sampardaye: Rachna te Vichar' (Gulabdasi Sect: Works and Ideas) (PhD thesis, Guru Nanak Dev University, 1984); Kapoor, *Sadhu Gulab Das Navaratan* (Patiala: Punjabi University, 1987). It was at Chathianwala that he composed his first two books of poetry: the love-lore *Shirin Farhad* and *Abla Nind*. Not long afterwards, under the influence of Jawahir Singh, formerly a follower of the Gulabdasi sect, he joined the Arya Samaj. But after entering into dialogue with Swami Dayanand on his visit to Lahore in 1877, he was drawn into the Sikh fold by Bhai Gurmukh Singh, then an active figure in the Singh Sabha movement. Ditt Singh's scholarly talents came in handy for the Sikh movement. The Lahore Singh Sabha floated a weekly newspaper, the *Khalsa Akhbar*, in 1886. He assumed editorship of the paper in 1887, which he continued till his death in 1901. A detailed account of Ditt Singh's contribution to Punjabi journalism is available in chapter 4, 'Giani Ditt Singh da Punjabi Patarkari nu Yogdan' (Contribution of Giani Ditt Singh to Punjabi Journalism), in Narinder Singh Kapoor, *Giani Dit Singh: Jiwan te Rachna* (Punjabi) (Patiala: Punjabi University, 1987), 98–124. Meanwhile, he was also appointed as a professor of Punjabi at the Oriental College. Even though a towering figure and leader in the limelight, he could not escape the overt and covert assault of untouchability from his fellow and follower Sikhs. For an early biography of Ditt Singh written from the angle of abolishing caste and untouchability from among the Sikhs, see Daljeet Singh, *Singh Sabha da Modhi arthat Jeevan Britant Giani Ditt Singh Ji* (The Founder of the Singh Sabha or the Life Description of Giani Ditt Singhji) (Amritsar: Shromani Khalsa Bradari Prabhandak Committee, n.d.). And it seems that despite being reminded that he belonged to an untouchable family, he was suffused with Sikh consciousness devoted as he was to the Sikh philosophy.

beyond devotional religiosity to seek liberation by enmeshing diverse spiritual traditions from Advaita to Sufi. Of the next two, while Ditt Singh grows from a Vedantist to an ardent spokesman of pristine Sikhism, becoming the pillar of the Singh Sabha movement, Daya Singh's didactic poetry is a fine example of the composite heritage of Advaitic 'Hinduism', Sufistic Islam and Sikhism. In our first and third poets, namely, Bhai Jaita and Giani Ditt Singh, we find complete devotion and dedication to Sikhism, while our second and fourth poets, both carrying the honorific title Sadhu, namely, Wazir Singh and Daya Singh, though deeply spiritual, reflect strong dissent within the dominant religious traditions; in the former, there is a definite stamp of dissent that persists through his life, and in the latter, the dissidence gets gradually dissolved into devotion to the Sikh philosophy. Indeed, the established and dominant literary and even historical tradition is hardly aware of this rich array of Dalit intellectual practice and even when it is known, it is not recognized. This essay will focus on the spirituality of Wazir Singh and Daya Singh expressed in their powerful poetry as they offer the best of 'devotion' and 'dissent' coming from the Punjabi Dalits in the nineteenth and first part of the twentieth centuries.

The Sikh Context

Questions of Dalit spirituality and of devotion and dissent within the Sikh tradition necessitate contextualization of the tradition itself. There is a broad understanding, if not complete consensus, among scholars that the Punjab had witnessed a substantial weakening of Brahmanical ideology with the emergence and growing strength of egalitarian religious currents and movements, such as Islam and the Sikh religion. Hence, the pain of untouchability for Dalits was far less severe here than compared to other regions of the subcontinent.[4] The Nath yogis, Hindu *sant*s, Sufi *pir*s and Sikh gurus had severally worked towards mitigating untouchability in Punjabi society. The Sikh gurus succeeded in articulating and putting together egalitarian ideas at one place. Guru Granth Sahib emerges as the world's unique text of spiritual wisdom. It comprises the compositions of six of the ten Sikh gurus and contributions of thirty-one *sant*s, Sufis and *bhatt*s of diverse socio-ethnic backgrounds. This makes the Guru Granth Sahib the most inclusive and non-sectarian expression of spirituality in history. Spread over 1,450 pages (5,894 verses minutely set to thirty-one

[4] See Harish K. Puri, 'Introduction', in *Dalits in Regional Context* (Jaipur and New Delhi: Rawat Publications, 2004), 323.

classical musical ragas or tones), the Guru Granth Sahib[5] seeks to sever the bondage of man-made ideologies and systems of thought and activates the dormant connection between each of us and the surrounding phenomena of life. Instead of giving a dogmatic or absolutist message, it seeks to build up spiritual awareness and searching through a life-long process of living and learning for the most liberating, empowered condition of human life. Nikky-Guninder Kaur Singh puts it aptly:

> The Guru Granth provided an excellent example of going beyond particular affiliations and loyalties into the universal basis of religion. 'There is One Being, Truth Is Its Name' forms the fundamental principle of Sikh scripture. The Sikh vision of the Ultimate encompasses and transcends all space, time, and gender, and cannot be imaged in any specific form. Such a perception shatters narrow and rigid barriers between peoples and enables an *inclusive* attitude towards followers from different religious and racial backgrounds.[6]

The Sikh religion, with Guru Granth Sahib, has been seen as 'emancipatory' by Gurnam Singh.[7] One possible way to reach out to the essence, the core

---

[5] See Gurinder Singh Mann, *The Making of Sikh Scripture* (New Delhi: Oxford University Press, 2001); Pashaura Singh, *The Guru Granth Sahib: Canon, Meaning and Authority* (New Delhi: Oxford University Press, 2002).

[6] Nikky-Guninder Kaur Singh, '*Gurbani* in English Translating Celestial Poetry', *Sikh Review*, June 2000, http://www.sikhreview.org/junc2000/heritage.htm; emphasis in original (accessed on: 4 February 2009).

[7] Gurnam Singh, 'Sikhism's Emancipatory Discourses: Some Critical Perspectives', *Sikh Formations: Religion, Culture, Theory* 2, no. 2 (2006), 135–151. This valuable suggestion came from Valerie Kaur in her thoughtful essay, 'A Liberation Philosophy and Border Thinking', that appeared in the November 2002 issue of *SikhSpectrum.com Monthly* (last accessed on: 24/03/2008). She introduces the Latin American thought as she opens up her essay: 'Latin American philosopher Enrique Dussel provides a philosophy of liberation that aims to empower and decolonize marginalized communities. His contemporary, Walter Mignolo, conceptualizes the role of border thinkers, intellectuals who move between dominant and marginalized communities in order to generate a process of intellectual, economic, and social liberation'. She argues that 'Latin American and South Asian scholars can understand the development of Sikhism, a Northern Indian religion born in the late 1400s, as a valuable kind of liberation philosophy and an instance of border thinking'. See *SikhSpectrum.com* 6 November 2002, http://www.sikhspectrum.com/112002/valerie_k.htm

of the gurus' message, is to see it as part of the 'philosophy of liberation' as propounded by Latin American philosopher Enrique Dussel. Dussel asserts:

> Philosophy of liberation is pedagogical activity stemming from a praxis that roots itself in proximity of teacher–pupil, thinker–people. Although pedagogical, it is a praxis conditioned by political (and erotic) praxis. Nevertheless, as pedagogical, its essence is theoretical and speculative. Theoretical action the poietic intellectual illuminative activity of the philosopher, sets out to discover and expose (in the exposition and risk of the life of the philosopher), in the presence of an entrenched system, all moments of negation and all exteriority lacking justice. For this reason it is an analectical pedagogy of liberation. That is, it is the magisterium that functions in the name of the poor, the oppressed, the other, the one who like a hostage within the system testifies to the fetishism of its totalization and predicts its death in the liberating action of the dominated.[8]

The very word 'Sikh' denotes a relationship between the guru (teacher) and Sikh (pupil). And the whole Sikh movement arose out of the proximity of thinker–people, an organic relationship between gurus and people, and at the height of thought, the merging of the two (*aape gur chela*). The Guru Granth Sahib is magisterial[9] that resists all systems of oppression and injustice especially perpetrated on the poor. As it speaks in the name of the low, the poor, the oppressed, Guru Granth Sahib envelops the philosophy of liberation. So much so that Guru Nanak, coming from the upper caste of Khatris, identifies completely with the lowest (Dalit) of the Indian social order as he says:

> *Neechan andar neech jati, Neechi hun ati neech*
> *Nanak tin ke sang sath, Vadian siyon kya rees*
> *Jithe neech sanmalian, Tithe nadr teri bakhshish*
>
> (I am the lowest of the low castes; low, absolutely low;
> I am with the lowest in companionship, not with the so-called high.
> Blessing of god is where the lowly are cared for)[10]

---

[8] Enrique Dussel, *Philosophy of Liberation*, trans. Aquilina Martinez and Christine Morkovsky (Maryknell, New York: Orbis Books, 1985), 178.

[9] Mann, *The Making of Sikh Scripture*, 133, says, it 'is treated in such a way as to manifest its royal status within the community. It is always robed in silk or expensive brocade and is displayed on a canopied throne, in a well-lit setting'.

[10] As cited in Harish K. Puri, 'Scheduled Castes in Sikh Community: A Historical Perspective', *Economic and Political Weekly* 38(26) (2003), 2694.

He challenges the Brahmanical dismissal of the low, the untouchable, by becoming one with the latter. He destroys the hierarchical systems – social as well as political. To Dussel, the 'praxis of liberation has been the cause of its unwelcome, its nonacceptance by the system'.[11] The Nanakian philosophy, the liberation philosophy, was unacceptable to the religious and political systems right from the beginning. Hence the persecutions: first of Nanak, then of Arjun and Teg Bahadur and finally, of Gobind Singh. These persecutions were symbolic of the subversion of the 'order' and 'law' that reached its climax in the system's war against Guru Gobind Singh as Dussel puts it:

> Thus when the oppressed who struggles against the death that the system assigns to him begins through the praxis of liberation the struggle for life, novelty erupts in history 'beyond' the being of the system. A new philosophy, a positive one, necessarily makes its appearance. The novelty is not original nor primarily philosophical; it is original and primarily historical and real; it is the liberation of the oppressed. It is secondarily a philosophical theory as a strategic 'instrument' or weapon of liberation itself.[12]

The outcome of such attempts to silence the liberation thought was the eruption of novelty, the 'weapon of liberation', the Khalsa.[13] The 'real' historical force emerged out of the long gestation of the liberation 'praxis' and 'philosophy' that not only fully integrated the 'untouchables' into the struggle for liberation but succeeded in abolishing the racist practice of untouchability in Sikh practice. But history had something else in store for the Dalits of Punjab as caste and untouchability was to re-enter the body politic of Sikh religion in the changed circumstances of Ranjit Singh's rule and subsequent colonial dispensation.

---

[11] Dussel, *Philosophy of Liberation*, 180.

[12] Enrique Dussel, 'Philosophy and Praxis (Provisional Thesis for a Philosophy of Liberation)', in *Philosophical Knowledge*, ed. John B. Brough et al. (Washington: Catholic University of America, 1980), 108–118.

[13] Uberoi highlights the multidimensional importance of the moment: 'The Khalsa was to be, since its inception, a society for salvation and self-realization, unitarian in religion, vernacular in culture and democratic in politics; this was in its nature, its constitution and its modernity of non-dualism'. See J.P.S. Uberoi, *Religion, Civil Society and the State: A Study of Sikhism* (New Delhi: Oxford University Press, 1996), 74.

Wazir Singh: Mid-nineteenth Century

In the dominant tradition of the history of Punjabi literature, what is less known and acknowledged is the third powerful literary current called '*sant sahit*', besides Sufi and '*gurmat*' literature. Most of these compositions by sadhus and *sant*s were either part of the established orders like Nath or Kanpata yogis, Udasi, Nirmala, Gulabasi, Seva Panthi, Suthra Panthi, Nirankari, Namdhari, Radhaswami, Kabir Panthi, Dadu Panthi and Ravidas Panthi, where the chances of survival of such literature were quite high due to continuity of succession, whereas in the cases of several independent and autonomous sadhus and *sant*s like Saeen Hira Das and Sadhu Wazir Singh, the availability of such literature would require conscious effort on the part of interested researchers.[14] This sant tradition, as part of the popular religion, has been fairly inclusive and the *dera*s were open to individuals belonging to all the caste communities. The fact that the study of the Vedas has been an integral part of much of the Sadh tradition has also been overlooked in the wake of the hegemonic tendencies of the established religiosity. This becomes clear in the nineteenth century tension and conflicts between the custodians of established religions and the followers of the non-conformist spirituality of Sadhu Wazir Singh and Gulabdas.

Sadhu Wazir Singh (c. 1790–1859) was born in a Dalit Mazhabi[15] Sikh family of Ferozepur district. Moving in the company of sadhus at an early

---

[14] Some earlier attempts to compile information about sant tradition in Punjabi were: Mahant Ganesha Singh, *Bharat Mat Darpan* (Amritsar: Bhai Budh Singh, 1926); and Sufi Sadhu Singh, *Jag Jeevan* (Amritsar, 1954) Punjab Commercial Press, Taran Taran. The latest compilation in Punjabi by Dharampal Singhal and Baldev Singh, *Baddan Punjabi de Sant Kavi* (New Delhi: National Book Trust, 2006) lists sixty-seven Punjabi saint poets and samples of their poetry. The Hindi works incorporating Punjabi sadhu and *sant* writings are: Pandit Chandrakant Bali, *Punjab Prantiya Hindi Sahitya ka Itihas* (New Delhi: National Publishing House, 1962); Acharaya Parshuram Chaturvedi, *Uttari Bharat ki Sant Parampara* (Prayag: Bharati Bhandar Leader Press, 1964).

[15] Mazhabi literally means 'of religious' or 'faithful'. The Hindu or Muslim *chuhra*s (scavengers) who had accepted Sikhism came to be known as Mazhabis. They were also known as Ranghretas. See E.K. Marenco, *The Transformation of Sikh Society* (New Delhi: Heritage Publications, 1976), 130–31; Pratap Singh Giani, *Jat-Pat te Chhoot-Chhaat sambandhi Gurmat Sidhant* (Amritsar: Shiromani Gurdwara Parbandhak Committee, 1933), 171–172; Karam Singh Historian, 'Ranghrete jan Mazhbi Singh', 5–8 in *Karam Singh Historian di Itihasak Khoj* (Amritsar: Shiromani Gurdwara Parbandhak Committee, 2005), 5–8; Arifi, *Ranghretian da Itihas*, 191–206, goes into details of the usage of these terms.

age eventually made him abandon his home in search of truth, and after much wandering, reading and learning, he settled down in Lahuke village, near Patti in Lahore district, around 1815–16, at the peak of Ranjit Singh's rule. There, he was absorbed in the study of the Vedas and Sufi thought and after a great deal of meditational practice, reached the stage of *Brahmgyani* and came to formulate his thoughts on non-dualism, the unity of god and man. And as word of his wisdom spread, multitudes of followers thronged the young sadhu. His growing fame as a *sant* using his poetry to teach also attracted some poets who became his disciples. All five of his identified poet disciples, including two young widows, came from the high castes. One of them, Vir Singh Sehgal, belonged to a well-to-do family of Amritsar, while Nurang Devi turns out to be the first woman Punjabi poet groomed under his tutorship.[16] He is credited with having composed massive tome of poetry; 930 *chhand*s in Punjabi and about 3,800 in Braj. Because of the volume of his work and the range of themes covered by him from the metaphysical to social and political, he has come to be recognized as *Mahan Kavi* (great poet) of his times.[17] He claims *Brahmgyan* at several places in his poetry. At one place he says:

> Te takk rahe jaan nakk ayee, rahe thakk na hakk nitaria si.
> Dhooni lae vibhut charae rahe, teerath naeh ke haal gujaria si.
> Parh pothian vekhian thothian ni, chare Bedan da bhed vicharia si.
> Mithe arifan aye Wazir Singha, sarup apna aap niharia si.[4]
>
> (I meditated for a long time and did not tire till I arrived at the truth. I covered my body with ashes and weak on pilgrimage; I carefully studied the sacred texts, till I discovered the secret of the tour vedas. After I realised the self, I felt the universe manifest itself in my own image.)
>
> Se sach di agg jan mach payee, jal bal gayee granthi karam di si.
> Jaan apna aap nishang hoye, chhuti kalapna maran te janam di si.
> Van trin parbat parbrahm jata, kiti dur dwait jo bharam di si.
> Ahn brahamgyan Wazir Singha, rahi kaid na baran ashram di si.[5]
>
> (When the fire of truth was ignited, the illusion of karma was burnt. The ecstasy of realising the Self freed me from the question of life and death. I found Brahma in everything; in mountains, woods and flora and removed the

[16] The small details about his life and works are given in the only monograph available, written by an eminent Punjabi writer, Samsher Singh Ashok. See Samsher Singh Ashok, *Siharfian Sadhu Wazir Singhji Kian* (henceforth *Siharfian Wazir Singh*) (Patiala: Publication Bureau of Punjabi University, 1988).

[17] Ashok, *Mazhabi Sikhan da Itihas*, 110.

illusion of dualism. Wazir Singh attained the brahmgyan after which there was no prison of vara-ashram.)[18]

In a sense, Wazir Singh is part of the Sant tradition of North Indian *nirguna bhakti*, yet, he seems to be going beyond set paths. He is radical and iconoclast like Kabir but, in addition, he brings in the question of gender equality. He is highly critical of establishments, whether social or religious. He boldly lashes out at Brahmanical structures of inequality manifested in *varnashrama* and *jaat-paat* and like Ravidas, envisions 'Beghampura', a liberated society. As a keen observer and widely travelled seeker of truth, he provides an interesting ethnographic account of Punjabi society, as he also his observations on different regions and people. He becomes an inspiring precursor to an intellectual 'Gulabdasi' movement led by Gulabdas, who graduated from being a Vedantis to an epicurean atheist.[19] Wazir Singh opens up possibilities of re-reading the history of the Punjab and its people.

His devotion to Almighty God, the formless, is total as he says:

Giving up all materials I have joined God in ecstasy.
One who is immersed in Him transcends caste differences.[20]

---

[18] Ashok, *Siharfian Wazir Singh*, 42, 12th siharfi.

[19] The Gulabdasi sect emerged as an intellectually vibrant sect in nineteenth century Punjab. The founder of the sect was one Gulabdas (1809–73), born in a Jat family of Ratola village near Taran Taran in Amritsar district. He had served as a trooper in Maharaja Sher Singh's cavalry, after but soon, he became a Sadhu, studied the Vedas and started his own establishment. He was an accomplished poet who had attained *Brahmgyan* (realization of the self and universe). He became an atheist and advocated an epicurean life. He shunned caste and gender differences and discrimination as untouchables and women became an integral part of his creed. The first woman Punjabi poet, Peero Preman (c. 1830–1872; former Aiysha, a Muslim prostitute), almost became the co-saint of his establishment. For details, see Sevak, 'Gulabdasi Sampardaye'; (Navratan Kapoor, *Sadhu Gulab Das: Jeevan te Rachna.* Patiala: Publication Bureau, Punjabi University, 1993); Bikram Singh Ghuman, *Kishan Singh Arif: Jeevan te Rachna* (Patiala: Publication Bureau, Punjabi University, 1987), 9–10. For details about Peero Preman, see Santokh Singh Shaharyar, 'Punjabi di Pahili Shaira: Peero Preman', *Ajoke Shilalekh*, January 1997, 5–8 and Swarajbir, 'Antika' (Epilogue), in *Shairee (A Play)* (Ludhiana: Chetna Prakashan, 2004), 185–197. For a scholarly treatment of Peero and her poetry, see Anshu Malhotra, 'Telling her Tale? Unravelling a Life in Conflict in Peero's *Ik Sau Sath Kafian (one hundred and sixty kafis)*', *Indian Economic and Social History Review* 46, no. 4 (2009), 541–578.

[20] Ashok, *Siharfian Wazir Singh*, 9, 3rd *chhand* in 3rd siharfi.

This moment of the day is auspicious when I have found my Beloved.
I am delighted in thought as I stand free from all illusions.
I see Him word in word, manifest in different forms.
Like water and wave O! Wazir Singh, He and I are the same.[21]

His poetry is suffused with negation of *varnashrama* (in Punjabi, quite often, *baran-ashram*) and *jaat-paat*, the pillars of Brahmanical Hinduism, which he denounces forcefully. A few samples would show his conviction:

Dualism was the source of arrogance and miseries, which the guru has removed.
The guru has severed the chains of casteism, baran-ashram and three-shames.
While distinguishing the Name, Form and Way the guru has emphasised the unity of soul.
Understand O' Wazir Singh! the existence is manifest in your image after duality is removed.[22]

Once I realised the self, I threw away the baran-ashram.
Shameless I am after breaking the three-shames and demolishing the ego.
Freed from caste-differences, I have transcended the Hindu-Turk differences.
Going beyond all O' Wazir Singh, I find everyone within me.[23]

Once you meditate on breaths you would get subsumed in Brahma.
Concentrate and see that there is nothing outside Brahma.
You see the truth about yourself once you see the unity in soul and Brahma.
By relinquishing baran-ashram O' Wazir Singh! You would sing of your omniscience.[24]

Ashiqs have no doubts as they have gone beyond the frame of all logic.
They have left behind distinctions of castes and baran-ashram, of Muslims and Hindus.
After practicing rituals, prayers and knowledge they have gone beyond all.
Realising all in the self O' Wazir Singh! They stand distinct from all.[25]

We have no shame either of lineage or people, nor do we recognise Vedas and Quran.
Neither have we bothered about Muslims or Hindus nor about baran-ashram.
We have gone beyond this or that world; we also don't differentiate jeev from eesh.

[21] Ibid., 15, 19th *chhand* in 4th siharfi.
[22] Ibid., 6, 9th *chhand* in the 2nd siharfi.
[23] Ibid., 15th *chhand*.
[24] Ibid., 9, 4th *chhand* in the 3rd siharfi.
[25] Ibid., 14, 12th *chhand* in the 4th siharfi.

> We relish the state of ecstasy O' Wazir Singh! beyond two there is no profit and loss.[26]

> Appreciate him as brave who has destroyed the illusion of pride.
> Who has crossed the boundaries of baran-ashram and annoyed others by abandoning three-shames.
> The One who has gone beyond concerns of Five-koshas, three-gunas and three stages.
> Being different from all O' Wazir Singh! You have passed the degree of self-realization.[27]

> Don't get self-conceited, give up your ego and listen to guru's counsel.
> Weigh the three-shames and baran-ashram in the scale of truth and decide.
> If you have a strong desire to play the love-game, carry your head on your palm.
> Guru sayeth to you O' Wazir Singh! you are god unto you.[28]

> Look! The enemy parents oppressively detain the child wanting to be free.
> He has been tied in the bonds of three-shames and trapped in baran-ashram.
> His body is trapped in the prison of caste identity.
> O' Wazir Singh! the man gets forcefully married at young age to this social trap.[29]

Wazir Singh's dissent to Sikhism is quite clear as he notices degeneration that was taking place in the Sikh religion during his time. He could perhaps be the first bold voice in this regard. He says:

> The Guru left the Granth and Panth under the care of sants to be rated above all.
> There are many sects now and the leaders stress their own codes of conduct.
> Bringing back the trap of baran-ashram, they also bind people with three-shames.
> By creating different Sikhis O' Wazir Singh, they have created cults around them.[30]

> They highlight their own sects and do not give clue to the common thread.
> They surround the unattached and trap a free soul into their narrow webs.
> Gurus are greedy and so are Sikhs, both reciprocating in their interests.
> The Sikhs become angry with their gurus who in turn keep pleasing their clients.
> Both accuse each other in public while people get surprises of this kind.
> O' Wazir Singh! these gurus and Sikhs have become worldly to the disenchantment of Sants.[31]

---

[26] Ibid., 20, 24th *chhand* in the 5th siharfi.
[27] Ibid., 21, 4th *chhand* in the 6th siharfi.
[28] Ibid., 24, 25th *chhand* in the 6th siharfi.
[29] Ibid., 54, 30th *chhand* in the 14th siharfi.
[30] Ibid., 66, 47th *chhand* in the 16th siharfi.
[31] Ibid., 48th *chhand*.

The lions that had eaten together with goats are devouring the goats and call themselves Singhs.
As a lion awakens another lion, O' Wazir Singh, Sikhs of Gurus should not forget their duty to awake others to fearlessness.[32]

His bold denunciation of established orders, old practices and new ones invoked strong reactions from a range of vested interests. One gets sufficient leads from Wazir Singh's compositions as to how his dissent and radical preaching invoked hostilities and opposition from several quarters. He refers to his own establishment:

The Sants reside in the tower of Lahuke, they do not hurt anyone nor do they allow others to hurt them.
Years have passed staying here but they never asked anyone for a penny.
People wonder from where we eat and how we survive.
Some speculate we have something O' Wazir Singh, some think we manufacture.[33]

Many crave for audience while others burn in envy at the blessed sight.
While many come full of love for us, others want to kill us.
Many worship in great devotion while some unnecessarily annoy.
O' Wazir Singh! while devotees bow their heads the opponents seek duels.[34]

He provides a graphic picture of one such skirmish in one of his compositions:

If you are really interested in knowing let us enter into questions-answers.
If you don't want to listen why should we waste our time; better be silent.
From wherever the Truth can be had we should touch the feet of the source, why fight?
Sayeth Wazir Singh! if interested we meet, else keep distance and do not hurt.[35]
They created ruckus and misbehaved with Sants.
These fools hurled abuses in hundreds on guru and women without discrimination.
They got back what they came intended and got thoroughly beaten.
Wazir Singh got a staff in his hands and gave them five to seven to get rid of.[36]

---

[32] Ibid., 93, 25th *chhand* in the 21st siharfi.
[33] Ibid., 51, 10th *chhand* in the 14th siharfi.
[34] Ibid., 52, 13th *chhand* in the 14th siharfi.
[35] Ibid., 94, 1st *chhand* in the 22nd siharfi.
[36] Ibid., 2nd *chhand*.

Wazir Singh's criticism does not stop at established religious practices but he extends his observations to castes and communities. He talks of Khatris, Jats, Julahas, artisan communities and shepherds. He is very critical of the dominant community of Khatris from which all the Sikh gurus came as he says:

> Bedis[37] are supposed to know Vedas but today's Bedis meaninglessly call them such.
> They are greedy and coax others' women while kill their own female infants.
> Wazir Singh! they claim gurus of the world but shamelessly commit sins.[38]

Giving the range of his knowledge from material to spiritual, social to religious, political to philosophical, it is not difficult to see him in the role of a preceptor, guide and *sant* philosopher. Luckily, we have compositions of his disciples expressing their gratitude towards their *guru*. There is no dearth of internal evidence, to which we would shortly turn, that shows that he had reached those heights to be considered a spiritual master and guru. Even though he stresses the importance of the *guru*, the preceptor, for paving the way to enlightenment, there is no clue to his personal guru. But he definitely got recognized as the *guru* by his followers and literal testimony is important in this respect. The use of the terms 'sant' and 'guru' needs some clarification in the context of Indian religions, especially *bhakti* traditions. Karine Schomer offers some clarification in the variety of usage in different traditions:

> Derived from Sanskrit *sat* ('truth, reality'), its root meaning is 'one who knows the truth' or 'one who has experienced Ultimate Reality', i.e. a person who has achieved a state of spiritual enlightenment or mystical self-realization; by extension, it is also used to refer to all those who sincerely seek enlightenment. Thus conceptually as well as etymologically, it differs considerably from the false cognate 'saint' which is often used to translate it. Like 'saint', '*sant*' has taken on the more general ethical meaning of the 'good person' whose life is a spiritual and moral exampler, and is therefore found attached to a wide variety of gurus, 'holy men' and other religious teachers. Historically, however, 'Sant' is the designation given to the poet-saints belonging to two distinct, though related devotional *bhakti* groups.[39]

---

[37] Guru Nanak was from the Bedi family.

[38] Ibid., 59, 4th *chhand* in the 16th siharfi.

[39] Karine Schomer, 'Introduction: The Sant Tradition in Perspective', 251–263 in *The Sants: Studies in a Devotional Tradition of India*, ed. Karine Schomer and W.H. McLeod (Delhi: Motolal Banarsidass, 1987), 2–3.

While distinguishing North Indian *nirguna* from the non-sectarian Vaishnava poet saints of Maharashtra, she is clear that the North Indian *sant*s defy classification within the usual categories of Hindu *bhakti*. Though in the Sikh usage, the word sant acquires a different and also changing meaning and the word guru carries the hierarchically higher status,[40] our poet of the paper was more in tune with Schomer's North Indian usage. Let us listen to Wazir Singh on what he has to say on who is a *sant*:

> The entire world lives in limits, only a Sant is abundantly shameless.
> He abandons parents, siblings and relatives and runs away from home.
> He breaks the trap of baran-ashram and shackles of three-shames.
> He boldly denies and defies caste-differences and untouchability.
> He is satiated in the company of truth-seekers and doesn't need anybody else.
> O' Wazir Singh! by getting the human form, You are adoring everywhere.[41]
> A Sant is full of knowledge, is beautiful surrounded by disciples and followers.
> Listening to his discourses, people start revering him as 'Sahib in bhakti'.
> Priests get extremely jealous on his being adored and served by people.
> A Sant is God (*parmeshwar*) manifested in him O' Wazir Singh.[42]
> A Sant is the one who is free of Three-shames and Hindu–Turk differences.
> People get furious in vain, on listening a Sant how outdated is baran-ashram.
> O' Wazir Singh! a Sant is liberated and carefree as he listens to his heart alone.[43]

Having reached that state of liberation for himself and his followers, as the realized goal, he is in a position to call it 'Beghampura' that had remained a utopia for Ravidas. This may be a small space, a commune, a liberated zone, but it is the realized one, the loved one. He describes it thus:

> Beghampura is our city in which we reside and speak truth.
> We care not about codes of conduct, we live as we desire.
> Devotees throng and serve us; they come with offerings but get fruits in return.
> O' Wazir Singh! The river of love flows here, lovers come and swim across.[44]

---

[40] W.H. McLeod points out that in the works of the gurus, the 'Sikh' and 'sant' are interchangeable, while the word 'gurmukh' is favoured to both. See W.H. McLeod, 'The Meaning of "Sant" in Sikh Usage', in *The Sants*, ed. Schomer and McLeod, 1–17.

[41] Ashok, *Siharfian Wazir Singh*, 67, 54th *chhand* in the 16th siharfi.

[42] Ibid., 83, 20th *chhand* in the 19th siharfi.

[43] Ibid., 86, 6th *chhand* in the 20th siharfi.

[44] Ibid., 98, 30th *chhand* in the 22nd siharfi.

Even though in the Punjab context, a guru stands higher than a sant in status (Sikh gurus, for example), Wazir Singh also attains that status as accorded by his disciples. The poetic compositions of Vir Singh Sehgal and Nurang Devi are full of adoration for him as guru. The former sings:

> The guru has awakened vairag in me which has come in full share to me.
> Without my going through meditation the guru has awakened me in a flash.
> He has filled me abundantly and allowed my entry into his good company.
> Wazir Singh has accepted me his servant O' Vir Singh! he has opened my eyes.[45]
>
> Throwing away the quilt of lineage-shame we accepted guru's words and got rid of our sorrows.
> Ignorant humans, we came to the guru who filled us with knowledge.
> The guru accepted our devotion and removed the difference of Jeev and Brahman for us; transformed we are from cowards to brave.
> Sayeth Vir Singh, the servant of Wazir Singh, he has removed our faults and made us popular.[46]

Nurang Devi, in her moving poetry, proclaims Wazir Singh as her guru with an élan:

> I had taken this birth to better the life but got trapped in the family web.
> I have met the enlightened guru and has passed the test by leaving the blind.
> O God! Destroy those sinners who prevented me from the truth.
> Nurang Devi beseeches Guru Wazir Singh to keep her as servant at his feet.[47]
>
> I have left the shelter of amateur guru and found the true guru.
> Amateur guru had raw ideas but now I have met the perfect guru.
> As the perfect guru has shown I have burnt the heightened ego and pride.
> Nurang Devi has left crafty guru behind while meeting the excellent guru.[48]

So much so that Vir Singh could not resist elevating Wazir Singh above the status of avatar when he says:

> Guru's charisma is so much and such, it is beyond my description.
> Four Vedas and Ten Avtaras are no parallel to the guru.[49]

---

[45] Ibid., 17, 1st *chhand* in the 5th siharfi.

[46] Ibid., 105, 24th *chhand* in the 23rd siharfi.

[47] Ibid., 25, 1st *chhand* in the 7th siharfi.

[48] Ibid., 4th *chhand.*

[49] 'Mahima guru ki adhik hai, keti kahun sunai| Bed char avtar das, e guru ke sam nahin', Ibid., 40, 11th siharfi.

Wazir Singh seems to have studied all the religious and spiritual literature available to him and is clear on most of the related questions. His dissent and assertion on going beyond the established religions is well captured in his 12th siharfi,[50] where he says:

> We don't need Koran as we also tear the useless granths.
> There is no desire for Rehras (allusion to Granth Sahib), as we burn temples and mosques.
> We have abandoned the Ganges, Gaya and Prayag, as we also do not worship the Dead.
> Becoming non-sectarian O! Wazir Singh, we keep a watch over the game both sides play.

Such a powerful voice of the nineteenth century as that of Wazir Singh remained unheard and unattended except for a sole monograph by Samsher Singh, and that also has escaped the attention of the academia. Another powerful Dalit voice to appear later in the century was that of Ditt Singh, but I have decided to skip it, as explained in the introduction. The one who connects well with Wazir Singh's legacy happens to be Daya Singh who was born in the closing decade of the nineteenth century.

Daya Singh: First Quarter of the Twentieth Century

Sadhu Daya Singh Arif conferred upon himself every part of his name during his journey towards self-realization when he was immersed in attaining temporal and spiritual insights. He was born to his mother, Ram Deyee, and father, Santa Singh, on 26 December, 1894, in Jalalabad Poorbi (East) village of Firozepur district. This landless, untouchable Mazhabi Sikh family gave him the name of Deva Singh at his birth. Quite contrary to the material as well as cultural condition of his Dalit family, he developed a keen interest in learning letters and clandestinely started going to his village Sikh temple, known as Baba Teja Singh's gurdwara, for the purpose. With his sharp intellect, he learnt to read *Panj Granthi* (five compositions of *Japji*, *Japu*, *Rehras*, *Sohila* and *Anand* from

---

[50] *Kaaf-kade Koran di lod naahin, vekh pothian thothian parde han*| *Rehras namaz di khahash naahin, dharamsal masit nun sarde han*| *Gang, Gaya Pryag nun tiyag keeta, gor marhi niyaz na charde han*| *Hoye aap nirpakh Wazir Singha, pakhan dohan di khed nun tarde han*, Ibid., 44, 12th siharfi.

Guru Granth Sahib)[51] at his village. Santa Singh, Daya Singh's father, was not at all enamoured by his son's craze for learning and had warned him to desist from wasting his time in the 'useless' pursuit. On Daya Singh's not paying any heed to his father's warnings, one day, he was pulled out from the gurdwara and thoroughly beaten up. That did not necessarily deter him from his passion. The beating had tremendous impact on his mind and he turned into a recluse. He left home and started living independently under a peepal tree outside the village where, eventually, he raised a *kutia* (cottage). At times, he would eat at the gurdwara, or he would also collect food in the village as a young sadhu.[52]

Living independently, Daya Singh was absorbed in reading and contemplation. For reading and understanding the entire Guru Granth Sahib, he started visiting Baba Hari Singh at a gurdwara in the adjacent village, Cheema, which was about 5 kilometres from his village. This step was facilitated by the fact that Baba Hari Singh also belonged to the Mazhabi caste. While studying the Sikh scripture, his curiosity and hunger to learn about religions increased several folds in a short time. As a result, he learnt Urdu from a local teacher in his village madrasa, Maulvi Ibrahim. His craze for knowledge and conversations with the learned soon became the 'talk of the town' and hence, he did not find major problems at learning Persian from Sunder Singh Patwari and Master Munshi Ram Khatri. The desire to learn about Islam became so strong that Daya Singh approached the local Sufi scholar, Shadi Khan.[53] Shadi Khan taught him with unreserved attention; the result was that Daya Singh emerged as a sound scholar of Arabic, Persian and Koran. This is reflected in his poetry where *aayet*s from Koran and wide references from Islamic traditions appear abundantly. At the end of the studies, Daya Singh convincingly demonstrated

[51] See http://www.thesikhencyclopedia.com/sri-guru-granth-sahib-and-guru-gobind-singhs-bani/panj-granthi.html.

[52] Atam Hamrahi, *Sadhu Daya Singh Arif*, Second Print (Patiala: Publication Bureau of Punjabi University, 1990), 4–6.

[53] Shadi Khan was a sound scholar of Islamic studies, including Koran, as he had studied religion at Deoband and Delhi. He had his own religious establishment (*takia* – rest house), in his own fields, amidst the agricultural land of the village where he was teaching several pupils. To teach Arabic and Koran, he put a condition of conversion to Islam for Daya Singh. In turn, the latter promised that on completion of his education in Islamic studies, if he finds Islamic principles sounder than those of Sikhism, he would surely accept the Semitic religion. Daya Singh's passion for knowledge and his logical mind convinced Shadi Khan to accept him as his pupil. Daya Singh was so dedicated in his pursuit that he also watered his ustad's orchard at night. See Ibid., 9.

that he found the Sikh principles sounder than Islamic and therefore, he should not be pressed relentlessly for conversion, which his ustad accepted. Learning Sanskrit from Baba Sawan Das who lived in the nearby town, Dharamkot, was not very difficult as the Sanskrit scholar was bowled over by Daya Singh's knowledge. The latter learnt Vedant from Baba Sawan Das' younger brother, Baba Prabhati Das, who had studied the Vedas in Kashi for ten years. It must be noted that Baba Sawan Das did not discriminate against anyone on caste lines as far as learning was concerned; but, here, Daya Singh also happened to be an exceptionally sound scholar, with whom teachers enjoyed sharing knowledge. Daya Singh possessed, to his credit, the appreciable traits of dedication, devotion, diligence and service.[54]

Thus, Deva alias Daya Singh acquired all his education in his teens. By mastering the Punjabi, Urdu, Persian, Arabic and Sanskrit languages, his major aim was to know the basic principles of all the major religions of the subcontinent. He used to regularly read the Koran and would complete a reading in one day. Finally, after learning Sanskrit, he studied the Vedas, Puranas and mythological aspects of the Hindu tradition and expressed, unambiguously, his dissent while standing by the philosophy of Sikhism. This is reflected in one of his unpublished compositions[55] where he elevates Guru Granth Sahib to the supreme position on a comparative scale where his devotion is abundantly evident:

> Studied all the Vedas and *Puranas,* are they the end of world's scriptures?
> Absorbing *Smriti* I have read countless Shastras, read and sung poems of numerous poets
> Nanak *bani* rendered by *nirankari* is the poetry of poetries it praises the Lord
> Neither seen, not to be seen Daya Singh, non-sectarian is the message of *Shri Guru Granth*
> Devoured many tomes including Manu *Smriti* which codifies the highs and lows
> Society divided in four *varnas,* Flouted thus are Creator's rules
> On reading *Bhagwat Garud*, duality enters distracting the thinking *sants*
> Neither seen, not to be seen Daya Singh, non-sectarian is the message of *Shri Guru Granth*

[54] See Ibid., 7–11.

[55] Cited in Atam Hamrahi and Surjit Chander, 'Sadhu Daya Singh Arif: Jeevan te Rachna', in *Arif Rachnavali: Sadhu Daya Singh Arif di Prapat Prakashit Rachna* (henceforth *Arif Rachnavali*), ed. Atam Hamrahi and Surjit Chander (Amritsar: Bhai Chatar Singh Jeevan Singh, 2002). *Arif Rachnavali* is an anthology of all the published works of Daya Singh. There is no running pagination for the authology; each work carries autonomous page numbers.

Daya Singh's desire to get to the core message of the major religions in the subcontinent turned him into quite a philosopher. After gaining insights into the theological aspects of religion, he turned to the secular literature of Punjab, especially the *kissa*s.[56] Long spells of solitude in his hut left ample time for Daya Singh to read. He would spend long hours in reading and contemplation, but this also led him to a state of madness that ultimately erupted in profound poetry. His first poetical work, *Fanah dar Makan*, was published in 1915 when he was 21 years old. This was written in *sadh bhasha*, the language of sadhus, and emphasized the quintessential element of human mortality. It is worth mentioning that his first work of poetry appeared under his given name Deva Singh. Due to the somewhat difficult language and style of composition, he was advised by Baba Sawan Das, his Sanskrit guru, to revise it and write in simple language. He was bursting with so much creative energy that he altogether produced another *kissa*, titled *Fanah da Makan*, which soon became very popular throughout Punjab.[57]

The work which made Daya Singh a household name through the width and breadth of the Punjab was *Zindagi Bilas*, which was completed on 23 August 1916. It is in this work where his vast religious, spiritual and secular knowledge is manifest. Following the ancient wisdom, as also recorded by Manu, that the average human life is of 100 years, Daya Singh composed lyrical poems on each year. The mortality of human existence is re-emphasized to impress upon the readers' mind the importance of good deeds and moral conduct. Overall, it is a touching didactic poem that caught the masses' imagination and became the most read or heard poetic creation next only to Waris Shah's *Heer*.[58] The impact of Daya Singh's poetry could be seen not only on commoners, who listened to all kinds of readers and singers, but also on the educated, including the creative writers. In this case, the testimony of celebrated Punjabi litterateur, Nanak Singh, is very instructive as he acknowledges Daya Singh's influence on his novels.[59] Daya Singh wrote his next major published poetic work, *Sputtar*

---

[56] See Hamrahi, *Sadhu Daya Singh Arif*, 11–12.

[57] See Ibid., 29.

[58] Even in the 1980s, the publishers of Bhai Pratap Singh Pritam Singh Press said that two Gurmukhi editions of either 3,300 or 4,400 were published every year. They were also selling 1,100 copies of the Devanagri edition every two years, while the same number was still sold in Persian script every four years. See Hamrahi and Chander, *Arif Rachnavali.*

[59] In his letter of 17 December 1967, Nanak Singh reminiscences: 'As much as I was a child to Sadhu Daya Singh in age, being 18–19 years, my work *Satgur Mahima*

Bilas', in 1922. Written in the same genre, this is also a didactic work of great aesthetic value addressed as it is to his eldest son, Kultar Singh. While he had sold the property rights of his early works to the publishers, he published and also used to sell *Sputtar Bilas* on his own.[60]

Daya Singh succeeds in reinforcing the moral thrust of the medieval spiritual saints in a fast-changing objective world when there was a rise in the acquisitive tendencies irrespective of the means adopted. His poetry is full of spiritual knowledge found in Islam, Hinduism, Sikhism and as also found in the works of Sufi poets and *bhagats*. He talks of the unity of the human soul with God and throws light on its philosophical dimension. His poetry is an effortless emphasis on mortality; the reader is constantly reminded of the greatest truth, death. Stress on good deeds and moral conduct is ineluctable. Though he could not find a scientific explanation for the prevalent Indian despondency, which was not his field any way, Daya Singh attributes the listlessness to a decline in spirituality and morality. His introverted nature made him seek answers in the subjective human makeup rather than in the objective material conditions.

His devotion to the divine is present in all his works, as is evident from his prayers before starting his works. He thus opens his first work, *Fanah dar Makan*, with these words:

> O! Lord, you bestow to all, the world stands ingratiated.
> The humble servant prays to you, thousands time over.
> I pray the creator of the universe, time and again.
> Him who is formless, casteless, without birth and self-created.

---

looked very small against his very big *granths*...Perhaps it was 1918–1919 when I first came to Amritsar from Peshawar. While daily going to Darbar Sahib (Golden Temple), I used to witness huge gatherings near Guru ka Bagh. One blind singer clad in saffron robe used to render Sadhu Daya Singh's *Zindagi Bilas* melodiously in touching voice. The entire *granth* was in his memory. Sometimes the strength of listeners would reach the critical number to jam the traffic. For one, I was soaked in *vairag* those days and to top that the poetry of *Zindagi Bilas* used to captivate me. The result was that sometimes I would forget going to Durbar Sahib...It would not be an exaggeration if I say that I could easily see the initial impact of Sadhu Daya Singh's poetry on my mind in my later novel writings. Half a century is not a small time. Even now when I remember the compositions of *Zindagi Bilas* and *Fanah da Makan*, my soul feels a special kind of freshness. A large part of these two epics is still fresh in my memory. And at times I would even sway while singing him in good moods.' See Hamrahi, *Sadhu Daya Singh Arif*, 130–131; my translation.

60 Ibid., 31.

I am without merit with least intellect; sinner, without character and hard.
The poor, lowly born has no shelter without You.[61]

In a similar way, he opens his last important work, *Sputtar Bilas*, with these lines:

O! Creator God, the benefactor of the humble humanity
You are remembered and prayed before beginning any work
You are worshipped inside homes before launching new ventures
The sant-poet prays to you for removing any obstacle in writing.[62]

His devotion to the Sikh gurus, at the same time, gets a clear expression in the concluding part of the introductory section:

O! Lord of the Universe listen to my prayer
I begin writing Sputtar Bilas under Your protection
I bow to the feet of Ten Gurus beginning with Satguru Nanak for their blessings.[63]

While not basing himself on mythology, legends and romance, Daya Singh made a break within the *kissa* tradition. He has used the genre for character building and cleansing of the inner self via spiritual regeneration. Among moral issues, he lays high premium on the ideal of 'truth', as it can be seen in his advice to his son in *Sputtar Bilas*:

Follow the second sermon of dervish, speak truth for the religious cause
Don't oppress in the world even once, good you do millions if you can sway
Not to let your mind astray to evil, turn to the good cause ever
Never mix with the mighty corrupt the whole life, after all the traitors must betray[64]

Daya Singh became acutely aware of the rising communal tide and like earlier *sant*s, raises his voice against division of people on religious lines. He makes his dissent and position clear in the closing composition of *Fanah da Makan* called Antim Bachan:

This world is city to me and I am constant traveller
No proximity to Hindus or enmity with Muslims I nurture
None is evil to me; the one who is will die of that poison

---

61 'Fanah dar Makan', in Hamrahi and Chander, *Arif Rachnavali*, 1.
62 'Sputtar Bilas', in Ibid., 1, Rasawal *chhand* 1.
63 'Dohira' in 'Sputtar Bilas', in Ibid., 1–2.
64 'Sukhan Dooja' in 'Sputtar Bilas', in Ibid.

To Daya Singh all humans are good; it's me only who's the Other
Four varnas but one script, useless is the talk of different faiths
Hindus are happy with me, Muslims detest me not.[65]

He transcended all the man-made divides as he came to realize the real self. This is reflected in his 'Thanks to the God' composition appearing after the conventional *Manglacharni* in *Zindagi Bilas*:

Discriminate? How do I? When the entire humanity is His
One Brahma point resulting in Creation, why accept caste or no-caste
Friends all – none left behind, Hindu–Sikh–Muslims alike
Questions of faith resolved all, religious conflicts left behind
Enemy none, Pundits and Mullas both are my friends
Duality Dissolved, cleanest is my internal as is external[66]

Daya Singh comes to the theme of prevailing communal division again and again. In his discourse on 56th Year in *Zindagi Bilas*, he sings:

Unity I see all around, wherever my eyes rove
Superior claims of faith, Hindus and Muslims fight over
Mere jugglery of words, as Essence of Ram and Rahim is the same
Of Casteist belief untouchability born, both made of the soil same
Children of same parents, if they just see Origins
Forsaking God, they worship false objects, get astray into aimlessness
Give up evils for salvation, devils you remain sans praxis
Daya Singh has left partisanship, in every sector, every deed[67]

Daya Singh was aware of all the competing revivalist tendencies and religious polemical wars around the turn of the century, as he says in the *Fanah da Makan*:

Varnas and religions all, exclusive claims of purity
Hindus with Har Narayan, hold their principles True
Pastors and Dayanandi Aryas pronounce, no deliverance without them
Exclusive rights in Heaven say Muslims, no place for Hindus there
God has no enmity with Hindus, keeps no exclusive place for Muslims
Fight they all over religion, without knowing the Unknown
Filthy n empty sans good deeds, paupers they are, without a penny
Daya Singh false claims the world may make; no recognition without actions[68]

---

65 *Zindagi Bilas* in Ibid., 32.

66 Ibid., 2.

67 'Condition of 56th Year' in Ibid., 38.

68 'Fanah da Makan', Ibid., 19.

His dissenting voice against all established religions is loud and clear. He is wary of differences created by different religions born of human minds as he says that no one is born with religion:

> The religions are man-made; the man is born a simple human.
> A Brahman is not born with a tuft on head nor is a Muslim born with circumcision.
> One adopts the religion of parents to which one is born.
> There is no caste, pure or polluted according to Vedas and Puranas.
> ...
> Those who test and recognise high and low are full of vanity and conceit.
> In no other country there is untouchability, only Hindustan is ruined by it.
> ...
> The arifs have transcended religions after reaching their spiritual destination.
> They have shed the illusion of dualism by crossing those boundaries.[69]

He holds Brahmanical ritualism with the same contempt as did *bhagat*s, *sant*s and Sufis. He is dead against idol worship. The Islamic influence on his mind is quite obvious as he has used eighteen *aayets* in his three works. Similarly, Sufi influence is manifest in his insistence on *murshid*, guru without whom the seeker cannot reach the Divine. The concept of *ishq* is present at several places in Daya Singh's works. Towards the close of *Zindagi Bilas*, in *Uttam Updesh No. 39*, he says:

> Creator is happy loving his Creation, be happy in the service of that creation
> There is no knowledge without guru, beseech *murshid* for the purpose
> Death is premium for lovers' union, emboldened you be like a true lover
> Be reformed thoroughly before counselling others with confidence
> Elated be not with worldly joys, be soaked in *ishq's* spring
> Reads He your heart's letters, send your sweetheart an urgent telegram[70]

And in one of his discourses to his son in *Sputtar Bilas*, he advocates living life like a possessed lover:

> Body sans love is skeleton, plunge and revive the deserted field
> You find beloved in truthfulness and honesty
> Ashiqs never look back, honourable death of Hindus and Muslims you die
> Your lover chops your body like a goat's? Be ready to offer your life
> Slice your thigh for beloved's dish, as Mahivaal did for Sohni[71]

---

[69] 'Sputtar Bilas' in Ibid., 42, 57th sukhan.

[70] *Zindagi Bilas*, in Ibid., 76, 'Uttam Updesh No. 39'.

[71] 'Sukhan Choutha', in Ibid., 8.

The importance of Sadhu Daya Singh is manifold. First and foremost, he is the first Dalit Punjabi poet to attain the widest possible popularity, the kind of popularity enjoyed by Waris Shah, in undivided Punjab. This, of course, was facilitated by the print culture of his time. Second, he gives the *kissa* genre a new twist and subject. Till his arrival on the scene, *kissa*s narrated stories of outstanding legendary heroes and heroines, whether they were *ashiq*s, *bhagat*s or brigands. He moves from the particular to general, the quintessential human life. Third, he brings moral and ethical for consideration by the common man. In this sense, he is thinking like Gandhi, his contemporary, but quite independently of the latter, as Gandhi till then had not become a public figure in India. Objectively speaking, in two centuries of political swings after the guru period, there had been a depletion of this force in the Punjabi society. Casteism, especially untouchability, that had substantially weakened in the seventeenth and the eighteenth centuries had not only raised its ugly head in Punjab but was also becoming virulent. Daya Singh's stress on the moral force in this respect was in a way to pose a challenge to the malaise. Fourth, Daya Singh's poetry is free from any kind of sectarianism and is thoroughly secular in the prevailing communal environment. His concern and message was universal in content; it is libertarian rather than restraining. Lastly, Daya Singh not only produces good poetry but also emerges as an intellectual of his age. Through the study of scriptures and traditions of major religions of the land, he arrives at his own understanding of human existence that he corroborates from his practical life and keen observation. He lays greater stress on practice than theory, on deeds than the scriptural knowledge. Here, his labour background provides him practical insights to talk about the class different stages of human life, diverse facets of existence and practical utility of ethical living.

Conclusion

Wazir Singh and Daya Singh offer interesting similarities separated even as they are by a century. Both were Dalits, born in Dalit Sikh (Mazhabi) families in Ferozepur district in the Malwa region of the Punjab. Both of them became mendicants at an early age and came to be known as sadhus. Both acquired great knowledge through meditation and vast readings as also from conversations with others. Both transcended the narrow sectarian pursuits of a particular religion and lived and preached cosmopolitanism where diverse religious and spiritual traditions came to be integrated. Both the poets emphasized what was moral and what was ethical, though Wazir Singh seemingly had more liberal concepts of what was moral. Both of them reached the stage of *Brahmgyan* through contemplation and reflected it in their rich and powerful poetry. Both were soaked in devotion to the divine power and yet, expressed their strong dissent not only with all the established religions that failed to mitigate differences of caste and class but also with the religion in which they were born. Both of them maintained their individual spirituality without becoming part of any of the numerous sects in currency. While both exhibited spiritual knowledge and poetic talent reminiscent of the early sants like Kabir or Ravidas, and came to enjoy fame in their own times, neither of the two got any biographer to write about their lives. While Wazir Singh succeeded in establishing a small establishment where his disciples would throng to seek his blessings, and these included some fine poets of the times (pre-print age in the case of Punjab), Daya Singh was a recluse by nature and attained his vast popularity through his powerful poetry printed over times. Both of them travelled far and wide and gained practical knowledge of lands and people; though Wazir Singh remained unmarried and settled in a different place than his birth place, Daya Singh settled down in his own village as a complete family man. In the former's case, dissent from family life sustained through his life, the latter, though became a dissident sadhu in his childhood, turned to be a devoted husband and father after attaining *Brahmgyan* and popularity. The given examination of their lives and poetry shows that devotion and dissent were not necessarily contradictory to each other but both appear to be complementary, even supplementary. Their devotion, in a way, strengthened their dissenting voice against all kinds of sectarian differences; devotion to the invisible benevolent apparently empowered their dissent to boldly dismiss the visible iniquitous and unjust. They quietly exhibit the creative potential systematically denied to their Dalit community and that they express in a bold manner of rejecting the dominant religious traditions, while showing the great value of the shared heritage of popular religiosity of the poor and lowly in the hierarchical social order.

References

Arifi, Naranjan. *Ranghrehtian da Itihas (Adi Kal ton 1850 Tak)*, Part I (Amritsar: Literature House, 1993).

Ashok, Samsher Singh. *Siharfian Sadhu Wazir Singhji Kian* (Patiala: Publication Bureau of Punjabi University, 1988).

______. *Mazhbi Sikhan da Itihas*, Second Edition (Amritsar: Bhai Chatar Singh Jeevan Singh, 2001).

Bali, Pandit Chandrakant. *Punjab Prantiya Hindi Sahitya ka Itihas* (New Delhi: National Publishing House, 1962).

Chaturvedi, Acharaya Parshuram. *Uttari Bharat ki Sant Prampara* (Prayag: Bharati Bhandar Leader Press, 1964).

Dussel, Enrique. 'Philosophy and Praxis (Provisional Thesis for a Philosophy of Liberation)'. In *Philosophical Knowledge*, edited by John B. Brough, Donald O. Dahlstrom and Henry B. Veatch (Washington: Catholic University of America, 1980).

———. *Philosophy of Liberation*. Translated by Aquilina Martinez and Christine Morkovsky (Maryknell, New York: Orbis Books, 1985).

Giani, Pratap Singh. *Jat-Pat te Chhoot-Chhaat sambandhi Gurmat Sidhant* (Sikh Principles about Caste and Untouchability) (Amritsar: Bhai Chatar Singh Jeevan Singh, 1933).

Gandiwind, Giani Nishan Singh. *Shaheed Baba Jeevan Singh: Jeevan, Rachna te Viakhia* (Amritsar: Bhai Chatar Singh Jeevan Singh, 2008).

Ghuman, Bikram Singh. *Kishan Singh Arif: Jeevan te Rachna* (Patiala: Publication Bureau, Punjabi University, 1987).

Hamrahi, Atam. *Sadhu Daya Singh Arif*, Second Print (Patiala: Publication Bureau of Punjabi University, 1990).

Hamrahi, Atam and Chander, Surjit (eds). *Arif Rachnavali: Sadhu Daya Singh Arif di Prapat Prakashit Rachna* (Amritsar: Bhai Chatar Singh Jeevan Singh, 2002).

Kapoor, Narinder Singh. *Giani Dit Singh: Jiwan te Rachna* (Patiala: Punjabi University, 1987).

Kapoor, Navratan. *Sadhu Gulab Das: Jeevan te Rachna* (Patiala: Publication Bureau, Punjabi University, 1993).

Kaur, Valerie, 'A Liberation Philosophy and Border Thinking'. *SikhSpectrum.com Monthly*, November 2000.

Malhotra, Anshu. 'Telling her Tale? Unravelling a Life in Conflict in Peero's *Ik Sau Sath Kafian (one hundred and sixty kafis)*'. *Indian Economic and Social History Review* 46(4) (2009), 541–578.

Mann, Gurinder Singh. *The Making of Sikh Scripture* (New Delhi: Oxford University Press, 2001).

Marenco, E.K. *The Transformation of Sikh Society* (New Delhi: Heritage Publications, 1976).

McLeod, W.H. 'The Meaning of "Sant" in Sikh Usage'. In *The Sants: Studies in a Devotional Tradition of India*, edited by Karine Schomer and W.H. McLeod. (New Delhi: Motilal Banarsidass, 1987).

Puri, Harish K. 'Scheduled Castes in Sikh Community: A Historical Perspective', *Economic and Political Weekly* 38(26) (2003), 2693–2701.

______. 'Introduction'. In *Dalits in Regional Context* (Jaipur and New Delhi: Rawat Publications, 2004).

Sahgal, Manmohan. *Sant Kavya ka Darshanik Vishleshta* (Chandigarh, 1965).

Schomer, Karine. 'Introduction: The Sant Tradition in Perspective'. In *The Sants: Studies in a Devotional Tradition of India*, edited by Karine Schomer and W.H. McLeod (New Delhi: Motilal Banarsidass, 1987).

Sevak, Gian Inder Singh. 'Gulabdasi Sampardaye: Rachna te Vichar' (Gulabdasi Sect: Works and Ideas). PhD Thesis, Guru Nanak Dev University, 1984.

Shaharyar, Santokh Singh. 'Punjabi di Pahili Shaira: Peero Preman'. *Ajoke Shilalekh*, January 1997, 5–8.

Singh, Baldev. *Panjwan Sahibjada* (Ludhiana: Chetna Prakashan, 2005).

Singh, Daljeet. *Singh Sabha da Modhi arthat Jeevan Britant Giani Ditt Singh Ji* (Amritsar: Shromani Khalsa Bradari Prabhandak Committee, n.d).

Singh, Gani Ditt, *Mera ate Sadhu Daya Nandji da Sambad* (Lahore: Khalsa Press, 1900).

Singh, Gurnam. 'Sikhism's Emancipatory Discourses: Some Critical Perspectives', *Sikh Formations: Religion, Culture, Theory* 2(2) (2006): 135–151.

Historian, Karam Singh. 'Ranghrete jan Mazhbi Singh'. In *Karam Singh Historian di Itihasak Khoj* (Historical Research of Karam Singh Historian), Part 3, edited by Hira Singh Dard (Amritsar: Shiromani Gurudwara Prabandhak Committee, 2005).

Singh, Mahant Ganesha. *Bharat Mat Darpan* (Amritsar, 1926).

Singh, Nikky-Guninder Kaur. '*Gurbani* in English Translating Celestial Poetry'. *Sikh Review*, June 2000. Available at http://www.sikhreview.org/june2000/heritage.htm.

Singh, Pashaura. *The Guru Granth Sahib: Canon, Meaning and Authority* (New Delhi: Oxford University Press, 2002).

Singh, Sufi Sadhu. *Jag Jeevan* (Taran Taran: Punjab Commercial National Book Trust, 1954).

Singhal, Darampal and Baldev Singh. *Baddan Punjabi de Sant Kavi* (New Delhi, 2006).

Somal, Karnail Singh. *Bhai Ditt Singh Gyani: Jeevan, Rachna te Sakhshiat* (Life, Works and Personality of Bhai Ditt Singh Gyani) Second Edition (Amritsar: Singh Brothers, 2005).

Swarajbir, 'Antika' (Epilogue). In *Shairee (A Play)*, 185–197 (Ludhiana: Chetna Prakashan, 2004).

Uberoi, J.P.S. *Religion, Civil Society and the State: A Study of Sikhism* (New Delhi: Oxford University Press, 1996).

Vaudeville, Charlotte. 'Sant Mat: Santism as the Universal Path to Sanctity'. In *The Sants: Studies in a Devotional Tradition of India*, edited by Karine Schomer and W.H. McLeod (New Delhi: Motilal Banarsidass, 1987).

CHAPTER

10

Protest and Counter-protest

The Nath Siddhas and Charpatnath

Mahesh Sharma

Historians are coming to terms with a comprehensive paradigm shift in early medieval India, which also has a bearing on the historiography of protest and revivalist movements. While there is an abundance of literature on the protest movements, and the dissidents as well, but the nature of protest, however, needs a critical review. This essay seeks to understand the process by which the 'protest' itself becomes dogmatic and therefore requires a protest and/or 'reform' to further revitalize the 'tradition'. Moreover, the protest in itself needs a cogent qualification: for a question arises about the protest being aimed against whom/what? We shall ask this twofold question from the non-conformist North Indian Nath Siddhas over a long period, from the tenth to the sixteenth centuries, reflected in the waxing and waning of the movement, particularly in the Punjab. Also, we shall contextualize the protest against the changing profile of ascetic institutions and their nexus with the state; as much as against the dominant medieval perceptions impacting the language, norms and issues of devotion and worship.

> O King! If you control the world,
> We control spirituality.
> You are worshipped by the rich and greedy,
> We, by those who strive to remove illiteracy/
> (We serve the knowledgeable).
> If you have no faith in us,
> We also have no sympathy for you ![1]

[1] Bhartṛharī, *Vairāgya Śataka*, verse 83. Translated by the author. Haridwar, Gorakh Mandir, n.d.; also, see Mahesh Sharma, *Western Himalayan Temple Records*: State, Pilgrimage, Ritual and Legality in Chambā (Leiden: Brill, 2009), 341.

The post-Gupta period in India is characterized by political fragmentation (particularly with the fall of the Palas, Pratiharas and Rashtrakutas), the crowning of the Puranic religion with profound impetus on temple activity – temple building, images and rituals – and the horizontal expansion of the ritually lower castes, the Shudras. The turbulence was such that the later Puranas predicted a systemic inversion, 'the chiliastic image of total cataclysm',[2] whereby the Brāhmaṇas will behave like Shudras and the Shudras like Brāhmaṇas; the kings will become paupers and the paupers, kings; the servants as masters and masters like servants. That such an assertion was made at a time when the economy was being feudalized – declining trade, increase in land grants, declining towns and enhanced dependence upon agriculture – things must have been desperate, as the positional inversion within the power structure is inbuilt in this argument. The most significant outcome of this dread was the rise of tantric practices, which changed the nature of ritual and the forms of image worship in the leading sectarian religions, be it Shaivism, Vaishnavism or Vajrayana Buddhism.[3] That Yuan Chwang was baffled at, and therefore criticizes, the conduct of Buddhist monks is a pointer to the changing ritual practices in northern India. It is against such a shifting background that the Nath Siddha protest may be understood. The varying direction of the spiritual discourse, frowned upon by the purists, is discernable in the *Caryagiti* and the *dohakosa* of the Mahasiddhas, the Tibetan school of the 'perfected masters', and a precursor to the Vajrayana Lamaic forms of Buddhism of Tibet and Central Asia.[4] That the paradigmatic figures of the Nath Siddhas and the Mahasiddhas are identical, which in a way contextualizes the extent of mutual borrowing,

[2] Such imagery is particularly articulated in the *Yuga Purana* and *Markandaya Purana*. For details, see, Mahesh Sharma, *The Realm of Faith: Subversion, Appropriation and Dominance in the Western Himalaya* (Simla: IIAS, 2001), 64–69.

[3] For a brief understanding of tantra, see George Feuerstein, *Tantra: The Path of Ecstacy* (Boston: Shambhala, 1998[2000, South Asia Edition]). For the analysis of the tantric literature, Teun Gourdiaan and Sanjukta Gupta, *Hindu Tantric and Sakta Literature* (Wiesbaden: Otto Harrassowitz, 1981); see particularly, the tantras devoted to Kali, 75–91 and the Kaulatantras, 92–104.

[4] For a succinct survey, David Snellgrove, *Indo-Tibetan Buddhism: Indian Buddhists and their Tibetan Successors* (Boston: Shambhala, 1987[2002]). Also, for general account of the Nath movement, see H.P. Dwivedi, *Nath Sampradaya* (1966), in *Hazari Prasad Dwivedi Granthavali*, No. 6, Second Edition. Delhi: Rajkamal, 1998; D. Yadav, *Vajrayani Siddha Sarhyada* (Shantiniketan: University Press, 1972).

support, sustenance and diffusion of ideas and practices, as has been so well documented by Davidson.[5]

The Nath Siddhas, who were prominent in North India by the turn of the first millennium CE, were the medieval renouncers who were characterized by the *haṭha* yogic and tantric practices aimed at gaining *siddhis* or perfections – which are mostly seen as bestowing magical powers. The early Siddhas were the demi-gods, as argued by David White, who lived in the rarefied air as the musical ministrants, the Gandharvas.[6] Flight was one of their accomplishments, as was commonly believed by the time of Kalidasa, the celebrated poet–playwright. The earliest usage is, however, in the *Yoga-sūtra* of Patanjali and the term *siddha* is prominently used by the *Arthashastra* for skilled ascetics as well as magical practitioners. The Jainas also employed the term *siddha*s for the *arhant*s, as in the Hāthigumphā inscription of Khārvela; while the CE 474 Manḍsor inscription makes an allusion to *siddha*s as those who obtain magical powers (*siddhī-arthin*).[7] The *siddha*, from root *sidh* – meaning accomplishment or achievement – was a term that seems to be of generic usage for the magical practices and practitioners, which was later radicalized by the Mahasiddhas and the Nath Siddhas to emphasize perfection. That they denoted themselves as the Siddhas sets them apart from other sectarians with/from whom they shared/borrowed certain rituals, ideas and concepts, like the Pāśupatas, the Kapālikas, the Māheśvaras and later, the Kaulas of Kashmir.[8] As far as the North Indian Siddhas are concerned, Kashmir was a prominent centre for learning. The Tibetan state continued to invite teachers or send its members to learn languages and also to acquire esoteric knowledge, like Vairocana or Naropa, among others.[9] This, however, was not a one-way street. For instance, Abhinavagupta, who wrote the famous *Tantraloka*, stayed in Punjab to learn from the Nath Siddhas.

---

[5] R.M. Davidson, *Indian Esoteric Buddhism: A Social History of the Tantric Movement* (New York: Columbia University Press, 2002).

[6] David G. White, *The Alchemical Body: Siddha Traditions in Medieval India* (Chicago: University of Chicago Press, 1996).

[7] Ibid., 173–176.

[8] For general history, David Lorenzen, *The Kāpālikas and Kālākukhas: Two Lost Śaivite Sects* (Delhi: Thompson Press, 1972).

[9] David Snellgrove, *Indo-Tibetan Buddhism*, 334; Herbert Guenther, *The Life and Teaching of Naropa: Translated from the Original Tibetan with a Philosophical Commentary based on the Oral Transmission* (Boston: Sambhala, 1999[1963]).

The paradigmatic Nath Siddhas, generally considered eighty-four in number, were organized into twelve horizontally linked clans, each owing allegiance to Gorakṣanāth, the progenitor of the movement. Gorakṣa, the medieval renouncer and author of *Gorakṣa Śataka* and the anthologized *Gorakh-Bāṇi*,[10] explicated the sectarian spiritual–ritual genealogy by associating with Matsyendranāth, who lived at least a couple of centuries earlier. The practitioner of eastern tantra, who is perhaps the same as Minapa in the Tibetan tradition, is an influential presence in the songs of contemporary Mahasiddhas. Matsyendranāth, who composed the masterpiece *Kaulajñānanirṇaya*,[11] perhaps systematized the clan-based practices of the esoteric knowledge of the flow of wind (through techniques such as *prāṇāyāma*, *kapālabheda* and *khecari mudrā*) through the six chakras or nerve plexuses – which is at the root of the *haṭha* yoga practices – a concept that was given a firm rooting in the *Kubjikāmatā Tantra*.[12] Abhinavagupta, who synthesized the Kaula doctrines in the beginning of the tenth century, mentions his debt to Matsyendranāth.[13] Significantly, he does not name Gorakṣa. That, in a way, settles the later origin of Gorakṣa as well.

The Kashmiri Kaula tradition had its link with the *āgamic* corpus and different Kaula groups (each of them a sacral lineage, hence *Kula*)[14] had

[10] There are number of works ascribed to him, written in Sanskrit, except for his anthologized sayings. Other major works are *Amarrodhaśāsanam, Avadhūtagītā, Gorakṣa Paddhati, Yogabīja, Siddha Sidhānta Paddhati*, etc.

[11] P.C. Bagchi, ed., *Kaulajñānanirṇaya and Some Minor Texts of the School of Matsyendra* (Kolkata: Metropolitan, 1934).

[12] Teun Goudriaan and Jan A. Schoterman, ed. and trans., *The Kubjikā Upaniṣad* (Groningen: Egbert Forsten, 1994).

[13] K.C. Pandey, *Abhinavagupta: An Historical and Philosophical Study* (Varanasi: Chowkhamba Sanskrit Series, 1963). Also, see Jayadeva Singh, trans., *Abhinavagupta: A Trident of Wisdom: Translation of Parātrīśikā Vivaraṇa* (Albany: State University of New York Press, 1989). For a succinct narrative on Kaula tantra rituals and positions, see D.G. White, *Kiss of the Yoginī: 'Tantric Sex' in the South Asian Contexts* (Chicago: University of Chicago Press, 2003).

[14] This fact is slightly recognized that all Kaulas were organized as different lineages associated to a particular *mātṛkā*, the goddess, called *kulaja*. These *kulaja*s would be exogamic units and people contracted marriages within the Kaula practitioners of different *kuluja* clans. Yet, caste and *gotra–pravara* rules applied along with this, perhaps to maintain the larger social norms. It is interesting to note that Brahmāṇī is the tutelary deity of Brahmapura, even though the Kula Devi (the goddess of the royal lineage) of Chamba's royal household is Bhadrakālī. We must remember that Brāhmaṇī is the early *mātṛkā*: the terrible power of the goddess that helped in the annihilation of the foes and cleaning up of the battleground.

a specific place of their own in the greater Shaivite canon, usually as the members of the *Bhairavastotras*. Their rites, to put it simplistically, were private (tantric) and were performed in lonely places, like forests. A variant of Kashmiri Shaivism that was more widely recognized after the tenth century, the Tṛkha Kaula, used the ritual to awaken and carry forward the serpentine force, the *kunḍalinī*, through the body path that would 'delight the senses and mind'. The *kunḍalinī* progresses by arousing the dormant psycho-spiritual points located in the body called chakras, leading to the bonding of the opposites, the fusion of the male–female polarities, the Shiva–Shakti, in the head.[15] In other words, as *Kaulajñānanirṇaya* defines, *Kula* was the 'embodied cosmos'[16] that unites things of the same 'order'. It rejects, therefore, the 'sense of plurality', which may be internally achieved by the fusion of the distinction perceived in the knower, the knowledge and the object of knowledge. In other words, the distinction between the subject and object is dispelled, leading to the cognizance of non-dual reality. The eastern tantric Siddha tradition therefore defines the *Kula* as, 'the state in which the mind and the sight are united, the sense-organs lose their individuality, *śakti* (power) becomes identical with the *jīva* (being) and the sight merges into the object to be visualised'.[17]

Ritually, the Nath Siddhas inherited the Kaula practices and modified them as they interacted with other tantrikas and alchemists, seeking to perfect the body and transmute it internally by practising *haṭha* yoga, as the alchemists sought to transform the material. This could lead to miraculous powers, the *siddhis*, which they tried to perfect during their lifespan. This form of yoga consisted of lifting the *kunḍalinī* force through the nerve plexus, the *naḍīs*, over various psycho-physical points, the *chakras*. The transmutation takes place in the mind, the *Brahmarandhra*, where the male–female (Shiva–Shakti) polarity merged, leading to the state of supreme consciousness, which casts off all distinctions and illusion; a state where microcosm and the macrocosm lose identity and became a singular reality. Let me illustrate this with a couple of verses from *Ātma-bodh*, the text attributed to Gorakṣa, which exemplifies

---

[15] For further details, see the second part of M.S.G. Dyczkowski, *The Canon of the Saivagama and the Kubjika Tantra of the Western Kaula Tradition* (New Delhi: Motilal Banarsidass, 1989).

[16] P.E. Muller-Ortega, *The Triadic Heart of Śiva: Kaula Tantricism of Abhinavagupta in the Non-dual Shaivism of Kashmir* (Albany: State University of New York Press, 1989), Chapter 5.

[17] Bagchi, *Kaulajñānananirṇaya*, 37–38.

the tantric–alchemical ritual and tangentially indicates the complex process of borrowing from diverse traditions, the Kaulas and the Tibetan Buddhist tantra being among them.

> Contrary to perception, the moon engulfs Rāhū
> The sun, in turn, engulfs Ketu.
> The sun stabilizes on the path of moon (that there is union of sun and moon)
> This is the realisation of the yogis' path [haṭha yoga][18]
>
> The union of mind and wind is difficult
> Until the moon and sun are tied in tight [but equal] embrace.
> It sucks in nine hundred and ninety waters
> The Jogī drains it and it fills again to drain.[19]

The Protest and Conformity

The Nath Siddhas were organized into twelve clans, which had strong spiritual kinship through the agency of a guru or the preceptor. As with all the esoteric sects, the guru played a major role in instruction and transmission of the spiritual knowledge and ritual practices.[20] Thus, the guru came to occupy a privileged position that linked the past and the future generations. These guru-centred families, where disciples–*chelas* were horizontally linked as *guru-bhāi*s or spiritual brothers descending from the same guru, formed different spiritual lineages, each specializing and emphasizing a particular cognitive spiritual process and ritual. As the Nath tradition was heavily influenced by the Tibetan Nyingma innovations, the role of the guru in determining the well-being of spiritual lineages was also influenced by it. The role was different for different disciples, dependent upon the maturity of the disciple–*chela*. The guru was simply a preceptor who initiated and ordained disciples into the sect and passed on its cherished instructions. However, for the realized disciple, the guru was the path itself, which one followed faithfully. The tribulations and tests devised, for instance, by Marpa for Milarespa or Naropa for Marpa (which included physical hardship), were a part of the complex coded instructions that signified

[18] *Ātma-bodh*: 6 Gorakhnath, *Atma Bodh* (Haridwar: Bhekh Barah Panth Series, 1986).

[19] Ibid., 12.

[20] For general discussion on the role of gurus in the medieval vernacular literature, Daniel Gold, *The Lord as Guru: Hindi Sants in North Indian Tradition* (New Delhi: Oxford University Press, 1987).

the ways of the path.[21] The ultimate aim was to fuse the mind of the disciple with that of the guru. In other words, the guru was conceived not merely as an instructor but was the path, which needed no instruction but pursuit. This is the process that liberated the disciple from the master, where he learnt to become his own guru.[22] In a certain sense, the duality between the guru and the disciple ends there. In other words, the guru is a path but the ultimate path is the realization of the 'self'.

> There is no Guru like knowledge (*jñāna*). No 'disciple' like conscience (*cita*).
> There is none like Mind (that realizes God and conscience).
> Gorakṣa, therefore, walks alone (he seeks his own path).
>
> *Sabadi* 189

In the end, one had to become one's own guru. The physical guru was merely a visualization of the spiritual; a visualization of the meditative/spiritual genealogy.[23] How important the institution of guru is in the Nath Siddha tradition may be comprehended from the fact that every fifth verse in the *Gorakh-Bāṇi*, directly or indirectly, speaks about the guru.

Closely allied to the position of guru was the concept of sound and language. Once again, it is pertinent to point out that the role of sound and 'word' was critically explored in salvific rituals, leading to a polemical binary in the South Asian devotional. The word and its sound were used as a cryptic code that determined the subtle variation in different rituals and visualizations involved in such rituals, particularly the tantric ones.[24] The words were not/cannot be

[21] Tsang Nyon Heruka, *The Life of Marpa the Translator: Seeing Accomplishes All* (Boston: Sambhala, 1982 [1999, South Asian Edition]); Lobzang Jivaka, *The Life of Milarepa: Tibet's Great Yogi* (condensed and adapted from the original), trans. W.Y. Evans-Wentz (New Delhi: Rupa, 1996[1928]).

[22] As observed in the commentary of verse 39 in the *Kāma-Kalā-Vilāsa*, 'Sadāśiva Himself remaining in the positions of (both) Teacher (Guru) and Disciple (Śiṣya), by words cast in the form of questions and answers brings down Tantra (on earth)'. *Kāma-Kalā-Vilāsa by Punyananda Natha: With the Commentary of Natananda-Natha*, Fourth Edition, trans. and commentary Sir John Woodroffe, 1921 (Chennai: Ganesh & Co., 1971), verse 39.

[23] For recent exposition of such practices in the Nyingma order, see Cortland Dahl, compiled, trans. and introduced, *Entrance to the Great Perfection: A Guide to the Dzogchen Preliminary Practices* (Ithaca: Snow Lion Publications, 2009).

[24] Each sound alphabet has a meaning and the word formed, cryptic or otherwise, has a complex meaning that is standardized in the language of ritual visualization. For instance, Hriṁ, the *bīja* (seed mantra) of Goddess Lalitā, is a verbal visualization

devoid of meaning. They were elevated to the spiritual level through the process of visualization. As suggested, for instance, in *Kāma-Kalā-Vilāsa*, 'Word (*vāka*) and its meaning (*artha*) are always united. They are Śiva and Śakti which are three-fold as Creation, Maintenance and Dissolution (*sṛṣṭisthitilayabhedau*), and as the three *Bījas*'.[25] This later resulted in the development of language as an ornament of ritual offering; as well as an instructive text that was the key to ritual performance. This development starts simultaneously with the early Puranic ritual image worship, which later matures into an elaborate ritual performance in the *saguna* Vaishnava devotionals, particularly the Kṛṣṇite sects that emerge and bloom in the first half of the second millennium CE. On the other hand, the Vajrayana Buddhist tantrikas, and concurrently, or subsequently, the 'Hindu' tantrikas, started exploring the relationship between the sound, word and language in raising the serpentine force or the *kuṇḍalinī*, as a process to access and advance the cognitive faculties beyond the normally accepted development.[26] All major tantric texts allocate extensive space to pinpoint the nature of sound and the letter/alphabet (*varaṇa*) correlates that would be used in the ritual. The Nath texts raise this to the level of alternative cosmogonic exploration, using such subtlety as *nāda*, *bindu*, *śabda-brahma* as the causative principle in the process of creation. The reverberation of the sound in the hollow of the mind is the archetype for the creation of the universe.

> The 'word' is the lock, it indeed is the key
> Only the word awakes the Word (*Nāda* or cosmic sound)
> The word is the basis of introducing the Word (the language)
> The word subsumes the WORD.
>
> *Sabadi* 21

The concept of sound is logically unified in the institution of guru. While the sound is divine, the guru is the one who achieves and leads to such spiritual

---

of her form. This may be encrypted as explained in *Tantrarāja Tantra*: '"H" stands for Prakāśa, because it is (the bīja of) Ākāśa which is Sphuraṇatmaka, "R" which is (the bīja of) Agni means Devouring (*grāsa*) because Fire devours; "I" is the Vimarśa (as it leads to oneness in the Supreme sense: *tādātmyaparamārthamelana*). By the Bindu (ṁ) is effected the Niphālāna of Realisation, of oneness of the Sādhaka with these'. *Tantrarāja Tantra: A Short Analysis*, Fourth Edition, introduction by Arthur Avalon (Madras: Ganesh & Co., 1971), XXXV: 24–25, 111.

[25] *Kāma-Kalā-Vilāsa*, verse 12.

[26] For a brief and modern exposition written primarily for the West, see Gopi Krishna, *Kundalini – The Secret of Yoga* (New Delhi: UBS Publishers, n.d).

levels that attains divinity. Through the words of the *guru*, one attains the divine.[27] However, the Nath tradition accentuates the significance of language when it says that it is through the objective language that the subtle yet subjective can be attained through the instructions of the *guru*.

When liturgical and spiritual treatises were written, these were written in a coded language, which could be decoded only by following the instructions of the guru, which were given orally. The oral thus complemented the written, which in fact was clueless and therefore incomplete without the oral component. Siddhas and tantrikas had realized the significance of language and sound and used it for ritual purposes, the *mantra-yaṇā*, for instance, but also to keep the esoteric knowledge secret. They, thus, developed a coded language, wrote in cryptic verses or *vyākulitākṣara*;[28] the language of absurd or *ulṭi-bāṇi*; and the twilight language or the *sandhā-bhāṣā*,[29] which shielded and empowered the ritually initiated from the uninitiated and the lay. In the process, the *guru* ensured a bonding within the clan as the oral liturgical transmission was restricted within the 'spiritual brotherhood' only. Through the usage of unique language and ritual and the agency of *guru*, both horizontal and vertical relations within the clan and sect were thus fostered and sustained. Let us sample a translated example of the Nath coded language:

> Sowed the seeds of *Āmalā* (sweet)
> It bore the fruits of *Neem* (bitter)
> Those who are wise, they find it sweet
> As the fruits (*prasāda*) bestowed by Guru.
> The camel became the food
> As it sat on the branch of a tree!
> The barren woman gave birth to son
> Merely by 'staring' at a man!

---

27 For instance, Guenther, *The Life and Teaching of Naropa*, XIII–IV, comments on Naropa's self-realization: 'The quest in a way brings about a significant distinction between the two paths of self-realisation. One is the path of knowledge, that Naro was adept in, he understood the meaning of the words, the noetic path of understanding the dharma. The other is more exalted, that he learns from Tilopa, the emotions behind the words. The second is the path of realisation.'

28 *Tantrarāja Tantra: A Short Analysis*; Mahamahopadhyaya Lakshmana Shastri, ed., *Tantrarāja Tantra* (Tantrik Texts), *Vol. III, Part I* (London: Luzac & Co.) 1919, 23–24; Chapter VIII, verses 72–90.

29 Agehananda Bharati, 'Intentional Language in the Tantras', *Journal of the American Oriental Society* 81(3) (1961), 261–270.

The wood drowned, the stone (*sila*) floated
The world comes to an end!
The big camel drowned in the flow
But it could not enter the subtle gate!
The fish climbed atop the mountain
The water caught fire!
The adept (*Jogī*) got free of illusion
The thorn got free of the thorny-bush.
Pada 20

That the language in this coded verse is symbolic is evident at the first reading itself. What is 'sweet' and 'bitter'; why a camel (what does it represent) sits on the tree; or the barren woman bears a son (daughter would represent a different meaning). How/why does the wood sink while the stone floats? Obviously, the key to all these (and such) symbols/symbolism rests with the guru. What, therefore, sounds 'absurd' might be sagacious once deciphered by the knowledgeable. Let us also consider the symbols in another example of the evocative 'absurd' *pada*:

O Avadhuta [the realized one]...,
The ants brought down the mountain
The cow lacerated the tiger!
The rabbit triumphed over the sea-waves,
The antelope killed the leopard! [*bāgh*]
Pada 57.2

The cryptic, coded and absurd language played a major role in the society of the medieval spiritualists. One, by singing such songs, these renunciates were seen as 'deranged' (mad, as it were) or, at best, as mystics whose language was difficult to comprehend. They, thus, were left alone by the lay people, which afforded them time and secrecy to perform some of their secret/prohibited/censured rituals.[30] Two, the codes were orally passed on by the gurus and were critical keys in the transmission of the prohibited or the esoteric content of the verses that could otherwise be sung openly as 'absurd'. What is being

[30] For example, consider this advice offered to the practitioners in the medieval text *Haṭhayoga Pradīpikā*: 'A yogi desirous of success should keep the knowledge of Hatha Yoga secret; for it becomes potent by concealing, and impotent by exposing'. Pancham Singh, trans., *The Haṭhayoga Pradīpikā of Atmā Rāma* (New Delhi: Indian Press, 1915), 11, Chapter I.

suggested is that the usage of the 'absurd' language was a well thought out textual strategy that ensured a faithful transmission of the oral tradition and its diffusion over space and time. Without the agency of the guru, however, the transmission process would lose its valuable key. No wonder, the literature underlines the significance of the guru in the spiritual growth of the disciple by narrating the coded dialogues and actions that purportedly took place between Matsyendra and Gorakṣa; and later, between Gorakṣa and other Nath Siddhas.[31] Theoretically, the dialogues are significant as they also invert the roles of guru and disciple, undergirding the fact that spiritual development is not bound by such relationships; that the disciple may become the guru of his guru and help him achieve his goal. The agency of the guru is, nevertheless, projected as an innovation, unique to the Nath Siddha order, later replicated by other Hindu sectarians. For instance,

> 'The Vaiṣṇavas need milk to survive; the Nāgā *sanyāsis* need wood to keep them warm. The silent ascetics (munis) depend on friends to express themselves. The Jogīs depend on his guru, for without him, there is no life'.[32]

The Nath Siddha protest was more real also because most of them belonged to different professions and castes, mostly from the ritually lower castes. They were shepherds, temple drummers, artificers, potters, weavers, tillers, hunters, etc. Charpatnath, whom we shall discuss shortly, was a *kahār* or the pall-bearer, the prerogative of the Jhīr caste men (Jhīvara or the fishermen and water carrier). It is perhaps because of their humble origin that the Nath Siddhas could understand and influence the folk–peasant societies.

> I am a shepherd, I drink milk like Him.
> Without love the mother dies; without father, the son.
> Of no caste, this shepherd looks after cows every day![33]

The Nath Siddha compositions integrated in its conceptual body everyday categories, giving precedence to lived experiences, which endeared them to the rural masses. The literature is aimed at an agrarian society, rather than urban masses.[34]

---

[31] See such texts and translations in Sashibhushan Dasgupta, *Obscure Religious Cults*, Third Edition (Calcutta: Firma K.L. Mukhopadhyaya Limited, 1976).

[32] *Naṭh Siddha Bani*, Vs no. 40, p.34.

[33] R.L. Srivastava, ed., *Gorakh Bani*, (Gorakhnath Mandir: Gorakhpur, 1978) verses 21, 165.

[34] Pitambardatta Barathwal, *Gorakh Bani: Jogesari Bani, I* (Prayaga: Chaukhamba Press, Vikrami Samvat 2003 (1946) 136–37, verses 1–4.

O distressed find a Guru, don't remain Guru-less
O brother, there is no redemption without Guru.
As the black cuckoo bird if bathed in milk [that is white], does not become white;
By adorning a garland of flowers the crow does not become a swan.
The crow took away my un-broken bread
My Guru asked where you sat to eat.
He comes from north, to the west he goes
My guru advised, there you should eat.

Pada: 34

My Guru sings only three verses.
I do not know where the guru has gone,
I cannot sleep (refrain)
In the house of a potter, the pitcher is
Illusion, as the milk is in the Ahīr's [buffalo/cow-herder].
In the house of a Brāhmaṇa, woman is illusion,
Hence the pitcher, milk and woman [all three are same].
In the house of a king, the lance is illusion,
In the house of a farmer, an oxen is illusion,
In the house of oil-presser (Telī), oil is illusion;
Oil, oxen and lance [are the same].
In the house of Ahīr, buffalo is illusion, as
Phallus (*linga*) in temple and asafoetida (*hīnga*) in a shop,
Hence, cattle, *linga* (icon) and asafoetida are same.
Though the concept is same, there are different ways to express,
Only God can realize this intricate notion of Illusion.

Pada: 52

There is a trenchant criticism, in the Nath Siddha literature, of various rituals and ritualists across religious boundaries. Therefore, they castigate the Brāhmaṇa clergy as well as the *maulvis*; the temple, as much as the mosque. The pilgrims and pilgrimage are taken to task. The 'realization' comes not from the place-of-power or ritual; rather, these are the ways of the unrealized.

The qāzī and mullah recites the Koran, Just as the brāhmaṇa recites the Veda.
Pilgrims and Sanyāsis (the followers of Śankracārya) live in the illusion of pilgrimages
None of them grasped the true meaning of salvation (*nirvāṇa*).

Sabadi: 96

The Nath Siddhas do not belong to a particular religion; they are in fact, as a late passage from the *Gorakh-Bāṇi* says: 'By birth we are Hindus, as practitioners,

Jogīs and by thought, Muslims [Sufis]'.[35] Similarly, we may take note of other musings of such gravity,[36] as:

> Hindus worship in the temple, as Muslims in the mosque.
> The Jogīs meditate on the Ultimate Truth, which requires neither a temple nor mosque.

Or,

> The Hindu calls Rāma, what the Muslims say is *Khudā* (*Allah*)
> The Jogīs meditate only on the Timeless (*alakha*)[37]

Most of the Nath ritual texts were written in Sanskrit. The popularity of the sect was, however, gained through the vehicle of vernacular compositions. It is interesting to note that the Nath Siddha compositions in vernacular languages are after the twelfth century, when Sanskrit was not the favoured language, or the court language, of the North Indian polity. The literature is particularly vibrant in medieval Punjabi, Braja, Marathi and Rajasthani. In the east, Bengali, and in the south, Tamil, was the medium of dissemination and popularization of the sect and its paradigmatic figures – the nine Naths. It is in this literature that we can see the amplification of the Siddha protest. However, the protest of the northern Nath Siddhas is not as virulent and evocative as their southern counterparts, recounted, for example, in the songs and poems translated by Kamil Zvevil ('We shall kindle the fire in the rift among castes/We shall plant our staff in open market...').[38] At the same time, it is not as 'ecstatic' and radical as the Kartabhaja Baul songs, which have been translated and analysed by Hugh Urban ('...There is no consideration of caste: ritual is empty;/...all low classes and untouchables; Brāhmaṇas and Kāyasthas; police chiefs and those who burn the dead/All together eat the same food').[39] The north, in

[35] Srivastava, *Gorakh Bani*, 6, verse 14.

[36] Ranghey Raghav, *Garakhnath aur unka Yuga* (New Delhi: Pustakmahal Publishers, 1963), 230.

[37] Ibid., *sabadi* 38 and 39.

[38] This is only an illustrative verse from the larger radical literature of the Tamil Siddhas, particularly Pāmpāṭṭic Cittar, who wrote *Cittarārūtam*. See Kamil V. Zvelebil, *The Poets of Power* (London: Rider and Company, 1973), 114.

[39] '...They are neither holy men nor atheists; they remain outside the door like hypocrites./They are neither Hindu nor Muslim weavers…/They overturn all Hindu religion...'. Hugh B. Urban, *The Songs of Ecstacy: Tantric and Devotional Songs*

fact, was a different integrating place for the Naths and Sufis, as the Buddhist Mahasiddhas earlier, resulting in the proliferation of alchemical practices and the development of power relations between the Nath Siddhas and the state. For instance, Dominique-Sila Khan has documented the mutual influence exerted upon these heterodox practitioners in Rajasthan, particularly the Ismaili Naziris and the Naths.[40] The frequent reference to the Muslim clergy, the holy book, Koran and the Sufis in the Nath Siddha literature, moreover, is an indicator of their social comfort and ease, in as much their vision of the society that was inclusive and composite. The interchanging suffix for the Naths by *Pir*, which was a common practice among the northern Naths, was one way of firming up this inclusive vision, just as saying that the Siddhas and the Auliyas or the Sufis were the same.

> Siddha Auliyā in this world are few.
> They move as a child, only few know them.[41]

Or, in the words of Rattan Hājjī (one who has undertaken the Haj pilgrimage), whose sayings are part of *Gorakh-Bāṇi*:

> The pīr (guru) is iron, the path (taqbīr) copper
> The prophet is silver, the gold, the God. Between these (variables) the world swims.
> We the timeless sit and watch (are impassive to the developments around us),
> Thus says the adept Rattan Hājjī.
> *Sabadi*: 118

Is there certain arrogance discernable in this verse? We may, however, observe that Prophet Mohammad is accorded both respect and space in the Nath texts. But just like the Brāhmaṇas, it is the clergy, the mullahs/*maulvi*s, who are disparaged for not comprehending in true perspective the nuances of his 'word', the true 'tenets' of Islam.

---

from Colonial Bengal (New York: Oxford University Press, 2001), 142; also, see Hugh B. Urban, *The Economics of Ecstacy: Tantra, Secrecy and Power in Colonial Bengal* (New York: Oxford University Press, 2001).

40 Dominique-Sila Khan, *Conversions and Shifting Identities: Ramdev Pir and the Ismailis in Rajasthan* (New Delhi: Manohar, 1997).

41 Shankaranath, ed., *Sri Mastnath Charit* (Haridwar: Behkh Barah Panth Mahasabha, 1990), 17.

> Do not repeatedly invoke the name of Muhammad, O *qāzī*, consider the depth of His words.
> If you were to put a sword in the hands of Muhammad, it would neither be moulded sharp nor made of iron (that the words of Prophet bonded the social, evoked spirituality of love, and were inclusive).
>
> *Sabadi*: 9

How different is this understanding from the positions taken by the Sufi orders, which were mostly at war with the established clergy? Is this a pointer to the mutual influence that the Sufis and the Nath Siddhas exercised over each other? Do they speak for each other, as it seems in the following verse:

> The 'word' gave birth to purity, the 'word' wiped out impurity (of knowledge and mortality), that is *pīr*, that is Muhammad.
> Do not live in illusion, O *qāzī*, do not forget that spirituality towers over the corporeal body – the brutal force.
>
> *Sabadi*: 10

> We took birth as Hindus but developed into *jogīs*, just like the *pīrs* among Muslims.
> Choose such a path O *Qāzīs*, *Mullahs* and Brāhmaṇas, which aspires to divinity.
>
> *Sabadi*: 14

There is unusual evidence from the Tibetan tradition that, in a roundabout fashion, indicates the common ground – of mutual borrowing and influence – of the soteriological praxis. Even in the late thirteenth century, there was some contact, though tangential, between the Tibetan and the Nath Siddha traditions, evident in the travels of one Götsangpa Gönpo Dorjé (CE 1189–1258). He travelled with his guru, Gar Lotsawa, to Jālandhara-pītha, the seat of the goddess, through Chamba. Interestingly, the king of Chamba received them thinking that they were *pir*s! Let me provide the passage referring to their journey to Chamba that was translated by Dan Martin for the Rubin Foundation in New York:

> Gar Lotsawa dismissed the idea that he could go to Jalandhara, 'You won't reach it. Food is hard to get. You don't know the language. The road is infested with death-happy bandits. On the one-in-a-hundred chance you do make it there, you will be blocked by the non-human spirits in the cemeteries.'
>
> But Götsangpa was so determined to go that Gar decided to go with him, which at least solved the problem of not knowing the language. The passes that both join and separate Lahul and Chamba would have proven impassible if it were not for the good fortune of meeting some local porters he called Mönpas

> (mon-pa). With pickaxes and ropes tied around their waists they helped them by making footholds in the mirror-smooth rock faces. Götsangpa said about these Mönpas that they had nothing to wear but deerskins and nothing to eat but buckwheat chaff. Meanwhile the two Tibetans had nothing at all to eat and were constantly passing out from hunger. After a twelve-day trek, thrilled to see just how green forests can be, and catching a first glimpse of the Indian plains 'as smooth as the palm of the hand' stretching out beneath them, they found themselves in the capital of the Chamba king.[42]

Does it not substantiate our hypothesis that the Sufis were held in great esteem by the people as peripheral as in the western Himalayas? Significantly, the Tibetan tantric practitioners continued to visit the sites of the goddesses in the Indian heartland, renewing their contacts with other practitioners – the Nath Siddhas. One may also commend the sensitivity of the guru, who undertook the difficult journey, despite his old age, to help his disciple in conformity with the sectarian ethos.[43] Our contention, however, is that the exchange between

---

[42] I am grateful to Dr Dan Martin of the International Institute for Asian Studies (IIAS), Leiden, for providing me with this information and translation of the passage that he did for the Rubin Foundation in New York. See also, Laxman S. Thakur, *Buddhism in the Western Himalaya: A Study of the Tabo Monastery* (New Delhi: Oxford University Press, 2001), 47, 48.

[43] I am grateful to Dr Dan Martin of IIAS, Leiden, for providing me his notes. He refers to the 'Collected Works (*Gsun 'bum*) of Rgod-tshan-pa Mgon-po-rdo-rje', reproduced from the manuscript set that once belonged to Rje Sâkya-rin-chen and preserved at Pha-jo-ldin Monastery, Kunzang Tobgey (Thimphu, 1976). Tucci translated passages on the trip to Jālandhara from a biography entitled, *Rgyal ba rgod tshang pa mgon po rdo rje'i rnam thar mthong ba don ldan nor bu'i phreng ba* (the one by Sangs rgyas dar po), which very closely corresponds to the same passage in this work. Chapter 4:

20.1. He goes to the headwaters of the Ganga, and meets the chief Dakini 'Gro-ba-bzang-mo. This place had been visited by Slob-dpon Nag-po-spyod-pa. This place is greater in blessing than others. He descends to Zhang zhung-gi-yul Gu-ge, where Atisa had stayed, then down to Zhang zhung-gi Tho-lding-gi gtsug-lag-khang, built by Lha btsun Byang chub'od.

20.4. He has a darshana of Kha-rag-pa when he arrives at the highlands of Bi-li-pi-chog. He had been a monk, but became a rten-dkar-po (white dresser). Requests teaching from him.

21.3. He travels upward and meets Grub-thob Brag-smug-pa. Although he was 84 years old, he retained his yogic posture.

the Nath Siddhas and the Tibetan Buddhist tradition was already waning, as both were being transformed, operating hence after within more rigid religious parameters. The tantric influence of the Tibetan tradition was gradually replaced by more material alchemy and other soteriological praxis that came along with the visitors from Central/West Asia and beyond, who are commented upon in the vernacular literature as recounted earlier. That these visitors could also open doors of patronage to the Nath Siddhas in the changing state system cannot be overlooked.

The Siddha literature is indicative of their social position, a protest that they were the carriers and product of. The Nath Siddha protest was ideologically compelling because they successfully used the vernaculars to transmit their message, a strategy that was later replicated by other sectarians. Their ideological position was also strengthened because they were challenged and

---

21.6. Then he goes to Gar-zha (Lahul). Then, Mt. Gan-dho-la. At its peak was a self-produced mchod-rten called Dharma-mu-tri.

22.3. Dge-bshes Mgar Lo-tstsha-ba had tried to convince him not to go to Dza-lan-dha-ra, on account of the rarity of food, not knowing the language, and the many murderous brigands.

22.6. He joins up with one Su-ru, a minister of the Lcam-be Rgyal-po. Three days journey from Gar-zha he comes up against a high glacier pass. Some heavily laden Mon pas head across it, so he thinks he can make it. An un-laden member of their group goes ahead with an axe and digs steps in the ice. It takes them half a day to reach the top of the pass. Then he travelled 11 days in Mon-yul. He describes the Mon people as dressing only in skin of mountain game. Describes their diet.

23.5. On the 11th day they reach the capital of Lcam-be. There all the mountains of Mon-yul come to an end. When arriving in India, the men and women all become mi 'bru (?) and therefore very handsome. They have rice for food. They dress in the Ca-ta-ras, a very fine cloth. The groves of sugarcane are extremely beautiful and pleasant feeling.

23.6. There was a king Be-khri-bra-ma with 7,000 ministers. Each minister had 7,000 families. The king had eleven wives.

The name of the Chamba king is Vaira[si] Varman. This does not match with the accepted chronology as he supposedly ruled around CE 1330, when a copper plate bearing his name was recovered from Chamba. 'Guroli Plate of Vairasivarman VS 1387', in *Antiquities of Chambā State, Part II*, B. Ch. Chhabra. Memoir of Archaeological Survey of India, No. 72 (New Delhi: Government of India Press, 1957), 21–23.

engaged by other sectarians and reformists/dissenting traditions. They are thus mentioned, even if in a dialogical defeat, by Guru Nanak, as in the Sikh canon, the Guru Granth Sahib (the *Ādī Granth*);[44] or in the war-of-miracles, as, for instance, in the Puṣṭimārga Vaishnavite literature.[45] Significantly, such textual strategies are indicative of the fact that the Siddhas, by the end of the fifteenth century, occupied a hegemonic space and needed to be challenged and confronted by other sects/sectarians, if these wanted to grow. It is also around this time that one realizes the gravity of decadence that had crept into their 'orders', which had become belligerent and militarized, as recounted, for instance, by Abul Fazl. There are pointers to the fact that a certain arrogance had crept in to their orders. These are subtle indicators of their entrenchment, yet non-conformist ways.

> The *Jogīs* are friend to none, one should know them warily.
> They do not consider the 'high' and 'low' and act as they please.[46]

By the end of the fifteenth century, the Nath Siddhas were assimilated into the social fabric of North India. So much so, in the fifteenth century social text, *Varṇa Ratnākara*, while describing the attributes or *guna*s of *nayaka* (the

---

[44] Gorakhnath and Charpatnath are mentioned in the celebrated debate between the Siddhas and Nanak, a textual strategy used to supplant and legitimate the new 'religious' ethos. 'Sidh Gośṭhī' – Conversations with the Siddhas: Section 22, Rāga Rāmakalī/63/ First Mahl, Śaloka 3; 78 First Mahl, Śaloka 5. Also, Piar Singh, *Guru Nanak Siddha Goshti (With a Comprehensive Introduction Text [Trilingual] Translation & Annotations)* (Amritsar: Guru Nanak Dev University, 1996), 22, 53. He says that only Gorakh and Charpat are named among the Siddhas. He also says that this portion was probably included by the third guru. Though the only verse bearing Charpat's name is on p. 73, Dr Jodh Singh refers to the reference made by Bhāī Gurdās to the dialogue between Guru Nanak and Charpatnath at Achal Baṭālā, in modern Punjab, in the first half of the sixteenth century. The Siddhas ask questions to which the guru answers in deferential terms to Charpati, while he is dismissive towards other Siddhas. This is an oblique reference to the status and stature of Charpati in the contemporaneous milieu. Jodh Singh, *The Religious Philosophy of Guru Nanak* (Varanasi: Sikh Philosophical Society, 1983), 22, 24, 28, 34, 71–75, 81–83.

[45] The purported defeat was inflicted in the Nath Siddha's den of Mount Srisailam. Damodar Sastri and Somesvara Sastri, ed. and trans., *Srimad Vallabhacarya Digvijayah* (Indore: Cartons and Printers, 1987).

[46] Shankranath, *Sri Mastnath Charit*, 178.

protagonist–hero), the possession of the eight siddhis (the magical powers) is considered a major attribute. In fact, it is through power relations, which were abhorred in the early Nath literature, that the Siddhas are held in awe by the rural population. These power relations were exhibited by an inane display of their *siddhis*, perhaps figuratively, by which they dominated the rural populace. The *siddhis* demonstrate their mastery over space (from finite to infinite), time (by flight), weight, to fulfilling desires, exerting perverse control over their immediate environment, subjection or fame.[47]

The frame stories also change. The legends of Gopichand, Pūraṇ Bhagat, Caurangīnāth or Guggā/Ghoḍā-colī/Munḍalīka, and the later cult of Balaknāth, pervasive in the entire North India, are indicative of the alchemical practices. In all these stories, following the argument of David White, the core of the legends is about the regenerative powers of the alchemical process, like Pūraṇ Bhagat becoming complete after the intervention of Gorakhnath. He was thrown into the well after dismembering his limbs and gouging out his eyes. He was restored to his former shape and glory by Gorakhnath.[48] Similarly, when a woman, whose cowherd Balaknāth was, accused him of negligence after she had raised him for twelve years, he took her to the well and asked her to take back all the 'bread' and 'butter-milk' that she had served. In fact, the forest, 'cave' or 'well' is a kind of a Siddha laboratory, like the crematorium for some tantrikas, from which the life is churned and reshaped, just like the base metals are transmuted into higher order by certain alchemical process. It is only after passing the test of the 'well', that one is pronounced a *Jogi*, be it Pūraṇ Bhagat or Balaknāth.

If people were in awe because of the miraculous powers that the Nath Siddhas allegedly possessed, they feared them for their eightfold ritual powers

---

[47] *The Padmāvatī*, written by Malik Muhammad Jaisi, tr. A. G. Shirraff (Kolkata: The Royal Asiatic Society of Bengal, 1944) p.25, has been used here because it is a contemporary of the Chamba genealogy process. Himself a mystic, he enumerated these siddhis as: (a) *Anīmā* or the power to become infinitesimally small; (b) *Mahīmā*, acquire gigantic proportions; (c) *Laghīmā*, become light weighted; (d) *Garīmā*, become really heavy; (d) *Prāptī*, to reach really far; (e) *Ichatva*, obtaining desired object; (f) *Prākmaya*, obtaining fame (sovereignty); (g) *Vacitiva*, the power to subjection; and (h) the power to conquer sense perception. The range and nomenclature of these siddhis or powers changed over time, but continue to emphasize the control of these adepts over the material and spiritual spheres that lead to awe and fear, often expressed in the idiom of respect or reverence.

[48] White, *The Alchemical Body*, 298–301.

(*siddhī-karma*) by which they could control and inflict death, hypnotize, cure/inflict disease, peace, etc.[49] In fact, by the late medieval times, the hutments of the Nath Siddhas were the popular centres for the cure of skin and eye diseases, psychic illness, snake bites, intestinal ailments, etc.[50] Most of the paradigmatic Siddhas were deified, or as White argues, they were considered demi-gods – a position they always aspired to attain by linking themselves through their professed *siddhis* to the Gandharvas and the Vidyādharas.[51] The places associated with such Siddhas, mostly the local Siddhas, became the popular pilgrimage places managed by the householder priests – the *Jogis*. The deified Siddhas manifested miraculous powers through the medium, the priests (called *celās*), of these shrines. People undertook pilgrimages to these centres to beget children, to seek protection from malevolent spirits, cure illness, for the recovery of sick cattle, for psychosis or 'possession syndrome' and faith healing, mental illness and to recover or overcome vicissitudes, as well as for a successful completion of life cycle rituals (except in the case of death).[52] Obviously, the role of the local Nath Siddhas had changed from protest to conformity.

The changed role of the Nath Siddhas is also underscored by their increased presence in the state apparatus as well. They were particularly associated with North Indian medieval polity, for example, the Guhilas;[53] later Mārwār;[54] and

---

[49] These eight are: *Siddhi karma*, *shanti karma*, *vidvesana karma*, *roga karma*, *marana karma*, *vasikarana karma*, *stambhana karma* and *ucattana karma*.

[50] H.A. Rose, *A Glossary of the Castes and Tribes of the Punjab and North-West Frontier Province*. 3 Vols. 1919 (Chandigarh: Punjab Language and Culture Academy, 1973 [Reprint]) I, 261–64, 279–80; H.S. Oberoi, 'The Worship of Pir Sakhi Sarver: Illness, Healing, and Popular Culture in the Punjab', *Studies in History* III, no. 1 (1987), 29–56.

[51] White, *The Alchemical Body*.

[52] Oberoi, 'The Worship of Pir Sakhi Sarver', 32, reports similarly about another cult.

[53] Nandini Sinha, 'A Study of State and Cult: The Guhilas, Pasupatas and Ekalingaji in Mewar, Seventh to Fifteenth Centuries A.D', *Studies in History* IX (1993), 161–182.

[54] The householder Jogis played a dominant role in the court of Man Singh (1803–1843) and were responsible for realigning of the Rajput nobility against the ruler who alienated them in favour of the Naths. These Jogis were accused of debauchery, kidnapping and killing by the British, and their influence waned after the 1850s. For a brief account, Debra Diamond, 'Painting, Politics, and Devotion under Maharaja Man Singh, 1803–43', in *Garden and Cosmos: The Royal Paintings of Jodhpur*, ed. D. Diamond et al. (Washington: Smithsonian Institution, 2008), 31–41.

as we shall discuss later, they played a pivotal role in the Chamba state;[55] or as Jakhbar records point out, and as Pinch demonstrates amongst the Mughals as well.[56] This assumption is supported by the incidents of sectarian rivalry between the Jogis and Sanyasis, leading to the militarization of their orders, as reported, among others, by Abul Fazl, the chronicler of Akbar.[57] These monastic orders, particularly the Sanyasis or Gosains, were also cash-rich organizations that were sustained by a brisk long distance trade, as demonstrated by Cohn and Kolff.[58] Therefore, these trader–soldier–ascetics legitimated and sustained the polity, the Mughals included, by providing both arms and cash. In turn, the state patronized them, thereby creating a symbiotic relationship of dependence and collaboration.

---

[55] Mahesh Sharma, *Western Himalayan Temple Records: State, Pilgrimage, Ritual and Legality in Chambā* (Leiden: Brill, 2009), 56–72.

[56] B.N. Goswamy and J.S. Grewal, *The Mughals and Jogis of Jakhbar* (Simla: Indian Institute of Advanced Study, 1967); W.R. Pinch, *Warrior Ascetics and Indian Empires* (Cambridge: Cambridge University Press, 2006); and David N. Lorenzen, 'Warrior Ascetics in Indian History', *Journal of the American Oriental Society* 98(1) (1978), 61–75.

[57] The skirmishes took place between the Jogis and Sanyasis around 1567, as informed by Nizam-ud-din Ahmed's *Tabaqat-i-Akbari*, where the Sanyasis were outnumbered by the Jogis by 300 to 500. Akbar surreptitiously supported the Sanyasis and with his aid, they emerged victorious in this conflict. Abul Fazl, in *Akbar-Nama*, calls this conflict between Puris and Giris, both the orders of the Sanyasis, which is unlikely. They must be Jogis and Sanyasis, perhaps of the Giri and Puri orders. Lorenzen, 'Warrior Ascetics in Indian History,' p.69. As Furquhar suggests, these disputes were largely because of the 'policing of the great religious fairs, and the collection of pilgrim dues'. See J.N. Furquhar, *An Outline of the Religious Literature of India* (London: Oxford University Press, 1920; (New Delhi: MLBD, 1967 [reprint]), 328).

[58] B.S. Cohn, 'Role of Gosains in the Economy of Eighteenth and Nineteenth Century Upper India', *Journal of Social Research* 17 (1974), 88–95; D.H.A. Kolff, 'Sanyasi Trader–Soldiers', *Indian Economic and Social History Review* 8 (1971), 213–18; also, see S.N. Gordon, 'Comment', *Indian Economic and Social History Review* 8 (1978), 219–20. Pinch writes that these 'ascetics' 'exercised broad political and economic influence as merchants, bankers, and, most importantly, soldiers. Powerful Mahants (abbots) speculated in real estate and engaged in extensive money lending activities in order to diversify monastic endowments in urban centres throughout the north, thus facilitating links between the increasingly regional political economies of the late Mughal era'. W.R. Pinch, *Peasants and Monks in British India* (Berkeley: University of California Press, 1996), 24.

While Pinch focuses on ascetic warlordism, and at times their nexus with the state as mercenaries, the hold of the Nath Siddhas over people was more pronounced because of their alleged miraculous powers, the *siddhis*, which they possessed. The quest for immortality and 'Power', while living (as against the ontological position of spirituality, that is empowered in death: attaining *mokṣa* or nirvana), epitomized in the attainment of six to nine *siddhis*, in a way defined these charismatic Nath Siddhas. It is this sway that paved way for their ideological penetration and hold over the North Indian polity, as recounted in the medieval royal Chamba genealogy. This is also an index of their popular appeal, where fear and awe inspired by their powers – the control over the material and the spiritual – was often described in the idiom of respect and reverence.[59] How these Siddhas were regarded may be gauged from the mid-sixteenth century account of Malik Muhammad Jaisi, written about the same time when the Chamba genealogy, which seeks legitimation by associating with the Siddhas – particularly Charpatnath – was in the process of compilation:

> …the Siddha is one who feels neither hunger nor confusion of thought. He whom the Lord has made a Siddha in this world, none can recognise him whether he be revealed or disguised…A Siddha wanders fearlessly by night and by day; where he has fixed his eyes, there he approaches. A Siddha is so fearless as regards to his own life that when he sees a sword he bows his neck. A Siddha goes verily to places where life is destroyed…Siddhas are immortal; their bodies are like mercury…Siddhas are like vultures, and can see to the ends of heaven.[60]

It is against this perception of dominance, ritualism and power-hungry mercenaries that popular protest finds a voice. This protest is both from within and from without. For example, Kabir, though arguably influenced by the

[59] Francois Bernier, who travelled across India in the seventeenth century, also observed the 'hideous to behold' 'Jauguis': 'In their trim I have seen them shamelessly walk, stark naked, through a large town, men, women, and girls looking at them without any more emotion than may be created when a hermit passes through our streets. Females would often bring them alms with much devotion, doubtless believing that they were holy personages, more chute and discreet than other men'. Francois Bernier, *Travels in the Mogul Empire*, trans. I. Brock and A. Constable (London: Oxford University Press, 1934; Delhi: Munshiram Manoharlal, 1994 [reprint]), 317.

[60] Jaisi, *Padmāvat*, 133: 22.6, 148: 24.2. For an outsider's view, see Francois Bernier above, note 59.

Nath Siddha ideology and practices, questions his contemporaries for their doublespeak:

> How will you cross, Nāth,
> How will you cross,
> So full of crookedness?
> Look how he meditates,
> Serves and prays…
> Mood of a snake, look:
> Utterly lewd,
> Utterly quarrelsome,
> Utterly shrewd.
> Look: a hawk's
> Face, and the thoughts of a cat
> Schools of philosophy
> Like a cloak furled.
> Look: the witch vanity
> Gulps down the world.[61]

Just as Nanak, who is reverential towards the paradigmatic Naths but is disdainful of the contemporaries, reminds them of their mission and goals that they set out to achieve but went astray in between and lost sight of their destiny.

> He alone is a Siddha, a seeker, a Yogi, a wandering pilgrim, who meditates on the One Perfect Lord. Touching the feet of the Lord Master, they are emancipated; they come to receive the Word of the Teachings.[62]

The Protest Within: The Inner Conflict

It would be methodologically fallacious to locate Charpati, who is a paradigmatic figure in the Nath Siddha order, as one of the nine principal Naths, as a dissenting voice and therefore, consider him outside the evolving tradition. Rather, his criticism should be taken as integral to the evolution of the tradition, that he was a part of, as an attempt to reform the decadent. Alternatively, by

---

[61] Linda Hess and Sukhdev Singh, *The Bījak of Kabir* (New Delhi: Motilal Banarsidass, 1986), Chapter 2, Verse 104.

[62] Section 22, Raag Raamkalee, Part 003.2. translation, http://www.hinduwebsite.com/sacredscripts/sikhscripts/guru922.htm.

incorporating him as a major sectarian figure, has the tradition co-opted/glossed over his criticism as well? The question is particularly significant because chronologically, Charpati lived when the tradition was stressed and challenged and conceding its social base in North India.

The precise history of Charpatnath, like other Siddha cultic figures, is doubtful. He is mentioned in the medieval *vaṁśāvalī* of the Chamba state, which refers to the pivotal role that he played in the state formation in the tenth century. This, however, seems a later interpolation (as discussed elsewhere)[63] as the genealogy was compiled in the sixteenth–seventeenth century and is influenced by the legend of Bappā Rāval of Mewār. He does not find mention in the prolific copper plates of Chamba, except in the late eighteenth century. The insertion of his name in the Chamba genealogy, nevertheless, is significant because it does speak about the influence that the Nath Siddhas exerted in the medieval polity, particularly in the peripheral hill states like Chamba and Mandi.[64]

Chronologically, he may be placed somewhere in the latter half of the thirteenth and the earlier decades of the fourteenth centuries. Even though he is mentioned in all major Mahasiddha and Nath Siddha compilations of the fourteenth–sixteenth centuries, there is no reference about him prior to the thirteenth century.[65] The efflorescence of Charpat legend is, therefore, somewhere in between, particularly in North India where he finds mention, among other texts, in the Guru Granth Sahib (the *Ādī Granth*), which was compiled in CE 1604.[66]

The hagiography of Charpat projects him as the disciple of Jālandharanāth and a preceptor of Dumari and Minapa, as well a pupil of a particular alchemist, Vyali-pa. Historically, his position oscillates between the Tibetan Vajrayani Siddhas and the Kānaphaṭā Jogis – the Nath Siddhas of Gorakṣanāth and Matsyendranāth, belonging to *Aī-panth* (one of the twelve sects associated with the Naths). He is variously named: Carapaṭipada, Carapaṭri, Carya-di-pa and

---

63 Sharma, *Western Himalayan Temple Records*, 15–74.

64 Ibid.

65 The prominent omission is in the *Lha-Khang* inscription, orthographically attributed to the eleventh–twelfth centuries by Francke, containing the names of Nāgārjuna, Āryadeva, Naropa, Tilopa, Luhipa, Dharmakīrtī and Śāntīpa. This is reflective of the chronology as far as Charpati is concerned, for he finds mention in the later *grub-thob* or the *Tibetan Book of Siddhas*. A.H. Francke, *Antiquities of Indian Tibet, I*, Archaeological Survey of India, XXXVII (New Delhi, 1975 [reprint]), 91.

66 See footnote 39.

C(K)a-rba-bi-pa.[67] It is pertinent to mention here the accounts of two Tibetan travellers, of the thirteenth century, who may have a bearing on the chronology of Charpat: rGod-tshan-pa (CE 1189–1258) and his disciple, Orgyan-pa (CE 1230–1309).[68] rGod-tshan-pa visited Spiti particularly to meet the great Siddha (*grub-thob chen-po*) named Kha-rag-pa (according to one legend, Charpati is Karpaṭi, born from the water taken from the loincloth of Gorakṣa). Significantly, he also visited Chamba from Lahul after crossing the Kugtī pass. Thereafter, he visited Kangra, the seat of Jvālāmukhi (*Dza-vā-lā-mu-gi*) – the goddess that offered *siddhis* as Siddhulā. The goddess was also associated with the Nath ascetics and the *pīṭha* (the seat of the goddess) was famed for its sulphur springs. As has been demonstrated by White , sulphur was associated with the goddess and played a significant part in the tantric *haṭha* yogic praxis.[69] Orgyan similarly followed his guru to Kangra, to meditate and offer prayers.

There are three unknown (?) texts attributed to Charpat in the Tibetan *bsTan-'gyur*: (a) *Caturbhūta-bhavābhivāsana-krama-nāma*; (b) *Āryāvalokiteśvarasya carpaṭiracita-stotra*; and (c) *Sarva-siddhi-kara-nāma*.[70] There are, however,

---

[67] Lama Taranath, *The History of Buddhism in India*, trans. Lama Chimpa and Alaka Chattopadhyaya (Kolkata: K.P. Bagchi & Co., 1980), 153. Also, Lama Taranath, *Mystic Tales of Lama Taranath: A Religio-Sociological History of Mahāyāna Buddhism*, trans Bhupendranath Dutta (trans. from German, *Edelstein-mine*; trans. Gruenwedel, 1914) (Kolkata: Ramakrishna Vedanta Math, 1944), 53–56. Also, see footnote 32.

[68] Thakur, *Buddhism in the Western Himalaya*, 47, 48.

[69] David G. White, *The Alchemical Body: Siddha Traditions in Medieval India*, (Chicago: UCP, 1996). Thakur (Ibid.) opines that they visited the shrine of Vajreśvarī in Kangra and wrongly ascribed it as *Dza-vā-lā-mu-gi*. I think that this type of omission by a practitioner is not possible. Moreover, these people were looking for the technique of calibrating mercury in sulphur, which the seat of Vajreśvarī did not offer. I am of the firm opinion that the shrine of Vajreśvarī did not exist at this time, as it is only towards the beginning of the sixteenth century that we start getting evidence about its existence, while all early chronicles associated with the Tughlaqs (fourteenth century) or Akbar (sixteenth century) write about Jvālāmukhi. See also Mahesh Sharma, 'Shaktism in Himachal', in *Religious Movements and Institutions in Medieval India, Vol. VII, Part 2*, ed. J.S. Grewal, (Delhi: Oxford University Press, 2006), 95–105; and 'Perspectives on the Himalayan Goddess: History, Myth and Practice', *Research Bulletin: VVRI* 4 and 5 (2006), 349–376.

[70] *bsTan-'gyur*, which lists Charpati at No. 64, mentions his works, No. 3253, 3546 and 5098; see J.B. Robinson, trans., *Buddha's Lions: The Lives of the Eighty-Four Siddhas* (Berkeley: Dharma Publishing, 1979), 304.

vernacular verses attributed to him, composed in the medieval western Punjabi and in old Rajasthani. There is a Sanskrit work, *Charpaṭśatakam*, that is also attributed to him. In the little-known couplets/verses that are attributed to Charpatnath, he ridicules the Jogi attire, the Nath tradition of splitting ears and questions their ways to achieve salvation. He emphasizes the tradition and role of '*Sata-Guru*' or 'the True Preceptor', like the Nath/Mahasiddha schools; cautions against tantrics; he is concerned with disease; he is passionate about health/healthy body; and he is an alchemist. He allegedly calls himself the '*ātmā-Jogī*' – the one who has realized the 'Soul' or 'Self' by perfecting yogic–alchemical techniques, emphasizing control over 'sense-organs' and 'mind'.[71] Alternatively, the '*ātmā-Jogī*' is an adept who has realized the *kuṇḍalinī* process – one who has attained the highest cognitive–spiritual sphere, the *Brahmarandhra*.[72] At the same time, an insignificant *stotra* – the hymn

71 Virnath, *Śrī Nāth Carita* (Haridwar: Behkh Barah Panth Mahasabha, 1988), 333; T.R. Punja, *Śaiva Mata aur Lokavaṇī* (New Delhi: Dharma Prakashan, 1979) 100; also, see, based on a manuscript from Lahore, Mohan Singh's book, *Gorakhnath and Medieval Hindu Mysticism* (Lahore: Oriental College, 1937). Kieth Dowman reckons that he is the same as Carparipā, the disciple of Jālandharanāth, and a preceptor of Dumapa as well Mīnapa, hailing from eastern India, from Magadha. See Kieth Dowman, *Masters of Mahamudra: Songs and Histories of the Eighty-Four Buddhist Siddhas* (Albany: State University of New York Press, 1985), 309–312; also, the same tradition in Abhayadatta, *Caturśīti-siddha-pravṛtti* or Robinson, *Buddha's Lions*, 205–207; Dwivedi, *Nath Sampradaya*. David G. White calls him an alchemist, recognizing the widespread provenance of his writings, some housed in Jodhpur, and to an allusion made to him in Chamba; see White, *The Alchemical Body*. Similarly, Davidson, *Indian Esoteric Buddhism*, too places him in the tenth century Chamba, along with the myth of the coming of the eighty-four Siddhas in Bhramaur, relying on the Genealogy, see, Vogel, J. Ph. *Antiquities of Chamba State*. Part I. Memoir of Archaeological Survey of India, No. 36. Calcutta: Government of India Press, 1911.and Hutchison, J. and J. Ph. Vogel. *History of the Panjab Hill States*. Vol. 1. Lahore: Government Press, Panjab, 1933; as does K.P. Sharma, *Manimahesh: Chamba Kailash* (New Delhi: Indus Publishing, 2001). The writings of Charpati also are of little help as they are located within the wider Nath Siddha tradition, a hagiographic corpus in Sanskrit, and vernacular languages – the themes cutting across, or blurring, sectarian lines.

72 This refers to the process of taking the *kuṇḍalinī*, the serpent force seated near the anus, through six chakras or psycho-mystical points seated in body. The lowest, in the hierarchy of progression, is called *Mulādhāra* and the highest is *Brahmarandhra* – symbolically depicted as a Lotus with thousand petals. Each chakra has its designated deity, the Shakti. See P.C. Bagchi, *Kaulajñānananirṇaya*, verses 14.15a

of praise – from Nepal, allegedly composed by Charpat (*Carpaṭīstutīpaṇī*), alludes to certain magical practices that he was dexterous in, firmly placing him within the larger Nath Siddha tradition. These would include 'levitation': '*añjanagutikāpādukasiddhi*' (the book of power to fly);[73] just as the tales of Lama Taranath, composed towards the end of the sixteenth century, inform us that he learnt the art of making 'quicksilver elixir' from Vyali, who also taught him the transmutation of base metals into gold.[74] A drive for such exoteric transmutation of metals has an esoteric spiritual parallel as well. In the words of Svoboda (writing for his Aghorī guru, Vimalānanda), there is a corresponding metamorphosis of the 'base metal of human consciousness into the gold of enlightenment, a state of unlimited consciousness'.[75]

According to the tradition explicated by Briggs, the followers of the Āī sect, in which Charpat is placed, are related to Gorakṣanāth through his disciple Bimlā Devī, affectionately called Āī, 'the mother'. Their names therefore end with 'āi'. Hence, Charpat would be Charpatai (Charpati), if we were to place his name according to the norms of Āī sectarians. The suffix 'nath' was accepted much later in this sect.[76] The sectarians believe in the goddess

---

onwards; or for Kashmir, *The Kulacūḍāmaṇi Tantra*, 1.34 onwards; see Louis M. Finn, tr. *The Kulacūḍāmaṇi Tantra and the Vāmakeśvara Tantra with the Jayaratha Commentary* (Wiesbaden: Otto Harrassowitz, 1986), Chapters I and II, for chakra ritual and language–yantra associations. The *Kubjikā Upaniṣad* emphasizes the control of breath (with the mantra: *haṃ-sa*), as underscored later in the Nath tradition, to power the sleeping *kuṇḍalinī* through these chakras to finally unite with the supreme Shiva in the *Brahmarandhra.* Goudriaan and Schoterman, *The Kubjikā Upaniṣad*, 7.29, 7.62.

[73] Giuseppe Tucci, 'Animadversiones Indicae', *Journal and Proceedings of the Asiatic Society of Bengal* XXXVI, no. 1 (1930), 139. He, however, accepts the tenth century dating and hopes to work out the chronology of others from this point of reference. Levitation was a particular Siddhi that was popular in the Himachal hills in the eighteenth century at least, as we know of Sidh Sen, the ruler of Mandi, who was one of its practitioners and claimed success. There is a painted tradition to this effect as well. See Kirandeep Gill, 'Raja Sidh Sen of Mandi' (M. Phil dissertation Punjab University, Chandigarh, 1989).

[74] Taranath, *Mystic Tales of Lama Taranath.*

[75] Robert E. Svoboda, *Aghora: At the Left Hand of God* (New Delhi: Rupa & Co., 2007[1986]), 9.

[76] G.W. Briggs, *Gorakhnath and the Kanphata Jogis* (New Delhi: MLBD, 1982 [reprint]), 67–68.

particle as the signifier of Sadāśiva. In other words, it is only by grasping and then transcending the material, signified by the Goddess Shakti, that it is possible to realize the supreme reality, the Sadāśiva. Thus the goddess, in her mother form, is the supreme motif for the Āī sectarians, which also explains why the Jogis of Chamba worshipped Mahākālī in the portal of Charpat. It is, therefore, interesting to observe that the *Haṭhayoga Pradīpikā* associates him with Manthanabhairava,[77] just as he is associated with Mahākāla in the *Śābara Tantra*.[78] These associations are usually in a dyadic relationship with the forms of Kālī or *Kālīkrama*; a pointer to the type of rituals practised by the adepts. The popular legend from Chamba obliquely refers to such practices. Just like the frame stories of Pūraṇ Bhagat or Gopichand, Charpati is also associated with a woman. According to the legend, the Chamba King, Sahilla Varman, suspected an unacceptable relationship between the Siddha and his daughter Campāvatī, who was his disciple. He once followed them to prove his suspicion. The legend has that the 'daughter' (the goddess incarnate) was enraged, so much so that she disappeared from earthly existence. We know that the temple of Campāvatī was erected in her honour, housing the demon-slaying goddess, Mahīṣamardinī.[79] The relationship is, at best, the cover for the tantric rituals (*sādhanā* worship) that these Siddhas believed in. Both these linkages, the Bhairava and with Campāvatī, tacitly explain why his legates were associated with Mahākālī or Bhadrakālī, the tutelary deity of the Chamba state as recounted in the royal medieval genealogy. Consider the following verses that are attributed to Charpat in this light.

> Fearless, unaccompanied, and firm in resolve,
> Surmounting insults or fame, winning over the 'Senses';
> Mind consumed by unmitigated Awareness,
> (Charpaṭ) proffers this as the path to Liberation (*Siddhī*).
> O Avadhuta! Seal the main door

[77] Singh, *The Haṭhayoga Pradīpikā of Atmā Rāma*, verse 6, 17. It associates Charpati, along with Siddhībuddha, Kanthaḍī, Korāṇṭaka, Surananda and Siddhīpāda, with Manthanabhairava.

[78] Sashibhushan Dasgupta, *Obscure Religious Cults*, Second Revised Edition (Kolkata: Firma K.L. Mukhopadhyaya, 1962[1956]). He is one of the twelve initiators and converters as per the list provided in *Śābara Tantra* and quoted in *Gorakṣa Siddhanta Samgraha*, 206–207.

[79] Hutchison and Vogel, *History of the Punjab Hill States*, 285.

And play there with the Sixty-Four.
Fever vanishes, disease withers away,
Charpaṭ marvels the ways of 'Union'.
Tie it firmly, seal and secure!
The Sun rules above, the Moon below;
On the new-moon night, Charpaṭ sips the nectar,
Neither the oil dries up
Nor the lamp blows off.[80]

More popular, however, are the vernacular couplets in the North Indian dialects attributed to Charpatnath.[81] Like other paradigmatic Siddhas, Charpat is more radical in his outlook and is outspoken. He is not only against the entrenched Brahmanical social order and clergy, but is also against the practices followed by the Jogis. It is because of the debased nature of the renouncers that he takes up upon himself to instruct the credulous; for instance, he instructs what the socially acceptable behaviour should be:

Listen, O respected! O truthful!
How to live in this world.
See with your eyes, Hear with your ears,
But, do not open your mouth.
A good listener to garrulous; humble to an arrogant;
A good disciple to guru.
Be steadfast to this advice,
Keep your Self to your Mind;

---

[80] Sharma, *Western Himalayan Temple Records*, 94; translated from Manuscript No. 5661 (not traceable now), from the Punjab University, Lahore; originally in Gurmukhi script. Mohan Singh provides the text in the Devanagari script in *Gorakhnath and Medieval Hindu Mysticism*, 22 (my translation, like all other verses of Charpat). The variant verses in Devanagari are published as 'Atha Charpaṭjī kī Sabadī', in Kalyani Mallik, *Siddha Sidhanta-Padhati and Other Works of the Nātha Yogīs* (Poona: Poona Oriental Book House, 1954), 72–79.

[81] I have translated all these verses, attributed to Charpati, from Manuscript No. 512, Hafiz-ul-Ulum, private collection, Lahore, dated S 1711 (CE 1654), by Mohan Singh, who provides their text in Devanagari script in *Gorakhnath and Medieval Hindu Mysticism*, 20–23. Also, see the English translation of some of the verses by Singh (Ibid., 68–71). Compare these with the Kartabhaja sectarian songs sung in Bengal; see Urban, *The Economics of Ecstasy*.

Reveal no secrets; speak sweet:
The antagonist may be Fire,
You, an adept, always Water be.
The world is a garden full of thorns,
Tread cautiously.
Charpaṭ says, listen O Siddhas!
Don't be stubborn in performing austerities.
Understand, O Knowledgeable,
That which is mis-said:
If one is a disciple, it is a station of profit.
If one is a guru, it is a position of loss.
If the 'interior' is dirty, the 'exterior' is dirty too,
Why do you forget this, O Charpaṭ, the blind?[82]

Why he is so incensed with the ascetics, particularly the Nath Siddhas, is because of their licentiousness, which is masked by the facade of ritual. It seems that the tantric and alchemical practices were more popular with the Nath Siddhas, as is evident from the rising corpus of the tantric and alchemical literature during this time, which most of them followed for negative reasons, thus bringing censure to the sect and losing the social base. Later, Guru Nanak too calls them debased (if not debauched) and questions the type of Yoga (interplay of words, as yoga is the 'union') that they practised and professed. The sayings of Charpati are more satirical than those of other Nath Siddhas, which make him more radical and popular.

An ascetic comes to our household!
Won't you serve him?
Spread the mattress, fluff and fluffy,
Let him sit on a pedestal high.
Get all the objects of leisure (*māyā*),
Smug, he sits, as if attained the Timeless.
The wife of disciple who serves him,
Seeing her shape, he desires her?
He cuddles the face of his disciple's daughter
Like the dog plays with marrow-bone!
The disciple dies, the guru cries,
The guiltless also mourn.

---

[82] Sharma, *Western Himalayan Temple Records*, 91; Mallik, *Siddha Sidhanta-Padhati*, 2.

He renounced one house, but got another;
He left that, but man lives in illusion.
Who could not even breed mercy,
Instead became a guru?
Says Charpaṭ, he has charted his way to Hell.[83]

He castigates the Nath Siddhas when he says that they are as hypocritical as the Brāhmaṇas or the clergy, who are more concerned with the external markers than the reform that was expected from them. In his perspective, these renouncers are as busy earning their living as the lay society, irrespective of the means employed to earn a livelihood.

Some wear ochre-robes,
Some are robe-less.
Some mark the forehead; wear sacred-thread;
Dangle long matted-hair.
Some are Faqirs; some Munis;
Some, split-eared Kānaphaṭas.
When the deathly storm shall blow,
Will blow away their external robes!
Those, who do not understand the Reverse Flow,
Charpaṭ ridicules them as Clowns with stomachs.
[Charpaṭ calls them as mere bread earners.][84]

Charpat is severe on the Naths who waste their lives following ascetic activities, which are mere ritualistic pretension without conviction. These activities are just like ritualized worship, which the Siddhas were so against, and serve no purpose if the mind is not disciplined.

Wandering in forest, eating roots and berries,
Austerity in water, wasting Time
In useless attachments;
Vigour of fire, wasted by thoughts
Of self-preservation;
The Self, atrophied by the haṭha-yogic rigour.

---

[83] Original text in Devanagari; Singh, *Gorakhnath and Medieval Hindu Mysticism*, no. 12; translation by Mahesh Sharma.

[84] Sharma, *Western Himalayan Temple Records*, 92.

Says Charpaṭ, one without Will over Mind,
Speaks like this![85]

Or,

Draping torn patched-garment,
Holding a begging bowl,
Wooden cloys on feet
Face smeared red.
Greedy eating! Thirsty drinking!
Yet an austere practitioner?
Charpaṭ asks: why bring bad name to ascetics.[86]

He reminds the community of renouncers how they should be: where the external are mere signs of the internal resolve; where the outer is the portrayal of knowledge and peace that is internal.

The renouncer's play is fearless!
His intellect rests upon the firm Belief.
He has won over Mind; reined in desires;
Continence is his way of life.
He has pierced the ears of awareness
Contemplating Knowledge.
Charpaṭ says, this is the Siddha doctrine.[87]

The Forms of Protest

The question of protest is in itself problematic; more so, when the protest is by the renouncers, a social category that exists in contravention to the rules and ethics of the society at large. In the Indian subcontinent, asceticism is understood as the social death of the person concerned. He/she is no longer regulated by its rules and organization. The question is further problematical in that the renouncers reinforce the values and norms of the society that they are opting out from, as has been argued by Romila Thapar.[88] It would be pertinent

[85] Ibid.

[86] Original text in Devanagari; Singh, *Gorakhnath and Medieval Hindu Mysticism*, no. 4; translation by Mahesh Sharma.

[87] Ibid., 91–92.

[88] Romila Thapar, 'Renunciation: The Making of a Counter-culture?', in *Ancient Indian Social History*, (Hyderabad: Orient Longman, 1978), 63–104.

to bring to the fore the distinction that Thapar makes between the renouncers and ascetics. She argues, and we agree, that the ascetics gave up the world and its ways in totality, abandoning the wherewithal of the social completely and dedicating themselves to the spiritual pursuits, without company and support. On the other hand, the renouncers' repudiation of the social was not absolute. They sought the support of lay people to accomplish the mission of their 'order'. With the reinforcement of the monastic organization and the militarization of these 'orders', the renouncers sought the patronage of the society and state that they ostensibly served. Thus, while they maintained their opposition with the householders, they interacted with and lived off the society. In their own enclaves, the monasteries, they had to promulgate and follow certain binding rules, conform to hierarchy and act towards the benefit of their order and monastery. Renouncers, in a sense, created an alternative society. Since this alternative was in negation to the values of the society that the ascetic/renouncers lived in, it marked the first protest against contemporary society. It is also within this context that the protest of the Siddhas, and later the vitriolic criticism of Charpat, may be understood.

It must be pointed out that the manuals of renunciation were still being written, like the *Nāradaparivrājaka* or *Śāṭyāyanīya*, which are assigned to CE 1150 and 1200 by Patrick Ollivelle.[89] External attributes of the ascetics/renouncers were explicated. Staff, water pot, loincloth, waistband and a garment were emblematic of the renouncers, according to the *Nāradaparivrājaka*. A water strainer, sling, ochre garment, a tripod, a pair of shoes and a begging bowl were recommended in addition to the above by the *Laghu Saṁnyāsa*. These texts were even now debating if the renouncer could give up his top-knot or not; how he should beg food; and his attitude towards food, caste and caste-related rituals. The dress codes were enunciated to distinguish the renouncers from lay people as well each other; the rules in general were to regulate their behaviour. The *Samnyasa Upaniṣadas*, and the related literature, is an attempt to socialize the renouncers according to the codes of the alternative society, which in turn is a response to the social acceptability of the society that they had opted out of. This is, of course, paradoxical, what Olivelle, borrowing Jan Heesterman's phrase, calls the 'inner conflict of tradition'.[90] When we are thinking of the remonstrations of Charpat, even if his protest is formulated

---

[89] Patrick Ollivelle, *Samnyasa Upanisads: Hindu Scriptures on Asceticism and Renunciation* (New York: Oxford University Press, 1992).

[90] J.C. Heesterman, *The Inner Conflict of Tradition: Essays in Indian Ritual Kingship and Society* (Chicago: University of California Press, 1985).

within the perspective of the Nath Siddhas and is aimed at them (though there are sayings which criticize the wider ascetic community as well), it acquires an added dimension as he stands up against such externalist notions that the renouncers were obsessed with. For instance, he says:

Becoming externalist!
I will not set out.
Why should I get my ears pierced?
I will not smear the ash
That wears out.
Damned, if I roll in ash like a donkey!
I will not sport Selī around my neck,
Nor the deer's skin.
The patched garment,
I will not wear, which is worn out.
I shall not worship the begging vessel,
Nor carry the staff;
I will not go begging like a dog,
Nor blow the horn before evening prayer.
I will not go from door to door,
Lighting smoke!
I do not want to be called the Jogī of Appearance,
Charpaṭnāth is the Jogī
Who has realized the Soul.
[Charpaṭnāth is the 'one' who can see into the 'Soul'.][91]

---

[91] Sharma, *Western Himalayan Temple Records*, 91. This seems a part of the larger discontentment with numerous practitioners using tantric rituals as part of physical entertainment. Moreover, monasticism also emphasized much on the external appearance that marked the distinct identity, differing not only from lay people but also competing ascetic orders. The discontentment, therefore, is voiced in various other texts as well. For instance, similar echoes can be comprehended in Taranath Vidyaratna, ed., *Kularnava Tantra*, intro. Arthur Avalon (New Delhi: MLBD, 1975[1916]). 'Liberation is not to be got by merely smearing oneself with ashes, feeding on herbs and water, exposure to heat and cold and the like. Donkeys and other animals go about naked. Are they therefore Yogins?' (Ibid., verse 113). Similarly, 'The yogis cannot enjoy; and he who enjoys cannot know yoga but in kaula dharma there is both *bhoga* and *yoga*' (Ibid., verse 23). Yet, he qualifies, 'But Kaula knowledge can only be gained by one whose mind is pure and who has controlled his senses' (Ibid., verse 33).

Such dissensions from within compel us to reconsider the dialectics of protest and reform. As evident from the given discussion, the protest/reform movement, in the long duration, develops into a conventional practice, socialized by the tradition it sets out to protest against, weighted down by the burden of its pernicious legacy of dissidence. The protest in itself constitutes a transformation, which requires constant scrutiny and contemplation; just as the 'protest movement' requires a periodic dissidence/reform to achieve its objective. In the social process, however, the objectives keep changing and receding into distance, thereby rendering the protest(s) a persistent strife in an unending journey. As to Charpat, the state of Chamba endowed his legates, who embraced matrimony and accepted ritually low social status in the local caste hierarchy, and were appointed as the priests of the tutelary deity of the erstwhile Chamba state, the Bhadrakālī, while managing the 'portal' of Charpat.[92] Almost five centuries after the times of the paradigmatic Siddha, Charpatnath, his legates initiated lawsuits to wrest control over the local Shaivite rituals from the low-caste shaman/oracle–*celās*; as also to appropriate land from the marginal sharecroppers and the ritually low-caste tenants.[93]

References

Gorakhnath. *Ātma Bodh* (Haridwar: Bhekh Barah Panth Series, 1986).

Bhartṛharī, *Vairāgya Śataka* (Haridwar: Gorakh Mandir, n.d).

Bagchi, P.C. ed. *Kaulajñānananirṇaya and Some Minor Texts of the School of Matsyendra* (Kolkata: Metropolitan, 1934).

---

[92] The insertion of Bhadrakālī in the genealogical record is significant on many counts. The goddess (as *Jayadurgā*) is worshipped particularly to gain victory in war, which the rulers of Chamba were in desperate need of in the sixteenth–seventeenth centuries. As she could only be worshipped by the non-Brāhmaṇas (*pāraśavaḥ*), the Jogis, who practised tantric rituals, became then priests. The Shaivite character of these priests was textually manipulated and they were known as *pāraśaivā* (literally, the foremost worshipper of Shiva): the title of those who have been consecrated as the officiants of the goddess. Alexis Sanderson, 'Atharvavedins in Tantric Territory: The Āṅgirasakalpa Texts of the Oriya Paippalāadins and their Connection with the Trika and the Kālīkula (With critical editions of the Parājapavidhi, the Parāmantravidhi, and the *Bhadrakālīmantravidhiprakaraṇ), in *The Atharvaveda and its Paippalāda Śākhā: Historical and Philological Papers on a Vedic Tradition*, ed. Arlo Griffiths and Annette Schmiedchen (Aachen: Shaker Verlag, 2007), 277, footnote 142.

[93] Sharma, *Western Himalayan Temple Records*, 304–339.

Barathwal, Pitambardatta. *Gorakh Bani: Jogesari Bani, I* (Prayaga: Chaukhamba Road, V.S. 2003 [1946]).

Bernier, Francois. *Travels in the Mogul Empire*. Translated by I. Brock and A. Constable (London: Oxford University Press, 1934; New Delhi: Munshiram Manoharlal, 1994 [reprint]).

Bharati, Agehananda. 'Intentional Language in the Tantras'. *Journal of the American Oriental Society* 81(3) (1961): 261–70.

Briggs, G. W. *Gorakhnath and the Kanphata Jogis* (New Delhi: MLBD, 1982 [reprint]).

Cohn, B.S. 'Role of Gosains in the Economy of Eighteenth and Nineteenth Century Upper India'. *Journal of Social Research* 17 (1974): 88–95.

Dahl, Cortland, compiler, trans. with introduction. *Entrance to the Great Perfection: A Guide to the Dzogchen Preliminary Practices* (Ithaca: Snow Lion Publications, 2009).

Dasgupta, Sashibhushan. *Obscure Religious Cults*, Second Revised Edition (Kolkata: Firma K.L. Mukhopadhyaya, 1962[1956]).

______. *Obscure Religious Cults*, Third Edition (Kolkata: Firma K.L. Mukhopadhyaya Limited, 1976).

Davidson, R.M. *Indian Esoteric Buddhism: A Social History of the Tantric Movement* (New York: Columbia University Press, 2002).

Diamond, Debra. 'Painting, Politics, and Devotion under Maharaja Man Singh, 1803–43'. In *Garden and Cosmos: The Royal Paintings of Jodhpur*. Edited by D. Diamond, C. Glynn and K. Jasol (Washington: Smithsonian Institution, 2008), 31–41.

Dowman, Kieth. *Masters of Mahamudra. Songs and Histories of the Eighty Four Buddhist Siddhas* (Albany: State University of New York Press, 1985).

Dwivedi, H.P. *Nath Sampradaya* (1966). In *Hazari Prasad Dwivedi Granthavali*, No. 6, Second Edition (New Delhi: Rajkamal, 1998).

Dyczkowski, M.S.G. *The Canon of the Saivagama and the Kubjika Tantra of the Western Kaula Tradition* (New Delhi: Motilal Banarsidass, 1989).

Feuerstein, George. *Tantra: The Path of Ecstacy* (Boston: Shambhala, 1998. South Asia Edition, 2000). Finn, Louis M. Translated. *The Kulacūḍāmaṇi Tantra and the Vāmakeśvara Tantra with the Jayaratha Commentary* (Wiesbaden: Otto Harrassowitz, 1986).

Furquhar, J.N. *An Outline of the Religious Literature of India* (London: Oxford University Press, 1920; Delhi: MLBD, 1967 [reprint]).

Gill, Kirandeep. 'Raja Sidh Sen of Mandi'. MPhil dissertation, Punjab University, Chandigarh, 1989.

Gold, Daniel. *The Lord as Guru: Hindi Sants in North Indian Tradition* (New Delhi: Oxford University Press, 1987).

Gordon, S.N. 'Comment'. *Indian Economic and Social History Review* 8 (1978), 219–20.

Goswamy, B.N and J.S. Grewal. *The Mughals and Jogis of Jakhbar* (Simla: Indian Institute of Advanced Study, 1967).

Gourdiaan, Teun and Sanjukta Gupta. *Hindu Tantric and Sakta Literature* (Wiesbaden: Otto Harrassowitz, 1981).

Goudriaan, Teun and Jan A. Schoterman, ed. and trans. *The Kubjikā Upaniṣad* (Groningen: Egbert Forsten, 1994).

Guenther, Herbert. *The Life and Teaching of Naropa: Translated from the Original Tibetan with a Philosophical Commentary based on the Oral Transmission* (Boston: Sambhala, 1999[1963]).

'Guroli Plate of Vairasivarman VS 1387'. In *Antiquities of Chambā State, Part II*, B.Ch. Chhabra. Memoir of Archaeological Survey of India, No. 72. (New Delhi: Government of India Press, 1957).

Heesterman, J.C. *The Inner Conflict of Tradition: Essays in Indian Ritual Kingship and Society* (Chicago: University of California Press, 1985).

Heruka, Tsang Nyon. *The Life of Marpa the Translator: Seeing Accomplishes All.* (Boston: Sambhala, 1982. South Asian Edition, 1999).

Hess, Linda and Sukhdev Singh. *The Bījak of Kabir* (New Delhi: Motilal Banarsidass, 1986).

Hutchison and Vogel, *History of Panjab Hill States.*

Jaisi, Malik Muhammad. *Padmāvatī.* tr. A.G. Shirraff (Kolkata: The Royal Asiatic Society of Bengal, 1944).

Jivaka, Lobzang. *The Life of Milarepa: Tibet's Great Yogi* (condensed and adapted from the original). Translated by W.Y. Evans-Wentz (New Delhi: Rupa, 1996[1928]).

Kāma-Kalā-Vilāsa by Punyananda Natha: With the Commentary of Natananda-Natha, Fourth Edition. Translated and commentary by Sir John Woodroffe in 1921 [Chennai: Ganesh & Co., 1971).

Khan, Dominique-Sila. *Conversions and Shifting Identities: Ramdev Pir and the Ismailis in Rajasthan* (New Delhi: Manohar, 1997).

Kolff, D.H.A. 'Sanyasi Trader–Soldiers', *Indian Economic and Social History Review* 8 (1971): 213–218.

Krishna, Gopi. *Kundalini – The Secret of Yoga* (New Delhi: UBS Publishers, n.d.).

Lama Taranath. *Mystic Tales of Lama Taranath: A Religio-sociological History of Mahāyāna Buddhism.* Translated by Bhupendranath Dutta (translated from German, *Edelstein-mine*; translated by Gruenwedel, 1914) (Kolkata: Ramakrishna Vedanta Math, 1944).

______. *The History of Buddhism in India.* Translated by Lama Chimpa and Alaka Chattopadhyaya (Kolkata, 1980).

Lorenzen, David. *The Kāpālikas and Kālākukhas: Two Lost Śaivite Sects* (New Delhi: Thompson Press, 1972).

______. 'Warrior Ascetics in Indian History'. *Journal of the American Oriental Society* 98(1) (1978): 61–75.

Mallik, Kalyani. *Siddha Sidhanta-Padhati and Other Works of the Nātha Yogīs* (Poona: Poona Oriental Book House, 1954).

Muller-Ortega, P.E. *The Triadic Heart of Śiva: Kaula Tantricism of Abhinavagupta in the Non-dual Shaivism of Kashmir* (Albany: State University of New York Press, 1989).

Oberoi, H.S. 'The Worship of Pir Sakhi Sarver: Illness, Healing, and Popular Culture in the Punjab'. *Studies in History* III, No. 1 (1987): 29–56.

Ollivelle, Patrick. *Samnyasa Upanisads: Hindu Scriptures on Asceticism and Renunciation* (New York: Oxford University Press, 1992).

Pandey, K.C. *Abhinavagupta: An Historical and Philosophical Study*. Varanasi.

Pinch, W.R. *Peasants and Monks in British India* (Berkeley: University of California Press, 1996).

______. *Warrior Ascetics and Indian Empires* (Cambridge: Cambridge University Press, 2006).

Punja, T.R. *Śaiva Mata aur Lokavaṇī*. Delhi.

Raghav, Ranghey. *Garakhnath aur unka Yuga* (Delhi, 1963).

Robinson, J.B. trans. *Buddha's Lions: The Lives of the Eighty-Four Siddhas* (Berkeley: Dharma Publishing, 1979).

Rose, R.A. *Glossary*, I, 261–64, 279–80.

Sanderson, Alexis. 'Atharvavedins in Tantric Territory: The Āṅgirasakalpa Texts of the Oriya Paippalāadins and their Connection with the Trika and the Kālīkula (With critical editions of the Parājapavidhi, the Parāmantravidhi, and the *Bh adrakālīmantravidhiprakaraṇ', in *The Atharvaveda and its Paippalāda Śākhā: Historical and Philological Papers on a Vedic Tradition*, edited by Arlo Griffiths and Annette Schmiedchen, 195–311 (Aachen: Shaker Verlag, 2007).

Sastri, Damodar and Somesvara Sastri, ed. and trans. *Srimad Vallabhacarya Digvijayah* (Indore: Cartons and Printers, 1987).

Shankranath, ed., *Sri Mastnath Charit* (Haridwar, 1990).

Sharma, K.P. *Manimahesh: Chamba Kailash* (New Delhi: Indus Publishing, 2001).

Sharma, Mahesh. 'Shaktism in Himachal', in *Religious Movements and Institutions in Medieval India, Vol. VII, Part 2*, edited by J.S. Grewal, 95–105 (New Delhi: Oxford University Press, 2006).

______. 'Perspectives on the Himalayan Goddess: History, Myth and Practice'. *Research Bulletin: VVRI* 4 and 5 (2006): 349–376.

______. *Western Himalayan Temple Records: State, Pilgrimage, Ritual and Legality in Chambā* (Leiden: Brill, 2009).

Singh, Jayadeva, trans. *Abhinavagupta: A Trident of Wisdom: Translation of Parātrīśikā Vivaraṇa (*Albany: State University of New York Press, 1989).

Singh, Jodh. *The Religious Philosophy of Guru Nanak* (Varanasi: Sikh Philosophical Society, 1983).

Singh, Mohan. *Gorakhnath and Medieval Hindu Mysticism* (Lahore: Oriental College, 1937).

Singh, Pancham, trans. *The Haṭhayoga Pradīpikā of Atmā Rāma.* New Delhi, 1915.

Singh, Piar. *Guru Nanak Siddha Goshti (With a Comprehensive Introduction Text [Trilingual] Translation & Annotations)* (Amritsar: Guru Nanak Dev University, 1996).

Sinha, Nandini. 'A Study of State and Cult: The Guhilas, Pasupatas and Ekalingaji in Mewar, Seventh to Fifteenth Centuries A.D.', *Studies in History* IX (1993), 161–182.

Snellgrove, David. *Indo-Tibetan Buddhism: Indian Buddhists and their Tibetan Successors* (Boston: Shambhala, 2002[1987]).

Srivastava, R.L., ed. *Gorakh Bani*. Gorakhpur, 1978.

Svoboda, Robert E. *Aghora: At the Left Hand of God* (New Delhi: Rupa & Co., 2007[1986]).

Tantrarāja Tantra: A Short Analysis, Fourth Edition. Introduction by Arthur Avalon. (Chennai: Ganesh & Co., 1971).

Thakur, Laxman S. *Buddhism in the Western Himalaya: A Study of the Tabo Monastery* (New Delhi: Oxford University Press, 2001).

Thapar, Romila. 'Renunciation: The Making of a Counter-culture?', in *Ancient Indian Social History* (Hyderabad: Orient Longman, 1978), 63–104.

Tucci, Giuseppe. 'Animadversiones Indicae'. *Journal and Proceedings of the Asiatic Society of Bengal* XXXVI, No. 1 (1930), 139.

Urban, Hugh B. *The Songs of Ecstacy: Tantric and Devotional Songs from Colonial Bengal* (New York: Oxford University Press, 2001).

______. *The Economics of Ecstacy: Tantra, Secrecy and Power in Colonial Bengal* (New York: Oxford University Press, 2001).

Vidyaratna, Taranath, ed. *Kularnava Tantra*. Introduction by Arthur Avalon (New Delhi: MLBD, 1975[1916]).

Virnath. *Śrī Nāth Carita*. Hardwar, 1988.

White, David G. *The Alchemical Body: Siddha Traditions in Medieval India* (Chicago: University of Chicago Press, 1996).

______. *Kiss of the Yoginī: 'Tantric Sex' in the South Asian Contexts* (Chicago: University of Chicago Press, 2003).

Yadav, D. *Vajrayani Siddha Sarhyada* (Santiniketan: University Press, 1972).

Zvelebil, Kamil V. *The Poets of Power* (London: Rider and Company, 1973).

CHAPTER

11

Fakirs of Bengal

Dissenters of Shariat and Challengers of Establishments

Sumanta Banerjee and Surojit Sen

Part I

A History of Protest from Past to Present

Sumanta Banerjee

The rise of the fakirs, who come mostly from the Muslim community, was not an isolated phenomenon in the history of Bengali society and religion. They were a part of a wider constellation of numerous syncretistic religious sects that shone over the Bengali popular religious scene during the sixteenth to seventeenth century. They continued to thrive in rural Bengal through the British colonial period, and still survive in the villages of Bengal. These sects occupy a special position in the history of Bengali popular religion, creating a subculture of their own. One nineteenth century Bengali scholar, Akshay Kumar Dutta, listed some fifty-odd syncretistic sects, which flourished all over India during his lifetime, and which originated in the seventeenth to the eighteenth centuries. Among them, at least forty were found in Bengal alone.[1]

---

[1] Akshay Kumar Dutta, *Bharatbarshiya Upasak Sampraday,* Vol. I (Kolkata, 1997 [1870]), 230.

The development and popularity of these syncretistic sects should be understood in a dual context: first, the socio-religious composition of Bengali society at the time of their birth; and second, the cultural tradition that continues down to the present times in rural society, where people require songs and music not only for entertainment but also for their deep spiritual needs.

To go back to the socio-religious past that gave birth to these sects and their songs, we should note that Bengali society at that time was occupied by the twin religious establishments: one ruled by the Brahmanical order according to strictly laid down hierarchical caste-bound norms for the Hindus; and the other by the *ashraf*s (Muslim aristocrats and clergy who claimed descent from the earlier Arab, Turkish, Afghan and Moghul settlers) for the Muslims. Both sought to institutionalize their own mechanisms of socio-religious control over their respective followers, with the aim of purging them of the many pre-Brahmanical and pre-Islamic beliefs and customs that they shared, to hegemonize them instead under their respective religious doctrines.

Below this horizontally stratified minority of the dominating Hindu and Muslim classes at the top, there was another and a larger world of lay members of society. Among the Hindus, starting from the bottom, they consisted of the traditional occupational castes like the Harhis (scavengers), Chamars (tanners) and Domes (who cremated dead bodies), who were relegated as untouchables in the Hindu religious hierarchical order. Then there were the farmers, agricultural labourers, artisans and small traders who came from the middle and lower-caste Hindu society. Among the Muslims also, although Islamic theology is against any discrimination among its followers, in practice in Bengal, the labouring *atraf* and *ajlaf* classes (ranging from cultivators to tailors, cobblers and washermen) and *arjal* (sweepers, scavengers and others engaged in occupations considered lowest in the hierarchy in the list of professions in contemporary Bengali Muslim society) were looked down upon by the *ashraf*s. Members of all these various rural lower orders could never be totally hegemonized by the orthodox religious establishments under their respective norms of doctrinal purity. They continued to lead an eclectic lifestyle – Muslims participating in Hindu religious festivities and vice versa; or both sharing religious practices and rituals of an animistic nature, which harked back to a tradition of collective memories (for example, worshipping godlings or *pir*s). It was these communities of the lower orders in Bengali society that formed the base of the popular syncretistic sects that developed in the past. Despite the 1947 partition of the Indian subcontinent that split them apart, and the later socio-economic changes that have taken place since then in the countryside of West Bengal and Bangladesh, these rural communities continue to sustain the culture of popular religion.

These syncretistic sects still share certain common characteristics from the past. First, most of them were founded (between the seventeenth and nineteenth centuries) by humble people of obscure origins belonging to the depressed and poorer castes among the Bengali Hindu and Muslim population, like Balaram Harhi (founder of the Balarami sect), Aulchand (of the Kartabhaja sect) and Shahebdhani (by whose name his sect is known), to mention a few.[2] Second, their belief systems and rituals lay stress on the equality of human beings, irrespective of their caste origins, religious denominations and gender differences. They generally renounce polytheism and formal observance of cast regulations. Women enjoy a more expansive space in their system of beliefs and rituals, compared to the position allotted to them in the orthodox Hindu, Islamic or Christian religious systems. To add a word of caution however – at the ground level, this space is also quite often intruded upon by the patriarchal tendencies that dominate these sects, almost all of them still being structured around subservience to their male founders – a guru or a *pir.*

A Rebellious Past

Interestingly enough, some of these sects had had associations with a tradition of armed rebellion – the fakirs being one of them. Apart from challenging the established socio-religious order (whether the hegemony of the Hindu orthodoxy or the Islamic clergy), they also fought against the British colonial order. In the early years of British rule – from the mid-eighteenth century to the turn of the nineteenth century – rural Bengal was overwhelmed by a series of peasants' revolts. Prominent among them was the uprising known as the Sannyasi and Fakir rebellion. According to contemporary official records, as well as oral folklore, organized armed bands of *sanyasis* and fakirs – both working in coordination – raided the *mofussil* factories and revenues offices of the East India Company, the *kutcheries* of rich landlords and the granaries of merchants between 1763 and 1800. The choice of their targets indicates that they were aiming against colonial institutions as well as indigenous feudal establishments, which were exploiting the rural poor and depriving them of their food and habitat.

A brief historical recapitulation of the role of the fakirs in the rebellion may be helpful in our understanding of some of the aspects of the present position

[2] For a historical analysis of the Kartabhaja sect, see Sumanta Banerjee, 'From Aulchand to Sati-Ma: The Institutionalization of the Karta-Bhaja Sect in Nineteenth century Bengal', in *Logic in a Popular Form*, (Kolkata, 2002).

of the fakirs in relation to the established political order in West Bengal. In the eighteenth century, the fakirs used to be a wandering group of Sufi mendicants moving all over India – visiting a network of *dargahs* of *pir*s stretching from North India to Bengal in the east. The Bengali fakirs mainly belonging to the Madari sect, followers of Saint Badi-uddin-shah-i-Madar (1315–1436), usually gathered around *dargahs* in north Bengal – Maldah, Pabna, Rangpur, Dinajpur, and Mymensingh.[3]

The British colonial authorities held such gatherings in suspicion. They imposed taxes on the movement of pilgrims, and extorted money from fakirs, *sanyasis*, *bairagi*s and various other wandering mendicants who earlier used to move freely all over India. This led to resentment among the fakirs – an otherwise peaceful Sufi community.[4] It was not only the interference with their free movement and violation of their religious rights that antagonized the *sanyasis* and fakirs but also the economic exploitation by the colonial authorities, which affected their occupations. They mainly belonged to the agricultural and artisan communities. The East India Company's rack-renting revenue collection methods and destruction of traditional crafts (like muslin weaving) left them destitute and resentful. Their plight became further aggravated by the terrible famine of 1770, which wiped out about 10 million people, almost one-third of the population of Bengal. The survivors, according to a contemporary British official account, 'formed themselves into bands of so-called houseless devotees (*sanyasis*) and roved about the country in armies fifty thousand strong…known under the name of Sanyasis or Faquirs…'.[5]

Official records as well as oral folklore confirm that a fakir leader, Majnu Shah – known as Majnu Fakir all over Bihar and Bengal – led this rebellion, along with a Hindu sanyasi called Bhabani Pathak. In 1771, Majnu Fakir sent a letter to Rani Bhabani, the zamindar of Natore in north Bengal, explaining why the mendicant fakirs had been forced to take up arms. He said in the letter:

> For a long time, we had been begging in Bengal, and Bengal also had welcomed us…We never abuse anyone, nor have we raised our arms against anyone. But despite that, some 15 innocent fakirs from our community have been killed… Earlier, the fakirs used to go around as individuals seeking alms. But now they

[3] Muhammad Enamul Haq, *A History of Sufism in Bengal* (Dhaka: Asiatic Society of Bangladesh, 1975).

[4] Suprakash Ray, *Bharater Krishak Bidroha O Ganatantrik Sangram* (Calcutta: DNBA Brothers, 1972).

[5] W.W. Hunter, *Annals of Rural Bengal* (Calcutta, 1883), 44.

> are moving around in groups. The British do not approve of this group solidarity of theirs. They are putting obstacles to the prayers of the fakirs...[6]

The Fakir rebellion of the late eighteenth century could thus be seen as an instance of how a peaceful Sufi community was forced to take up arms against colonial rule. However, several questions still remain to be answered. Are the present fakirs of Bengal descendants or disciples of the religious leaders of the Fakir rebellion of the past? In their present-day songs or narratives, do they ever hark back to the exploits of Majnu Fakir, Mushah Shah, Cherag Ali and other fakir leaders who led the rebellion? Is there a disjuncture in the history of the fakirs between the eighteenth century and the present? These questions raise problematic issues that need further research by scholars working in the field of popular Islam and Bengali folk religion. In the meantime, awaiting the results of such future research, at the moment we can only assume that following the defeat of the Fakir–Sannyasi rebellion by the end of the eighteenth century, these Sufi communities returned to their old belief systems and practices.

The Language of Enigma

But henceforth, the fakirs had to follow their religious practices in a more secretive manner, since they were under a cloud – in the eyes of the colonial rulers. We thus find, from the nineteenth century onwards, that they had begun to use an enigmatic language of codes in their songs. Their songs were made up of words that were loaded with symbolic and suggestive connotations. This was described as *sandhya bhasha* (often translated as 'twilight language', that is, half-expressed and half-hidden. The term is also interpreted as a derivation from *abhisandhi*, which when translated loosely, means a secret plot). The young Bengali scholar, Surajit Sen, has examined some of these songs (both old and new) and explained the hidden meanings that the words convey to those initiated into the beliefs and practices of the fakirs.[7]

The recourse to the enigmatic idiom of *sandhya bhasha* could have also been forced upon them by pressures from the orthodox religious establishment. It is significant that like the Bengali Bauls (another syncretistic sect of folk minstrels, primarily deriving inspiration from the Hindu Vaishnavite philosophy) who faced persecution from the Hindu theological establishment, the Bengali Sufi

---

[6] *Calendar of Persian Correspondence,* Vol. III, 198, quoted in Ray, *Bharater Krishak Bidroha*, 29.

[7] Surojit Sen, ed., *Fakirnama* (About Fakirs) (Kolkata: Gangchil, 2009).

fakirs were also hounded by the puritanical Islamic clergy. The syncretistic creed of both, based on an eclectic adoption and adaptation of beliefs and customs from different religious sources, was frowned upon by the orthodox theocracy which felt that the purity of religious doctrine was being diluted and distorted by these dissident groups. Besides, they also posed a threat to the hegemony of the upper castes in Bengali society. As mentioned earlier, most of the founders of the popular religious syncretistic sects came from the depressed castes. They empowered their followers (again from the lower orders) with a faith that helped them to assert their freedom as individuals, since these gurus and *pir*s (respected by both Hindus and Muslims) taught them that humanity could not be divided along caste or religious lines. Such self-assertion by the lower orders often posed a challenge to the upper-caste Bengali landlords in nineteenth century Bengal. We hear of an incident in a village in Nadia, where the Brahmin landlord took offence at the temerity of a lower-caste member of the Balarami sect who did not bow his head to show him respect. Despite a thrashing by the landlord's men, he kept on saying that he would never bow his head to anyone except his guru, Balaram Harhi, the founder of his sect.[8]

Threatened by the spread of such beliefs and actions, the upper-class/upper-caste establishment launched a systematic campaign against *bauls*, fakirs and other similar eclectic and syncretistic sects in Bengal in the nineteenth century. The fakirs, in particular, became targets of attacks by the orthodox Islamic clergy and their followers. In the course of the Wahabi and Ferazi rebellions in the nineteenth century Bengal (peasant uprisings mainly inspired by Islamic millenarian ideals, which were aimed at overthrowing the British colonial order), some of the local Muslim leaders, devoted to their Wahabi preacher Syed Ahmad, undertook the mission of purifying the Bengali Muslim community by purging it of Sufi influences (like singing songs) and eclectic practices (like their participation in Vaishnavite *bhakti* festivals). They wanted to re-establish a sort of pure Islamic order in the hybrid, conglomerate rural Bengali Muslim society – trying to impose on them a purist Islamic identity over their local Bengali cultural identity that had been formed over generations, cutting across religious differences.

In their campaign, these Bengali Muslim religious preachers damned the fakirs as apostates and renegades who had deserted from the path of the Shariat. All through the nineteenth and early years of the twentieth centuries, the Islamic clergy and their Bengali spokesmen came out with pamphlets attacking the

---

[8] Re: Dinendra Ray's article published in the journal *Aryavarta,* 1910.

fakirs. They bracketed them with *bauls* – the other heretic sect in the Hindu Vaishnavite stream, which defied the orthodox norms of the Hindu religious establishment and followed their independent lifestyle that cut across religious, caste and gender barriers. One of the most aggressive campaigners against the fakirs was Munshi Meherulla who, towards the end of the nineteenth century, published a pamphlet in poetic verses entitled *Meherul Eslam* (1897) where he accused the fakirs of converting men into beasts. Meherulla's programme of anti-fakir campaign was followed by a generation of Bengali Islamist pamphleteers in the twentieth century, notably among whom were Fazlur Rahman (who wrote *Bhanda Fakir* – meaning 'a hypocrite fakir' – in 1914) and Sheikh Reajuddin Ahmad (who wrote *Baul Dhangsho Fatwa*, an Islamic mandate calling upon all to destroy the *bauls*, brought out sometime in the early twentieth century, which had a second edition in 1925).[9]

The Current Situation

This brings me back to the research by Surajit Sen on the present condition of the fakirs in West Bengal. His findings have revealed widespread persecution of fakirs in the countryside even today, by the orthodox mullahs and rural landed interests as well as local government officials. Some typical instances are cited here. In February 2003, in the Nadia district of West Bengal, in Arangsharisha village, a fakir called Aynal Sheikh hired a van to take his relative to the hospital. The local Muslim clergy threatened the van driver with social boycott for helping the fakir. Another fakir, Madhu Sheikh, was fined Rs 2,000 for marrying his sister to someone against the wishes of the clergy who issued a fatwa against him. Jalil Sheikh, a fakir, even after paying Rs 1,200 to the Muslim elders, was not allowed to collect the harvest from his field. A fakir called Asan Sheikh could not find a bridegroom for his daughter, since the mullahs imposed a social boycott on his family. Because of the persecution faced by them as a result of their refusal to surrender to the diktats of the orthodox Shariat laws, many fakir families were forced to leave their homes and fields in Arangsharisha and seek refuge in the neighbouring village of Pitambarpur. When asked by a newspaper reporter why the clergy were targeting the fakirs, the imam of the mosque in Arangsharisha village, Ali Sheikh, announced arrogantly: 'In our (Muslim) community, every one will have to obey the Shariat laws'. When asked to protect the fakirs, the local police station officer-in-charge (of Chapra police station)

---

[9] Wakil Ahmed, *Unish Shatoke Bangali Musalmaner Chinta-Chetonar Dhara,* Vol. II (Dhaka, 1983), 83–84.

said: 'The fakirs refuse to accept the injunctions of their (Muslim) society. As a result, they have entered into a conflict with the elders of their society. We, the police cannot solve it.' The local political leaders of the village – belonging to the Communist Party of India (Marxist) or CPI(M) and the Congress – chose to remain indifferent to the problem. In a last desperate step, the fakirs sent a petition to the then West Bengal Chief Minister, Buddhadeb Bhattacharya, and the State Human Rights Commission.[10]

The above-mentioned incidents highlight certain interesting facets of the socio-religious situation and political compulsions that prevail today in West Bengal. The historians of popular religion should note the continuity of two main trends in the narrative of the fakir movement. One, there remains, in fakir beliefs and practices (all through the last three centuries), a running thread of rebellion against the orthodox rules and norms of the Islamic religious establishment, an assertion of humanist values that cut across caste, religious and gender barriers. Two, precisely because of their rejection of the dogmatic and puritanical Shariat laws and assertion of a pluralistic vision of society, there had emerged the other trend of violent opposition to them from Islamic fundamentalists – a trend that had run concurrently all through the centuries.

Given their past history of rebellion against religious orthodoxy and the colonial order, and their present adherence to religious harmony as practitioners of a lifestyle that cuts across caste and gender barriers, one would have expected the present Left Front government of West Bengal to accept and protect the fakirs as its natural allies. Yet, the Left Front administration bows down to the power of the orthodox Muslim clergy, which ostracizes and persecutes the fakirs. Here is a paradoxical situation. The fakirs are ideologically closer to the liberal and reformist views that are professed by the Left. Yet, because they are a numerical minority as a dissident group (within the Muslim community), the Left political parties in West Bengal refuse to stand by them against the numerically larger Muslim followers of the Shariat, and are reluctant to oppose the socio-religious hegemony of the powerful mullahs over the rural Muslim community – for fear of losing Muslim votes in elections.

Losing hope of getting any support from the existing secular political establishment, or the Left government, the fakirs of West Bengal have begun to organize themselves (as they did some 200 years ago, under Majnu Shah and others – but in a peaceful form today). From an existence of solitary bands, they are emerging into an organized force. Along with their fellow travellers

---

[10] *Anandabazar Patrika*, Kolkata, 23 February 2003.

in the Hindu Vaishnavite community – the *bauls*, who are also dissidents – the fakirs are active in an organization called the Baul–Fakir Sangha (formed in 1973). Their objectives are spelt out in a pamphlet released on the occasion of their annual conference during 5–6 March 2004, held in a village in Nadia. They stated:

> ...We want to project another India...in opposition to those who fight over temples and mosques, those who taint the sacred soil of India with the blood of human beings in the spiteful riots that they provoke in the name of caste difference ('"jater namey bajjatir" danga'...the words used in the pamphlet, recalling a famous poem of the Bengali rebel poet Kazi Nazrul Islam)...We regard human beings as one kind...We don't reject any one of the numerous manifestations of the universe created by the One and unique Creator. We are opposed to imprisoning within walls the One who inhabits the entire world. We do not support the division of human beings according to the Koran or the Puranas. We Bauls and Fakirs do not divide people along the lines of religious scriptures, castes, gender and class. We announce – 'The human being is the only truth.' We are beginning to build a paradise of peace and happiness on this earth itself – not in the 'paraloke' of the world beyond death...We, the Bauls and Fakirs, possessing nothing, depending only on our physical toil, are giving the call for the globalization of the equality of all human beings, against the profiteers who take away the last morsel from the hungry and against the deception of the consumerist culture. Let there be an end to all divisions and bloodshed among human beings. We have to get together to fight against abominations, injustice and exploitation...[11]

Can this not be a manifesto for those among us who are seeking changes in the present dismal socio-religious and political scenario?

Part II

Dissenters of Shariat

Surojit Sen

The Marfati fakirs or sexo-yogic worshippers of Bengal have deviated from institutional Islam as propagated by the clerics and in the mosque. Rather, they

[11] Quoted in Sen, *Fakirnama*, 61–62.

have developed their own philosophy based on the concept of universal human love and compassion attained through sexo-yogic principles of worshipping the human body. They believe that Allah or the Supreme Being resides in every human body, and thus by knowing the human body and the soul, one can realise Allah.

The guru or the preceptor is the only person who can impart this knowledge upon the disciple, as Prophet Hazrat Mohammad had imparted the knowledge upon his disciple and son-in-law, Hazrat Ali. This philosophy has been passed on through generations and transgressed borders following the tradition of the *preceptor* and the *disciple*. After the demise of Hazrat Mohammad, institutional Islam (Shariat) took the path of hegemony to dominate the world by converting people to Islam through religious wars. As a counterpoint, Marfat or non-institutional Islam, in its own mystic way, reached far and wide by spreading the message of love and compassion.

A song by the late Ghulam Shah Fakir of Birbhum district can be mentioned in this context. The song says, '*Alef-Lam-Mim holo jakhon/Hukum Dilen Sain Niranjan/Sejda kore Ferestagan/Shey Manush Ashilen Jabe*' (When *Alef, Lam, Mim* happened/The God had given his command/The angels show their obeisance/When the man had arrived). The whole song is like this. This song is written by Mahammad Shah, who was a very well-known guru of Bardhaman district of West Bengal:

> Everyone cries for humanity but to reach out enter his inner soul
> The self dwells in anonymity within the being – subtle and in stupor
> Reach out to him and feel the being within you
> Shred all your mundane chores as the self is waiting for you to behold
> Reach out to the Self who resides in a vibrant world, found in the kalma (sexo-yogic practice)
> Else your human birth will go astray, and at the end will have to repent.
> When Alef, Lum, Mim happened the Lord has given him command, the Angels show their obeisance
> When the man had arrived,
> Muhammed takes to the feet of guru Fakir Sha and cries
> 'I can see all this as the being provides me with all my inner visions'[12]

The Koran starts with the three words: *Alef, Lam* and *Mim*. The fakir says that the entire mystery lies in these three words. *Alef* signifies Allah; *Mim* signifies

---

[12] Mahammad Shah, 'Everyone cries for humanity but to reach out enter his inner soul', Field Recording.

Mohammad, Rasul or Prophet; and *Lam* signifies *Adam* or the man. *Alef* is on the right side, *Mim* on the left and in the centre is the seat of *Adam* or the man. It is only the man who can lift the veil between Allah and *Nabi.* The man is Allah's finest creation, and even the angels have shown their obeisance towards man being commanded by Allah. Guru is the one who can lift the veil and take the disciple to the other side.

Fakirs of Bengal believe that they had North Indian Sufi connections in the past, which is true. The Sufis remain the main face of non-institutional Islam. They had good relations with the rulers. The Sufi saints had first come down to northern India. They had reached Bengal by the end of the eleventh century. We don't know why many Sufi worshippers had come down to Bengal from as far away as Persia, Samarkhand or Bokhara; maybe, they were attracted by the riverine landscape and a primarily agricultural society offered by Bengal. When the Sufis came down to Bengal, it was already a seat of learning for sexo-yogic principles of the *Sahajiya Deha Sadhana*, which had taken a concrete shape completing a historic turbulent journey since the pre-Buddhist era.

The study of the body or the sexo-yogic practice was the most public and popular religion of Bengal during the entire 400 years of the Pal rule spanning the eighth century AD to the twelfth century AD, from Gopal (AD 750) to Madanpal (AD 1140). Incidentally, the Pals were Buddhists by religion, though the practice was not supported by the state. In the history of Bengal, the Pal era is known as the golden age. The Pals were sons of the soil and they were not known for their pedigree. They took over as the representatives of the people to save the land from a very chaotic and violent era known as the era of '*Matsyonyay*' (the era of bigger fishes eating smaller fishes). And Bengal reached the height of excellence in religion, philosophy, literature and arts during the Pal rule.

One more thing has to be said about the fakirs of Bengal. They were referred to as 'Nerar fakir'. *Nera* in Bengali means a person with shaven head. A shaven head is one of the important symbols of the Buddhist saints. Even now, the *sraman*s shave their heads regularly. The Bajrajana and the Sahajjana sects of Buddhists were popular during the four centuries of Pal rule. Innumerable subaltern people were followers of these sects. When the Muslims took over Bengal, a large number of the people took to Islam formally but did not give up their old rituals. Rather they continued with it, even if secretly. The study of the body of the Buddhist Sahajiyas and that of the fakirs is hardly any different. The underlying meanings of the verses of the *Charyapadas* by the Buddhist saints and Lalon's lyrics are proof enough of this fact. After that, in the wake of various social changes, this religion from disappeared public view but continued to be practised by various sects secretly. People from the social mainstream looked scornfully at this practice of the study of the body but its importance in the history of Bengal is undeniable.

Anyway, during the initial years, the Sufis of Bengal maintained a symbiotic relationship with their North Indian counterparts. However, as they went deeper into the principles of sexo-yogic worship, the guru took the place of the Supreme Being in their worship. The guru does not sell his knowledge; he takes care of his disciples and imparts upon them the knowledge of sexo-yogic practices. Only the guru can impart the knowledge of the cosmos residing in a man's body. Thus, these people started meditating upon the face of the guru rather than on the formless Supreme Being, since it was the guru who showed them the way to the One. These worshippers transcended the barriers of worshipping any formless Supreme Being. The guru, with his mortal form, interposed between the worshipper and the formless god. Not only this, but the ancient elements are: *mati* (earth), *rasa* (water), *rup* (fire) and *rati* (air). Thus, *charchandrabheda* or the four-moon method entered into the practices of the fakirs in Bengal. According to Sahajiya traditions, the four moons signify *raja*, *virya*, *veeshtha* and *mutra*. *Raja* signifies the vaginal fluid; *virya*, the semen; *veeshtha* signifies human faeces; and *mutra* is urine. *Raja* signifies form, *virya* is conceived as libido, faeces is earth and urine is water. The fakirs believe that the human body is made up of four basic elements: *aab* (water), *aatas* (fire), *khaak* (earth) and *baat* (air). The metaphoric depiction of regaining the body elements that are lost in the natural process and converting them into energy through chemical synthesis thereby gaining vital life force is the main aim of the four-moon tradition. The references to the four-moon method came into the work of the mendicant poets.

The four-moon references can be traced out from a song written by Baharuddin Fakir and sung by Shanti Fakir. When you hear the song written by Baharuddin, one is unable to trace any antecedent of the character Baharuddin. In Bengal, there are many such poets of Dehattathya (sexo-yogic practice).

> The body is made up of a little fire, a little earth and a little bit of water.
> But it is very difficult to understand the dynamics of it all
> O! my frenzied mind
> It so hard to understand it all
> The eye-eid (refers to the vagina due to its similar shape)
> that resides in our body

Which moon signifies the namaaz
Which one the bakri-eid (the moon of eid signifies the three days of the menstrual cycle with different coloured bodily fluids flowing out on each day)
Which moon signifies the beginning of creation
Which moon signifies the God
O! my frenzied mind
It so hard to understand it all
The four sounds that originate from this body
There are four masjids at four places
And there are four differently coloured Fakirs
Which fakir would show me the God
O! my frenzied mind
It so hard to understand it all
There are four wise men in the body
The only ones who know how to reach the God
Fakir Baharuddin is engulfed in thoughts
It so hard to understand it all.[13]

The world is used to one side of Islam, and the fakirs of Bengal are another face. This side of Islam seeks to endear itself to people through love, music and their way of life, irrespective of the man-made boundaries of caste, creed and culture. The fakirs are like any other ordinary labourer, fishmonger or farmer. When they sing, some of them do their *alkhallah*s, some don't. Otherwise, it is not easy to recognize them by their vestments. Unlike the followers of the Shariat, they don't frequent the mosques, nor read *namaz*, nor observe *roza*. For them, the human body is their mosque where they read their *namaz*, and according to the rules of which they keep *roza*.

The fact that the fakirs in Bengal had tried to interpret the Koran in a different way – took up the ancient Sahajiya tradition of the four moons and converted non-institutional Islam into a *Guruvadi* or oral tradition based on the importance of the guru – was disdained by the institutional Islam. They thought that the fakirs of Bengal had distorted Islam, and thus the fakirs of Bengal have had to face a lot of ire from the Shariatis.

A little before the beginning of the nineteenth century, many lower-caste Hindus and Shariati Mussalmans of west and northern Bengal took up the fakiri tradition from the gurus to live freely and escape the dogmas that shrouded both these religions. They created a society within, with liberal and non-communal

[13] Baharuddin Fakir, 'The body is made up of a little fire, a little earth and a little bit of water', Field Recording.

living. At that time, the fakirs in Bengal numbered approximately sixty to seventy million. Shariati violence was inflicted upon these people. It can be said that for more than the past 100 years, the fakirs of Bengal have had to live as a marginalized sub-cult due to instances of regular violence that were inflicted upon them.

The importance of the guru or *murshid* reached such colossal status among the fakirs of Bengal that during the practice of sexo-yogic principles, they remembered the face of the guru, rather than that of Allah, to calm their minds. Next, we discuss Lalon Fakir.

Lalon Fakir (1774–1890) is arguably the best saint poet of the *baul*–fakir genre. He is certainly the most popular among all the fakirs. He lived in the village of Cheuria, the area known as Nadia in the Bengal Presidency of British India, corresponding to the district of Kushtia in present-day Bangladesh. Till this date, his songs are sung all over Bengal, blurring the political border dividing the two Bengals. There are reasons to believe that Lalon's compositions had a lasting influence on Rabindranath Tagore. His ashram or *khanqah* at Cheuria in Kushtia came under the Tagore zamindari of Silaidaha, and Tagore is the first documented collector of Lalon songs. The unfinished portrait of Lalon by Jyotirindranath, Tagore's beloved elder brother, is the only image of the great saint poet. Lalon left behind over 600 mesmerizing songs. At the time of his death in 1890, the number of his direct disciples went well past 10,000.

Lalon wrote many songs denouncing casteism. He himself was a victim of Hindu–Muslim discrimination. There is no reliable biography of Lalon. In the words of Lalon's biographer, Basanta Kumar Pal, he was by birth a Hindu. He accompanied his neighbours to the adjacent district of Murshidabad on foot for a holy dip in the sacred Ganga. On his way, he caught the deadly pox and nearly died. His companions thought death was imminent and tied him to a raft made of banana plants and threw him in the Ganga. However, Lalon was found by a Muslim woman from the weavers' community. The woman tended him for a long time and Lalon recovered and went back to his family. In the meanwhile, Lalon's neighbours had gone back to his village and announced the his death, following which his mother and wife completed his *shradh*. Now, when Lalon came back, his family was happy, but after hearing that he stayed with a Muslim family, went for the verdict of the Brahmins or the influential people of the society. The verdict was that Lalon could not be taken back by his family. Lalon's mother and wife could not ignore the verdict. After this rejection, Lalon went back to the weaver family. A fakir called Siraj Sain used to frequent the place. Lalon was baptized (given *diksha*) by him into the Marfati fold.

Lalon never discriminated on religious or caste grounds. The uniqueness of Lalon is that, to him, Allah and Krishna were the same and Chaitanya and Mohammed were both inspired by the same godly powers. In both, the god expressed himself fully. Both of them were whom the Sufis called *Insaan-ul-kamel*. He thought these were the *sadguru*s, the torchbearers. In his songs, Lalon sought blessings from both of them.

Lalon has written many songs in reverence to guru or *murshid*, and one such is:

Don't worry, this boat, a morphed human body will not sink
You, who want to get ashore, come to prophet's boat
The infidel oarsmen will perish at the stroke of the deluge
What your badar gazi will do, where he will be
Where badar gazi will be
You, who want to get ashore, come to prophet's boat
The infidels are the wretched of this world
Their worship is futile,
The scriptures don't indicate
You, who want to get ashore, come to prophet's boat
He is the guru, He is the Prophet
There is no confusion
In the form of Ahmmed he is the Supreme Being
This is what Quran tells, not Lalon
You, who want to get ashore, come to prophet's boat[14]

How beautifully Lalon captures the fact that this boat (made of a morphed human body with flesh and blood) will not sink (to get trapped in the libido) as this boat is guided by Prophet (Hazrat Mohammad). But one has to remember that Lalon talks about the Prophet of the Marfati way, not as in Shariat. Then he says that the infidel (who doesn't follow Shariat) oarsmen will die in the deluge (libido). How so they chant the name of Badar Gazi (the saviour of river). Here, Lalon has inverted the Shariat–Marfat discourse.

He claims Marfat (sexo-yogic practice) and only Marfat is the real scripture and the institutional Islam is *Beshra* (not following Shariat). He continues by saying that those who don't go by the Prophet (the Prophet of Marfat), they are the real *kafer* (infidel). It transpires that practising this way will not take anyone to god and the scripture (Koran) doesn't indicate it. At the end, Lalon

[14] See Abul Ahsan Choudhury, ed., *Lalonsamagra* (Lalon – Collected Works) (Dhaka: Pathok Samabesh, 2008).

comes out of the metaphor and says that he who is *murshid* (guru) is Rasul (Prophet). And there is no mistake in this realization. In the form of Ahammed (the other name of Hazrat Mohammad), he is the Supreme Being also, because *murshid* or guru helps one to find the way to God. And he who gives the way to the unknown is the Supreme Being because the Supreme Being only can bring out the self within; merely, he has taken the form of the guru.

The entire Marfati philosophy and doctrine is propagated through song. One point must be made about the songs of *dehatattwa* or the sexo-yogic practice. The subject of these songs is more or less the same, the same *sadhana*, the same guru-ism, the same study of the body. So, this is limited to particular sects and is monotonous. The difference lies in the language and the presentation. The lyrics get precedence over the melody, thus they are known as word songs or *shabda gaan*, because the words lay down the method of *sadhana*. These songs have been written by the so-called uneducated or partially educated people from villages in a way that best suited the spontaneous expression of practitioners and believers of a simple religion. The imageries draw heavily on various directly material experiences of daily life. Often, they are dialectal. Like the natural resources, the songs of *dehatattwa* are natural, easy and untended.

For the Marfati fakirs, playing music is singing paean to Allah. Probably, they have taken this tradition from the Chistiya and Suhrawardiya Sufis for whom music is an inseparable part of life. These Sufis used music to lift the mind beyond the chores of normal life and attuned it to a higher philosophical plane where they could connect with God. At times, when these Sufis reached a state of ecstasy – called *halka* – with the song and dance, their disciples had to bring them down to a normal earthly plane of thought by using different means. The fakirs of Bengal also use music to worship Allah. This is in counterpoint to Shariat, where music is considered vile or *haram*, and is one of the main reasons behind the ire and oppression of the Shariati clerics the fakirs have to face. However, the fakirs have carved out their space very subtly amid all the hostility. I relate one incident from Akkas Fakir's festival in Gorbhanga village in the Nadia district of Bengal, where the fakirs had stopped the music during the hours when *namaz* was held at the nearby mosque.

Again, we will talk about Lalon Fakir, in the context of gender, who bears a speciality in the sense that he transcended the gender barrier and brought femininity into his realm. As the following song written by Lalon Shah says:

> The indomitable Cupid doesn't leave me alone
> How can I be a true devotee?
> The Cupid sets his kingdom in this body

And collects the revenue ruthlessly
So allure the crooked Cupid
Because he keeps secret vigil
How can I be a true devotee?
What a strange game this is to use a thief to catch theft
You don't answer to my posers
The mendicants outsmart the thieves in their art and the thieves run away scared
To a nothingness
How can I be a true devotee?
Lalon Sain humbly stays at the feet of guru Siraj Sain
If my husband ditches me, where to seek justice?
My husband is my soul mate, how can I meet up his desire
Yet keep my virginity
How can I be a true devotee?[15]

Lalon Fakir says that inside the human body resides *Kamadeva Madan* or the god of sexual impulses. One has to play hide and seek with him all the time, so that one does not fall prey to his chores, notably the sexual impulses. If one does fall prey to the sexual impulses, then his worship is rendered useless. The sadhus or mendicants commit stealth by controlling the sexual impulses through regulation of the breathing process. The sexual impulses thus get transformed into vital air which comes out through the breath after moving upward. In the song, Lalon Fakir imagines himself as a female disciple who was initiated by a guru along with her husband. Both the husband and the wife follow the sexo-yogic principles of worship as taught by the guru. However, as the husband controls the entire process, she is afraid of what would happen to her if her husband gets entrapped by the sexual impulses while performing the sexo-yogic rituals ('ejaculation' has been compared to death among mendicants.) She asks her guru, whom she would complain to, if she suffers *death* at her husband's hand. If she refuses her husband, then he would question her chastity, and if she gives in to his demands, she deviates from the path shown by the guru. She cannot find wisdom or become a *prem-rasika.* This is the dilemma of this song.

The sexo-yogic principles expound the philosophy of *purusha* or the masculine assuming a *prakriti* or feminine trait. It also says that the feminine trait is of attraction and the masculine that of repulsion. Thus, if the masculine can attain a feminine trait, then he can convert the downward flow of semen or vital fluid into an upward movement, thereby controlling the ejaculation.

---

[15] Ibid.

Lalon extrapolated this theory and imagined himself as a woman and has written this song:

Always I get into the vile acts
Will the Guru allow me to be a maid at his service?
I came into this world through the pangs of birth
And through the darkness of the black-hole
Forgotten all those
I have forgotten everything
Once I came into this world.
Will the Guru allow me to be a maid at his service
I failed to recognise the Guru Vastu
Abstained from worshipping it
I have to retrace the circle of eighty-four million births
Will the Guru allow me to be a maid at his service?
He, whose self is entwined to the image of Guru
Is fearless to the eventuality
Lalon says Oh! My mind you make me the sinner
Will the Guru allow me to be a maid at his service?[16]

Lalon Fakir says in this song that, in our daily lives, we commit so many vile acts that the guru would not give her/him a place as a maid servant at his feet. And if one does not find a place at the feet of the guru, then one cannot know the different stages of meditation. After so much of pain I was born out of the black-hole (compared to the vagina), however I get enamoured in the earthly pleasures of life and forget its true existence. If I cannot understand the meaning of *Guru Vastu (notably Veerya and Raja),* if I cannot worship it properly, then I am bound to regress into the cycle of eighty-four million births to be reborn as a human being again. However, one who has understood the significance of the *guru*, in whose heart resides the omnipresent image of the *guru* can avoid death. Lalon repents, O my mind you make me the sinner.

This is a small reflection on the sexo-yogic practices of the Marfati fakirs in Bengal and the ways in which they can be seen to be dissenters against the Shariat.

References

Bhattacharya, Upendranath, ed. *Banglar Baul o Baul Gaan* [Bauls and Baul songs of Bengal] (Kolkata: Orient Book Company, 2001).

[16] Ibid.

Chattopadhyay Debiprasad, *Lokayata Darshan* [Pagan Philosophy] (Kolkata: New age Publishers Pvt. Ltd, 1956).

Dasgupta Sashibhushan, ed. 1983. *Boudha Dharma o Chorjageeti* [Buddhism and Charja songs], Orient Book Company, Kolkata.

Ghani Osman, ed. 2005 . *Hazrat Ali* [Life of Hazrat Ali], Mallick Brothers, Kolkata.

Haq Enamul Mahmmad, ed. 2006. *Bonge Sufi Probhab* [Sufi influence in Bengal], Ramon Publishers, Dhaka.

Ahmed, Wakil. *Unish Shatoke Bangali Musalmaner Chinta-Chetonar Dhara,* Vol. II (Dhaka, 1983).

Anandabazar Patrika. Kolkata, 23 February 2003.

Banerjee, Sumanta. 'From Aulchand to Sati-Ma: The Institutionalization of the Karta-Bhaja Sect in Nineteenth century Bengal', in *Logic in a Popular Form*. Kolkata, 2002.

Choudhury, Abul Ahsan, ed. *Lalonsamagra* (Lalon – Collected Works) (Dhaka: Pathok Samabesh, 2008).

Dutta, Akshay Kumar. *Bharatbarshiya Upasak Sampraday,* Vol. I (Kolkata, 1997 [1870]).

Haq, Muhammad Enamul. *A History of Sufiism in Bengal* (Dacca: Asiatic Society of Bangladesh, 1975).

Hunter, W.W. *Annals of Rural Bengal* (Kolkata, 1883).

Ray, Suprakash. *Bharater Krishak Bidroha O Ganatantrik Sangram* (Kolkata: DNBA Brothers, 1972).

Sen, Surojit, ed. *Fakirnama* (About Fakirs) (Kolkata: Gangchil, 2009).

CHAPTER

12

Music in Chishti Sufism

Raziuddin Aquil

> *Kushtagan-i khanjar-i taslim ra*
> *Har zaman as ghayb jaan-i digar ast*
> [The victims of the dagger of submission
> Get a new life from the unseen every moment]

Khwaja Qutb-ud-Din Bakhtiyar Kaki, a music aficionado and second in a chain of five great Chishti Sufis who flourished in the Delhi Sultanate in the thirteenth and fourteenth centuries, died in 1235, after bouts of ecstasy caused by the above couplet recited by the *qawwal* in a *mahfil-i-sama*, music assembly, organized by the Khwaja himself. Chishti memory recounts that the Khwaja was in rapture for over three days, and every time he would regain consciousness, he would ask the *qawwal* to recite the same couplet. Eventually, the Khwaja breathed his last in that state of bliss, ascending to the heaven in anticipation of achieving union with his beloved Allah. He was buried at a site selected by him in advance and the shrine soon became a major centre of pilgrimage. This was a perfect finale to a Muslim mystic's career devoted to God, marked by night-long prayers and meditation, a refined taste for poetry and music, an informed understanding of the classical traditions of Islam and occasional performance of miracles either as an expression of benevolence towards the faithful or to silence the antagonists, especially the aggressive Sunni Hanafi *ulama* of the Delhi Sultanate, who sought to censor the ways of the Sufis. It was no coincidence that the five great Chishti masters and the later upholders of Chishti traditions shared their love for poetry and music as central to their spiritual activities.[1] There can be no mysticism without some degree of ecstatic

[1] For a general history of Chishti Sufism, see Carl W. Ernst and Bruce B. Lawrence, *Sufi Martyrs of Love: The Chishti Order in South Asia and Beyond* (New York: Palgrave Macmillan, 2002).

expression of devotion for God (*haal*) and a desire to dance your way up to heaven (*raqs*). Seen in simple terms by theologians, the conscience keepers of Islam, dance and music are marks of vulgarity and uncontrolled fun, which must be stopped.

This essay is part of my larger study of Chishti Sufis of the Sultanate period, which aims at a critical appreciation of Sufi practices and the whole argument on their lawfulness in the light of the sources of Islamic traditions (Koran, *Hadis* and antecedents from the lives of early exemplars). Before we get into the details of one of the most contested practices, music, it will be useful to have a quick look at the historical legacies of Sufism. Why does Sufism continue to be a vibrant tradition and how have Sufi institutions commanded a wide following and respect even in contexts when several other ways of practising Islam are attacked or disliked? How has Sufism not only survived the onslaught of the reformist *ulama* but also made itself meaningful in disparate Indian environments, which is no less challenging?

Sufism and its Contested Legacy

Sufism began as a spiritual revolt against the worldliness and rampant materialism in the Ummayad and Abbasid Caliphates in the Middle East within the first centuries after the emergence of Islam (seventh and eighth centuries CE). Famous early figures such as Bayazid Bustami, Rabiya Basari and Hasan Basari led simple, ascetic lives and aspired to achieve union with God through meditation and other spiritual disciplines. The early Muslim mystics, who were often charismatic leaders with popular appeal, were eventually organized or institutionalized in *silsila*s, or orders, branching into quite a few competing strands.[2]

Prophetic tradition refers to three dimensions of Islam: *islam*, or 'submission', forced by the jurists; *iman*, or faith, preached by theologians; and *ihsan*, to do beautiful things, practised by the Sufis (making the latter appear as the best of the Muslims). The main objective of the Sufis is to seek nearness or union with a merciful and loving God, through prayers, remembrance, meditations and spiritual exercises (some of which may not have been approved by the *ulama*, or theologians). This third dimension, *ihsan*, constituted the heart of religion, marked by sincerity, love, virtue and perfection, which the Sufis aspired for.[3]

[2] For a good introduction to the formative phase of Sufism, see Ahmet T. Karamustafa, *Sufism: The Formative Period* (Edinburgh: Edinburgh University Press, 2007).

[3] William C. Chittick, *Sufism: A Short Introduction* (Oxford: Oneworld Publications, 2007).

Typically, Sufis began with shunning the anxieties of attachment to this world, whether private or public. They called for soul searching, remembrance of God beyond ritual prayers in mosques, meditation in solitude and wandering around as dervishes to Muslim cities and non-Muslim or semi-Islamized hinterlands. At the end of it, they would 'come back' with claims of personally experiencing the truth of Islam, of the loving God and the righteousness of the path of the Prophet (strengthening here the position of the Sunni *ulama*). As religious exemplars, then, Sufis were supposed to guide Muslims, ignoring or tolerating human weaknesses, and also bring non-Muslims to the fold of Islam. Thus, the Sufi movement was an established stream within Islam before the emergence of various Muslim Sultanates in the Indian subcontinent in the thirteenth century.

Much of what we know about Sufism is derived from the carefully crafted Sufi literature in Persian and vernacular languages. Sufi sources included: (a) *malfuzat* (discourses of a Sufi compiled by a disciple, *murid*, generally in the lifetime of the Sufi himself); (b) *maktubat*, or letters, written by a Sufi to his disciples; (c) mystical treatises on Sufism prepared by a Sufi shaikh; (d) compilations of Sufi poetry; and (e) *tazkira*s, or hagiographies of Sufis, compiled generally after the death of a Sufi. Important information on Sufi activities may also be found in court chronicles and general histories, particularly on matters relating to Sufis' relations with the rulers. The anecdotes of Sufi miracles and other popular narratives also throw immense light on the valuable presence of Muslim mystics in various localities. Though historians might find it difficult to judge the historicity of myths and legends associated with saintly figures like *ghazi*s and *shahid*s, the claims of the paranormal powers enjoyed by mystic figures and their perceived ability to help those in distress form the core of Sufis' role in society in which they flourished.

Of the Sufi orders that emerged, four of them enjoyed considerable importance in India. While Chishtis and Suhrawardis flourished in the Sultanate period, the other two, Qadiris and Naqshbandis, became significant in Mughal India. Many branches of these Sufi orders proliferated in various regions over the centuries. To start with, the living Sufi master guided followers or visitors at his hospice, but later the shrines (*dargahs*) of Sufis of the previous generations became important and grew into places of pilgrimage, eventually carving a whole sacred geography of Sufism, called *wilayat*, which involved a lot of struggle and competition for control of territory, followers and resources. Spreading in regions such as Bengal and the Deccan from roughly the thirteenth century, Sufis of the orders like the Chishtis attempted to guard the grand tradition they had inherited from their great preceptors of North India and, at the same time, got themselves entrenched in the local religious milieu and shaped local mystical traditions. The dual process of identifying with the tradition which flourished outside and recognizing, or adjusting to, local realities may have led to make compromises by the Sufis, which may not have been acceptable to the Shariat-driven *ulama*, the watchdogs of Islam.[4]

What distinguished Sufism from other forms of Islam was its belief that a human soul could achieve union with God, a belief formulated in the doctrine of *wahdat-ul-wujud* (unity of existence, or monism as a reality) by the thirteenth century Sufi master Ibn-i-Arabi. This doctrine often brought Sufis into conflict with Islamic orthodoxy (represented by the Sunni Hanafi *ulama*). The latter believed that God was unique and, therefore, to suggest that a human soul could achieve union with God was to imply that there was no distinction between the creator and this creation. It is for this reason that Sufis were occasionally attacked and persecuted. Sufis were also targeted by the *ulama* for their occasional indifference to formal religious practices such as regular congregational prayers (*namaz/salat*), instead focusing on meditation and spiritual exercises which included music. The legitimacy of the latter, that is, listening to music in *sama* or *qawwali*, was a major source of confrontation between the *ulama* and Sufis.

As we shall see in the next part of this essay, despite oppositions from sections of the *ulama*, Sufi orders such as the Chishtis used song and dance techniques for concentration and for creating spiritual ecstasy. The Sufis also played a significant role in the growth and development of vernacular languages and literature. By contrast, the court culture facilitated the spread and dominance of Persian as the language of power and government. Sufism, therefore, contributed greatly to the development of both Indian folk and classical culture.

The belief in *wahdat-ul-wujud* and several forms or techniques of meditation brought Sufis spiritually very close to certain strands of non-Muslim religious traditions. For example, Advaita Hinduism claimed that *atma* (a human soul) and *parmatma* (God) were one and the same, a theory similar to *wahdat-ul-wujud*. Also, Sufis found much to learn from Hindu spiritual disciplines, such as yoga, which influenced their meditation and other spiritual practices. Mention may be made here of the popular practice of *pranayam*, breath control, and the more spectacular *chilla-i-makus*, hanging oneself upside down with a branch of tree on the mouth of a well, though generally conducted in private and in the darkness of night.

---

[4] See the important contributions of Richard M. Eaton, *Sufis of Bijapur, 1300–1700, Social Roles of Sufis in Medieval India* (Princeton: Princeton University Press, 1978); *Essays on Islam and Indian History* (New Delhi: Oxford University Press, 2002).

If Sufis learnt from non-Muslim traditions, local non-Muslim traditions were also powerfully affected by the principles of Islam as represented by Sufi saints. The criticism of idol worship, of 'useless' ritual, emphasis on equality, worship of and excessive devotion for one God, which are central to many strands of medieval Bhakti movements, can be traced to Sufism. Sufism's greatest contribution to Indian culture is considered to be the example it set in the field of religious and cultural coexistence, traditionally articulated by scholars as syncretism and synthesis. Whatever may be the accurate term, Sufi orders showed that Muslim and non-Muslim religious traditions could prosper side by side and learn from each other – subconsciously or strategically.

Though scholars of Sufism and Vaishnava Bhakti generally tend to study the two broad religious movements in isolation, a closer look might reveal not only similarities at the level of spiritual practices and devotionalism, but also a kind of competitive spirituality at work.[5] The leaders of various competing movements may be found devising various strategies of prestige, such as performing better miracles, defeating antagonists in miraculous combats and presenting a critical reading of each others' scriptures to prove one's superior intellect and thus superiority and righteousness. Yet, Sufis and their competitors assimilated or borrowed ideas from each other both to inform themselves better and to attract devotees or followers in large numbers. The influence of Sufism or similarities between Sufism and mysticism of the *bauls* and strands of Vaishnavites in Bengal are clearly discernible in the literature of these devotional movements. Often, the commonalities between the mystics of diverse traditions (fakirs, dervishes, Nathas, Goswamis) would blur the fine distinctions they would have otherwise liked to maintain and strive for.

The closeness to non-Muslim traditions helped Sufis play an important role in conversion and Islamicization, even if many of them might not be working with an explicit agenda of this kind. Yet, the presence of Sufis was the main factor in the conversion of large sections of the population to Islam. To start with, Sufi institutions, *khanqahs*/*dargahs*, became centres where Muslims and non-Muslims gathered for worship, meditation or spiritual experience and sought blessings and benediction from Sufi masters. The process of conversion started with devotion towards a particular Sufi, leading to the emergence of syncretic sects, symbolizing only half or partial conversion. Eventually, there

[5] For more on the competition, see the works of Aziz Ahmad 1999 and Simon Digby 1994 (Digby, Simon. 1994. 'To Ride a Tiger or a Wall? Strategies of Prestige in Indian Sufi Legend', in Winand M. Callewaert and Rupert Snell, eds, *According to Tradition: Hagiographical Writing in India.* Wiesbaden: Otto Harrassowitz.)

emerged communities of Muslims who professed Islam formally, but continued with their practice of local customs and traditions, which were condemned by the puritanical, reformist Islam. Be that as it may, many communities of Muslims attribute their conversion to the blessings of Sufi masters. It is possible that communities emerged around the shrines of Sufi saints over centuries of cultural accretion.

The shrines of *ghazi-baba*s and *shahid*s, which dot the landscape, have also played meaningful roles in the lives of the people without demanding formal conversion and yet, they did succeed in winning converts to Islam. Apart from performing miracles of a universal nature to be found in mystical hagiographies, Sufis are especially venerated for their ability to master the environment in which they settled down and protect the people by such activities as controlling a demon or taming a tiger, besides helping the poor through charitable endeavours and political interventions.

Despite the fact that Sufis have been careful not to stray outside the pale of Islam, while attempting to integrate themselves in the society in which they flourished, the *ulama*'s attitude towards Sufi orders has generally been hostile, for the former considered many Sufi ideas and practices as heretical from the point of view of their own interpretation of the Shariat, Islamic law. Even as the *ulama* were concerned with guarding orthodoxy than spreading Islam and their contact with non-Muslims was limited and perhaps unproductive, the role played by Sufis in conversion and Islamicization was not counted as important by the *ulama*, for they thought that the quality of Islam practised and preached by the Sufis was inadequate and inferior. In fact, the *ulama* attacked many Sufi practices, condemning them to be un-Islamic. For this purpose, they often used political power also.

It is generally suggested that the relationship between Sufi orders and the state was distant. Orders like the Chishtis refused to accept money or support from the ruler. They believed that involvement in politics led to materialism and worldliness, which they wished to avoid. However, this attitude varied from order to order and between Sufis within an order also. Whereas the Chishtis recommended aloofness from the state, the Suhrawardis had no qualms about associating with the sultan's court. The Naqshbandis and the Qadiris were also known for their political involvement in the Mughal period, though the representatives of the two *silsila*s displayed remarkable divergence in their approach to contemporary social and political issues. In general, the rulers needed the support of the Sufis and other holy men to legitimate their political authority. On the other hand, the leading mystic figures looked for political patronage and support and attempted even to influence the rulers to be able to dominate over their rivals. Though the preoccupations of the mystics, seen wandering around in search of God or truth, might appear to be other-worldly, many of them could also be found deeply involved in this-worldly concerns, often embroiling them into political controversies.

The occasional political interventions apart, Sufi traditions continue to practice and preach in the language of love and peace at a time when most forms of Islam are identified or confused with violence or terrorism. Tolerant, accommodative and popular branches of Sufism, like that of the Chishtis, originating in a region which is now infamous for violence, Afghanistan, have shown that it was possible to lead a good Muslim life even as one can reach out to a larger humanity and attract them to their fold without using force or political power. The Sufis, both living masters and later inheritors as well as keepers of the shrines, *dargahs* and their practice of Islam (love for God, often like a Majnun would do for Layla; respect for the traditions of Prophet Mohammad and aspiration to follow his path; and service to humanity and not of Muslims alone), command a lot of respect. Sufi shrines are flourishing in a context in which mosques can be destroyed at will, state machinery permitting.

Despite opposition from various quarters, Sufism remains a vibrant movement, attracting devotees from across various strata of society: rural–urban poor, thugs, criminals, politicians and ministers can be seen offering ritual Sufic *chadar*s and prostrating in the *dargahs*. It is the ability of the Sufis to speak in the language of the masses, local dialects and the perceived paranormal powers that have attracted people, some for following the ways of the Sufis, but mostly for blessings and benedictions.

Qawwali and other song and dance techniques are central to most forms of devotional religion. In his lifetime, the leading Chishti Sufi, Nizam-ud-Din Auliya, himself fought a bitter struggle with the *ulama* of Delhi in the early fourteenth century, who contested the legitimacy of his practice of organizing musical sessions. For the theologians professing Hanafi interpretation of mainstream Sunni Islam, music is *haram*, or a forbidden act. For most Sufis, on the other hand, music is one of the most effective and perfectly valid ways to remember Allah and achieve ecstasy.

Sufi Music as a Legitimate Spiritual Activity

Compared to the Qalandars, Madaris and such other 'heterodox' Sufi groups, the Chishti Sufis actually conformed to the traditional Islamic norms of conduct at the social level. However, their non-conformism was reflected at the level of their defiance of the rigid interpretation of Islam by the dominant Sunni *ulama* (theologians) of the Hanafi school of jurisprudence. Apart from other aspects of their religious or spiritual practices, which were often questioned by the antagonists, the use of music (*sama* or *qawwali*) in Chishti devotionalism was a cause of major tension between the Chishti Sufis and the *ulama* in the Delhi Sultanate. Whereas for the Chishtis, music was central to their expression of love for God, the Hanafi *ulama* condemned song and dance techniques in Sufi spirituality as illegal or *haram*. At the centre of the intense debate was no less a figure than Nizam-ud-Din Auliya, who flourished in the late thirteenth and the early fourteenth centuries.

In this section, we shall look at the various forms of music recommended in Chishti Sufi circles of the Delhi Sultanate and the arguments defending their legitimacy in the light of the classical sources of Islam (Koran and *Hadis*), amidst the clamour for their suppression. In particular, the focus will be on Nizam-ud-Din Auliya's practice of organizing music assemblies, the Sunni Hanafi *ulama*'s opposition to music and the resultant inquest at Sultan Ghiyas-ud-Din Tughluq's court. Though I have previously published some of the details relating to the controversy concerning Sufi music, an attempt here is made to reread a chapter of *Siyar-ul-Auliya* devoted entirely to *sama*, which especially refers to Nizam-ud-Din's defence of music and his curse, which, the Sufi fraternity believed, led to the elimination of the antagonists and destruction of the city of Delhi. We shall also refer to Nizam-ud-Din's own subtle remarks and distinctions found scattered in the pages of *Fawa'id-ul-Fu'ad*, identified by historians as an authentic collection of his *malfuzat*. (The distinctions between good music and vulgar forms, which were informed by classifications and justifications in mystical treatises, may be further cross-checked with an important work like *Kashf-ul-Mahjub* of Ali Hujwiri; a text Nizam-ud-Din himself used and referred to during the course of his conversations.)

According to Amir Khwurd, Nizam-ud-Din identified four kinds of musical practice: *halal* (lawful); *haram* (forbidden); *makruh* (abominable); and *mubah* (permissible). If the connoisseur (*sahib-i wajad wa haal*) is fairly attracted towards the divine, then his practice of *sama* is *mubah*; if he is inclined more towards *majaz*, then it is *makruh*; if his interest is entirely for *majaz*, then it is *haram*; and if he is fully devoted to god, *sama* is *halal* for him. The practitioner of music (*sahib-i sama*) should be capable of understanding these distinctions.[6]

[6] Amir Khwurd Kirmani, *Siyar-ul-Auliya*, trans. Islamuddin Nizami (in Urdu) (New Delhi: Islamuddin Nizami, 2002), 645.

Amir Khwurd further writes, quoting from Nizam-ud-Din's remarks (recorded in *Fawa'id-ul-Fu'ad*), that the singer (*musma*) should be an adult male and not a boy or woman. The heart of the listener (*mustama*) should be full of love and devotion for God. The content (*masmu*) should not be vulgar (*fahash, hazal*). Musical instruments (*ala-i sama*) such as chang and rabab should not be used in *majlis-i-sama*.[7] Nizam-ud-Din emphasized during his conversations with his disciples that whatever was being heard was for remembering God (*yaad-i-haqq*), and thus, a valid (*halal*) act.[8] Nizam-ud-Din was also reported to have outlined the *adab* for *sama*: it should be held at an appropriate time when the heart is free from any anxiety; it should be held at a place where the environment is soul refreshing; and the participants should belong to the same group of male adults known for their addiction (*zauq*) for *sama*, which in practice was a blend of poetry, music and dance. At the time of settling down in the *majlis*, musical assembly, one should wear a neat and perfumed attire.[9]

The above norms are further supplemented with suggestions made by Fakhr-ud-Din Zarradi, a *khalifa* (one of the spiritual successors) of Nizam-ud-Din Auliya, who actively participated in the discussion on the legitimacy of Sufi music. According to Zarradi, *sama* should be listened to with full attention. The participants of the *majlis* should not look at each other or be conscious of each other's presence. Clearing one's throat and yawning should be avoided. The heads should be lowered and completely lost in contemplation. There should not be any movement of the body and one should keep one's *nafs* (sensual aspect of one's being) in control so that dancing and clapping are avoided. However, if one is so lost or moved, while listening to music, that one suddenly starts crying, shaking or dancing and his intention is not marred by any sense of ostentation or hypocrisy, then his actions will be treated as *mubah*. For, crying and wailing drown one's sorrows (*gham*) and dancing is equivalent to *sarur* (cheerfulness, exhilaration) which is a valid movement or activity.[10] Among the recommended norms in *adab-i-sama* included the suggestion that if a fellow participant stands up in *wajd*, moved or transported in an ecstasy of love for God, then others in the *majlis* should follow him in standing up to be

[7] Ibid., 646; *Fawa'id-ul-Fu'ad*, conversations of Nizam-ud-Din Auliya, compiled by Amir Hasan Sijzi, Persian text with Urdu translation by Khwaja Hasan Sani Nizami (New Delhi: Urdu Academy, 2001), 418–419.

[8] Ibid., 419.

[9] Kirmani, *Siyar-ul-Auliya*, 647.

[10] Ibid., 648.

by his side. And, while dancing in ecstasy (*raqs*), one should maintain a certain degree of grace so that others are not put off by his movements and intention.[11] Though it takes two to tango, but the dance companions' role should be to help him reach out for Allah.

Nizam-ud-Din is also quoted as saying: the body movement that is generated in remembering God in ecstasy is *mustahab* and if the intention is for some carnal pleasure (*fasad*), then it is *haram*.[12] However, if a person gets really ecstatic (*raqs* and *harkat*) in *sama* and even tears his clothes, he may be treated as someone overpowered by ecstasy. Thus, he may not be questioned, but those who pretend to be lost in ecstasy just to show off their spiritual bent of mind will be accused of indulging in *haram*.[13] Sufi circles did identify the pretenders who would be the cause of embarrassment, especially when the *ulama* were ready to interrogate anyone departing from norms of proper conduct. Qalandars and related groups particularly attracted attention for their behaviour, which could be identified as deviance. Also, Nizam-ud-Din's followers themselves would be reported to be part of musical jamborees, where not only instruments were used but also women present; much to the disappointment of the shaikh. However, it might appear that Nizam-ud-Din maintained some ambiguity in the matter, or at least let the followers decide for themselves what was good for them: recalling here reports of Amir Khusrau inventing not only ragas, *khayal* and *tarana* but also being instrumental in creating sitar, sarod, etc.

Amir Khwurd has noted that certain jurists and *ulama*, who were opposed to *sama*, would also come to observe the *majlis* organized by Nizam-ud-Din Auliya. Looking at the manner in which the shaikh would be standing at a place, crying silently and wiping his tears, even as the singers – two of whom are named as Hasan Paihadi and Samat Qawwal – were reciting heart-rending Persian poetry in their distinctive intonations, the *ulama* would fall at his feet and accept as legitimate what they would otherwise condemn as un-Islamic.[14] Despite being deeply touched by the poetry of love being recited by the singers and all but lost in the thought of the divine, Nizam-ud-Din would not only come out of the hall, taking a break at the time of prayers, but also kept a watch on the activities of the other participants. He once noticed Amir Khusrau raising his hands during *raqs* as a Sufi would do and asked him not to do so as he was

---

[11] Ibid., 648–649.

[12] Ibid., 658; *Fawa'id-ul-Fu'ad*, 419.

[13] Kirmani, *Siyar-ul-Auliya*, 658.

[14] Ibid., 664–665.

attached to this-worldly concerns. Thenafter, Khusrau would dance with his hands down and wrists closed, appearing as if his hands were tied and, unlike the Sufi, unable to break free and reach out for Allah.[15]

Nizam-ud-Din's interest in music and particular verses, which touched his soul and created ecstasy in him, would become very popular in the large circle of his followers. Some very good singers attached themselves to the shaikh; they would spend a lot of time to train themselves, compose new ghazals, create new ragas, and took the art to newer heights.[16] According to reports, not only the sophisticated Persian poetry of love, but also Hindi *jigri* would create ecstasy for Nizam-ud-Din. On one occasion, the shaikh was overwhelmed with ecstasy (*haal*) for a long period after listening to a *jigri* composed by one of his *khalifa*s, Maulana Wajih-ud-Din Yusuf, which was something like this: '*beena ban bhaaji aisa sukh seen baason*'.[17] This is one of the early examples of a Hindi verse touching the soul of the Sufis of the Delhi Sultanate, which become more prevalent from the latter half of the fourteenth century onwards.

Also, not only poetry sung by an accomplished singer but also an excellent work of prose can sound like music to the discerning. Nizam-ud-Din reports that once his preceptor, Shaikh Farid-ud-Din Ganj-i-Shakar, was overwhelmed by the desire for *sama*, but a singer was not available. The shaikh asked his disciple, Badr-ud-Din Ishaq, who was in his service, to bring the bag containing the letters he had preserved and take out and read aloud one letter he had received from the Suhrawardi Sufi, Qazi Hamid-ud-Din Nagauri. As Badr-ud-Din stood up and began to read the first line: '*faqir, haqir, za'if, nahif muhammad ata ke banda'i darweshan ast wa az sar o dida khak qadm-i ishan...*', by the time Farid-ud-Din heard the above expression, he was transported into ecstasy (*hali wa zauqi paida shud*).[18]

Further, like Farid-ud-Din's love for music, the encouragement provided to music by Nizam-ud-Din created a flutter in Delhi. The *ulama* had not succeeded in stopping Qazi Hamid-ud-Din Nagauri, the Suhrawardi Sufi who could float in the Chishti circle of Delhi in the early thirteenth century, and Nizam-ud-Din's preceptor, Shaikh Farid-ud-Din Ganj-i-Shakar, from organizing *mahfil-i-sama*, despite some fatwas issued against them. They did not succeed in preventing Nizam-ud-Din Auliya from listening to music at the time of the Khalji sultans, Ala-ud-Din and Qutb-ud-Din Mubarak-shah, despite some misunderstanding

[15] Ibid., 662, 665.

[16] Ibid., 666–667.

[17] Ibid., 667–668.

[18] *Fawa'id-ul-Fu'ad*, 254–255.

and difficulties in the relationship between the shaikh and the sultans. However, they were able to drag Nizam-ud-Din Auliya to the court of Sultan Ghiyas-ud-Din Tughluq, forcing him to participate in an inquest and defend his practice of organizing music assemblies. According to Amir Khwurd, the ulama were actually jealous of, or threatened by, the wide popularity Nizam-ud-Din had gained across various strata of society in the late thirteenth and early fourteenth century Delhi Sultanate. Nizam-ud-Din was not only able to unleash a whole new movement of popular piety amongst Muslims, reflecting in increased interest in *namaz* and other formal rituals or prayers, but also able to fill the hearts of his followers with love for God.[19]

Eventually, the Naib Hakim of the Sultanate under Ghiyas-ud-Din Tughluq, Qazi Jalal-ud-Din Lawanji, who was opposed to the lovers of God (*ahl-i-ishq*), encouraged Shaikhzada Husam-ud-Din, a disgruntled disciple of Nizam-ud-Din Auliya who had access to the Sultan's court, to build a case against the shaikh. It was reported to the sultan that Nizam-ud-Din, who was a leading religious personality of the time, indulged in music, which was considered *haram* in the *mazhab* of Imam Abu Hanifa, founder of the Hanafi school of jurisprudence, which the Sultanate ulama followed in their practice of Islam. The sultan was told that following Nizam-ud-Din, thousands of others were fascinated by the unlawful practice of music. According to Amir Khwurd, Sultan Ghiyas-ud-Din had no idea of the unlawfulness (*halal/haram*) of music and, therefore, wondered how was it that a leading religious authority could indulge in an un-Islamic (*ghayr mashru*) act.[20]

In order to convince Sultan Ghiyas-ud-Din, Nizam-ud-Din's opponents collected the works relating to the Shariat, which were used to issue fatwas against Hamid-ud-Din Nagauri and presented to the ruler. The sultan, who was in fact uncomfortable with Shaikh Nizam-ud-Din's attitude, especially over the dispute regarding the recovery of cash grants doled out by the usurper Khusrau Khan, announced that if the *ulama-i-din* have issued fatwas against the legality of *sama*, then the shaikh be brought to his presence and the leading *ulama* of the city be also summoned so that the matter is discussed or debated in an assembly of the learned and the truth of the matter is established. Nizam-ud-Din's followers who were employed in the sultan's court reported the matter to the shaikh, who apparently did not show any concern over the development.[21] However, a number of other leading religious scholars of the time, who had

[19] Kirmani, *Siyar-ul-Auliya*, 684–685.

[20] Ibid., 686.

[21] Ibid.

joined the discipleship of Nizam-ud-Din Auliya, such as Maulana Fakhr-ud-Din Zarradi and Maulana Wajih-ud-Din Pa'ili, began to scan the relevant texts to collect arguments in favour of the validity of the practice of *sama*.[22]

When Nizam-ud-Din eventually appeared in the court on the appointed date, Fakhr-ud-Din and another leading scholar of the age, who was superior in reputation to the Naib Hakim, Qazi Jalal-ud-Din, accompanied the shaikh. As the discussion began, Qazi Jalal-ud-Din lectured the shaikh on the need to mend his ways and warned him of being punished if he continued to organize music assemblies. Amir Khwurd notes that Nizam-ud-Din silently listened to all the accusations levelled in a harsh language, but Jalal-ud-Din's warning of punishment provoked the shaikh to curse the opponent, first, for his removal from his position of the Naib Hakim, and death soon after. Whatever may be the rationale, historical arguments, Jalal-ud-Din actually lost his position and died not long after the inquest.[23]

To return to Amir Khwurd's report, as the debate proceeded in front of the leading *ulama* of the city and a full house of nobles, Shaikhzada Husam-ud-Din took over from the silenced Qazi Jalal-ud-Din and asked the shaikh whether he would organize *sama* in his assemblies in which the participants danced, cried or raised slogans. Nizam-ud-Din advised Husam-ud-Din (a former disciple turned antagonist, as mentioned previously) to refrain from showing his overenthusiasm and instead of making unnecessary statements, he should explain what did he mean by *sama*. Nizam-ud-Din's question on the need to first clarify the meaning of the term *sama* itself would test any theoretical grounding of the opponents in the terms and categories being deployed by them. Instead of offering any insight on his understanding of the validity or otherwise of music, Husam-ud-Din continued to be in rhetorical mode and said that he did not know the meaning of *sama*, but so many big *ulama* have said that it was *haram*. Nizam-ud-Din replied that if Husam-ud-Din did not know the meaning of *sama*, he was not fit enough to discuss the matter. Thus, the main opponent in the case was also silenced.[24]

Amir Khwurd records that Ghiyas-ud-Din Tughluq was all along carefully following the debate and was asking the noisy opponents to keep quiet and listen to what the shaikh was saying. Of all the ulama present there, Maulana Hamid-ud-Din and Maulana Shahab-ud-Din Multani were silent; they did not say anything scandalous from the point of view of the Sufi facing the inquest.

[22] Ibid., 687.

[23] Ibid.

[24] Ibid., 688.

According to Amir Khwurd, Hamid-ud-Din, in fact, intervened to say that the reports of the opponents regarding the details of the activities in Nizam-ud-Din's *majlis* were not true and he had himself closely observed the participants, including shaikhs and dervishes. During the course of the discussion, another official *alim*, Qazi Kamal-ud-Din, interjected by saying that he had seen a report quoting Imam Abu Hanifa that *sama* was *haram* and *raqs* was *fasq*. Nizam-ud-Din replied that there was prohibition in the matter.[25]

As the arguments and counter-arguments were continuing, Maulana Ilm-ud-Din, a grandson of Baha-ud-Din Zakariya (the thirteenth century Suhrawardi master of Multan) arrived at the court. The sultan turned towards Ilm-ud-Din and, referring to him as a scholar and traveller, inquired whether *sama* was *halal* or *haram*. Ilm-ud-Din replied that he had written a tract on the issue, wherein he has collected all the arguments, for or against, music. His conclusion was: *sama* is permissible (*mubah*) for those who take it as a matter of heart; and it is unlawful (*haram*) for those who indulge in it to satisfy their *nafs*. The sultan further asked Ilm-ud-Din whether during his travels to Baghdad, Damascus and Rum, he had seen the Sufis of those cities listening to music and whether anyone stopped them from doing so. Ilm-ud-Din said that the Sufis of those cities did listen to music, which was sometimes also accompanied with instruments like *daf* and *Shababa* (*shahnai*), but no one prevented them from following this practice, which was inherited from the time of Shaikh Junaid and Shibli. The sultan was silenced on hearing this response from Ilm-ud-Din, but the Naib Hakim spoke again, insisting that the sultan must announce a ban on music, keeping in mind Imam Abu Hanifa's opinion in the matter. However, the sultan eventually followed Shaikh Nizam-ud-Din's request not to issue any order in this regard, and thus concluded, for Nizam-ud-Din on a happy note, the acrimonious debate in the durbar, which lasted for roughly the whole of the first half of the day, from *chasht* to *zuhar* prayers.[26]

Amir Khwurd's above-mentioned narrative on the sultan being favourably disposed towards Nizam-ud-Din and his accepting the shaikh's suggestion not to issue an order is derived from a reliable report of Fakhr-ud-Din Zarradi, who was present in the inquest and recorded the details in a text of his own. Amir Khwurd notes that, according to another, less reliable report, the sultan had ordered that Nizam-ud-Din could continue with his practice of *sama* and no one should prevent him from doing so, but others like the Qalandars and

---

[25] Ibid.

[26] Ibid., 688–689.

Haidaris, who were suspected of listening to music for fun, should be prevented from doing so.[27] According to another report, unlike Imam Abu Hanifa who was reported to have disapproved of *sama* as a whole, Imam Shafi'i, the founder of the Shafi'i school of Sunni jurisprudence, not only considered *sama* a legitimate devotional practice but also approved the use of instruments like *daf* and *shababa*.[28]

Referring to Ziya-ud-Din Barani's report, in his *Hasrat-nama*, Amir Khwurd further writes that after returning from the sultan's court at the time of the *zuhar* prayer, Nizam-ud-Din called Maulana Muhi-ud-Din Kashani and Amir Khusrau and told them of the disgusting behaviour of the *ulama*, not only their personal opposition to him but also of their disrespecting prophetic traditions (*Hadis*) by privileging a report of a jurist, Imam Abu Hanifa. All the *Hadis* referred to by Nizam-ud-Din were dismissed as important only for Imam Shafi'i and the Shafi'i school of jurisprudence was characterized as in opposition to the Hanafi *mazhab* followed by the official *ulama* in Delhi. Expressing his concern that the ulama's approach could mislead the people into not having enough respect for the prophetic reports, Nizam-ud-Din prophesied that there would be a divine retribution for the wrong faith of the *ulama* of the city.[29]

Amir Khwurd concludes that within a period of four years, all the *ulama* of the opposing group were forced to migrate to Deogiri, most of them dying there. The city itself was faced with famine and epidemic. The shaikh's prophecy proved true, and the legitimacy of his practice was not only approved by the sultan but also confirmed through divine intervention.[30]

Irrespective of what happened subsequently and whether those developments were related to Nizam-ud-Din's curse, what cannot be denied is that the shaikh was considerably irritated by the opposition to his mystical practices. In *Fawa'id-ul-Fu'ad* itself, which was being compiled by Amir Hasan Sijzi during period that coincided with the debate in Ghiyas-ud-Din's court, the shaikh is found explaining his position in self-restrained agitation (neither cursing nor abusing the antagonists, but deploying the language of the jurists). It is recorded that one of the members of the audience mentioned that the ruler had given orders to the effect that the shaikh could listen to music whenever he liked and that it was lawful (*halal*) for him. Nizam-ud-Din replied that what was *halal* could not become *haram* and vice versa just because someone has issued

[27] Ibid., 689–690.

[28] Ibid., 690.

[29] Ibid., 690–691.

[30] Ibid., 691.

orders to this effect. However, the shaikh added, in a case like the then current controversy over *sama* and the ruler's order, since Imam Shafi'i has termed *sama* as *mubah* (permissible) even when accompanied with instruments like *daf* and *chaghana*, which is not in conformity with the majority Hanafi position, it was the ruler's discretion to follow whichever position he found appropriate in his opinion.[31] Ghiyas-ud-Din clearly followed the Shafi'i position in the matter, allowing the shaikh to continue with his practice, despite the initial hostility between the Sufi and the sultan.

Yet, in continuing to defend the legitimacy of music, Nizam-ud-Din insisted that musical instruments, such as *chang* and *rabab*, should be completely avoided. When reported that some dervishes were found dancing (*raqs*) in a musical programme in which instruments were used, Nizam-ud-Din maintained that it was not the right thing to do. He was informed that when confronted, the dervishes explained that they were so lost (in remembering God) that they had no idea of musical instruments being played there. According to Nizam-ud-Din, this justification was not valid and could be used for covering any *gunah*, or sin.[32]

Further, referring to the differences of opinion within Sufi fraternities on the validity of music as a legitimate spiritual exercise, Amir Hasan mentions that he participated in the ongoing discussion at Nizam ud Din's *jama'at-khana* by mentioning how one could understand the *ulama's* opposition to *sama*, but how should one explain certain Sufis be opposed to the practice. This and Amir Hasan's additional remark that even if some Sufis considered *sama* as *haram*, they may avoid it and not fight with fellow Sufis, which was not the way of the dervishes, was apparently liked by Nizam-ud-Din. The latter added that there were so many *ulama* who were not saying anything and an ignorant fellow (*na-waqif*) was fighting (the shaikh was clearly referring to the disgruntled disciple who had lost the case in the Sultan's court).[33] Amir Hasan further noted that the shaikh liked his remark that the opponents of *sama* were known to him and that they would not have taken any interest in music even if there were no two opinion on its lawfulness. Nizam-ud-Din opined that such people actually lacked the *zauq* for music and had no basis or orientation for its appreciation.[34] The pleasure of music is appreciated better by some one who is filled with pain (*dard*) for the divine beloved and endured it gracefully. In exceptional cases, an outward expression of madness, as in Majnun's love for Layla, is also recommended.

---

[31] *Fawa'id-ul-Fu'ad*, 384.

[32] Ibid., 384–385.

[33] Ibid., 385–386.

[34] Ibid., 386.

Discounting for the *ulama*'s tirade and some Sufi groups distancing themselves from controversial practices, the popularity of music is not only to be found in the Chishti circles but also in a much larger devotional milieu across Sufi fraternities historically. In modern times, Sufism has been under attack from reformist Islam of various hues, such as the puritanical Tablighi Jama'at and the political Jama'at-i-Islami. Sufi practices like listening to music, adaptations from Hindu mystical traditions and any other innovations in the Indian environment are condemned and the Sufis' claims that it was because of them that Islam could spread so rapidly is mocked. In addition, though extremist or militant forms of political Islam generally draw on the Wahabi kind of reformism or Islamism, Muslims adhering to devotional Islam or Sufism are not innocent to international politics involving Muslims. In hostile political contexts, the Sufi-oriented Islam can be as aggressive as any other group, even as, culturally, it is not averse to appropriating from diverse mystical traditions and adapting to the demands of time and space. In doing so, however, the Sufis knew the difference between *bhajan* and *kirtan* on the one hand, and *ghazal* and *shahnai*, on the other.

References

Chittick, William C. *Sufism: A Short Introduction* (Oxford: Oneworld Publications, 2007).

Eaton, Richard M. *Sufis of Bijapur, 1300–1700, Social Roles of Sufis in Medieval India* (Princeton: Princeton University Press, 1978).

———. *Essays on Islam and Indian History*. Delhi: Oxford University Press, 2002.

Ernst, Carl W. and Bruce B. Lawrence. *Sufi Martyrs of Love: The Chishti Order in South Asia and Beyond* (New York: Palgrave Macmillan, 2002).

Fawa'id-ul-Fu'ad. Conversations of Nizam-ud-Din Auliya, compiled by Amir Hasan Sijzi. Persian text with Urdu translation by Khwaja Hasan Sani Nizami (New Delhi: Urdu Academy, 2001).

Karamustafa, Ahmet T. *Sufism: The Formative Period* (Edinburgh: Edinburgh University Press, 2007).

Kirmani, Amir Khwurd. *Siyar-ul-Auliya*. Translated by Islamuddin Nizami in Urdu (New Delhi: Islamuddin Nizami, 2002).

CHAPTER

13

Dissenting the Dominant

Caste Mobility, Ritual Practice and Popular Sufi Shrines in Contemporary Punjab

Yogesh Snehi

Popular Sufi shrines and the practice of saint veneration have a significant bearing on the social formation of contemporary Punjab. In the centuries before the British arrived, networks of shrines loosely linked within the Sufi orders spread through much of the province as the descendants and successors (*khalifa*s) of many of the major saints established their own *khanqahs*[1] (hospices), which in turn developed into new Sufi shrines. Besides these imposing Sufi shrines, there was an emergence of 'lesser shrines' dedicated to one or many, major or minor Sufi centres of medieval Punjab.[2] The networks became particularly dense in parts of the Indus Valley; in south-western Punjab, the shrines of the descendants of Syed Jalaluddin Bukhari of Uch dotted the countryside when the British arrived. Though loosely linked, each of these shrines maintained its distinctive identity and apparently played a crucial role in the Islamization of new territory.[3]

---

[1] The construction of Sufi *khanqahs* (hospices), and later Sufi tombs, produced symbolic cultural outposts of the power of Islam and of the Muslim in a world where local, tribal identities continued to be of vital importance. Imposing Sufi tombs, constructed by Muslim sultans, underscored the importance of Islamic shrines as sites of access to transcendent spiritual authority. See David Gilmartin, *Empire and Islam: Punjab and the Making of Pakistan* (New Delhi: Oxford University Press, 1989), 41–42.

[2] Ibid.

[3] Ibid., 43–45.

To the Muslim rulers, these shrines represented the local outposts of Islam, and to the population at large, they represented sources of power to all in need of superhuman intervention. They were open to people from all religious persuasions. Liebeskind terms this all-inclusive approach as the local face of Islam.[4] There was yet another practice of constructing 'memorial shrines', which gradually developed into distinctive centres of cultural practices, often denoting local as well as long-term geographical influences. These memorial shrines existed in the realm of the popular and inspired many folk writers of medieval and modern Punjab, evolving into a distinct form of 'saint veneration'.[5] Significantly, these popular shrines emerged as centres of inter-communal dialogue and evolved into a distinct form of cultural practices. One particularly distinct character of this social formation was that while western Punjab (now in Pakistan) became a major centre of emergence and dissemination of Sufism in the medieval period, it was eastern Punjab (India) which was the recipient of the vast influence of sacred shrines in Sind, Multan, Bahawalpur and Montgomery districts of colonial India.

The frontier districts of eastern Punjab had a direct influence of the major shrines of Shaikh Baha-ud-Din Zakariya at Multan, Shaikh Farid-ud-Din Ganj-i-Shakar (popularly known as Baba Farid) at Pakpattan, Shaikh Ali Hujwiri (popularly known as Hazrat Data Ganj Bakhsh) and Hazrat Mian Mir at Lahore. Besides, the shrines associated with Ajmer Sharif and the Chishti *silsila*s of Delhi (Shaikh Nizam-ud-Din Auliya and Qutb-ud-Din Bakhtiyar Kaki), Kaliyar (Sabir Pak) and Panipat (Bu Ali Qalandar Panipati) continued to influence the

---

[4] Claudia Liebeskind, *Piety on its Knees: Three Sufi Traditions in South Asia in Modern Times* (New Delhi: Oxford University Press, 1998), 2. It is significant to elaborate the term 'local Islam' here. In this essay, this term is used as representing the articulation of belief systems at the popular level. Alternatively, the term syncretism could have been utilized but it assumes that dominant identities are the core determinant of popular identities and thus discounts the academic understanding of the latter.

[5] Literary representation in Punjabi popular narratives, such as *Hir–Ranjha*, suggests that people participated in saint veneration without recourse to or invoking pre-existing religious identities. The practices involved the reinterpretation of piety and constituted beliefs that stood alongside formal categories of religious identity, without necessarily being in conflict with them. The repeated depiction of this form of devotional practice in the most ubiquitous Punjabi cultural form suggests the importance of this social formation in Punjab popular imagination, and in Punjab's religious and cultural history. Farina Mir, 'Genre and Devotion in Punjabi Popular Narratives: Rethinking Cultural and Religious Syncretism', *Society for Comparative Study of Society and History* 48(3) (2006), 755.

popular beliefs of colonial Punjab. But the form in which Sufism came and was disseminated in these regions was different from the major centres. The central and southern districts of Punjab were not known for major centres of Sufi mystics. Rather, minor/memorial shrines dedicated to either major Sufis or the more popular saints emerged as a source of veneration. Often, the local Hindu deities, or later, even Sikh gurus, came to be associated with these 'lesser shrines' and led to the emergence of popular ethos. These forms of social interaction can be best understood through the writings of folk writers like Waris Shah, Bulleh Shah and others.[6]

The Partition of Punjab in 1947 into eastern and western Punjab led to the emergence of immense social complexities. We saw an unprecedented migration of millions of people across the Radcliffe Line. It gave rise to the exodus of non-Muslims from western Punjab and Muslims from eastern Punjab.[7] This migration not only reconfigured demographic, economic and political settings but also led to a serious break in that social thread of Punjab which had been woven through centuries of social and political changes. It led to the creation of boundaries in a social milieu, which developed out of a long tradition of exchange between cultures and communities. While colonial Punjab was characterized by multifaceted identities from different socio-religious groups, the Partition almost dissolved these identities. The Partition of the provinces also led to the systematic communalization of social and political spheres.[8] But the memories of a shared cultural past continued to live in the Punjabi psyche and folklore.

---

[6] For a fascinating account on social interaction in *Hir Waris*, see Ishwar Dayal Gaur, *Society, Religion and Patriarchy: Exploring Medieval Punjab through* Hir Waris (New Delhi: Manohar, 2009); and for *qisse* tradition in medieval and modern Punjab, see Mir, 'Genre and Devotion in Punjabi Popular Narratives'. For an overview of folk writers of Punjab, see Surinder Singh and Ishwar Dayal Gaur, *Popular Literature and Pre-modern Societies of South Asia* (New Delhi: Pearson Longman, 2008); ed., *Sufism in Punjab: Mystics, Literature and Shrines* (New Delhi: Aakar, 2009).

[7] Soon after the announcement of the boundary award in mid-August 1947, the trickle of uprooted persons developed into a spate and they started pouring in and going out in an unending stream. *Punjab District Gazetteer, Firozpur District* (Chandigarh: Revenue Department, Punjab, 1983), 57.

[8] The state politics, which became more pronounced on the question of language and religious identities, also affected the historiographical tradition of the region. It led to the emergence of a majoritarian and communal construction of the region's history which, after 1966, almost abandoned any understanding of the ancient and medieval history of Punjab. For an insightful understanding of the limits of the post-Partition historiography of Punjab, see Singh and Gaur, *Sufism in Punjab*, 31–37.

Folk and popular tradition constitutes a major repository of generally unexplored domains of Indian historiography. The growth of these traditions cannot be straightjacketed into fixed frames of medieval or modern history. The Partition attempted to bring a break in the social milieu of pre-Partition Punjab but the creation of physical boundaries did not deter people from carrying 'memorial' traditions to new lands. Thus, oral history and the working of cultural production, their narratives and counter-narratives are crucial to the recovery of such marginal voices of history and their memory which also constitutes a significant process of this historical formation. It is significant to analyse how groups and/or individuals negotiate their subjectivities with the historical processes. Thus, the memory of refugees and the displaced also becomes an important aspect of social formation. Recent scholarship on popular culture in India has treated oral and popular traditions as a significant resource of interpreting modern and contemporary social formations. The contributions of Ishwar Dayal Gaur,[9] Surinder Singh and Ishwar Dayal Gaur,[10] Tahir Mahmood,[11] Shail Mayaram,[12] Dominique-Sila Khan,[13] Christian W. Troll,[14] Shahid Amin,[15] Richard M. Eaton,[16] Harjot Oberoi,[17] Dirk H.A. Kolff[18] and

---

[9] Gaur, *Society, Religion and Patriarchy*.

[10] Singh and Gaur, *Popular Literature and Pre-modern Societies* and *Sufism in Punjab*.

[11] Tahir Mahmood, 'The Dargah of Saiyid Salar Masud Ghazi in Bahraich: Legend, Tradition and Reality', in *Muslim Shrines in India: Their Character, History and Significance*, ed. C.W. Troll (New Delhi: Oxford University Press, 2003), 24–43.

[12] Shail Mayaram, 'Beyond Ethnicity? Being Hindu and Muslim in South Asia', in *Lived Islam in South Asia: Adaptation, Accommodation and Conflict*, ed. I. Ahmed and H. Reifeld (New Delhi: Social Science Press, 2004), 18–39.

[13] Dominique-Sila Khan, *Conversions and Shifting Identities: Ramdev Pir and the Ismailis in Rajasthan* (New Delhi: Manohar, 2003).

[14] Christian W. Troll, *Muslim Shrines in India: Their Character, History and Significance* (New Delhi: Oxford University Press, 2003).

[15] Shahid Amin, 'On Retelling the Muslim Conquest of North India', in *History and the Present*, ed. P. Chatterjee and A. Ghosh (New Delhi: Permanent Black, 2002), 27–38.

[16] Richard M. Eaton, *Essays on Islam and Indian History* (New Delhi: Oxford University Press, 2000).

[17] Harjot Oberoi, 'Popular Saints, Goddesses, and Village Sacred Sites: Rereading Sikh Experience in the Nineteenth Century', *History of Religions* 31, no. 4 (1992), 363–384; *The Construction of Religious Boundaries: Culture, Identity, and Diversity in the Sikh Tradition* (Chicago: The University of Chicago Press, 1994).

[18] Dirk H.A. Kolff, *Naukar, Rajput and Sepoy: The Ethnohistory of the Military Labour Market in Hindustan 1450–1850* (Cambridge: Cambridge University Press, 1990).

Asim Roy[19] have laid emphasis on an understanding of popular culture for a critical reconstruction of historical processes.

This essay seeks to investigate the nature of popular Sufi shrines and the practice of saint veneration in contemporary Punjab. After a brief lull in the post-Partition scenario, many older shrines managed by the Muslims of Punjab were taken over by non-Muslims, though the ones managed by non-Muslims continued. These shrines have been a place of veneration for people of diverse faiths. While some of them are identified largely with Sufi mystics, others are an intriguing admixture of Hindu deities and popular saints. Translation of such centres into the popular domain was made possible through Sufi terminology like '*pir*s', '*khanqah*' and '*dargah*'. In the backdrop of the communalization of social spaces in contemporary Punjab, how do we understand the continuation, evolution and development of recent shrines as new forms of social articulations? The narratives of the caretakers, the ritual practices and the profile of pilgrims suggest that these popular spaces are not just centres of veneration but dissent against the dominant religious discourse and also present an alternative expression of caste mobility. Significantly, these narratives appropriate and interweave the liberal discourse of the Chishtis with the Nath and *bhakti* tradition, and emphasize the continued relevance of these articulations in contemporary social formation.

Locating Pre-Partition Milieu

It would be useful to underline two significant accounts to articulate an alternative understanding of the pre-Partition social milieu in Punjab: Gaur's recent work on exploring medieval Punjab through *Hir Waris*; and Oberoi's seminal work on the nature of Sikh religious practices before the Singh Sabha movement.[20] These works provide us with a significant glimpse into the nature of social formation in pre-Partition Punjab by analysing folk literature and popular belief systems, and critique such dominant and communal understanding of colonial and pre-colonial Punjab which treat religious categories as real and fixed and classify popular traditions as deviant and fictitious.

Oberoi remarks that the historiography of the Sikh experience in the nineteenth century – rituals and quotidian practices that constituted the Sikh

---

[19] Asim Roy, *The Islamic Syncretistic Tradition in Bengal* (Princeton: Princeton University Press, 1983).

[20] Gaur, *Society, Religion and Patriarchy*; Oberoi, 'Popular Saints, Goddesses, and Village Sacred Sites'.

tradition – is based on two principles: one of absence and the other of negation.[21] While the historical texts are virtually silent about nature worship, witchcraft, sorcery, spirits, festivals, exorcism, astrology, magical healing, omens, wizards, miracle saints, goddesses, ancestral spirits, divination and village deities among the Sikhs, official Sikh historiography goes on to establish that Sikhs were delivered from the bondage of these un-Sikh beliefs by the intervention of the late nineteenth century Singh Sabha movement.[22] The Sikh literati who emerged under the shadows of the Raj were powerfully influenced by the European discourse on their religion and in due course, began to exhibit a similar intolerance towards many aspects of the Sikh tradition.[23]

Like the Europeans, they began a journey in search of 'authentic' texts so that the 'correct' articles of faith could be established. Much like the European scholars or late nineteenth century Sikh reformers, contemporary scholarship either tends to ignore vast terrains of Sikh life in the nineteenth century or views it as a superfluous addition that has to be ignored.[24] Oberoi emphasizes that religious boundaries in nineteenth century Punjab were highly flexible and the categories 'Sikh', 'Muslim' and 'Hindu' semiotically did not have the same implications as they do today.[25] He emphasizes the significance of popular centres of devotion like the shrines dedicated to Sakhi Sarwar[26], Gugga Pir and goddesses, among others, as shared sites for the people of pre-Partition Punjab. The movement for reform and 'textual revivalism' of dominant religious traditions critiqued these shared popular edifices.

Gaur problematizes the watertight compartmentalization of the term Muslim in medieval and colonial Punjab. With the partition of Punjab in 1947, the problem arose of defining, determining and demarcating Punjabi identity (or the description of culturally circumscribed characteristics), and that of its component social sections, labelled in religious terms. Since then, the

---

[21] Ibid., 363.

[22] Ibid., 364. It is significant to note that the nature of the critique presented by ardent Singh Sabhaites like Giani Ditt Singh (1852–1901), who was himself a Dalit, in his work *Gugga Gapoura*, is in contradiction with popular practices among ritually low castes and dominant Jats until the late nineteenth and early twentieth century. Ditt Singh, *Gugga Gapaura* (Amritsar: Kendri Sri Guru Singh Sabha, 1902[1976]).

[23] Oberoi, 'Popular Saints, Goddesses, and Village Sacred Sites', 365.

[24] Ibid., 365.

[25] Ibid., 366–367.

[26] Sakhi Sarwar, also known as Lakhdata or the Giver of Lakhs, Lalanwala Pir, He of the Rubies, or Rohianwala or He of the Hills, was widely spread among the Sikhs. Ibid., 366.

problem has persisted. The politicization and communalization of the identity, both in east and in west Punjab, have thus transfigured the socio-cultural differences. Like religion, state, nation and nationality have been presented as single organic wholes.[27] Such (mis)appropriation of the religious traditions of Hinduism, Sikhism and Islam, made by the communitarian forces, poses a perennial challenge to the concept of vernacular Punjabi identity, both in India and in Pakistan.[28] Gaur emphasizes that the people of Punjab, in view of their respective great religious traditions and their historically evolved common indigenous culture, constituted a pluralistic–cultural Punjabi whole, not a multi-communitarian society ridden with socio-cultural conflicts.[29]

A study of the folk legend of *Hir* enables us to draw a distinction between the conscious projection of a culture and its spontaneous expression.[30] The representation of *pir* cult, which is prominent in *Hir Waris*, was a significant feature of popular religion in the Sultanate period.[31] Besides, *Hir* presents Waris

---

[27] Gaur, *Society, Religion and Patriarchy*, 17–18.

[28] Ibid., 19.

[29] It is in this holistic space that cultural praxis of the people of Punjab took birth and was manifested in sacred spaces (*khanqahs*, *gurudwaras*); at fairs and festivals (*Jarag Da Mela*, *Chhapar Da Mela*, *Jagravan Di Roshni*, *Haider Shaikh Da Mela*, *Hola-Mohalla*, *Baisakhi*, *Teeian*, *Gugga Naumi*, *Basant*, *Lhori*, *Diwali*, etc.); in specific literary genres (such as *qissa*, *kafi* and *baramaha*); in folk religion (the worship of local, tiny brick mausoleums, that is, *marhi*s, of Sitla Devi, Sanjhi Devi, Gugga Pir, Khawaja Khizar and of elders, that is, *jathere*, and ancestors, that is, *pittar*); in the veneration of folk heroes (like Raja Rasalu and Dulla Bhatti); in folk dance (*giddha*, *bhangra*, *luddi*, *jhumar*, *samin*); and in folk art (like *phulkari*). Ibid., 21.

[30] The former tends to cause communitarian biases and boundaries of the craft of writing history. Unlike the spontaneous expression, it remains remote from the lived experience. It needs to be realized that both the nature of the source material selected for the construction of the said craft and the language of narration play a vital role in constituting the craft of history writing and its ideological nature. Due to the manipulation of these two factors, the true holistic cultural picture of a society becomes distorted and splits into sectarian cultures. As a matter of fact, the way the phenomenon of socio-cultural fusion evolved in the land of the five rivers is something a student of cultural history discovers by using people's sources rather than the official sources of the archives. Ibid., 23.

[31] They cured ailments and suffering and infused new energy into people. In the Hindu popular/folk religious domain, they might be minor deities who were the guardians of the people against evil spirits and calamities of nature, particularly of agrarian and pastoral society, but in the popular Muslim folk realm, they assumed the status of *pir*s, as Islamic orthodoxy did not approve of deities but somehow tolerated the cult of *pir*s. Ibid., 52–53.

Shah as the protagonist of inter-cultural dialogue, who implicitly conveys that no culture or religion is a system totally closed within itself, or an independent reality. He is not comfortable with degenerate persons who are at the helm of religious affairs, as is evident from the encounters with the mullah, the *qazi* and *jogi* Balnath. At the beginning of the *qissa* , Ranjha debunks the corrupt character of the mullah of a village mosque.[32] Mir emphasizes that the centrality of saint veneration in Punjabi *qisse* tradition bears no direct relation to Islam, Hinduism, Sikhism or any other religion. The way saint veneration is represented in various texts on the Hir–Ranjha tradition points to an independent or parallel set of beliefs that are neither in conflict with Punjab's major religions traditions nor coterminous with them. She also underlines the limitation of the term syncretism to represent such beliefs systems as they are neither an amalgam of Hindu and Muslim practice, nor does Hir's participation in the religious world of the shrine appear in any way predicated on her religious identity as a Muslim.[33]

Thus, medieval and colonial Punjab was significantly different from the communal perspective presented for the partition of Punjab. The intriguing example of *Hir* exemplifies a cultural scenario where the writer draws characters from Punjabi folk tradition and continues to have an indelible imprint on the social psyche of Punjab.[34] The pertinent question which intrigues a historian at this point is to locate that cultural archaeology and landscape in contemporary Punjab which is significantly represented in the popular literature and belief systems in the pre-Partition scenario. Twentieth century Punjab experienced three significant turning points – socio-religious reform and revivalism; the Partition and, subsequently, continued construction of communal identities; and the turbulent phase of Sikh militancy – which attempted to destabilize the popular edifice of the region.

What happened to these shrines when attempts were made to dissuade Sikhs and Hindus from their veneration of popular saints by Singh Sabha, Gurudwara

---

[32] Ibid., 109.

[33] Mir, 'Genre and Devotion in Punjabi Popular Narratives', 754.

[34] Waris Shah was born in the village Jandyala Sher Khan near Gujranwala and studied at Qasur under Hafiz Ghulam Murtaza. In his youth, he fell in love with a village girl of Pakpattan. Scandalized by a Saiyid stooping to such depths, the villagers drove him out of their village and Waris Shah was forced to retire to a village in the Sahiwal district. There he found spiritual comfort by versifying the romance of *Hir–Ranjha*. Although several other re-versifications exists – one of them by the sixteenth century poet, Damodar (1556–1605) – it is the artistry of Waris Shah in the eighteenth century which has made his *Hir–Ranjha* immortal. Rizvi (1983), 447.

reform, Anjumans and Arya Samaj movements? What was the fate of popular shrines which were left behind when the Muslim population was virtually wiped off as a result of migration? How did these shrines manifest in the context of the threat posed by militants? It becomes significant to probe the nature and role of such shrines and practices in contemporary social formation. How did such popular practices reconfigure themselves when the larger centres of Sufism were left behind in west Punjab (now Pakistan)? This essay shall probe these questions through case studies on some popular shrines in the towns of Abohar, Makhu and Amritsar along the Indo-Pak border and situate ritual practices in an understanding of contemporary Punjab.

Case Study 1 – *Pirkhanas* in Southern Punjab

The practice of constructing *pirkhana*s in Punjab has been recorded by colonial ethnographers.[35] The Punjabi landscape was dotted with saints' shrines called *pirkhana*s. Built on the boundaries of the village, out of plastered hollow brick cubes, they were 8–10 feet in each direction, covered with a dome and with low minarets or pinnacles at the four corners. In front was a doorway, which generally opened out to a plastered brick platform.[36] This case study focuses

[35] Sakhi Sarwar, popularly known as Lalanwala or Lakhdata Pir, was the most popularly revered saint of Punjab in the nineteenth century. The following of Sakhi Sarwar must have been sizeable, for his adherents were known by varied names in different localities: Sarvaria, Sewak Sultani, Hindu Sultani, Nigahia, Sarvar Sakhi, Sarvar Sagar, Sultani Ramrae, Sarvar Panthi, Guru Sultania, Khawaja Sarvar and Ramdasia Sultania. Three major fairs which were held in the Sarvar calendar in the colonial Punjab – in Dhaunkal in Gujranwala; the *Jhandamela* at Peshawar and *Kadmon ka Mela* at Lahore – were complemented by similar festivities on a lesser scale at local shrines, whose formation and endowment manifest the nature of the customary culture of Punjab and the extensive worship of the *pir*. The myths and literary narratives illustrating the life of Sakhi Sarwar link him to deities like Bhairava, a manifestation of the Hindu god Shiva, and he was often represented in the legends as a messenger of the saint. Similarly, Dani, the wife of a Sidhu peasant, is among the ones who were blessed by the saint with a male child. The local votaries offered grain at each harvest, and at the fair, visitors were fed free. H.A. Rose, *A Glossary of the Tribes and Castes of the Punjab and North-West Frontier Province* (Lahore: Superintendent, Government Printing Punjab, 1919), 566.

[36] Beyond the doorway, there were two or three niches for lamps, but otherwise the shrine was kept empty. Every Thursday, the shrine was swept and lamps were lit. The same day, the guardian of the shrine, a *bharia*, collected offerings from the village

on two such *pirkhanas* in Abohar and Malout towns of south Punjab. Most of these *pirkhanas* are concentrated in the adjoining regions of Punjab, Haryana and Rajasthan and are controlled and managed by Aggrawal Sabhas.[37] There are *pirkhanas* at Malout (which is believed to be 70 years old and is among the oldest in this region), Gidderbaha, Bhatinda, Bhuchho Mandi, Rampura Phul (around 27 years old), Barnala, Muktsar, Maur and Tapa in Punjab; Sirsa, Kalanwali and Dabawali in Haryana; and Hanumangarh, Ganganagar, Padampur, Suratgarh, Gharsana and Pilibangan in Rajasthan.[38]

Fig. 13.1: Shrine at Pirkhana, Malout

to the sound of the drum. These were mostly grain and came especially from the women. W.E. Purser, *Final Report of the Revised Settlement of the Jullundur District* (Lahore: Civil and Military Gazette Press, 1892), quoted in Oberoi, 'Popular Saints, Goddesses, and Village Sacred Sites', 371.

[37] Though other castes like Aroras are also associated with these shrines, it is the presence of Punjabi Aggrawals which is visibly marked. A survey was conducted at an annual *darbar* on 20 May 2010 at Sri Peerkhana Sabha, Abohar.

[38] These *pirkhanas* are primarily located in the southern part of Punjab and adjoining areas in Rajasthan and Haryana. However, such practices were popular in other parts of Punjab too. Sunil Aggrawal of Amritsar narrated how his father organized a *durbar* at their house in the walled city, which was attended by relatives and people from the community. Sunil Aggrawal was interviewed on 10 June 2010 at Shimla.

Most of these *pirkhana*s emerged in the post-Partition period and owe it to the tradition of venerating *pir*s in the pre-Partition times. Baba Makhan narrates that in his family, there was a tradition to visit and give thanks to Shaikh Haider of Malerkotla at the birth of a son, the occasion of marriage, etc.[39] Dr Darshan narrates that once his father had a *paun*[40] (revelation) of 'unconscious mistakes committed by their family' which have led to enormous difficulties in their lives. He adds that until 1940, his great grandfather (Kahn Mal) was rich and prosperous, and when his great grandmother stopped worshipping *pir*s and lighting *chirag*, the family suffered losses and was reduced to penury during 1958–60. Later, his father (Tirath Chand, d. 78 years in year 2000, a resident of village Dyalpura-Bhaika in Rampura Phul) restarted the practice of venerating *pir*s. His father left home for Lahore at a very young age. He came back home after two to three months and narrated that he had a *paun* (revelation) where the Baba of Malerkotla had asked him the reason why his family stopped worshipping *pir*s in the post-Partition scenario.[41]

In 2004, Master Shambu Nath arrived at the house of Dr Darshan Paul during a *chauki* chaired by Baba Krishan Lal of Rampura Phul and offered a piece of land to establish a *pirkhana* at Abohar. The Punjabi Aggrawal Sabha did not find the place suitable for establishing a *pirkhana* since it was located in a Dalit colony. Later, after two years, Master Shambu offered the land once again and it was finally decided to establish a *pirkhana* at the same place on 17 May 2007. The chairman of Shri Peerkhana Sabha, Abohar, says that in a span of two years since the establishment of the shrine, an amount of Rs 25,00,000 has been spent on the expansion of the *pirkhana*.[42] Baba Makhan Lal instructs

---

[39] Baba Makhan Lal Bansal (50 years, younger sibling of Dr Darshan and originally a native of a *qasba* Bhagtan) was interviewed on 29 December 2009 at Abohar. He acts as an intermediary between the *pir* and *murid*s. He frequently visits the *dargah* of Haider Shaikh at Malerkotla and Nigaha at village Langiana.

[40] Haider Shaikh is believed to reveal himself through his spirit, which in Hindi is termed as *paun* and in Arabic as *ruh*, which enters and manifests through certain devotees who in turn dispense advice, treatments and blessings. Anna Bigelow, 'Saved by the Saint: Refusing and Reversing Partition in Muslim North India', *The Journal of Asian Studies* 68(2) (2009), 449.

[41] Dr Darshan Paul Bansal (60 years), an RMP and President of Shri Peerkhana Sabha, Abohar, was interviewed on 29 December 2009 at Abohar.

[42] Mr Suresh Kumar Bansal (Chairman, Shri Peerkhana Sabha, Abohar) and Naresh Bansal were interviewed on 26 December 2009 at Abohar. They also narrated the association of their family with Baba Malerkotla since their grandfather's time.

the visitors according to their religious affiliations, irrespective of caste and religious barriers. Dr Darshan had been to Goddess (*mata*) Chintpurni and says that fakirs have no caste. A *sanjhi gaddi* is held primarily by him every Thursday at the *pirkhana*. Baba Harbans Lal Garg from Mandi Dabawali and Baba Suresh Kumar from Hanumangarh also preside over *sanjhi gaddi* from time to time.

There is a practice of lighting *diyas/chirag* everyday at the central shrine in *pirkhana*. A *bhandara/langar* is organized every third Thursday. The weekly *chauki* is associated with *bhajans* and *bujhe*. People from various hues come with problems relating to marriage, business, children, family dispute, etc., and seek solutions at the *sanjhi gaddi*. The caretaker of the shrine says that, generally, Banias flock to the shrine. Besides, the residents of the locality (Rajiv Nagar), which include Dhanuk, Kumhar and Valmikis, also frequent the shrine.[43] During the annual *mela*, exhibits of Radha, Krishna and Sudama, or a sadhu standing on the ice slab, are also displayed outside the *pirkhana*. *Bhajans* in Punjabi are sung and the *langar* goes on from 8 p.m. till midnight. The *Pirkhana* has memorials for various *pirs*, fakirs and goddesses. These include a central shrine with a photograph of six popular saints of the region,[44] a memorial grave on the left dedicated to Shaikh Haider of Malerkotla and covered with a blue *chadar* (cloth), an enclosed grave of Baba Lakhdata (Sakhi Sarwar) covered with a green *chadar*, Mata Masani (Sitala Mata),[45] Khan Doda Pir who is believed to be the young brother of Baba Lakhdata and Bhairon Chadi, who was supposedly the wazir of Baba Lakhdata.

When asked about the resurgence of the veneration of *pir*s in recent times, Baba Makhan Lal says, 'If a customer goes to the market to purchase things he/she looks for the cheapest and the most durable (*kifayati*) store. *Pirkhanas* are also more *kifayati* centres for the fulfilment of wishes of individuals.' Significantly, he had earlier been associated with the Rashtriya Swayamsevak Sangh (RSS) and served as *mukhya shikshak* and *karyavar* since 1984. But,

---

[43] Mr Anant Ram (45 years, Sevadar, Shri Peerkhana Sabha, Abohar – a migrant and originally a resident of Etawa district in Uttar Pradesh) and Akshaya (14 years, a visitor) were interviewed on 27 December 2009 at Abohar.

[44] The photograph contains references to six popular saints of the region, which include Hazrat Ghaus Pak (Abdul Qadir Gilani), Hazrat Bu Ali Sharaf (Bu Ali Qalandar), Hazrat Mahbub-i-Ilahi (Nizam-ud-Din Auliya), Hazrat Khwaja Gharib Nawaz (Muinuddin Chishti), Hazrat Khwaja Qutb-ud-Din (Qutb-ud-Din Bakhtiyar Kaki) and Hazrat Baba Farid Shakar Ganj (Shaikh Farid-ud-Din Ganj-i-Shakar).

[45] Shaikh Haider's *shagird*, Rode Shah, had a revelation of Mata Masani.

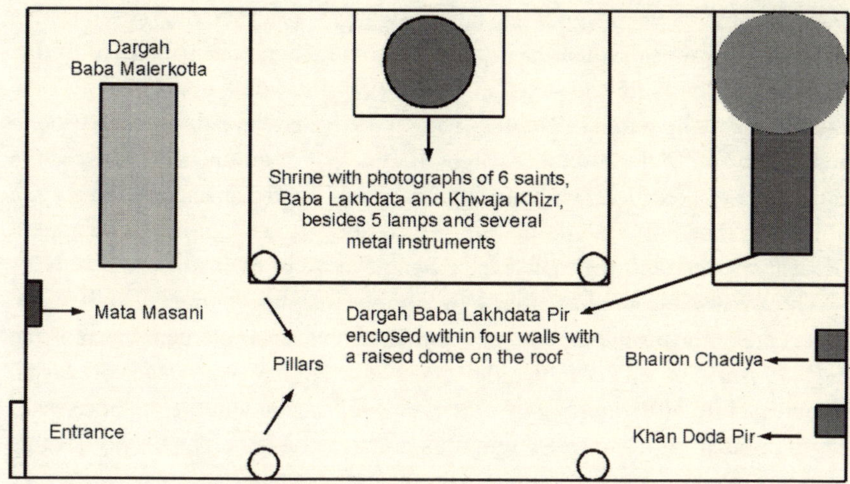

Fig. 13.2: Layout of Shri Pirkhana Sabha- Abohar

lately, he has not been going to the meetings of the organization, primarily because of his association with the *pirkhana*. The local members of the RSS had also categorically pointed out his association with *pir*s and regarded it as inappropriate. Baba Makhan amusedly says that even now, some members of the RSS (like Faqir Chand Goyal who has consistently been elected for his ward in the local municipal elections) come to him for solutions to their financial and personal difficulties.

There is another variety of a small *pirkhana* at Abohar, personally run and managed by Ved Prakash Kukkad, an Arora by caste.[46] His family has supposedly been worshipping Haider Shaikh for the past 300 years and he acts as an intermediary between the visitors and the *pir*. His mother (Bhagwanti Devi) performed the *sewa* of the *pir* for fifty years and later, he also joined the *sewa* and has been associated with it for the past forty years. This *pirkhana* was established by his mother in the month of December 2001. She used to organize a *chauki* every Thursday until she died in late 2004 (*dhanteras*). He

[46] Sevadar Ved Prakash Kukkad was interviewed on 29 December 2009 at Abohar. An Arora by caste, Ved Prakash was earlier employed with the Abohar Cooperative Cotton Marketing and Spinning Mill for 29 years and later, supposedly resigned (though his uncle says that the mill he was working in was shut down). He is currently unemployed and runs the *pirkhana*. One can see that he owns a motorbike and a shabbily kept house. One of his two sons has some neurological disorder. His wife is a double MA and BEd and worked as a teacher, but has also resigned from her service.

narrates that 300 years ago, their family (which was a tribe then) used to live at Sardargarh in Rajasthan. Every month, someone in their tribe used to die. One day, a fakir came and said that their entire tribe would eventually become extinct due to the wrath of a curse. The fakir advised the elders of the tribe to go to the *pir* of Malerkotla who might offer help. For around four months, the entire tribe walked along with the fakir and finally paid obeisance at the *dargah* of Haider Shaikh in Malerkotla. Since then, they lit two lamps at Sardarsgarh (Rajasthan) and their tribe survived from the curse of extinction.

Three years ago, he established a twenty-one member committee to look into the affairs of the *pirkhana*, but later abolished it as it was allegedly against the *hukm* (wishes) of the Baba. People come to him for marriage issues or marital disputes, child birth, etc. Significantly, he emphasized that the *pir* never asks any individual to leave one's religious practices but can supposedly change the ways of gods (ritual hierarchy). He emphasizes that he accepts no offerings except rice and that Baba only gives in to the wishes of *murid*s and never asks for offerings. Ved Prakash claims that if someone bestows faith in the *pir* of Malerkotla, he/she bears a son (emphasizes that this is 101 per cent true) but he should not drink alcohol. When asked how, being a Hindu, he is serving a Muslim saint, he said that no one is a Hindu or a Muslim; religious distinctions are man-made. He exaggerates his claims of worship and his popularity world over and emphasizes that even temples in trouble come to seek solutions to declining attendance and offerings, etc. He frequents Malerkotla once in every two months.

Case Study 2 – Khanqah Chishtiya, Makhu

The emergence of Sufi shrines in post-Partition Punjab has been an intriguing phenomenon. Until the last decade of the twentieth century, the Partition historiography communalized the forced migration and presented a picture of break and trauma. Current trends in the historiography of Punjab, similarly, negate and restrict the history of Punjab to an understanding of dominant Sikh traditions,[47] thus ignoring an objective and meaningful analysis of those popular traditions which were crucial to the growth of Sikhism. The continuity and re-emergence of Sufi shrines in this scenario is crucial to our understanding of contemporary Punjab.

[47] Singh and Gaur, *Sufism in Punjab*, 33, underline the tendency of framing the syllabus on the history of Punjab which reduces it to the history of Sikhs. The two terminal dates are 1469 and 1849; the former indicating the birth of the first Sikh Guru and the latter marking the extinction of the Sikh Kingdom.

Khanqah Chishtiya at Makhu in Punjab emerged in the last decade of the twentieth century. The narrative associates the emergence of this centre with Bohar (aged 32 years in 2009).[48] Bohar belongs to an orthodox Christian family. Bohar's father's name is Bahadur and mother's name is Bibi Shahido. He is the only son in the family and has two sisters. His elder uncle's name is Barkat and aunt's name is Bibi Jijo. His parents and grandparents were associated with and periodically frequented the shrine of Pir Haider Shaikh of Malerkotla. Before 1995, his father was a contractor loading goods trains with materials, but he later suffered a loss because, on the occasion of a family marriage, he consumed liquor due to which Baba of Malerkotla was supposedly offended. Bohar was pursuing graduation at Khalsa College (Sarhali) until he too started getting ill very often. He was taken to the shrine of the Baba of Malerkotla at village Sodhan on several occasions but his health showed no signs of improvements.

In the year 1995, Bohar had a 'revelation' (*hazari*) of Anant Nath who was a Nath saint of Makhu and apparently the 213th disciple of Gorakhnath.[49] According to this revelation, Bohar was actually a reincarnate/rebirth of Anant Nath. He also had a revelation of the mortal remains of Anant Nath, which were reportedly dug up in the main town of Makhu and a memorial (locally called *dargah*) was constructed over it in the narrow lanes of the town. Later, he had a revelation of the Baba of Malerkotla, and then of Sakhi Sarwar/Lalanwala Pir. In 1996–97, he had another revelation which said that all that has been happening to him is at the behest of Khwaja Muinuddin Chishti of Ajmer. Since 1995, he started frequenting (almost once in two months) the shrines of Nizam-ud-Din Auliya (Delhi), Qutb-ud-Din Bakhtiyar Kaki (Mehrauli), Hazrat Bu Ali Qalandar (Panipat), Hazrat Saiyid Alauddin Ali Ahmed Makhdum Sabir Pak (Kaliyar) and Shaikh Muinuddin Chishti (Ajmer).

The narrative around Anant Nath relates him to the Khatri caste. At the age of 12 years, he apparently became a disciple of Gorakhnath and started living in Kasi. His desire to achieve mystical revelation remained unfulfilled in the association of Gorakhnath and his other disciples. His wandering spirit was assisted by Muinuddin Chishti who helped him in 'meeting god'. Later, Bohar, who now came to be known as Babaji, visited the shrine at Ajmer, and in the

---

[48] Harjinder Singh Bittu (30 yrs), *khadim* at Khanqah Chishtiya and a Jat agriculturist, is a local resident of Makhu. He was interviewed on 23 August 2009, and subsequently on 3 December 2009, at Makhu. His father was a friend of Bohar's (now known as Ghulam Farid Chishti) father (Bahadur).

[49] He could have been a regional Nath saint and constructing a lineage must have been a local attempt to relate Anant Nath to the larger and dominant identity of Gorakhnath.

year 1999, read *kalmia* and converted to Islam. He assumed a new name, Sufi Ghulam Farid Chishti, and was also handed over the Chishti *gaddi* at Makhu by Saiyid Nasiruddin Niyazi, a Diwan of the Ajmer *gaddi*. The narrator of the version claims that this is the only Chishti *gaddi* outside Ajmer in India. The shrine follows the *maryada* of Ajmer Sharif and an annual fair is held once a year in the memory of Shaikh Muinuddin Chishti. *Roshni* is read in the morning and evening each day and a white *chadar* (*nima*) from Ajmer Sharif is also offered at the memorial grave of Muinuddin Chishti at Khanqah Chishtiya, Makhu.

Fig. 13.3: Memorial Grave of Muinuddin Chishti at Khanqah Chishtiya, Makhu

Gradually, with the assistance of local *lalas*/Mahajans, the scale of the fair over the grave of Anant Nath became large. Later, a 'Sikh' *murid* who was blessed by Baba Bohar and subsequently went to America, donated a piece of land (1/2 *kila*) to construct a larger *khanqah* outside the city. The foundation of the *khanqah* was laid on 12 February 2003 and it was decided to dedicate it to Shaikh Muinuddin Chishti. On 3 August 2006, the first *Urs* was celebrated at the new *khanqah*. A stud farm was later established along with the new *khanqah* and the proceeds from the sale of horses bred there is utilized for the purpose of the maintenance, upkeep and development of the *khanqah*. In 2009, the annual *Urs* was organized from 1 to 3 July (first three days of the second week of Rajab, 1430 AH).

The newly constructed shrine complex, though incomplete, has an imposing arched gateway through which one large dome of the main complex is visible. There is a beautifully decorated memorial grave dedicated to Shaikh Muinuddin Chishti inside the sanctum. On the wall outside the grave is an engraved, brief description of the saint written in Punjabi. The names of the significant Islamic saints, Khwaja Usman Haroni, Bibi Fatima, Ali, Muhammad, Shaikh Muinuddin Chishti, Allah, Hasan and Hussain, are also engraved separately on the three walls around the grave. Outside the sanctum is a hall which is marked by the *gaddi* of Ghulam Farid Chishti, the *gaddi-nishin* of Makhu.

This entire narrative around Khanqah Chishtiya engages and weaves early medieval interaction between Naths and Chishtis. From the eleventh century, the Nath yogis began to spread throughout northern India, and from their centre at Peshawar, moved to all parts of Central Asia and Iran, at the same time influencing Qalandars and Sufis.[50] The Naths initiated members of all castes, including those outside the Hindu caste system, such as Chandalas and sweepers, into their non-hierarchical order.[51] The *Siddha Siddhanta Paddhati*, and some authentic works of Gorakhnath's followers, formed the basis of the doctrines of the puritanical Naths and offered a common ground for exchange of ideas with such Sufis as Shaikh Hamid-ud-Din Nagauri and Baba Farid.[52] Shaikh Abdul Quddus's *Rushd-Nama* (or *Alakhbani*), which consists of his own verses, identifies Sufi beliefs based on the *wahdat-ul-wujud* with the philosophy and practices of Gorakhnath.[53]

The narrator also associates Anant Nath with Bhagat Puran, both of whom are said to be contemporaries. He also draws parallels and associates the former with the episode of meeting between Ranjha and Balnath, under whose guidance the famous love martyr of Punjab becomes a Nath *jogi*.

Case Study 3 – Contemporary Sufi Practices in Amritsar and Batala

Amritsar has a wide variety of popular shrines and centres associated with Khwaja Khizr, Baba Lakhdata, Zahrah Pir, etc. Khwaja Khizr, popularly known as Jhule Lal, is the mythical saint who is associated with the trading

---

[50] Saiyid Athar Abbas Rizvi, *A History of Sufism in India* (New Delhi: Munshiram Manoharlal, 2003), 332–333.

[51] Ibid., 332.

[52] Ibid., 333.

[53] Ibid., 336. All the verses by Shaikh Abdul Quddus relating to the simile of the mirror and the polishing of the heart are based on ideas expressed by Ibn Arabi and Gorakhnath (Ibid., 341). The Shaikhs' interest in Nath teaching was not merely theoretical. In several ways, he found Nath ascetic exercises compatible with Chishti practices (Ibid., 342).

classes among Hindus, Muslims and Sikhs, and continues to be a major source of veneration in the walled city, which is dotted with various shrines in nooks and corners of the city, managed by Hindu *sewadar*s, including Dalits. Another saint, Zahrah Pir, who is associated with Gaus Pak (Shaikh Abdul Qadir Jilani, founder of Qadiri Silsila in India) has a shrine at the Hall Gate and is venerated along with a number of other popular saints and goddesses. These include Khwaja Khizr, Goddess Durga, Shiva along with Parvati and Ganesha and Sai Baba, among others. Zahrah Pir is represented as riding a white horse. Both Hindus and Sikhs flock the shrine every Thursday.

Fig. 13.4: Gugga Pir, Khwaja Khizar and Shiv Parivar at a Shrine at Khu Kaudiyan in the Walled City of Amritsar

Besides the popular veneration of shrines, the walled city is also known for organizing *Urs* in the memory of Baba Lakhdata. One of such *Urs* has been annually organized by Sai Baba Gope Shah Chishti Faridi Sabiri in the walled city for the past eleven years.[54] In 2007, the practice of organizing a *qawwali*

[54] 11th Urs Mubarak in the Memory of Lakhdata Sakhi Sarwar Sultan on 20 January 2010 at Chowk Telephone Exchange, Amritsar. Organized by Mahatma Ashwini Sabiri, Babbi Sabiri, Bagga Sabiri, Jimmy Sabiri, Prince Sabiri, Pamma Pehalwan Sabiri, Gurdip Pahelwan Sabiri, Bau Ram Sabiri, Rocky Sabiri, Vikas Sabiri, Sham Lal Sabiri, Manjit Singh Sabiri, Tinku Sabiri, Jivan Sabiri, Billa Sabiri, Vijay Sabiri,

durbar was also started. Since then, Daman Sabri, the *darbari qawwal*s of Kaliyar Sharif, sing *qawwalis* on the occasion from 9:30 p.m. to 4:00 a.m. On the occasion of the annual *Urs* organized in 2010, Sufi Rashid Mian (Delhi), Sai Baba Mheshi Shah Chishti Faridi Sabiri (Batala Sharif) and Baba Gope Shah (Amritsar) were present. Eight years ago, 'Gulamane Anjuman Chishtiya', an organization of Chishtiya *murid*s, was founded by Hazi Baba Gulam Gilani Khadime Khas Dargah Kaliyar Sharif Sabir Pak. The present President of the organization is Dr Kittu Grewal (Jalandhar). The organization consists of 'Hindus' (Brahmins, Khatris, Mahajans and Valmikis), 'Christians' and 'Sikhs'. The branch at Amritsar does not consist of 'Muslims'.

Another *Urs* shamiana was organized by Savita Baba at Chowk Passian in the walled city of Amritsar on 29 April 2010. Savita Baba is a woman *sewadar* who also runs a *gaddi* and organizes a *chauki* (gathering) dedicated to Sabir Pak at her residence in the locality. Before the beginning of the *Urs* celebrations, Rashid Mian (*khadim* at the dargah of Hazrat Saiyid Roshan Ali Shah Shahid Baba, New Delhi) read several vows for the gathering at the residence of Savita Baba and later, read a *kalmia* in the Islamic fashion, though uniquely popular in its own sense, to initiate the congregation in the Sabiri tradition. The *Urs* was organized opposite to a 'Hindu' temple at Chowk Passian. *Qawwal*s led by Rashid Mian and Baba Gope Shah (Amritsar) sat opposite the *darbar* decorated with the pictures of popular saints, such as Baba Lakhdata, Khwaja Khizr and Zinda Pir, which were placed on a green *chadar* (sheet) printed with images of a crescent moon and star and other Islamic symbols. The programme began with an Islamic prayer by Rashid Mian, which was followed by a speech by Harish Sabiri, a local Patwari who highlighted the relevance of the shared '*sant'* (saint) traditions of Punjab. He emphasized that saints 'don't have any religion' and did not see any conflict between an individual's reverence for one's *ishta* (deity) and its relation with shared Sufi traditions.[55] There was a large presence of women in the gathering.

The foundation of a minor shrine in the memory of Sabir Pak was laid near Lahori Gate on 25 December 2007 and a *chirag* (lamp) was lit by Hazrat Shah Jilani Sabiri Chishti of Kaliyar Sharif. Harish Sabiri has been instrumental

Ashwini Sabiri, Gulshan Sabiri and D.K. Sabiri. Interview conducted with Prince (Bharadwaj) Sabiri (40 years) who is a government parking contractor and Pamma Pahelwan (Valmiki) Sabiri (39 years) who is an Assistant Sub-Inspector (ASI) in Punjab Police, on 20 January 2010, at Chowk Telephone Exchange.

[55] Survey conduced at the annual *Urs* at Chowk Passian on 29 April 2010.

in establishing this shrine.[56] Morning and evening prayers at this shrine are performed in the Sabiri tradition.[57] Every year, on the same day, an *Urs* is organized by the community of the area which comprises primarily of Dalits. The youth of the area organize regular pilgrimages to several places associated with Chishti Sufis like Kaliyar Sharif (Roorkee), the shrine of Shamsuddin Panipatti and Bu Ali Qalandar (Panipat), Nizam-ud-Din Auliya (New Delhi) and Muinuddin Chishti (Ajmer). Several Dalit families of the locality have been venerating *pir*s since the time of their grandparents and have dedicated a corner of their house to *pir*s.[58] Among the followers of this tradition, there is also this practice of using the surname Sabiri.[59]

The *Dargah* of Buddhu Shah at Batala is associated with an obscure pre-Partition saint and is currently under the supervision of Baba Mheshi Shah Chishti Faridi Sabiri who associates the present *gaddi* with the tradition of Kaliyar Sharif. This *gaddi* is related to the *gaddi* of Baba Mast Diwani Bulleh Shah at the dargah of Pir Bhikham Shah, village Ghuram, district Patiala. Baba Mheshi emphasizes the unity of all religions and gives examples of legends from Hinduism (Krishna and Rama), Koran (Mohammad and Fatima), Sikhism (Nanak and Guru Gobind Singh), Saint Valmiki, etc. Significantly, he conceptualizes Guru Granth Sahib as a sacred text evolving from the times of with Shaikh Farid, Kabir, Guru Ravi Das and later, Guru Nanak until the tenth Sikh Guru Gobind Singh. He also lays emphasis on the fact that all holy books are essentially shared, and prominently uses Islamic legends in his discourse.[60]

---

[56] Harish Sabiri, who is a Patwari by profession and also associated with Hind-Pak Dosti Manch, Amritsar, was interviewed on 29 April 2010 at the shrine outside Amrik Singh Nagar, Lahori Gate, Amritsar.

[57] One is amazingly struck with constant repetition of verse, '*data karim sabir, maula karim sabir*' (Sabir is the giver and master), by the disciples who are primarily non-Muslims. Survey conducted at the memorial shrine of Sabir Pak at Lahori Gate, near Amrik Singh Nagar, on 29 April 2010.

[58] At the house of Rohit Kumar Mattu (22 years), who works as a sweeper at DAV College, Amritsar, there is a *darbar* (shrine) dedicated to Baba Farid, Hazrat Ali Sahib (Shere Khuda), Baba Shah Jilani of Kaliyar Sharif, Khwaja Khizr, Sabir Pak shrine, Pir Baba Nazir Shah Chishti at Kot Khalsa (Amritsar) and Hindu deities, Bhole Nath and Parvati. Interviewed on 29 April 2010 at his residence outside Amrik Singh Nagar, Lahori Gate, Amritsar.

[59] Karan Bhatti Sabiri (23 years) has been to Kaliyar Sharif several times since 2007, the year he assumed the surname Sabiri. Interviewed on 29 April 2010 at his residence outside Amrik Singh Nagar, Lahori Gate, Amritsar.

[60] Interview conducted with Baba Mheshi Shah Chishti Faridi Sabiri on 7 February 2010 at Batala Sharif.

Fig. 13.5: Left to Right – Baba Mhcshi Shah and Baba Gope Shah at an Annual Qawwali Darbar at Telephone Exchange in Amritsar

Dissenting the Dominant

The dominant discourse of Sufism in India has, until recently, focused its discussion on the major *silsilas*, their shrines and *khanqahs*, *sama*, *qawwali* and rituals, Sufi philosophy and *sajjada nishins*. The large number of 'lesser' shrines dedicated to rural and popular Sufis and/or local belief systems, and often constructed as memorial shrines, mark the landscape of numerous towns and villages of the Indian subcontinent and constitute the unexplored margins of Sufi idioms in India. These localized shrines have often been labelled as 'fake and fictitious'. Asim Roy categorizes some of these 'lesser' traditions as 'fictitious pirs' who sought to be Islamized through the protean process of pirification.[61] Rizvi says that

> the lack of literary evidence is the most formidable obstacle to the presentation of any picture of village *khanqahs* where the tombs of local pirs and fictitious *dargahs*, ascribed to eminent Sufis…and the graves of the local martyrs both real and unreal had been – and still are – the sole comfort of their inhabitants in their sufferings and anguish.[62]

---

[61] Roy, *The Islamic Syncretistic Tradition in Bengal*, 207–248.

[62] Rizvi, 2002, 458.

Contemporary research on Sufism in Punjab has failed to give a satisfactory explanation of the manner in which essentially esoteric mystical traditions might have filtered down to commoners in some sort of comprehensible and appealing form.[63] Eaton says that one likely reason for the failure to explain the attraction of Hindu non-elites (and Sikhs) to Sufis has been the tendency among scholars of Sufism to concentrate almost exclusively on the mystical literature, as opposed to folk literature, as representing the sum and substance of the Sufi movement. This essay is an exercise to understand the agency of the shrines and their subaltern devotees, their belief systems, social interaction and situating their role as significant participants in historical processes.

Thus, besides the discursive practices in the form of stories and written histories, bodily practices like rituals, pilgrimages and physical presence, located in the shared space of a shrine, are also important in understanding the popular veneration of *pir*s. The tomb cult is central to this process, as spaces associated with the holy dead are also locations for the circulation of capital – social, political and spiritual, as well as financial. Because caste and religious divisions are no barrier to attendance at most *dargahs*, these shrines facilitate interpersonal engagement across social and religious lines.[64] Hindus and Sikh devotees often employ a Muslim style of prayer, holding their hands before their faces in the typical posture of *dua*, or supplicatory prayer. Many Sikh devotees perform *sewa*, or service, at the tomb, mopping, sweeping and cleaning it after festivals. Thus, the processes of interaction, identity formation and conflict pluralize the repertory of language, behaviour, knowledge and power and do not denote distinct groups that define themselves as Muslim, Hindu or Sikh. Members of these communities must be understood in the context of the historical circumstances in which they lived. These circumstances include the entire range of context-specific interests with which these particular identities interacted, as well as the larger contexts that framed various categories of identity.[65]

In the context of Deccan villages, Eaton suggests that until the twentieth century, when radio and cinema took its place, the folk poetry of Sufi origin had occupied a dominant position in the folk culture and became a link between

---

[63] Eaton raises this pertinent question in the case of studies on Sufism in India. He tries to fill this gap through a discussion on the role of Sufi folk literature in the expansion of Islam in Deccan. Eaton, *Essays on Islam and Indian History*, 189–99.

[64] Bigelow, 'Saved by the Saint', 436.

[65] Jackie Assayag, 'Can Hindus and Muslims Coexist?', in *Lived Islam in South Asia, Accommodation and Conflict*, ed. I. Ahmed and H. Reifeld (New Delhi: Social Science Press, 2004), 41.

the religious philosophy and the popular religion of Islam.[66] However, Eaton cautions, this process should not be construed as 'conversion' to Islam, nor should the Sufis themselves be considered as Muslim 'missionaries'.[67] The debate on the role of shrines in conversions to Islam should be analysed through varied dimensions. The proximity and reach of a particular shrine tradition at the popular domain indeed played a crucial role in Islamization. But, as Robinson argues, the taking on of Islam in many cases where large-scale conversions seem to have occurred came about by other processes.[68] In fact, adoption of certain symbols associated with Islam should not be construed as conversion per se. Anthropological understanding of colonial and post-Partition Punjab illustrates that individuals and families generally have plural religious affiliations, half Hindu–half Sikh, or half Hindu–half Muslim, or partially Hindu, Sikh and Muslim at the same time.[69] Besides, almost all communities throng the sacred shrines associated with *pir*s.[70]

The intriguing question of the continued existence of Sufi shrines and the emergence of newer centres forces us to rethink the conventional and dominant discourse on Sufism in India. Shrines were earlier considered symbols of the distant yet transcendent cultural authority of the Muslim state. Moini says that irrespective of social and cultural divisions, the people of Punjab signed bonds (*vikalatnama*s) – individually and collectively – particularly during the eighteenth century. They had been inspired by the Chishti exemplars of Punjab to develop intimate devotional links with the shrine of Khwaja Muinuddin Chishti

[66] Eaton, *Essays on Islam and Indian History*, 190–191.

[67] The main problem is that both the terms 'conversion' and 'missionaries' carry connotations of a nineteenth and twentieth century Christian movement in India, a context in which 'missionary' denoted a self-conscious propagator of the Christian faith and 'conversion', a self-conscious turning around in religious conviction. Ibid., 199.

[68] Rowena Robinson, 'Modes of Conversion to Islam', in *Religious Conversion in India: Modes, Motivations, and Meaning*, ed. R. Robinson and S. Clarke (New Delhi: Oxford University Press, 2007), 24.

[69] The fascinating outcome of the Anthropological Survey of India's survey in various states of India reveals a composite structure of religious identities in India. There are eighty-seven communities in India that follow both Hinduism and Sikhism; 116, Hinduism and Christianity; thirty-five, Hinduism and Islam; twenty-one, Hinduism and Jainism; and twenty-nine, Hinduism and Buddhism. K.S. Singh, *People of India: Introduction* (New Delhi: Oxford University Press, 2002), 89.

[70] Ibid., 112.

at Ajmer, which emerged as a centre of spiritualism and communal harmony.[71] These were related to the dominant Muslim consciousness in colonial Punjab. But how do we explain the post-independence scenario in Punjab where the majority population constitutes non-Muslims? Quoting S. Nurul Hasan, Gaur says that the understanding of the significant trends of historical change in the country (India) would remain sadly incomplete unless the details are studied at the regional level, through the dialectical evolution of culture.[72]

The gradual reinvention of these centres, and the development of memorial shrines and fairs dedicated to popular Sufi saints in Pakistan, forces us to rethink the communal perspectives in any understanding of social formation in contemporary Punjab. The post-Partition scenario amply illustrates that popular traditions could have been altered or abandoned altogether but nevertheless, continued to be a vibrant force of social formation. Even in the context of debates on Islamization, an obvious distinction needs to be made between conversion that is fabricated as a 'rupture' and conversion that is an addition to existing social life. One needs to know that the dialectics of culture do not subscribe to the 'total' negation of the previous cultural phase.[73] The communal representation of the Partition negates these organic linkages of people's history. What is also significant is that besides popular shrines which were managed by non-Muslims, shrines in the post-Partition scenario are almost exclusively managed by them. It is also important to take into consideration the role of merchants and traders as well as of state practices, which were geared towards the production of economic benefit and political influence rather than religious transformation per se.[74]

Popular culture is strikingly communitarian in nature and acculturation has an organic relationship with the lives people lead. Popular Sufi shrines were centres of shared cultural ethos and hence, even while they played a significant role in upward social mobility, they primarily existed as wish-fulfilling shrines. *Dargahs* and folk literature have to be understood as a gradual and ongoing process of Islamic acculturation through adaptation of symbols of dress, food, speech, etc. It is in this context that the role of Punjabi folk culture needs to be understood. A socio-anthropological analysis of these shrines strengthens

---

[71] Syed Liyaqat Hussain Moini, 'Devotional Linkages of Punjab with the Chishti Shrine at Ajmer: Gleanings from the Vikalatnamas', in *Sufism in Punjab: Mystics, Literature and Shrines*, ed. S. Singh and I.D. Gaur (New Delhi: Aakar, 2009), 390.

[72] Gaur, *Society, Religion and Patriarchy*, 22.

[73] Ibid., 128–129.

[74] Robinson, 'Modes of Conversion to Islam', 24.

the argument that the post-Partition scenario of the continued popularity of such *dargahs* is an expression of a pre-Partition milieu of shared cultural sites. These *dargahs* could have played an important role in Islamization, yet, they existed as 'cult centres' and 'principal deities' for Sikhs and Hindus alike. Significantly, these shrines had earlier existed independent of state control, in the popular domain of society, and the *wilayat* of such shrines extended beyond the political boundaries of either medieval or modern states, providing an alternative expression of social space.[75]

Concentrating on perhaps the most famous such tomb–shrine in the Punjab, that of Farid-ud-Din Ganj-i Shakar (d. 1265), popularly known as 'Baba Farid', Eaton seeks to connect the processes of Islamization and peasantization in western Punjab. Specifically, he asks why and how Jat tribesmen, as they abandoned pastoral nomadism for settled agriculture between the thirteenth and nineteenth centuries, gradually took on an Islamic identity.[76] The case study of Khanqah Chishtiya illustrates the tendency of an upward social mobility of ritually low castes, reconfiguring their relationship with high-caste Jat agriculturalists and other ritually high castes in contemporary Punjab. Shrines emerge as an alternate representation of the structures of power and authority. It also represents an inter-communal dialogue and dissent from the existing and oppressive discourses of caste and class hierarchies. While Bohar is a Dalit 'Christian', his family frequents the Sufi shrine of Malerkotla. He manifests himself as a reincarnation of Anant Nath who was a 'Hindu'. Bohar later converts to 'Islam'.[77] These case studies amply illustrate the significance of establishing an organic relationship between the human past and archives. The actual but hidden long-standing relationship between the two gets debunked when one comes across the popular literature of divergent people and divergent cultures.[78]

While the general distinction between religious identities is informed by different sets of belief and ritual systems, religion also includes everyday life

---

[75] Yogesh Snehi, 'Historicity, Orality and Lesser Shrines: Popular Culture and Change at the *Dargah* Panj Pir at Abohar', in *Sufism in Punjab: Mystics, Literature and Shrines*, ed. S. Singh and I.D. Gaur (New Delhi: Aakar, 2009), 418–419.

[76] Eaton, *Essays on Islam and Indian History*, 4.

[77] The dominant religious identities have been marked in inverted commas to emphasize and problematize the fixed notion of identities in the contemporary context. It is significant to underline that identities in contemporary Punjab are fluid, and though social mobility reflects upon a tendency for appropriation of liberal spaces, it does not necessarily mean conflict of one against the other.

[78] Singh and Gaur, *Popular Literature and Pre-modern Societies of South Asia*, 4.

and social exchange.[79] Even within the fixed framework of Hindu, Islamic and Sikh norms, we need to understand the discrete processes of identity formation and the constant interplay and overlap between different religious worldviews.[80] The Sufis had an amicable relationship with the *jogis*, and both enjoyed the veneration and confidence of simple folk. The love legend of Hir–Ranjha testifies to this. In the popular imagination, Sufi and *jogi* were identical. Both were detached, both practised renunciation of worldly possessions, both lived in a sort of trance or absorbed in the Supreme Reality, both observed service and submission to a *pir* or guru and both observed *zikr* or the recitation of the sacred word. Both adopted the use of the rosary, and believed in union with the Supreme Being. Both believed in the toleration of other religions and advocated universal love and *bhakti*.[81] This ethical and sacred milieu is significantly visible in all the popular Sufi shrines of Punjab. The case study of *pirkhana* at Abohar illustrates how various castes came to be associated with the veneration of *pirs* in the late medieval and colonial times. Thus, terms of identity are invariably shaped by the larger frames of knowledge in which they are embedded. It is thus in the interaction between the particular and the general that we must embed the analysis of identity.[82]

Critiquing the construction of popular identity, Assayag says that the presumptions projecting a syncretistic phenomenon as non-competitive is based on the assumption that a hybrid construction is itself a single identity.[83] Despite borrowing the practices of the other community in specific religious contexts, Hindus and Muslims continue to retain their separate identities. For these caste Hindus and Muslims, visiting places of worship belonging to the other community, acculturation is 'dissociative by differentiation'; he uses the typology devised by the ethno-psychiatrist Devereux, who explains it as 'the adaptation of the average to the manifest culture, but not the underlying culture'. Hindus perform a Hindu rite to propitiate a Muslim saint as if he were a Hindu deity. Even though they respect the rituals associated with the worship of the Muslim saint, for example, by offering sugar instead of rice and absorbing a portion of his divine power (*baraka*), they do not touch his tomb as Muslim worshippers would in a *dargah*. By the same token, when Muslims visit a

---

[79] David Gilmartin and Bruce B. Lawrence, *Beyond Turk and Hindu: Rethinking Religious Identities in Islamicate South Asia* (New Delhi: India Research Press, 2002), 1.

[80] Ibid., 2.

[81] Gaur, *Society, Religion and Patriarchy*, 51–52.

[82] Gilmartin and Lawrence, *Beyond Turk and Hindu*, 3.

[83] Assayag, 'Can Hindus and Muslims Coexist?', 43, footnote 6.

temple, they follow Hindu practices in order to obtain a view (*darshana*) and the blessings of the divine power.[84] In the context of this critique, it would be pertinent to locate identity formation in a scenario where the Muslim population does not exist and understand it in relation to the continued relevance of popular Sufi shrines in Punjab.

A significant question here pertains to the strength or fragility of these social identities. How strongly would these manifest and assert their identities in troubled times? Assayag further suggests that we must, therefore, be prepared to suspend the ideological debate and concentrate on cultural dynamics and socio-genetic aspects that have created the communal mosaic or 'composite culture' peculiar to India and shaped by bilateral relations between Hindus and Muslims.[85] Better still, despite the existence of a network of exchanges and reciprocal actions and the absence of a clear and definitive conceptual boundary between them, this process allows members of these communities to periodically withdraw into themselves whenever the situation (dramatized by social agents) requires them to affirm their social identity vis-à-vis the other community. Hindus and Muslims have been able to achieve this not by enunciating basic spiritual truths, but through seemingly insignificant, though decisive, signs, cobbling together 'little bits of truth', as observed by Sigmund Freud, during the displacement and readjustment of traditions.[86]

In the context of the shrine of Haider Shaikh at Malerkotla, Bigelow says that mere existence of a popular shrine does not prevent the growth of communalism and religious violence. Yet, because saints' tombs attract those who reject unitary religious identities and loyalties, they are important indices of the quality of inter-religious relations in a given locale.[87] Ian Talbot warns that pre -Partition Punjabi culture should not be idealized as free of religious communalism but does single out *dargahs* for the integration. It was only in the celebrations of the Sufi shrines that 'distance' was broken down between communities who were otherwise near neighbours, but living in separate worlds.[88] In the context of shrines in Punjab in general, it should be noted that not only do Hindus, Muslims and Sikhs visiting such places verbally validate one another's presence, but also adopt each other's ritual practices, attend the same spiritual gatherings, visit at the same time of day, make the same offerings, consult the same ritual

[84] Ibid., 44–45.

[85] Ibid., 54.

[86] Ibid., 55.

[87] Bigelow, 'Saved by the Saint', 440.

[88] Ibid., 442.

specialists and in some cases, become possessed by the saint's spirit. These exchanges and encounters reject communalism.[89] In the post-Partition scenario, a majority of popular shrines are associated with ritually low castes, though the visitors include high-caste Hindus and Sikhs. Case studies of *pirkhanas*, however, illustrate the popularity and almost complete identification of the *pir* as a personal deity. These places also dissent against the dominant and often communal symbols and practices of dominant religiosity.

What is equally significant is that the adoption and identification with Islamic idioms like *pir*, *dargah*, *khanqah*, *barkat* and *ibadat*, and even construction of mosques and *pirkhanas*, is almost universal in the contemporary popular landscape of Punjab. In the post-Partition milieu, especially after militancy in Punjab, these idioms have emerged as significant symbols of identity formation. Several *qawwali darbar*s organized at Amritsar bring together people from varied caste and religious affiliations, in different strata of social hierarchy, and adopting symbols of an alternative identity. Kaliyar Sharif has emerged as a major marker of this unique identity, which has been playing a significant role in the new wave of Chishti movement in contemporary Punjab. While earlier the veneration of popular Punjabi saints, like Shaikh Farid and Shaikh Haider, and various Qadiri affiliations continue to be associated with Sufi shrines in the state, the emergence of Sabiri branch of Chishtis is most prominent. Also, the assertion of pre-Partition social identities in present times is an exercise in reconfiguration of the communal discourse of the Partition. The emergence of *pirkhana*s and the reconfiguration of the association of Aggrawals with Baba Lakhdata and Shaikh Haider is a crucial process of counter-hegemony and a reinstatement of pre-Partition social consciousness. Another significant dynamic in the shaping of a contemporary social formation is the political economy associated with such shrines which, again, are premised on the popular veneration of saints and play a critical role in the articulation of the power structures of caste and class hierarchies of Punjab.

Emergence of new *khanqah*s and *dargahs* is another feature of contemporary Punjabi consciousness. In significant cases, it is the Jat veneration of Sufi saints which is playing an important role in the emergence of the cult of Baba Lakhdata or Khanqah Chishtiya. The emergence of new lineages and successions has led to invention of fairs and festivals in the memory of popular saints, which mark the rural and urban landscape of Punjab. Significantly, shrines associated with these popular practices have not been affected by the recent incidence of caste

[89] Ibid., 440.

violence in Punjab, attesting its shared value for inter-communal dialogue. The identity of Guru Granth Sahib as a popular text conceptualized from the times of Shaikh Farid and completed by Guru Gobind Singh, besides rejection of caste and religious differences, is a crucial element of this enterprise. The formation of the Gulame Anjuman Chishtiya represents new form of dissenting associative identities in contemporary Punjab.

References

Ahmed, Imtiaz and Helmut Reifeld, eds. 2004. *Lived Islam in South Asia: Adaptation, Accommodation and Conflict* (New Delhi: Social Science Press).

Amin, Shahid. 'On Retelling the Muslim Conquest of North India'. In *History and the Present*, edited by P. Chatterjee and A. Ghosh, 27–38 (New Delhi: Permanent Black, 2002).

Assayag, Jackie. 'Can Hindus and Muslims Coexist?' In *Lived Islam in South Asia: Adaptation, Accommodation and Conflict*, edited by I. Ahmed and H. Reifeld (New Delhi: Social Science Press, 2004).

Bigelow, Anna. 'Saved by the Saint: Refusing and Reversing Partition in Muslim North India'. *The Journal of Asian Studies* 68(2) (2009): 435–464.

Chatterjee, Partha and Anjan Ghosh, eds. 2002. *History and the Present* (New Delhi: Permanent Black).

Eaton, Richard M. *Essays on Islam and Indian History* (New Delhi: Oxford University Press, 2000).

Gaur, Ishwar Dayal. *Society, Religion and Patriarchy: Exploring Medieval Punjab through* Hir Waris (New Delhi: Manohar, 2009).

Gilmartin, David. *Empire and Islam: Punjab and the Making of Pakistan* (New Delhi: Oxford University Press, 1989).

Gilmartin, David and Bruce B. Lawrence. *Beyond Turk and Hindu: Rethinking Religious Identities in Islamicate South Asia* (New Delhi: India Research Press, 2002).

Khan, Dominique-Sila. *Conversions and Shifting Identities: Ramdev Pir and the Ismailis in Rajasthan* (New Delhi: Manohar, 2003).

Kolff, Dirk H.A. *Naukar, Rajput and Sepoy: The Ethnohistory of the Military Labour Market in Hindustan 1450–1850*. Cambridge: Cambridge University Press, 1990.

Liebeskind, Claudia. *Piety on its Knees: Three Sufi Traditions in South Asia in Modern Times* (New Delhi: Oxford University Press, 1998).

Mahmood, Tahir. 'The Dargah of Saiyid Salar Masud Ghazi in Bahraich: Legend, Tradition and Reality', in *Muslim Shrines in India: Their Character, History and Significance*, edited by C.W. Troll, (New Delhi: Oxford University Press, 2003), 24–43.

Mayaram, Shail. 'Beyond Ethnicity? Being Hindu and Muslim in South Asia'. In *Lived Islam in South Asia: Adaptation, Accommodation and Conflict*, ed. I. Ahmed and H. Reifeld, 18–39 (New Delhi: Social Science Press, 2004).

Mir, Farina. 'Genre and Devotion in Punjabi Popular Narratives: Rethinking Cultural and Religious Syncretism', *Society for Comparative Study of Society and History* 48(3) (2006): 727–758.

Moini, Syed Liyaqat Hussain. 'Devotional Linkages of Punjab with the Chishti Shrine at Ajmer: Gleanings from the Vikalatnamas'. In *Sufism in Punjab: Mystics, Literature and Shrines*, edited by S. Singh and I.D. Gaur, 378–401. New Delhi: Aakar, 2009.

Oberoi, Harjot. 'Popular Saints, Goddesses, and Village Sacred Sites: Rereading Sikh Experience in the Nineteenth Century'. *History of Religions* 31(4) (1992): 363–384.

———. *The Construction of Religious Boundaries: Culture, Identity, and Diversity in the Sikh Tradition* (Chicago: The University of Chicago Press, 1994).

Punjab District Gazetteer, Firozpur District (Chandigarh: Revenue Department, Punjab, 1983).

Purser, W.E. *Final Report of the Revised Settlement of the Jullundur District* (Lahore: Civil and Military Gazette Press, 1892).

Rizvi, Saiyid Athar Abbas. *A History of Sufism in India* (New Delhi: Munshiram Manoharlal, 2003).

Robinson, Rowena. 'Modes of Conversion to Islam'. In *Religious Conversion in India: Modes, Motivations, and Meaning*, edited by R. Robinson and S. Clarke (New Delhi: Oxford University Press, 2007).

Robinson, Rowena and Sathianathan Clarke, eds. 2007. *Religious Conversion in India: Modes, Motivations, and Meanings* (New Delhi: Oxford University Press).

Rose, H.A. *A Glossary of the Tribes and Castes of the Punjab and North-West Frontier Province* (Lahore: Superintendant, Government Printing Punjab, 1919).

Roy, Asim. *The Islamic Syncretistic Tradition in Bengal* (Princeton: Princeton University Press, 1983).

Singh. Ditt. *Gugga Gapaura* (Amritsar: Kendri Sri Guru Singh Sabha, 1902[1976]).

Singh, K.S. *People of India: Introduction* (New Delhi: Oxford University Press, 2002).

Singh, Surinder and Ishwar Dayal Gaur. *Popular Literature and Pre-modern Societies of South Asia* (New Delhi: Pearson Longman, 2008).

———, ed. *Sufism in Punjab: Mystics, Literature and Shrines* (New Delhi: Aakar, 2009).

Snehi, Yogesh. 'Historicity, Orality and Lesser Shrines: Popular Culture and Change at the *Dargah* Panj Pir at Abohar'. In *Sufism in Punjab: Mystics, Literature and Shrines*, edited by S. Singh and I.D. Gaur (New Delhi: Aakar, 2009), 402–429.

Troll, Christian W., ed. *Muslim Shrines in India: Their Character, History and Significance* (New Delhi: Oxford University Press, 2003).

CHAPTER

14

Devotion and Dissent within the Catholic Church in Late Colonial Bengal

G. Gispert-Sauch, S.J.

The Roman Catholic tradition has a solid reputation, at least within the Christian world, of conservatism and lack of flexibility. Even in contemporary media, the memory of the Grand Inquisitor is never far from the background of the frequently presented figure of the present Pope. With its doctrine of 'infallibility' and authoritarian structure, Catholicism seems to throttle any attempt to express dissent not only in religious matters but, often enough, also in social movements. The history of the last two centuries shows how often official teachings have tried to support the established order and block change in religion. As evidences, one need only read the famous *Syllabus of Condemned Errors*, issued by the Vatican authority in 1864. In more recent times, the rejection of priestly ordination for women seems to be another case in point.

However, even within this conservative tradition, there are always movements rooted in new understandings of devotion and faith that make space for themselves within the church, often with difficulty. I would like to present here two important movements in Indian Catholicism, one at the opening and the other at the close of the twentieth century, and in this context, examine how the Indian Catholic Church has been coping with change and has strengthened its identity.

Brahmabandhab Upadhyay was a Bengali Brahmin, son of a police officer of the Raj, a contemporary and friend of Swami Vivekananda and member, at one time, of the circle of Keshab Chandra Sen's followers. He was born in 1861 and was initiated early in his life into a double devotion: to the country and to Kali. In his original name, 'Bhavanicharan' suggests Kali, while the 'Banerjee' of Bengal suggests patriotism. University studies opened his horizons and he became interested in the field of religion as *karma marga*, *bhakti marga* and *jnana marga*.

Bhavanicharan Banerjee, therefore, was born in a key time of transition not only in his Bengal but also in other parts of India. Politically, the British Parliament took over the direct control of the administration of India and the Raj was established. It would lead to Queen Victoria (1837–1901) proclaiming herself the Empress of India in 1876. But the Raj begot its own antibodies, a new Indian nationalism that found expression in the 1857 uprising.

The transition was not only political but also cultural and religious. Not in vain has it been called a time of the 'Hindu renaissance'! Two powerful cultural and religious movements were trying to woo the soul of India. They may be considered movements of political and cultural dissent. In the east, the Brahmo Samaj, conceived by Raja Rammohan Roy (1772–1833), had arrived at its maturity in the middle of the century with the help of the Tagore family. The Brahmo Samaj itself also experienced dissent, especially in Keshab Chandra Sen (1838–84), at one time guru of Upadhyay and others. The Samaj was a rather intellectual and reformist movement. Its roots were in the Upanishads and the Gita, reinterpreted in modern language, although it did not entirely forget the popular and the emotional factors. The other powerful revivalist movement was found in north-west India, the Arya Samaj, led by Swami Dayananda Saraswati (1825–83), rooted firmly in the Vedas, again as reinterpreted by the founder, to the exclusion of all later literature. Its main concern was to overcome the influence, on the masses, of Islam, Christianity and any Western influence.

The second half of the nineteenth century, up to the partition of Bengal in 1905, was a time of lively cultural, political and religious debate in India, especially in Bengal. One can sense this in the many journals and magazines that sprouted at the time. Nationalism was becoming the new creed of India. After the partition, the debate became purely political.

The Indian Christians were naturally affected by the nation's mood. There was a nationalist movement within the church which led to attempts to establish Indian churches (for example, the Christo Samaj in Calcutta in 1887 or the National Church of Madras in 1886). These were basically movements of dissent in the Protestant Churches of India against the dominance of the foreign missionaries over the local pastors, or priests, and the local congregations.

In the Catholic Church, there had been, much earlier – in the seventeenth century – a similar movement of dissent which did not however lead to schism. Interestingly, Upadhyay referred a number of times to this movement. It was initiated by Roberto de Nobili (1557–1656), an Italian missionary educated during the European Renaissance, who realized soon that the missionaries under the Portuguese *Padroado* were misguided in the way they reproduced Western Christianity in India. Citing the teachings of the ancient writers and decisions of the authorities of the Western church, he insisted that Indian Christians should conserve as much as possible their own valuable languages and cultures and should develop a theological understanding according to their traditions. He himself adopted the lifestyle of a sanyasi and learned Sanskrit, Tamil and Telugu. He gave Jesus the title of 'Sadguru', in preference to the 'Lord' of Western origin. He was thus the father of the movement we today call 'interculturation'.[1] A good number of missionaries agreed with the inspiration of de Nobili and thus, in practice, promoted a parallel 'Indian Catholic Church' different from the church that followed the Latin traditions of Europe. Not surprisingly, the two forms of the church lived in tension. The matter was referred first to Goa, then the seat of the bishop of the Western church in India, and later, to Rome. Both centres of authority dithered, first in favour, later against. Rome eventually stopped the 'experiment' of the Indian rites, as it is called, and ended what could have been a creative moment for Christianity. Upadhyay revived the idea two centuries later.

The Brahmo Samaj circles Upadhyay frequented had been interested in the figure of Jesus Christ ever since the founder, Raja Rammohan Roy, had published *The Precepts of Jesus* in 1820. Keshab developed this line of religiousness and exalted the figure of Jesus not only as a teacher of humanity but also as especially relevant for India. Bhavanicharan – first an admirer, later a critic of Keshab – separated definitely from him after reading a doctrinal and apologetic book by an Italian priest, Faa di Bruno's *Catholic Belief*. After much reflection and discussion, he accepted the faith in Jesus Christ as proposed by the church and entered into the Catholic community in 1891, while he was employed as a teacher in a school at Hyderabad, Sindh.

His exile from Bengal to Sindh was a consequence of the death of Keshab Chandra Sen in 1884 that left the Brahmo Samaj in a deep crisis of leadership. Hiranand Saukhiram Advani, a Sindhi student in Calcutta and fellow member of the Arya Samaj, had gone back to Sindh and from there, invited Bhavanicharan to join him to start a new school in Hyderabad, Sindh, for the revival of Hinduism. There were plenty of Brahmo Samajis in Sindh and they disagreed profoundly with the local Arya Samaj movement. Upadhyay would teach

[1] For a deeper understanding of this term, see C. Joe Arun, ed., *Interculturation of Religion – Critical Perspective on Roberto de Nobili's Mission in India* (Bangalore: Asia Trading Corporation with de Nobili Research Centre at Chennai, 2007).

Sanskrit and other matters, and be in charge of sports. Upadhyay was glad to escape the situation in Bengal and to cooperate in an adventure that was according to his ideals. He proved a popular teacher and a powerful orator. He remained away from Bengal for about fifteen years. There, he understood Christ better. His father died in Multan, not far from Hyderabad, and at that time, he decided to become a Christian and take a new name.

Though he remained at heart a firm believer in Jesus Christ, Upadhyay's position in the church was precarious. His stand was that he was both a Hindu by birth and culture, and a Christian by faith and sacramental rebirth. He was a hyphenated Hindu-Christian. To the end of his life, he maintained this double belonging: and if in the first decade after his baptism, he wrote mostly on his Christian faith, he also wrote interpretations of Hindu doctrines and practices from the point of view of Indian Christianity. He wanted the church in India to be what it professed to be, 'Catholic', that is, universal in its self-understanding and practice, which for him meant that it needed to integrate and preserve the cultural and religious values traditional in India. In many senses, he was conservative, though he pioneered strong religious and political action with far-reaching social consequences.

He was also a dissenter on several accounts. In his conversion, he partially broke from his ancient upbringing and with many friends, including his own brother, who vehemently tried to prevent it. The conversion cost him his job. He had also parted from Ramakrishna Paramahamsa in favour of Keshab Chandra Sen. Politically, he rejected the 'acceptable' middle position of the freedom movement, the compromise of accepting 'Home Rule' rather than independence. As a young man, twice he had attempted to join the army of the Maharaja of Gwalior, hoping that it would become strong enough to defeat the British. When this proved an illusory dream, he took to the pen instead of the gun. He would bring people to his views through journalism. In the church, he rejected the accepted entente cordial with the Raj: he thought that, at that moment, the authorities of the community, mostly the foreign bishops, were far too sympathetic to the British rule in the country. Change in the church was only possible by a deep reshaping of its life.

Not strangely, the church authorities reacted negatively to the views of a recent member who had no recognized theological or philosophical training in the Christian tradition, though he had read a good deal of the available literature. He was looked upon suspiciously by the authorities, especially when he changed his clothes into *kavi* dress and began to publish his views. Monsignor Ladislaus M. Zaleski, originally from the Lithuanian nobility, was at the time an authoritarian Papal Delegate to the Catholic Church in India (from 1892 to 1916). He took the initiative of forbidding Catholics from subscribing to the journals published by Upadhyay in the last decade of the nineteenth and the first decade of the twentieth centuries. He, thus, financially sank the projects and silenced a new lay voice in the Indian Church. Eventually, Upadhyay, always professing Catholic obedience to the church authorities, tried to bolster up his legitimacy by a journey to England that would also enable him to visit the Pope in Rome. But this visit did not take place, and the trip to Britain was only partially successful.

Upadhyay was essentially a journalist and a teacher. These were the main activities most of his life. In the beginning of the century, he established close contact with Rabindranath Tagore, whose poetic and mystical genius Upadhyay was the first to recognize in a review of the Bengali book, *Naibedya*, the forerunner of the widely read English *Gitanjali* that won for Tagore the 1913 Nobel Prize in literature. Upadhyay, like Tagore, was sceptical about the value of the 'English education' being implanted in India at the time, and wanted to recover the ethos and values of the traditional Indian educational system. For this purpose, he started a new kind of school on updated traditional lines. He agreed to support Tagore's own effort to do the same at Shantiniketan.

On his return to India early in the new century, Upadhyay devoted himself to political activism, supporting, and in a sense leading, the *garam dal*, the group of freedom fighters who opted for direct and even violent action, rather than following the slow path of political activism. Upadhyay was convinced that the church had to do away with the incubus of the British Raj that blocked any hope for the freedom to become what God wanted it to be, an 'Indian Church' – not indeed cut off from the church elsewhere and certainly not from the Church in Rome, but an authentic Indian expression of the Catholic faith. Upadhyay did not see it happen. In the final years of his life, he took ambiguous decisions that shocked some of his most loyal friends. For one, he decided to request a social purification for having broken the Brahmanic rule of not travelling away from the *punyabhumi*, that is, India. His *shuddhi* was interpreted by many as a renunciation of his Christian faith and a 'return' to the Hindu fold.

There was no question of a return because Upadhyay had always claimed to be both a Hindu and a Christian. There was no renunciation of this Christian faith, for he made it clear that what he was doing was fulfilling a social duty as a member of his Brahmin caste. He did not frequent the church services now, as he had done so enthusiastically in the first decade after his baptism. But he did remember, and in a sense follow, the liturgical times like Lent and Holy

Week. He died, technically, as a prisoner of the Raj, from an attack of tetanus that overtook him after a session of a court trial for 'sedition' against the British government. His last words in the intense suffering of his final attack of tetanus were, 'Thakur! Thakur!', the title he had used for Jesus ever since he believed in him. His Hindu friends took his body from the hospital where he died and cremated it with Hindu rites.

What did Upadhyay achieve? One may say both 'little' and 'much' at one and the same time. In Sindh, he started a small Christian movement that attracted a number of conversions to Christianity. The movement died a couple of decades after his death. He also began writing theological tracts and articles that, in a sense, were the starting point of what can be called the movement of an Indian Christian theology in the Catholic Church. Politically, though he seems to have been the first freedom fighter to demand total *svatantra* from the Raj, not merely Home Rule; he did not see independence coming nearer. Yet, he surely helped to deepen the will for independence in the country, for his daily evening paper was extremely popular in Bengal. Yet, independence would come only forty years after his death!

Nor did he see a church fiercely proud of its Indian character. Yet, he started a new consciousness within it that many consider the starting point of the Catholic Indian theology movement that has certainly changed the sense of self-identity in the community. The issues of *Sophia* which he published were preserved and well read in training centres of the Catholic clergy. In 1922, the Jesuits of Calcutta started a monthly journal that lasted till 1946, which recovered and made public the legacy of Upadhyay. In 1938, a journal for priests was started by the Archbishop of Madras, today continuing as the *Vidyajyoti Journal of Theological Reflection*, which keeps alive and develops the idea of an authentic Indian Church. 'Inculturation' is a key word that has captured the attention of the church, not only in India but elsewhere in Asia and indeed in the world, and was partially accepted by the movement started by Vatican II. It sums up the goal of Upadhyay's life and action.

The move towards an 'inculturation' of the church had been started by de Nobili in the seventeenth century, two centuries before Orientalism was even thought about. But the movement had remained low key in the apogee of the British rule in the country. Upadhyay revived it and gave it a clearer focus. It has continued to change the church of the twentieth century, but always in tension with the conservative tradition. By the time of independence, out of fifty-one Catholic bishops in India, only nineteen were Indians, the rest were born elsewhere. Today, all the active 180 bishops are Indians. Not all this is due to Upadhyay, of course, but he did contribute to create an atmosphere favourable to this 'Indianization' of the church.

However, not all that Upadhyay did and stood for was acceptable. One important issue was that of the caste in India. For him, as for Gandhiji after him, caste was an essential part of the Indianness of our culture, and it was essential to keep it, although in a modern form. Without accepting legal untouchability and willing to receive Holy Communion together with outcaste members in a community of faith, Upadhyay defended that the social structure of India needed to keep the traditional roles assigned by tradition to the members of the four *varnas*. With the Gita, he argued that the mixture of castes could only hasten the destruction of the country.

He called one of his short-lived journals, *The Twentieth Century*. By the end of that century, new movements emerged within the church in total disagreement with Upadhyay's vision and ferociously fighting its effect in the community. They became what, today, we call the Christian Dalit movement, which in the church, spawned also a Dalit Christian theology, a new version, with its own characteristics, of the better-known liberation theology promoted by Gustavo Gutierrez in Latin America. As is well known, the national Dalit movement started in the nineteenth century by Mahatma Phule and was strengthened in the twentieth by the leadership of Dr B.R. Ambedkar. In the second half of the twentieth century, the Dalits of Maharashtra awakened and gelled into the movement of Dalit Panthers, partly inspired by the Black Panther movement in the United States; one product of this had been the publication of *Black Theology of Liberation* by James Cone, one year before the more famous *Liberation Theology* of Gutierrez appeared in the bookshops and galvanized the popular church of South America.[2]

Tamil Nadu has, by Indian standards, a respectable presence of Christians (Orientals, Catholics and Protestants), about 6.5 per cent of the population. According to some statistics, about 70 per cent of this Christian population would be of Dalit origin. Not surprisingly, the new awareness created by the Dalit movement all over the country also affected the Tamil Christian communities, and they engaged in a vigorous protest movement against their

[2] The Reverend James Cone is the founder of black liberation theology linked to the Black Rights movement of the 1960s. In an interview with Terry Gross, Cone explains the movement, which has roots in the 1960s civil rights activism and draws inspiration from both the Reverend Martin Luther King, Jr and Malcolm X, as 'mainly a theology that sees God as concerned with the poor and the weak'.

marginalization in the authority structures of the church. There was much research and writing on the reasons of their situation: why in spite of their numerical superiority, there was no Dalit bishop in the country even near the end of the twentieth century (in contrast, perhaps, with the tribal bishops that had been appointed already from the early 1950s)? The Brahmanic sources of social untouchability were exposed, ancient myths challenged and the question asked why this social sin had infected the church already in the early times of colonialism. There was not only research and writing on the subject but also movements of social protest, including *gheraos* and letters of protest and appeals to the Vatican. At present, one may be able to count about a dozen bishops of Dalit origin, by no means a satisfactory situation, but whatever it may be, this is partly due to the protests.

The movement also extended to other parts of India. Even today, a group of concerned Christians and sympathizers run a Centre of Dalit/Subaltern Studies, near Dwarka, New Delhi, with numerous activities and extensive contacts with other parts of the country. At the moment, it is engaged in publishing the first Dalit commentary of the Bible, of which the New Testament is already available and the Old Testament is in active preparation. The Catholic Dalit community in Bihar has also been affected by this movement: there, too, demands for positions of responsibility within the community are being felt. The commanding position of ancient Christians coming to Bihar from other parts of the country is no longer accepted easily. The new bishops are generally from the soil. At the organizational levels, the Catholic Bishops' Conference of India (CBCI) has now departments for Dalit and for tribal concerns. Dissent has produced some results.

There is no doubt that both Upadhyay and the Dalit movement drew and draw inspiration from the deepest resources of their Christian faith. They have managed to change, to some extent, not only the externals of the community leadership but also the ways of community's perception of reality and of their own role in it. They have pioneered important ideas like those of cultural identity, double religious 'membership', Christian ashrams, activist social reform and political involvement. If today, individual 'conversions' are not the primary objective of the major churches, it is not out of infidelity to the gospel but out of an awareness that the culture and the social structures of the country need to be changed before we can authentically practice the primary command of the gospel, that is, that we love one another in a community that upholds the values of justice, equality, freedom and fraternity, which are the foundation of our national life.

References

Arun, C. Joe ed.. *Interculturation of Religion – Critical Perspective on Roberto de Nobili's Mission in India* (Bangalore: Asia Trading Corporation with De Nobili Research Centre at Chennai, 2007).

Cone, James, H. Black, *Theology and Black Power*, 1997, Orbis Books, New York.

Gutierrez Gustavo, A., *Theology of Liberation: History, Politics and Salvation* (New York: Orbis Books, 1988).

Lipner, Julius J. and Sauch, Gispert, G., 1991, *The Writings of Brahmabandhab Upadhyay (1862–1907):A Resume of His Life and Thought,* United Theological College, Division of Research and Post Graduate Studies, Bangalore.

Lipner, Julius J., *Brahmabandhab Upadhyay: The Life and Thought of a Revolutionary* (Cambridge University, UK, Delhi: Cambridge University Press, 1999).

Rajamanickam, Svarimuthu, *Roberto de Nobili on Indian Customs,* 1972, De Nobili Research Institute, Palayamkottai.

Roy, Raja Rammohan and Marshman Joshua, *The Precepts of Jesus:Second Appeal to the Christian Public* (New York: B. Bates, 1825).

Tagore, Rabindranath, *Noibedya*, 1965, Visva-bharati, West Bengal.

Journals

Vidyajyoti Journal of Theological Reflection, founded in 1938 and currently published by Vidya Jyoti, New Delhi.

CHAPTER

15

Narratives of Travel, Voices of Dissent and Attacks on the Colonial Church Fabric of the European Missionaries

A Study on the Varthamanapusthakam

Pius Malekandathil

Varthamanapusthakam, which was written in the 1790s by Father (Fr) Thomas Paremakkal as an account of his travel along with his friend Mar Joseph Kariyattil to Madras, Africa, Brazil, Portugal and Rome and often hailed as the first travelogue in an Indian language, has been used as a literary medium by the author to ventilate his dissent and anger against the hegemonic attitude and the colonial fabric which the European religious missionaries set up for the church in India, particularly for the St Thomas Christians of Kerala. Arguing vehemently that India should be ruled by Indians and not by foreigners, he demands, as early as 1785, that Indian Christians should be ruled not by European religious missionaries but by Indians. Within the larger format of a travelogue detailing meticulously the socio-economic and political processes of the several countries he visited in Africa, South America and Europe, he argues his case by showing how the foreign missionaries, fearing reduction of the span of their power and authority, did not want to have another bishop for the St Thomas Christians and how the innocent priests of this community were brutally killed (as in the case of Chacko Kathanar of Edappilly, who was starved to death in their jails) and the very community often fined for the blunders and crimes of omissions and negligence of these foreign missionaries.

Fr Thomas Paremakkal and Fr Joseph Kariyattil made their travels to Portugal and Rome based on the decision of the general body of the St Thomas Christians taken at Angamaly, for the purpose of informing the Pope and the queen of Portugal of the various discriminations, sufferings and difficulties that this community experienced over a considerable period of time from the foreign Carmelite missionaries working in Kerala. As the general meeting of the representatives of this community at Angamaly was dominated by feelings of anger and animosity against the European religious missionaries and the European bishop working in Kerala, the travelogue has anti-Europeanism as its basic thread, critiquing the hegemonic and colonial fabric of the church set up by the European missionaries. Stressing the need for going back to the pre-Portuguese days when democratic institutions of *yogams* (representative body at the grassroots levels), *mahayogams* (representative bodies at higher levels) with *jathikkukarthaviyan* (head of the community) existed among this community for their administration, instead of one-man centred or European notion of bishop-centred administration, the travelogue challenges the notion of authority that the European missionaries had set up within the colonial fabric they had created for the Church of the St Thomas Christians.

Interestingly, the narratives in this book, with copious accounts of hardships that the St Thomas Christians had to face from the church fabric set up by the European missionaries in Kerala, soon formed an inspiring literary device for this community in their later clamour for having Indian bishops for them instead of European bishops, and also for reviving their age-old liturgical traditions, customs and ritual practices. The central purpose of this essay is to see how the European version of Christian experience and church administration was challenged by Indians with alternative faith experience and administrative formats, and also to see how the web of travel narratives was used as a powerful medium for getting ventilated and disseminated the spirit of dissent and meanings of Indian alternatives to the larger collectivity of the community.

Historical Setting

The period from 1750 till 1830, which is often referred to as the period of revolutions and regime change all over the world, was also a period of political fluidity in India, particularly in South India, where regime changes coincided with attempts for cultural appropriations and ethnic mutations. St Thomas Christians, who usually trace back their origin to the preaching of

St Thomas and are often known as Syrian Christians or Nazarenes,[1] form a unique community in India that was increasingly subjugated to ethnic mutations because of the processes of cultural appropriations and colonial grafting that happened during this period. In fact, the St Thomas Christians, who numbered about 60,000–75,000[2] in the beginning of the sixteenth century, were estimated to be about 1,00,000 by the second half of the sixteenth century.[3] By the 1830s, their number increased to 3,50,000.[4] However, by this time, the community was literally fragmented into different pieces and groups by the foreign ecclesiastical administrators mutating their identities. On the one hand, there was an attempt from the West Syrian bishops to extend their jurisdiction over the non-Catholic segment of St Thomas Christians by grafting the cultural elements of West Syriac liturgy and ritual practices onto them from 1748 onwards.[5] On the

[1] For details, see Eugene Tisserant, *Eastern Christianity in India*, trans. E.R. Hambye (Kolkata: Orient Longman, 1957); Placid Podipara, *The Thomas Christians* (Mumbai: St. Paul Publications, 1970); A.M. Mundadan, *History of Christianity in India*, Vol. I (Bangalore: Church History Association of *India*, 1989); Joseph C. Panjikaran, 'Christianity in Malabar with Special Reference to the St. Thomas Christians of the Syro-Malabar Rite', *Orientalia* VI (1926), 89–136.

[2] Tome Pires, *A Suma Oriental de Tome Pires e o Livro de Francisco Rodrigues*, ed. Armando Cortesão (Coimbra: Universidade de *Coimbra*, 1978), 180; João Teles e Cunha, 'De Diamper a Mattancherry: Caminhos e Encruzilhadas da Igreja Malabar e Catolica na India: Os Primeiros Tempos (1599–1624)', *Anais de Historia de Alem-Mar* V (2004), 283–368; João Paulo Oliveira e Costa, 'Os Portugueses e a Cristandade Siro-Malabar (1498–1530)', *Studia* 52 (1994), 121–178.

[3] Josef Wicki, ed., *Documenta Indica, Vol. VI* (Roma: Institute of Historical Society, 1948), 180; Ibid., Vol. VII, 475.

[4] According to the account of William Horsely, there were about 1,74,566 Syrian Christians (56,184 Romo-Syrians and 1,18,382 Syrians) in Travancore in 1836. W.H. Horsley, *Memoir of Travancore, Historical and Statistical, Compiled from Various Authentic Records and Personal Observations* (Trivandrum: Government Press, 1838), reproduced by Achuth Sankar S. Nair, ed., 'William Henry Horsley's Memoir of Travancore (1838): Earliest English Treatise on the History of Travancore', *Journal of Kerala Studies* XXXI (2004), 63. Almost the same number of Syrian Christians lived in the kingdoms of Cochin and Calicut. By 1891, the number of Syrian Christians in Travancore increased to 2,87,409. See George Mathew, *Communal Road to a Secular Kerala* (New Delhi: Concept Publishing Company, 1989), 52.

[5] The West Syrian ritual practices were grafted on to the non-Catholic fraction of the St Thomas Christians with the arrival of Mar Ivanios, a West Syrian bishop, in 1748. He shaved the head of the priests and ordained priests without the consent

other hand, the British wanted to anglicize this community by introducing Anglican theology and ritual practices through the instrumentality of Anglican missionaries, particularly the Church Missionary Society (CMS) from 1815 onwards.[6] The Catholic segment of the St Thomas Christians was in no way exempted from this fragmentation process. On the one side, there was the Portuguese Church administrative system called *Padroado*, which appropriated a major chunk of Catholic St Thomas Christians under its jurisdiction,[7] while the remaining Catholic fraction of St Thomas Christians was controlled by a non-Portuguese Church administrative system called Propaganda Fide, established under the Pope in 1622.[8] This community was Literally torn into four different fractions by the various church administrative systems from outside, and each category of church administrators wanted to perpetuate its domination over this indigenous Christian community without allowing the members to come together under their own bishop. Interestingly, the Jacobites, or the non-Catholic segment of the St Thomas Christians, had their own indigenous bishop from

---

of the indigenous bishop, Mar Thoma V, and also burned crucifixes and images of saints used in the churches. The second team of West Syrian bishops came under Mar Baselius Sakrallah in 1751, who introduced the Jacobite ideology and West Syrian ritual practices. See also Paulinus Bartholomeo, *India Orientalis Christiana* (Rome: Propaganda Press, 1796), 86.

[6] W.S. Hunt, *The Anglican Church in Travancore and Cochin 1816–1916* (Kottayam: C.M.S. Press, 1918).

[7] For details on *Padroado* system, see Thomas Pallippurathukkunnel, *A Double Regime in the Malabar Church* (Alwaye: Pontifical Institute of Theology and Philosophy, 1982), 3–4. See also Isabel dos Guimaraes Sa, 'Ecclesiastical Structures and Religious Action', in *Portuguese Oceanic Expansion, 1400–1800*, ed. Francisco Bethencourt and Diogo Ramada Curto (Cambridge: Cambridge University Press, 2007), 255–80; João Paulo e Costa, 'The Padroado and the Catholic Mission in Asia during the 17th Century', in *Rivalry and Conflict: European Traders and Asian Trading Networks in the 16th and 17th Centuries*, ed. Ernst van Veen and Leonard Blusse (Leiden: CNWS Publications, 2005), 71–88.

[8] The defects in the functioning of the *Padroado* system made Pope Gregory XIV set up Propaganda Fide in 1622 and entrusted a major portion of Asia under the ecclesiastical administrative arrangement of Propaganda Fide. The *Padroado* system was suppressed by the Pope in 1838, despite the severe opposition from the Portuguese crown, and the strained relationship between Rome and Portugal continued up to 1886. For more details, see C.D. Dominic, 'The Latin Missions under the Jurisdiction of Propaganda (1637–1838)', in *Christianity in India*, ed. H.C. Perumalil and E.R. Hambye (Alleppey: Prakasam Publications, 1972), 102–103.

1666 onwards.[9] However, later, from 1748 onwards, the indigenous bishop, Mar Thoma VI , was sidelined in church matters by the new West Syrian bishops who arrived from Babylonia, who eventually secured support from some local clergy for introducing the West Syrian liturgy and ritual practices among them.[10] Being highly ignored and peripheralized by the new West Syrian bishops, Mar Thoma VI wanted to reunite with the Catholic Church by the 1770s. However, the European Carmelite missionaries and the European Bishop of Verapoly working under the church administrative system of Propaganda Fide were reluctant to accept Mar Thoma VI to Catholicism as they were suspicious of the genuineness of his intentions.[11]

The Catholic St Thomas Christians, who had earlier been ill-treated by the European Carmelite missionaries on several other occasions, got all the more offended by their refusal to accept Mar Thoma VI to Catholicism. They immediately called a meeting at Angamaly, of the representative body of this Christian community, known as *mahayogam*, with delegates from seventy-two churches, to chart out their course of action.[12] In this meeting, the members ventilated their anger and frustration against the Carmelite missionaries for the various types of ill-treatment and discriminations that the community had had to face from the missionaries. In the *yogam*, a decision was taken to send a few representatives from this community to submit, before the Pope and the ruler of Portugal, their grievances and complaints about the Propaganda missionaries,

---

[9] See Joseph Thekkedath, *History of Christianity, Vol. II*, Bangalore: Church History Association of India, 1988), 98; and *The Troubled Days of Francis Garcia S.J., Archbishop of Cranganore (1641–59)*, (Analecta Gregoriana, 187, Sectio B, n.31) Gregorian University Press , Rome.

[10] See footnote 5.

[11] Paremakkel Thommakathanar, *Varthamanapusthakam*, 61; See also Antoney George Pattaparambil, *The Failed Rebellion of Syro-Malabar Christians: A Historiographical Analysis of the Contributions of Paulinus of St. Bartholomew*, Rome, 2007, pp 241–3. Quoting the letter of Fr.Paulinus of St. Bartholomew, he says that Mar Thoma VI while trying to get reunited with Catholic Church , secretly contacted the Jacobite Patriarch of Baghdad for assistance. Ibid., 243. We do not know whether it was actually true or a biased view of Paulinus, who worked almost as a leader of the European missionaries opposing the admission of Mar Thoma VI to Catholicism.

[12] Paremakkal Thomakathanar, *Varthamanapusthakam* (Malayalam), Janatha Books, Thevara ed. Thomas Moothedan (An English translation of the book was edited by Placid Podipara and published by Oriental Institute, Rome, 1971) (Ernakulam, 1977), 33.

besides seeking permission for admitting Mar Thoma VI to Catholicism. The delegation was taken from both the Catholic groups belonging to the *Padroado* administrative system and the Propaganda Fide administrative system and both the groups advanced money for travel.[13] In fact, the money needed for travel was raised from the members of the community by selling or pawning their jewellery and property;, however, due to the lack of sufficient funds, finally, only two delegates, Fr Thomas Paremakkal and Fr Joseph Kariyattil, decided to travel to Europe.[14] *Varthamanapusthakam* is an account of their travel to Europe, written by Fr Thomas Paremakkal.

Structure of the Book

Though the book consists chiefly of an account of a journey to Portugal and Rome, it gives detailed information about the socio-economic and political processes that they witnessed during the period from 1778 to 1786 at Tuticorin, Madras, Cape of Good Hope, Venguela, Bahia, Lisbon, Catalonia, Genoa, Liberno, Pisa and Rome.[15] There are seventy-eight chapters running into 363 pages; however, the travel narratives begins only from the seventeenth chapter. Each chapter has got two parts: (a) the first part is an account of everything that happened around them or what they heard or saw during their travel; and (b) the second part of each chapter consists of reflections on their observations. The second part is titled 'thoughts or reflections' and forms, invariably, an assessment and evaluation of personalities, events and institutions that the author describes in the first part of every chapter.

The content of the book gives the impression that it was written to justify everything that they had done in Portugal and Rome to defend the cause of the community and in that sense, it meant instant circulation and reading by the members of the community.[16] The original Malayalam manuscript of the

[13] Ibid., 126.

[14] The delegation consisted initially of twenty-two people; however, for want of sufficient funds to pay the ticket charges, only two, Joseph Kariyattil and Thomas Paremakkal (besides two seminarians), left for Europe. Ibid., 65.

[15] They left Madras on 14 October 1778 (Ibid., 68). In 1779, they crossed Cape of Good Hope and reached Venguela (Ibid., 102). In the same year, the delegation reached Bahia in Brazil and Lisbon in Portugal (Ibid., 109, 118–119).

[16] This is evident from the fact that on several occasions, the author says that he is narrating the developments so that the members of the community may know of it. Thomakathanar, *Varthamanapusthakam*, 134.

book was obtained from the descendants of Thachil Mathu Tharakan, who was the principal trader for the Travancoreans and the English in Trivandrum in the second half of the eighteenth century and who had actually borne the major share of their travel expenses.[17] Though it was printed for the first time in 1936, copies of the manuscript were being made and circulated even before that year.[18] Joseph Kariyattil and Thomas Paremakkal, who went to Portugal and Rome as priest delegates of the community, were not really dissidents of the church, even though they were highly critical of the European missionaries. They were very much a part of the church as Kariyattil was later made the Bishop of Cranganore in Portugal in 1783 and, on his death in 1786, Paremakkal became the governador of the diocese from 1786 till 1799.

Grievances and Anger

The tone of the book is set in the very first page of the narrative, where the author depicts the way the St Thomas Christians were humiliated before the large crowd assembled for the burial of Bishop Florentius of Verapoly in 1773. The bishop actually belonged to the ecclesiastical administrative system of Propaganda Fide and most of the St Thomas Christians who went for the funeral of the bishop were from the jurisdiction of the *Padroado* administrative system. On seeing them, the provincial superior of the Carmelites came out to them and said: 'What business have you got here? Your bishop is in Porcad. This is our bishop and his burial is not something that matters you…Hence I want that you better leave the place and allow us to bury our bishop.'[19]

The author and the members of the community were deeply pained by these words and equally by the denial of a chance to participate in the funeral rituals of

[17] Ibid., 18–19.

[18] There were at least four copies of *Varthamanapusthakam* in circulation in the 1970s. One, prepared by Fr Ouseph Vezhaparambil in 1898; the second one was transcribed by the Carmelites of Mary Immaculate (CMI) priests in 1902; and the third one was made by Fr Mathai Paremakkal in 1903. However, the copy with the Tharakan family is considered to be the original work of Fr Thomas Paremakkal. See Ibid., 17. The first printing of this work was done in 1936 by Plathottathil Luka Mathai. However, the printing from the original was done in 1977 by Janatha books, Thevara. Nevertheless, an English translation of the book was already published by Placid Podipara from the Oriental Institute of Rome, in 1971.

[19] Ibid., 27–28; but later, the missionaries sent an envoy expressing their regret for having sent out the St Thomas Christians from the funeral of the bishop and they were ready to do penance for it. Ibid., 33–34.

the bishop for the simple reason that they belonged to a different administrative organ of the same Catholic Church.[20] The community immediately called for a general meeting of the *mahayogam*, consisting of representatives from seventy-two churches in 1773.[21] Despite the attempts of the European missionaries of Verapoly to prevent the St Thomas Christian representatives from coming together,[22] a large number of priests and community members assembled at Angamaly. The representatives came with rice and food materials, while the local Christians of Angamaly gave salt, oil and firewood to them for cooking their food, as the meeting lasted for several days. Seeing the unprecedented flow of people to Angamaly, the missionaries of Verapoly sent their own spies to keep track of the deliberations taking place in the meeting.[23]

The initial tempo of the meeting was dominated by spiritual readings, speeches, prayers and meditation, which were later followed by vociferous outbursts of emotions.[24] The mood began to change with the enumeration of different types of discriminations and injustices that the St Thomas Christian community had to face from the European missionaries.[25] The representatives from Edappilly narrated how the European missionaries put their parish priest to death. Paremakkal writes:

> On the feast-day of Theresa of Avila there was a forty-hour adoration at Verapoly. Fr. Jacob Puthenpurackal, the parish priest of Edappilly church also went for the adoration and returned to his parish church along with other people. The European Carmelite missionaries forgot to lock the church after dinner and on the next day the gold monstrance was found to be missing. Suspecting Fr. Jacob to be the thief, he was taken by force to Verapoly by the missionaries and was denied food for several days. He fell ill and died. His last request before death for communion too was denied. He was also denied a church burial, as his body was wrapped in a mat and buried near a pond.[26]

[20] Ibid., 27–28.

[21] Ibid., 185.

[22] Ibid., 30.

[23] Ibid., 30, 33. After the beginning of the *yogam*, three European missionaries came to Angamaly to keep track of the situation and they were secretly put up in the presbyteral house by the supporters of the European missionaries.

[24] Ibid., 31, 34.

[25] Ibid., 28–29.

[26] Ibid., 36–38. For having killed Fr Jacob, the Travancorean government later punished two European missionaries, namely, Fr John and Fr Paulinus.

Citing the incident, Paremakkal says that this happened because of the 'helplessness of the people of Malankara (Kerala)' and 'the might and power of the missionaries and their bishop'.[27] He refers to this incident repeatedly in his travelogue, whenever he felt that the missionaries were obstructing the moves of the St Thomas Christian delegation in Europe.

The *yogam* also discussed the arrogance of the European missionaries and the lead roles that they always wanted to appropriate in churches. One among them was the case of festal processions in the churches, in which the European missionaries used to lead the procession without allowing the indigenous priests to take the lead with monstrance or cross, even if the latter were the celebrants.[28] With the discussions of the *yogam* turning out to be highly anti-missionary in nature, the representatives of the European missionaries in the *yogam* finally agreed for a compromise, accepting many of the demands of the St Thomas Christians, and the agreement between the two came to be called '*Angamaly Padiyola*'.[29]

Paremakkal says that the European missionaries gave little value to this agreement, as Fr John de Santa Margarita, one of the missionary signatories of the document, himself arrested Fr Vargese Panachikal from Malayattoor church at midnight for having taken the cross to lead the festal procession. Paremakkal writes: 'Fr. Varghese Panachickal was arrested and tied to a cot and was beaten by the Vadukas employed by the missionaries and was then carried by force to Verapoly, which was the seat of the Carmelite missionaries in Kerala'.[30] Paremakkal also refers to the strong resistance that the community of St Thomas Christians staged against Fr Santa Margarita for the atrocities committed against Fr Panachickal. The St Thomas Christians, in retaliation to this, prevented Fr Santa Margarita from entering the church of Parur to celebrate Holy Mass.[31] Paremakkal congratulates the *yogam* for having taken such a bold decision against the erring missionaries and views that the abuses of European missionaries could be checked only by strengthening the power of the *yogam*.[32]

Meanwhile, the indigenous bishop, Mar Thoma VI, of the non-Catholic faction of St Thomas Christians, who was opposed and sidelined by the West Syriac Jacobite Bishop, Mar Gregorios, and his allies in Kerala like

---

[27] Ibid., 38–39.

[28] Ibid., 41.

[29] Ibid., 42

[30] Ibid., 42–43, 54.

[31] Ibid., 54–55.

[32] Ibid.

Kattumangattu Rabban, wanted to be reunited with Catholic Church along with 80,000 of his followers.[33] However, the missionaries refused to accept him to Catholicism saying that his intentions were not genuine and his emissary was vehemently abused and humiliated.[34] On hearing about the abuses that the European missionaries showered on the emissary, Kallarackal Tharakan, Paremakkal writes:

> If a white carpenter or a cobbler comes before them (missionaries) they receive these guests with respect and offer them chairs, while the emissary from the bishop was humiliated and abused and this is happening because of the helplessness of our community and because of the might and evil of the European missionaries.[35]

The author empathizes with the community and translates its feelings of helplessness and emotions of anger into his travelogue, which are later developed as a significant layer of his narrative with certain arguments for indigenization.

Against the Abuses of European Missionaries

Paremakkal vehemently attacks the European missionaries for their high-handedness. The missionaries who are frequently attacked in his travelogue are the Carmelite missionaries working under Propaganda Fide. However, they were not monolithic in composition; they had different layers. Most of them were from Italy, as a result of which they were not obedient to bishops and authorities from other nationalities, as it happened in 1775, when the Italian missionaries refused to collaborate with the new German bishop appointed by Propaganda Fide. As the bishop, Francis de Sales, was a non-Italian, the Carmelite missionaries started writing denigrating and slanderous letters about the bishop to Rome. Since the bishop was not of their choice, they wanted him to leave Kerala. The bishop sought the help of Fr Joseph Kariyattil who was a Professor in the seminary at Alengad, narrating in tears the injustice being done to him by the Carmelite missionaries. On the initiative of Fr Joseph Kariyattil and Thachil Mathu Tharakan, who had by this time become the principal trader for the Travancorean ruler and the English, the St Thomas

---

33 Ibid., 125.

34 Ibid., 61.

35 Ibid.

Christians took him in a solemn procession to Alengad.[36] However, later, the missionaries of Verapoly complained about it to the Diwan of Travancore who, siding with the missionaries, punished the St Thomas Christians with a fine of 12,000 *kalipanams*.[37] Not desiring to antagonize the missionaries any further, the German bishop, Francis de Sales, did not divulge the truth, which resulted in the St Thomas Christians being forced to pay the fine. Commenting on the huge amount of money that the community had to pay as fine because of the missionaries, Paremakkal says: '…the drum gets the beatings while the drummer gets the money…we pay the money while they are there only to occupy positions; they alight from the palanquins, while we are there to carry it…'.[38]

On another occasion, in the same mood, Paremakkal writes that, for all the blunders that the European missionaries committed in Kerala, the St Thomas Christians had to pay the penalty. Thus, he says that the church of Malayattoor had to pay a fine to the local ruler for a European missionary priest who released a robber arrested by the local ruler. On another occasion, a missionary priest kicked a faithful (Koonan Varkey) in the church while Bishop Francis de Sales was listening to the account of the church of Malyattoor and the St Thomas Christians were made to pay a fine for this atrocity as it was in their church.[39]

Later, when Joseph Kariyattil was made the Bishop of Cranganore in 1783 in Lisbon, a strong anti-Kariyattil lobby of the Carmelite missionaries complained against him saying that he would bring division within Kerala Christians. Paremakkal retaliates by saying:

> …it is you and your ancestors who brought division and conflicts to Kerala, which now nobody can solve…[40]…You take the hand of one to beat the other and take his hand to beat the first person. You make us fight among ourselves so that we may always remain subjugated to you.[41]…You divide the Christians of Malabar into *Mundukar*, converted Christians, *kuppayakar* and put them into different groups, and thus people of Malabar who form one flesh and one

[36] Ibid., 49–51.

[37] Ibid., 62–63.

[38] Ibid., 64.

[39] Ibid., 329. The church of Malayattoor had to pay a fine imposed by the local ruler for the release of a robber by a European missionary called Padre Clemis. Actually, he was tied there in the vicinity of the church by the local ruler on the feast day of Malayattoor church and for the arrogant behaviour of the missionary, the faithful had to pay the fine.

[40] Ibid., 327.

[41] Ibid., 315.

> blood are divided into different groups in such a way that nobody can ever rectify it.[42]

When Paremakkal saw that the Carmelite missionaries had complained against an Indian (Joseph Kariyattil) becoming a bishop for a diocese in Kerala, he criticizes them severely:

> if these European missionaries are coming to India to suffer for Christ, why did not they go to China or any other similar country. If they go there it is sure that they would get beatings and thrashes[43]...In India who is giving you the suffering, whether it is our king or whether it is from us. We the St. Thomas Christians and the kings respect you[44]...When you come to our church we and our yogams accept and respect you so much; but in turn you give back to us suffering, thrashings and atrocities and we used to bear it in the name of the Lord without complaining to anybody.[45]

However, these were not mere reflections confined to his travelogue. Joseph Kariyattil and Thomas Paremakkal made a representation to Pope on reaching Rome in 1780. In the representation, they requested the Pope to contact Propaganda Fide authorities and the General Superior of the Carmelite Order to ensure that the Carmelite missionaries behave properly when they reach Kerala.[46]

Criticizing the arrogance of the European missionaries, Paremakkal writes on another occasion:

> ...you wrongly think that you (European religious missionaries) are much nobler than us because when you come to our churches we stand with respect and obey you and carry you on palanquins and our priests and the people walk in procession before you and you wrongly think that we show respect and obeisance to you because we are less noble than you...We are showing this respect not because of the fact that we are less noble nor because of your superiority, but because we have learnt from our parents that the priests and religious teachers are to be respected and revered in the name of almighty God.[47]

---

[42] Ibid., 327–328.

[43] Ibid., 328.

[44] Ibid., 328–329.

[45] Ibid., 329–330.

[46] Ibid., 188.

[47] Ibid., 318–319.

Paremakkal and Kariyattil placed a request before the queen of Portugal that no European religious missionary should be sent as bishop to Kerala. Paremakkal says:

> ...because they never would send a good and God-fearing person to India... Moreover only those who would love to dominate over others would often depart from the European religious houses...Even if the religious priest is a good person we do not want him to be our Archbishop. Because just like a fish outside water, a religious priest outside the control of the senior priests of the religious congregation would find himself in utter confusion and danger...[48]

The antipathy towards European missionaries appears often as a strong strand in the travel narrative of Paremakkal. On their way back from Rome to Portugal, Joseph Kariyattil and Thomas Paremakkal stayed in a religious house, whose members asked their help for finding a place to do missionary work in India. Paremakkal looks at their request with his usual critical language:

> See how the European religious missionaries are coming to India for their own interests and those of their religious houses. Had it been for proclaiming the gospel of Jesus then why should they request for places for their religious house alone, why not for other religious houses, as well.[49]

The travelogue, in the form of indicating the various abuses and defects of individual European missionaries working not only in Kerala but also in other places, is eventually transformed into a literary mechanism for spreading anti-Europeanism among his readers in Kerala.

Indianness and Indian Alternatives

Paremakkal, who had also written a book titled *India for Indians* in the 1780s, is highly critical of the European domination over the St Thomas Christians. He feels that the head of the church should be from the same nationality. He writes:

> The foreign missionaries do not respect the feelings of the community, as it now does not have its own leader.[50] Earlier when it had its own leader, no foreign

[48] Ibid., 135–136.

[49] Ibid., 232–233.

[50] The reference is to *jathikkukarthaviyan* or Archdeacon. For details on the institution of Archdeacon, see Jacob Kollaparambil, *The Archdeacon of All India*, Kottayam: Catholic Bishop's House, 1972; Thekkedath, *The Troubled Days of Francis Garcia S.J.*

> missionary dared to do any injustice or evil to this community.[51] ...In Europe, in Italy, France, England and Portugal, the kings and ecclesiastical heads are made from their own nationality. Even the Christians under the Turks have got their own rulers and bishops. In Kerala too, except in the case of St. Thomas Christians, the leaders of different communities are from their own communities.[52]

His view is that the community gets power only if the leader comes from the same community.[53] He also stresses the fact that the community had lost its oneness and unity because it did not have its own leader from among the community members.[54]

Varthamanapusthakam gives the impression that Joseph Kariyattil and Thomas Paremakkal defended the cause of the reunion of Mar Thoma VI with the Catholic Church in the royal court of Lisbon and papal court of Rome for the purpose of having an Indian as the ecclesiastical head for the church in Kerala. Paremakkal perceives that the Propaganda refused to accept Bishop Mar Thoma VI to Catholicism because if he would become a Catholic, then the division of St Thomas Christians into Jacobites and Catholics and the division of Catholics into *Padroado* and Propaganda administrative jurisdictions would cease to exist as they would all accept him as the legitimate bishop and then, the vicar apostolic sent by Propaganda Fide would have no right to stay in Kerala and consequently, the Propaganda would lose its control and power over these Christians.[55] On another occasion, Paremakkal writes that acceptance of Mar Thoma VI to Catholicism was feared by the European missionaries because they thought that the presence of an Indian bishop in Kerala would reduce their power in Kerala.[56]

These delegates earnestly wanted Rome to give permission for accepting Mar Thoma VI to Catholicism. Paremakkal says that their request was not the words of two priests alone, it was the voice of seventy-two churches of Kerala.[57] He argues that the community of St Thomas Christians would make progress only if the person who rules it would be from the same community and nationality.[58]

---

[51] Thomakathanar, *Varthamanapusthakam*, 32.
[52] Ibid., 32–33.
[53] Ibid., 55.
[54] Ibid., 32.
[55] Ibid., 171.
[56] Ibid., 207.
[57] Ibid., 208.
[58] Ibid., 322.

Paremakkal opposes the European ecclesiastical structural formats and develops arguments for Indian alternatives for church administration not only due to anti-Europeanism but also from feelings of patriotism and nationalism. The discourse on nationalism is set against the background of ill-treatment that Paremakkal and his colleagues experienced from the European missionary priest of Veerapandianpattinam on their way to Madras in 1778. The missionary priest did not permit Joseph Kariyattil and Paremakkal to celebrate Holy Mass in the church of Veerapandianpattinam. On hearing this, the parishioners and the faithful were very sorry and later, came out to meet the St Thomas Christian delegation and said that the church actually belonged to them and not to the missionary and offered every possible help to the delegation. On this, Paremakkal writes in his book:

> ...these believers were sad not because they had known us, nor because we had done some good things to them – but because we all belong to one nationality; that is we are all Indians. It is this love for people of the same nationality that actually moved their hearts.[59]

Later, in 1780, Joseph Kariyattil entered into a long and heated debate with Monsignor Borgio, the Secretary of Propaganda Fide in Rome, to get the Indian bishop, Mar Thoma VI, reunited with Catholic Church. Towards the end of the discussion, Monsignor Borgio told Kariyattil that if a bishop from the same nationality is appointed over the St Thomas Christians (evidently referring to Mar Thoma VI), then who among the Propaganda missionaries would be able to stay there in Kerala and who would listen to them?[60]

Paremakkal is also highly critical about the one-man-centred or bishop-centred church administrative system that the European missionaries introduced in India. He is a staunch supporter of the democratic institution of *yogam* or *palliyogam* which formed an important ingredient in the church administration of St Thomas Christians. He projects *yogam* as the Indian alternative to church administration. The administration of the St Thomas Christians was carried out by *jathikkukarthaviyan* (community leader) in agreement with the *yogam* (the representative body of the community). This type of administration provided space for individual initiatives of the leader strengthened by the wisdom of the representatives. Moreover, such an administrative system accommodated the grassroots-level demands and aspirations of the members.

---

[59] Ibid., 71.

[60] Ibid., 171.

The *jathikkukarthaviyan*, however, could not act independently of the *yogam* or act against the *yogam*, as he was bound by the majority decision of the representative body. On another occasion, while replying to the complaints that the Carmelite missionary bishop of Cochin raised against Joseph Kariyattil, Paremakkal writes about the power of the *yogams*, the representative body of the community:

> ...Our churches were built not by you nor by your ancestors; nor did we sell ourselves nor our church people to you. If our *yogam*, is willing to accept you, we would accept. If our *yogams* do not want to accept you, you cannot forcefully make us accept you.[61]

Paremakkal is battering the Western notion of a single person exercising hegemonic control over the community, without allowing space for the voice of the community to be heard through their representatives. As a proud Indian, he is highly critical of the feelings of subjugation and subordination that the European missionaries attempted to construct among the St Thomas Christian community. He writes:

> Don't think that the two bottles of Mass wine and three quarter kilogram of wheat that you (European missionaries) supply to priests for making host for Mass would be sufficient to get the priests of St. Thomas Christians subjugated to you.[62] If we can sustain ourselves and our churches with our own efforts and with our hard work, we can raise money from our own efforts for the bread and wine for Mass[63]...Before your coming to Kerala, the church, the bishops and the priests were maintained not by your subsidy but with the donations that we and the yogam used to make.[64]

When Joseph Kariyattil was made the Bishop of Cranganore in 1783, Jose de Solidade, the Carmelite missionary Bishop of Cochin, sent a letter to Portugal saying that the two priests went to Rome on their own and that if Kariyattil would reach Kerala, there would be a lot of conflicts and tensions among the Christians, as the people of Kerala did not know how to rule, and moreover, Keralites would not submit themselves to a bishop of the same nationality.[65]

---

[61] Ibid., 331.

[62] Ibid., 324.

[63] Ibid.

[64] Ibid., 325.

[65] Ibid., 306.

This touched the pride of the author, who writes: '…you say that Keralites do not know how to rule…don't say that...our king (evidently referring to the king of Travancore) would not tolerate this, as he is also a Keralite'.[66]

Paremakkal then goes on to compare Joseph Kariyattil with Moses who liberated Israelites from the slavery of Egypt and says that Kariyattil will liberate the Kerala people (evidently referring to the St Thomas Christians) from the bondage of European missionaries.[67] He banks upon the power and authority of the representative body, the *yogam*, and further says that they did not go to Rome on their own, but because of the mission that *yogam* gave to them and that it is the *yogam* that sent them to Rome.[68]

Thus, though *Varthamanapusthakam* is a travelogue by its literary feature, it reflects the intensity of conflicts and dissent that arose among the St Thomas Christians in the third quarter of the eighteenth century. Paremakkal, representing the dissenting voices, puts them in black and white and adds them as a substantial layer of his narrative of travel. While attacking the paradigms of the European missionaries, Paremakkal attacks not from outside as a heretic or a schismatic, but writes from inside as an administrator of the church, both as a reformer suggesting Indian alternatives and as a patriot bringing Indianness to the domains of church. However, the words and the language of attack that Paremakkal uses against the European missionaries are sharper than those of critics and enemies of missionaries; moreover, it should be said that they flow from the fire of suffering that this community was made to undergo during the period of colonial interventions and cultural mutations. From the same fire of suffering and tribulations emerged his notions of nationalism and arguments for India to be handed over to Indians.

References

Bartholomeo, Paulinus. *India Orientalis Christiana*. Rome: Propaganda Press, 1796.

Costa, João Paulo Oliveira e. 'Os Portugueses e a Cristandade Siro-Malabar (1498–1530)', *Studia* 52 (1994): 121–178.

———. 'The Padroado and the Catholic Mission in Asia during the 17th Century'. In *Rivalry and Conflict: European Traders and Asian Trading Networks in the 16th and 17th Centuries*, edited by Ernst van Veen and Leonard Blusse, 71–88 (Leiden: CNWS Publications, 2005).

[66] Ibid., 321.

[67] Ibid., 301.

[68] Ibid., 306–309.

Cunha, João Teles e. 'De Diamper a Mattancherry: Caminhos e Encruzilhadas da Igreja Malabar e Catolica na India: Os Primeiros Tempos (1599–1624)', *Anais de Historia de Alem-Mar* V (2004): 283–368.

Dominic, C.D. 'The Latin Missions under the Jurisdiction of Propaganda (1637–1838)'. In *Christianity in India*, edited by H.C. Perumalil and E.R. Hambye, 102–128 (Alleppey: Prakasam Publications, 1972).

Hunt, W.S. *The Anglican Church in Travancore and Cochin 1816–1916* (Kottayam: C.M.S. Press, 1918).

Kollaparambil, Jacob. *The Archdeacon of All India* (Kottayam: Catholic Bishop's House, 1972).

Mathew, George. *Communal Road to a Secular Kerala* (New Delhi: Concept Publishing Company, 1989).

Mundadan, A.M. *History of Christianity in India,* Vol. I. (Bangalore: Church History Association of India, 1989).

Nair, Achuth Sankar S., ed. 'William Henry Horsley's Memoir of Travancore (1838): Earliest English Treatise on the History of Travancore'. *Journal of Kerala Studies* XXXI (2004): 1–66.

Pallippurathukkunnel, Thomas. *A Double Regime in the Malabar Church* (Alwaye: Pontifical Institute of Theology and Philosophy, 1982).

Panjikaran, Joseph C. 'Christianity in Malabar with Special Reference to the St. Thomas Christians of the Syro-Malabar Rite', *Orientalia* VI (1926): 89–136.

Pires, Tome. *A Suma Oriental de Tome Pires e o Livro de Francisco Rodrigues*. Edited by Armando Cortesão (Coimbra: Universidade de *Coimbra*, 1978).

Podipara, Placid. *The Thomas Christians* (Mumbai: St. Paul Publications, 1970).

Sa, Isabel dos Guimaraes. 'Ecclesiastical Structures and Religious Action'. In *Portuguese Oceanic Expansion, 1400–1800*, edited by Francisco Bethencourt and Diogo Ramada Curto, 255–80 (Cambridge: Cambridge University Press, 2007).

Thekkedath, Joseph. *The Troubled Days of Francis Garcia S.J., Archbishop of Cranganore (1641–59)* (Rome, 1972).

______. *History of Christianity,* Vol. II (Bangalore: Church History Association of India, 1988).

Thomakathanar, Paremakkal. *Varthamanapusthakam* (Malayalam). Edited by Thomas Moothedan (An English translation of the book was edited by Placid Podipara and published by Oriental Institute, Rome, 1971) (Ernakulam, 1977).

Tisserant, Eugene. *Eastern Christianity in India*. Translated by E.R. Hambye (Kolkata: Orient Longman, 1957).

Wicki, Josef, ed. *Documenta Indica, Vols VI and VII* (Roma: Institute of Historical Society, 1948).

CHAPTER

16

Devotion and Dissent in Narayana Guru

S. Omana

In the history of India, particularly of South India, we see the remarkable life and teachings of Narayana Guru. He confronted the course of history and shook the conscience of the very people who had been exercising the worst kind of social iniquity on the authority of an assumed caste superiority. He boldly encountered the orthodoxy and performed the miracle of arousing self-esteem among the downtrodden. Out of the clutches of an age-old custom, he brought out a new civilization, which is fighting for equality of opportunity and social justice in its own right even today.

Narayana Guru was one of the epoch-making seers of the modern era, who has dynamically effected a radical change in the social, moral and spiritual value–visions and behavioural patterns of his contemporaries in India.[1]

In this essay, an earnest attempt is made to focus on the originality and scientific validity of the Vedantic teachings of Narayana Guru, by examining how he looked at religious differences and casteism, exploring possibilities of impacting discourses on religion and caste, in order to animate processes to undermine religious feuds and caste prejudices. The Guru's religious and social reform activities were an outright application of his philosophy of 'Oneness of Consciousness' (according to Narayana Guru – the ultimate reality is *arivu* or consciousness). But this real causal force behind them is not observed by the historians and people of India. The Guru was a living example of his own highest

[1] S. Omana, *The Philosophy of Sree Narayana Guru* (Varkala: Narayana Gurukula, 1984), 6.

The Editor would like to thank Anna Verghese, her PhD student, for refining and fine tuning this essay.

ideal. So, before understanding his reform activities, a brief outline is being given of his life, the then social conditions of South India and his philosophy.

Caste in Kerala

During the days of Narayana Guru, caste differences were very rigid in Kerala. Hindus, Christians and Muslims lived almost as exclusive communities. Hindus had, among them, Brahmins and non-Brahmins. Even among the Brahmins, there were sharp divisions based on their linguistic origin. Non-Brahmins ranged from the most touchable to the least touchable. No rational sociological norm was implied in this classification. These castes evolved and crystallized in relation to hereditary trades and work opportunities. Caste in Kerala had nothing or very little to do with what is popularly known as the fourfold division of Brahmanas, Kshatriyas, Vaisyas and Sudras. Besides Brahmins, there were Nairs, Varriers, Pisharadis, Marars, etc. All of them enjoyed certain social privileges, which were not shared by the rest of the Hindu community. There was also a large community that acted as a buffer group between the touchables and the untouchables. They are known in Travancore as Ezhavas; in Cochin, Chovas; and in Malabar, Thiyas.[2] Then there came the poorest of the poor, who were real children of the soil – the *Bhūmiputrās*. They were branded as untouchables. Kuravas, Pulayas, Parayas and tribals; all have their own traditions reaching back to antiquity. Socially and economically, they were underprivileged. There was not only untouchability but also unseeability. It was into this dark chapter of Indian history that Narayana Guru came in the 1850s. He belonged to the Ezhava caste. The Guru once described the Ezhavas as an unrecognized seed in the garden of caste scruples.[3]

Narayana Guru was born on 14 September 1856 in Vayalvaram house at Chempazhanthy, 5 kilometres away from Thiruvananthapuram, the capital of Kerala. His father was Madan Asan and his mother was Kutty Amma. The Guru's parents called him 'Nanu'. He was a smart, handsome, witty child who was very perceptive about all that was happening around him. Even as a child, Nanu had a natural ingenuity in discerning right from wrong and the essential from the non-essential. When Nanu's parents kept fruits and sweetmeats for divine offerings (puja), he did not hesitate to partake of it before the puja was performed. When he was called to account for his action, his plea was that

[2] K.P. Padmanabha Menon, *History of Kerala,* Vol. III (Ernakulam: Government Press, 1933), 343.

[3] Ibid.

God would be happy if he made himself happy.[4] When Nanu's uncles were meticulous in enforcing the customary convention of untouchability, the child showed the silliness of it by running around and embracing all who were tabooed as untouchables.[5]

There is a touching story of Nanu's childhood in relation to injustice which also reveals his consistency in opposing injustice with passive spiritual force. One day, when Nanu was going to school along with the other village boys, a *sanyasin* with matted hair, clad in rags, was also on the road. The unusual look of the mendicant intrigued the mischievous imps. They started jeering and throwing stones at him. The *sanyasin* walked on as if he was not aware of what was happening. When Nanu saw this, he burst into tears. The *sanyasin* turned back and spotted Nanu walking behind him in tears. The kind mendicant asked Nanu why he was crying. Nanu said that he was crying because of his inability to stop the village urchins from pelting stones at such a good man. Hearing this, the *sanyasin* lifted the boy to his shoulders and brought him back to his parents. He blessed Nanu and said that he would one day become a great man (*mahātma*).[6] The incident narrated symbolizes hundreds of other acts of injustice against which Narayana Guru protested in his life. He always employed a passive dynamism whereby he brought the powers of the heavens to the earth to correct the ills of the world.[7]

Nanu had his primary education in the one-teacher school (Kudipallikudam) of Chempazhanthy Pillai, and his higher education in Sanskrit and Vedanta was under Kummanpilli Raman Pillai Asan at Cheruvannur Gurukulam in Karunagapally district. [8]After completing his studies, he started one-teacher schools in many places in Thiruvananthapuram for the so-called untouchables like Pulayas, Parayas and Kuravas. In his free time, he visited the houses of the low-caste people to teach them lessons of neatness and of prayer. At night, he devoted himself to self-discipline. He became more and more withdrawn from home and also from social gatherings. He left his home and wandered aimlessly. During the period he had his yogic training under Thycaud Iyer Swamikal. His thirst for enlightenment was increasing. He went

---

[4] K.K. Panikkar, *Sree Narayana Paramahamsan* (Alleppy: Vidyarambam, 1976), 76.

[5] K. Balarama Panikkar, *Sree Narayana Vijayam* (Thiruvananthapuram: M.M.S.B. Printers, 1974), 30.

[6] Sanoo M.K., Narayana Guruswami, Irinjalakuda, 1976, 42.

[7] Omana, *The Philosophy of Sree Narayana Guru*, 12.

[8] Nitya Chaitanya Yati, Guru. *The Life and Teachings of Narayana Guru*. U.P., 1995, 4.

to Marutvamalai, which is not far from Kanyakumari, and in a cave at the top of the hill, known as *Pillathadam*, he performed *thapa*s for years. How long he remained in the cave and how he managed to sustain himself physically can only be guessed at today. It is presumed that the Guru had his awakening during his solitary penance there. Of course, the Guru had the intuitive experience, vision of the ultimate reality. He became one with that reality. As he became an Advaita *darsi*, he spoke of his realization in poignant words in *Atmopadesa Satakam*, as noted next:

> A very waste land suddenly
> flooded by a river in spate thus come the sound
> that fills the ears and opens the eye of the one who is never distracted;
> such should be the experience of the seer par excellence.[9]

The great awakening was bestowed upon the Guru as an all-inclusive vision of unity. A man who saw the one Absolute that transcends the phenomenal may feel tempted to withdraw himself from the maddening crowd of humanity into the silence of a cloister. But Narayana Guru experienced the vision of unity in a very different manner. The immanent and all-pervading Absolute in its purest aspect is the blissful awareness of eternal existence. But it, very often, occurs to us as an ill-fed child, a crying mother, a downtrodden man in the street or a neglected member of an outcaste society. He decided to return to the world from which he had withdrawn to seek the mystery of life.

It was not possible for the Guru to return to the society all at once. He, therefore, chose to live in a thick jungle at Aruvipuram on the banks of Neyyar, 5 kilometres away from the township of Neyyattinkara. He spent a considerable time in a cave there till the news leaked out that a saint was living in the forest. Soon people rushed there with fruits and other offerings to the Guru and he became the centre of attraction. More and more devotees gathered for worship and it became necessary to have a temple for the visitors. In 1888, the Guru installed a *Sivalinga* for them. It was a landmark in the social and spiritual history of India. At that time, only the Brahmins had the right to install deities in temples. The Guru was neither a Brahmin nor a Sudra. He came from a community which was totally outside the fourfold *varnas*. In winding up the

---

[9] Narayana Guru. *Atmopadesa Satakam* (Varkala: Narayana Gurukula, 1960), verse 16, 124.

proceedings of this memorable day, the Guru proclaimed a message to the crowd:

> Devoid of dividing walls
> Of caste or race
> Or hatred of rival faith,
> We all live here
> In Brotherhood
> Such, know this place to be!
> This Model Foundation [10]

This message soon overflowed the limits of the province and spread its seed far and wide. Sree Narayana Dharma Paripalana (SNDP) Yogam was organized for the propagation of Sree Narayana Dharma in 1903.

In 1904, the Guru chose Varkala Sivagiri, a coastal suburb of Quilon, as the next centre of his public activity. Here, the Guru founded an ashram and consecrated two temples (Shiva and Sarada Devi). The one dedicated to Sarada (Devi) in 1912 is distinguished by exquisite architecture, as also by the simplicity in the construction and in the form of worship maintained as per the instruction of the Guru. In Sivagiri Mutt, the Guru also founded an English school and an industrial school. It was here in Sivagiri that Rabindranath Tagore and Mahatma Gandhi visited Sree Narayana Guru. Later, Jawaharlal Nehru, Indira Gandhi, Rajiv Gandhi, K.R. Narayanan and Dr Abdul Kalam also visited Sivagiri Mutt. In 1912, the Guru founded an Advaita Ashram at Kaladi in Alwaye. And it was here that the Guru organized the Parliament of Religions in 1924. The Guru spent a great deal of his time in Sivagiri Mutt until his *mahasamadhi* in 1928. The Guru's Mahasamadhi Mandir is on the beautiful peak of Sivagiri. Many worship him as God. The beauty and serenity of the location impresses everybody and Sivagiri gradually got transformed into a place of pilgrimage, worship and meditation.

The Guru was a *vedantin*. Vedantic wisdom took shape originally in the Upanishads. A long line of masters redefined this wisdom, making it more precise, keeping in mind the exigencies of their times. Narayana Guru continued this tradition, restating and redefining Vedantic wisdom in line with the mindset of the Age of Science in which he lived. Hence, his philosophy is at once traditional and modern, scientific and religious, which makes it all comprehensive and universal.

---

[10] Nataraja Guru. 'The life and teachings of Narayana Guru', Fern Hill, East-West University (revised 1990), 24.

Guru's Concept of Religion

Narayana Guru's most important maxim is, 'Man is of One Caste, One Religion, and One God'.

Guru's concept of god is given in one of his most important works, entitled *Atmopadesa Satakam (One Hundred Verses of Self Instruction,* verses 44–49), which is known as Guru's critique of religion. According to Guru, all religions in their content are essentially seeking happiness; everyone seeks happiness for once. This is the one religion of the Guru (*eka matam*). The existing prominent religions were Judaism, Christianity, Islam, Hinduism and Sikhism. The founders of all religions were enlightened persons who have the intuitive experience of God. What they have seen and experienced is beyond words and certainly beyond the comprehension of a relativist vision. When these great masters disseminated the truths, their wisdom was misunderstood because the minds of the recipients were not so enlightened as those of their masters. As a result of this, feuds and conflicts arose among the followers of all masters. Guru says in his *Atmopadesa Satakam*:

> The many faiths have but one essence;
> not seeing this, in this world, like the blind men and the elephant,
> many kinds of reasoning are used by the unenlightened who become distressed;
> having seen this, without being disturbed, remain steadfast.[11]

Guru declared openly in this verse that the content of all religions is essentially one and the same. Those who argue for or against any particular religion are compared to the well-known story of a few blind men seeing an elephant. One religion becomes respectable and another despicable only because of the partial understanding that people have about religion.

It is not possible to defeat any religion through fighting, for every religion has, for its strength, at its core, the high value factor that makes of it a religion. So, fighting over religion results not in the destruction of the targeted religion, but only of the persons who fight. This is stated in Guru's verse 46, p.130:

> It is not possible to vanquish any religion by fighting it.
> By becoming competitive and fighting each other's
> religion, the adherence of the members of the persecuted
> religion only becomes increased in its fanatic zeal. By

[11] Ibid., verse 44, 130.

> promoting religious feuds one is only destroying his own integrity and succumbs to the evils of hatred. This should never be forgotten.[12]

Religions and the Overall Aim of Happiness

All religions when viewed horizontally as different from another in expression reveal many features that make for contrast. When we take a vertically inclusive or contemplative dialectical view of the same situation, the overall aim and end of all religions, however diverse, is none other than happiness in life, here, or hereafter or both. Verse 49 enunciates this unequivocally as follows:

> All beings, at all times, everywhere, are exerting themselves to attain happiness. This quest for happiness is the 'One Religion' in the world, of which no one has any dispute. Knowing this, one should restrain from being turned into any sin of fighting one's own fellow beings.[13]

Happiness, in other words, refers to a supreme human value in whose light all other motives are only secondary considerations or particular instances. Happiness as the aim of man gives unity to human purpose and brings all religions, faiths or creeds under its single sway.

The Guru not only presents here the happy prospect of one religion for all mankind in a scientific or public sense, but more pointedly than that, asks each man to adopt this attitude so that he could find peace of mind for himself and attain the goal of happiness. The one religion of mankind would thus be followed as night, the day or as a natural corollary to the common human goal of happiness as the highest of unitive human values. The Guru's well-known dictum, 'whichever the matam, it suffices if it betters man', is to be understood in this light.

All Religions Conference

In 1893, the First Parliament of Religions was held in Chicago. Swami Vivekananda was one of the delegates from India. The very first speech of Swami Vivekananda in the Parliament of Religions opened up the possibility

[12] Ibid., verse 46.

[13] Ibid., verse 49, 130.

of meaningful dialogue between the East and the West, and his persuasive logic was effective to make cracks in the walls of exclusiveness which kept one religion separated from another.

In 1923, thirty years after this epoch-making gathering of the world community in Chicago, Narayana Guru organized an 'All Religions Conference' in Alwaye. This was the first of its kind in India. The Guru's dream of the people of all the races and religions coming together to share the light of love and spiritual insight had thus become a reality. Though the conference did not catch world attention like the Parliament of Religions held in Chicago, it turned out to be a great seed of unity sown in the right soil at the right time.

At the entrance of the venue were written – specially directed by the Guru – the words, 'meant not for arguing and winning, but for knowing and letting known'. At the conclusion of this conference, the Guru decided to start an advanced study centre for religions at his own headquarters in the ashram at Sivagiri. The materialization of this wish actually took form as the East–West University of Brahmavidya, which is a part of the Narayana Gurukula movement.

Bhakti or Devotion

Bhakti or devotion is considered to be the best of all tools for god-realization. *Bhakti* is a word derived from the verb root *bhaj*, meaning 'to do service by sitting nearby' (*bhaj sevayam*). This sitting nearby, doing service, need not necessarily be a physical act. The more virtual rather than actual it is, the more is it sublime. The root also denotes to be seated nearby, to partake of something to mediate, to attain, to accept, to worship, none of which needs to be excluded from the sense of bhakti understood here.

Bhakti is defined as *parama–prema* in the *Narada Bhakti Sutras*, one of the best Indian treatises on *bhakti*. *Parama* means 'beyond, the Absolute, the supreme'. *Prema* means 'an intense uplifting love'. *Prema* should not be equated with the English word 'love', for more is implied here than that. *Bhakti*, therefore, is that *prema* or kind of love which is at once a yearning and an ecstasy of fulfilment; it is a search and a seeing; it is a holding on and a being held; it is a giving and a receiving. *Bhakti* is meditation on the Self. The Bhagavad Gita (111.17) underlines the truth that a man who is always interested in the Self and satisfied in it has nothing else to do.

Sri Shankara in the *Vivekachudamani* (verse 32) also says that *bhakti* is the meditation on the true form of one's Self. Narayana Guru also gives a high place to *bhakti* in his *Darsana Mala*, entitled 'Bhakti Darsanam' (Vision by

Contemplation).[14] *Bhakti* is defined as *atmanusandhana* (constant contemplative adoration of *atma*). And this *atma* is nothing but Brahman in essence. *Bhakti*, then, could also be defined as *Brahmanusandhana* (constant, contemplative adoration of Brahman).

Atma or Brahman is sought by a seeker aiming at happiness (*ananda*). Therefore, *bhakti* could be defined also as meditation on *ananda*. A real *bhakta* is one who is fully convinced of the oneness of *atma*, Brahman and *ananda*. He always remains filled with the feeling, 'I am *atma*', 'I am Brahman', 'I am *ananda*'. When seen as meditation on *ananda*, it does not exclude from its scope the adoration a husband has for his wife and vice versa, one's love for God, for one's guru, father, mother, king and the like.

In short, whatever it is that we love, the basic usage behind that feeling is our love for ourselves, the love for *atma*, a ceaseless urge in all beings. This self-love, instead of turning towards something external, could directly turn towards *atma* itself, towards the most lovable content of our own being, towards *paramatma*, and that is considered the best kind of *bhakti* called *para-bhakti*.

God-realization, which is conceived of in experiential terms, is portrayed by Guru in his *Janani Navaratna Manjari*.

> The ever appearing and ever disappearing experiences emerge first, and then they sway back and forth assuming the forms both of mind and matter. And thus the Real becomes darkened (as apparent forms) in a thousand ways, and then all of them roll back to their restful abode, finally to merge in its own splendour. Even philosophically perceiving thus is not wisdom. One should, instead, become a bee that gently falls into the honey-filled core of the lotus (God) and with its gentle murmur be there forever in the ecstasy of blissfulness.[15]

Congregation Prayer as a Pathway to God

Prayer is a religious observance and it is found in one way or the other in all religions. It prevails even in religions that do not admit the existence of God or souls. Even atheists and nihilists seem to have some sort of prayer like observances. In short, prayer is a psychological phenomenon that manifests in all humans, the religious as well as non-religious.

Prayer is the incessant effort made by the people to keep their will always attuned to the will of God. And *advaitin*, being a non-dualist, in reality needs no prayers, for in his perception, there is no duality between the supplicant

[14] Narayana Guru, *Darsana Mala* (Varkala: Narayana Gurukula, 1960), Chapter VIII.
[15] Narayana Guru, *Janani Navaratna Manjari* (Varkala: Narayana Gurukula, 1954), 3.

and perfection of wisdom. Still, he needs a prayer. Such a prayer should be a means to attain the highest of non-dualistic perception.[16] Though almost all the available prayers and hymns composed by the great masters are philosophically sound, such a one addressed to one God and not to any particular deity, such as Brahma, Vishnu, Shiva and so, on can hardly be found. Viewed from this perspective in the vast panorama of the spiritual literature of India, from the most modern age, it was the pen of Narayana Guru that blessed not only the Indian spiritual tradition in general, but also all with a philosophically profound prayer addressed directly to the one God.

We have seen that devotion is the best of all tools for realization. The realization that one gains by resorting to *bhakti* has five aspects. They are: (a) *saranagati*, surrendering oneself absolutely to the Divine; (b) *stuti*, praising god; (c) *dayana dheya pārasparya*, cultivating a bipolarity between the meditating person and that which is meditated upon, as, for instance, in the bipolarity between man and god; (d) *arthana*, praying making requests; and (e) the final one is *santi*, the peace that one gets by disciplining oneself this way.

Daiva Dasakam of Narayana Guru is a prayer which has all these five principles implied in it.[17] God is here recognized as one God, not as the god of any place or religion. That Absolute is related with everything that depends on the Supreme. This prayer begins with the word '*daivam*' which means, 'Oh, God'. It ends with the word '*sukham*', which means 'happiness'. Literally, the word *daivam* means 'light', the light of lights. The aim of all religions is to attain happiness. This prayer is for the seeking of happiness. The means for gaining happiness is by turning to God. That God is described here as means and end. When end and means are unitively recognized and understood, it is called yoga. In that sense, this prayer is a prayer of yoga.

In the heart of this prayer, we can find the secret of unitive understanding. The Guru addresses the God as, 'you are truth, knowledge and happiness'. Further, the identity of the person who prays and to the Supreme to which the prayer is implied; if properly considered; is none but you. Thus, this is a prayer of non-dual wisdom. When we critically examine it, it will become evident that this is a prayer which is philosophically sound, emotionally rich and scientifically structured. This prayer was composed by the Guru keeping in mind his close devotees and disciples. Nowadays, in the morning and evening hours, one can hear this prayer being recited in many homes in South India.

---

[16] Narayana Prasad, Guru Muni, *The Philosophy of Narayana Guru* (Varkala: Narayana Gurukula, 2003), 222.

[17] Narayana Guru, *Daiva Dasakam* (Varkala: Narayana Gurukula, 1961).

Jnana Karma Samanvaya

Narayana Guru was a *jnānin*, a wisdom teacher par excellence. Yet, he was not totally against rituals. In every human civilization in the world, we can observe some symbolic actions that prevail. Such actions of symbolic significance are called rites. Every ritualistic action thus has something sublime to convey to us. Rediscovering this wisdom, we realize the significance of rituals and their necessity. The *Chandogya Upanishad* puts forth an attempt, in an elaborate way, to recover the forgotten wisdom and significance of the simple rite of *udgita* –chanting that forms part of the ritual known as *Somayaga*. The Upanishad, by accomplishing this, unfolds the entire spectrum of the highest wisdom known as *Brahma-vidya* or *Atma-vidya*.

Bhagavad Gita also recommends the integration of karma and *jnana* to attain the goal. Narayana Guru has the same attitude towards rituals. The Guru revisualized fire sacrifice, for which he composed a new mantra, entitled *Homa Mantra*. In this work, the Guru shows how karma could be made use of as a means for imparting wisdom, by the harmony of karma and *jnana*, a means that will be called *jnana karma samanvaya*.

The revisualization and revaluation of the very ancient ritual of fire sacrifice which forms part of the Vedic culture is accomplished by Narayana Guru in this work. Ritualism is not altogether ruled out in the present work which is to be chanted while performing the sacrifice. The Guru admits it and shows that each element of the ritual helps to lead to the highest realm of non-dual wisdom. This perception also reveals a philosophical understanding that life and day-to-day values become inseparably one.

Temples as Gateways to the Knowledge of Non-duality

Temples are considered as mediums through which devotees approach the godhead, which cannot be otherwise comprehended or grasped directly as we do with the world around us. When we worship at a temple, we temporarily step out of the limitations of worldly life and try to have glimpses of transcendental reality. The deity, which is the object of devotion and worship, guides the devotees in their pious life. Thus, temples bring devotees close to the divine.

The deity installed in a temple is not just meant for worshipping and asking for favours. Every deity in his/her perception is a visual means that helps the suppliant to attain the non-dual experience. The deity installed in a temple is a symbol. A symbol is a known idol representing the unknown idol. The symbol helps the supplicant to reach the higher spirituality. The art of god symbolism helps both the literate and illiterate. The illiterate derives at least some idea of the supreme truth through the symbols which help him/her to maintaintheir ancient culture and heritage. As for the literate, the understanding of the inner significance of the symbols establishes a greater conviction of the truth that they represent.

Illumination in the hearts of the devotees was Guru's concept about the purpose of the temple. A notable change is reflected in Narayana Guru's attitude towards idol worship. He wanted to elevate man to god, to sublimate idolatry to the pure level of abstract values, to lead the stem of devotion to the bondless ocean of Brahman, the changeless and imperishable, '*Tat Tvam Asi*' and '*Aham Brahmasmi*'.

In the perception of Guru, temples are not merely the places of worship. They are also there to serve as the focal point for the cultural advantage of the localities concerned. Each temple should have an open area for people to get together formally and informally to discuss matters of higher values. This is to be supported by the addition of a library attached to the temple. Narayana Guru installed various deities such as Shiva, Devi, Subramanya in temples and composed hymns in praise of them. His installing many gods does not mean that he admits to more than one god. The Guru sees many gods as representatives of the one Brahman or *arivu*.

A number of temples in Kerala and a few in Tamil Nadu and Karnataka were founded by the Guru. Some scholars of his time who were influenced by the Arya Samaj of Dayananda Saraswati even suspected that the Guru was in favour of idolatry. Some others thought of Narayana Guru as a Hindu revivalist wanting to protect the masses from being converted to Christianity and Islam. In fact, all these are mistaken notions. He was always willing to give his guidance and blessings when people wanted to walk in the right direction. The temples governed by orthodox theocrats were inaccessible to most of the working-class people. Even though their offerings in money and kind were always accepted, such shameless exploitation of the poor by their superiors in caste needed to be met with in a telling manner. The answer lay in the founding of counter temples, which were open to all irrespective of caste or religion. Narayana Guru thought that if temples were the culprit in subjecting these people to such oppression and misery, he must use the very same temple to resurrect the people from these miseries.

Guru brought about certain specific reforms in connection with the consecration of the new temples. Guru consecrated higher gods in the newly founded temples in the place of the lower ones. In those days, the *avarna*s were allowed to worship only inferior local deities like Chathan, Maruta and

Yakshi. Their offerings were also crude items like meat, fish, liquor and other intoxicating drinks, and also animal sacrifices like goat, cock and so on. They were not allowed to make sober offerings like flowers, fruits and delicious food items as the caste Hindus. This was certainly an instrument to keep their morale at a lower level. Narayana Guru stopped all these crude offerings and animal sacrifices. He appointed *sanyasin*s and young men trained at Sivagiri Mutt as priests of the new temples, instead of the traditional Brahmin priests. Thus, he showed that birth as a Brahmin is not a necessary qualification to function as a priest.

Narayana Guru proclaimed that all had equal right to enter any place of worship and they had the right to enjoy the resources of religious literature, which were monopolized by the caste Hindus. In the Vidikamadam of the Sivagiri Mutt and the Sanskrit school of Alwaye ashram, all were admitted as students irrespective of caste or religion. Even Muslims and Christian students studied there. In his ashram, Guru taught Vedas and Upanishads to the so-called untouchables. The Guru instructed that temples should be kept clean and should be beautiful places where the people should come with clean bodies and minds. Most of the temples built under his supervision had good gardens, libraries, industrial schools and Sanskrit schools. Some of the temples set models for constructing schools and colleges, for example, Poonthotta temple and Muthakunnam temple founded by the Guru in Ernakulam district.

Guru advised his disciples to build new temples in a simple and less expensive way so that the energy and money could be utilized for useful purposes. He made changes in the form of offerings also. Any ritual that will make the premises dirty was prohibited. The rituals prescribed by the Guru were simple enough for the common people to follow. The Sarada temple was consecrated by the Guru in 1912 at Sivagiri Mutt and was built in an octagonal pattern. This was essentially different from the other traditional patterns of temple architecture in Kerala. He advised that no money should be spent for elaborate festivals, especially for its pomp and paying for the burning of fire crackers.

Sarada Mutt at Sivagiri was installed by Narayana Guru on his own desire and initiative. The deity installed was Sarada, goddess of wisdom and learning, bearing testimony to the importance Guru gave to knowledge. Thereafter, at one stage, he publicly declared that people needed more schools than temples. Even the temple concept of the Guru was becoming more and more sublime, making him bold enough to install a mirror with the letters 'Aum' etched therein, in the place of an idol, or even a lighted lamp. All these reflect Guru's concern for leading people towards the light of wisdom with temple worship simply as a means. The hymns composed by him also do the same.

Eighty-five temples were consecrated by the Guru. They may be classified into Shiva temples, Devi temples, Subramanya temples, Vinayaka temples and the temples in which, in the place of idol, a mirror with the letters 'Aum' etched therein or a lighted lamp was placed. The first one was the Shiva temple at Aruvippuram in Thiruvananthapuram district. From Rameswaram to Kailas, there are thousands of temples dedicated to Shiva but Narayana Guru picked up a stone from the river Neyyar and installed it on a pedestal with a silent prayer. This *Sivalinga* is more talked about than the *Sivalinga* of Rameswaram, installed by Sri Rama himself. It is probable that the caste tradition was not so rigid in the days of Rama so that no Brahmin questioned the right of a Kshatriya to install a *Sivalinga*. The Guru was very particular that the temples he founded were all to be on spots of great scenic beauty. Such a place is Aruvippuram. The Guru knew how temples would become instrumental in changing the lifestyle of people, for example, the regular temple goers become cleaner in their habits. Once in Trichur, the editor of a progressive journal asked the Guru about his attitude towards temples. The Guru said that a clean temple situated in a hygienic place with water and fresh air would inspire people to come and spend their time in prayer and meditation. An open place dedicated to God is free of parochial feelings. It can be a good stepping stone for a more serious search into the higher values of life. The editor asked him if it was good to propitiate stone image. In reply, the Guru said, 'When a man goes to a temple, he is only thinking of God and not of stone images. They are confused only if people like you ask them to look for stone images. Nobody worships stone.'[18] Pointing to the newly built temple at Trichur, the Guru continued, 'Make good gardens around temples and plant trees around'.[19] In every temple, there should be a good library and arrangements for teaching the fundamentals of living a virtuous life. A well-conceived temple will be of great help to the public. The Guru knew in his mind that the *Sivalinga* he installed was only a stone. In the tenth verse of the 'Astya Dersana' of *Darsana Mala*, the Guru writes:

> One (alone) is real, not a second
> What is unreal indeed seems as being real
> The Sivalinga is stone itself not a second made by the mason [20]

[18] Parameswaran P., *Sree Narayana Guru Swamikal,* (Calicut: 1971), 121.

[19] Ibid., 122.

[20] Narayana Guru, *Darsana Mala*, Chapter 3, verse 10.

The Shiva in the *Sivalinga* is projected on it by the devotee. The image serves the purpose of the language of iconography. This is true of all the idols of Subramanya, Devi, Vinayaka and even the lighted lamps installed in temples. Side by side with the religious reforms, Narayana Guru worked incessantly for social reforms. The social problems were mainly two: first, caste-based social prejudices; second, prevalence of certain social customs that were impoverishing those who were already poor.

Narayana Guru's Concept of Caste

Casteism: Varna and Jati

Casteism is a perplexing social phenomenon peculiar to India, having some parallels with the racism practised in some other parts of the world. Whatever its origins may be, the undeniable fact is that the senseless caste system and its discriminations existed, and continue to exist, as a social reality.

Varna is yet another word understood as much related to, and often mixed up with, *jati*. *Varna*, literally meaning 'colour', is purely a psycho-local factor, not of any sociological bearing. It shows the mental nature of each individual person. It means the characteristic traits of individual beings. Such personal traits are classified in the Bhagavad Gita as four – Brahmana, Kshatriya, Vaisya, Sudra – and are admitted as pertaining to the Absolute, meaning it is just part of *prakriti*. One has to be fully aware of what kind of person one is to enable oneself to live a happy life in which one gets maximum opportunity to give expression to one's characteristic personal traits, and thus find the joy of actualizing oneself. The distinguishing marks of each *varna* are fully described in the last chapter of the Gita. The varna concept of the Gita thus does not have anything to do with any social hierarchical order .[21] *Varna* gained the status of social stratification later, especially after the advent of the epics, Puranas and *smriti*s. *Manu Smriti* is wherein *varna* distinction gains a fully social dimension, causing much confusion, and is mixed up later with *jati*.

Caste discrimination forbids marriage between people of different caste groups, and their cooking and dining together. Those of the lower caste were not to enter the houses of the upper-caste people. Untouchability and unseeability was prevalent. Economically, those of the higher strata owned all landed properties and the others had to be satisfied with being labourers, mainly in agriculture.

[21] Narayana Prasad, *The Philosophy of Narayana Guru*, 103.

Guru's enlightenment that everything is but one *atma* became manifested and it could not tolerate any social discrimination among humans whether based on caste, religions, race or any other consideration. In his *Jati Lakshana (Kind Defined)* and *Jati Mimamsa* or *Critique of Caste*, Narayana Guru states there was actually no difference between man and man. Caste distinctions have no basis in actuality. Subjected to the most drastic of scientific tests, *homo sapiens* falls within the human species. Castes such as Brahmin and Pariah have no reality; man should realize his true humanity and unitive solidarity, and realize also that terms like 'Brahmin' and 'Pariah' are ideas superimposed on this reality, that is, human nature which is essentially one and fundamentally the same.

In the fifth verse of his critique of caste, the Guru quotes the example of Parasara and Vyasa to reveal to all that the saintly characters, Parasara and Vyasa, who are recognized everywhere as ancestors of holy cherished memory and worshiped as such by all castes in every home in the Hindu world, are themselves outstanding reminders that mere prejudices lingers around the notion of caste, since they come from much absurd and misunderstood Pariah line and not from the Brahmin stock at all; hence, here is the ultimate contradiction to be faced of the Brahmin not only accepting and adopting the Pariah guru but putting him on the topmost pedestal as a sage of supreme value from the Vedic point of view. In the contradictory absurdity thus proved, all caste prejudices based on heredity, dynasty and blind tradition must be dispelled, and the social atmosphere of the present, ultimately and finally, be cleared of this major caste impediment.[22]

All caste prejudices have ignorance and selfishness for their basis. Identity with such caste, which is born due of ignorance, is to be given up by becoming enlightened about our one and only identity, our natural and real identity, with one *atma*. Human beings in no way are of different kinds, but are of one self-fraternity (*atam sahodarar*). Proclaiming this eternal and unquestioned truth, Narayana Guru said: 'Those discerned differently as that person or this person, when given thought to, are revealed to be one primeval self alone appearing in various forms'.[23]

Of these different appearances of one's Self, none is superior or inferior to another. No one desires to do anything harmful to oneself. Seeing oneself alone in everything brings about a total change in the mode of one's activities. What one does for one's own happiness naturally ensures the happiness of

---

[22] Narayana Guru, *Jati Mimamsa* (Varkala: Narayana Gurukula, 1954), verse 5.

[23] Narayana Guru, *Atmopadesa Satakam*, verse 24, 125.

all else, for the others are not different from oneself in essence. Guru points out how realization of oneness of the Self becomes reflected in actual life as follows: 'Whatever is performed for the sake of one's happiness should be for the happiness of others as well'.[24] Thus, Narayana Guru's notion of dharma was founded on strong ethical foundations.

The Guru's Directives

The Guru directed his followers to ignore *jati* conscientiously. Hence, he gave the directive, 'Do not ask caste, do not tell caste, do not think caste'. He visualized a slow and steady educational process for this, including doing away with reference to caste in official records.

Inter-dining and Inter-caste Marriages

There are three main sources of traditional customs. One is symbolic customs, like rituals, which are often introduced with a view to enlighten the public on the need to find their oneness with nature. Such customs or rituals become part of the social system.

There are three kinds of customs; first, symbolic customs to enlighten the public; second, customs required to stabilize the society, And, third, there are certain religious practices that are simply meant to show the extravagance which the rich can afford. Such practices, psychologically, make the poor also follow them at the cost of making themselves poorer. In course of time, such customs got mixed up, making it impossible to discern which were meaningful and purposeful and which were otherwise. As a result, people took them as necessary for the upkeep of social integrity.

At the time of Narayana Guru, there were three ancient customs among the *avarna*s which were causing decay in their social life. They were *talikettu* (child marriage), *thirandukuli* (a puberty festival for girls) and *pulikudi* (a festivity associated with the first pregnancy). Narayana Guru opposed celebrating these customs because they were very expensive at times and had no religious value attached to them at all.

Talikettu was a costly festival connected with marriage of girls, at various ages, from one to nine. If a girl was not married according to the customary practice, her parents had to bear the reproaches of their neighbours and faced exclusion from social privileges, such as attending feasts of marriage

---

[24] Ibid, verse 22, 125.

celebrations and the social gathering attached to it. The whole *talikettu* celebrations lasted for about a week. The bridegroom, who married a girl in infancy, usually did not live with her afterwards. The actual marriage ceremony usually took place after the girl attained puberty.

Thirandukuli was a bathing ceremony held at puberty, so that all might know that a girl had reached puberty. *Pulikudi* was drinking of a juice when a woman became pregnant for the first time after her marriage. These age-old ceremonies were expensive because they had to be conducted in such a way that, often, poor families sold their properties so that they could successfully celebrate these ceremonies.

Narayana Guru enlightened the people as to the meaninglessness of these practices and discouraged them from extravagant spending of wealth. He did, of course, encourage all healthy and educational practices. His enlightened conviction made him bold enough to declare such things openly in public. And the people, in return, could not but abide by his authoritative directives. He, on the strength of his wisdom and holistic perception of life, served as a catalyst for a total change in the perception and practices of the people at large, particularly of the lowest stratum of society.

Narayana Guru propagated his message of reform through the help of his close associates and the SNDP Yogam. Abolition of alcoholic drink is another subject which always attracted Narayana Guru's attention. The evils of drink, such as drunkenness, violence, loss of work and money wasted, were harming the lower castes. The Guru attacked this evil habit incessantly throughout his life. In 1921, Guru proclaimed a message: 'Liquor is poison. It should not be manufactured, should not be given to others or used by oneself. The tapper's body stinks, his clothes stink, his house stinks; whatever he touches stinks'.[25]

Narayana Guru proposed three essential steps for social progress, namely, organization, education and industrial development. The Guru thought of the necessity of an organization for the propagation of his teachings and for the eradication of the evil social customs prevalent in the society. It was with this intention that SNDP Yogam was organized and registered in 1903.

Guru believed that only through education could people imbibe the right perspective about a good life. A study of his concept of education reveals that it was aimed at realization of certain objectives, such as freedom of the individual, occupational mobility, equality of status, of opportunity and general progress.

---

[25] Parameswaran, P., *Sree Narayana Guru Swamikal* (Calicut, 1971), 130.

He emphasized the necessity of English education, Sanskrit education and industrial education. The Guru himself started an English school and a Vedic school at Sivagiri Mutt and a Sanskrit school in Alwaye ashram. He exhorted the rich to provide for the education of poor children who had an aptitude for learning. He encouraged students to go abroad for advanced study. He also advocated equal educational opportunities for women. The Guru called upon the rich to start schools for the weaker sections.

Economic development was another major concern of Narayana Guru. He inspired his followers to start small-scale industries. The Guru also inspired them to organize agro-industrial exhibitions all over Kerala to enable the people, especially the *avarna*s, to learn about the technological progress and its impact on production. Thus, the Guru's reforms were directed towards the emancipation of the totality of the human life, of the body, mind and spirit.

Sree Narayana Dharma Paripalana Yogam

The SNDP Yogam was founded and registered on 28 March 1903 (M. E. 1078 Dhanu 23) . Narayana Guru was the President of the Yogam for life; Kumaran Asan was the first secretary of the Yogam. The constitution and by-law of the SNDP Yogam were read out to the Guru by the general secretary. The Guru objected to the definition of the word 'community' (*samudayam*) that was given in the constitution. It was limited to those communities known as Ezhava, Tiya, Billava and Nadar. He wanted it to be changed into the community of the human family. His followers thought it was not pragmatically feasible to have such a global basis for their organization.

The Yogam engaged itself in the laudable efforts of eradicating untouchability and voicing the fundamental human rights of the working class. These efforts actually paved the way for many of the Guru's followers to later accept the Marxian interpretation of socialism as their most acceptable ideal. Under the aegis of Dr Palpu, Kumaran Asan, T.K. Madhavan, C.V. Kunjiraman, Mulur Padmanabha Panicker, K. Ayyappan and others, several drastic changes were brought about in the social structure and texture of the Kerala community. The role Narayana Guru played was only of catalyst and not as a fighter in the frontlines. To others, he set an example by his own personal life. His great dignity and sense of oneness with mankind did not allow him to give vent to anger or protest against any particular person or community. He believed that there was only one caste for man and that was humanity. In this, he was uncompromising. The Yogam grew very fast. It still remains as a large and very influential social organization in the state. Now, it has its branches all over India and a few branches outside India.

Sree Narayana Dharma Sangham

Narayana Guru was not very happy with the way in which his disciples were conducting their life mission. He would not accept anything less than a world community of the human family. He hated the very idea of caste and man's adherence to such a totally irrational social prejudice and psychic colourization, so he decided to trust the materialization of his teachings in the hands of his *sanyasin* disciples who came from all classes and communities and included even Westerners. This newly organized institution of *sanyasin*s was called Sree Narayana Dharma Sangham. The Sangham was registered in Thrichur on 11 January 1928. After the registration of the Dharma Sangham, the Guru instituted a will and a testament by which all the ashramas, *mutt*s and temples founded by the Guru were transferred to the care and custody and administration of the Dharma Sangham. The Guru nominated Swamy Bodananda to be his successor and Nataraja Guru to be the advisor of the Dharma Sangham.

Narayana Gurukula

The only organization that works as an international movement is the Narayana Gurukula, founded by Nataraja Guru – a direct disciple and spiritual successor of Narayana Guru – in 1923 at Fernhill, Nilgiris, with the blessings of the Guru. The Gurukula has expanded its function by founding the East–West University, a unique educational movement which is very much more a university of people anywhere than one managed by a group of people somewhere. After Narayana Guru's *samadhi*, Guru Nithya Chaithanya Yati was the head of the Gurukula. The present head of the Gurukula is Guru Muni Narayana Prasad. The main Gurukula centres are in India, Singapore, Malaysia, Fiji, Australia, Europe and America.

Another powerful expression of Narayana Guru's call for one world came through the sacrifices of the world citizen, Garry Davis.[26] The World Service Authority and the world government for world citizens, now having bases in Washington, London, Paris and Basel, are gaining momentum as a refuge for the stateless people of the world.

---

[26] Garry Davis, *My Country is the World* (London: McDonald, 1962), 29–30.

The gesture of truth can be simple and yet its message can triumphantly go over the frontiers of time and space. Jesus broke the five loaves of bread and two fish given by a willing donor and fed the multitude. To every Christian, this has become a source of inspiration and a model of sharing irrespective of the meagreness of one's resource. Mahatma Gandhi walked to the seashore and processed an ounce of salt from the saline water of the ocean to prove to the British imperialists that the right of man to share the bounty of nature cannot be stifled by anybody's gun. Even so, Narayana Guru picked up a rolling stone, licked into shape by the stormy river at Aruvipuram, and placed it on an altar to prove to the conceited world of crafty priesthood that there is no need for a middle man for the common folks to see the luminous manifest in whichever medium they choose. When Narayana Guru's prerogative was questioned by the traditionalists, his protest and chastisement of orthodoxy came in the form of gentle humour. He said that he did not install a Namboothiri Siva. The latest echoes of the challenge and response thus initiated in Aruvipuram were recently heard when the United Nations confronted the World Service Authority, which is founded on Narayana Guru's maxim of 'One mankind; one common interest and one country', for issuing World Passports to identify half a million stateless people who are pushed around mostly in African countries. When those who sit on the highest seat of justice asked world citizen, Garry Davis, to show his mandate to issue World Passports, he said that the passport was only a plea of one man to his fellow men to be the caretakers of their brothers and sisters. In these days of bickering and spite that are ever growing between man and man in the name of caste, colour, language, race, nationality, political ideology and sex, there is a challenge to man wherever he turns to reclaim the solidarity of the one human family, for which Narayana Guru raised his voice and lived in the eloquent science of his dedication. Hence, there is no doubt that the future of Narayana Guru's philosophy is not a matter of conjecture but is an assured fact that is proving itself by the earnest effort of every man who spontaneously aspires to peace, justice and human welfare.

The Bhagavad Gita closes with the verse 78 of chapter 18:

> Where there is Krishna, the Lord of Yoga, where there is Partha (Arjuna) the Archer, there (will be) prosperity, victory, progress and well-established justice: such is my (Samjaya's) belief.

In the same way, we also say: 'Where there is reprisal of human freedom, the denial of man's natural right for justice and the need for man to overcome force for the realization of his higher values, the wisdom of Narayana Guru will always shine as a clear light and it will be an inspiration for ever'.[27] Such is our belief.

References

Parameswaran P., *Sree Narayana Guru Swamikal* (Calicut, 1971), 121.

Nataraja Guru. 'The life and teachings of Narayana Guru', Fern Hill, East-West University (revised 1990) 24

Sanoo M.K., Narayana Guruswami, Irinjalakuda, 1976.

Balarama Panikkar, K. *Sree Narayana Vijayam*. Thiruvananthapuram: M.M.S.B. Printers, 1974, 30.

Davis, Garry. *My Country is the World* (London: McDonald, 1962), 29–30.

Narayana Guru. *Atmopadesa Satakam* (Varkala: Narayana Gurukula, 1960).

______. *Daiva Dasakam* (Varkala: Narayana Gurukula, 1961).

______. *Darsana Mala* (Varkala: Narayana Gurukula, 1960).

______. *Jati Mimamsa* (Varkala: Narayana Gurukula, 1954).

______. *Jati Mimamsa* (Varkala: Narayana Gurukula, 1954). The critique of caste is another name for Jati Mimamsa, verse 5, 177.

______. *Jununi Nuvuratna Manjari*. Varkala: Narayana Gurukula, 1954 verse 3, 93.

Narayana Prasad, Guru Muni. *The Philosophy of Narayana Guru* (Varkala: Narayana Gurukula, 2003).

Nitya Chaitanya Yati, Guru. *The Psychology of Darsanamala* (Varkala: Narayana Gurkula, 1987, 6)

Nitya Chaitanya Yati, Guru. *The Life and Teachings of Narayana Guru* (U.P., 1995), 4.

Omana, S. *The Philosophy of Sree Narayana Guru* (Varkala: Narayana Gurukula, 1984), 12.

Padmanabha Menon, K.P. *History of Kerala*, Vol. III (Ernakulam: Government Press, 1933, 343.

Panikkar, K.K. *Sree Narayana Paramahamsan* (Alleppy: Vidyarambam, 1976), 343.

---

[27] Nataraja Guru, The Bhagavad Gita: Trans and Commentary, (New Delhi: RK Publishing, 1973), 712.

CHAPTER

17

Sree Narayana Guru's Idioms of the Spiritual and the Worldly

Udaya Kumar

Devotion and dissent, the two principal ideas around which this volume is organized, seem at first sight to indicate opposite attitudes: while the former brings to mind pictures of loyalty and voluntary submission, the latter points to contrasting images of disagreement and opposition. However, on a closer look, the difference may not be so stark; both these postures denote forms of agency, for devotion too is positive action for the subject even though acts of devotion can often be self-effacing. The word 'agency' in English, interestingly, contains a sense of these contrarieties: although derived from the Latin word *agere* which means 'to act' and used often in the sense of a full capacity for action, the word 'agent' in ordinary usage often refers to contexts where the subject acts on behalf of someone else, under an authority that is located outside. Agency does not always point to autonomous and full originators of actions; agents are more accurately described as authorized performers – and not necessarily authors – of actions. This brings questions of authority to the centre of the very conception of agency. The juxtaposition of devotion and dissent as genres of action enable not only a deeper understanding of devotional practice but also a re-evaluation of the nature of agency that finds its expression in acts of dissent. The diverse registers of spiritual and communitarian practice in Sree Narayana Guru's life and writings insistently foreground an interplay between these tropes.

Sree Narayana's published writings consist mostly of devotional or spiritual–metaphysical poems. In addition to these, he also authored a rather small corpus of poems, instructional writings and messages, as well as a few prose texts. These writings have come to us surrounded by a dense thicket of discourses –

biographical accounts, stories about Sree Narayana's extraordinary powers as a spiritual practitioner and anecdotes that testify to his acerbic, at times almost dark, humour. Sree Narayana Guru's writings, however, pose some difficulties for the contemporary, historically inclined reader. It is not always easy to see in his philosophical or religious compositions, the historical signature that their author has come to acquire: the originality and innovativeness of his anti-caste initiatives do not always find a direct textual correlate with his writings. Although Sree Narayana's texts are marked by a profound engagement with reflective and poetic traditions in Sanskrit and Tamil, his philosophical arguments or devotional idioms do not always directly display dramatic individual departures from his predecessors or contemporaries. Is his originality then to be found in the unusual conjunction of his authorship with his lower-caste origins? Is dissent then external to the content of his metaphysical and devotional writings, rather to be seen in the adoption of postures and discourses of devotion not permitted to him by virtue of his caste status? When do such unauthorized performances acquire the status of new subjectivities? This brief chapter has the modest aim of indicating these lines of inquiry in the form of a postscript to the longer, more detailed discussion of Sree Narayana's work in this volume by S. Omana (Chapter 16).

The scholarship on Sree Narayana's metaphysical writings has predominantly identified him as a thinker in the Advaita Vedanta tradition. This is clearly borne out by the arguments he proposed in texts such as *Atmopadesastakam*, *Darsanamala* and *Advaitadeepika*. From the perspective of a critical history of thought, it may be rewarding to consider this characterization as a point of departure rather than arrival in inquiring into the singularity of Sree Narayanan's interventions. The nineteenth century saw a wide range of thinkers from different parts of India invoke Advaita arguments, not only in metaphysical inquiries but also in new formulations about worldly life and social initiatives. These figures displayed a wide range of stances in their interventions in the specific contexts of their life and thought, and an excessive emphasis on their doctrinal consistency with a single line of philosophical thought may limit our understanding of what was new and distinctive about each of them. Their singularity is to be found not in their adherence to philosophical doctrines derived from tradition but in the way they invoke and re-cite these in order to make new discursive moves. This does not mean that the reference to doctrines is instrumental or strategic, external to the aims they are made to serve; the repetition of doctrines by these thinkers involves difference and creativity, which may be recognized only inadequately by a logic of sameness. Doctrines from tradition acquire new lives and forms when they authorize unprecedented statements and actions within the space and time of worldly life.

Sree Narayana's complex relationship to cosmopolitan and vernacular idioms of thought and articulation is symptomatically manifest in several anecdotes surrounding his life. Gandhi visited him in Sivagiri in March 1925 and wished to converse with him without the aid of interpreters. When asked whether he could speak English, Sree Narayana is said to have replied in the negative and proposed Sanskrit as an alternative medium – Gandhi declined this offer due to his inadequate command over the language.[1] However, in discussions with Brahmin scholars opposed to the Guru's move to establish a temple in Tellicherry, Guru insisted – in spite of his disciple Kumaran Asan's readiness to engage them in debate in Sanskrit – that the debates be conducted in Malayalam.[2] During the First World War, he famously urged his devotees to pray for the success of the English: 'they are our *gurus*,' he said, 'it is they who gave us *sanyas*', referring to the Brahmanical interdiction against lower castes engaging in spiritual practice.[3] These stories give us a glimpse into the Guru's complex sense of location in his discursive and practical initiatives.

Sree Narayana's compositions span three languages: Sanskrit, Tamil and Malayalam. He received his early education in the Tamil and Sanskrit traditions. It is difficult to make easy connections between Sanskrit learning and Brahmanism in the context within which Narayana Guru grew up. K. Muthulakshmi, in a recent study, has highlighted a long-standing tradition of non-Brahmanical participation in Sanskrit scholarship in Kerala, probably owing its origins to the largely forgotten history of Buddhism in the region.[4] Narayana Guru received Sanskrit education from Kummanpilli Raman Pillai Asan (1845–1911), a well-known Nayar instructor at Varanappally. The story of Narayana Guru's literary and philosophical apprenticeship is not fully known. The compositions attributed to his early years show the strong influence of the Tamil *siddhar*s and poets from the Shaivite traditions. This was probably not uncommon at that time, as Raman Pillai Asan's own compositions included

[1] M.K. Sanu, *Narayanaguruswamy* (Kottayam: Sahitya Pravartaka Cooperative Society, 1976 [reprint, 1986]), 439.

[2] J. Reghu, 'Kshetranirmana Prasthanathinte Pratidharmikata' (The Counter-ethics of the Temple Construction Movement), *Madhyamam Weekly*, 12 March 2004, 44.

[3] Sanu, *Narayanaguruswamy*, 306.

[4] K. Muthulakshmi, 'Samskrtapadanam Keralathil: Sangharshavum Samanvayavum', in *Samskarapadanam: Charitram, Siddhantam, Prayogam*, ed. Malayala Padana Sangham, (Kalady: Malayala Padana Sangham, 2007) 306–328.

not only *Prabodhachandrodayam* and *Dasakumaracharitasamgraham* but also *Pattanathupillayar Pattu*. T. Bhaskaran, in his commentary on Sree Narayanan's writings, has drawn attention to the influence of Shaiva Siddhanta thought and the writings of the Tamil *siddhar*s.[5]

These connections may be profitably understood in the context of Sree Narayanan's close association with Chattampi Swamikal, Thycaud Ayya and the spiritual traditions in Southern Travancore towards the end of the nineteenth century. Guru had his yogic training under Thycaud Ayyaswamikal. Ayya and Chattampi Swamikal, and scholars such as Professor P. Sundaram Pillai, were part of a group called 'Jnanaprajagaram', organized around Pettayil Raman Pillai Asan in Trivandrum, to discuss philosophy, literature and spiritual matters.[6]

Narayana Guru appears to have known many of these figures. Thycaud Ayya was a disciple of Vaikundaswamy or Ayya Vaikuntanathar from Tirunelvelli, a spiritual leader with a millenarian, egalitarian vision.[7] Both Vaikundaswamy and Ayya came from strands of anti-Brahmanical lower-caste spiritual practices in Tamil Nadu. These thinkers drew upon and contributed to a Tamil tradition of thought which combined elements from Advaita Vedanta with Shaiva Siddhanta and the practice of the *siddhar*s. There are several stories of Sree Narayana's travels in southern Tamil Nadu and his interaction with practitioners of this strand. Chattampi Swamikal's writings, ranging from explications of Advaita Vedanta in *Advaitachintapaddhati* and *Nijanandavilasam* to contributions to non-Brahmanical Dravidian thought in *Pracinamalayalam*, *Vedadhikaranirupanam* and *Adibhasha*, also show a close familiarity with the

---

5 *Sreenarayanaguruvinte Sampurnakritikal* (Sree Narayana Guru's Complete Works), ed. T. Bhaskaran (Calicut: Mathrubhumi, 1995).

6 R.Raman Nair and L. Sulochana Devi, eds., *Chattampi Swami: An Intellectual Biography* (Trivandrum: Centre for South Indian Studies, 2010), 65–66.

7 For a discussion on Ayya Vaikuntanathar, see M.S.S. Pandian, 'Meanings of Colonialism and Nationalism: An Essay on Vaikundaswamy Cult', *Studies in History* 8 (1992), 167–85; G. Patrick, *Religion and Subaltern Agency: A Case-study of Ayya-Vali, A Subaltern Religious Phenomenon in Southern Travancore* (Chennai: Department of Christian Studies, University of Madras, 2003); and P. Sundaram Swamikal and K. Ponnumani, *Ayya Vaikuntanathar (Jeevacharitram)* (Ayya Vaikuntanathar: A Biography) (Kanyakumari: Ayya Vaikuntanathar Siddhasramam, 2001). An account of Thycaud Ayya's life may be found in *Brahmasree Thykkattu Ayyaswamikal (Jeevacharitram)* (Thycaud Ayyaswamikal: A Biography), Revised Edition (Thiruvananthapuram: Sri Ayya Mission, 1997[1960]).

Vedantic and the Tamil Siddha traditions.[8] In the light of these connections, it might be useful to see Sree Narayana's thought and writings in their relationship to a vernacular context of spiritual initiatives in Southern Travancore in his times. This may help in understanding the transactions between his metaphysical writings and his practical social initiatives in complex, locally situated interconnectedness. It is important to see Sree Narayana's instructions to his followers, conversations and anecdotes – all of them deeply embedded in a sense of context – as an essential part of his thought.

Gandhi's conversation with Sree Narayana Guru in 1925 gives us an insight into the relations between spiritual and social life in the Guru's thought. In response to Gandhi's enquiry whether he permitted religious conversion, Sree Narayana replied: 'It is often seen that those who convert to other religions are able to obtain freedom. Seeing this, it becomes difficult to criticize people for speaking in favour of religious conversion.'[9] Gandhi probed further: 'Do you consider the Hindu religion sufficient for the attainment of spiritual liberation (*adhyatmikamayamoksham*)?' 'Other religions too possess paths for liberation (*mokshamargam*),' replied the Guru. 'Let us leave aside other religions. Is it your view that the Hindu religion is adequate for the attainment of *moksha*?' 'For attaining spiritual liberation, the Hindu religion is amply adequate. However, it is worldly liberty (*laukikamayaswatantryam*) that people desire more.[1]'

The two conceptions of freedom, spiritual and worldly, and their mutual linkage, remained an important concern in Sree Narayanan's thinking. He wrote a short note by way of an instructional message at the founding of the Sivagiri Muth; this was published under the title 'Advaita Jeevitam'.[10] Sree Narayanan began by highlighting well-being or *sukham* as that which is desired by all human beings. The human soul yearns for eternal, spiritual well-being rather than that of a transient, sensory nature. Sree Narayanan made an interesting move in the argument here by introducing a worldly, social dimension and stressing the impact of internal reforms of communities on the attainment of this objective.

For a community to achieve prosperity of all sorts – related to the body, the mind and the soul – the religious and moral rectitude of its members could

[8] See, for a discussion on Chattampi Swamikal's engagement with Vedanta and Shaiva Siddhanta, Pandit C. Ramakrishnan Nair, 'Chattampi Swamikalum Thrithapada-sampradayavum', in *Sree Chattampi Swami Satabdismaraka Grantham* (Kollam: Sreeramavilasam Press, 1953), 70–71.

[9] Sanu, *Narayanaguruswamy*, 440.

[10] 'Advaita Jeevitam', in *Sreenarayanaguruvinte Sampurnakritikal*, 1.

be a source of great help. Temples and places of worship may be useful for developing these qualities in everyone within the community. However, the economic prosperity of the community's members is equally essential. For this, we need to reform agriculture, trade and technical education, among other things.

The move from temples and worship to agriculture, trade and technical education anticipates the convergence stated in the concluding lines of the note:

> The worldly and the spiritual are not two separate things. In reality, both work with the same aim. The body enjoys well-being thanks to the harmonious functioning of all its parts. Similarly, the harmonious functioning of various spiritual and worldly arrangements is necessary for the human community to attain its ultimate goal of well-being.[11]

The passage moves from the individual to the community and then, to the human species. The spiritual practices of the individual are considered as analogous to the worldly, social reform initiatives of communities, and both these find their final elaboration in the idea of the human community, which is no less than the entire species considered as a community. Well-being or *sukham* is understood as arising from the harmonious working of parts within a whole, and the model for such accord is the human body. The body and worldly life figure prominently – not as a subordinate element, but as an equal partner and even as a model and figure – in this description of non-dualistic life. The human body is an important presence in Sree Narayana's devotional and metaphysical writings. The body is a site of complex ambivalence in these texts: it appears negatively as a sign of sensual attachment and mortality; and positively as opening a path to true knowledge and as a site of self-practices. Metaphors and arguments are drawn from diverse philosophical traditions – Advaita, Shaiva Siddhanta and Buddhism – to produce this complex invocation of the body.[12]

Sree Narayanan used the image of the human body not only in his devotional and metaphysical compositions; they performed an important role in his arguments on worldly life and human collectivities. Sree Narayanan's writings on caste, such as 'Jatinirnayam' and 'Jatilakshanam', proposed a redefinition of

---

[11] 'Advaita Jeevitam', *Sreenarayanaguruv Sampurnakritikal*, 1.

[12] See, for a more detailed discussion on these arguments, Udaya Kumar, 'Self, Body and Inner Sense: Some Observations on Sree Narayana Guru and Kumaran Asan', *Studies in History* 13(2) (1997), 247–270.

caste as human species.[13] Relying on the etymological connection between the word *jati* and the idea of birth, Narayanan argued that beings that can reproduce together belong to the same *jati*. The fact that two individuals from different castes like Chandala and Brahmin can procreate together demonstrates that these castes are false categories; the only true caste is *manushyajati*, or the caste of all human beings. This argument is also found in some Buddhist and Tamil Siddha texts.[14] *Jati* is identified here with the human species, and the individual human body with its reproductive capacity, and its necessary presupposition of other human bodies, is the privileged visible sign of this.

The body in this sense signifies a minimal threshold for the human, freed from historical and cultural ascriptions. At the same time, it is also a site of worldly inhabitation in the sense that it necessarily orients the individual to other species members and to collective endeavours. *Samudayam* or community may be seen as the principal site of collective efforts. In Sree Narayanan's writings and pronouncements, *samudayam* functions in contrast to collectivities grounded in ascribed caste identities: thus, Ezhava *jati* is a false denomination; the discourse of *samudayam* may address the same individuals, but as potential members of a group engaged in voluntary collective efforts. Communities have their specific locational and historical conditions, including ascribed identities, as their starting point; however, the ultimate orientation of the concept *samudayam* is towards the *manushyasamudayam* or that collectivity which is grounded in our belonging to the human species. This seems to be the sense in which 'human community' appears towards the end of *Advaitajeevitam*.

Collective worldly efforts, in this conception, are compelled to negotiate tensions between their particular conditions and universalizing aspirations. Sree Narayana Guru's interventions, pronouncements and decisions in the context of collective efforts give us some fascinating insights into the specific, contextual character of these negotiations. He strongly opposed the identification of Ezhava as a caste category, and even the use of 'Ezhava' as a name for the community. The word 'Ezhava' was considered as referring to the place of origin of the community, in accordance to the belief that Ezhavas came to Kerala from Ceylon. The Guru felt that even if this were true, since the community has been in Kerala for centuries, an appellation like 'Malayali' would be more appropriate.[15] At the same time, the early issues of *Vivekodayam* record some

---

[13] See 'Jatinirnayam' and 'Jatilakshanam', in *Sreenarayanaguruvinte Sampurnakritikal*, 496–500 and 501–506, respectively.

[14] See Kumar, 'Self, Body and Inner Sense', 257.

[15] M.K.Sanu,Narayanaguruswamy (Kottayam: Sahitya Pravarthaka Co-operative Society, 1976, reprint. 1986), 431.

decisions by the Guru in community matters, which indicate a conception of the *samudayam* involving sharply defined borders. In relation to some Ezhavas who converted to Christianity but pretended in public that they were still Hindus, the Guru is reported to have recommended that 'believers in other religions should not be allowed to attend the functions of the caste (*jati*), and that if they renounce in writing their new religions then there is no objection to their participation'.[16] Similarly, in response to a question concerning a woman who had intimate contact (*samsargam*) with a man from another religion, Sree Narayana is reported to have ordered that

> the woman should be made an outcaste, depending on the seriousness of the evidence of the contact. On the basis of a penalty commensurate with her fault, she may also be pardoned and purified. The money paid as penalty should be kept as common property.[17]

It is difficult to determine with certainty the authorship of these decisions: we do not know whether they were made solely by Sree Narayana Guru or by larger organizational structures, and what procedures were adopted in decision making. It is also difficult to assess whether the penalties prescribed were aimed at punishing transgression or finding some acceptable means for facilitating reintegration. The more prominent thrust in Sree Narayana's discourse on the community was to redefine its identity and to alter its inherited features; exclusion and purification were also invoked as instruments for this transformation. Sree Narayana rejected toddy tapping, an occupation associated with the ascribed caste identity of the Ezhavas, as dirty, and suggested that toddy tappers should be expelled from the community and reinstated after purification if they gave up this occupation.[18]

Several statements ascribed to Sree Narayana in anecdotes and conversations recounted by his followers show the Guru's cheerful distrust of fixed identities and his ironic disregard for rigid prescriptions of 'proper' practice. This can be seen in his efforts to open the places of worship he founded to everyone, including those from Dalit castes, sometimes in the face of opposition from orthodox Ezhava followers. As for religious identity, Sree Narayana gave a literal interpretation of the Malayalam word for religion, '*matham*', as opinion

---

[16] "Christian Ezhavar" [Christian Ezhavas], *Vivekodayam*, 1(2) (1905), 41.

[17] "Oru Samsaya Nivritti" [The Resolution of a Doubt], *Vivekodayam*, 1(2) (1905), 41.

[18] Sanu, *Narayanaguruswamy*, 540.

or belief, and argued that this is subject to constant transformation in all thinking individuals.[19] He also felt that if several different schools of thought could be placed under the rubric of the Hindu religion, it should be possible to consider Christianity, Islam, Hinduism, Buddhism and other faiths as belonging to one religion. Both these lines of thought saw fixed religious identities as an invalid ground for differentiation. However, the reformed rituals Sree Narayana instituted often rejected the vernacular deities and spirits traditionally worshipped by the Ezhavas in favour of more 'mainstream' Hindu deities like Shiva, Subrahmanya and Devi.[20] The temples he founded were dedicated to these deities, but at times he also abandoned idols altogether in favour of lamps or mirrors as the principal objects of worship within the sanctum. He stated that he had founded temples in response to the desire of some Hindus and that he was prepared to found places of worship for Christian and Muslim communities too if they so wished.[21]

Sree Narayana's legacy compels a rich conception of the transactions between the spiritual and the worldly domains. While the philosophical doctrines in his metaphysical writings no doubt provide intelligible grounds and authorizing sources for his unorthodox worldly initiatives, the latter merit study on their own in their diversity and complexity as an integral part of his thought. A move beyond familiar distinctions between doctrines and practices is essential for understanding Sree Narayana Guru's singularity in the history of devotion and dissent in Kerala.

References

Balakrishnan, P.K., ed. *Narayanaguru* (Trichur: Kerala Sahitya Akademi, 2000 [1954]).

Brahmasree Thykkattu Ayyaswamikal (Jeevacharitram) (Thycaud Ayyaswamikal: A Biography), Revised Edition (Thiruvananthapuram: Sri Ayya Mission, 1997 [1960]).

---

[19] P.K. Balakrishnan, ed., *Narayanaguru* (Trichur: Kerala Sahitya Akademi, 2000 [1954]), 172–173.

[20] See, for a detailed discussion, Roby Rajan and J. Reghu, 'Backwater Universalism: An Intercommunal Tale of Being and Becoming', in *Political Hinduism: The Religious Imagination in Public Spheres*, ed. Vinay Lal (New Delhi: Oxford University Press, 2009), 66–67.

[21] *Desabhimani*, 15 July 1916, cited in C.R. Kesavan Vaidyar, *Sree Narayana Guruvum Kumaran Asanum* (Sree Narayana Guru and Kumaran Asan) (Kottayam: Current Books, 1993), 6.

Kumar, Udaya. 'Self, Body and Inner Sense: Some Observations on Sree Narayana Guru and Kumaran Asan', *Studies in History* 13, no. 2 (1997), 247–270.

Muthulakshmi, K. 'Samskrtapadanam Keralathil: Sangharshavum Samanvayavum', in *Samskarapadanam: Charitram, Siddhantam, Prayogam*, edited by Malayala Padana Sangham (Kalady: Malayala Padana Sangham, 2007), 306–328.

Nair, Pandit C. Ramakrishnan. 'Chattampi Swamikalum Thrithapada-sampradayavum', in *Sree Chattampi Swami Satabdismaraka Grantham* (Kollam: Sreeramavilasam Press, 1953), 68–75.

Pandian, M.S.S. 'Meanings of Colonialism and Nationalism: An Essay on Vaikundaswamy Cult', *Studies in History* 8(2) (1992), 167–185.

Patrick, G. *Religion and Subaltern Agency: A Case-study of Ayya-Vali, A Subaltern Religious Phenomenon in Southern Travancore* (Chennai: Department of Christian Studies, University of Madras), 2003.

Rajan Roby and J. Reghu. 'Backwater Universalism: An Intercommunal Tale of Being and Becoming', in *Political Hinduism: The Religious Imagination in Public Spheres*, edited by Vinay Lal (New Delhi: Oxford University Press, 2009), 58–95.

Reghu, J. 'Kshetranirmana Prasthanathinte Pratidharmikata' (The Counter-ethics of the Temple Construction Movement), *Madhyamam Weekly*, 12 March 2004, 42–46.

Sanu, M.K. *Narayanaguruswamy* (Kottayam: Sahitya Pravartaka Cooperative Society, 1976 [reprint, 1986]).

Sreenarayanaguruvinte Sampurnakritikal (Sree Narayana Guru's Complete Works). Edited by T. Bhaskaran (Calicut: Mathrubhumi, 1995).

Swamikal, P. Sundaram and K. Ponnumani. *Ayya Vaikuntanathar (Jeevacharitram)* (Ayya Vaikuntanathar: A Biography) (Kanyakumari: Ayya Vaikuntanathar Siddhasramam, 2001).

Vaidyar, C.R. Kesavan. *Sree Narayana Guruvum Kumaran Asanum* (Sree Narayana Guru and Kumaran Asan) (Kottayam: Current Books, 1993).

Vivekodayam 1(2) (1905).

Contributors

Raziuddin Aquil is Associate Professor in the Department of History, University of Delhi. His research interests include Sufism and the making of Islam in the Indian subcontinent. He has extensively published on Islamic religious movements, literary and historical traditions, comparative historiography and political culture in medieval and early modern India. His publications include: *Sufism, Culture, and Politics: Afghans and Islam in Medieval North India*; *In the Name of Allah: Understanding Islam and Indian History*; *Sufism and Society in Medieval India* (OUP Debates in Indian History Series) and *History in the Vernacular*, co-edited with Partha Chatterji. 'Beloved of Allah: The Chishti Sufis of the Delhi Sultanate', is under preparation.

Sumanta Banerjee is a researcher in social history and commentator on current political developments, based in Dehradun. His publications include: *In the Wake of Naxalbari* (2010); *The Wicked City: Crime and Punishment in Colonial Calcutta* (2008); *Logic in a Popular Form: Essays on Popular Religion in Bengal* (2002); and *The Parlour and the Streets: Elite and Popular Culture in Nineteenth Century Calcutta* (1989). He is, at present, a Fellow in the IIAS, Shimla.

Ranjeeta Dutta teaches at the Department of History and Culture, Jamia Millia Islamia. Her specialization is religion and society in pre-colonial South India. She was a Fellow at the Indian Institute of Advanced Studies (IIAS), Shimla, from 2009 to 2011. She has published articles on pilgrimage, community identities, textual tradition and hagiographies. She has also co-edited a book with R.P. Bahuguna and Farhat Nasreen, *Negotiating Religion: Perspectives from Indian History* (New Delhi: Manohar, 2012).

G. Gispert-Sauch S. J. is Professor Emeritus at Vidyajyoti College of Theology, Delhi. Born in 1930 in Catalonia, Spain, and sent to India by the Society of Jesus in 1949, Professor George Gispert-Sauch has been teaching theology and interreligious dialogue at the St Mary's College, Kurseong, which in 1972 became the Vidyajyoti College of Religious Studies. He writes preferably in the areas of Hindu–Christian encounter and Indian theology. He has also been editor of *Vidyajyoti: Journal of Theology Reflection*, for many years. His publications include: *God's Word among Man* (New Delhi: Vidyajyoti Institute of Religious Studies, 1971); *Gods and Men* (Bombay: Popular Book Depot, 1962); *Bliss in the Upanishads* (Delhi: Orient Publishers, 1977) and, with M. Amaladoss and T.K. John, *Theologizing in India: Selection of Papers Presented at the Seminar Held in Poona (Pune), 1978* (Bangalore: Theological Publications in India, 1981).

Robert P. Goldman is Professor of Sanskrit at the University of California, Berkeley. His areas of scholarly interest include Sanskrit literature and literary theory, Indian Epic Studies and psychoanalytically oriented cultural studies. He has published widely in these areas, authoring several books and dozens of scholarly articles. He is perhaps best known for his work as the Director, General Editor and a principal translator of a massive and fully annotated translation of the critical edition of the *Valmiki Ramayana*. His work has been recognized by several awards and fellowships, including election as a Fellow of the American Academy of Arts and Sciences.

S. Gunasekaran teaches history at Hindu College, University of Delhi. His specialization is in the pre-modern socio-economic history of South India. His current research interests are frontier histories, peasant studies and mapping a range of historical experiences, including memory, dissent, eroticism and suicide. A bilingual scholar, he writes and publishes in Tamil and English.

Raj Kumar Hans was born and educated in rural Punjab and graduated in History from Guru Nanak Dev University, Amritsar. With a doctorate degree on the nineteenth century agrarian economy of South Gujarat from M.S. University of Baroda, he has been teaching there since 1983. Several articles and papers of his have been published in journals and books. Shifting his research from economic to social history, he has been working on the history of Panjabi Dalits. A monograph on 'Literary Creativity of Punjabi Dalits', a result of a fellowship at the IIAS is almost ready for the press. Another monograph on the history of dalits in Sikh religion is also in progress. He has participated in several national and international conferences in India and abroad.

Udaya Kumar is currently Senior Fellow at the Nehru Memorial Museum and Library, New Delhi, and Professor of English at the University of Delhi. He is the author of *The Joycean Labyrinth: Repetition, Time and Tradition* *in 'Ulysses'* (Oxford: Clarendon, 1991) and several papers on contemporary literary and cultural theory and Indian literature. His research interests include autobiographical writing, cultural histories of the body and the shaping of modern literary cultures. He is currently completing a book on modes of self-articulation in modern Malayalam writing, and working on the emergence of new idioms of vernacular social thought in early twentieth century Kerala.

David N. Lorenzen is a Professor at El Colegio de Mexico in Mexico City. His recent publications include a collection of his essays, *Nirgun Santon ke Swapna* (2010), and an edited book, *Yogi Heroes and Poets* (2011). His current project is an edition–translation of a 1751 Christian–Hindu dialogue in Hindustani by an Italian missionary.

Pius Malekandathil is Professor at the Centre for Historical Studies, Jawaharlal Nehru University, New Delhi. His major publications include: *The Germans, the Portuguese and India* (Münster, Germany: LIT Verlag, 1999); *Portuguese Cochin and the Maritime Trade of India, 1500–1663* (A Volume in the South Asian Study Series of Heidelberg University, No. 39, Germany) (Delhi: Manohar, 2001); *Jornada of Dom Alexis Menezes: A Portuguese Account of the Sixteenth Century Malabar* (Cochin: LRC Publications, 2003); *Maritime India: Trade, Religion and Polity in the Indian Ocean* (Delhi: Primus Books, 2010); *The Mughals, the Portuguese and the Indian Ocean: Changing Imageries of Maritime India* (Delhi: Primus Books, 2013); *The Portuguese, Indian Ocean and European Bridgehead: Festschrift in Honour of Prof. K.S. Mathew* (Lisbon: Fundação Oriente, 2001) (co-editor with T. Jamal Mohammad); *The Portuguese and the Socio-Cultural Changes in India:1500–1800* (Tellicherry, India: MESHAR and Lisbon: Fundação Oriente, 2001) (co-editor with K.S. Mathew and Teotonio R. de Souza); *The Kerala Economy and European Trade* (Muvattupuzha: Nirmala and Research Publications, 2003) (co-editor with K.S. Mathew); *Goa in the Twentieth Century: History and Culture* (Panaji: Institute Menezes Braganza, 2008) (co-editor with Remy Dias).

Rohini Mokashi-Punekar is Professor at the Department of Humanities and Social Sciences, Indian Institute of Technology, Guwahati. Besides several papers in books and journals, she is the author of *On the Threshold: Songs of Chokhamela* (Walnut Creek, CA: Altamira Press, 2005 and Delhi: The Book Review Literary Trust, 2002); *Untouchable Saints: An Indian Phenomenon* (Delhi: Manohar, 2005), which she co-edited with Eleanor Zelliot and *Vikram Seth*: *An Introduction* (Cambridge University Press, 2008). She is currently engaged in translating medieval Varkari poetry from the Marathi, an anthology of which will be published by Penguin in their Black Classics series.

S. Omana retired as Head of the Department of Philosophy, University College, Thiruvananthapuram, Kerala. She has several publications to her credit – books and periodicals on Narayana Guru and his philosophical visions. *One Caste, One Religion and One God* (1971), *The Philosophy of Sree Narayana Guru* (1984), *Advaita in Malayalam – Narayana Guru* (2000), *Epistemology of Narayana Guru* (2011) and *Life and Teachings of Narayana Guru* (2012) are some of her works. It is her discipleship under Nataraja Guru, the direct disciple of Narayana Guru (along with other disciples, namely, Guru Nithya Chaitanya Yati and Guru Muni Narayana Prasad), which made her conscious of the importance of an independent study on the philosophy of Narayana Guru and its relevance in the present world.

Vijaya Ramaswamy is Professor of History at Jawaharlal Nehru University, New Delhi. Currently she is Senior Fellow at Nehru Memorial Museum and Library, New Delhi. She teaches economic history of early India, a seminar course in religion and society in early India and a lecture course on 'Devotion and Dissent in Indian History'. Ramaswamy's most recent book is *The Song of the Loom* (Delhi: Primus Books, 2013). Her other publications include: *The Historical Dictionary of the Tamils* (Lanham, Maryland: Scarecrow Press Inc., 2007); *Textiles and Weavers in Medieval South India* (Delhi: Oxford University Press, 1985 and 2006); *Divinity and Deviance: Women in Virasaivism* (Delhi: Oxford University Press, 1996); *Re-searching Indian Women* (Delhi: Manohar, 2003); *Walking Naked: Women, Society, Spirituality in South India* (Shimla: Indian Institute of Advanced Study [IIAS], 1997 and 2007); and *A to Z of the Tamils* (Lanham, Maryland: Scarecrow Press Inc., 2010).

K. T. S. Sarao is Professor of Buddhist Studies at the University of Delhi. He has doctoral degrees from the universities of Delhi and Cambridge. He has written fourteen books and published over 150 research papers and articles. The Preah Sihanouk Royal Buddhist University, Phnom Penh (Cambodia), conferred the degree of D.Litt. (*honoris causa*) on him in 2011 for his special contribution to Buddhism studies.

T. S. Satyanath is Professor in the Department of Modern Indian Languages and Literary Studies, University of Delhi. He has taught comparative Indian literature and Kannada language and literature for the last 35 years. Comparative Indian literature, translations studies, folklore studies and cultural studies are his areas of interest and he has published extensively in these areas. He was a visiting scholar at the University of Pennsylvania, Philadelphia, and University of Guyana, Georgetown, and a visiting professor at Kannada University, Hampi.

He is also associated with Delhi Comparatists, a group of faculty and students engaged in comparative Indian literary studies on the campus of University of Delhi.

Surojit Sen is a graduate of Calcutta University. He works as a researcher for documentary films and also writes scripts for film and television. He has written articles in the Bengali newspaper, *Ei Samay*, on film, literature, art and culture. He has also written non-fiction prose in Bengali periodicals. He has a special interest in subaltern religious movements in Bengal, like the Bauls and Fakirs.

Arvind Sharma is the Birks Professor of Comparative Religion at McGill University, Montreal, Canada. Sharma's works focus on comparative religion, Hinduism and the role of women in religion. Some of his more famous works include *Our Religions* and *Women in World Religions*. *Feminism in World Religions* was selected as the Outstanding Academic Book (1999). He has held fellowships at the John F. Kennedy School of Government, the Center for the Study of World Religions, the Brookings Institute, the Center for the Study of Values in Public Life and the Center for Business and Government. He was also elected a Fellow of the Royal Asiatic Society.

Mahesh Sharma is Professor of History at Punjab University, Chandigarh. He was a Fulbright Senior Fellow at the University of California, Los Angeles (UCLA); Fellow IIAS (Shimla); and visiting faculty at University of North Florida (UNF), Jacksonville. He is the author of *Western Himalayan Temple Records: State, Pilgrimage, Ritual and Legality in Chambā*, Brill's Indological Library, 31: Brill, Leiden/Boston, 2009, and *The Realm of Faith: Subversion, Appropriation and Dominance in the Western Himalaya*, Indian Institute of Advanced Study, Shimla, 2001.

Yogesh Snehi teaches history at the School of Liberal Studies, Ambedkar University Delhi (AUD). He has been engaging with critical debates on the Punjab region and has published research, organized workshops and conducted surveys on themes related to diversity, sexuality, region formation, identity and communalism, piety and orality at popular Sufi shrines and social reform in colonial Punjab. Through a Tasveer Ghar Fellowship, he has created a digital repository of images that are in circulation at popular Sufi shrines in contemporary Punjab.

Index